W9-BGC-989

JAN   2013

BANNED BOOKS

LITERATURE SUPPRESSED ON
Social Grounds
Third Edition

DAWN B. SOVA

Preface by
KEN WACHSBERGER

An Infobase Learning Company

Banned Books: Literature Suppressed on Social Grounds, Third Edition

Facts On File, Inc.
An imprint of Infobase Learning
132 West 31st Street
New York NY 10001

Library of Congress Cataloging-in-Publication Data

Sova, Dawn B.
Literature suppressed on social grounds / Dawn B. Sova. — 3rd ed.
p. cm. — (Banned books)
Includes bibliographical references and index.
ISBN 978-0-8160-8228-5 (acid-free paper) 1. Censorship—History. 2.
Prohibited books—History. 3. Social problems—United States—History.
4. Social problems—History. 5. Social problems in literature. I.
Title.
Z658.U5S69 2011
363.31'09—dc22   2010038222

Facts On File books are available at special discounts when purchased in bulk quantities for businesses, associations, institutions, or sales promotions. Please call our Special Sales Department in New York at (212) 967-8800 or (800) 322-8755.

You can find Facts On File on the World Wide Web at
http://www.infobaselearning.com

Text design by Cathy Rincon
Composition by Publication Services, Inc.
Cover printed by Yurchak Printing, Landisville, Pa.
Book printed and bound by Yurchak Printing, Landisville, Pa.
Date printed: June 2011

Printed in the United States of America

10 9 8 7 6 5 4 3 2 1

This book is printed on acid-free paper.

There is no freedom either in civil or ecclesiastical [affairs],
but where the liberty of the press is maintained.
—Matthew Tindal

If all mankind minus one were of one opinion, and only one person
were of the contrary opinion, mankind would be no more justified
in silencing that one person, than he, if he had the power,
would be justified in silencing mankind.
—John Stuart Mill

Dare to think for yourself.
—Voltaire

*To my son, Robert Gregor,
and to all young people who will try
to make the world they have inherited a better place.*

CONTENTS

ACKNOWLEDGMENTS

The long history of censorship has created many heroes, both famous and obscure, who have dared to defy the restrictions of their times to write and publish the truth as they understood it. Some are discussed in this volume, but many more have been silenced, their works destroyed. To all, however, this book owes both life and purpose. Had they acquiesced to those who suppress, censor, and ban ideas or language that displeases powerful authorities, smug majorities, or vocal minorities, our intellectual universe would be significantly smaller.

I treasure my association with Bert Holtje, whose support and advice as both literary agent and friend helped me to maintain perspective throughout this lengthy project. His insight and literate commentary helped to resolve seemingly insurmountable problems. Gene Brissie, of James Peter Associates, brought his patience and his considerable knowledge of the publishing world to ensuing editions of the work. I am grateful to know him.

My sincere gratitude also belongs to former Facts On File editors Gary M. Krebs, who saw potential in the idea and courageously proposed a censorship series, and Drew Silver, who provided substance and direction to the work. My greatest appreciation, however, goes to Jeff Soloway, for his skill in suggesting changes to improve the work—and for his patience.

Some of the works discussed in this volume have been difficult to locate. I would have been unable to locate this literature without the efforts of I. Macarthur Nickles, director of the Garfield (New Jersey) Library, a man whose professional expertise and insight were invaluable. He made certain that my sometimes obscure research requests were satisfied and introduced innovations in my hometown library. I am also grateful to reference experts Kathleen Zalenski and Karen Calandriello, who tracked down unusual books, odd quotations, dates, and notes, always persevering long after I had given up the chase.

In my personal life, no one has meant more to me than my son, Rob Gregor, who helped me to organize my thoughts, contributed insights on various works, and kept me human. I appreciate greatly the continued support of my parents, my mother Violet Sova and my late father Emil Sova, whose pride in my accomplishments and unwavering confidence in my abilities have always sustained me.

Finally, although I can never meet them, I appreciate the efforts of the many authors over centuries who risked their lives and livelihoods to stand against those who would oppress and silence them.

—D. B. S.

PREFACE

We Americans are proud of our Constitution, especially its Bill of Rights. The First Amendment right to freedom of speech and religion has inspired dissenters and nonconformists everywhere. Censored writers such as Salman Rushdie, Pramoedya Ananta Toer, and Aleksandr Solzhenitsyn have looked to our country's example for strength as they battled for their rights to express their own thoughts, and that of others to read them, even at the risk of their lives.

Yet censorship has been a major part of American history from the time of Roger Williams and other early colonial freethinkers. Many of our richest literary works—*Adventures of Huckleberry Finn*, *The Color Purple*, *The Grapes of Wrath*, *The Jungle*, *Uncle Tom's Cabin*, *Tropic of Cancer*—have been censored at one time or another. Even today, school boards, local governments, religious organizations, and moral crusaders attempt to restrict our freedom to read or to learn alternative viewpoints. Witness the Texas State Board of Education's attempts to revise American history and tear down the wall separating church and state through its revisionist textbooks. Advancing technology has provided more diverse targets—the record, film, and television industries and the Internet—for the censors and would-be censors to aim at, as they work their strategies to restrict free expression and the freedom to read, watch, and listen, dumbing down material in order to shield their children, and you, from original or disturbing thoughts.

In this third-edition volume of books censored for social reasons, Dawn B. Sova shows that puritanical views continue to motivate censors, who often object to depictions of youthful sexuality (*The Absolutely True Diary of a Part-time Indian*) or graphic descriptions of bodies (*The Earth, My Butt, and Other Big Round Things*). Books that deal with themes of violence (*The Kite Runner*) also face the social censor's wrath. A prominent theme among the new books of the previous edition, objection to depictions of loving same-sex relationships, continues in this edition, with the discussion of *And Tango Makes Three*, a true story about two male penguins and their adventures hatching and raising a chick. Other books new to this edition—though not at all new to the literary community—include novels widely regarded as literary triumphs, such as *The Old Man and the Sea*, *Beloved*, *The Great Gatsby*, and more.

Fortunately, our country has a strong tradition of fighting censorship as well. Groups such as the National Coalition Against Censorship, the American Library Association's Office for Intellectual Freedom, People for the American Way, the American Civil Liberties Union, the PEN American Center, and the National Writers Union exist to defend the First Amendment and support independent writers, through legal action and by raising public awareness.

The first edition of the Facts On File Banned Books Series came out as a four-volume hardcover set in 1998. The second edition, which was published in 2006, added 50 additional titles to the list. The four volumes in this dynamic revised and expanded third edition add to our rich First Amendment tradition by spotlighting approximately 500 works that have been censored for their political, social, religious, or erotic content, in the United States and around the world, from biblical times to the present day. While many of these have been legally "banned"—or prohibited "as by official order"—all indeed have been banned or censored in a broader sense: targeted for removal from school curricula or library shelves, condemned in churches and forbidden to the faithful, rejected or expurgated by publishers, challenged in court, even voluntarily rewritten by their authors. Censored authors have been verbally abused, physically attacked, shunned by their families and communities, excommunicated from their religious congregations, and shot, hanged, or burned at the stake by their enemies, who thus made them heroes and often enough secured their memory for posterity. Their works include novels, histories, biographies, children's books, religious and philosophical treatises, dictionaries, poems, polemics, and every other form of written expression.

It is illuminating to discover in these histories that such cultural landmarks as the Bible, the Qur'an, the Talmud, and the greatest classics of world literature have often been suppressed or censored from the same motives, and by similar forces, as those we see today seeking to censor such books as *Daddy's Roommate* and *Heather Has Two Mommies*. Every American reading these volumes will find in their pages books they love and will be thankful that their authors' freedom of expression and their own freedom to read are constitutionally protected. But at the same time, how many will be gratified by the cruel fate of books we detest? Reader-citizens capable of acknowledging their own contradictions will be grateful for the existence of the First Amendment and will thank its guardians, including the authors of this series, for protecting us against our own worst impulses.

It is to Facts On File's credit that they have published this new version of the original Banned Books series. May the day come when an expanded series is no longer necessary.

* * *

To prevent redundancy, works banned for multiple reasons appear in only one volume apiece, based on the judgment of the editor and the volume authors. The alphabetical arrangement provides easy access to titles. Works whose titles appear in SMALL CAPITAL LETTERS within an entry have entries of their own elsewhere in the same volume. Those whose titles appear in *ITALICIZED SMALL CAPITAL LETTERS* have entries in one of the other volumes. In addition, each volume carries complete lists of the works discussed in the other volumes.

—Ken Wachsberger

Ken Wachsberger is a longtime author, editor, educator, and member of the National Writers Union. He is the editor of the four-volume Voices from the Underground series, a landmark collection of insider histories about the Vietnam era underground press (www.voicesfromtheundergroundpress.com).

INTRODUCTION

The broad nature of obscenity laws has made possible a wide interpretation of what constitutes an essentially "obscene" literary work. The language of American law stresses work that "depicts or describes sexual conduct in a patently offensive manner." The law also specifies that the "average person, taking contemporary community standards, would find that a work, taken as a whole, appeals to the prurient interest." Often what this has meant in reality is that works containing words deemed "vulgar" by specific members of a community or presenting interracial, homosexual, or other relationships that are unacceptable to the standards of a given community acquire the label "obscene." These are social factors, the topic of this volume, and they are distinctly different from erotic, religious, and political content.

Censors have so frequently applied such general guidelines to published writing that a wide range of literature has been declared "inappropriate" or "obscene." This volume avoids such generalization. Instead, the books discussed in this volume are literary works that have been banned, censored, or challenged because of language, racial characterization, depiction of the drug use, social class or sexual orientation of characters, or other social differences that their challengers have viewed as harmful to readers. Thus Mark Twain's *Adventures of Huckleberry Finn* is included, while D. H. Lawrence's *Lady Chatterley's Lover* is not, even though both have been banned in the past for being "obscene"; the first has attracted the label because of its language and depiction of race while the second contains graphic sexual description and has been banned for its erotic content. The books discussed in this volume have been censored because their subject matter and characters do not conform to the social, racial, or sexual standards of their censors.

There are currently no books in print that systematically examine and describe the content and controversy surrounding books that have been banned, censored, or challenged specifically because they contain socially unacceptable ideas or speech. A survey of the literature on censorship reveals that many texts of the past that were condemned for "vulgar" and "offensive" language, portrayals of lesbian or homosexual relationships, racially volatile incidents or themes, or socially offensive behavior such as drug use were condemned under the broad laws governing obscenity. Thus, while their subject matter, intention, and presentation might differ substantially, such works as Ray Bradbury's *Fahrenheit 451* and D. H. Lawrence's *Lady Chatterley's Lover* were both condemned as obscene. This study separates the two.

Most books on the topic are concerned with defining what is obscene and describing the litigation and court decisions, rather than with examining the censored writings from a particular vantage point. Much commentary was published during or soon after the issuance in 1973 of the Report of the 1970 United States President's Commission on Obscenity or soon after the 1986 U.S. Attorney General's Commission on Pornography released its findings. Thus, books on the subject of pornography became plentiful. However, little attention was paid to nonerotic books that have been censored as "obscene" and condemned under the same laws for social factors characterized as "offensive" by individuals or communities.

The goal of this volume is to identify and discuss books that have been censored as obscene, in centuries past as well as the present day, either because the authors or the works did not conform to the social expectations of their censors or because they contain socially unacceptable ideas or speech. Several works, despite limited censorship histories, are included to exhibit the lengths to which censors' fears will take them, as in the case of *Alice's Adventures in Wonderland* and *The Adventures of Sherlock Holmes.* Other works have extensive histories of censorship, exhibiting the multiplicity of reasons that motivate censors. Taken as a whole, the entries provide a fascinating view of socially motivated censorship.

NOTE ON THE THIRD EDITION

This new edition adds 10 new entries and many updates to the censorship histories of existing entries. Much of the material reflects a changed climate in censorship. Most books challenged for social reasons in the past century have suffered because of the language used or the racial relationships portrayed within. Certainly, these reasons underlie the challenges to some of the newest entries in this volume. Language, particularly the use of the N-word, and unflattering portrayals of ethnic groups have motivated challenges to such disparate books as *Uncle Remus, The Old Man and the Sea, Mother Goose,* and *Freakonomics,* although they are centuries apart in their origins and appeal to widely diverse audiences. The numerous efforts to ban *A Light in the Attic* are evidence that communities still fear perceived challenges to parental authority and the possibility that adolescents will act out the disrespect and bad behavior displayed in books, which have made *The Catcher in the Rye* a perennial member of the list of books challenged annually. However, there is also a new definition of "obscene," which emerged in the last decade of the 20th century and continues to the present and appears to emphasize the discussion or the depiction of homosexual relationships, minus any mention of sexual interaction. Such books as *Am I Blue?, Baby Be-Bop, King & King,* and *Unlived Affections* have experienced numerous challenges and requests for their removal from both public and school libraries because they depict same-sex relationships. Overt sexuality does not appear, no appeal is made for readers to enter the homosexual lifestyle, and nothing offensive in language or illustration is portrayed. For challengers, however, none of the preceding occurrences are needed. Rather, the mere suggestion that healthy relationships might be forged between partners of the same sex and that families might consist of something other than mother-father-child provokes many to challenge such books.

The meaning of "obscene" remains fluid, changing with the rise and fall in power of social groups. What must remain constant, however, is a steadfast resistance to all those who would restrict our freedom of expression.

WORKS DISCUSSED IN
THIS VOLUME

THE ABSOLUTELY TRUE DIARY OF A PART-TIME INDIAN
Sherman Alexie

ADVENTURES OF HUCKLEBERRY FINN
Mark Twain

THE ADVENTURES OF SHERLOCK HOLMES
Sir Arthur Conan Doyle

THE ADVENTURES OF TOM SAWYER
Mark Twain

ALICE'S ADVENTURES IN WONDERLAND
Lewis Carroll

THE AMBOY DUKES
Irving Shulman

*THE AMERICAN HERITAGE DICTIONARY OF THE
  ENGLISH LANGUAGE*

AM I BLUE?
Marion Dane Bauer

AND STILL I RISE
Maya Angelou

AND TANGO MAKES THREE
Justin Richardson and Peter Parnell

HEATHER HAS TWO MOMMIES
Leslea Newman

A HERO AIN'T NOTHIN' BUT A SANDWICH
Alice Childress

HOWL AND OTHER POEMS
Allen Ginsberg

I KNOW WHY THE CAGED BIRD SINGS
Maya Angelou

IN THE NIGHT KITCHEN
Maurice Sendak

INVISIBLE MAN
Ralph Ellison

JAKE AND HONEYBUNCH GO TO HEAVEN
Margot Zemach

JAMES AND THE GIANT PEACH
Roald Dahl

JAWS
Peter Benchley

JUNKY
William S. Burroughs

KING & KING
Linda de Haan and Stern Nijland

KINGSBLOOD ROYAL
Sinclair Lewis

THE KITE RUNNER
Khaled Hosseini

LAST EXIT TO BROOKLYN
Hubert Selby, Jr.

LEAVES OF GRASS
Walt Whitman

OF TIME AND THE RIVER
Thomas Wolfe

THE OLD MAN AND THE SEA
Ernest Hemingway

ONE FLEW OVER THE CUCKOO'S NEST
Ken Kesey

ORDINARY PEOPLE
Judith Guest

THE OX-BOW INCIDENT
Walter Van Tilburg Clark

THE RED PONY
John Steinbeck

THE SCARLET LETTER
Nathaniel Hawthorne

A SEPARATE PEACE
John Knowles

SISTER CARRIE
Theodore Dreiser

SOUL ON ICE
Eldridge Cleaver

STEPPENWOLF
Hermann Hesse

STRANGE FRUIT
Lillian Smith

STRANGER IN A STRANGE LAND
Robert A. Heinlein

THE SUN ALSO RISES
Ernest Hemingway

TO HAVE AND HAVE NOT
Ernest Hemingway

LITERATURE
SUPPRESSED ON
SOCIAL GROUNDS

THE ABSOLUTELY TRUE DIARY OF A PART-TIME INDIAN

Author: Sherman Alexie
Original date and place of publication: 2007, United States
Original publisher: Little, Brown and Company
Literary form: Young adult novel

SUMMARY

The Absolutely True Diary of a Part-Time Indian is a semiautobiographical novel that relates the hopes, fears, disappointments, and eventual triumphs experienced by the 14-year-old budding cartoonist Arnold Spirit, Jr. (better known as Junior), who lives on the Spokane (Washington) Indian Reservation ("the rez"). He dreams of becoming a wealthy and respected artist and draws because "I feel like it might be my only real chance to escape the reservation." Despite his talent, displayed in cartoons scattered throughout the novel, Junior's problems appear to be insurmountable, and he views himself as "really just a poor-ass reservation kid living with his poor-ass family on the poor-ass Spokane Indian Reservation." Junior was born with too much cerebral fluid in his skull that leaves him "susceptible to seizure activity" and brain damage that makes him "nearsighted in one eye and farsighted in the other, so my ugly glasses were all lopsided because my eyes were so lopsided," a mouth containing 42 instead of 32 teeth, huge hands and feet paired with a too-skinny body, and a lisp and a stutter. Although "Dad is a drunk and Mom is an ex-drunk," they love their son and want him to escape the cycle of poverty and despair that destroyed their dreams, so they agree to allow him to transfer to Reardon, a small school in "a rich, white farm town" 22 miles away that will provide him with an excellent education. *The Absolutely True Diary of a Part-Time Indian* is the story of Junior's freshman year at Reardon.

The first four chapters—"The Black-Eye-of-the-Month Club," "Why Chicken Means So Much to Me," "Revenge Is My Middle Name," and "Because Geometry Is Not a Country Somewhere Near France"—provide readers with depressing views of Junior's life on the rez. His schoolmates humiliate him, call him names, stuff his head into toilets, and beat him up regularly, "at least once a month." He copes with this abuse by staying at home as much as he can, and he draws "all the time." His lisp and stutter make spoken communication difficult, "words are too unpredictable . . . words are too limited," but "when you draw a picture, everybody can understand it." Junior also suffers because his family is poor, although he acknowledges that most of the Indian families on the reservation are poor. He occasionally misses a meal "and sleep is the only thing we have for dinner," but he reassures readers that "sooner or later, my parents will come bursting through the door with a bucket of Kentucky Fried Chicken. Original Recipe." The lack of money forces Junior to face a heartrending tragedy when he does not have the money for medical attention for his "best friend Oscar," an adopted stray dog who develops seizures, vomiting, and diarrhea and who whimpers in pain while his "red, watery, snotty eyes" plead for help. Junior's parents cannot afford the cost of a veterinarian, and he realizes that there was nothing he could do to save Oscar. "Nothing. Nothing. Nothing." His father offers the only solution he can, to end Oscar's misery by shooting him, a solution that first infuriates Junior, then reinforces his feelings of despair. "So I heard the boom of my father's rifle when he shot my best friend. A bullet only costs about two cents, and anybody can afford that."

Junior turns to his "best human friend" Rowdy, "the meanest kid on the rez," after Oscar dies. Rowdy is "mean as a snake" and fights with others constantly, but he is protective of Junior, whose home is a safe place where he can avoid his father's hard drinking and brutal beatings. Rowdy takes revenge on the 30-year-old Andruss triplets after Junior tells him that they played catch with him "and then kneed me in the balls." He waits until they fall into a drunken stupor and then shaves their eyebrows and cuts off their braids that have taken five years to grow. In a prelude to discussing his first day of high school, Junior reveals that he spends "*hours* in the bathroom with a magazine that has one thousand pictures of naked movie stars. *Naked woman* + *right hand* = *happy happy joy joy*." Addressing the reader, Junior becomes expansive:

> Yep, that's right, I admit that I masturbate.
>> I'm proud of it.
>> I'm good at it.
>> I'm ambidextrous.
>> If there were a Professional Masturbators League, I'd get drafted number one and make millions of dollars.
>> And maybe you're thinking, 'Well, you really shouldn't be talking about masturbation in public.'
>> Well, tough, I'm going to talk about it because EVERYBODY does it. And EVERYBODY likes it.
>> And if God hadn't wanted us to masturbate, then God wouldn't have given us thumbs.
>> So I thank God for my thumbs.

Despite the poverty, humiliation, and abuse, Junior seems relatively accepting of life until his first day as a high school freshman. He looks forward to geometry class, but his excitement turns to anger when he receives his book and finds his mother's maiden name written inside the cover. He loves his mother, who gave birth to him when she was 30, but her name on the book means that the textbook is at least 30 years old, a fact that hits his heart "with the force of a nuclear bomb" and makes him feel his poverty and sense of hopelessness more keenly. Without thinking, he throws the book at his teacher Mr. P, breaking his nose and earning a suspension from school. The action serves as the turning point in Junior's life.

In "Hope Against Hope," the fifth chapter, Mr. P visits Junior at home, speaks about the incident, and commends him for having retained the spirit and hope for change that most of the reservation residents, including Rowdy and Junior's parents and older sister Mary, have lost. Mr. P reveals that Mary, once his student who now spends most of her day in front of the television in the basement with no ambition to do anything else, "was the smartest kid" he had ever had in class. Much to Junior's surprise, Mr. P says that she had wanted to be a writer, but "she always thought people would make fun of her." Mr. P counsels Junior to leave the reservation and to save himself rather than to give up as everyone else, including the white teachers, have. "You're going to find more and more hope the farther and farther you walk away from this sad, sad reservation." In the following chapter, "Go Means Go," Junior tells his parents that he wants to transfer out of his reservation school and into Reardan, located in a town "filled with farmers and rednecks and racist cops who stop every Indian that drives through." Junior's father had been stopped in Reardan five times in one week for DWI: "Driving While Indian." Despite their fears and the difficulty of transporting him 22 miles each way, and while acknowledging that many residents of the reservation will be angry and resentful, Junior's parents agree that he can transfer schools. Rowdy, however, is not happy, and the two exchange insults in "Rowdy Sings the Blues," one calling the other "dickwad" to the response "kiss my ass." Junior exudes praise for his soon-to-be schoolmates, which Rowdy counters by shouting, "you retarded fag."

Once at Reardan, Junior learns that, aside from the school mascot, he is the only Native American. The girls ignore him, as did girls on the reservation. The boys do not physically attack him, but they call him such names as "Chief," "Tonto," and "Squaw Boy." Addressed by his true name Arnold in class and by Penelope, with whom he becomes infatuated, Junior is intimidated and awed by the tall white farm boys until one, Roger, steps over the line with what he calls a joke: "Did you know that Indians are living proof that niggers fuck buffalo?" Junior lashes out in blind anger, "defending Indians, black people, *and* buffalo," and punches Roger in the face, knocking him to the ground. The farm boy is stunned and surprises Junior in return by refusing to agree to the challenge to meet after school to finish the fight. In a later discussion with his grandmother about the incident, Junior realizes that his rash move has gained him respect.

As the school year progresses toward Thanksgiving, Junior remains physically safe at the high school but also very lonely, a major hazard because "whenever I get lonely, I grow a big zit on the end of my nose." He realizes that he does not feel fully comfortable either at school or at home: "Zitty and lonely, I woke up on the reservation as an Indian, and somewhere on the road to Reardan, I became something less than an Indian. And once I arrived at Reardan, I became something less than less than less than an Indian." His father becomes unreliable in driving Junior to school, so some days he hitchhikes, other days he takes the bus, and on several occasions he walks the 22 miles home. Although everyone and everything seems to turn against Junior, he persists in attending Reardan. He learns that his sister Mary, a persistent runaway, has left for Montana and married a Flathead Indian, and the knowledge buoys him because he feels it means that she has not given up on life. Mary sends letters filled with glowing accounts of her new home and life, which Junior learns later are fiction. The large "gorgeous" home she claims to have is actually a cramped trailer, and her new life is simply a continuation of the old. He also becomes study friends with Gordy, an acknowledged genius at Reardon, but as much of an outsider as Junior. In one silly exchange the two discuss "a metaphorical boner," by which Gordy means joy but which Junior understands "in the sexual sense." Junior also learns that Penelope, with whom he has been in love since his first day at Reardan, is bulimic, and sharing this secret forges a friendship between them, despite threats by her father Earl. At school, Junior, whom Penelope prefers to call Arnold, is suddenly popular, and he enjoys his new celebrity, even though he knows it is fleeting. Gordy brings him down to earth by telling him that adoring the pretty, blonde Penelope "means you're just a racist asshole like everybody else."

Junior's parents try to help him to retain his pride at Reardan by giving him as much spending money as they can, although it is far less than other students have. Fearful of being exposed as poor, he tries to keep up and to impress Penelope, but when the group goes out to eat after the prom to which Junior has worn with great success his father's bell-bottomed leisure suit, Roger reveals that he has known all along that Junior has financial difficulties and he kindly offers $40 to cover dinner. The same night, Roger also drives Junior home to the reservation, and he does so for many nights following. This leads Junior to state, "If you let people into your life a little bit, they can be pretty damn amazing."

Through the remainder of the school year, Junior continues to move between his life on the reservation and his newfound life in Reardan. While in the computer lab with the genius Gordy, Junior opens an e-mail from Rowdy who "was exactly the kind of kid who would e-mail his bare ass (and bare everything else) to the world." When Gordy asks if the image is a "posterior," he responds, "That is a stinky ass. You can smell the thing, even through the computer." Gordy learns that Rowdy is angry with Junior, whom he considers to be an "apple," red on the outside and white on the inside. Gordy explains to Junior that the evolution of both boys in relation to the concept of tribe is completely to be expected.

Major changes occur in rapid succession in Junior's life. He tries out for the high school basketball team—dreaming big as his father advised—and makes the team; the later stars when Reardan plays against the team from his reservation school. His chronically drunk father disappears on Christmas Eve, yet manages to keep $5 aside to give Junior when he returns the day after New Year's Day. Sadly, his beloved grandmother is killed by a drunk driver, and when Junior attends the wake he is fearful of the reaction of the other 2,000 Indians who attend. He is surprised and pleased to hear no harsh words and no criticism because he has left the reservation. His father's friend Eugene is shot in the face and killed by another friend named Bobby in a fight over a bottle of wine. In jail, Bobby hangs himself using a bedsheet. Junior watches as his father reacts by going on "a legendary drinking binge" and his mother goes to church every single day. "It was all booze and God, booze and God, booze and God." A few months later, Junior is taken out of school early and told that his sister has died. Alcohol has been responsible for her death, as well. His father tells him through tears, "They had a big party . . . And your sister and her husband passed out in the back bedroom. And somebody tried to cook soup on a hot plate. And they forgot about it and left. And a curtain drifted in on the wind and caught the hot plate, and the trailer burned down quick." Rowdy lashes out at Junior, blaming him for Mary's death, telling him that Mary would not have run away from the reservation and married so quickly if Junior had not left to attend Reardan. Unable to face a house full of grieving friends and family who "would be drinking booze and getting drunk and stupid and sad and mean," Junior returns to Reardan where the students and teachers greet him and let him know that they care about him and are sorry his sister died.

When the school year ends, Junior reacclimates himself to being home on the rez. He joins his parents in cleaning the family gravesites, and he mourns the "ten or fifteen more Spokanes [who] would die during the next year, and that most of them would die because of booze." He also recognizes that his journey from the reservation toward a better education and future is no different from the journey taken by millions of immigrants "who had left their birthplaces in search of a dream." He also thinks about the many people on the reservation who would not survive, and Rowdy comes to mind. He recalls their friendship and their summers spent swimming, watching television, playing video games, and insulting each other. In one exchange, after Junior looks at the "monster pine tree" and says he loves the tree, Rowdy calls him a "tree fag." When Junior denies this, Rowdy asks, "Then how come you like to stick your dick inside knotholes?" to which Junior replies, "I stick my dick in girl trees." Junior feels that those times together are over, but Rowdy surprises him soon after the school year ends. The two make peace, and Rowdy admits that he is happy for Junior and wishes him a successful future.

CENSORSHIP HISTORY

The Absolutely True Diary of a Part-Time Indian was awarded the National Book Award for Young People's Literature in 2007 and was named one of the *Los Angeles Times*'s Favorite Children's Books of 2007 and one of the *New York Times*'s Notable Children's Books of 2007. Further, the audio version earned the Odyssey Award in 2009, but such honors have not insulated the novel against controversy. Parents of students attending Antioch (Illinois) Community High School, located in a predominantly lower-middle-class Chicago suburb halfway between Chicago and Milwaukee, asked school officials in

June 2009 to remove the novel from the summer reading list and claimed to be "appalled by certain passages." Jennifer Andersen, whose son would be a freshman at the high school in September 2009, said that she was "stunned by descriptions of masturbation, racist language, graphic depictions of sex, and references to bestiality." She read the book so that she could help her son with discussion of the content, but "I wasn't prepared for what I read. It was shocking. If there were just swear words, I could deal with that. But sections of this book are just vulgar." In an interview with the *Chicago Tribune*, Andersen said that she understands that children use profanity but protested that if it is part of the curriculum, the students will believe the school condones it. Six other parents joined Andersen to formally petition the school board to remove the book and contacted local news media to air their complaint. The novel had been selected by a committee of English teachers at the high school and approved by John Whitehurst, chairman of the English department, who defended the book and asserted that the passages condemned by parents "need to be read in context." He praised the novel for its "life-affirming values" and reminded parents that even in the controversial paragraphs the words are authentic. "This is honest and realistic language for a boy of this age. Though he has sexual thoughts, he records them but doesn't act on them." Whitehurst also reminded parents that the novel has "a strong anti-drug, anti-alcohol message." The English committee admitted to selecting the novel specifically to appeal to boys who often do not like to read. "We were looking for a book that is engaging for boys. We wanted a main character that they could relate to." The school district offered parents an alternative reading, *Down River*, until the controversy could be settled. The Antioch school superintendent Jay Sabatino told parents that he wanted to complete reading the book before making a decision, and he asked school board members to also read the book before meeting to decide the fate of the novel. Although the superintendent was sensitive to the concerns of parents, he stated, "We don't want to make a knee-jerk reaction." While she awaited the decision of the board, the parent who initiated the controversy sent an e-mail to high school principal Michael Nekritz telling him that, at the very least, she "would have appreciated a warning from school officials about the potentially offensive content." Andersen said that she wanted this protest to begin a national conversation about placing warning labels on books. "We rate movies and put warnings on music and TV. What about books? There is no warning whatsoever if there is vulgar language in a book."

In a closed meeting a week later, the superintendent and the school board of School District 117 "voiced strong support for the book as an educational tool that engages young readers," but they also decided to write a letter to parents of incoming students and invite them to discuss any concerns they may have. They also offered all students the opportunity to read the alternate selection, *Down River* by John Hart. Further, the district will form a committee made up of parents, teachers, and administrators that will meet each March to review books and to select summer reading titles. Jennifer Andersen praised the school board for proposing the committee, but she remained adamant in her disapproval of *The Absolutely True Diary of a Part-*

Time Indian and told reporter Lisa Black, "There are so many great stories out there without the vulgarity—Why bother with this book? I don't believe we need swear at our kids to get them engaged."

In an interview with *Publishers Weekly*, the English department chairman John Whitehurst said that there had been opposition in the past to books selected by the faculty for required reading, but "talking to the parents about the selection and offering an alternative has always defused the situation. But it didn't satisfy them this time around." In response to the decision by the school district to retain the novel, the publisher Little, Brown and Company released a statement that it "applauds the school board's decision to have the book remain on the Antioch High School summer reading list for the incoming freshman class. Based on his own experience of growing up, *The Absolutely True Diary of a Part-Time Indian* is ultimately a story about hope, resilience and self-discovery."

FURTHER READING

Black, Lisa. "Antioch School Won't Ban Book: District Calls It a Valuable Read but Offers Alternative." *Chicago Tribune*, June 23, 2009, p. 18.

Fuller, Ruth. "Some Parents Urge Board to Ban Book: School Official Says Book Is Relevant to Incoming Freshmen." *Chicago Tribune*, June 22, 2009, p. 18.

Kirch, Claire. "Chicago School Keeps Alexie Novel on Summer Reading List." *Publishers Weekly* (June 25, 2009). Available online. URL: http://www.publishersweekly.com/article/CA6666906.html?nid=2788&source=title&rid=630002055. Accessed December 15, 2009.

Pierri, Vincent. "Books Stirring Controversy at Antioch High School." *Daily Herald*, June 19, 2009. Available online. URL: www.dailyherald.com/story/?id=302477. Accessed December 16, 2009.

"Recorded Book Wins 2009 Odyssey Award for *The Absolutely True Diary of a Part-Time Indian*." *Young Adult Library Services* 7, no. 3 (Spring 2009): 18–19.

"Sherman Alexie Gets National Book Award." *Seattle Post-Intelligencer*, November 15, 2007, p. C-1.

ADVENTURES OF HUCKLEBERRY FINN

Author: Mark Twain (Samuel Langhorne Clemens)
Original date and place of publication: 1884, London
Original publisher: Self-published
Literary form: Novel

SUMMARY

This novel relates the adventures and struggles of a rambunctious young southern boy in the early 19th century. Told from the first-person point of view, *Adventures of Huckleberry Finn* portrays river life in a developing America and young Huckleberry Finn's adventures while on the journey from boyhood to manhood. The story begins with Huck's escape from his brutal father and follows him up the Mississippi River as he and his slave friend Jim run from authorities and various other scoundrels.

As the novel opens, Huck reminds readers that many of his adventures have already been detailed in Mark Twain's THE ADVENTURES OF TOM SAWYER. He states that the $12,000 that he and Tom had found in the previous novel was invested for them and was earning interest. Huck, who now lives with the Widow Douglas and Miss Watson, expresses annoyance with the amount of concern placed on making him conform to society. Huck sees no point in this lifestyle and yearns to be a rambunctious youth, as is his nature.

As the narrative progresses, Huck's father, the town drunk and a general burden on society, learns of Huck's recent wealth. He kidnaps Huck and holds him hostage in a shack in a remote area outside the town. While Huck waits to be either freed or rescued, his father repeatedly beats him, leaving Huck convinced that escape is the only feasible solution. To accomplish this, he conjures up a plan to make it appear that he has been murdered. Succeeding in his plan, Huck flees to safety on Jackson's Island, where he is reunited with Miss Watson's runaway slave, Jim. Jim is also hiding, fearful that he will be caught and punished for leaving his mistress. Huck agrees not to speak of Jim to anyone, and the two become partners. Aware that men are looking for Jim, the two decide to leave the island in search of adventure and the free states.

They board a raft that they found on the island and begin their journey. By day they hide on land, and by night they travel on the river. All goes well until one night when, during a violent storm, the raft is torn apart by an oncoming steamship. This experience not only almost ends Huck's young life, but it also separates him from Jim.

Huck swims to shore and finds himself in the midst of a feud between two families, the Grangerfords and the Shepherdsons, and he is immediately attacked by members of the Grangerford family. He states his name as George Jackson and explains quickly that he fell off a riverboat and was washed ashore. He stays with the family for a short time, enjoying their lifestyle and making new friends along the way, and he even manages to be reunited with Jim. When the family feud escalates and Huck and Jim watch numerous members of both families die, they decide to resume their adventure on the river, where they meet two men known as the Duke and the King. The unscrupulous men specialize in robbery and deceit, and they do not hesitate to pose as a dead man's next of kin in order to receive a rather large inheritance. The innately moral Huck refuses to cooperate, and he reveals the Duke and the King's deceit. The scoundrels flee, but they first sell Jim to Silas Phelps.

Seeking to obtain Jim's freedom, Huck visits the Phelps farm, where he is mistaken for Tom Sawyer, who is expected to arrive the same day. Huck allows the deception to continue, then meets with the real Tom, who agrees that Huck will continue to pose as Tom, and Tom will pose as his brother Sid. The two also agree to free Jim as soon as possible. After many attempts, Jim finally escapes, but Tom is accidentally shot in the leg during the effort.

Although Jim has been portrayed as ignorant throughout the novel, he is a morally decent man who temporarily puts aside his dreams of freedom to nurse Tom back to health.

The novel closes as Jim and the boys learn that Jim is already a free man, as decreed by the last will and testament of Miss Watson, his former owner. This puts an end to all escape plans and allows Jim to be the one thing that he has always wanted to be, free. Huck also decides to leave and wander on his own, convinced that the civilized world is no place for him.

CENSORSHIP HISTORY

The novel excited controversy from the outset, when Concord (Massachusetts) Public Library banned the book in 1885, charging that the novel was "trash suitable only for the slums." Conventional morality was offended by the street vernacular spoken by Jim and Huck, as well as by their coarse behavior. Denver Public Library banned the novel in 1902, and Brooklyn (New York) Public Library removed it from the children's room on the charge that "Huck not only itched but he scratched, and that he said sweat when he should have said perspiration." In 1930, Soviet border guards confiscated the novel, along with *The Adventures of Tom Sawyer*.

In the United States, the furor quieted down for five decades, as the novel became an American classic and a mainstay of school reading lists. A new challenge emerged in 1957, when the National Association for the Advancement of Colored People protested the racist aspects of the book and demanded that it be removed from high schools in New York City. African-American author Ralph Ellison noted that Huck's friendship with Jim demeaned the stature of black males, because the adolescent Huck is portrayed as equal or superior to the adult Jim in decision-making capability. In 1969, Miami Dade (Florida) Junior College removed the novel from the required reading list, charging that the book inhibited learning in black students by creating an emotional block.

In 1973, the Scott, Foresman publishing company yielded to the demands of school officials in Tennessee and prepared a version of the novel that omitted material to which officials objected. The version omits the passage in Chapter 18 in which the young men of the Grangerford family toast their parents each morning with alcohol. It appears in *The United States in Literature*, a textbook distributed and used nationally.

The most frequent objection to the novel has been its language in reference to African Americans. Yielding to pressures from school districts across the nation, textbook publishers up to 1975 met challenges by substituting euphemisms for the term *nigger*. Scott, Foresman rewrote passages to eliminate the word, Singer replaced the term with *slave*, and McGraw-Hill replaced the term with *servant*. In a 1975 dissertation, Dorothy Weathersby found that Ginn and Company was the only textbook publisher to retain the word, but their textbook included an essay by Lionel Trilling to explain the need to include the word in the novel.

The novel has been frequently banned or challenged by school districts for its language, particularly its racial references and the use of the slur *nigger*. A significant number of such challenges have come from well-educated, middle-class, African-American parents who wish to prevent their children from exposure to such insulting references. The Winnetka (Illinois) school district challenged the novel as being racist in 1976, as did school districts in Warrington, Pennsylvania, in 1981; Davenport, Iowa, in 1981; Fairfax County, Virginia, in 1982; Houston, Texas, in 1982; State College, Pennsylvania, in 1983; Springfield, Illinois, in 1984; and Waukegan, Illinois, in 1984.

In 1988, Rockford (Illinois) public schools removed the book from their required reading list because it contained the word *nigger*. Berrien Springs (Michigan) High School challenged the novel that same year, while Caddo Parish (Louisiana) removed the novel from both its school libraries and required reading lists, charging that it contained racially offensive passages. The following year, the novel was challenged at Sevierville County (Tennessee) High School due to perceived racial slurs and the use of ungrammatical dialect.

The 1990s brought new challenges and continued antagonism to the novel. Citing derogatory references to African Americans, parents challenged its inclusion on the supplemental English reading list in Erie (Pennsylvania) High School in 1990. That same year, the novel was challenged as being racist in Plano (Texas) Independent School District.

In 1991, citing the repeated use of the word *nigger*, parents in Mesa (Arizona) Unified School District challenged inclusion of the novel in the curriculum and claimed that such language damaged the self-esteem of young African Americans. For the same reason, that year the novel was removed from the required reading list in the Terrebone Parish public schools in Houma, Louisiana. Also in 1991, it was temporarily removed from the Portage (Michigan) curriculum after African-American parents charged that the portrayal of Jim and other African Americans made their children "uncomfortable."

In 1992, the school superintendent of Kinston (North Carolina) School District removed the book from the middle school in the belief that the students were too young to read a work containing the word *nigger*. Concern with the same word, as well as additional "offensive and racist language," motivated a 1992 challenge to including the novel on the required reading list in Modesto (California) High School. In 1993, challengers charged in the Carlisle (Pennsylvania) school system that the racial slurs in the novel were offensive to both African-American and Caucasian students. In contrast to other areas, the Lewisville (Texas) school board retained the novel on school reading lists in 1994, despite challenges of its racism. The most comprehensive objection to the novel regarded its use in English classes at Taylor County (Butler, Georgia) High School in 1994, when challengers not only claimed that it contained racial slurs and improper grammar, but it also did not reject slavery.

Also in 1994, in Enid, Oklahoma, a group called the Southern Heights Ministerial Alliance challenged the novel as required reading in American literature classes and brought the issue to the textbook review committee. The committee recommended that the book be restricted to students taking advanced-placement American Literature classes, a move that the school board soundly rejected in a 7-0 vote. Instead, the board passed a resolution to keep the book in the curriculum and enacted a measure to require teacher training to be led by Harvard professor and African-American Twain scholar Jocelyn Chadwick.

In 2002, an African-American student in Portland, Oregon, challenged the use of the novel as a required reading and claimed that he was offended by the use of ethnic slurs in the novel. The board considered the challenge and voted to retain the novel.

In 2003, parents of students in the Community High School in Normal, Illinois, sophomore literature class challenged use of the novel in the curriculum. They asserted that the novel is degrading to African Americans. The school board considered the challenge and decided to retain the novel in the curriculum and to offer students an alternative. Students who do not feel comfortable reading *Adventures of Huckleberry Finn* are given the option of reading *The Chosen* by Chaim Potok.

In October 2003, an African-American student and her grandmother in Renton, Washington, complained to school officials that the novel degraded all African Americans and their culture. Calista Phair and Beatrice Clark objected to the use of the word *nigger*, and they contended that the book "reinforces institutional racism." The novel was not required reading, but it was on the supplemental reading list for approved assignments to 11th-grade students in the three high schools in the Renton district; thus, students who objected to being assigned the book could be excused from reading it and were permitted to select an alternate work. Phair and Clark demanded the removal of the work throughout the district. In response, school administrators ordered the book removed from the readings lists in the three high schools and asked teachers to stop teaching it until guidelines could be developed. The district formed a committee of language arts teachers, chaired by Ed Sheppard the district curriculum director, to work with the education chairman of the Seattle branch of the National Association for the Advancement of Colored People (NAACP) to develop guidelines for teaching the novel. The resulting one-half-inch thick book of guidelines was distributed to the teachers and posted on the Renton district Web site. The guidebook included information on the history of the objectionable word and explained the place of Huck Finn in the canon of Western literature, information bolstered by articles from educational journals and diverse sources instructing how to teach the novel. Roy Matheson, a Renton school district spokesperson, said that the district did not ever consider banning the book from the curriculum, because doing so would force the school district to consider eliminating such works as *BLACK BOY* by Richard Wright or *Narrative of the Life of Frederick Douglass, an American Slave*, which also contain the racial epithet. The novel was reinstated on the supplemental reading list.

The controversy over the N-word and the portrayal of African Americans in the novel has continued. In 2007, African-American parents of students attending St. Louis Park High School in Minneapolis challenged the mandatory reading of *Adventures of Huckleberry Finn* in a 10th-grade honors English class and asked the school to remove the novel from the required reading list. Parents Kenneth and Sylvia Gilbert, the main opponents of the requirement, claimed that they did not want the book banned from the school, but they did not want it to be required classroom reading. Mr. Gilbert told school officials that the novel is "a racial issue," and the use of the racial epithet "brings you to a lower level. . . . It makes children feel less equal in the classroom." In response to the parents' protests, a 12-member committee composed of parents, teachers, a community member, and a school administrator reviewed the request and reevaluated the book for classroom use. They determined that the novel should remain. Students at the high school actively opposed removal of the book. Some created posters saying "Save Huck Finn" and others posted a Web site that supported retention of the novel. In a letter to parents, St. Louis Park High School principal Robert Laney wrote that the committee acknowledged that some of the language in the novel is offensive but determined "the literary value of the book outweighed the negative aspect of the language employed." Parents appealed the decision, but the district retained the book as required reading.

The responses to complaints regarding the racial stereotyping and racial epithets in the novel have changed significantly in the last two decades. Rather than remove the book permanently—or for long periods of time—from the classroom or library until the furor has abated, school districts have chosen to place a hold on teaching the novel while assembling committees that are representative of the community to formulate plans to retain the work while making it an effective and acceptable teaching tool. A recent widely publicized challenge provides an example. In 2008, a group of African-American parents in Manchester, Connecticut, challenged the use of the novel as required reading in Manchester High School. The school administrators asked teachers to stop teaching the book until the district could devise a series of seminars that would provide them with the tools to deal with the issues of race before bringing the book back into the classroom. The seminars were presented with the assistance of Reverend John Selders, of the Amistad United Church of Christ, who worked with teachers to handle class discussions about the book. School administrators viewed the seminars as a means of putting the book into perspective and of providing the opportunity to "create a dialogue on race, white privilege, satire and stereotyping." The assistant school superintendent Anne Richardson praised the retention of the book as providing "a very good platform to talk about racial issues," and Manchester High School principal Kevin O'Donnell expressed the belief that the seminars would provide students "with a new opportunity to have those courageous conversations about race and all of the elements that surround race, as difficult as they might be." Reverend Selders was less expansive in his praise of the results of the committee and noted that some teachers "may need to do some more work," although he expressed optimism that the new approach to the novel would be beneficial and justified its retention.

In February 2011, NewSouth Books, a publisher based in Alabama, released a new and more politically correct edition of Twain's classic work in which the word *nigger* was replaced by *slave* and the word *Injun* by *Indian*. Auburn University professor Alan Gribben, who edited both *Adventures of Huckleberry Finn* and *The Adventures of Tom Sawyer* and combined both works into a single volume entitled *Mark Twain's Adventures of Tom Sawyer and Huckleberry Finn: The NewSouth Edition*, claimed in interviews with various news media that his work is not an attempt to censor Mark Twain. He said that he produced the edited version because he had become increasingly worried in recent years that Twain's works were being removed from reading lists in schools because of the 219 uses of the word *nigger* and other racial slurs and felt that his version would revive interest in teaching the work at the high school level.

In an interview with the *New York Times*, Gribben claimed that he had not changed the essential character of Twain's work. "I'm by no means sanitizing Mark Twain," he said. "The sharp social critiques are in there. The humor is intact. I just had the idea to get us away from obsessing about this one word, and just let the stories stand alone."

Reactions to the revised edition have been diverse. Some critics have seen the move as unconscionable censorship or bowdlerization, while others contend that the modifications to the novel will make it more accessible to a wider audience. To date, the planned print run is only 7,500 copies, and Gribben admits that no school districts have expressed plans to reintroduce the book into their curricula because of the revisions. The *New York Times* reported that NewSouth received a large number of negative e-mails after plans for the new edition were announced.

FURTHER READING

Bach, Deborah. "'Huck Finn' Back in Renton; School District Now Provides More Guidance to Teachers." *Seattle Post-Intelligencer*, March 17, 2004, p. B2.

Beam, Alex. "In Other Words . . . , Why Stop with Mark Twain's 'Huckleberry Finn'" *Boston Globe*, January 11, 2011, p. G23.

Bosman, Julie. "Publisher Tinkers with Twain." *New York Times*, January 5, 2011, p. A12.

Bradley, Julia T. "Censoring the School Library: Do Students Have the Right to Read?" *Connecticut Law Review* 10 (Spring 1978): 747–771.

Cloonan, Michele. "The Censorship of the Adventures of Huckleberry Finn." *Top of the News*, Winter 1984, pp. 191–194.

Geller, Evelyn. *Forbidden Books in American Public Libraries, 1876–1939: A Study in Cultural Change.* Westport, Conn.: Greenwood Press, 1984.

Greenlee, Steven. "Sanitized Huck Finn." *Boston Globe*, January 8, 2011, p. G 4.

Leider, Paula. "Does Huck Finn Belong in My Classroom? Reflections of Curricular Choice, Multicultural Education, and Diversity." *Multicultural Education* 13, no. 4 (Summer 2006): 49–50.

Nelson, Randy F. "Banned in Boston and Elsewhere." *The Almanac of American Letters.* Los Altos, Calif.: William Kaufman, 1981.

Newsletter on Intellectual Freedom (May 1969): 52; (July 1976): 87; (September 1976): 116; (November 1981): 162; (January 1982): 11, 18; (May 1982): 101; (July 1982): 126; (September 1982): 171; (January 1984): 11; (May 1984): 72; (July 1984): 121–122; (November 1984): 187; (January 1985): 38; (September 1988): 152–153; (November 1988): 201; (January 1989): 11; (March 1989): 43; (May 1989): 94; (January 1991): 17–18; (March 1991): 43–45, 64; (May 1991): 90–92; (July 1992): 126; (September 1992): 140; (May 1993): 73; (May 1994): 99–100; (March 1995): 42; (July 2000): 125; (January 2003): 11–12; (May 2004): 91; (January 2009): 22–3).

People For the American Way. *Attacks on the Freedom to Learn, 1990–91.* Washington, D.C.: People For the American Way, 1991.

Reichman, Henry. *Censorship and Selection: Issues and Answers for Schools.* Chicago: American Library Association; Arlington, Va.: American Association of School Administrators, 1993. A joint publication.

Teachout, Terry. "Unpleasant Truths." *Wall Street Journal,* January 16, 2011, p. A22.

Tucker, Cynthia. "The Error of Editing History." *The Atlanta Journal-Constitution,* January 16, 2011. p. A22.

Wascoe, Dan, and *Minneapolis Star Tribune.* "'N-word' Fight over Classic: Couple Want 'Huck Finn' Off Reading List." *The Record* (Bergen County, N.J.), March 23, 2007, p. A20.

Weathersby, Dorothy T. *Censorship of Literature Textbooks in Tennessee: A Study of the Commission, Publishers, Teachers, and Textbooks.* Ed.D. dissertation, University of Tennessee, 1975.

THE ADVENTURES OF SHERLOCK HOLMES

Author: Sir Arthur Conan Doyle
Original dates and places of publication: 1892, England; 1892, United States
Original publishers: George Newnes Ltd.; Harper & Row
Literary form: Short story collection

SUMMARY

The 12 short stories contained in the collection first appeared in *The Strand Magazine* during the 1880s: "A Scandal in Bohemia," "The Red-Headed League," "A Case of Identity," "The Boscombe Valley Mystery," "The Five Orange Pips," "The Man with the Twisted Lip," "The Blue Carbuncle," "The Adventure of the Speckled Band," "The Adventure of the Engineer's Thumb," "The Adventure of the Noble Bachelor," "The Adventure of the Beryl Coronet," and "The Adventure of the Copper Beeches." Narrated by John Watson, M.D., they relate the activities of Sherlock Holmes, who functions as a scientist of crime, approaching his adventures with the objectivity and caution of a man of science.

His creator, a physician like Watson, made Holmes the perfect Victorian hero who remains unmoved by emotion and invulnerable to passion. Single-minded in his devotion to the detection of crime, Holmes examines even the most minute piece of evidence, leaving nothing to chance. Thus he can tell by examining ashes the type of tobacco a man smoked, which leads to the place where such tobacco might be sold. Dust and soil particles at a crime site yield information about a region the criminal has recently visited. In his daily life, Holmes is condescending toward ordinary mortals, yet to carry out his investigations he often assumes disguises that allow him to appear among common men, as a tramp, opium addict, minister or other figure of daily life. A more damaging vice than condescension is Holmes's cocaine addiction, which he works hard to eliminate.

The main concern of many of the stories is to prevent scandal, an important preoccupation of Victorian England. All begin similarly, with Watson reminiscing about cases to date. Holmes may be performing chemical experiments or sitting in his study and smoking his pipe as he waits for the next client to appear. Once a client is shown to the rooms at 221B Baker Street, Holmes dazzles his visitor by using careful observations of the individual's clothing, speech, appearance and mannerisms to reveal aspects of the client's profession and personal background. The client then tells his story and Holmes gets to work.

The stories are influenced by the interests of their creator, and Doyle's early dabbling in spiritualism and interest in the occult enter several of the stories. These interests do not dominate the stories, but they become points of reference against which Holmes exhibits his own seemingly mysterious skills.

CENSORSHIP HISTORY

The censorship history of *The Adventures of Sherlock Holmes* is brief, and it is not based upon the main character's cocaine addiction, as might be expected. Rather, in 1929, the USSR banned the short story collection because references to the occult and spiritualism are made in several of the stories. The Soviet authorities viewed such references as contradictory to their ban on religion and dangerous to maintaining order.

FURTHER READING

Cox, Don Richard. *Arthur Conan Doyle*. New York: Frederick Ungar, 1985.

Lamond, John. *Arthur Conan Doyle: A Memoir*. Port Washington, N.Y.: Kennikat Press, 1972.

Orel, Harold, ed. *Critical Essays on Sir Arthur Conan Doyle*. New York: G. K. Hall, 1992.

Weil-Norden, P. *Sir Arthur Conan Doyle*. Centenary edition. Garden City, N.Y.: Doubleday & Company, 1959.

THE ADVENTURES OF TOM SAWYER

Author: Mark Twain (Samuel Langhorne Clemens)
Original date and place of publication: 1876, United States
Original publisher: Self-published
Literary form: Novel

SUMMARY

The novel is a first-person account of the life of young Tom Sawyer along the banks of the Mississippi before the Civil War.

When the novel begins, Tom is missing, and his Aunt Polly is worriedly searching for him. She is furious when she learns that he has been swimming all day instead of attending school. As punishment, Tom must whitewash a fence on Saturday, instead of playing as usual, but he tricks his friends into doing the job.

After Tom shows off "his" work on the fence, Aunt Polly agrees to let him play for the remainder of the day. Tom later spots Becky Thatcher and attracts her attention with flamboyant antics, earning a flower from her as his reward.

In catechism class the next morning, Tom receives a Bible for having enough tickets to indicate that he memorized 2,000 passages in the Bible. But Tom cheated and traded various items with friends in order to amass the correct number of tickets. When the Sunday School teacher asks him to answer a Scripture question, he is unable to do so. Later that morning, Tom creates chaos in church when his pinch bug attacks a wandering dog.

On Monday, Tom once again attempts to avoid school, but Aunt Polly forces him to go. On the way, Tom meets Huckleberry Finn, and the two plan to take the corpse of a cat to the cemetery at midnight in order to cure warts. Once Tom reaches school, he is automatically punished for his tardiness and made to sit in the female section of the schoolroom. Tom sits next to Becky, but she acts repelled by his presence. As soon as they can, Tom and Joe Harper leave and take the rest of the day off.

That night Huck and Tom go to the cemetery with the cat. While there, the two boys see Dr. Robinson, Injun Joe, and Muff Potter unearthing a recently interred body. The three men argue and struggle, leaving Muff Potter unconscious, after which Injun Joe stabs Dr. Robinson to death and leaves. The frightened boys swear never to tell anyone about the murder, even when they hear the next day that Injun Joe has named Muff Potter as Dr. Robinson's slayer.

Tom, Huck, and Joe Harper decide to become pirates for a short while, so they run away to Jackson's Island. Days go by, and the boys continue to enjoy their carefree, adventurous life, while the townspeople frantically search for them. After their efforts prove fruitless, the townspeople legally declare the boys dead and plan a memorial service. On a brief return to his house to leave his Aunt Polly a note, Tom hears that there will be church services the following Sunday for the repose of the three boys' souls. The three guests of honor interrupt the services and casually stroll down the main aisle of the church.

The boys agree to retire from piracy and to return home. Back in school, Tom continues his courtship of Becky, finally winning her admiration by taking the blame and the punishment for something that she does. Tom and the others are able to have their revenge when, on the last day of school, Tom humiliates the schoolmaster by exposing his bald head to the entire school.

When Muff Potter is placed on trial for the murder of Dr. Robinson, Tom is called as a surprise witness. He tells the court that it was not Muff Potter but Injun Joe who ruthlessly murdered Dr. Robinson, and Injun Joe escapes the court and imprisonment by jumping through a window and fleeing.

Days later, Tom and Huck are exploring an abandoned house when two men enter, one of whom is Injun Joe disguised as a Spaniard. The men take gold and silver coins to use at a tavern, and the boys overhear Injun Joe state that he isn't going to leave the area until he can take revenge upon the boys.

At a picnic a few days later, Tom and Becky become lost in McDougal's cave. Later that night, Huck overhears Injun Joe plot to attack the Widow Douglas in retaliation for a whipping that he received from her late husband. After Huck informs Mr. Jones of the plot, Injun Joe and his companion are quickly driven off. Huck then becomes ill, but the Widow Douglas takes care of him.

The townspeople discover that Tom and Becky are missing and search for the two children. In the cave, Tom sees Injun Joe, who is in hiding. The two children finally find a back opening to the cave and return to town. After hearing about Tom and Becky's ordeal, Judge Thatcher orders the cave sealed, unintentionally trapping Injun Joe. When Tom learns that the cave has been sealed, he tells Judge Thatcher that Injun Joe is inside, and Injun Joe's body is later found near the cave entrance.

Tom and Huck return to the cave to recover $12,000 of treasure, which is divided between the boys and invested for them. Tom returns to live with Aunt Polly, and Huck is taken into the Douglas home, to be educated in the moral lifestyle by the Widow Douglas. He agrees to this ordeal and seems placated as long as he can join Tom's newly established robber gang.

CENSORSHIP HISTORY

The novel was censored from its first publication, although it has not provoked as much controversy as Twain's later novel, ADVENTURES OF HUCKLEBERRY FINN. In 1876, Brooklyn (New York) Public Library banned the book from the children's room; that same year, Denver (Colorado) Public Library removed it from the library shelves. Five decades later, in 1930, guards at the USSR border confiscated the novel, along with *Adventures of Huckleberry Finn*.

The novel proceeded to earn a reputation as an American literary classic and remained unchallenged until 1985, when education officials in London removed the novel from all school libraries after determining that the book was "racist" and "sexist." In 1990, the novel was challenged, along with

Adventures of Huckleberry Finn, as being racist in the Plano (Texas) Independent School District. In the O'Fallon (Illinois) schools in 1992, parents challenged the inclusion of the book on the required reading list and charged that the use of the word *nigger* was degrading and offensive to black students. They won the right to request that an alternative reading choice be offered. In 1994, parents of seventh-grade students in the West Chester (Pennsylvania) schools claimed that the book contained an abundance of racially charged language, and it was removed from the curriculum.

FURTHER READING

Burress, Lee. *Battle of the Books: Literary Censorship in the Public Schools, 1950–1985.* Metuchen, N.J.: Scarecrow Press, 1989.

Geller, Evelyn. *Forbidden Books in American Public Libraries, 1876–1939: A Study in Cultural Change.* Westport, Conn.: Greenwood Press, 1984.

Newsletter on Intellectual Freedom (September 1985): 156; (January 1991): 18; (March 1991): 45–46; (May 1991): 92; (May 1992): 97; (September 1994): 152.

ALICE'S ADVENTURES IN WONDERLAND

Author: Lewis Carroll (Reverend Charles Dodgson)
Original date and place of publication: 1865, England
Original publisher: Macmillan
Literary form: Novel

SUMMARY

Lewis Carroll's *Alice's Adventures in Wonderland* began as an amusing story created especially for Alice Liddell, the young daughter of the author's Oxford colleague, Henry Liddell; it first appeared as a handwritten manuscript entitled *Alice's Adventures Under Ground.* Although the work is filled with numerous parodies of his age, puns, mathematical puzzles, and turns of phrase, contemporary interpretation has concerned psychoanalytic and allegorical meaning. In addition, much attention has been paid to the author's numerous and intense friendships with young girls. The sequel, *Through the Looking Glass and What Alice Found There*, was published in 1871.

Set in Victorian England, the story relates the dream of a curious young girl named Alice who dozes off and, in her dream, catches sight of a white rabbit, whom she follows into the strange and exciting world of Wonderland. In this world, ordinary logic fails to apply, and Alice can find little pattern or order in the events that befall her. She finds a key to open a necessary door, but she is too large to fit through the doorway. A magic elixir in a bottle marked "Drink Me" shrinks her to the correct size, but she becomes too small to reach the key. Alice consumes a cake marked "Eat Me," hoping that it will make her grow a little. Instead, her neck grows until her head reaches the ceiling, as she cries large teardrops. As she attempts to come to terms with the chaotic environment, Alice converses with numerous animals. The White Rabbit reappears and drops his fan and gloves in fear, as Alice sits in a pool of her own tears and meets a parrot-like creature named a Lory, with whom she discusses the proper way to dry off. A mouse attempts to dry everyone off by interpreting a "dry" history of the Archduke of Canterbury, and the Dodo suggests that they have a Caucus-Race in which the contestants run for however long and far they wish, stop whenever they like, and all win.

The surroundings become even more chaotic as the White Rabbit reappears and orders Alice to retrieve a fan and pair of gloves from his home. Alice drinks from a bottle marked "Drink Me" and immediately grows to an enormous size, leading the White Rabbit to scold Alice and attempt to evict her from the house by ordering a serpent gardener to forcefully move her. The serpent and a lizard, the rabbit's servant, hit Alice with pebbles, but the stones become cakes as they hit the ground. Alice eats one and shrinks, then runs off in fear and finds herself under a mushroom on which a caterpillar reclines. The caterpillar tells her the secret of the mushroom before she leaves, which is that one side will make her taller and the other, smaller. She nibbles the magic mushrooms for a while and learns to control their enlarging and reducing effects.

Alice next meets the Duchess, who is nursing an infant, and the famous Cheshire Cat. When Alice makes a snide comment that offends the Duchess, she sentences Alice to be beheaded. The Duchess tosses the baby to Alice, and the baby immediately is transformed into a pig, which runs off squealing. Alice focuses on the Cheshire Cat, but he appears to speak in riddles.

Alice wanders to the home of the March Hare, who is having a tea party with the Dormouse and Mad Hatter. The tea party is dominated by horrible puns and insane behavior, and Alice leaves, only to find herself in the original hallway with the glass table. She eats more of the mushrooms and shrinks to a size that allows her to enter a garden where she meets the King and Queen of Hearts, who look like oversize playing cards, playing croquet. Alice offends the Queen and is sentenced to death, along with many of the other cards. The Queen then orders all of the croquet players except Alice to be taken away and executed, thus leaving the King, herself, and Alice to play for the remainder of the afternoon.

The Knave of Hearts is brought before the Queen, accused of stealing tarts. After emphatically denying this heinous crime, he is proved guilty by "solid" evidence and executed. This upsets Alice, who pleads with the Queen, then suddenly finds herself back in her world, where she awakens and contemplates the dream of Wonderland.

CENSORSHIP HISTORY

Despite the concerns raised in the author's own time regarding his apparent lack of maturity and the questions of possible sexual impropriety, the novel has not been challenged for either of these reasons. The sole ban occurred in 1931, when the governor of Hunan Province in China ruled that the book was unacceptable because it portrayed animals using human language. The censors asserted that "it was disastrous to put animals and human beings on the same level," because it showed disrespect for humans.

FURTHER READING

Bjork, Christina. *The Other Alice: The Story of Alice Liddell and Alice in Wonderland.* New York: R&S Books, 1993.
Cohen, Morton N. *Lewis Carroll: A Biography.* New York: Alfred A. Knopf, 1995.
Lennon, Florence Becker. *The Life of Lewis Carroll.* New York: Dover Publications, 1972.
Wullschlager, Jackie. *Inventing Wonderland: The Lives and Fantasies of Lewis Carroll, Edward Lear, J. M. Barrie, Kenneth Grahame and A. A. Milne.* New York: Free Press, 1995.

THE AMBOY DUKES

Author: Irving Shulman
Original date and place of publication: 1947, United States
Original publisher: Bantam Books
Literary form: Novel

SUMMARY

The novel, which gained a large following among high school students when it was first published, offers a sordid and realistic look at the sad and aimless lives of young men growing up in the slums of a big American city during World War II. Left largely to fend for themselves and to create their own moral code, as they see little of their parents who work in the large defense plants, the boys develop a herd instinct that leads them to form a gang, the Amboy Dukes. Although the novel was written in the mid-1940s, the bleak portrait of slum life and the pervading sense of hopelessness transcend the time period and apply as well to today. The actions of the members of the Dukes, and the reactions of others around them, make them the precursors of the highly popularized "juvenile delinquents" of books and movies of the 1950s.

The author explains the elements of gang life through each of his characters, and he portrays these unsupervised young misfits as being as much the victims of their environment and of society in general as they are of callous families and indifferent social institutions. To portray the gang members realistically, Shulman peppers their speech heavily with vulgarities. They use crude terminology in referring to relations with women. Their appearance and attitude are provocative, but the author also includes incidents in which individual adolescent gang members suffer harassment from the police as well as from school officials, with little hope of recourse. The lives of teenagers are presented in a sympathetic manner, with an attempt at gritty reality, and the author offers a strong indictment of the conditions that lead these boys to crime and brutality.

Despite his empathy with members of the Dukes, the author graphically portrays the toll of their abandonment by established society, and the subsequent formation of their own gang society, on both the boys and those with whom they come into contact. Robberies, fighting, muggings, and other crimes pervade the novel. In one episode, the gang members pay a girl to have sex with all of them, then forcibly try to take their money back from her. The novel ends with no solutions to the problems it exposes. There are no happy endings for members of the Amboy Dukes.

CENSORSHIP HISTORY

The novel was severely criticized from the outset and blamed for promoting delinquency among poor young slum dwellers. In 1949, the book was challenged as obscene in Brantford, Ontario (Canada), but Judge D. J. Cowan cleared the bookseller and the book of obscenity charges when the case came to trial. That same year, local authorities in Milwaukee, Detroit, and Newark (New Jersey) challenged sales of the book, claiming that it was obscene, but no formal charges were lodged.

In 1952, the Gathings Committee Report criticized the book for contributing to juvenile delinquency, a conclusion that made the novel a favorite target of attempted but unsuccessful censorship in the 1950s. In a statement to the Gathings Committee, Judge James V. Mulholland of the New York Domestic Relations Court supported restriction of the novel and stated that two recent cases involving juveniles, one a boy who viciously attacked several other children and the other a 14-year-old girl who had committed incest, could be directly linked to the influence of the book. In 1954, the novel was placed on the disapproved list of the National Organization for Decent Literature.

FURTHER READING

Burress, Lee. *Battle of the Books: Literary Censorship in the Public Schools, 1950–1985.* Metuchen, N.J.: Scarecrow Press, 1989.

Loth, David. *The Erotic in Literature.* New York: Dorset Press, 1961.

Select Committee on Pornographic Materials, House of Representatives, 82nd Congress. *Report of the Committee on Pornographic Materials.* House Report No. 2510. 1952. (Known as the Gathings Committee Report because E. C. Gathings was chairman).

THE AMERICAN HERITAGE DICTIONARY OF THE ENGLISH LANGUAGE

Author: American Heritage Publishing Company
Original date and place of publication: 1969, United States
Original publishers: American Heritage Publishing Company and
   Houghton Mifflin
Literary form: Dictionary

SUMMARY

The American Heritage Dictionary of the English Language is a comprehensive lexicon containing over 170,000 entries. The words defined range from the common and conventional to slang and technical jargon. Many of the entries give word origins, as well as meanings, along with sample phrases to show the different meanings in context. Entries seek to explain all connotations of the word.

CENSORSHIP HISTORY

In June 1976, a group of parents who were members of People for Better Education complained that *The American Heritage Dictionary* was obscene and demanded that all copies be removed from classrooms in Anchorage, Alaska. They cited as offensive the entry for "bed," defined as a noun meaning "a place for lovemaking" and "a marital relationship with its rights and intimacies," and as a verb meaning "to have sexual intercourse with." They also objected to "knocker," "balls," and "nuts" being defined with their slang meanings. The assistant superintendent headed a review committee that examined the dictionary and approved it unanimously. In reporting the committee findings, the assistant superintendent stated that the dictionary provided children with the opportunity to look up the designated words, which "helped diffuse excitement and curiosity about them." The committee further defended *The American Heritage Dictionary* as being "an excellent reference for advanced students, especially for scientific terms." The school board ignored the defense and, citing their list of definitions taken from the dictionary, voted to remove it from the schools.

In September 1976, parents in Cedar Lake, Indiana, complained that 70 or 80 words in the dictionary were obscene or otherwise inappropriate for high school students to see, and they demanded that *The American Heritage Dictionary* be removed from the schools. The word "bed" was again the most frequently criticized entry. The school board voted to remove the dictionary from the high school, and the board president refused to listen to the protests of teachers, whom he characterized as "unqualified to select learning materials." In mid-November 1976, the school board reversed its decision by a 3-2 vote and allowed the dictionary to be used in the senior

English classrooms. This action was taken after counsel advised the board that the dictionary could not be considered obscene. In April 1977, 24 parents of junior high school students in Eldon, Missouri, signed a complaint in which they listed 39 words in *The American Heritage Dictionary* that were objectionable. One parent was quoted on page 1 of the *St. Louis Post-Dispatch* for April 18, 1977, as stating, "If people learn words like that it ought to be where you and I learned it—in the street and in the gutter." The school board agreed with the parents and voted to remove the dictionary from the junior high school. In later cases, the school library in Folsom, California, removed the dictionary from its shelves after parents issued complaints, and the dictionary was challenged but retained in the Churchill County, Nevada, school libraries in 1993. That same year, the Washoe County, Nevada, school district removed the dictionary from classrooms, then reinstated it a short time later.

A more extensive case of dictionary censorship occurred in Texas in 1976. *The American Heritage Dictionary* was one of five dictionaries recommended by the State Textbook Committee that the Texas State Textbook Commission banned because they contained definitions that the commission viewed as obscene. The other four were *The Doubleday Dictionary, The Random House College Dictionary*, revised edition; *Webster's New World Dictionary of the English Language*, college edition; and *Webster's Seventh New Collegiate Dictionary*. The move was spearheaded by Mel and Norma Gabler, who operated Educational Research Analysts, a tax-exempt organization that initiated local censorship efforts and sent out textbook reviews pointing out what they viewed as questionable material. They had numerous supporters, among them the Texas Society of the Daughters of the American Revolution, whose textbook chairperson stated in a Bill of Particulars to the Texas commissioner of education, "Reviewer is shocked that a supposedly reputable publisher would offer for adoption a book which is debasing the English language. Students need the basics rather than sub-standard language." Her remarks were in reference to *Webster's New World Dictionary of the American Language*. In addition to citing the obvious words, such as "cunnilingus," "fart," "fuck," "piss," "screw," and "shit," the report also noted that the following words in the five dictionaries were objectionable; the reason cited for the objection appears in parentheses: "across-the-board" (betting on horse racing in Texas was illegal); "Arab" (incomplete definition); "ass" (unnecessary); "attempt" (ties word into subject of murder); "banana republic" (insulting to Latins); "bawdy house" (unnecessary); "bed" (Why is sexual intercourse mentioned?); "the big house" (slang, unnecessary); "block busting" (inaccurate and unnecessary); "boob" (a female breast); "brain" (denotes violence); "bucket" (slang for buttocks); "butt" (slang for the buttocks); "cherry" (the hymen; virginity); "clap" (slang for a brothel and gonorrhea); "coke" (slang for cocaine); "crocked" (slang for intoxicated); "deflower" (to cause loss of virginity); "dyke" (a female homosexual); "fag"/"faggot" (slang for male homosexual); "fairy" (slang for male homosexual); "gay" (slang for male homosexual); "G-string" (slang, unnecessary); "head" (slang for one who uses or is addicted to a drug); "hooker" (slang for prostitute); "horny" (slang for sexually excited); "hot" (slang for sexually excited); "john" (slang for a customer of a prostitute); "john" (slang for toilet); "keister"/"keaster" (slang for buttocks or rump); "kinky" (slang for sexually abnormal); "knock" (slang for to make pregnant); "queer" (homosexual; a contemptuous term); "rubber" (slang for a condom); "shack"/"shack up with" (slang for to share living quarters with one's lover); "slut" (a dirty, untidy woman; slattern; a sexually immoral woman); "tail" (slang for the buttocks); "tit" (a breast). In efforts to sell their books, the publishers of the dictionaries wrote to the Texas commissioner of education to defend the inclusion of these words, citing their appearance in classic literature and the Bible, as well as highly reputable contemporary books and publications. Despite their efforts, the dictionaries were placed on the "no-purchase" list.

FURTHER READING

Hechivger, Fred M. "Censorship Rises in the Nation's Public Schools." *New York Times*, January 3, 1984, p. C-7.

Hung, Pham Thien. "Parents Protest Textbooks." In *Censorship and Education*, edited by Eli M. Oboler, 135–139. New York: H. W. Wilson Company, 1981.

Kakutani, Michiko. "The Famed Will Gather to Read the Forbidden." *New York Times*, April 5, 1982, p. C-11.

Massie, Dorothy C. "Censorship in the Schools: Something Old and Something New." *Today's Education*, November 1980, pp. 56–60.

Newsletter on Intellectual Freedom (September 1976): 115–116; (November 1976): 145; (January 1977): 7; (July 1977): 101; (March 1983): 39; (March 1991): 71.

AM I BLUE?

Editor: Marion Dane Bauer
Original date and place of publication: 1994, United States
Original publisher: HarperCollins
Literary form: Short story anthology

SUMMARY

Am I Blue? was the first anthology of young adult fiction to contain stories devoted solely to gay and lesbian themes. The 16 stories are all written by notable young adult or children's fiction writers, and all feature at least one character who is gay or lesbian. The intention of the anthology was to provide adolescents with the realization that they are not alone, unique, or abnormal in their sexual orientation, and the works included all provide readers with positive and credible gay role models. The stories center on themes of coming to terms with homosexuality and, as such, contain diverse views of love, coming of age, adventure, and self-discovery. As editor Marion Dane Bauer writes in her introduction, while the stories will help those young people who are struggling with their sexual identity, they will also provide those who are firmly heterosexual with a means of understanding what others are going through. She writes, "The power of fiction is that it gives us, as readers, the opportunity to move inside another human being, to look out through that person's eyes, hear with her ears, think with his thoughts, feel with her feelings."

The stories in this anthology contain a fairy godfather ("Am I Blue?"), a gay father, and the tender awkwardness of teenage boys bonding ("Holding"), as well as a story that takes place in Vietnam ("In the Tunnels"), another that examines the world of 1951 ("Three Mondays in July"), and still another that takes place in a mythical kingdom called The Dales where women live together in communities ("Blood Sister"). The authors of the stories are homosexual and heterosexual, and their goals in writing these stories are to present realistic human beings experiencing life.

Included in this anthology are the following stories: "Am I Blue?" by Bruce Coville, "We Might as Well Be Strangers" by M. E. Kerr, "Winnie and Tommy" by Francesca Lia Block, "Slipping Away" by Jacqueline Woodson, "The Honorary Shepherds" by Gregory Maguire, "Running" by Ellen Howard, "Three Mondays in July" by James Cross Giblin, "Parents' Night" by Nancy Garden, "Michael's Little Sister" by C. S. Adler, "Supper" by Leslie Newman, "Holding" by Lois Lowry, "Blood Sister" by Jane Yolen, "Hands" by Jonathan London, "50% Chance of Lightning" by Cristina Salat, "In the Tunnels" by William Sleator, and "Dancing Backwards" by Marion Dane Bauer.

CENSORSHIP HISTORY

Am I Blue? became the source of controversy in 2004 in Solon, Iowa, after seven parents with children in the school district filed complaints about use of the book in the middle school classroom and demanded that middle school teacher Susan Protheroe cease using any books in her classroom that contain gay, lesbian, or transgender characters. Only one of the parents had a child in Protheroe's classroom, but the group complained that *Am I Blue?* "has no instructional value for her class" and asserted that "it is about controversial areas that should be discussed within families, and it is not appropriate for middle school–aged students." The parents also condemned the book as promoting bias and prejudice, arguing that the book "promotes intolerance through use of slanderous and racist terms, perpetuates gay stereotypes, and promotes homosexuality." One father told a reporter for the *Iowa City Press-Citizen* that "the material directly contradicts and undermines the beliefs and teachings of our faith. It introduces a very adult situation and mature subject to an inappropriately young audience. It is likely to introduce sexual confusion to a group of children who are just becoming sexually aware."

During a meeting held in late October 2004, parents presented their complaints to the nine-member Materials Review Committee (MRC), which by school board policy has the function of reviewing materials that have met with objections from parents or from other school district residents. The meeting was attended by more than 100 people, mostly parents. As the local newspaper reported the next day, parents were extremely upset by the existence of the book in the curriculum. One parent accused the school district of being "disrespectful of parents" and condemned the school administration for not having told parents the content of the stories in the book. Another parent quoted by the local paper claimed that the stories in the book promote a "gay agenda" and that they "advocate promiscuity and gay fantasies." Several former and current students of the Solon Middle School spoke in support of the book and requested that parents should have "respect for their innate intelligence to be able to deal with controversial material in a mature manner." Eight of the nine committee members voted to retain the book in the eighth-grade curriculum, but the board as a whole also recommended that the district institute a policy of informing parents of controversial materials before each school year. The school board accepted the recommendations of the MRC, and one board member told parents who vowed they would appeal the decision: "If your goal out there is to take your personal views and instill them in your children and also force them on all children, then the road to the state school board is open to you in Des Moines."

FURTHER READING

Bello, Deidre. "Parents Want Gay Literature Removed." *Iowa City Press-Citizen*, October 23, 2004.
———. "School Group OKs Gay Literature." *Iowa City Press-Citizen*, October 29, 2004.
———. "Solon Debates Class Material." *Iowa City Press-Citizen*, October 27, 2004.
"Book Ban Stopped." *The Advocate*, December 21, 2004, p. 14.
Broz, William J. "Defending *Am I Blue?*" *Journal of Adolescent & Adult Literacy* 45 (February 2002): 340–350.

AND STILL I RISE

Author: Maya Angelou (Marguerite Johnson)
Original date and place of publication: 1978, United States
Original publisher: Random House
Literary form: Poetry collection

SUMMARY

And Still I Rise is a collection of 31 autobiographical poems that celebrate life and the survival of the human spirit. The subject matter ranges from the author's proud examination of her powers to attract men, through references to the range of roles that women, especially African-American women, have been forced to assume throughout time. Angelou speaks in rhyme and rhythm as they suit the specific subject of a poem, and the diction ranges from the lofty speech of a sermon to the vernacular of a welfare mother challenging the system. She challenges readers in her references to rape as well as in her frank statements regarding exuberant sexuality.

In "Remembrance," the poet states that "mystery rapes my reason," and she speaks of feeling melancholy after a lover leaves her bed, "when only the smell of your love lingers between my breasts." The harshly analytical "Men" speaks of the "breasts of a young girl" and the betrayal of the young persona, "Fifteen years old and starving for them [men]," who learns that the soft romanticism of the initial encounter will result in her body being "slammed shut. Forever." The soft caresses give way to the unpleasant physical reality that "it is your juice that runs down their legs." In "Lady Luncheon Club," a male speaker at a woman's club attempts to relate to his bored audience as "he sighs for youthful death and rape at ten," while the mother in "Momma Welfare Roll" is "too fat to whore."

On a more positive note, Angelou celebrates her sexuality and that of all African-American women in "Through the Inner City to the Suburbs" as she speaks of "the juicy secrets of black thighs." This celebration of the self reaches its peak in "Still I Rise," in which the author challenges readers, "Does my sexiness upset you? / Does it come as a surprise / That I dance like I've got diamonds / At the meeting of my thighs?"

CENSORSHIP HISTORY

And Still I Rise has been challenged both for its language and for the "suggestive sexuality" contained in many of the poems. In 1982, parents at Northside High School in Lafayette, Louisiana, demanded that the book be withdrawn from the high school library because of its references to rape and sexual activity, but the book was retained. In 1987, a Wake County High School parent group approached the school board in Raleigh, North Carolina, and protested that the work was unsuitable to be required reading for junior-level English classes. Among their concerns were the mentions of rape and the references to the breasts of young girls and to their sexual awareness. Critics also protested that several of the poems exhibited a "bitterness and hatred toward whites." The board sided with the parents and removed the work from the required list. Protests by parents in Longview (Washington) School District in 1987 resulted in the temporary removal of the collection from high school reading lists until the school board could consider claims that "some students could be harmed by its graphic language." The book was retained on the reading list, but students were provided numerous alternative reading choices.

FURTHER READING

Kallen, Stuart A. *Maya Angelou: Woman of Words, Deeds, and Dreams.* Minneapolis: Abdo and Daughters, 1993.
Newsletter on Intellectual Freedom (May 1982): 83; (May 1987): 91; (September 1987): 195.
Pettit, Jayne. *Maya Angelou: Journey of the Heart.* New York: Lodester Books, 1996.
Spain, Valerie. *Meet Maya Angelou.* New York: Random House, 1995.

AND TANGO MAKES THREE

Authors: Justin Richardson and Peter Parnell; illustrated by Henry Cole
Original date and place of publication: 2005, United States
Original publisher: Simon & Schuster Children's Books
Literary form: Children's picture book

SUMMARY

And Tango Makes Three is a charming children's picture book based on the true story of two chinstrap penguins living in the Central Park Zoo who adopt a rejected egg, work together to hatch it, and raise the little girl chick together. The book's watercolor illustrations depict the activities of the two adult penguins, whom the zookeepers admit are "a little different." Roy and Silo do everything together. They cuddle, they play together, they bow to each other, and they look lovingly at each other. "They sang to each other. And swam together. Wherever Roy went, Silo went too."

The two male penguins also share a nest that they realize is very different from the nests of other penguin couples, because their nest is empty. They watch as female penguins sit on their nests and hatch fertilized eggs, and they wait futilely for their nest to fill. The illustrations portray the two bewildered penguins craning their necks toward their nest, which was "nice, but a little empty." After a long while, they drag an egg-sized rock to their nest and try to hatch it, but they are unsuccessful.

The zookeeper watches as Roy and Silo try desperately to hatch the rock, caring for it and keeping it warm, and he sees their frustration and sadness when they are unsuccessful. Once he realizes what they have been trying to do, he helps them. He finds a female penguin with two fertilized eggs, one that she is ignoring, and places the egg in Roy and Silo's nest. The two immediately tend to the egg, taking turns to keep it warm and safe, until their penguin girl chick emerges to greet the two loving fathers who "knew just what to do." The zookeeper gives the baby penguin her name, "We'll call her Tango, because it takes two to make a Tango." The illustrations both on the cover and in the book show the happy family of three, the two loving male penguins and their downy chick Tango, "the only penguin in the Central Park Zoo with two daddies."

CENSORSHIP HISTORY

And Tango Makes Three was the most frequently challenged book in the United States in 2006, and its presence in school and public libraries continues to create controversy. Parents demanding its removal have labeled the book "brainwashing" and condemned what one parent in Lodi, California, characterized as its "homosexual story line that has been sugarcoated with cute penguins." The president of the California-based Campaign for Children and Families, Randy Thomasson, told a *Los Angeles Times* reporter that "The huge majority of parents would avoid this book if they knew it was brainwashing their children to support and experiment with homosexual behavior." Marketed toward children ages 4 through 8, the book has also received extensive praise from educators and parents who endorse its role in opening up a discussion of diverse lifestyles and who view it in a positive light. Christine Jenkins, associate professor at the Graduate School of Library and Information Science at the University of Illinois, asserted in an interview with a reporter for the *St. Louis Post-Dispatch*, "It's different from many other gay-themed children's books because it was published by the mainstream press, and homosexuality isn't a source of conflict." Instead, "The characters are just gay and living their lives. The plot doesn't grapple with being homosexual as do many books for youths of the same nature."

In 2006, parents of students attending Shiloh Elementary School in Shiloh, Illinois, questioned the "appropriateness of the subject matter" and asked school officials to move the book from the regular shelves in the school library to a restricted section "for mature issues." Lilly Del Pinto, the parent who first complained, told school officials that she was surprised by the content. "When it came to the point where the zookeeper saw that the penguins were in love I redirected [my daughter]. That was the end of the story for her." Del Pinto and "a group of like-minded parents" approached the school board and asked to have the book removed to a separate shelf that required parental permission before checkout. School Superintendent Jennifer Filyaw opposed the plan but did concede that "parents could restrict their children from checking out certain titles, and this request would appear when the librarian scans the student's card."

The book did not fare as well that same year in two Rolling Hills Consolidated Library branches in Savannah and St. Joseph, Missouri, after two parents expressed concern about its content. The library director Barbara Read moved the book from the children's fiction to the children's nonfiction section after having read the book and "consulted with zoologists about penguin behavior." The American Library Association's *Newsletter on Intellectual Freedom* reported in its May 2006 issue that, despite Read's claim that she moved the book because it tells a true story, she originally told a local newspaper that she had reshelved *And Tango Makes Three* in juvenile nonfiction because "Given that patrons rarely browse the nonfiction section, there was less of a chance that the book would 'blindside' someone."

In December 2006, Peter Gorman, the superintendent of schools in Charlotte, North Carolina, ordered the district school libraries to remove the book after several parents voiced concerns and after he received an e-mail from Republican county commissioner Bill James. The commissioner, who had read an article online about the book, told a reporter, "I am opposed to any book that promotes a homosexual lifestyle to elementary school students as normal." James contacted the school superintendent and on November 30, 2006, top school officials sent a memo to principals and media specialists in the district explaining the decision to ban the book. "First, it is a picture book that focuses on homosexuality. Second, we did not feel that such information was vital to primary students. Next, we did not believe the book would stimulate growth in ethical standards, and the book is too controversial." Parents who opposed the ban placed pressure on school officials to reconsider their decision and to let a committee review the decision, but the book would remain inaccessible until the committee had reached a decision and their recommendation would be accepted by the school officials.

In 2007, Johanna Habeisen, a school librarian in Southwick, Massachusetts, received an intimidating letter from her principal Kimberley Saso after a substitute teacher took *And Tango Makes Three* to Saso and questioned its appropriateness. In her letter, Principal Saso warned Habeisen against use of the book. "Hopefully you will take this matter seriously and refrain from disseminating information that supports alternative styles of living. Further infractions may result in discipline up to and including suspension and/or termination of employment." *School Library Journal* reported that Saso considered the book "questionable for young readers." She said, "I'm not against alternate lifestyle. I'd love that to be available for counselors that work with families that maybe have this situation. But in this society here, in this town anyways, I don't know if it's our job to expose children." Ms. Habeisen said in the same article that after the challenge to *And Tango Makes Three*, she began "pulling everything that had any reference to families with two moms and dads." She remarked that the irony was not lost on her that such a challenge could occur in Massachusetts, a state in which same-sex marriage has been legal since 2004. In March 2007, the *Newsletter on Intellectual Freedom* reported that the Charlotte-Mecklenburg school district received extensive negative international news coverage after the ban. After the reporters working for the *Charlotte Observer* questioned the ban, Superintendent Gorman returned copies of the book to the school libraries and determined that "the book will be reviewed only if parents ask for its removal."

Parents have had strong negative reactions to the book that are not always shared by school and library officials. In April 2007, Stephanie Bramasco, the parent of a 17-month-old child in Lodi, California, spoke at a public meeting and asked the Lodi Public Library board of directors to remove *And Tango Makes Three* after she admitted that she did not check the book out but "had a stronger urge to present the issue to the board of directors than her friend did." Bramasco charged that the illustration of the two adult penguins and the baby penguin on the book cover was deceptive because it "does not indicate the adult penguins are a same-sex couple." She further admitted that she "struggles with the idea of explaining to her 17-month-old the reasons why two male penguins would be unable to hatch an egg on their own or why two male penguins would have such an intimate relationship together." In a 4-1 vote, the library board of directors refused the request to ban the book.

Parents in Chico, California, in 2009 complained that *And Tango Makes Three* is offensive, and three challenged shelving of the book in the library among picture books and easy-to-read children's literature. After the district received formal complaints from parents at two elementary schools in the Chico Unified School District, officials formed a review committee composed of parents, teachers, librarians, and school administrators, which decided unanimously to retain the books on their current shelves. Also in 2009, in Prince Frederick, Maryland, parents complained to the Calvert County Board of Library Trustees and asked that it be removed. Beth Bubser, a parent who filed a formal complaint, expressed concern that there "is no warning on the book that it is about same-sex parents." The library board reviewed the complaint and the book and decided to keep the book in the children's section, a decision that Bubser and three other mothers appealed. The women expressed dismay that the book would remain in the library and "expressed concerns about their young children being exposed to information contrary to their values, such as homosexuality." Patricia Hoffman, the library director, was supported in her decision by library trustees who concluded that the job of a library is to disseminate information and not "take the role of a parent." As library trustee Laura Holbrook stated about segregating books such as *And Tango Makes Three*, such actions would be the equivalent of passing value judgments of same-sex families and "would censor what readers could easily find in the library."

In Ankeny, Iowa, school board members voted 6-1 to keep the book in circulation at two elementary school libraries. At the same meeting, the board also voted to develop a new process for selecting materials for the school libraries. Controversy began in the school district when a kindergarten child checked out the book from the East Elementary School library, where it was in open circulation. Parents Cindy and James Dacus asked the school board to place the book in "a parents-only section" and argued that it "normalizes homosexuality for children who are too young to understand the risky lifestyle." The challenge attracted the attention of national advocacy groups that sent letters to the district, urging officials to keep the book available to students. Dr. Justin Richardson, a coauthor of the book, expressed skepticism about the suggestion made by Ankeny school superintendent Matthew Wendt and the school board to institute a new process for selecting school library materials. While admitting that he did not know the superintendent's intentions, Richardson told a reporter for the *Des Moines Register*, "It's more troubling to think a school might screen out a book because a parent might complain about it in the future. That could really limit the kinds of books that children have access to."

FURTHER READING

"'And Tango Makes Three' Prompts Serious Challenge in Massachusetts School." *School Library Journal*. Available online. URL: http://www.schoollibraryjournal. com/index.asp?layout=articlePrint&articleID=CA6440187. Accessed January 6, 2010.

Levantis, Angie, and *St. Louis Post Dispatch*. "Children's Book on Gay Penguins Has Parents Concerned." *The Record* (Bergen County, N.J.), December 8, 2006, p. A27.

McClatchy Newspapers. "Schools Chief Bans Book on Penguins." Available online. URL: http://www.boston.com/news/nation/articles/2006/12/20/schools_chief_bans_ book_on_penguins?mode=PF. Accessed January 15, 2010.

"Success Stories: Libraries." *Newsletter on Intellectual Freedom* 56, no. 2 (March 2007): 71–72.

"Success Stories: Libraries." *Newsletter on Intellectual Freedom* 56, no. 4 (July 2007): 163–164.

"Success Stories: Libraries." *Newsletter on Intellectual Freedom* 57, no. 3 (May 2008): 115–117.

"Success Stories: Libraries." *Newsletter on Intellectual Freedom* 58, no. 1 (January 2009): 21–22.

"Success Stories: Libraries." *Newsletter on Intellectual Freedom* 58, no. 2 (March 2009): 55–56.

Swanson, Stevenson. "Penguin Papas Lead a List of Literary Controversies." *Los Angeles Times*, October 7, 2007, p. A20.

ANNE FRANK: THE DIARY OF A YOUNG GIRL

Author: Anne Frank
Original date and place of publication: 1947, The Netherlands
Original publisher: Contact
Literary form: Diary

SUMMARY

Anne Frank: The Diary of a Young Girl is a compilation of the notebooks and papers left behind by a 15-year-old Jewish girl, Anne Frank, when she and her family were taken from their hiding place in Amsterdam by German soldiers during the Nazi occupation of the Netherlands in World War II. The hiding place was a "secret annex," a group of rooms at the top and back of a building that served as a warehouse and office for a Dutch-owned business. Those hiding remained quiet by day, while business was conducted in the lower part of the building, but they moved freely at night when the building was deserted. After the Frank family was taken, members of the Dutch family that had sheltered them gathered the papers and hid them in a desk without reading them. When Otto Frank, Anne's father and the only one of the family to survive the war, returned from the death camps, he took the papers and sought to publish them. He would thus fulfill his late daughter's dream for her work and make her live again through her writing.

The final published diary is the combination of Anne's original text with the later edited version that she began, modifying her earlier, more childish phrasing. She also used pseudonyms for the other occupants of the annex, as well as for their protectors, to prevent hurt feelings in instances in which she is critical of them. She writes at several points in the diary that she wants it to live on long after her death and would like it published as *Het Achterhuis* (The house behind), the title under which the work first appeared.

The small, red-checkered diary, which Anne named "Kitty," was a present from her father on her 13th birthday, June 12, 1942, less than a month before they would enter the annex. She began the diary on her birthday, writing in it and in notebooks for the family's 25 months in hiding, from July 5, 1942, through August 1, 1944, three days before Gestapo sergeant Silverbauer and four soldiers broke in and took them away. In the diary, Anne followed the course of the war and recorded her hopes, dreams, fears, and desires, as well as her observations of daily life. The increasingly bad news brought by their protectors, as well as what they heard on the English radio, also prompted Anne's reflections.

Anne's observations about her family as well as the dentist, Mr. Dussel, and the Van Daan family (a father, mother, and 16-year-old son), who share the annex with the Franks, are followed in the diary. She irritably records Mrs. Van Daan's attempts to flirt with Otto Frank, noting that "she strokes his face and hair, pulls her skirt right up, and makes so-called witty remarks," and registers her relief that her father "doesn't play ball." She also records the idiosyncrasies of the other inhabitants, as well as her coldness toward her mother. The reader also learns that the three young people managed to read a lot during their stay and even completed a correspondence shorthand course. Anne also manages to maintain her sense of humor as conditions worsen, remarking at one point when food becomes scarce, "Whoever wants to follow a slimming course should stay in the 'Secret Annexe'!"

CENSORSHIP HISTORY

Censorship of *Anne Frank: The Diary of a Young Girl* began with its initial publication in the Netherlands. Anxious to spare the feelings of their protectors and the memory of the other occupants, Otto Frank excised details of the squabbling among the occupants of the annex and sections in which Anne complained about the selfishness or insensitivity of others. Because she viewed the diary as her private writing, Anne frequently expressed unadorned thoughts and concerns and used the diary as a means of venting her frustrations with the situation. Her father removed such passages without changing significantly the overall representations of the others or their relationships.

Once Otto Frank sought a publisher, additional censorship was required. The Dutch publisher, Contact, required the removal of certain passages that the editors viewed as "tasteless" or "unseemly." These included Anne's references to her and her sister's menstruation. Anne's growing sexual curiosity was also deemed unacceptable, despite the naturalness of such curiosity in an adolescent. Therefore, a passage in which she recalls a friend's developing breasts and muses about wanting to touch them was removed. The publisher also asked that Otto Frank delete all "offensive" remarks made by Anne about her mother.

In 1950, the German publishing firm of Lambert Schneider commissioned a German translation, and additional censorship occurred. The Critical Edition notes that material that would have been especially offensive to German readers was removed. One such passage written by Anne related the rule in the annex that everyone was required "to speak softly at all times, in any civilized language, therefore not in German," which Lambert Schneider changed to "All civilized languages . . . but softly."

The 1952 publication of the diary in England restored most of the excised material. More recent challenges have focused on Anne's growing sexual awareness. In a January 5, 1944, entry Anne recollects sleeping with a girlfriend and having "a strong desire to kiss her," which she did. She states further that she was terribly curious about the other girl's body, "for she had always kept it hidden from me. I asked her whether, as proof of our friendship, we should feel one another's breasts, but she refused. I go into ecstasies every time I see the naked figure of a woman, such as Venus, for example. . . . If only I had a girl friend!" At the same time, she develops a crush on Peter Van Daan, who shows her "the male organs" of a cat, and with whom she experiences her first ardent kiss on the mouth, questioning if she "should have yielded so soon." She also observes increased flirting between the dentist and Mrs. Van Daan and notes that "Dussel is beginning to get longings for women."

In 1982, parents in Wise County, Virginia, challenged the use of the book in school and asserted that Anne's discussion of sexual matters was "inappropriate" and "offensive" and that the criticism of her mother and of the other adults "undermines adult authority." Others have objected to the discussion of "the mistreatment of the Jewish people," and one parent of Arab ancestry objected to the portrayal of a Jewish girl. In 1983, four members of the Alabama Textbook Commission wanted to reject the title for use in the schools because it was "a real downer."

FURTHER READING

Frank, Otto. "Introduction." In *Anne Frank. The Diary of a Young Girl: The Definitive Edition*, edited by Otto Frank and Mirjam Pressler. New York: Doubleday, 1995.

Newsletter on Intellectual Freedom (March 1983): 39.

Wisse, Ruth. "A Romance of the Secret Annex." *New York Times Book Review*, July 2, 1989, p. 2.

ANNIE ON MY MIND

Author: Nancy Garden
Original date and place of publication: 1982, United States
Original publisher: Farrar, Straus & Giroux
Literary form: Young adult novel

SUMMARY

Annie on My Mind details what happens to two teenage girls who recognize that they love each other. Students at different schools who start out as friends, Annie and Liza meet at a museum and share a common interest in art and the Middle Ages. Annie is the daughter of minimally educated Italian immigrant parents and attends an inner-city school. In contrast, Liza is from an affluent family. Her parents are professionals, and she attends Foster Academy, a private school where she is student council president.

The main setting of the book is Foster Academy, run by a headmistress who demands that even minor infractions of rules be disciplined. The academy is in financial trouble, and a fund drive is in progress, a complication that requires that all hint of scandal be eliminated or the academy will suffer.

The love between Annie and Liza develops gradually. They have difficulty admitting their feelings because of the stigma attached to their love, and there is no place for them to become physically intimate. When two of the academy's best-liked teachers, Ms. Widmer and Ms. Stephenson, who share a house, go on vacation, Liza offers to care for their cats, then realizes that she and Annie can be alone there. Liza also discovers that the two teachers are lovers when she explores the empty house, sees books about lesbians in the master bedroom and notices the bedroom furnishings. During that spring vacation, Liza and Annie meet at the house and explore their sexual relationship. They are discovered by another student and a nosy school secretary who tells the headmistress and exposes the two teachers as well.

Liza is suspended from school and required to attend a disciplinary meeting of the school's board of trustees, who will decide if the incident should be placed on her permanent record and if the board should inform the Massachusetts Institute of Technology, which has accepted Liza as an architectural student. Annie attends another school, so she is spared the humiliation and her parents never learn about the incident. The academy board takes no disciplinary action, but Liza must bear nasty remarks and whispering when she returns to school. The two teachers, however, lose their jobs because the school mistakenly believes that they influenced the girls.

Annie attends the University of California at Berkeley on the West Coast, while Liza remains on the East Coast and attends MIT in the fall. Annie writes Liza a letter, but Liza does not answer it. Finally, after realizing that she does love Annie, Liza telephones her, and they decide to get together during Christmas vacation.

CENSORSHIP HISTORY

The novel has frequently been attacked on the grounds that it promotes, idealizes, or encourages homosexuality. Challengers who have not read the book mistakenly charge that it contains explicit sex. Other critics cannot accept the positive portrayal of the gay characters, who are not psychological misfits, nor are they condemned. Yet the book makes a compelling point that homosexual behavior risks harsh consequences and may often result in pain and suffering for individuals who dare to challenge the majority.

In 1988, patrons of Cedar Mill Community Library in Portland, Oregon, challenged the book because it portrays lesbian love and sex as being normal. The book was removed temporarily from shelves, then returned. In 1990, a parent in Sedgwick, Maine, became upset when she learned that the novel was included in the seventh- and eighth-grade library. She objected to the lesbian relationship portrayed. The matter was referred to the school board because the school district did not have a complaint policy in place. The board created a review committee consisting of board members, educators, and parents, who voted to retain the book in the library.

In 1991, *Annie on My Mind* disappeared mysteriously from two high school libraries in San Ramon, California. The librarians later discovered that the vice principals of the two high schools had taken the book from the libraries, claiming to want to examine them. The copies had been donated by a community member, who publicly accused the vice principals of censorship and stated, "They might as well burn the books; clearly the intent is to deny students books having a gay or lesbian theme." Although the vice principals denied censoring the books, a representative of the American Civil Liberties Union determined that this had been the intent and stated that "a school district cannot exclude the topic of homosexuality from a school library."

In 1992, librarians at Colony (Texas) Public Library received numerous requests to remove the novel because "it promotes and encourages the gay lifestyle." After receiving the first complaint, the library board members voted unanimously to retain the book in the library and issued a statement that it was not the job of the library to tell children what they could read, "it is the parents' job." The board maintained that position when other complaints followed and encouraged parents to evaluate the materials to which their children were exposed.

In 1993, parents of students at Bend (Oregon) High School challenged the book in their school library because it "encourages and condones" homosexuality. The school board considered the complaints and voted to retain the book. That same year the book was also challenged but retained in the Lapeer (Michigan) West High School library. Several Kansas school districts also experienced challenges in 1993 after the schools received a donation of library copies of the novel from a national group that sought to give young adults "fair, accurate, and inclusive images of lesbians and gay men." The book was first removed, then returned to general circulation in the library in Shawnee Mission School District. Copies of the book were doused with gasoline and burned by a minister and his followers in the Kansas City School District, but a copy of the novel was retained in the high school library, and the school district donated the novel to the city's public library.

In 1994, the novel was banned from the libraries of five junior high and three senior high schools in Olathe, Kansas, by the superintendent of schools with the backing of the school board. When the district refused to return the book to the school libraries, six students and their families contacted the American Civil Liberties Union and filed a lawsuit against the school. The case was decided in December 1995, when a U.S. district judge ruled that the school board and superintendent had violated the First Amendment of the United States Constitution by removing the novel from the school libraries. The judge ordered the district to return copies of the novel to the school libraries and to pay legal fees and expenses for the plaintiffs.

The novel was also removed from the Chanute (Kansas) High School library in 1994, after parents challenged the work. Librarians returned the book to a limited-access shelf and made it available only to those who had written parental permission.

FURTHER READING

"Annie Goes Back to School." *School Library Journal* 42 (January 1996): 13.
Cart, Michael. "Carte Blanche Winning One for the First Amendment." *Booklist* 92 (April 15, 1996): 1,431.
Newsletter on Intellectual Freedom (January 1990): 4–5; (January 1992): 5–6; (July 1992): 125–126; (September 1993): 158–159; (November 1993): 191–192; (January 1994): 13; (March 1994): 51–52; (May 1994): 84; (July 1994): 129; (September 1994): 140–141; (March 1995): 40.
Olson, Renee. "Battles over Books Usher in New School Year." *School Library Journal* 41 (October 1995): 10–11.

ANOTHER COUNTRY

Author: James Baldwin
Original date and place of publication: 1962, United States
Original publisher: Dial Press
Literary form: Novel

SUMMARY

The novel is set in New York City and moves freely from Greenwich Village to Harlem, as it recounts a year in the lives of the seven major characters. *Another Country* spotlights the interrelationships and artistic careers of African-American jazz drummer Rufus and his sister Ida, a singer, with those of five white characters: Vivaldo, Ida's lover and a would-be writer; Yves, a young Frenchman, and his lover, Eric, an actor; Richard, a pulp novelist, and his wife, Cass. Through the often complex interaction of the characters of both races set in the period of the mid-1950s, the author investigates the deep racial wounds suffered by both groups. He experiments with the concept of equality by placing his characters on roughly similar levels, then examines the reasons for their failure to remain at these levels. Baldwin seeks to shatter prevailing social concepts as he erases established color and sex lines and bends social expectations of the period by the freedom with which he writes of interracial sex and homosexuality.

Written in social-realist style, the novel examines the lives of its characters at a specific moment in time; in so doing, it successfully re-creates the people, streets, stores, apartments, and sounds of the city, its glory, as well as its more sordid aspects. In keeping with the stress on reality, the characters speak as their real-life counterparts speak, expressing their fears, frustrations, desires, and emotions in street vernacular and sprinkling their conversations with obscenities. White characters are sexually attracted to African-American characters, men are drawn to men, and the surrounding city casts a squalid gloom on all their lives.

From the outset, despite their efforts, the characters are doomed to succumb to a fate beyond their control. Rufus Scott, a talented and successful musician, internalizes the low opinion of African-American men held by the society of his time. When his white lover, Leona, professes her love and seeks his approval, his lack of self-esteem and inability to overcome the pain of former rejections prevent him from returning her love. Instead, he labels her "white trash" for loving a black man, physically abuses her, and accuses her of sneaking out with his male friends. Unable to deal with the hopelessness of his fate, Rufus, the most fully developed character in the novel, commits suicide by jumping off the George Washington Bridge in the first fifth of the novel. In the remaining four-fifths, the rest of the characters cope with their loss, recalling from their unique perspectives their relationships with Rufus and their own frustrations in life.

Although reviewers criticized his unconventional sexual pairings in the novel, the public made it a success, and *Another Country* became the second-best-selling novel of the year when it came out in paperback in 1963.

CENSORSHIP HISTORY

Upon publication in 1962, the novel caught the attention of the Federal Bureau of Investigation, which viewed it as being similar in many ways to Henry Miller's *TROPIC OF CANCER* and *TROPIC OF CAPRICORN*. The novel was considered of sufficient importance by the bureau that it warranted a separate file, *FBI HO 145-2625*, apart from their main file on Baldwin. On September 19, 1962, FBI director J. Edgar Hoover sent the novel to the

FBI laboratory to be "examined," expressing particular concern regarding its interracial and homosexual sex scenes. The General Crimes Section returned an unexpected decision, declaring that the novel "contains literary merit and may be of value to students of psychology and social behavior."

In 1963, a New Orleans bookseller was arrested for stocking copies of the novel in violation of city ordinances related to the sale of obscene literature, but the Louisiana district attorney dropped the case. That same year, the New Orleans Public Library asserted that the novel was obscene and banned it. The case went to court and, after a year of litigation, the book was restored.

In 1965, the FBI received a letter from a Fort Worth (Texas) citizen, claiming that the novel contained "sex perversion at its vilest" and demanding action to curtail the sale of the novel, which was available at stores throughout the city. Hoover replied to the writer, assuring him that the FBI appreciated his concern but stated that the author had not yet broken any federal laws. The air of tolerance is subverted by an entry made in the 1969 FBI summary on the author, which included the suggestion of an informant that Ku Klux Klansmen obtain copies of the novel "to determine whether it is suitable reading for college students."

FURTHER READING

Campbell, James. *Talking at the Gates: A Life of James Baldwin.* New York: Penguin Books, 1991.

Nelson, Emmanuel. "Critical Deviance: Homophobia and the Reception of James Baldwin's Fiction." *Journal of American Culture* 14 (Fall 1991): 91–96.

Robins, Natalie. *Alien Ink: The FBI's War on Freedom of Expression.* New York: William Morrow, 1992.

Rowden, Terry. "A Play of Abstractions: Race, Sexuality, and Community in James Baldwin's *Another Country.*" *Southern Review* 29 (Winter 1993): 41–50.

APHRODITE

Author: Pierre Louÿs
Original date and place of publication: 1896, France
Original publisher: Privately published
Literary form: Novel

SUMMARY

Aphrodite, a novel set in Alexandria, Egypt, in 57 B.C., recounts the adventures of a courtesan in the pagan, decadent society that preceded the reign of Cleopatra. Chrysis, one of 1,400 courtesans in the city, relentlessly pursues sensual pleasures that include orgies, lesbian encounters, and "all dangerous feats of passion before which the living recoil." The novel also includes instances of extreme cruelty, including a crucifixion.

Chrysis attracts the attention of Demetrios, a sculptor who is also the lover of Queen Berenice. Before she will promise to spend the night with him, Chrysis demands that he exact revenge for her by stealing three treasures: a rare silver mirror from a courtesan named Bacchis who recently took away an admirer, a precious comb from the wife of the high priest, and a necklace made of seven strands of pearls from the statue of the goddess Aphrodite. Demetrios carries out her wishes, and his acts help to reveal the inhumane and unfeeling nature of Chrysis, as well as his obsession with her. When a young and beautiful slave who is supposed to be freed is accused of stealing the mirror, Chrysis fails to correct the error and allows the girl to be crucified for the crime. The comb can only be obtained by cutting off the hair of the high priest's wife, and Chrysis knows that Demetrios must first stab the woman to death to accomplish this. Obtaining the necklace requires that Demetrios desecrate the temple of Aphrodite.

The novel includes several types of exotic sexual behavior. Hermaphrodites guard the temple, Scythian courtesans who couple "only in the attitude of the beasts" are discussed, and gay and lesbian relationships are identified. While he is obtaining the articles, Demetrios visits a 10-year-old courtesan who professes to know all of the arts of love, and Chrysis romps in bed with two adolescent lesbian companions. When the philosopher Naucrates visits Chrysis to invite her to Bacchis's feast, he finds her naked and in bed with the two young girls and protests that too many women have been taking girl lovers. He notes, "Already a great many women achieve perfect pleasure only with their own sex. Soon you will refuse to receive us entirely, even as a makeshift." Chrysis informs him, "Only a woman knows how to love. Only a woman knows how to be loved. Therefore, an amorous couple made up of two women is perfect; if there is only one woman, it is only half as good; and if there is no woman it is perfectly idiotic."

After meeting Chrysis's demands, Demetrios realizes the gravity of what he has done and grows to hate Chrysis. As he coldly rejects her, Chrysis protests wildly that she really loves him and wants him to stay with her forever. To prove her love, she dresses herself in the stolen items and appears to the throng of people gathered at the temple of Aphrodite. Chrysis is charged with the crimes and sentenced to die. In her jail cell awaiting her death by poison, the courtesan begins to chant half-remembered prayers from her childhood in Galilee, verses from the Old Testament. Demetrios visits her and watches her drink the cup of hemlock, then later poses her body and makes a clay model of it. At the end, Chrysis's two young lesbian lovers claim the body and bury it.

CENSORSHIP HISTORY

Aphrodite, along with Louÿs's *The Songs of Bilitis* and *The Twilights of the Nymphs*, was banned in 1929 by the United States Customs Bureau for being lewd, lascivious, corrupting, and obscene. Although none of the three books contains explicit sexual content, all three portray lesbian relationships and advocate an unrestricted sensuality among women and, to a lesser degree, between women and men. In the preface to the original work, Louÿs asserts that "it is, then, by conscious and willful fraud that modern educators from the time of the Renaissance to the present day have presented ancient ethics as the inspiration of their narrow virtues." He declares, instead, that "there is nothing under the sun more sacred than physical love, nor more beautiful than the human body." In this spirit, Louÿs aims to return with his reader in *Aphrodite* to "a time when the most sensual love, the divine love of which we are born, was without blemish, without shame, and without sin."

The first English translation was made in 1925 and published in an edition limited to 1,000 copies in the United States and 500 copies in Great Britain. In 1930, John S. Sumner, secretary of the New York Society for the Suppression of Vice, seized 54 copies of the book from New York book dealer Earl Marks and filed a complaint against Marks and his distribution company, the Mutual Circulation Company. The New York City magistrate who bound Marks over for trial claimed to have read *Aphrodite* and declared it to be "filthy" and too obscene for his daughter to ever read. The case was heard in June 1930 before three Special Sessions judges who refused to concur with Marks's defense that the book was a recognized classic and, as such, could not be viewed as obscene. Marks lost the case and paid a fine of $250 for violating state laws against objectionable literature, but he was spared the 60-day jail sentence. Marks immediately found a position as circulation manager for *The American Hebrew*, and his probation officer Jacob Lichter reported that Marks had held jobs successfully for 19 years with various magazines.

Two years later, the Liveright Publishing Corporation included the 1925 translation in its *Collected Works of Pierre Louÿs* without challenge. In 1933, the Modern Library edition translated by Lewis Galantiere appeared and also remained unchallenged, but U.S. Customs prevented attempts to import a deluxe edition in 1935. At the time of the ban, however, the novel was freely advertised in the *New York Times Book Review* for 49 cents per copy, with mail delivery anywhere in the United States for only an additional 10 cents. As recently as 1954, the novel was condemned by the National Organization for Decent Literature and placed on its blacklist, where it remains.

FURTHER READING

"*Aphrodite* Brings Fine." *New York Times*, June 24, 1930, p. 8.
"Book Scored, Seller Held." *New York Times*, March 5, 1930, p. 25.
"Class *Aphrodite* as Indecent Book." *New York Times*, June 14, 1930, p. 12.
Louÿs, Pierre. "Preface." *Aphrodite*. Translated by Lewis Galantiere. New York: Modern Library, 1933.

APPOINTMENT IN SAMARRA

Author: John O'Hara
Original date and place of publication: 1934, United States
Original publisher: Harcourt, Brace Publishing
Literary form: Novel

SUMMARY

Appointment in Samarra, O'Hara's first novel after the successful publication of short stories, covers three days during the Prohibition era in the lives of the country club set in the fictional town of Gibbsville, Pennsylvania. The characters are driven by money, status, and sex, and they worry continuously about which clubs, prep schools, colleges, and other associations bring high social status.

The main plot concerns the social and moral disintegration of Julian English, son of a woman of means and a respected physician who heads the staff of the Gibbsville Hospital. Wealthy from childhood and well liked by women, Julian is married to Caroline Walker, to all appearances the ideal wife, but their marriage is strained by Julian's drinking and womanizing. The seemingly prosperous head of a Cadillac automobile dealership, Julian has mismanaged funds and must borrow $20,000 from a newly rich member of the country club, Harry Reilly. Resentful of the obligation and drinking heavily one evening, Julian throws a drink in Harry's face, blackening his eye with an ice cube. Rebuffed when he tries to apologize the next day, Julian then drinks even more heavily and commits suicide by sitting in his car in a closed garage with the motor running. Survivors are mystified because they cannot see that Julian was any more unhappy than they.

Although no graphic sex scenes occur, sexual references are made and offensive ethnic comments appear throughout the novel. A character kids his wife that the newspaper reports that straitlaced Mervyn Schwartz has been "shot in a whorehouse last night." He then teases her that he plans to take his six-and-a-half-year-old son "out and get him laid tonight" and brags "when I was Teddy's age I had four girls knocked up." When a young woman rejects Julian's sexual advances, he has the desire "to call her all kinds of bitches." Throughout the novel, characters drink liquor heavily, and there are numerous instances in which they are drunk. The mobsters in the town are of Italian background, and they are also grade-school dropouts with long arrest records.

Anti-Semitism is even more pronounced. A character awakens on Christmas morning, thinks disparagingly about Mrs. Bromberg across the street, feels momentarily guilty, then reminds herself that "Jews do not observe Christmas, except to make more money out of Christians, so you do not have to treat Jews any different on Christmas than on any other day." She considers that having the Bromberg family on their street has "hurt real estate values" and expresses concern that others will move into the neighborhood. "Pretty soon there would be a whole colony of Jews in the neighborhood, and the Flieglers and all the other nice children in the neighborhood would grow up with Jewish accents." At the hearing where Julian's death is ruled a suicide by the coroner, Dr. Moskowitz, Julian's father sees the verdict as revenge for having excluded Moskowitz from a dinner at the country club for the County Medical Society and thinks, "let the little kike quack Moskowitz have his revenge."

CENSORSHIP HISTORY

Appointment in Samarra aroused criticism when it was first published from those who believed that it contained "thoroughgoing vulgarity . . . an insufferable vulgarity, which has crept into many of our supposedly advanced novels that someone not squeamish, nor unread in earlier literatures, must protest against. . . ." Aside from sporadic and weakly enforced pressure placed by the Watch and Ward Society on Boston booksellers to curtail sales of the novel because of its risqué language and situations, *Appointment in Samarra* was openly sold for nearly seven years without major protest.

In 1941, the novel was declared not mailable because of "obscene language," after the solicitor to the U.S. Department of the Post Office reviewed a copy of the novel. He then advised O'Hara's publisher of the ban, the impetus for which was a complaint brought by the New York Society for the Suppression of Vice that charged the book with being "of an obscene character" because of its sexual references and slurs on various ethnic groups. The post office department would not permit the work to be mailed, and the publisher was told that copies of the book would be confiscated. The novel remained on the U.S. Post Office's index of banned books through the mid-1950s.

The novel also attracted the attention of the National Organization for Decent Literature (NODL), a Roman Catholic organization that identified "objectionable" literature and advised members against reading "offensive" and "obscene" novels. In 1953, NODL found the novel to be "objectionable" and placed it with O'Hara's TEN NORTH FREDERICK on their list of blacklisted books. The list was then sent to cooperating book dealers who agreed to remove the book from their racks. Such NODL blacklists resulted in elaborate collegial pressure among booksellers, although not legal enforcement against the work. Instead, the organization supplied cooperating booksellers with a certificate to display, containing the following notice: "This store has satisfactorily complied with the request of the Committee [the local committee of the NODL] to remove all publications listed as 'OBJECTIONABLE' by the National Organization for Decent Literature from its racks during the above month." As a result of NODL action, the work was banned from sale in St. Cloud, Minnesota; Port Huron, St. Clair County, Michigan; and Detroit. Sales were limited in numerous other cities, through the efforts of local chapters, until the demise of the organization in the late 1950s.

FURTHER READING

Bruccoli, Matthew Joseph. *The O'Hara Concern: A Biography of John O'Hara.* New York: Random House, 1975.

Paul, James C. N., and Murray L. Schwartz. *Federal Censorship: Obscenity in the Mail.* New York: Free Press of Glencoe, 1961.

Podhoretz, Norman. "Gibbsville and New Leeds: The America of John O'Hara and Mary McCarthy." *Commentary*, March 1956, pp. 493–499.

Trilling, Lionel. "John O'Hara Observes Our Mores." *New York Times Book Review*, March 18, 1945, pp. 1, 9. Reprinted as the introduction to *Selected Short Stories of John O'Hara.* New York: Random House, 1956.

AS I LAY DYING

Author: William Faulkner
Original date and place of publication: 1930, United States
Original publisher: Jonathan Cape & Harrison Smith, Inc.
Literary form: Novel

SUMMARY

The novel tells the story of a poor, white Mississippi farm family, the Bundrens, in which the mother, Addie, is dying. Using multiple points of view and short, quick-paced chapters, the author chronicles and examines the feelings and reactions of each character to her dying as well as to the death itself. The feelings portrayed are raw and often selfish, as Faulkner uses regional dialect, stream-of-consciousness, and interior monologue to provide a realistic view of a family in crisis. As the novel progresses, ensuing sections reveal the basic selfish feelings of the family members, including those of the dying woman, and of others who make up this microcosm.

Surviving family members consist of Addie's husband, Anse, her four sons, and one daughter who must all deal with the struggle between their self-centered natures and their obligations to fulfill their late mother's final wish to be buried in the family cemetery in Jefferson. The cemetery is a day's ride from their farm, and several seasonal obstacles must be overcome. Heavy rains and an overflowing river upset their wagon and drown their mules. In the process, the coffin containing Addie falls off the wagon and nearly washes down the river. After substantial frustration and significant effort on the part of all family members, Addie's final wish is granted, and she is buried in the family cemetery. By the time the process is complete, Addie has been dead for 10 days, and the decaying body has become odorous in the Mississippi heat, a fact that the author notes frequently.

Throughout the story, each character reflects upon his or her past, using occasional epithets in realistically portrayed inner monologues. Addie is revealed to be a former schoolteacher, whose married life and drudgery made her an embittered and controlling woman even to the end. Her son Cash builds the coffin outside his dying mother's window, because she wants to make certain of the quality of the finished product. That same son appears to be more interested in crafting a perfect coffin than in grieving for his mother. Addie's daughter eagerly supports the trip to Jefferson to bury her mother, despite the effort and sacrifice, because she is secretly pregnant and the town of Jefferson will offer the opportunity for an abortion. Anse, Addie's husband, professes great love and devotion to his late wife, but he is more interested in going to Jefferson to be fitted for false teeth. Addie's other children recall their own fears, doubts, and anxieties, at times questioning the mercy of God for allowing suffering, both their mother's and theirs. At the end of the novel, only a short while after the decomposed body has finally been buried, Anse marches toward his children, with newly bought false teeth in his mouth and the next Mrs. Bundren following close behind.

CENSORSHIP HISTORY

In 1986, Graves County School District, in Mayfield, Kentucky, banned the novel from the school classrooms and libraries, charging that it used "offensive and obscene passages referring to abortion and used God's name in vain." The ban was heartily supported by the Graves County Baptist Association, an organization that represented the 41 Baptist churches in the county. Two weeks later, after the story of the ban had been in numerous newspapers and the American Civil Liberties Union had intervened, the school board reversed the decision, and the novel returned to the curriculum.

The following year, parents challenged the inclusion of the novel as required reading in the advanced English class at Pulaski County High School in Somerset, Kentucky. They claimed that the book was inappropriate because of its profanity and the contemplation of masturbation by one character. The book was retained. It was also challenged and then retained in the Carroll County, Maryland, school district, where in 1991 two school board members expressed concern regarding the use of coarse language and uneducated southern dialect by the characters, despite the realism of the portrayals.

In 1994, the novel was banned for a few months by officials at Central High School, in Louisville, Kentucky, due to its profanity and the questions that various characters express regarding the existence of God.

FURTHER READING

Blaine, Diana York. "The Abjection of Addie and Other Myths of the Maternal in *As I Lay Dying*." *Mississippi Quarterly* 47 (Summer 1994): 418–419.
Hale, Dorothy J. "*As I Lay Dying*'s Heterogeneous Discourse." *Novel: A Forum on Fiction* 23 (Fall 1989): 5–23.
Hayes, Elizabeth. "Tension between Darl and Jewel." *Southern Literary Journal* 24 (Spring 1992): 49–61.

Kincaid, Nanci. "As Me and Addie Lay Dying." *Southern Review* 30 (Summer 1994): 582–595.

Newsletter on Intellectual Freedom (November 1986): 208; (May 1987): 90; (March 1992): 64; (November 1994): 189.

Noble, William. *Bookbanning in America: Who Bans Books?—And Why?* Middlebury, Vt.: Paul S. Eriksson, 1990.

Reichman, Henry. *Censorship and Selection: Issues and Answers for Schools.* Chicago and Arlington, Va.: American Library Association and American Association of School Administrators, 1993. A joint publication.

THE AUTOBIOGRAPHY OF BENJAMIN FRANKLIN

Author: Benjamin Franklin
Original date and place of publication: 1791, France
Original publisher: Buisson
Literary form: Autobiography

SUMMARY

The Autobiography of Benjamin Franklin is an honest and sometimes lusty chronicle of a man who lived life fully. Franklin originally began to write his memoirs for his son, William Franklin, from whom he later became estranged. The *Autobiography* relates the author's rise from poverty as the youngest of 17 children of a soap and candle maker through his apprenticeship as a printer and to his role as Pennsylvania's agent in England in 1757. Franklin provides details regarding his constant struggle to improve himself in education and in business and explains his passion for improvement, of both self and the public. The *Autobiography* ends when Franklin's activities reach an international scope, and he becomes a truly public figure.

Despite the emphasis upon moral improvement in much of the *Autobiography*, Franklin also admits to human failings. He acknowledges that the "hard-to-be-governed passion of youth had hurried me frequently into intrigues with low women that fell in my way, which were attended with some expense and great inconvenience, besides a continual risk to my health by a distemper." He also admits that he has been the victim of passionate bouts of indulgence and that he has not always stood by his beliefs. Instead, he changed "opinions which I had thought right but found otherwise."

In one episode, Franklin speaks of his hasty departure from Boston in 1723 and writes that he left people to speculate that his exit was because he "got a naughty Girl with Child." In a later episode, Franklin recounts the incident that caused a breach with a friend named James Ralph, who left behind a wife and child when he traveled to England with Franklin to find work. Ralph began an affair with a young Englishwoman, Mrs. T., and they had a child. Unable to find work teaching in London, Ralph left to teach in a country school and asked Franklin to look after Mrs. T. Franklin lent her money and responded to her frequent calls for assistance. On one of those visits, he "attempted familiarities, which she repulsed with proper resentment," and later told Ralph.

The *Autobiography* presents a very human view of a well-known historical figure.

CENSORSHIP HISTORY

Franklin's *Autobiography* is one of the most frequently expurgated books ever published in America, and it was censored from its first publication. In 1789, Franklin sent copies of the manuscript to friends Benjamin Vaughn and Guillaume Le Veillard, the mayor of Passy, France, asking for their advice. After Franklin died in 1790, a pirated edition of the book appeared in France. With the goal of publishing a more "acceptable" version, Franklin's grandson, William Temple Franklin, edited the French version, which he published in 1818 as part of the comprehensive *Works*. This edition made 1,200 changes in the phrasing of the original *Autobiography*, with the expressed aim of modernizing the language for the 19th century. Instead, the changes altered Benjamin Franklin's sometimes salty tone and word choice, providing a vastly different view.

In 1886, Houghton Mifflin published an edition of the *Autobiography* that included the story of James Ralph's affair with the young woman but removed Franklin's admission of a sexual advance. Instead, the editor inserted this explanation of the strained relationship between the old friends: "In the mean time other circumstances made a breach." In 1888, Ginn & Company removed the entire episode. Houghton Mifflin retained the expurgated account in its 1892 edition, but the editor, Middlebury College professor Julian Abernethy, changed the substituted statement to read, "In the mean time another matter which gave offense made a breach." The publishers justified these and similar changes in nearly a dozen editions on the grounds that they were meant for high school students, who must be protected.

Franklin published more overtly bawdy works that earned the approval of his peers but which are not frequently found among suggested readings. In his "Advice to a Young Man on the Choice of a Mistress," Franklin suggests that more pleasure can be found with an older woman than with a younger because "regarding what is below the Girdle, it is impossible of two Women to tell an old one from a young one" and "They [old women] are so grateful!" In "Polly Baker's Speech," printed in *Gentleman's Magazine* in 1747, he purports to speak as a New England woman who defends herself for being brought to trial, yet again, for having another illegitimate child. Franklin takes flatulence as his subject in "To the Royal Academy at Brussels," in which he parodies scientific reports in the suggestion that chemical additives to food might make "Wind from bowels" less offensive and puns using the slang term *fart*.

As Chief Judge Clarke noted in *Roth v. United States*, 345 U.S. 476 (1957), the discussed works by Franklin "which a jury could reasonably find 'obscene,' according to the judge's instructions in the case at bar" would also have subjected a person to prosecution if sent through the mails in 1957 and "to punishment under the federal obscenity statute." The judge further noted that Thomas Jefferson wrote approvingly of "Polly Baker's Speech" and that James Madison not only praised Franklin's humor but also wrote similarly Rabelaisian anecdotes. That Franklin is popularly known as "the father of the Post Office" (he was designated postmaster general by the First Continental Congress) is ironic, because his own works, with their tongue-in-cheek sexual references, would have been considered too obscene to mail according to federal statutes such as the Comstock Act, which applied to such matters until recent years.

FURTHER READING

Haney, Robert W. *Comstockery in America: Patterns of Censorship and Control.* Boston: Beacon Press, 1960.

Larabee, Leonard W., ed. *The Autobiography of Benjamin Franklin.* New Haven, Conn.: Yale University Press, 1964.

Padover, Saul Kussiel. *The Complete Jefferson.* New York: Duell, Sloan & Pearce, 1943.

———. *The Complete Madison.* New York: Harper & Brothers, 1953.

Perrin, Noel. *Dr. Bowdler's Legacy: A History of Expurgated Books in England and America.* Boston: David R. Godine, 1992.

Van Doren, Carl. *Ben Franklin.* New York: Bramhall House, 1987.

THE AUTOBIOGRAPHY OF MALCOLM X

Author: Malcolm X, with Alex Haley
Original date and place of publication: 1965, United States
Original publisher: Grove Press
Literary form: Autobiography

SUMMARY

The autobiography articulates the anger, the struggle, and the beliefs not only of Malcolm X but also of many African Americans during the 1960s. The work charts the development of the African-American leader from his birth as Malcolm Little in 1925 in Omaha, Nebraska, to his assassination in New York City in 1965. Throughout, he uses fiery rhetoric to preach revolution to African Americans as the only means by which they can achieve full social equality.

As background to his beliefs, he relates the main abuses that occurred in his own life. He recalls his father's adherence to the philosophy of black separatist Marcus Garvey and relates the threats he and his seven siblings endured because of his father's fiery preaching. The work not only chronicles the author's life, but it also presents a sociological examination of the changing roles and growing social and political awareness of African Americans in the United States over four decades.

Particular bitterness is aimed at the welfare system, with its white caseworkers, which strikes a final blow against his family. After their father is murdered, his mother is left a widow with eight children to support, and she works hard at whatever jobs are available to keep the family together. Yet intrusive caseworkers keep a constant watch on the Little home, finally placing the children in foster care and committing Mrs. Little to the state mental hospital at Kalamazoo, Michigan, after she has a mental breakdown when her children are removed. Such images stayed with the author, despite his early efforts to be a "good Negro" and to play the role that white society expected of him.

The autobiography candidly admits that he "tried to be white," like many other lighter-skinned African Americans of his day. From having his hair "conked" (straightened) to buying a "zoot suit," to conducting a five-year affair with a blonde white woman, he allows himself to be "brainwashed." He becomes involved in substantial illegal activity, from running a numbers racket to pimping, selling drugs, and committing robberies. When caught, he claims that he received a much longer jail term than usual because he was involved with a white woman.

At the age of 21, he begins serving seven years in jail, where he learns about the Nation of Islam and becomes a member of the Black Muslim faith. After his conversion and release from prison, the author drops the name Little, his "slave name," and takes "X" to denote an unknown quantity as his last name.

The second half of the autobiography relates the author's efforts to advance the Black Muslim cause, his gradual disillusionment with Black Muslim leader Elijah Muhammad, and his eventual expulsion from the Nation of Islam. He describes his experiences in visiting Africa as well as in the United States, speaking frequently at college campuses and influencing new converts. He also relates the betrayal that he experienced when rumors of an assassination plot surfaced from within the Nation of Islam.

The final three chapters of the work detail the reasons why Malcolm X left the Nation of Islam to form his own organization, Muslim Mosque, Inc. Later called the Organization of Afro-American Unity, its tone was one of militant black nationalism. As threats on his life occurred, the author became certain that the Nation of Islam was the source of the various attacks and threats. In the Epilogue, Alex Haley notes that Malcolm X became convinced that he would be murdered and felt that he would be a martyr "in the cause of brotherhood." His final hope for the autobiography was that it would motivate social action.

CENSORSHIP HISTORY

The Autobiography of Malcolm X was deliberately kept out of classrooms and school libraries when it first appeared because the work openly criticized the role of white society in restricting the achievements and accomplishments of African Americans in the United States. Parents complained that the language was "filthy" and "racist," and the work was viewed for years largely as a radical text that had no place in the high school curriculum, although it enjoyed substantial popularity on college campuses during the 1960s and 1970s. Librarians used "selection" as the criterion for excluding the work from public libraries in predominantly white communities. By the 1980s, the work had come to be viewed as a historical work, and the language and situations, including those in which Malcolm X uses street vernacular and candidly describes the illegal and immoral activities of his early life, seemed commonplace. The 1992 film, *Malcolm X*, directed by Spike Lee, reawakened interest in the book, and high schools added it to their reading lists.

In 1993, parents in the Duval County (Florida) public schools challenged the use of this book in the curriculum, charging that the anti-white racism and the violence espoused by the assassinated Black Muslims leader were disruptive of racial harmony. Citing passages from the book, the parents identified "vulgar" language and "criminal" acts that they felt did not provide decent models for their children to emulate.

The Jacksonville (Florida) school district restricted the availability of the book in the middle school libraries in 1994, after parents complained to the school board that the book was a "how-to" manual for crime and that it represented white people as racist in their views. Only students who had notes from their parents were allowed to take out the book.

FURTHER READING

Carson, Clayborne. *Malcolm X: The FBI File*. New York: Carroll & Graf, 1991.
Dyson, Michael Eric. *Making Malcolm: The Myth and Meaning of Malcolm X*. New York: Oxford University Press, 1994.
Early, Gerald. "Their Malcolm, My Problem." *Harper's* 285 (December 1992): 62–74.
Newsletter for Intellectual Freedom (September 1993): 147; (May 1994): 83.
Vincent, Ted. "The Garveyite Parents of Malcolm X." *Black Scholar* 20 (March 1989): 10–13.

THE AUTOBIOGRAPHY OF MISS JANE PITTMAN

Author: Ernest J. Gaines
Original date and place of publication: 1971, United States
Original publisher: Bantam Books
Literary form: Novel

SUMMARY

Written from the point of view of a 110-year-old former slave, *The Autobiography of Miss Jane Pittman* is a novel that celebrates the life of a woman from her birth into slavery to the beginning of the civil rights movement in the United States. Divided into parts entitled "The War Years," "Reconstruction," "The Plantation," and "The Quarters," the episodic novel is structured as an oral history project undertaken by an African-American history teacher interviewing Miss Jane, whose voice and personality direct the story.

The novel opens with a young Jane, still bearing her slave name Ticey, serving water to a Yankee soldier on a Louisiana plantation near the end of the Civil War. The soldier tells her that she should replace the name Ticey with the more attractive Jane, which she does and for which she later suffers a beating from her mistress, who tries to force Jane to respond to the old slave name. The change of name corresponds to a change of attitude as the formerly mischievous slave girl becomes self-reliant and assumes responsibility for herself as well as for young Ned Douglass, whose mother is beaten to death by racist vigilantes. Hoping for a better life, she flees to the North with the child but finds the promised land to be only an illusion. Jane returns to Louisiana, where she meets and falls in love with horse trainer Joe Pittman, whose name she takes when they live together. The two are happy together for seven years despite Jane's inability to have children, but Joe is killed trying to tame a wild black stallion.

In the years that follow, Jane experiences the dehumanizing effects of institutionalized racism and loses her beloved Ned, who is murdered by white racists after he begins speaking out about racial dignity and assertiveness. A half century passes and the civil rights movement erupts in Louisiana, led by young civil rights worker Jimmy Aaron, who is following the example of Dr. Martin Luther King. Successful in mobilizing African-American citizens in a nearby town, Jimmy becomes a threat and is also murdered by white racists. The novel ends with the 110-year-old Jane Pittman preparing to go into town to lend her support to the civil rights movement by attempting to drink from a "whites-only" water fountain.

The novel contains numerous instances of language unfavorable to African Americans, spoken by both races. As Miss Jane herself says approvingly of Louisiana governor Huey Long at one point, "When he said nigger he said, 'Here a book, nigger. Go read your name.' When the other ones said nigger, they said, 'Here a sack, nigger. Go pick that cotton.'" The offensive term and other words of derision are spoken by white characters who aim insults at African Americans. In addition, characters of both races use a range of slang terms and insults.

CENSORSHIP HISTORY

The novel has frequently been the source of complaints from both white and African-American parents and students who charge that *The Autobiography*

The plaintiffs in the case alleged that the decision of the defendants to remove the books from the library violated the free speech provision of the First Amendment to the United States Constitution. On February 26, 1999, the school district and the ACLU entered into an agreement that Judge Crabb approved; the agreement stipulated the school district would return *Baby Be-Bop* and *The Drowning of Stephan Jones* to the library shelves until the lawsuit was resolved. In an interview published in the *Duluth News Tribune* on March 2, 1999, district officials said they had agreed to reshelve the books only "to avoid unnecessary litigation and not as a concession to the people who have sued." In response, the ACLU said "the district moves were an indication of how strong the lawsuit against the district is." After eight months, the lawsuit was settled on October 8, 1999, with district officials agreeing to retain the four gay-themed books in the high school library. The executive director of the ACLU of Wisconsin, Chris Ahmuty, concluded, "This settlement restores not only the books to the library shelves, but also the district's credibility and good name."

In February 2000, school officials of the Bonsall Union School District in California removed *Baby Be-Bop, Question Quest,* and *Just Friends* from the school library. The books were part of a mandatory reading program at the Norman L. Sullivan Middle School. The officials charged that the books contained sexually explicit material unsuitable for children 11 and 12 years old. The superintendent of schools, John Heckman, removed the books after receiving complaints from parents that the books contain language that "if children used, they would be kicked out of school." Heckman also stated in an interview with the *North Country Times* that parents found the sexual content "amoral, demeaning or just inappropriate" for fifth-grade students. The district claimed that it was unfamiliar with the content of the books, and it believed that the books were screened by the company that created the accelerated reading program, Advantage Learning Systems. A representative of the company stated that the books were screened only to identify grade-level reading difficulty, not for content, which is left to the school district.

At a March 8, 2000, meeting, school board members and parents debated the decision to remove the three books from the library, and many parents supported the decision because the books were part of a mandatory literacy program in the district. The board promised parents that school trustees would create a set of standards to determine which books are suitable for children and that the library staff would be more thorough in reviewing books bought by the district. School board president Richard Olson stated in an interview in the *North Country Times*, "There are going to be books that this board will not allow in the program. If it has the 'F-word' 63 times in the first two sentences . . . it won't be here." The school board decided at the May 10, 2000, meeting to abandon the idea of creating a list of vulgar or obscene words and subjects to use in determining if a book is appropriate for adoption. Instead, with the support of parents, the board instituted a policy requiring children to obtain written permission from their parents to check out any young adult book from the library.

The book also created difficulties for the West Bend Community Memorial Library which, in February 2009, received a complaint from representatives Ginny and Jim Maziarka of the West Bend Citizens for Safe Libraries asking that the library remove *Baby Be-Bop* from the collection. The Maziarkas complained that the book is "sexually explicit," as well as "crude and raunchy." During the course of the controversy, in April 2009 four library trustees were denied reappointment and rebuked by city council members because they failed to comply immediately with the Maziarkas' requests; instead, they adhered to the library's reconsideration process. On June 2, 2009, the library trustees, including those who were not reappointed but remained to serve out their terms, met to listen to citizen comments for and against restricting the book and to vote. The West Bend Citizens for Safe Libraries presented the trustees with a petition containing 700 signatures asking the library to restrict the novel and other gay-themed works. Countering the challenge, the West Bend Parents for Free Speech presented a petition against restricting the works that contained 1,000 signatures. The trustees voted 9-0 to maintain the young adult collection as it is "without removing, relocating, labeling, or otherwise restricting access" to any books. After the vote, the West Bend Citizens for Safe Libraries condemned the library board for "submitting to the will of the American Library Association and the American Civil Liberties Union" and declared that the group "would let people know that the library was not a safe place unless it segregated and labeled YA titles with explicit content."

Baby Be-Bop continued to generate controversy in West Bend, Wisconsin, after the library board vote. On April 28, 2009, Milwaukee resident and Christian Civil Liberties Union (CCLU) member Robert C. Braun of West Allis, Wisconsin, and three other plaintiffs filed a claim for damages with the city. Braun, Joseph Kogelmann, Reverend Cleveland Eden, and Robert Bough asserted that their mental and emotional well-being were damaged by being exposed to the book in a library display and they sought the right "to publicly burn or to destroy by another means" the library's copy of the book. They sought "damages and relief pursuant to Wisconsin Statute Section 893.80," specifically, compensatory damages in the amount of $120,000 and the resignation of West Bend mayor Kristine Deiss. The CCLU legal claim described the novel as "explicitly vulgar, racial, and anti-Christian" and "inappropriate for the elderly and their minor grandchildren, and degrades the community." The four complainants asserted that *Baby Be-Bop* contains "the 'n' word and derogatory sexual and political epithets that can incite violence and put one's life in possible jeopardy, adults and children alike." The CCLU complaint further cited what it termed "Wisconsin's sexual morality law" and requested that the city attorney Mary Schanning impanel a grand jury to examine "whether the book should be declared obscene" and if making it available constitutes a hate crime. Speaking to an ABC News reporter on June 19, 2009, Braun cautioned, "We will have demonstrations if they don't remove it. . . . It has to be out of the library. If that doesn't happen, I will be out there burning."

FURTHER READING

American Civil Liberties Union of Wisconsin. "ACLU of Wisconsin Fights School Censorship of Gay-Themed Books." Press Release. October 6, 1998. Available online. URL: www.qrd.org/qrd/education/1998/misc.news-10.08.98. Accessed December 10, 2009.

———. "ACLU of Wisconsin Files Free Speech Lawsuit over School's Censorship of Gay-Themed Books." Press Release. February 16, 1999. Available online. URL: http://www.aclu.org/LesbianGayRights/LesbianGayRights.cfm?ID=8406&c= 102. Accessed December 10, 2009.

———. "ACLU to Sue WI School District for Censoring Gay-Themed Books." Press Release. December 22, 1998. Available online. URL: www.theroc.org/roc-news/school.html. Accessed December 11, 2009.

———. "Gay-Themed Books to Remain on High School Library Shelves after Barron, Wisconsin Lawsuit Settled." Press Release. October 8, 1999.

American Library Association. "Banned Barron Books Are Back for Now." Available online. URL: http://www.ala.org/ala/alonline/currentnews/newsarchive/1999/march1999/bannedbarron.cfm. Accessed December 10, 2009.

"Books on Gays Return to Library, at Least Temporarily." *Duluth News Tribune*. March 2, 1999.

Dorning, Anne-Marie. "Library Book Riles Small Wisconsin Town: 'Baby Be-Bop' and Its Gay Teen Angst Too Much for Christian Civil Liberties Union." *ABC News* (June 19, 2009). Available online. URL: http://abcnews.go.com/US/story?id=7874866. Accessed December 12, 2009.

Goldberg, Beverly. "Milwaukee Group Seeks Fiery Alternative to Materials Challenge." American Libraries Online. Available online. URL: http://www.ala.org/ala/alonline/currentnews/newsarchive/2009/june2009/westbendbabybebop060309.cfm. Accessed December 12, 2009.

THE BASKETBALL DIARIES

Author: Jim Carroll
Original date and place of publication: 1978, United States
Original publisher: Tombouctou Books
Literary form: Autobiography

SUMMARY

The publication of Jim Carroll's diary, entitled *The Basketball Diaries: Age Twelve to Fifteen* (1978), had been eagerly awaited. The book, which is generally referred to by its main title alone, had started appearing in excerpt form throughout the late 1960s and early 1970s in various literary publications. Carroll claimed that the diaries were written at the time in which the events related took place. However, some critics wondered how much the diaries were edited before publication, especially since the book includes many outrageous incidents. Regardless of its authenticity, the book made a statement when it was published, because Carroll's gritty diary was explicit, and it took readers inside the real world of drug addiction, male prostitution, and crime in 1960s New York. *The Basketball Diaries* has become Carroll's best-known work, especially after the release of a 1995 film adaptation starring Leonardo DiCaprio. In 1987, Carroll published a sequel, *Forced Entries: The Downtown Diaries, 1971–73*.

In the first entries, Carroll is a 13-year-old who has had limited experience with sex, drugs, and crime. He is also a novice basketball player in his first organized league. All of these aspects of his life change rapidly. He becomes a star basketball player, winning a scholarship to a rich private school, then becomes heavily involved in heterosexual experiences and hard drugs. His heroin addiction starts out small, and he lies to himself about being able to control it. However, as his addiction grows, it changes the quality of every other aspect of his life. He starts committing crimes, including stealing cars, in order to finance his drug habit. In addition, he makes money by selling his body to homosexuals and older women. His increased heroin use is supplemented by other drugs, including various kinds of pills, methadone, cocaine, and LSD. His massive drug use destroys his dream of playing professional basketball and eventually lands him in juvenile prison. Carroll tries to give up heroin abruptly several times and describes his withdrawal symptoms in detail, but each time he returns to using. In the last diary entry, Carroll surfaces from a four-day heroin high and laments about how low he has sunk in life. He says that he only wants to be pure.

Over the course of the diaries, Carroll is exposed to several cultural and political issues. He makes scathing attacks on hypocrisy and condemns the U.S. use of the communist scare as a justification for building more nuclear weapons and engaging in the Vietnam War. He bemoans the reality that poor junkies do not have the same treatment programs or escape options as middle-class or rich junkies, and he exposes the hypocrisy of narcotics police, whom he claims keep confiscated drugs for themselves—to sell on the streets. Ultimately, he predicts the publication of *The Basketball Diaries*, in which he intends to expose these views and facts.

The Basketball Diaries is composed of 10 sections, one for each season— in some cases two seasons—from fall 1963 to summer 1966. Each section is composed of five to 26 separate entries, and, collectively, these entries describe Carroll's coming-of-age transformation, from a healthy, relatively naive juvenile delinquent into a strung-out, culturally aware, heroin-addicted criminal.

The Basketball Diaries is conspicuous for its graphic profanity, used to describe sexual acts and for emphasis, even when describing relatively normal events. Carroll also includes a lot of slang; he refers to sexual intercourse as "nooky," calls condoms "scumbags," and refers to breasts as "knocks." Marijuana is "weed" or "grass," while heroin is "scag." A "spiller" is someone who acts like he has drunk more than he has, and someone who is drunk is "smashed."

The imagery in the diaries is violent and explicit. Carroll describes his sexual experiences in detail. For example, as he is about to say good-bye to his girlfriend before basketball practice one day, he states that she "socks her tongue in my mouth and grinds her sweet bottom up against me." Since Carroll has forgotten to wear a jock strap that day, his resulting erection makes it look "like [he] was shoplifting bananas." Drug imagery is also graphic, particularly the images associated with shooting up heroin. On one occasion, Carroll describes what it looks like when he shoots up: "Just such a pleasure to tie up above that mainline with a woman's silk stocking and hit the mark and watch the blood rise into the dropper like a certain desert lily."

CENSORSHIP HISTORY

The Basketball Diaries received negative criticism because of the book's striking depictions of sex, violence, and drug use. On June 8, 1998, the Gwinnett County Library Board in Georgia, with one member out of town, voted 2-1 to remove the book from library shelves "until a legal determination could be made of whether the book is harmful to minors under state law." The board asked the county solicitor Gerald Blaney to make a determination. The board also voted to create a parental advisory section in the library and to place *The Basketball Diaries* into that section if the book was not determined to be harmful to minors. The call for a ban was initiated by parents who were members of Citizens for Family Friendly Libraries, the Gwinnett affiliate of a national group. Judy Craft, cofounder of the local group, told a reporter for the *Atlanta Journal-Constitution*, "I think it was a good decision made for the families of Gwinnett County and for the well-being of our children."

The two board members who voted to ban the novel were Jennifer Toombs, a cofounder of Citizens for Family Friendly Libraries, and Ann MacLeod, owner of a Christian bookstore, who called the book "porno" and told a reporter, "It's filthy." Local citizens who were in favor of keeping the book were disappointed because the absent board member would have made the vote a 2-2 tie, and the chairman, Andy Touchier, was expected to have broken the tie in favor of keeping the book on library shelves.

In August 1998, Blaney told the library board that the state law standard for determining whether a book is harmful to minors—if it appeals to lewd interest, is offensive to most adults, and lacks artistic merit—applies only to booksellers and not libraries. He recommended that the library should have better procedures for dealing with controversial materials, "particularly books that fall in the grey areas, like *The Basketball Diaries*." The book has remained in circulation during the controversy. MacLeod, one of the board members who voted in favor of the ban, said that she is satisfied whatever the outcome of future votes because parents have been made aware of the book and "The message has already been sent."

The 1995 film version of *The Basketball Diaries*, starring Leonardo DiCaprio, ignited controversy in 1997. In the novel, Carroll writes in the "Winter '65" and the "Winter '66" entries about his fantasy to randomly shoot people in his school. He fantasizes that he will get to class early in the morning and "take a machine gun and start firing like mad toward my right side . . . my fantasy that always creeps up my back when I'm sitting there each morning . . . just wanting to whip out a tommy gun and blast away (Nothing less will do, no pistols, nothing else but rat-a-tat-tat, dig?)." The movie version depicts these actions as a dream sequence and makes clear that Carroll is not actually carrying out the action, simply fantasizing. In 1997, 14-year-old Michael Carneal of Paducah, Kentucky, opened fire in his school lobby, killing three female classmates and wounding five other students; he claimed that he had been influenced by the movie. Parents of the girls subsequently sued the makers of the film. On April 20, 1999, two teenage students, Eric Harris and Dylan Klebold, carried out a shooting rampage at Columbine High School in Colorado, killing 12 students and one teacher and wounding 24 others, before committing suicide. Harris and Klebold had left notes about having seen the movie. The family of Dave Sanders, a teacher who was killed that day, sued the filmmakers, but U.S. district judge Lewis Babcock dismissed the lawsuit in 2002, stating that the two gunmen were responsible for the deaths.

FURTHER READING

Carter, Cassie. " 'A Sickness That Takes Years to Perfect': Jim Carroll's Alchemical Vision." *Dionysos: Literature and Addiction Quarterly* 6 (Winter 1996): 6–19.

Carter, Nick. "Linking of 'Basketball Diaries,' Columbine Shootings Upsets Author." *Milwaukee Journal-Sentinel*, May 6, 1999.

Ippolito, Milo. "Board Members Expect Book to Remain on Shelves." *Atlanta Journal-Constitution*, August 3, 1998, p. JJ-03.

———. "Book-Banning Vote Not Likely until August." *Atlanta Journal-Constitution*, July 14, 1998, p. JJ-02.

———. "Library Board Wants Book Out: Removal to Rest on Legal Call." *Atlanta Journal-Constitution*, June 9, 1998, p. JJ-01.

———. "Library Votes Rare Wins for Conservatives." *Atlanta Journal-Constitution,* June 14, 1998, p. JJ-01.

James, Jamie. "Review of *The Basketball Diaries.*" *American Book Review* 2 (February 1980): 9.

Kirschenbaum, Gayle. "*The Basketball Diaries* Gets Bounced around in a Georgia Public Library." *School Library Journal* 44 (October 1998): 18.

BEING THERE

Author: Jerzy Kosinski
Original date and place of publication: 1970, United States
Original publisher: Harcourt Brace Jovanovich
Literary form: Novel

SUMMARY

Being There is a cynical look at the American political and intellectual scene as viewed through the eyes of Chance, a man whose whole life has been spent in tending a garden and passively watching television. He is a man without a past whose identity is formed by circumstances, and his perceptions of the world and of others reflect what he has seen on television. When he is forced to leave his home and to navigate the modern world, his simple answers related to gardening are taken by statesmen, financiers, and the news media to be brilliant assessments of the political and economic scene. Within four days of leaving his anonymous existence, he is considered as a candidate for vice president of the United States.

At the outset, Chance maintains the garden and grounds for a wealthy patron called simply Old Man. An orphan, his mother died when he was born, and he never learns the identity of his father. Chance cannot read or write and brain damage from birth has limited him to life in his quarters and the garden. He must do exactly as told or risk being sent to a home for the insane where, as the Old Man tells him, he would be locked in a cell. Thus, his only contact with the outside world is through the large color television in his room. In this surreal world, Chance controls life by rapidly turning the television dial to make images flip past each other and raising and lowering the volume at will.

Once the Old Man dies, estate lawyers determine that no record of Chance exists. He has no birth certificate, and he has never paid taxes, served in the army, or visited a doctor or dentist. Forced to leave his home, Chance dresses in one of his late employer's expensive suits, packs an expensive leather suitcase, and steps into the street, where he is promptly hit by the luxurious limousine of wealthy Elizabeth Eve Rand. Married to the much older, ailing Benjamin Rand, EE, as she is called in the novel, insists that "Chance, the former gardener," whose name she misinterprets to be Chauncey Gardiner, go home with her to receive medical attention and to have a place to recuperate. Her husband is a close adviser to the president of the United States, who visits the day after Chance arrives. When both men invite Chance to air his views regarding the nation's economy, he responds in terms of gardening with what appear to be highly appropriate metaphors to the two powerhouses. The president later quotes Chance in a televised speech, and the media mistakenly assume that he is a major financier, statesman, and presidential adviser. Asked to escort EE, head of a major United Nations committee, to a United Nations function, Chance attracts the attention of the Russian ambassador, who mistakenly believes that he not only speaks Russian but is pro-Soviet in his political and economic sympathies. The ambassador also quotes Chance in a televised speech.

As Chance hobnobs with important people, his physical attractiveness draws both male and female admirers. At one official reception, a well-dressed, silver-haired man suggests a sexual encounter, but Chance does not understand what he means because nothing of the sort has ever appeared on television. Thus, he tells the man that he chooses to watch, not participate. As they ride in the elevator, the man "thrust his hand into Chance's groin." Chance remains the spectator, watching as the man "cupped his own flesh in a hand, groaning and jerking and trembling as he did so . . . the erect extended part grew stiffer . . . a white substance coursed forth in short spurts." Chance also tells EE that he wants to watch when she approaches him for sex, and she masturbates as he watches her writhing with pleasure. Afterward, she compliments him for uncoiling her wants, for with him "desires flow within me. . . . You make me free." At one point, Chance examines his body to see how his sexual organ compares with those pictured in the pornography that a maintenance man had once shown him, but finds that "his organ was small and limp; it did not protrude in the slightest . . . . Though Chance prodded and massaged his organ, he felt nothing . . . his organ refused to stiffen out; it gave him no pleasure at all."

As Chance's detached attitude in his sexual encounters passes for experience, his lack of involvement and total obliviousness to the prevailing political and social realities pass for wisdom. At the end of the novel, the president decides to choose Chance as his running mate because the lack of any past makes him the perfect candidate with no sins to live down.

CENSORSHIP HISTORY

Being There has been challenged in high schools for containing "inappropriate images" and for its depiction of masturbation and the homosexual near-experience of the main character. Critics have charged that the book is "sex-oriented" and that the sexual content and "suggestive language" are unsuitable for high school students.

Parents of students attending Crete (Nebraska) High School in 1989 criticized the inclusion of the book as a reading assignment for the 11th-grade

English class and requested that the requirement be changed. School board officials determined that the book should remain as one of several choices of reading assignment, with suitable alternatives provided to those who preferred not to read it. Also in 1989, parental objections to the homosexual encounter of the main character resulted in the removal of the book from Mifflinburg (Pennsylvania) High School classes. After reconsideration of the text and the removal of the book from the recommended list, the book was reinstated for use as an alternative reading choice.

In 1993, parents of students enrolled in a senior advanced English course in the Davenport, Iowa, high school challenged the inclusion of the work as a required reading, claiming that the description of masturbation was too graphic and unnecessary to the text. After reconsideration, school board officials reversed themselves, and the teacher removed it from the required list.

FURTHER READING

Newsletter on Intellectual Freedom (May 1989): 79, 93; (July 1993): 105.

Sloan, James Park. *Jerzy Kosinski: A Biography*. New York: E. P. Dutton and Company, 1996.

———. "Kosinski's War." *New Yorker*, October 10, 1994, pp. 46–53.

Straus, Dorothea. "Remembering Jerzy Kosinski." *Partisan Review* 60 (Winter 1993): 138–142.

THE BELL JAR

Author: Sylvia Plath
Original date and place of publication: 1963, United Kingdom
Original publisher: William Heinemann Ltd.
Literary form: Novel

SUMMARY

The Bell Jar, first published under the pseudonym of Victoria Lucas, is a thinly veiled autobiographical account of the inner conflict, mental breakdown, and later recovery of a female college student in the 1950s. The novel covers approximately eight months in the life of Esther Greenwood, the 19-year-old narrator, and the plot is divided into three parts. In the first part, Esther embarks on a one-month residence in New York City as a guest editor for the college issue of a fashion magazine. Once in the city, she recalls key incidents from the past, exhibiting her emotional and mental disintegration as the recollections become more real and meaning-filled to her than incidents in her daily life. Her unsatisfactory relationships with men dominate her thoughts, and the reader learns of her disappointing date with Constantin, who makes no attempt to seduce her; the brutal

Female in America and the novel *The Stepford Wives* from the reading list. The books were removed because "someone in the community might be offended by their criticism of traditional roles for women." By mid-October, the principal demanded that Go Ask Alice also be removed from the list because it contained "dirty" words. In November, the principal directed that Burnau remove *The Bell Jar* from her list, after reviewing the book and determining that it was "inappropriate" because it spoke of a birth control device (the diaphragm) and used "profanity." Burnau's written protest brought the warning that she would be dismissed for insubordination if she included that book. Although Burnau complied with the demand and dropped the book, the principal later wrote in her evaluation that she exhibited "resentment and a poor attitude" when told not to use *The Bell Jar*. The school board did not rehire Burnau, giving only the reason that she failed to meet her responsibilities and displayed "a poor attitude."

A 17-year-old Warsaw Community High School student and her family challenged the decision of the board. In early 1979, Brooke Zykan, her brother Blair, and her parents became the plaintiffs in a suit that charged the school district with violating the First and Fourteenth Amendment rights of students and called for the court to reverse the school board decision to remove the books, which also included *The Feminine Plural: Stories by Women about Growing Up* and *The New Women: A Motive Anthology of Women's Liberation*. A group called People Who Care was formed to deal with the controversy and to further the aim of removing "filthy" material from the classroom and to press their agenda. One member stated, "School decisions should be based on the absolutes of Christian behavior." In *Zykan v. Warsaw (IN) Community School Corporation and Warsaw School Board of Trustees (1980)*, the plaintiffs claimed that the school board had removed the books from classrooms because "words in the books offended social, political, and moral tastes and not because the books, taken as a whole, were lacking in educational value."

The American Civil Liberties Union attorney associated with the case hoped that the state would recognize academic freedom as a First Amendment right. The suit charged that the school officials had violated students' "right to know" and the constitutional guarantee of academic freedom, but on December 3, 1979, the Indiana District Court rejected these claims and dismissed the suit. The plaintiffs appealed the decision, but the Court of Appeals sided with the school board and proclaimed that the school board had not violated anyone's constitutional rights because the right of "academic freedom" is limited at the secondary school level. On August 22, 1980, Judge Walter J. Cummings of the Seventh Circuit Court determined that "the student's right to and need for such freedom is bounded by the level of his or her intellectual development" and noted that the local school board has many powers to regulate high school classrooms. This case further strengthened the authority of school boards to select and remove books from and woman-hating Marco, who beats her up; and her conventional and ordinary college boyfriend Buddy Willard, who wants marriage and a traditional life. At the end of the first part, her last night in New York, Esther throws all her clothes off the hotel roof in a mock ceremony that reveals her disorientation.

In the second part, covering chapters 10 through 13, Esther's psychological deterioration continues as she returns home to see the "white, shining, identical clap-board houses with their interstices of well-groomed green [that] proceeded past, one bar after another in a large but escape-proof cage." Increasingly depressed, Esther cannot work or sleep, and she refuses to wash her hair or to change her clothes. Shock treatments deepen her depression and increase her obsession with death and suicide. At the end of this part, Esther visits her father's grave, then crawls beneath her house and consumes sleeping pills until she becomes unconscious.

The third section of the novel, chapters 14 through 20, details Esther's slow and painful recovery after the suicide attempt. She resists all efforts to help her when first hospitalized in the psychiatric ward of a public facility, but her move to a private mental hospital produces great progress. During short leaves from the hospital, she goes to Boston and obtains a diaphragm, then experiences her first sexual encounter, a wholly unpleasant experience. Despite this disillusionment, and despite the death of Joan, another mental patient to whom she has become close, Esther looks forward to leaving the mental asylum and returning to college. Yet she remains unsure if she will have another breakdown: "How did I know that someday—at college, in Europe, somewhere, anywhere—the bell jar, with its stifling distortions, wouldn't descend again?"

CENSORSHIP HISTORY

The Bell Jar has been challenged for its characters' discussions of sexuality and because it advocates an "objectionable" lifestyle. In one instance, the main character observes that her boyfriend's genitals are disappointing because they remind her of "turkey neck and turkey gizzards." The young college women yearn for sexual experience, and the main character purchases a diaphragm and seeks an anonymous sexual encounter. Beyond perceived obscenity, the novel aroused challenges because it openly rejects traditional marriage and motherhood. Characterizing marriage as a prison of dull domestic duties, Plath describes mothers as drudges with dirty, demanding children, while wives are subservient and inferior to their husbands.

In 1977, in Warsaw, Indiana, Teresa Burnau, a first-year English teacher at Warsaw Community High School, was assigned to teach an elective course entitled "Women in Literature" using texts that had previously been approved and ordered for the course. Before school began in September, the principal ordered Burnau to remove the literary anthology *Growing* school libraries and classrooms and provided warning to individuals who sought academic freedom within the school structure.

FURTHER READING

Alexander, Paul. *Rough Magic: A Biography of Sylvia Plath.* New York: Viking Press, 1991.

Butscher, Edward. *Sylvia Plath: Method and Madness.* New York: Seabury Press, 1975.

Hawthorn, Jeremy. *Multiple Personality and the Disintegration of Literary Character: From Oliver Goldsmith to Sylvia Plath.* New York: Ballantine Books, 1983.

MacPherson, Pat. *Reflecting on the Bell Jar.* New York: Routledge, 1991.

Newsletter on Intellectual Freedom (March 1980): 40; (July 1981): 102.

BELOVED

Author: Toni Morrison
Original date and place of publication: 1987, United States
Original publisher: Alfred A. Knopf
Literary form: Novel

SUMMARY

Beloved opens with an ominous message, the declaration that ". . . 124 was spiteful. Full of a baby's venom" and alerts the reader to the sadness and loss that the novel will reveal. Mirrors shatter without reason, and tiny handprints appear in cake icing in a house where no baby lives any longer, while kettles of chickpeas are mysteriously dumped on the floor to join soda crackers that have been crumbled and lined up meticulously along a door sill. The home at 124 Bluestone Road, a seemingly innocuous gray-and-white residence in Cincinnati, Ohio, in 1873, has lost most of its inhabitants to either death or flight due to fear. The sole inhabitants are former slave Sethe and her 18-year-old daughter Denver, whom many believe to be mentally slow, and the constant presence of Sethe's long-dead baby girl Beloved. The often surreal narrative, a complex blend of events past and present told from diverse viewpoints, examines the profound influence of the past on the lives of the characters.

Divided into three parts, the novel relates in flashbacks a story that begins five years before the start of the American Civil War and continues into the decade following the war's end. Part I is nearly twice as long as Parts II and III and provides an account of the years Sethe spent as a slave, recounts the details of her escape and her murder of her infant daughter Beloved and the attempted murder of her sons that led the community to shun her, and provides an account of her reawakening to life through the appearance of Paul D. Part I also relates the appearance of a young woman who seems to be the adult embodiment of her dead daughter Beloved. She is the person to whom

Denver turns in an obsessive manner for companionship and attention. In Part II, Sethe's re-entrance to the outside world is reversed, as Paul D leaves and the young stranger Beloved dominates both Denver and Sethe, who believes her to be the reincarnation of her infant daughter. Stamp Paid, who reveals the newspaper clipping that results in Paul D's exit from 124 Bluestone Road, tries to visit Sethe, but the door remains closed to his knocking and he hears voices, "loud, urgent, all speaking at once" that he attributes to ghosts of black people that have suffered at the hands of whites. Paid also attempts to find a home in the community for Paul D, who lives in the church basement after leaving Sethe's home and who finds himself unable to forgive her for her crime nor forgive himself for allowing the young stranger to seduce him repeatedly and, as he claims to himself, against his will. He admits to being afraid of Sethe because of her crime and cries out despondently to Paid, "How much is a nigger supposed to take?" to which Paid responds, "All he can."

In Part III, what began as a happy bonding among the three women—Sethe, Beloved, and Denver—turns bitter as Sethe lavishes love on the woman she believes to be her long-dead daughter and the closeness of the two closes out Denver. Beloved voices recriminations for Sethe's actions, expressing anguish for what she has suffered, thus leading Sethe to plead for forgiveness and to protest that she used a handsaw to try to kill her sons and succeeded in killing her daughter because of her great love for them and the desire to keep them from being taken into slavery when the schoolteacher arrived to recapture her. Sethe's obsession with Beloved leads her to report to work at Sawyer's restaurant later each day, until she is fired. With no income, the household nearly starves, until Denver takes control, searches for a job, and, through her efforts, reignites the concern and respect of the community, which brings the family food. The extent to which Sethe has become mentally unhinged is clear when Denver's new employer, a white man named Bodwin, arrives to drive Denver to work. Sethe attacks him with an ice pick, because she believes him to be one of the men who had walked the same path to the house 18 years earlier as they came to enforce the Fugitive Law and to return her to slavery. While women who had crowded into the yard after hearing the altercation wrest the pick from Sethe's hand, Beloved leaves the porch and disappears. When Paul D later returns to the house to Sethe, he finds her lying in Baby Suggs's bed, looking confused and ready for death. She cries out to him that she has lost her "best thing," Beloved. Paul D holds her hand and responds, "You your best thing." The novel closes with her question, "Me? Me?"

The sometimes harsh details of the characters' experiences reveal the multiple indignities and the suffering the characters endured while slaves and continue to endure in the aftermath of the war when seemingly freed. Aside from setting the historical context of the main character's actions and the brief mention of sons who said they left to fight, Morrison makes no use of the war in developing her characters and in explaining their circumstances. Rather, she castigates the system of slavery for its role in destroying black families, separating children from their "ma'ams," setting a value on black women as breeders and black men as studs, and treating them as nothing more than livestock to be bought, sold, and bartered for the profit of "whitepeople."

Sethe, a "used-to-be-slave woman," and Denver live in isolation at 124 Bluestone Road, a formerly happy house that once served as a way station for slaves running away to freedom in the North and that was often filled with friends of Sethe's mother-in-law, Baby Suggs, a "holy" woman. They have become used to hearing the sounds of the spirit baby crawling up the stairs that were painted white especially for her many years before and of cleaning up the damage and resituating furniture moved by the spirit.

When the novel begins, Baby Suggs has been dead for nearly a decade, Sethe's sons have left out of fear of the seemingly malevolent spirit of their baby sister Beloved, and the other "coloredpeople" in the town refuse to go near the house. The sudden appearance of Paul D, who knew Sethe and Halle at Sweet Home, and who is one of the few "Sweet Home men" still alive, angers the spirit into a violent rage of thrown objects and furniture. Paul D fights back and succeeds in driving the spirit from the house, leaving Denver feeling deprived of a presence that had lessened her loneliness. Only days later, when the three return from a carnival, they find a young woman wearing a black dress and new shoes sitting on the stump in their yard. She professes to have no memory of her past and claims that her name is Beloved.

Eighteen years before the novel opens, Sethe, in the later stages of her pregnancy carrying Denver, sent her two sons and baby daughter Beloved to the safety of Baby Suggs's house, expecting to follow soon after with her husband Halle, Baby Suggs's son. Sethe was living in Sweet Home, a plantation formerly owned by a benign master whose death brought his sadistic brother-in-law the schoolteacher as overseer, who made the worst abuses of slavery a reality for the plantation inhabitants. While preparing to run, Sethe was caught and abused by the schoolteacher's nephews and learns later from Paul D that Halle had watched the attack, too frightened to intervene, and had later gone mad from the knowledge. The memory of the experience haunts her. "I am full God damn it of two boys with mossy teeth, one sucking on my breast the other holding me down, their book-reading teacher watching and writing it up. I am still full of that, God watching, above me in the loft—hiding close by—the one place he thought no one would look for him, looking on what I couldn't look at all. And not stopping them—looking and letting it happen."

Paul D also reveals a range of indignities that he and other former slaves have suffered. Incarcerated in Alfred, Georgia, as part of a chain gang, he was weakened and exhausted by the heavy chains on his legs and wrists, and "his hands quit taking instruction. They would not hold his penis to urinate or a spoon to scoop lima beans into his mouth." He thinks of the steel bit that he has worn in his mouth, like a restrained horse, and he is bitter when he recalls the sexual abuse perpetrated by white chain gang guards.

> Kneeling in the mist, they waited for the whim of a guard, or two, or three. Or maybe all of them wanted it. Wanted it from one prisoner in particular or none—or all.
> "Breakfast: Want some breakfast, nigger"
> "Yes, sir."
> "Hungry, nigger?"
> "Yes, sir."
> "Here you go."
> Occasionally a kneeling man chose gunshot in his head as the price, maybe, of taking a bit of foreskin with him to Jesus. Paul D did not know that then. He was looking at his palsied hands, smelling the guard, listening to his soft grunts so like the doves', as he stood before the man kneeling in the mist on his right. Convinced he was next, Paul D retched—vomiting up nothing at all. An observing guard smashed his shoulder with the rifle and the engaged one decided to skip the new man for the time being lest his pants and shoes got soiled by nigger puke.

References are made throughout the novel to the violence that slaves endured at the hands of their white masters and the white authorities on a routine basis and of Baby Suggs for whom slave life had "busted her legs, back, head, eyes, hands, kidneys, womb and tongue." Sethe recalls the whipping she endured and describes the scars that remain on her back, branching out like a tree up her spine and across her shoulder blades.

One of the most graphic descriptions of violence is of Sethe's use of a handsaw to murder her baby daughter Beloved by slicing under her tiny chin, her attempted murder of her sons, and their discovery.

> Inside, two boys bled in the sawdust and dirt at the feet of a nigger woman holding a blood-soaked child to her chest with one hand and an infant by the heels in the other. She did not look at them; she simply swung the baby toward the wall of planks, missed and tried to connect a second time.

Such passages have created consternation in parents who seek to remove the novel from school reading lists.

CENSORSHIP HISTORY

Beloved has been challenged in school districts because of the violence that permeates the novel. In 1995, parents of students attending St. Johns County Schools in St. Augustine, Florida, challenged the use of the book as part of the required reading, but the school board voted to retain the book after receiving recommendations from a review committee composed of parents, teachers, and administrators. In 1996, parents of students attending the

Round Rock, Texas, Independent High School submitted a formal complaint to the school board and asked to have the book removed from the required reading list because it is too violent. After reviewing recommendations by a committee composed of students, teachers, and administrators, the school board voted to retain the novel on the district required reading list. In 1997, a member of the Madawska, Maine, School Committee challenged the use of the book as a required reading in the advanced placement English classes. The book had been a required reading for six years and had not previously been the object of complaints. The school district board honored the recommendations of an especially created committee composed of parents, teachers, and school administrators to retain the book. In 1998, a parent of a student attending the Sarasota County, Florida, schools filed a complaint requesting removal of the novel from the reading lists because it contained "inappropriate sexual material." The school board voted to retain the book.

In 1998, the Anaheim Union High School District school board in Illinois banned *Beloved* from the school district curriculum in a 4-1 vote because a member of the community complained that the novel contained material that was "too graphic." The novel, originally approved by an instructional materials review committee, was removed from the proposed reading list for advanced placement English classes. Commenting on her vote to ban the novel, school board trustee Katherine Smith told a reporter for the *Chicago Tribune*, "I think that there are so many other wonderful creative works of literature out there we could use. . . . We need literature that is uplifting and positive."

More recently in 2006, *Beloved* was among nine books on the required reading list that were challenged in the second-largest high school district in Illinois, an act that "triggered debate over whether works praised in literary circles are high art or smut." The controversy began when Leslie Pinney, a Township High School District 214 board member, identified books on the reading list that she considered to "contain vulgar language, brutal imagery or depictions of sexual situations inappropriate for students." The novels Pinney identified as inappropriate reading material, in addition to *Beloved*, are SLAUGHTERHOUSE-FIVE by Kurt Vonnegut, THE THINGS THEY CARRIED by Tim O'Brien, THE AWAKENING by Kate Chopin, FREAKONOMICS by Steven D. Levitt and Stephen J. Dubner, THE BOTANY OF DESIRE: A PLANT'S EYE VIEW OF THE WORLD by Michael Pollan, THE PERKS OF BEING A WALLFLOWER by Stephen Chbosky, FALLEN ANGELS by Walter Dean Myers, and HOW THE GARCIA GIRLS LOST THEIR ACCENTS by Julia Alvarez. The school board member admitted that she had not read most of the books she targeted and claimed that she did not want to ban the books from the district libraries, but in class she wanted "to replace them with books that address the same themes without explicit material." Her objection to *Beloved* focused on an early scene in the book in which Paul D remembers the way in which the five "Sweet Home" men, deprived of the company of women, left Sethe alone when "the iron-eyed girl" arrived as "a timely present" for their master's wife Mrs. Garner. "They were young and so sick with the absence of women they had taken to calves. . . . And so they were: Paul D Garner, Paul F Garner, Paul A Garner, Halle Suggs, and Sixo, the wild man. All in their twenties, minus women, fucking cows, dreaming of rape, thrashing on pallets, rubbing their thighs and waiting for the new girl. . . . She waited a year. And the Sweet Home men abused cows while they waited for her." The challenges were the first in more than 20 years that someone had attempted to remove books from the reading lists in the Arlington Heights–based district, which employed an extensive review process based on established reading lists. In defense of the choices, English and Fine Arts department head Chuck Venegoni told a reporter for the *Chicago Tribune*, "This is not some serendipitous decision to allow someone to do what they felt like doing because they had something about talking about something kinky in front of kids. It's insulting to hardworking people who really do care about kids." He criticized Pinney's approach of taking a few passages out of context to condemn entire books and observed, "there is nothing in any of those books that even remotely approaches what an objective person would call pornography." Although the school district had an opt-out clause that allowed parents to request that their child read another book if they find the assigned material objectionable, Pinney found the current measures ineffectual "because unless you're digging around the student's backpack, looking at the books and reading them, how exactly will you know what your student is reading?"

Five hundred people attended the school board meeting on Thursday, May 25, 2006, to debate whether to keep *Beloved* and the other novels on the school reading lists. Supporters of the ban asserted that their efforts were "to protect students from smut" and some people, such as Arlington Heights resident Brude Ticknell, claimed that "teachers promoting the books were motivated by their own progressive social agendas." Students took the debate to the social networking site MySpace.com, and sophomore Scott Leipprandt placed a petition against the ban on the Prospect High page, which nearly 500 students and alumni from the six high schools in the district signed. Leipprandt told a *Chicago Tribune* reporter that fighting the banning of books is important. "It's important because it shows us things. All these things happen in real life. By banning it, it doesn't give us the opportunity to talk about it before we encounter it in real life." After a long meeting during which hundreds of people spoke, the school board voted 6-1 in favor of approving the required reading list without change.

FURTHER READING

Doyle, Robert P. *2007 Banned Books Resource Guide*. Chicago: American Library Association, 2007.

Francisco, Jamie. "Book-Ban Debate Is Long, Impassioned: More Than 350 Sign Up to Speak to School Board." *Chicago Tribune*, May 26, 2006.

———. "Explicit Move Is Made to Ban Books from Reading List." *Chicago Tribune*, May 24, 2006.

Keilman, John, and Jamie Francisco. "Book-Ban Fights Are Far from Over: Reading Lists Face Scrutiny across the State." *Chicago Tribune*, May 28, 2006.

"School Board Bans Morrison's 'Beloved.'" *Chicago Tribune*, May 17, 1998.

THE BEST SHORT STORIES BY NEGRO WRITERS

Editor: Langston Hughes
Original date and place of publication: 1967, United States
Original publisher: Little, Brown & Company
Literary form: Short story collection

SUMMARY

The work is a collection of 47 short stories, which form a comprehensive anthology of writings by African Americans, ranging in time from the first well-known writers Charles W. Chesnutt and Paul Laurence Dunbar through such popular writers of the 1960s as Ronald Milner, Robert Boles, and Alice Walker. Also included are works by such noted African Americans as Jean Toomer, Richard Wright, Zora Neale Hurston, Ralph Ellison, Willard Motley, John A. Williams, Frank Yerby, and James Baldwin.

The subject matter of the stories ranges widely, from the fears, violence, and lynchings experienced in the Deep South to the glittering interracial parties in the North during the Harlem Renaissance. They contain characters as diverse as the tragically overworked sharecroppers and the well-dressed, glamorous Harlem dancers. Characters in these stories exhibit the range of African-American experience in the United States over seven decades. The settings are equally diverse, including as they do the South, North, East, West, Panama Canal Zone, Chicago Loop, and Harlem. The writers use dialect and realistic dialogue to provide a true-to-life portrayal of African Americans whose lives cover time periods from the Reconstruction through the Harlem Renaissance, the Depression, World War II, and the 1960s.

In faithful renderings, the writers also reveal society across time without a polite veneer to soften the criticism. White Americans are not spared their criticism but neither are African Americans. People are portrayed both in their ordinary, day-to-day pursuits and in pursuits that are unique to their history. Several of the stories present light-skinned characters who "pass" to avoid discrimination and to gain a toehold in white society, but stories also appear whose characters wear their color proudly.

CENSORSHIP HISTORY

In 1976, the school board of Island Trees (New York) Union Free District removed the short story collection from the junior and senior high school libraries along with BLACK BOY, THE FIXER, GO ASK ALICE, SLAUGHTER-HOUSE-FIVE, DOWN THESE MEAN STREETS, A HERO AIN'T NOTHIN' BUT A SANDWICH, LAUGHING BOY, THE NAKED APE, SOUL ON ICE, and *A Reader for Writers*. The books were charged by complainants with being immoral, anti-American, anti-Christian, or "just plain filthy." As entered in the court record, the specific objections to *The Best Short Stories by Negro Writers* concerned the use of street vernacular, as well as such allegedly obscene passages as the following: "You need some pussy. Come on, let's go up to the whore house on the hill." "She first became aware of the warm tense nipples on her breasts. Her hands went up gently to calm them." "In profile, his penis hung like a stout tassel. She could even tell that he was circumcised."

The books had been removed after several board members attended a conference of a group called Parents of New York United, in Watkins Glen, New York. When parents and students opposed the move, school board members returned *Laughing Boy* by Oliver LaFarge and *Black Boy* by Richard Wright to the libraries. In March 1976, a group of residents of the Island Trees School District joined to write a letter to protest the action to New York State Education Commissioner Ewald B. Nyquist.

In deference to the protests of parents and students, the school board appointed a committee made up of parents and teachers to review the books and to determine which, if any, of the books had merit. The committee recommended that seven of the books be returned to the library shelves, that two be placed on restricted shelves, and that two be removed from the library, but the school board ignored these recommendations and voted to keep all but one of the books off the shelves.

Five students challenged this censorship, claiming that the school board had violated their constitutional rights under the guise of protecting their social and moral welfare. On January 4, 1977, they filed a lawsuit against the Island Trees School Board to have the books returned to the bookshelves. The suit, filed on behalf of the students with the state supreme court in Mineola by the New York Civil Liberties Union, maintained that the ban violated their freedom of speech and academic freedom. The executive director of the New York Civil Liberties Union called the Island Trees action "part of a recent epidemic of book censorship in New York" and other states initiated by "self-appointed vigilantes who do not have the insight to understand their educational mission." The United Teachers of Island Trees also filed a grievance with the state, asserting that the academic freedom of the teachers had been violated. The case, *Board of Education v. Pico*, 457 U.S. 853, 102 S.Ct. 2799, 73 L.Ed.2s 435 (1982), was heard before a federal district court, which ruled in favor of the school board. The court declared that the Island Trees School Board did not violate the First Amendment of the United States Constitution by banning books from its libraries. In a 25-page decision rendered in Westbury, U.S. district court judge George C. Pratt determined that removal of the books "fell within the broad range of discretion to educational officials who are elected by the community." He wrote, "While removal of such books from a school library may, indeed, in this court's view, reflect a misguided educational philosophy, it does not constitute a sharp and direct infringement of any First Amendment right."

The students appealed the decision, and the appellate court remanded the case for trial before the U.S. Supreme Court, which determined that the district court had acted without authority in rendering a summary decision against the students. The justices were sharply divided and, in a 5-4 decision, upheld the right of the students to challenge the board's actions. The majority decision determined that a school board had the right to use its discretion in deciding issues within its district, but such decisions must be made within the boundaries of the First Amendment. In announcing the decision, Justice William J. Brennan wrote, "Local school boards have broad discretion in the management of school affairs but this discretion must be exercised in a manner that comports with the transcendent imperatives of the First Amendment; the First Amendment rights of students may be directly and sharply implicated by the removal of books from the shelves of a school library; and local school boards may not remove books from school library shelves simply because they dislike the ideas contained in those books."

In their dissenting opinion, Chief Justice Warren Burger and Justices Sandra D. O'Connor, Lewis Powell, and William H. Rehnquist issued a warning as to the role of the Supreme Court in making local censorship decisions: "If the plurality's view were to become the law, the court would come perilously close to becoming a 'super censor' of school board library decisions and the Constitution does not dictate that judges, rather than parents, teachers, and local school boards, must determine how the standards of morality and vulgarity are to be treated in the classroom." Thus, in their reluctance to place the Supreme Court in the position of local censor, the conservative justices recommended that the task of setting local community standards remain in local hands.

The U.S. Supreme Court ruled against the school board on June 25, 1982, in *Board of Education, Island Trees Union Free School District No. 26 v. Pico*, and the books were returned to the libraries.

FURTHER READING

Goldman, Ari L. "After 14 Months, a Vote on 'the Books.'" *New York Times*, May 22, 1977, p. 50.

Hurwitz, Leon. *Historical Dictionary of Censorship in the United States.* Westport, Conn.: Greenwood Press, 1985.

Jenkinson, Edward B. *Censors in the Classroom: The Mind Benders.* Carbondale: University of Southern Illinois Press, 1979.

"L.I. Parents Draft Protest to Nyquist on School Book Ban." *New York Times,* March 24, 1976, p. 41.

"L.I. Schools Press Effort to Avert Book Ban Trial." *New York Times,* March 8, 1981, p. 40.

"L.I. Students File Suit to Overturn School Book Ban." *New York Times,* January 5, 1977, p. 23.

Newsletter on Intellectual Freedom (May 1978): 57; (November 1982): 197.

Silver, Roy R. "High Court Appeal Likely on Book Ban." *New York Times,* August 5, 1979, p. 17.

———. "L.I. School Board Bans Nine Books." *New York Times,* July 29, 1976, p. 37.

Williams, John A. "Blackballing." In *Censored Books: Critical Viewpoints,* edited by Nicholas J. Karolides, Lee Burress, and John M. Kean, 11–18. Metuchen, N.J.: Scarecrow Press, 1992.

BLACK LIKE ME

Author: John Howard Griffin
Original date and place of publication: 1961, United States
Original publisher: Houghton Mifflin
Literary form: Journal

SUMMARY

Written in journal form, the personal narrative presents an introspective look at racism, examining its consequences in a chronicle of the experiences of a Caucasian social scientist who darkens his skin, shaves his head and assumes the life of an African-American man in the Deep South in 1959. The author acknowledges that as the result of this experiment his life and his views of both races must change forever. Griffin learns that, after having immersed himself in black culture and dealt with the white world as an African American, he can never again live completely as a Caucasian, for his views regarding his own race have changed.

In the opening pages of the work, the author identifies the background of his study and explains his reasons for concern with skin pigmentation. He rationalizes that, even though he is considered to be an expert on racial issues, he has no real idea of what it is like to be an African American and to live in the Deep South. After arranging funding with the magazine *Sepia,* the author travels to New Orleans, where he locates a doctor and begins to undergo the skin-darkening treatments that will change his racial appearance.

Griffin examines his anxiety once the dosage is stabilized and he completes his transformation. Wandering the New Orleans streets, he talks to people with whom he had spoken when he was white and observes a difference in their response now that he approaches them as an African American. He identifies the issues and problems that come with his new, nonwhite identity. First and foremost is the unwritten line between the black and the white races that he violates when he mistakenly allows a white woman to sit near his fellow blacks on a bus. His efforts to deal with the sometimes confusing segregation laws involving rest-rooms and restaurants offer a strong indictment against a society that rigidly controlled the access of African Americans to necessities that white Americans could take for granted. In contrast, Griffin enjoys the acceptance of his newly adopted race when the one man in whom he confides his secret eases the transition by teaching him the informal rules of "Negro" behavior.

The author observes that life as an African American is difficult and that security and the respect of others are determined by skin color. As an African American, he is a more frequent target of violence and looked upon as little more than trash by society as a whole. By day he hunts for the jobs available to him as a black man and for a semblance of humanity from the society in which he lives. By night, he roams the New Orleans pavements, falling deeper and deeper into his blackness. The author finds that other blacks treat him with a great deal of respect and kindness, more so than when he was white. But he also finds that white individuals have lost the humanity and respect they showed when he was white.

Griffin's divergent experiences lead him to postulate that the problem of the "Negro" is twofold. African Americans confront the racism and prejudice of white society, and they must also deal with self-hatred, low self-esteem, and loss of pride. He suggests that the two races will be able to live in harmony only when these two ills are eradicated from society.

Griffin reports both blatant and subtle differences in the way that white society in New Orleans treats each race. In one instance, a woman who had conversed with him pleasantly when he was white refuses to cash a traveler's check for him when he is black, even though the transaction involves no financial risk. He observes that instances such as this are common for the black man and learns that most cafés and bathrooms become off-limits to him due to his dark skin color.

In order to widen the significance of the study, Griffin extended the setting to other cities in the South. His reported observations show that the response to his new identity remained relatively consistent. Griffin records that he was addressed by whites as "boy" or "nigger" and that the actions of whites grew increasingly difficult to tolerate as he experienced the persecution and bigotry of segregation and racism. In Mobile, Alabama, white men demanded to know his business in the area and threatened him with death should he cause trouble.

Griffin reports that the way in which the threats were expressed strongly suggested that, if he were murdered, nothing would be done to identify his killers because of his race.

Shortly before terminating his one-month odyssey, the author experienced a revealing incident regarding the nature of white liberalism. Griffin visited the Tuskegee Institute for a day and met a visiting white academic who insisted on proving that he was a trustworthy white whom blacks should not fear. Despite good intentions, his ingrained prejudice emerged all too clearly when he suggested that a black man who was legitimately selling turkeys on the street might have stolen them.

The author reports in the final entries of the work that his experiment elicited hostility from people all over the country. He and his family received death threats and were forced to leave their home.

CENSORSHIP HISTORY

The book has been one of the 30 most frequently attacked books in the United States since its first, partial appearance in 1960 as an article in *Sepia* magazine and its publication as a book in 1961. The principal charge, in most challenges, has been obscenity. Researchers, however, postulate that more likely the truth is that those who challenge the book are opposed to books about African Americans or other minorities. One teacher stated in a 1982 nationwide survey conducted by Lee Burress, "In a rural community, people don't care to have their children read about Negroes." This position is supported by an examination of the 20 most frequently attacked titles between 1965 and 1977. One-third depict individuals belonging to a minority group in strong protest against racism.

In 1966, the paperback edition of the novel was widely attacked as being unfit for children to read. In Wisconsin, a man sued the local school board, claiming that the book contained obscene language, that it was integration-centered, vulgar, filthy, and unsuitable for any age level. He further charged that his child was damaged by having read the book as an assignment in English class. The court dismissed the case.

In 1967, the parent of an Arizona high school student challenged the use of the book in the classroom because of its obscene and vulgar language and the situations depicted. The school board removed the book from the classroom. Language, particularly "four-letter words," was the charge leveled in 1977 by a Pennsylvania parent and a clergyman, but the challenge was denied. An objection to the subject matter was similarly denied in a 1982 challenge of the book in Illinois. In Missouri in 1982, however, the material was placed on a closed shelf when a parent challenged the book on the grounds that it was obscene and vulgar and "because of black people being in the book."

FURTHER READING

Burress, Lee. *Battle of the Books: Literary Censorship in the Public Schools, 1950–1985.* Metuchen, N.J.: Scarecrow Press, 1989.

Farrell, Walter C., Jr. *"Black Like Me:* In Defense of a Racial Reality." In *Censored Books: Critical Viewpoints,* edited by Nicholas Karolides, Lee Burress, and John M. Kean, 117–124. Metuchen, N.J.: Scarecrow Press, 1993.

Griffin, John Howard. *Racial Equality: The Myth and the Reality.* ERIC Education Document Reprint Series, No. 26 (March 1971).

Sharpe, Ernest, Jr. "The Man Who Changed His Skin." *American Heritage* 40 (February 1989): 44–55.

BLESS THE BEASTS AND CHILDREN

Author: Glendon Swarthout
Original date and place of publication: 1970, United States
Original publisher: Doubleday & Company
Literary form: Novel

SUMMARY

Swarthout's *Bless the Beasts and Children* is a novel that identifies the fears of six boys, ages 13 through 17, and examines how they bond to face these fears. The story takes place in the Box Canyon Boys Camp, a dumping ground for the misfit children of wealthy parents who are too busy with their own lives to give their own children attention, and describes how six losers become winners on one supreme mission of peace and love.

The novel begins on a warm summer night, as Cotton, the leader of a group called the Bedwetters, is awakened by a bad dream in which he imagines the boys as hunted animals. He learns that one of the boys, Lally 2, is missing, so he awakens Lally 1, the missing boy's brother, and the rest of the Bedwetters.

Cotton informs the others that Lally 2 is missing, and the group leaves camp to find him. When they find Lally 2 near the main road, he refuses to go back with Cotton because of what he and the others had seen earlier that day. The reader is not yet made aware of the incident.

Cotton and the boys discuss breaking camp and completing a life-or-death mission. They vote, and the decision to go on with the mission is unanimous. Cotton gives the boys five minutes to return to the tent and pack for the long trip. They then push one of the trucks out of camp for Teft to hotwire but abandon this scheme when the incline becomes too steep. Instead, they ride horses into town, where Teft hotwires a pickup truck that they steal.

On the road, the six boys, none of whom possesses a driver's license, fear the police and keep a low profile to avoid arousing suspicion. They stop to eat at an all-night diner, where they are harassed by a couple of cowboys who joke about their ages. To avoid trouble, the boys return to the truck and drive off, but the two cowboys follow them. The two men run the pickup truck off the road and taunt the boys until Teft takes out a rifle and shoots the tires of the cowboys' car. This silences the two men and allows the boys to exit the scene with a modicum of pride.

As they near their destination, the pickup truck runs out of gas. Cotton tells them that they have an important decision to make. If they continue by foot and succeed at their mission, they will be found truant from camp and incarcerated. However, if they head back to camp, there is a good chance that they will not get caught. This is when the reader learns the purpose of the mission and the horror the boys had seen on the previous day. While returning from a camping excursion, they had gone to view some buffalo, but, to their utter dismay, it was slaughtering day for the poor beasts. People had been randomly chosen to kill the animals. This sent terror through the boys' hearts and motivated them to rescue the remaining buffalo.

Cotton votes to go back, but the rest of the boys vote to persevere and save the beasts, so Cotton joins them. They reach the buffalo preserve where, after a failed rescue attempt that almost kills five of the boys, Cotton devises a plan that will save the buffalo.

Teft will drive a game preserve truck through the field while several of the boys throw hay to entice the buffalo out of the pen. The buffalo will follow along while eating until they reach the distant fence that separates them from freedom and capture. This plan is automatically implemented, but the fence proves too strong for them to break through.

The boys also hear vehicles in the distance. Cotton orders Teft to fire the rifle at these vehicles in order to buy him some time. As Teft complies, Cotton boards the truck and revs the engine. Then, followed by about 40 buffalo, he crashes the truck into the fence, knocking it down and freeing the buffalo. He does not stop but continues along at full speed until the truck overturns and he is killed. The other vehicles arrive at the scene to find the buffalo free and the five boys crying.

CENSORSHIP HISTORY

The ingenuity and independence of the boys have motivated parents and school officials to charge that the book is critical of parents and that it encourages critical attitudes toward authority. In addition, parents have charged that the book contains questionable subject matter, regarding the issues of bed-wetting and running away, as well as "objectionable" language.

In 1978, parents in Waukesha, Wisconsin, complained that the novel was "psychopathically sick" and should not be required reading for students in the course entitled "Perspectives on Death and Aggression." The issue was heard by the school board, one member of which stated that endorsing the novel would be akin to "putting a rubber stamp" on violence. Although the boys are on a quest to save the buffalo from needless slaughter, the board member cited the descriptions of the slaughter and the boys' plan to rescue the buffalo as being unnecessarily "graphic." The school board voted to allow the course to continue but determined not to buy enough copies of the book for all enrolled students, so the teacher could not assign it to the class as a whole. Thus, while the board agreed that existing copies of the book would remain available for use by students in the course, their decision not to purchase enough books effectively prevented the entire class from discussing it.

In 1987, parents in Dupree, South Dakota, complained to the school board that the novel should not be allowed in the classroom because of its violent descriptions and obscene language. After considering the complaint, the school board banned the novel from all high school English classes, charging that it contained "offensive language and vulgarity."

FURTHER READING

Jenkinson, Edward B. *Censors in the Classroom: The Mind Benders.* Carbondale: Southern Illinois University Press, 1979.
Newsletter on Intellectual Freedom (January 1988): 12.
"Using Adolescent Novels as Transitions to Literary Classics: *Bless the Beasts and Children.*" *English Journal* 78 (March 1989): 83–84.

BLUBBER

Author: Judy Blume
Original date and place of publication: 1974, United States
Original publisher: Bradbury Press
Literary form: Young adult novel

SUMMARY

Blubber teaches a lesson to all those children who take pleasure in tormenting an easy victim, by showing them that today's tormentor can easily become tomorrow's tormented. The novel opens in a fifth-grade classroom as students take turns giving oral reports on mammals. Students sitting in their seats pass around notes and pictures, look at the clock, and yawn openly while Mrs. Minnish, the teacher, tries hard to look interested. Linda Fischer, "the pudgiest girl in our class, but not in our grade," is the last to report, and her study is about whales. She covers the topic methodically, then speaks about the removal and uses of whale blubber and shows the class a picture of blubber.

This gives her classmate Wendy an idea. She writes "Blubber is a good name for her" on a scrap of paper and passes it to Caroline, who then passes it to Jill Brenner. The note soon makes its way halfway around the class, creating a disruption as Linda tries valiantly to finish her report. On the bus after school, Jill and the other students tease Linda, calling her "Blubber," taking her jacket, and covering her hair with spit balls.

Halloween is near, and Jill decides to be a "flenser," a person who strips the blubber off whales, a term that she learned from Linda's report. The students wear their costumes to school, and when Jill, Caroline, and Wendy encounter Linda in the girls' room they strip off her costume cape and threaten to strip her entirely because Jill is dressed as a flenser "and the flenser's the one who strips the blubber." They rip open her blouse and pull up her skirt. Then Wendy, dressed as a queen, commands Linda to kiss her sneaker. The frightened and crying girl obeys. That night, the girls wind toilet paper through the trees of the Fischer house, spray plastic string on the house, and write "Blubber lives here" in blue chalk on the sidewalk.

At school, the fifth-grade students blame Linda for everything bad that happens to them, from low grades to being punished for talking. The abuse escalates until the class, usually left unmonitored in their room during lunch, decides to place Linda on trial. Wendy declares herself the judge and demands that Linda not have a lawyer. Jill, whose father is a lawyer, protests the "legality" of the trial and, with a sudden feeling of fair play, releases Linda from a locked closet.

The following day, Jill learns that Wendy has retaliated by declaring that she and Linda are now "best friends," and Jill becomes the class scapegoat. Labeled "B.B." for "Baby Brenner" because she refused to participate in the terrorizing, she is ostracized and mocked. Although despondent at first, Jill eventually resumes friendships with some of her less popular classmates.

CENSORSHIP HISTORY

Blubber is one of many books written by Judy Blume that have been challenged in schools and libraries. Some of the challenges, notably those regarding FOREVER, *Deenie*, and THEN AGAIN, MAYBE I WON'T, have resulted in restrictions and banning because of their sexual content that mirrors the realistic thoughts and actions of teenagers. Other books by Blume, such as *It's Not the End of the World, Starring Sally Freedman as Herself, Superfudge*, and *Tiger Eyes*, have been challenged and banned because they contain what one community or another deems to be "objectionable" or "indecent or inappropriate" language or because the characters do not exhibit model behavior. *Blubber* is in the second category. Challenges to this novel have arisen, in part, because of the determined nastiness of the characters and the unwillingness of adults to stand up to these nasty children. Many people who have challenged the book also admit to having "a problem with the language."

In 1980, *Blubber* was removed from all of the elementary school libraries in Montgomery County, Maryland, and in 1981, the novel was temporarily banned in Sunizona, Arizona. In 1983, parents of students in the Des Moines, Iowa, schools challenged the book because of "objectionable" language, the same year that parents of students at Smith Elementary School in Del Valle, Texas, challenged the book because it contained the words *damn* and *bitch*. They further complained that the book sets a bad example because it shows children cruelly teasing a classmate. The book was retained in both districts. Also in 1983, parents of students in the Xenia (Ohio) School District called for the removal of the novel from the school libraries, claiming that it "undermines authority since the word 'bitch' is used in connection with a teacher." It was also challenged in the Akron (Ohio) School District, where parents requested its removal from the school libraries. It was retained in both cases.

The novel was placed in "restricted areas" of the elementary school libraries in Lindenwold, New Jersey, in 1984, because of "a problem with language." In the same year, parents of students in the Peoria (Illinois) School District complained that the novel contains "strong sexual content" and "obscene language" and cited its alleged "lack of social or literary value" in requesting its removal from the school libraries. After the book was considered by a specially created review committee, the school board voted to restrict it to students whose parents had given them written permission to take out the book.

In another 1984 incident, the novel was removed from Hanover (Pennsylvania) School District elementary and secondary school libraries, after parents challenged the book as being "indecent and inappropriate." The school board considered the book and decided to authorize its placement on the "restricted shelf." That same year, the book was also challenged but retained in the Casper, Wyoming, school libraries. In 1985, *Blubber* was challenged as "profane, immoral, and offensive" but retained in the Bozeman, Montana, school libraries.

In 1986, parents of students in Muskego (Wisconsin) Elementary School asked to have the book removed from the reading list because "the characters curse and the leader of the taunting [of an overweight girl] is never punished for her cruelty." A similar complaint was voiced in 1991 by parents of students at the Perry Township, Ohio, elementary schools who demanded the removal of the book from the school libraries; they claimed that the book contained no moral message. "Bad is never punished. Good never comes to the fore. Evil is triumphant." In both cases, the school boards decided that the book should remain.

FURTHER READING

Clark, Elyse. "A Slow, Subtle Exercise in Censorship." *School Library Journal* 32 (March 1986): 93–96.

Donelson, Kenneth L., and Alleen Pace Nilsen. *Literature for Today's Young Adults.* Glenview, Ill.: Scott Foresman, 1989.

Klein, Norma. "Some Thoughts on Censorship: An Author Symposium." *Top of the News* 39 (Winter 1983): 137–153.

Newsletter on Intellectual Freedom (May 1980): 51; (March 1982): 57; (May 1982): 84; (July 1982): 124, 142; (May 1983): 73, 85–86; (July 1983): 121; (September 1983): 139, 153; (November 1983): 197; (November 1984): 185; (January 1985): 8–9; (March 1985): 3, 42, 58; (July 1985): 112; (January 1987): 31; (March 1992): 41; (July 1992): 124.

Webb, C. Anne. "The Battle Continues." *English Journal* 84 (September 1995): 123–124.

BRAVE NEW WORLD

Author: Aldous Huxley
Original date and place of publication: 1932, England
Original publisher: Chatto & Windus Collins
Literary form: Novel

SUMMARY

Brave New World is a satire in which science, sex, and drugs have replaced human reason and human emotion in the "perfect" society to which Huxley gives the name "Utopia." The novel depicts an orderly society in which scientifically sophisticated genetics and pharmacology combine to produce a perfectly controlled population whose entire existence is dedicated to maintaining the stability of society. People are genetically engineered to satisfy the regulated needs of the government in regard to specific mental and physical sizes and types. Sexual promiscuity is demanded by the state for the sake of pleasure, not procreation, and women are equipped with contraceptive cartridge belts to avoid pregnancy. The only respectable way to enter the world is through incubation in a bottle—people are decanted rather than born—and learning occurs through preconditioning.

Inhabitants are created and conditioned to fit into specific social slots. Thus, in the Hatchery and Conditioning Center, varying amounts of alcohol are placed into the decanting bottles that contain the embryos to stunt mental growth and create a hierarchy of genetic classes.

Those who will be conditioned to do the monotonous and hard labor of this society receive the highest doses of alcohol to create a low mentality. Labeled in descending order of intelligence as Gammas, Deltas, and Epsilons, they are the most numerous and are produced by subjecting the fertilized egg to the Bokanovsky Process, a budding procedure that enables division of the egg into as many as 96 identical beings from one egg and up to 15,000 brothers and sisters from a single ovary. The Alphas and Betas, who carry out the work of the government, remain individualized, yet they, too, are manipulated through early conditioning. The concept of family is unknown, and the words *mother* and *father* are viewed as smut. In this systematically promiscuous world, men and women are encouraged to experience many sexual partners to avoid the development of intimate emotional relationships that might threaten their obsessive loyalty to the state.

The expected ills of human life have all been eliminated, and inhabitants of this brave new world have been freed of the worries of disease, pain, unhappiness, old age, and death. Disease has been eradicated through sterilization, and pain and unhappiness are easily banished by liberal doses of *soma*, a drug that provides a high without side effects. Smaller dosages are used to counteract depression, while larger dosages are taken to provide a long-term sense of euphoria, described by one character as a two-week vacation. Blind happiness is necessary for social stability, so all emotions are dulled. Even death takes on a new appearance. People are given treatments that keep them youthful-looking until they near the age of 60, at which time their bodies are allowed to experience a brief, soma-controlled period of aging before they disappear into the prominently placed crematoria that turn human bodies into phosphorus to be used in fertilizer.

Huxley exhibits the undesirable aspects of such a world through the characters of the Alpha-class misfit Bernard Marx and the savage John, who lives on the Savage Reservation, a pre-civilized region that has been preserved for study. John is the son of the director of Hatcheries and Conditioning (DHC) and a Beta woman who was left on the reservation by the DHC. Taken to England by Marx, John is highly uncomfortable in the emotionless and intellectually vacuous Utopia. He wants love and rejects the promiscuity of Lenina Crowne, a Utopian woman to whom he is sexually attracted but whose morals are repugnant to him. Treated as a curiosity by Utopians who clamor to see him and who gawk at him, John finds only misery in this brave new world and decides that suicide is his only solution.

CENSORSHIP HISTORY

Brave New World has evoked a range of responses from those who are made uncomfortable by Huxley's satire of society. The novel has been charged with being sordid, immoral, and obscene, and it has been condemned for vilifying the family, for giving too much attention to sex, and for encouraging illegal drug use. Many cite the sexual promiscuity of the Utopians, as did the Board of Censors of Ireland when it banned the novel in 1932, yet the novel contains no graphic scenes of sexual behavior. For the most part, people who seek to ban the novel believe that *Brave New World* is "depressing, fatalistic, and negative, and that it encourages students to adopt a lifestyle of drugs, sex and conformity, reinforcing helpless feelings that they can do nothing to make an impact on their world."

The novel has been frequently challenged in schools throughout the United States. In 1965, a teacher of English in Maryland claimed that the local school board had violated his First Amendment rights by firing him after he assigned *Brave New World* as a required reading in his class. The district court ruled against the teacher in *Parker v. Board of Education*, 237 F. Supp. 222 (D.Md) and refused his request for reinstatement in the teaching position. When the case was later heard by the circuit court, *Parker v. Board of Education*, 348 F.2d 464 (4th Cir. 1965), the presiding judge affirmed the ruling of the lower court and included in the determination the opinion that the nontenured status of the teacher accounted for the firing and not the assignment of a particular book.

In 1979, a high school principal in Matthews County, Virginia, requested that a history teacher in the high school withdraw an assignment that included *Brave New World*. The teacher assigned it anyway, and the school board terminated the teacher's contract. No further actions were taken by either party.

Use of the novel in the classroom was challenged in 1980 in Miller, Missouri, where it was removed from the curriculum, and in 1988, parents of students at Yukon (Oklahoma) High School demanded the removal of the book as a required reading because of its "language and moral content." In 1993, parents challenged the novel as a required reading in Corona-Norco (California) Unified School District based on charges that it "centered around negative activity." After consideration by the school board, the book was retained on the list, but students who objected to the novel were given alternative choices.

In September 2000, the *Mobile Register* reported that *Brave New World* was removed from the Foley High School Library after parent Kathleen Stone complained. Stone asserted that the novel, which was assigned reading in one 11th-grade English class, showed contempt for marriage and family values. High school officials removed the book from the library pending review and, as the newsletter *Intellectual Freedom* reports, emphasized that the book was not banned, but removed.

In 2003, parents of students attending a summer science academy in the South Texas Independent School District in Mercedes, Texas, challenged the use of this novel and STRANGER IN A STRANGE LAND by Robert Heinlein in the curriculum. They objected specifically to the themes of sexuality, drugs, and suicide in the novels and asserted that such adult themes were inappropriate for students. School officials retained the novels in the summer curriculum. The school board considered the matter further and voted to require school principals to automatically offer an alternative to any challenged books in order to provide parents with greater control over their children's readings.

FURTHER READING

"Another Furor over Books." *Ohio State University Monthly* 55 (December 1963): 8–12.

Bedford, Sybille. *Aldous Huxley: A Biography.* 2 vols. London: Chatto & Windus Collins, 1973–74.

Massie, Dorothy C. "Censorship in the Schools: Something Old and Something New." *Today's Education* 69 (November/December 1980): 56–62.

Matter, William W. "The Utopian Tradition and Aldous Huxley." *Science Fiction Studies* 2 (1975): 146–151.

Nahmod, Sheldon H. "Controversy in the Classroom: The High School Teacher and Freedom of Expression." *George Washington University Law Review* 39 (July 1974): 1,031.

Newsletter on Intellectual Freedom (May 1980): 52; (September 1981): 127; (July 1988): 140; (January 1994): 14; (March 1994): 70; (November 2000): 193; (November 2003): 249–250.

BRIDGE TO TERABITHIA

Author: Katherine Paterson
Original date and place of publication: 1977, United States
Original publisher: Thomas Y. Crowell Company
Literary form: Novel

SUMMARY

Bridge to Terabithia is a Newbery Award–winning novel that relates the adventures and tragedy of a 10-year-old farm boy in contemporary rural Virginia who makes an unexpected new friend, then loses her to a drowning death for which he blames himself. The fastest runner in the fifth grade, Jesse Aarons has a lively imagination and loves to draw. Leslie Burke, the new girl in school, shares his imaginative view of life and challenges his position as the fastest runner in the fifth grade. She and her parents have moved from the city, hoping to find tranquillity in rural life. Despite the taunting of his schoolmates, Jesse becomes friends with the unusual newcomer who prefers to wear sneakers and blue jeans and who has a firm and extensive knowledge of literature. Her parents, whom she calls by their first names, are writers who have moved to the country because they are "reassessing their value structure." For them and for Leslie, that means a simplified life that excludes television but includes an expensive stereo set and a small, expensive Italian sports car. The two friends find a secret hiding place, where they create their imaginary world of Terabithia. To inform Jesse of the way a magic kingdom runs and how rulers behave, Leslie lends Jesse her books about Narnia. Later, Leslie tells Jesse stories that she has read in the numerous literary works owned by her parents. When a seventh-grade girl steals Twinkies from Jesse's little sister May Belle, Leslie devises a suitably sneaky revenge to humiliate the older girl.

Terabithia becomes a haven for Leslie and Jesse, and they build a bridge of tree branches to cross the creek into their secret world. On Easter morning, after heavy rains, Jesse heads for Terabithia to meet Leslie, but he turns back after he sees that the creek is nearly overflowing its banks. Later that day, he learns that Leslie has drowned in the creek after the rope on which she was swinging broke. He runs away as guilt and anger overwhelm him, but his father finds him and makes him return. Weeks later, he takes May Belle to the site and she nearly falls into the creek while trying to cross the fragile bridge. Jesse rescues her and later builds a sturdy bridge over the creek with lumber that Leslie's parents buy for him. He also vows to share the magic of Terabithia with May Belle.

CENSORSHIP HISTORY

Bridge to Terabithia was challenged in 1986 as recommended reading for the sixth-grade curriculum in the Lincoln, Nebraska, schools because it contained "profanities" and unsuitable expletives. In 1990, the parent of a Burlington, North Carolina, fifth-grade student demanded that the book be removed from the reading list, alleging that it contained profanities, violence, and disrespect for authority. When school officials offered an alternative selection, the parent declined, stating, "We care about not only what our daughter reads, but what other children read as well." Other parents called for the creation of a review committee to systematically review books in the school curriculum to root out "anything that in any way seeks to erode traditional, moral values," but the school denied their request.

The same year, parents of children in Harwinton, Connecticut, challenged the use of *Bridge to Terabithia* and other books in the classroom, claiming that they offered a negative view of life to impressionable students and that their language and subject matter set bad examples for young people. A review committee disagreed, and the books were retained. Vulgar language was similarly the basis for a 1991 challenge in Apple Valley (California) Unified School District. A district review committee recommended that the novel be retained, citing its literary value and the strong interest in it by parents and students. The district board of trustees refused to ban the novel and, instead, offered students an alternative selection.

In 1992, parents in the Mechanicsburg (Pennsylvania) Area School District requested that the novel be removed from the school library because it contained offensive language and encouraged a morbid fascination with death. One objector cited four instances in which "damn" is used, two of "hell" and one of "bitched," and several objectors demanded that all material in the library should reflect the opinions of parents. The superintendent agreed with an especially formed review committee which decided unanimously that the novel should be retained and defended the language, stating that it was not meant to be disrespectful and that it was integral to the purpose of the story. That same year, parents in the Cleburne (Texas) Independent School District cited the profane language in the book and demanded that it be removed from the school libraries. The novel was retained in the libraries but removed from the required reading list.

Parent concerns in 1993 regarding alleged "obscenities" in the novel led the Oskaloosa (Kansas) school district board of education to enact a new policy regarding the assignment of books in the curriculum. Teachers were made responsible for examining each of the required texts used in their classes to determine the number of profanities included in each. They must now list each profanity and the number of times that it appears in the book, then send the list home for parents to review. Before any given book can be used in the classroom, parents must provide written permission for their children to read it. Parents in Gettysburg, Pennsylvania, also challenged use of the book in 1993, voicing a similar concern for the use of offensive language by characters in this book and in *Jacob Have I Loved*, by the same author.

In 2002, parents of students attending a middle school in Cromwell, Connecticut, challenged use of the book in the middle school curriculum. They expressed concern that the book "promotes witchcraft and violence." The matter was reviewed by a district committee, which voted to retain the book.

FURTHER READING

Newsletter Intellectual Freedom (March 1987): 67; (March 1991): 44; (May 1992): 95; (September 1992): 162–163; (November 1992): 198; (March 1993): 45; (July 1993): 105–106; (March 1994): 55; (September 2002): 197; (November 2002): 257–258.
People For the American Way. *Attacks on the Freedom to Learn: 1990–1991 Report.* Washington, D.C.: People For the American Way, 1991.

CAIN'S BOOK

Author: Alexander Trocchi
Original date and place of publication: 1960, United States
Original publisher: Grove Press
Literary form: Novel

SUMMARY

Cain's Book recounts in journal form the sordid activities of a heroin addict who lives on a garbage scow on the Hudson River in New York. The preface disclaims any association between the author's life and the narrator's heroin use and illegal adventures, but Trocchi permits his narrator a family that resembles his own. In addition, like the narrator of the novel, Trocchi had also served in the Royal Navy and had a more than passing familiarity with Edinburgh and Paris.

The first chapter opens with the words "Half an hour ago I gave myself a fix" and proceeds in a prose style that seeks to mimic the musings of a man whose mind is unhinged by the effects of hard drugs. In language that is sometimes philosophical but more often anarchical, Cain rants and raves about a system that condemns his heroin use. He states broadly, "I say it is impertinent, insolent and presumptuous of any person or group of persons to impose their unexamined moral prohibitions on me." To those who would deny him or anyone else access to the drug, Cain angrily issues the challenge, "To think that a man should be allowed a gun and not a drug. . . . I demand that these laws be changed."

The narrator relates what led him to his present drug-addicted life, including memories of his adventures as a seaman during World War II. In one particularly bleak passage, Cain describes his first sexual experience with a prostitute, which took place on the stone steps of an air raid shelter during a wartime blackout in Edinburgh. Devoid of any attempt at erotic arousal on the part of the reader, the incident is presented in stark naturalistic detail in which the narrator observes of his sexual companion, "I had never seen such ugly thighs nor ever imagined it like that, exposed for me in matchlight, the flaccid buttocks like pale meat on the stone stairs . . . ." His account and others throughout the book punctuate the journal and his continuing defense of his drug use.

The novel also incorporates the author's defense of art. The narrator muses that art should be free of prohibitions, and he expresses the essential value of drugs in stimulating creativity in the artist. Overall, the narrator is not remorseful about his addiction nor does he speak against the use of heroin. Instead, Cain's journal is a polemic that condemns the prohibitions that society places both on the artist in society and on the individual who makes a conscious choice to use hard drugs and who rejects all efforts to rehabilitate him and to deny him the right of his addiction.

CENSORSHIP HISTORY

The censorship of *Cain's Book* is significant because the judge's 1964 decision that the book was obscene marked the first time a judgment of obscenity had been made based not on the vulgar language, depiction of sexual activity, or depravity in a work but on the lifestyle it advocated. The novel was published in the United States by Grove Press in 1960, but the little-read author stimulated only minimal interest with it. By 1963, when John Calder issued *Cain's Book* under his imprint, Trocchi had gained a following in the United Kingdom as a poet and a leading figure of the beat movement. At first little known for his fiction, Trocchi became well known after his highly publicized argument with Scottish poet Hugh MacDiarmid at the 1962 Edinburgh Festival Writers' Conference. The younger poet's arguments against Scottish chauvinism brought international attention and resulted in the publication of *Cain's Book* in the United Kingdom.

The publisher limited distribution of the book to established bookstores, in an effort to avoid the crackdown on books that had followed earlier convictions for the sale of *FANNY HILL*. The novel was kept out of less reputable stores that dealt in sexy photographs, condoms, and pornography to avoid its being scooped up in police raids, but the effort failed. In February 1964, police in Sheffield, England, raided a number of bookstores and confiscated *Cain's Book* along with numerous other novels and magazines. Police defended their seizure of the novel on the grounds that it "seems to advocate the use of drugs in schools so that children should have a clearer conception of art."

In the subsequent trial, which began in April 1964, the publisher defended the literary merit of the novel. Calder stated to the jury that the novel was "one of the most important books written by a British author that has an affinity with the beat movement which is a revolt against conventional values." The prosecution claimed that the book was obscene. Among the witnesses for the prosecution was the Sheffield city librarian, who testified that the library owned 20 copies of *Cain's Book*, "kept in a reserve category available only for adults." After only 45 minutes of deliberation, the jury gave its verdict that the book was obscene and that it was too offensive to remain available to citizens. All copies of *Cain's Book* in Sheffield were ordered confiscated. At the Edinburgh Festival in September 1964, Trocchi and his supporters devised a protest against the verdict, a public burning of copies of *Cain's Book* in a large bonfire to which were added fireworks.

An appeal filed later in 1964 was unsuccessful, and the judge dismissed the case with costs going against the publisher. In rendering his decision in December 1964, Lord Chief Justice Parker determined that the narrator's heroin addiction was the reason for censoring the book. He stated ". . . the book, highlighting as it were the favourable effects of drug taking, so far from condemning it, advocates it and . . . there is a real danger that those into whose hands the book comes might be tempted, at any rate, to experiment with drugs and get the favourable sensations highlighted by the book."

FURTHER READING

Blythe, Will. "Heroin Is Habit-Forming . . . Rabbit-Forming, Babbit-Forming." *Esquire* 118, no. 5 (November 1992): 51–52.

Campbell, James. "Alexander Trocchi: The Biggest Fiend of All." *Antioch Review* 50, no. 3 (Summer 1992): 458.

O'Higgins, Paul. *Censorship in England.* London: Nelson, 1972.

Robertson, Geoffrey. *Obscenity: An Account of the Censorship Laws and Their Enforcement in England and Wales.* London: Weidenfeld & Nicolson, 1979.

Sutherland, John. *Offensive Literature: Decensorship in Britain, 1960–1982.* London: Junction Books, 1982.

Ulin, David L. "Book Reviews—*Cain's Book* by Alexander Trocchi, with an Introduction by Richard Seaver and a Foreword by Greil Marcus." *Review of Contemporary Fiction* 12, no. 3 (Fall 1992): 209.

CAMILLE

Author: Alexandre Dumas, Jr.
Original date and place of publication: 1848, Brussels
Original publisher: Meline, Cans
Literary form: Novel

SUMMARY

Known by the title *La Dame aux camélias* when originally published, the novel is a sensitive and sympathetic portrayal of Marguerite Gautier, a French courtesan who dies young of consumption. The work gained early notoriety because it is drawn from life and features a main character who is the thinly veiled fictional version of an actual courtesan named Marie Duplessis. Her lavish lifestyle and many relationships with men are presented in the nonjudgmental narration of her life and death. Dumas purifies the courtesan's image and plays down her true-life desire to accumulate wealth and jewels. As such, it offered for its time a new treatment of social and moral problems.

Marguerite is so sensitive that she cannot even endure the scent of flowers; thus, for her adornment she selects the lush yet delicate camellia, which has no scent. This theme of simple yet lavish beauty characterizes Marguerite, with whom the 25-year-old Armand Duval remains deeply in love, even after her death at the age of 23.

The novel is framed as a story being told to the narrator by Duval, a now-impoverished former lover of the high-living courtesan. Dumas does not glorify her life; rather, he exhibits her effect upon others, especially her negative effect upon Duval. Of all her many lovers, Duval is the only one who places flowers (camellias) on her grave, even after she has ruined him financially. He is also the only person who seeks to move her body from its place in a cemetery plot with only a five-year lease to a large plot having a perpetual lease. When Duval becomes seriously ill with "brain fever," the narrator nurses him and, thus, learns the entire story as Duval narrates it to him.

Mingled with accounts of Marguerite's frivolous life and conspicuous luxury is the poignance of her realization that being a courtesan makes her of interest to others only as long as she can "serve the vanity or the pleasure of . . . lovers." She warns her young admirer Duval at the outset of their acquaintance that her lavish lifestyle is expensive to maintain and that she must continue her liaisons with older rich men in order to survive. Soon after they meet, Duval learns that Marguerite has been coughing up blood, yet she continues to meet and to fascinate her wealthy lovers. He becomes obsessed with her. He learns that she is 40,000 francs in debt and spends hundreds of thousands of francs annually. As his own health deteriorates, Duval is also drawn into debt as he borrows money and gambles to try to pay Marguerite's debts. After enduring months of working to convince the courtesan to give up her wealthy suitors and lavish lifestyle, Duval is successful, and they go to live in the country in a home that was purchased for her by a wealthy and elderly duke. Duval and Marguerite live together openly, supported by the profits from the sale of her numerous jewels and possessions.

After four months of remaining faithful to her young lover, Marguerite returns to her old life, more ill with consumption than before yet still able to attract a wealthy count who buys back for her the horses, carriage, and jewels that she had pawned. In revenge, Duval takes a new mistress, upon whom he lavishes money and jewels to make Marguerite jealous, thus driving himself even further into debt. When Marguerite dies, Duval is devastated and becomes ill shortly thereafter.

CENSORSHIP HISTORY

The novel has drawn criticism as much for its sympathetic portrayal of a courtesan as for the wisdom that Dumas expresses through the character of Armand Duval: "To be loved by a pure young girl . . . is the simplest thing in the world. But to be really loved by a courtesan, that is a victory of infinitely greater difficulty." Duval refers casually to Marguerite as "a kept woman," and he has Marguerite solemnly swear to him, "I gave myself sooner to you than I ever did to any man."

In 1850, the performance of the opera *La Traviata*, based on the novel, was permitted, but the translation of the text as a libretto was forbidden. In France, from 1849 through 1852, the play *La Dame aux camélias*, based on the novel, was forbidden on the Paris stage. Finally, in 1852, an influential government minister in the cabinet of Napoleon III intervened, and the play was produced.

The novel was singled out in 1857 by Lord Campbell, the lord chief justice of England, when he introduced to the House of Lords a bill that was aimed at strengthening the law of obscenity and made books liable to destruction by the magistrates. He assured his peers that the law was aimed at eliminating those works "written for the single purpose of corrupting the morals of youth and of a nature calculated to shock the common feelings of decency in a well-regulated mind." As he presented his arguments, he held a copy of *Camille* in his hands and referred to it with horror as an example of literary works of a polluting character that must be stopped. The bill became the Obscene Publications Act of 1857.

In 1863, all of Dumas's works were placed on the Vatican's list of forbidden books, and he was identified as one of only 11 authors whose total works had been condemned by the Roman Catholic church for emphasizing the treatment of impure love. As recently as 1948, all of Dumas's works were listed in the Vatican's Index librorum prohibitorum and declared to be forbidden to Catholics throughout the world and in every translation.

FURTHER READING

Burke, Redmond A. *What Is the Index?* Milwaukee, Wis.: Bruce Publishing Company, 1952.

Index of Prohibited Books. Revised and published by the order of His Holiness Pope Pius XII. Vatican: Polyglot Press, 1948.

Saunders, Edith. *The Prodigal Father.* New York: Longmans, Green and Company, 1951.

THE CANTERBURY TALES

Author: Geoffrey Chaucer
Original date and place of publication: 1387–1400, England
Original publisher: Unknown
Literary form: Short story collection

SUMMARY

The Canterbury Tales is a group of stories, mostly in verse, written in the closing years of the 14th century. Chaucer establishes the framework for the book in a lengthy prologue, in which he describes the 29 individuals who meet with their host at the Tabard Inn in preparation for a pilgrimage to the popular shrine of Thomas à Becket at the Canterbury Cathedral. They agree that, to pass the time on the journey, each pilgrim will tell four stories, two on the way to the shrine and two on the way home. The host will judge the best tale, and the winner will receive a sumptuous feast at the inn. Chaucer originally planned a book of 120 tales but died in 1400 before completing the work. Only 24 of the tales remain. Of these, 20 are complete, two are deliberately left incomplete because the pilgrims demand that the tellers cease, and two others were left unfinished by Chaucer's death.

The pilgrims extend across all levels of 14th-century English society, from the nobly born Knight, Squire, and Prioress to the low-born Miller, Cook, and Yeoman. None are spared Chaucer's critical examination of the human condition as he uses his characters and their tales to expose the absurdities and inadequacies of all levels of society. The travelers quarrel, interrupt, and criticize each other; become drunk; and provoke commentary. Members of the religious hierarchy are shown to be corrupt, women are lusty, and the dark underbelly of society is exposed. The tales reflect the tellers, from the gentle Knight, "modest as a maid," who describes an abstraction of womanhood in his pure Emily, to the bawdy Miller, who describes his Alison as a highly provocative physical object.

Risqué language and sexual innuendo pervade most of the tales. "The Cook's Tale" describes "a wife [who] whored to get her sustenance." In "Introduction to the Lawyer's Prologue," provocative images of incest emerge in "Canace, who loved her own blood brother sinfully" and "wicked king

Antiochus [who] bereft his daughter of her maidenhead." "The Reeve's Tale" tells of a miller named Simpkin whose wife "was a dirty bitch" and whose daughter was "with buttocks broad and round breasts full and high." "The Wife of Bath's Tale," one of the two most commonly anthologized of all the tales, offers an extraordinary view of women and sexuality. Described in the prologue as having had five husbands, "not counting other company in her youth," the Wife of Bath questions the concern over virginity and asks "Tell me also to what purpose or end the genitals have been made?" She lustily promises, "In wifehood I will use my instrument as freely as my Maker has sent it."

The second of the two most popularly anthologized stories is "The Miller's Tale," a story about adultery. Alison, an 18-year-old woman married to a middle-age miller, is courted by Absalom the parish clerk, but she is already having an affair with the boarder, a student named Nicholas. Absalom serenades her outside her window and promises to leave her alone only if she will let him kiss her. She agrees and, when he arrives at her window in the dark, she offers "her naked arse," which he kisses. He soon realizes the trick, for "it seem somehow amiss, for well he knew a woman has no beard; he'd felt a thing all rough and longish-haired." Seeking revenge, Absalom returns to the Miller's house carrying a red-hot poker from the fireplace and calls to Alison for another kiss. This time Nicholas, who "had risen for a piss," decides "to have his arse kissed" to carry on the joke. And, "showing the whole bum," he is shocked when Absalom "was ready with his iron hot and Nicholas right in the arse he got." Later, John, the other student boarder, mistakenly climbs into bed with Alison, who thinks it is Nicholas, and he "pricked her hard and deep, like one gone mad."

CENSORSHIP HISTORY

Canterbury Tales has been expurgated since its first appearance in the United States in 1908 in the Everyman's Library edition. Seventeen of the tales were translated into modern English with extensive expurgation, and seven were left intact but in the original Middle English language. In 1953, the tales were innocent victims of the "Red Scare," when critics approached the Texas State Textbook Commission and demanded that the commission bar the Garden City editions of *Canterbury Tales* and *Moby-Dick* from their schools. The two works were illustrated by Rockwell Kent, charged by critics with being a communist.

For the most part, however, the off-color references of the original text and blunt "Anglo-Saxon" terms related to the anatomy or to bodily functions have raised concerns among parents and those who select textbooks. Thus, they are routinely omitted from most editions, as are curses or oaths uttered by characters in the original tales. Editing has led to such absurdities as "He caught her by the queynte" being transformed into "He slipped his hand intimately between her legs." Challenges to the inclusion of "The Miller's Tale," "The Wife of Bath's Tale," and even the "Prologue" have sought to remove the readings from classrooms because of the "unhealthy characters" and the "nasty words" of the text. Risqué language and characters have made the tales a ready target for textbook evaluators and community and school watchdogs.

In 1986, a lengthy case arose over the use of a textbook that included "The Miller's Tale" and Aristophanes' play *Lysistrata* in an elective humanities course for Columbia County High School students in Lake City, Florida. The tale appeared in *The Humanities: Cultural Roots and Continuities Volume I*, a state-approved textbook that had been used for 10 years without incident. In 1985, the daughter of a fundamentalist minister had enrolled in the course and objected to the two selections, even though they were not assigned readings but portions referred to and read aloud by the teacher. In lodging a formal complaint, the minister identified "sexual explicitness," "vulgar language," and "the promotion of women's lib" as his reasons for demanding that the text be withdrawn from use. His specific objections identified concern over the inclusion of the terms "ass" and "fart" in "The Miller's Tale," as well as the jocular way in which adultery appears to be treated. An advisory textbook committee made up of Columbia County High School teachers read and discussed the two selections, then recommended that the textbooks be retained and that the two selections not be assigned. The school board rejected their suggestions and voted to confiscate all copies of the book and to lock them in the book room. Anxious to avoid the charge of censorship, board members also voted to allow a copy to remain in the high school library, but it was placed on "the mature shelf."

In 1988, the American Civil Liberties Union submitted an initial brief against the school board in *Virgil v. School Board of Columbia County*, 677 F. Supp. 1547, 1551-51 (M.D. Fla. 1988) and argued that the actions of the board in removing the textbook from the classroom suppressed the free thought and free speech of students. The ACLU based its arguments on decisions made in *Board of Education, Island Trees Union Free School District No. 26 v. Pico*, 457 U.S. 853, 102 S.Ct. 2799, 73 L.Ed.2d 435 (1982), in which the court decided that school boards violate the First Amendment rights of students when they arbitrarily remove books. (See BLACK BOY) The defense attorney for the school board relied on *Hazelwood School District v. Kuhlmeier*, 484 U.S. 260, 108 S.Ct. 562, 98 L.Ed.2d 592 (1988) in presenting the case, although the case applied to the right of school administrators to censor articles in a school newspaper that was produced as part of a high school journalism class.

The case went to court, and in deciding *Virgil v. School Board of Columbia County*, 862 F.2d 1517, 1525 (11th Cir. 1989), the judge determined that the *Hazelwood* case was the relevant precedent. The limited scope of that case in interpreting the First Amendment rights of students influenced the court to decide in favor of the school board. In the *Virgil* decision, the U.S. Court of Appeals for the 11th Circuit concluded that no constitutional violation had occurred and the school board could decide to remove books from the class-room provided that the removal was "reasonably related" to the "legitimate pedagogical concern" of denying students exposure to "potentially sensitive topics." The written contention of the board that the two selections contained "explicit sexuality" and "excessive vulgarity" was judged to be a sufficient basis for the removal of *The Humanities: Cultural Roots and Continuities* from the classroom. The plaintiffs decided to appeal the case to the United States Supreme Court and directed the ACLU attorney to file a Petition for Writ of Certiorari in 1988. After more than a year passed, the plaintiffs learned that the Supreme Court had never received the petition because a secretary newly hired in April 1989 by the office of the ACLU attorney had never sent it out. The plaintiffs decided not to pursue the matter because the changed character of the higher court did not promise success even if the motion to argue the case were approved.

In September 1995, parents of seniors in the Eureka, Illinois, High School complained to the Eureka School Board that parts of this classic are "too racy." Board members directed the teacher, Nancy Quinn, to stop teaching the work until the board could review the material further. School Board president Eric Franz stated that the parents were particularly concerned with classroom discussions about marriage and adultery that were prompted by the tales. He characterized the action of the board as "about education, not censorship" and said that the board had to determine "whether the community's standards are violated by any particular piece of literature." The board voted to ban the full version of *The Canterbury Tales* and to replace it with an expurgated version, which they described as "annotated."

FURTHER READING

"The Censor's Tale." *St. Louis Post-Dispatch*, September 25, 1995.
"Chaucer's Tales Get Suspension from Illinois High School Class." *St. Louis Post-Dispatch*, September 22, 1995.
Johnson, Claudia. *Stifled Laughter: One Woman's Fight against Censorship*. Golden, Colo.: Fulcrum Publishing, 1994.
Scala, Elizabeth. "Canace and the Chaucer Canon." *Chaucer Review* 30 (1995): 15–39.

CAPTAIN UNDERPANTS (SERIES)

Author: Dav Pilkey
Original date and place of publication: 1997, United States
Original publisher: Scholastic Books
Literary form: Illustrated children's books

SUMMARY

The *Captain Underpants* series consists of eight books aimed at a readership of children ages eight to 12. Librarians and the publisher report that boys are the major fans of the books. The heavily illustrated books are divided into short chapters and contain pages that are half text and half cartoon. Most also include a "Flip-O-Rama" section of successive pages that create a rough impression of action when the reader flips them back and forth. The series plays to an interest in scatological humor, and the text and cartoon balloons contain such terms as *barf, pee-pee, butt,* and *poopy,* as well as sections devoted to "boogers," "wedgies," and flying excrement. The books contain names such as Ivana Goda de Bafroom and Pippy P. Poopypants, and villains are said to be able to "leap tall buildings with the gassy aftereffects of their 'Texas-style' three-bean chili con carne."

The premise for the series is that George Beard and Harold Hutchins, two rambunctious fourth-grade students who are enrolled in a "remedial" physical education class and who draw comic books about epic adventures, accidentally make their school principal, Mr. Krupp, into a superhero, whose adventures they then chronicle. Mr. Krupp is a crabby bureaucrat whose frequent disciplining of the boys finally moves them to obtain "a magic 3-D Hypno-Ring," which they use to hypnotize him into believing he is a superhero named "Captain Underpants" who wears cotton briefs and a red cape and whose motto is "Truth, Justice, and all that is Pre-shrunk and Cottony." A snap of anyone's fingers turns Krupp into the superhero and leads him to champion justice in seven books: *The Adventures of Captain Underpants; Captain Underpants and the Talking Toilets; Captain Underpants and the Invasion of the Incredibly Naughty Cafeteria Ladies from Outer Space (and the Subsequent Assault of the Equally Evil Lunchroom Zombie Nerds); Captain Underpants and the Perilous Plot of Professor Poopypants; Captain Underpants and the Wrath of the Wicked Wedgie Woman; Captain Underpants and the Big, Bad Battle of the Bionic Booger Boy: Part I: The Night of the Nasty Nostril Nuggets;* and *Captain Underpants and the Big, Bad Battle of the Bionic Booger Boy: Part II: The Revenge of the Ridiculous Robo-Boogers.* The superhero persona fades and Mr. Krupp returns when even a small amount of water falls on his head. Also part of the series is *The Adventures of Super Diaper Baby,* which is presented as one of the comic books written and drawn by George and Harold.

Throughout the books, teachers, school secretaries, and other adults suffer disgusting experiences. Miss Anthrope, school secretary, is "covered in snot"; Mr. Meaner, a sadistic physical education teacher, is swallowed by a talking toilet; and Miss Singerbrains, the school librarian, finds a "purple potty" in her library. George and Harold play numerous pranks and generally take every opportunity to torment the adults in their lives, but every action is epic in proportion, if ridiculous. To make certain that readers are aware of the mock epic intent of each novel, each book contains a clear label at the bottom of the cover: "The First Epic Novel," "The Second Epic Novel," and so on.

Although the books contain silly illustrations and plots and scatological terms, they also function as an effective learning tool. Pilkey uses such vocabulary words as *merciless, gullible, hideous,* and others throughout the series, and the works contain compound sentences and significant use of synonyms and alliteration. In addition, the popularity of the books has motivated interest among many formerly reluctant readers.

CENSORSHIP HISTORY

The *Captain Underpants* series has evoked ardent proponents and opponents. Many librarians and parents have defended the books, echoing the opinion expressed by one mother in an interview conducted by CNN: "'The content IS sometimes vulgar, scatological, rude—but so are 9-year-old boys,' said Mary Jo Dickerson, whose son Ian reads the books out loud to her. 'I say any book that encourages my son to read is worth its weight in gold.'"

Opponents of the book are equally ardent. In 2000, Principal Rebecca Sciacc, of the Maple Hill School in Naugatuck, Connecticut, removed *The Adventures of Captain Underpants* from the elementary school library. Superintendent of schools Alice Carolan supported the decision and noted in an interview, "These Captain Underpants books are clearly inappropriate for an elementary school library. All of their humor comes from the bathroom and bodily functions. There's a fine line between censorship and selection. It comes down to what you think. I call this selection, you might consider it censorship."

In 2002, Dawn Ihry, a parent and former teacher, in Page, North Dakota, submitted a formal complaint to the school board of the Hope-Page Consolidated School District requesting that the school remove *Captain Underpants and the Perilous Plot of Professor Poopypants* from the Page elementary school library. In the complaint, Ihry wrote, "I didn't care for the language. I didn't care for the innuendo." The district materials-review committee rejected the challenge but offered Ihry a compromise that would have allowed the book to be retained in the library placed on a "restricted" shelf and available only to older students. Ihry rejected the offer, and the issue went to the district school board, which voted to uphold the challenge and to remove the book from the school library. The controversy motivated the school board to examine the district selection policy. On March 11, 2002, the board approved a policy requiring that the consolidated school board approve all library purchases and allowing them to reject materials "that label or characterize undeserving individuals in a derogatory manner."

In 2003, Pam Santi, a businesswoman and grandmother raising four grandchildren, filed a complaint with the Riverside (California) Unified School District calling for the removal of *The Adventures of Super Diaper Baby* from the Madison Elementary School library. She became upset when she found her grandson drawing a picture of one of the characters, Deputy Doo-Doo: "He was drawing a piece of poop." In her complaint, Santi charged that the 125-page book also shows "irreverence to authority," contains a large number of intentional misspellings, and offers a 12-point lesson on how to draw Deputy Doo-Doo, "sheriff's hat and all." She also asserted, "There's just no moral value to that poop character." The complaint was submitted for a decision to the materials review committee, a seven-member committee composed of parents, teachers, and administrators chaired by district librarian Christine Allen. The committee rejected the challenge in a 5-2 vote. One of the committee members, Linda Wallis, a second-grade teacher at Madison, who voted in favor of the ban, stated in an interview with the *Los Angeles Times:* "There is not one teacher I know who wants [*Super Diaper Baby*] out there . . . . This is not the type of humor we promote at school. It's putting down kids to say this is what they like to read."

FURTHER READING

Brown, Marian Gail. "Captain Underpants Stirs Controversy in Naugatuck: Captain Underpants Banned." *Connecticut Post*, February 10, 2000.

Goldberg, Beverly. "Captain Underpants Yanked Again." *American Libraries* 33, no. 5 (May 2002): 23.

Martinez, Al. "Life Support: A Home for 'Captain Underpants'—Where Do the Scatological Children's Books Belong? Not in the School Library, Says Captain Grandma." *Post-Gazette Lifestyle*, July 14, 2003. Available online. URL: http://www.post-gazette.com/lifestyle/20030714life6.asp. Accessed December 12, 2009.

Nissen, Beth. "Captain Underpants: The Straight Poop on a Grossly Entertaining Series of Children's Books." *CNN.com Book News*, July 11, 2000. Available online. URL: http://www.cnn.com/2000/books/news/07/11/captain.underpants. Accessed December 12, 2009.

Sauerwein, Kristina. "Irate Grandma Fights 'Captain Underpants.'" *Los Angeles Times*, June 4, 2003, p. 21.

———. "Super Diaper Baby Survives; A Riverside Schools Committee Rejects a Request to Ban the Toilet-Humor Tome." *Los Angeles Times*, June 13, 2003, p. B1.

Shen, Fern. "Is Series of Books Too Hot to Handle?" *Lubbock Avalanche-Journal*, August 1, 2002.

CATCH-22

Author: Joseph Heller
Original date and place of publication: 1961, United States
Original publisher: Simon & Schuster
Literary form: Novel

SUMMARY

Catch-22 is a comic novel about World War II that literary critics have described as among the best to have come out of that era. The novel concerns the efforts of Capt. John Yossarian, a bombardier with the 256th U.S. Air Force Squadron, to be removed from combat duty after he witnesses numerous friends being killed in action. He acts insane to achieve his goal, but his efforts are thwarted by military regulation number 22, which states that no sane person would willingly go into combat. Thus, anyone who seeks to avoid combat duty must be considered sane.

Set on the fictional Mediterranean island of Pianosa, from which the squadron makes regular bombing runs to southern France and to Italy, the novel contains graphic descriptions of sex and violence and exhibits strong rebellion against authority. Yossarian lies, sabotages military procedures, and exhibits gross irresponsibility. He also walks around naked for a few days, even when he is being awarded a medal. Given light duty censoring letters written by enlisted men, Yossarian plays games and blacks out words randomly, sometimes adding the chaplain's signature to romantic letters home. The unpleasant experience of his tent mate Orr in a brothel is carefully detailed, as the "whore" beats him with her high-heeled shoe. Readers learn that the two are naked and of "her wondrously full breasts soaring all over the place like billowing pennants in a strong wind and her buttocks and strong thighs shim-sham-shimmying this way and that way." Another character visits a brothel in the Eternal City, then kills the prostitute because she might damage his reputation should she tell others about their encounter. Throughout the novel, the men casually refer to and address each other as "son of a bitch," "prick," or "bastard." At one point, Yossarian loses his temper and rants, "That dirty goddam midget-assed, apple-cheeked, goggle-eyed, undersized, bucktoothed, grinning, crazy sonofabitchinbastard!"

The women in the novel are largely stereotypes to whom other characters refer as "whore." The woman whom "he had longed for and idolized for months" is "perfect for Yossarian, a debauched, coarse, vulgar, amoral, appetizing slattern . . . . She was interested in fornication." However, he also hopes that "Nately's whore" will find him a woman who is just as eager for sex as she. At the end of the novel, as Yossarian leaves the base to run off to Sweden, "Nately's whore was hiding out just outside the door." She attempts to kill him, but he escapes.

CENSORSHIP HISTORY

Catch-22 is part of the school censorship case that set precedent by supporting the student's right to know. In 1972, the Strongsville, Ohio, board of education used its discretionary power over textbook selection to disapprove purchase of *Catch-22* and Kurt Vonnegut's *God Bless You, Mr. Rosewater,* despite faculty recommendation. The board refused to allow teachers to use the books as part of the English curriculum, charging that they were "completely sick" and "garbage." The board then ordered the two books and

CAT'S CRADLE, also by Vonnegut, removed from the high school library and "all copies disposed of in accordance with statutory procedure."

Five high school students and their families brought a class-action suit against the school district, the school superintendent, and the board of education, claiming that their rights under the First and Fourteenth Amendments had been violated. The families argued that the board had not followed proper procedure and had not given good reason for rejecting the novels. In 1974, the U.S. District Court for the Northern District of Ohio ruled that the board did not violate First Amendment rights because it had followed the law. Ohio law granted school boards the authority to select textbooks, and the board had held open meetings and consulted enough teachers, administrators, and citizens to make a reasonable decision. The judge dismissed the complaint of the families regarding the removal of the books from the school library.

The case was then heard in 1976 by the U.S. Court of Appeals for the Sixth Circuit, and a different decision emerged. The court upheld the right of the school board to determine the choice of textbooks, but it stood firmly against the right of the school board to remove already purchased books from the school library.

> A public school library is also a valuable adjunct to classroom discussions. If one of the English teachers considered Joseph Heller's Catch-22 to be one of the more important modern American novels (as, indeed, at least one did), we assume that no one would dispute that the First Amendment's protection of academic freedom would protect both his right to say so in class and his students' right to hear him and to find and read the book. Obviously, the students' success in this last endeavor would be greatly hindered by the fact that the book sought had been removed from a school library.

The court also chastised the school board for withdrawing books from the school library. Stating in the decision that "a library is a storehouse of knowledge," the presiding judge warned that libraries are created by the state for the benefit of students in the schools. As such, they are "not subject to being withdrawn by succeeding school boards whose members might desire to 'winnow' the library for books the content of which occasioned their displeasure or disapproval." The judge ordered the Strongsville school board to replace the books in the school library. In response, the school district appealed to the U.S. Supreme Court, but the court refused to hear the case.

The use of the word *whore* at several places in the novel to refer to women resulted in challenges in the Dallas (Texas) Independent School District in 1974, where parents demanded that the novel be removed from all of the high school libraries. The same objection motivated a challenge in the Snoqualmie Valley (Washington) School District in 1979. Critics observed that the use of *whore* and Heller's failure to name one woman, calling her only "Nately's whore," represented a stereotyping of women that was harmful to students. In attempts to remove the novel from use in the school system as well as from the Mount Si High School library, critics also cited the "overly descriptive passages of violence" and the increasingly bizarre threats by squadron members against each other. The efforts to remove *Catch-22* were unsuccessful.

FURTHER READING

Green, Daniel. "A World Worth Laughing At: *Catch-22* and the Humor of Black Humor." *Studies in the Novel* 27 (Summer 1995): 186–196.

Moore, Michael. "Pathological Communication Patterns in Heller's *Catch-22.*" *Et Cetera* 52 (Winter 1995): 431–459.

Newsletter for Intellectual Freedom (January 1975): 6; (July 1979): 85.

O'Neil, Robert M. *Classrooms in the Crossfire: The Rights and Interests of Students, Parents, Teachers, Administrators, Librarians, and the Community.* Bloomington: Indiana University Press, 1981.

Pinsker, Sanford. *Understanding Joseph Heller.* Columbia: University of South Carolina Press, 1991.

Potts, Stephen. *Catch-22: Antiheroic Antinovel.* Boston: Twayne, 1989.

———. *From Here to Absurdity: The Moral Battlefields of Joseph Heller.* San Bernardino, Calif.: Borgo Press, 1982.

THE CATCHER IN THE RYE

Author: J. D. Salinger
Original date and place of publication: 1951, United States
Original publisher: Little, Brown and Company
Literary form: Novel

SUMMARY

The Catcher in the Rye tells the story of a middle-class, urban, late-adolescent boy in the 1950s who confronts crisis in his own life by escaping into the disordered and chaotic adult world. The story, told from the first-person point of view of Holden Caulfield, details 48 hours in his life and describes how he views and feels about society and the world in which he lives. As Holden experiences his misadventures, he muses about sex, society, and American values. He seeks to remain idealistic, but he is confronted at every turn by the phoniness of society.

Holden narrates his story while in a rest home in California, and the reader becomes aware that he is relating a story from his recent past. He flashes back to his school days, in particular to Pencey Prep, where he was a student until his expulsion. It is just after this expulsion that the action takes place. For most of the novel, Holden appears to search for someone or something in which to believe, but he finds that his generally pessimistic view of human nature and human values is reinforced rather than refuted.

Before Holden makes the decision to leave school, he visits his history teacher for one last time and receives a lecture regarding his lack of motivation and poor scholarship. Mr. Spencer even goes so far as to read Holden the last examination he took. The disappointments accrue, as Holden returns to his room in the dormitory and learns that his roommate, Ward, has a date with a girl whom Holden had wanted to date. To compound the pain, Ward asks Holden to write a composition, which he later criticizes severely. After an ensuing physical fight, Holden packs a bag and leaves the campus.

Holden boards a train bound for New York City and registers at a hotel upon arrival. When loneliness sets in, he makes several telephone calls without success, then visits a crowded nightclub, but he still cannot fill the void he feels inside. When Holden returns to the hotel, he asks the doorman to arrange for a prostitute, but he sends her away unpaid because he is too scared and too depressed to enjoy her. The doorman and prostitute later awaken him and demand the five dollars, and the doorman beats Holden to obtain payment.

After meeting a friend at a bar and indulging in underage drinking, Holden sneaks into his family's apartment to see his younger sister, Phoebe, with whom he discusses his fears that he may "disappear" into himself. He tells her that he has a mission in this world: "I keep picturing all these little kids playing some game in this big field of rye and all . . . . And I'm standing by on the edge of some crazy cliff. What I have to do, I have to catch everybody if they start to go over the cliff." In his further idealism, he becomes upset when he finds "Fuck You" scrawled on the walls of Phoebe's elementary school and on the wall of the museum where Phoebe will meet him.

Holden plans to hitchhike to the West but changes his mind and agrees to return home when Phoebe packs a suitcase and insists on going with him. He later watches Phoebe ride the carousel in Central Park and realizes that he really cannot protect her from all of the world's abuses and that he has to let her take chances without interfering.

By the end of the novel, after fending off the advances of a male former English teacher and reviewing his disappointments with the adult world, Holden appears resigned in the rest home and predicts that he will soon be returning to school.

CENSORSHIP HISTORY

The novel has long ignited disapproval, and it was the most frequently banned book in schools between 1966 and 1975. Even before that time, however, the work was a favorite target of censors. In 1957, Australian Customs seized a shipment of the novels that had been presented as a gift to the government by the U.S. ambassador. The books were later released, but Customs had made its point that the book contained obscene language and actions that were not appropriate behavior for an adolescent. In 1960, a teacher in Tulsa, Oklahoma, was fired for assigning the book to an 11th-grade English class. The teacher appealed and was reinstated by the school board, but the book was removed from use in the school.

The following year in Oklahoma City, the novel became the focus of a legislative hearing in which a locally organized censorship group sought to stop the Mid-Continent News Company, a book wholesaler, from carrying the novel. Members of the group parked a "Smutmobile" outside the capital building during the hearing and displayed the novel with others. As a result of public pressure, the wholesaler dropped the criticized novels from its inventory. In 1963, a delegation of parents of high school students in Columbus, Ohio, asked the school board to ban Catcher in the Rye, BRAVE NEW WORLD, and TO KILL A MOCKINGBIRD for being "anti-white" and "obscene." The superintendent of schools and the school board refused the request and expressed confidence in the ability of their teachers and librarians to choose reading material for the school system.

After a decade of quiet, objections again arose in 1975 in Selinsgrove, Pennsylvania, and the novel was removed from the suggested reading list for an elective course entitled "Searching for Values and Identity Through Literature." Based on parents' objections to the language and content of the book, the school board voted 5-4 to ban the book. The book was later reinstated in the curriculum when the board learned that the vote was illegal because a two-thirds vote was needed for removal of the text.

In 1977, parents in Pittsgrove Township, New Jersey, challenged the assignment of the novel in an American literature class. They charged that the book included considerable profanity and "filthy and profane" language that promoted premarital sex, homosexuality, and perversion, as well as claiming that it was "explicitly pornographic" and "immoral." The board of education had originally approved the novel for study. After months of controversy, the board ruled that the novel could be read in the advanced-placement class for its universal message, but they gave parents the right to decide whether or not their children would read it.

In 1978, parents in Issaquah, Washington, became upset with the rebellious views expressed in the novel by Holden Caulfield and with the profanity he uses. The woman who led the parents' group asserted that she had counted 785 uses of profanity, and she alleged that the philosophy of the book marked it as part of a communist plot that was gaining a foothold in the schools, "in which a lot of people are used and may not even be aware of it." The school board voted to ban the book, but the decision was later reversed when the three members who had voted against the book were recalled due to illegal deal-making. In 1979, the Middleville, Michigan, school district removed the novel from the required reading list after parents objected to the content.

Objections to the novel were numerous throughout the 1980s. In 1980, the Jacksonville-Milton School libraries in North Jackson, Ohio, removed the book, as did two high school libraries in Anniston, Alabama. In 1982, school officials removed the book from all school libraries because it contained "excess vulgar language, sexual scenes, and things concerning moral issues." In 1983, parents in Libby, Montana, challenged the assignment of the book in the high school due to the "book's contents." Deemed "unacceptable" and "obscene," the novel was banned from use in English classes at Freeport High School in De Funiak Springs, Florida, in 1985, and it was removed from the required reading list in 1986 in Medicine Bow, Wyoming, Senior High School because of sexual references and profanity. In 1987, parents and the local Knights of Columbus chapter in Napoleon, North Dakota, complained about profanity and sexual references in the book, which was then banned from a required sophomore English reading list. Parents of students attending Linton-Stockton (Indiana) High School challenged the book in 1988 because it "undermines morality," and profanity was the reason why the book was banned from classrooms in the Boron, California, high school in 1989.

The challenges to the novel continued well into the 1990s. In 1991, the novel was challenged at Grayslake (Illinois) Community High School for profanity, and parents of students in Jamaica High School in Sidell, Illinois, cited profanities and the depiction of premarital sex, alcohol abuse, and prostitution as the basis for their 1992 challenge. Three other major challenges to the novel occurred in 1992. The novel was challenged and removed from the Waterloo, Iowa, public schools and the Duval County, Florida, public school libraries because of the "lurid passages about sex" and profanity, and a parent in Carlisle, Pennsylvania, objected to the book because it was "immoral" and contained profanity. In 1993, parents in the Corona-Norco (California) School District protested the use of the novel as a required reading because it was "centered around negative activity." The school board voted to retain the novel but instructed teachers to select alternative readings if students objected to it. The novel was challenged but retained for use in select English classes at New Richmond (Wisconsin) High School in 1994, but it was removed as mandatory reading from the Goffstown, New Hampshire, schools the same year because parents charged that it contained "vulgar words" and presented the main character's "sexual exploits."

In May 2000, *American Libraries* magazine reported that the Limestone County School District (Alabama) voted on attempts to ban the book from high school library collections. Elkmont High School parent Mike Taylor had challenged use of the book, complaining that "the Lord's name is taken in vain throughout." The move had the support of Joel Glaze, a board member, who asserted that the book is "teaching debauchery" and stated that a nearby Bible school refused to teach the book. On March 13, 1999, the school board voted 4-3 to retain the book.

In 2001, parents of students in the Dorchester District 2 school in Summerville, South Carolina, complained to the school board that the novel is immoral and asked for the school officials to remove it. The school board reviewed the book and voted to remove it from the school, with one school board member supporting the decision and stating it "is a filthy, filthy book." The same year, a school board member in Glynn County, Georgia, challenged use of the book because of the profanity, but school district officials voted to retain the book.

In 2004, parents of students attending Noble High School in North Berwick, Maine, challenged the use of the novel as an assigned reading. School officials decided to retain the novel, but they planned to create a program in which teachers would provide more information to parents regarding why certain books are studied.

FURTHER READING

Alvino, James. "Is It Book Burning Time Again?" *New York Times*, December 28, 1980, pp. 11, 18.

"Another Furor over Books." *Ohio State University Monthly* 55 (4): 8–12.

Booth, Wayne C. "Censorship and the Values of Fiction." *English Journal* 53 (March 1964): 155–164.

Corbett, Edward P. J. "Raise High the Barriers, Censors." *America* 54 (January 7, 1961): 441–444.

Newsletter on Intellectual Freedom (November 1978): 138; (January 1980): 6–7; (May 1980): 51; (March 1983): 37–38; (July 1983): 122; (July 1985): 113; (March 1987): 55; (July 1987): 123; (January 1988): 10; (September 1988): 177; (November 1989): 218–219; (July 1991): 129–130; (May 1992): 83; (July 1992): 105, 126; (January 1993): 29; (January 1994): 14; (March 1994): 56, 70; (May 1994): 100; (January 1995): 12; (July 2000): 123; (November 2001): 246–247, 277–278; (January 2005): 8–9; (March 2005): 73–74.

Oboler, Eli M. "Idaho School Librarians and Salinger's *Catcher in the Rye:* A Candid Report." *Idaho Librarian* 15 (October 1963): 137–139.

THE CHOCOLATE WAR

Author: Robert Cormier
Original date and place of publication: 1974, United States
Original publisher: Pantheon Books
Literary form: Novel

SUMMARY

The Chocolate War is the story of a young boy's struggle against the conformity imposed on him by the restrictive atmosphere of an all-male Catholic prep school as well as by the demands of the Vigils, a secret group that the school does not officially condone but whose existence and infractions it ignores. Jerry Renault, a freshman, has just lost his mother to cancer when the novel opens, and his father is too deep in grief to offer any solace or guidance. Singled out by the Vigils, a secret society at Trinity that manipulates and intimidates students to follow the group's dictates, Jerry is given the assignment by the group to oppose for 10 days the annual chocolate sale at the school and to make a public demonstration of his opposition. The annual chocolate sale, said to be voluntary even though pressures are exerted to participate, is vital to the financial well-being of Trinity, and each boy must sell 50 boxes at $2 each for the school to achieve the necessary level of profit. Knowing that a successful sale is critical for Brother Leon, the leader of the Vigils decides to turn this to an advantage for the group. Brother Leon has already approached Archie, the Assigner of the Vigils, to gain support for the chocolate sale from the group, which he does not name, and Archie hints that they expect certain favors from Brother Leon in return.

When the 10 days end, Jerry, whose locker contains a poster that reads "Do I Dare Disturb the Universe?" continues his refusal to sell chocolates, despite the insistence by the Vigils that he now participate. He insists on the voluntary nature of the project and tries to gain control over his life by bucking the system, but his refusal influences other students to make little effort in the project. The Vigils place relentless pressure on Jerry, Brother Leon glares at him in a menacing manner, and other students give him the silent treatment and fear associating with him, but he continues in his refusal to sell chocolates.

Even as he receives brutal punishment in football practice and deals with threats on the telephone, Jerry stands firm on his decision. At the end of the novel, he must take part in a boxing match staged by the Vigils in the football stadium in front of the entire student body and out of sight of the school faculty. The rules demand that both fighters follow directions for blows that students have written on slips of paper. As Jerry is pummeled to near death, students catch sight of Brother Leon standing on the hillside and watching with approval.

CENSORSHIP HISTORY

The Chocolate War was frequently challenged throughout the 1980s and 1990s for reasons ranging from objections to the vocabulary and "pervasive vulgarity" to outcries regarding perceived themes of rape, masturbation, violence, and degrading treatment of women. In 1981, officials in two Lapeer, Michigan, high schools challenged the novel and temporarily removed it from the English curriculum, charging that it contained "offensive language and explicit descriptions of sexual situations." In 1982, it was removed from the classroom in Liberty High School in Westminster, Maryland, when critics charged that the novel portrayed violence and the degradation of schools and teachers and that it contained "foul language." The language was also the main complaint in 1983 when parents of students at Richmond (Rhode

Island) High School demanded that the book be removed from the classroom because of the "repulsive" and "pornographic" text.

In 1984, the novel was banned from the middle school libraries of the Richland Two School District in Columbia, South Carolina, due to "language problems," but the book was later reinstated for use by students in the eighth grade. That same year, school officials removed the novel from the freshman reading list at Lake Havasu (Arizona) High School. When teachers protested the ban, the school board censured the teachers for failing to set good examples for their students and for fostering disrespect in the classroom by failing to support the board in its decision.

In 1985, the novel was removed from the Stroudsburg (Pennsylvania) High School library after the school board determined that it was "blatantly graphic, pornographic and wholly unacceptable for a high school library." Similar charges were made in 1986, when the book was challenged at Barnstable High School in Hyannis, Massachusetts, for its profanity, as well as for "obscene references to masturbation and sexual fantasies" and "ultimately because of its pessimistic ending." Complainants charged further that the novel painted authority and school systems in an unfavorable light and provided a negative impression of religious schools. "Offensive" language motivated the removal of the novel from the Panama City, Florida, school classrooms and from its libraries in the same year. In 1987, parents cited the "profanity, sexual situations, and themes that allegedly encourage disrespectful behavior" in their demand that the novel be removed from school libraries in the Moreno Valley, California Unified School District. A West Hernando (Florida) Middle School principal recommended in 1988 that the novel be removed from the school library shelves because it was "inappropriate" for middle school readers.

In 1990, Methodist minister R. Lee Smith demanded that the novel be suspended from the required reading list for the ninth-grade class in Woodsville High School in Haverhill, New Hampshire, and the school superintendent withdrew the book from use until a district committee could meet. The novel had been on the required reading list for 13 years at the time of the challenge. At the first school board meeting, the minister identified numerous passages from the novel containing expletives, references to masturbation and sexual fantasies, and derogatory characterizations of a teacher. After consideration, the superintendent and the school board removed the novel from the required reading list. Similar charges were cited that same year when the novel was challenged in the Harwinton and Burlington, Connecticut, schools, where parents charged that it contained subject matter that set bad examples and gave students negative views on life.

In 1991, a minister in Paola, Kansas, joined the parent of a child in the school system to protest the use of *The Chocolate War* as part of the ninth-grade curriculum. The challengers charged that the novel contained curse words and depicted sexual desires. A review committee, appointed to study the issue, recommended that the novel be retained, and the school board voted 4-3 to affirm the decision of the review committee. The board also reaffirmed its policy of offering an alternative reading assignment to students who objected. That same year, a seventh-grade language arts teacher in Augusta, Maine, requested that the novel be removed from the middle school library and placed in the high school, alleging that the novel lacked positive role models and that it had an unhappy ending. The district superintendent followed the recommendation of a district review committee to retain the book in the middle school library.

Parents of eighth-grade students in New Milford, Connecticut, challenged the inclusion of the novel on the required reading list in 1992, citing negativism, as well as vulgar language, sexual references, and violence that are harmful to students. The assistant superintendent defended the novel and a language arts coordinator supported inclusion of the book as a means of helping eighth-grade students to deal with peer pressure. A districtwide review committee recommended that the novel be retained but at a higher grade level. The suggestion was countered by parents who opposed the book ban and who claimed that the book addressed issues that were important to middle school children's lives. After hearing discussion, the school board voted 9-1 to retain *The Chocolate War* on the required reading list.

A 1993 challenge to the novel in the Kyrene, Arizona, elementary schools identified the masturbation scene as the sole basis for requesting removal of the novel. The novel was temporarily removed from the 10th-grade reading list at Hephzibah High School in Augusta, Georgia, after a parent complained, "I don't see anything educational about that book. If they ever send a book like that home with one of my daughters again I will personally burn it and throw the ashes on the principal's desk." In 1994, critics identified recurring themes of rape, masturbation, violence, and degrading treatment of women in their challenge to the appearance of the novel on the required reading list in the Hudson Falls, New York, schools.

In 2001, parents of students attending Dunedin Highland Middle School in Dunedin, Florida, submitted a complaint to school district officials objecting to the use of the novel in the middle school curriculum. They expressed concerns regarding profanity in the book and scenes that contain sexual fantasy and references to masturbation. The complaint also asserted that the book contains segments that degrade women and girls.

In 2002, *The Chocolate War* was challenged in Fairfax County, Virginia, by parents Richard and Alice Ess, who are members of Parents Against Bad Books in Schools (PABBIS). The group complained that the book contains "profanity and descriptions of drug abuse, sexually explicit conduct, and torture" and asked the school district to remove the novel from the school district libraries. The school board reviewed the complaint and decided in a 7-4 vote to retain the novel in only one of the seven elementary school libraries, the Halley Elementary School.

In May 2005, the *Newsletter on Intellectual Freedom* of the American Library Association announced that *The Chocolate War* "tops the list of the most challenged books of 2004."

FURTHER READING

Donelson, Kenneth L., and Alleen Pace Nilson. *Literature for Today's Young Adults.* Glenview, Ill.: Scott, Foresman and Company, 1989.

Lewis-House, Nancy. "Books Worth Teaching Even Though They Have Proven Controversial: *The Chocolate War* by Robert Cormier." *English Journal*, April 1993, p. 88.

McGee, Tim. "The Adolescent Novel in AP English." *English Journal*, April 1992, pp. 57–58.

Nelms, Elizabeth D. "Reading in the Classroom: *The Chocolate War*/'The Chocolate War.' " *English Journal*, January 1991, p. 85.

Newsletter on Intellectual Freedom (March 1981): 48; (September 1982): 156; (September 1983): 152; (September 1984): 138; (January 1985): 10; (March 1985): 45; (May 1985): 79; (November 1986): 209; (July 1987): 125–128; (September 1987): 168–169; (March 1988): 45; (May 1990): 87; (March 1991): 44; (May 1991): 90; (May 1992): 96–97; (January 1994): 34; (July 1994): 130; (November 1994): 190; (January 1995): 13; (March 1995): 55; (January 2002): 49–50; (January 2003): 10; (May 2005): 97–98.

A CLOCKWORK ORANGE

Author: Anthony Burgess (John Anthony Burgess Wilson)
Original date and place of publication: 1962, United Kingdom
Original publisher: William Heinemann Ltd.
Literary form: Novel

SUMMARY

A Clockwork Orange is a futuristic warning against both mindless violence and the mechanical reconditioning that is often proposed as society's solution to its ills. It offers a horrifying view of a future England in which gangs of hoodlums, or "droogs," roam the streets freely, robbing, fighting, raping, and consuming illegal drugs and alcohol. Society is limp and listless, a socialist world in which no one reads anymore, despite streets named Amis Avenue and Priestley Place. The teenage language, "Nadsat," consists largely of English mixed with Russian and quasi-Russian words, and the current music star is a "Russky" singer named Jonny Zhivago. The rule of society is that everyone "not a child nor with child nor ill" must work, yet the prisons are overcrowded and officials work to rehabilitate criminals to make room for the large number of expected political prisoners. Even with regular elections and opposition, the people continue to reelect the current government.

Alex, the 15-year-old cocky and self-indulgent main character, is both a product of and a reason for the continued breakdown of social institutions. Deteriorating urban life, ineffective law enforcement, the failure of officials to create order from the chaos, and sexual violence characterize this world, in which social ills perpetuate the violent behavior and prevent cohesion. It is a nightmarish place in which the droogs drive over a big, snarling, toothy thing and "odd squealing things" in the road throughout the night, accompanied by screams and squelches. The young hoodlums drink doped milk, and before committing robberies Alex and his fellow droogs put on their "maskies," faces of historical personalities: Disraeli, Elvis Presley, Henry VIII, and "Peebee" Shelley. Women exist for the droogs only as objects of rape and other violence, and sex has also taken on a mechanical characteristic that is reinforced by the term to describe the sex act, "the old in-out in-out." Even classical music, usually viewed as a sign of civilized taste, gains a new character in the novel. Symphonic music is Alex's passion, and he retreats frequently to his speaker-filled room to lie naked on his bed and listen to the music of Mozart, Beethoven, or Bach. As the music swells, he fantasizes about raping and terrorizing young girls and grinding his boot heel into the faces of helpless victims.

The novel is divided into three parts. In the first part, Alex simply does whatever he wants without guilt or concern for others, and he experiences joy in violence of every kind, from destruction or theft of objects to every form of sexual and nonsexual assault. He is free to choose whatever pleasures he desires, however destructive to society they might be. However, because his choices are harmful, society asserts its right to deprive Alex of his freedom. Sentenced to 14 years for the murder of an old woman during a burglary, Alex is placed into prison, where he kills a fellow inmate. This ushers in the second part of the novel. The murder focuses attention on him and makes him the likely choice for an experimental treatment that will leave him "transformed out of all recognition" and make him unable to choose any socially deleterious course of action afterward. In essence, he is injected with a drug, strapped into a chair, and forced to watch films of Japanese and Nazi atrocities during World War II, as well as specially made films that combine with the drug to condition him against all thoughts of violence. His progress is measured with electronic devices that are wired to his body. The conditioning works, and the doctors declare Alex cured of his violent desires and now "your true Christian . . . ready to turn the other cheek, ready to be crucified rather than crucify, sick to the very heart at the thought even of killing a fly."

In the third part of the novel, the rehabilitated Alex, now a harmless citizen, returns home to find that his parents have rented out his room to a lodger and that his stereo equipment has been confiscated by the police and sold to provide food for the cats of the woman he murdered. He is attacked by a group of old men whom he had victimized earlier, then rescued by three policemen, two of whom are former gang members who tell him that the government has been cleaning up the streets and hiring former hoodlums as police. Rather than help Alex, they beat him severely, leaving him to crawl to a nearby cottage. There, he is bandaged and fed by a man whom he had once attacked and whose wife he had brutally raped and beaten, but the man does not recognize him at first. Instead, F. Alexander sees in Alex an opportunity for propaganda against the government. Professing that "a man who cannot choose ceases to be a man," he calls together his friends but soon realizes that Alex is his wife's murderer. He tortures Alex by playing symphonic music loudly, and Alex tries to commit suicide by jumping out a window. Days later, he awakens in the hospital, completely swathed in bandages, and realizes that he has regained his violent nature. The doctors and government officials are happy because they are now free of the charges that they had perpetrated a criminal reform scheme and violated Alex's rights. While he was in a coma, they used "deep hypnopaedia or some such slovo" to restore his former depraved nature and his appetites for Beethoven and violence. As the old thoughts of violence fill Alex's head, he declares himself "cured all right."

CENSORSHIP HISTORY

A Clockwork Orange has motivated debate since its publication, and the controversy has centered on the language of the book as well as on the brutality and sexual violence of the first third of the novel. In 1973, a book dealer in Orem, Utah, was arrested for selling three purportedly obscene books: *Last Tango in Paris* by Robert Ailey, *The Idolators* by William Hegner, and *A Clockwork Orange*. Using the 1973 Supreme Court "local standards" decision, *Miller v. California* (June 21, 1973), the town passed a very specific obscenity ordinance under which police charged bookstore owner Carole Grant. The charges were later dropped, but Grant was forced to close the store and relocate to another city.

In Aurora, Colorado, in 1976, the school board at a regularly scheduled meeting approved 1,275 books for use in the high school, but they disapproved *A Clockwork Orange* and the following nine books: *The Exorcist* by William P. Blatty, *The Reincarnation of Peter Proud* by Max Ehrlich, *New American Poetry 1945–1960* by Donald Allen, *Starting from San Francisco* by Lawrence Ferlinghetti, *The Yage Letters* by William Burroughs and Allen Ginsberg, *Coney Island of the Mind* by Lawrence Ferlinghetti, *Kaddish and Other Poems, 1958–1960* by Allen Ginsberg, *Lunch Poems* by Frank O'Hara, and *Rosemary's Baby* by Ira Levin. The books had already been included by teachers in their course reading lists, but on January 13, 1976, the school board issued a statement to teachers directing that the books "will not be purchased, nor used for class assignment, nor will an individual be given credit for reading any of these books." The school board did not rule that the books were legally obscene nor did it remove the books from the school libraries. The teachers challenged the decision of the board, and the case went to court, where, in *Bob Cary, et al. v. Board of Education of Adams-Arapahoe School District 28-J, Aurora, Colorado*, 427 F. Supp. 945, 952 (D. Colo. 1977), they argued that the decision had impinged on their academic freedom. In his decision, Judge Matsch observed that the board had committed itself to offering students "an opportunity to engage actively in the free exchange of ideas" by offering the courses as electives. He stated, "It is enough to conclude that having granted both teachers and students the freedom to explore contemporary literature in these high school classes, the school board may not now impose its value judgments on the literature they choose to consider." Despite his stated position, the judge was forced to rule against the teachers because the teachers had bargained away their rights to academic freedom in this matter with a specific clause in their master contract.

In Westport, Connecticut, in 1977, parents approached members of the school board to protest the use of the novel in the high school classroom. They cited "objectionable" language in their complaints. The work was removed from the classroom. In Anniston, Alabama, in 1982, protests resulted in the temporary removal of the novel from the school libraries, but the work was later reinstated with the restriction that students would need parental permission to take out the book.

FURTHER READING

Aggeler, Geoffrey. *Anthony Burgess: The Artist as Novelist.* Birmingham: University of Alabama Press, 1979.
Coale, Samuel. *Anthony Burgess.* New York: Frederick Ungar, 1981.
Modern Fiction Studies (special Burgess issue) 27 (Autumn 1981).
Newsletter on Intellectual Freedom (May 1976): 70; (January 1977): 8; (March 1983): 37.
Pace, Eric. "Fears of Local Censorship Haunt the Book Trade." *New York Times,* January 8, 1974, p. 26.

THE COLOR PURPLE

Author: Alice Walker
Original date and place of publication: 1982, United States
Original publisher: Harcourt Brace Jovanovich
Literary form: Novel

SUMMARY

The Color Purple, winner of the 1983 Pulitzer Prize for Fiction and the American Book Award, is composed of personal letters written by the main character, Celie, to God and to her sister Nettie. Written in the vernacular of poor Southern African Americans, the letters allow Celie to tell the story in her own words and permit the author to describe the community of women who support and eventually rescue each other from the restrictions placed on them by society.

The primary setting of the novel is Georgia in the years between World War I and World War II. The novel opens with the first letter written to God by 14-year-old Celie, the victim of continual sexual abuse by her stepfather Alphonso, whom she and her sister call "Pa" and whom they believe to be their natural father. When he first rapes her, he tells her to tell no one but God, and so begin her tragic and painful letters. Poor, uneducated, and unattractive as Celie believes herself to be, she finds no means of preventing the abuse to herself, but she strives to protect her younger sister, Nettie, from becoming a victim. Celie's two children born of the sexual abuse by her stepfather are taken from her and adopted by missionaries bound for Africa, a couple who also befriend Nettie and take her with them. Soon after, Celie is forced into a harsh and poverty-stricken marriage with Albert, a much older widower who mistreats her, leaving her letters to God and to Nettie as her only comfort. She never receives Nettie's responses because Albert hides the letters for years.

Victimized by men and by the failure to resist her ill treatment, Celie can conceive of no other life and views herself as ugly, talentless, and insignificant until the beautiful, sensual, confident, and independent Shug Avery enters her life. Albert's former lover and the mother of three of his children years earlier, Shug is a flamboyant blues singer. She returns as Albert's lover, then becomes Celie's lover, awakening her to experience love for the first time and to truly value her body and her talents. After learning that Albert has hidden her sister's letters for years, Celie leaves Albert to live with Shug and discovers her creative talent as she begins a pants company in Memphis. Years later, having become a confident and valued human being, Celie returns to Georgia to claim her family home. Her sister Nettie returns from Africa with Celie's children, and the family celebrates the survival of the human spirit.

CENSORSHIP HISTORY

The novel has been criticized for including such taboo themes as incest, birth of children outside of marriage, rape, sexual pleasure, and lesbian activity. Aggressive Shug Avery has not only given birth to three children outside of marriage, but she later becomes sexually intimate with both her former lover and his present wife, Celie. Critics of her behavior emphasize that she shows no remorse for her moral transgressions and, instead, exhibits daring boldness in her pleasure seeking. Some members of the African-American community find the novel insulting to African-American males with its emphasis on Celie's sexual abuse by her stepfather and her physical abuse at the hands of her husband. Parents have also objected to the lesbian theme within the novel, claiming that the book would not have been acceptable for use in schools had the lesbian characters been white. In only rare instances have critics challenged the book for its language, but those who have cite the several instances in which such terms as *tits* and *pussy* appear as the cause of their objections.

The novel was first challenged in 1984, when parents of students in the Oakland (California) High School honors English class complained that the book was inappropriate reading because of its "sexual and social explicitness," especially its "troubling ideas about race relations . . . and human sexuality." The book was removed from the classroom, pending review by the Oakland board of education. After nine months of discussion, the board reluctantly gave approval for use of the book in the honors curriculum. The following year, school trustees in Hayward, California, rejected a purchase order for copies of the novel based on their views that it contained "rough language" and "explicit sex scenes." In 1986, school librarians in Newport News, Virginia, removed the novel from the open shelves because of its "profanity and sexual references." The work was made available only to individuals over age 18 or to students who provided written permission from their parents. In 1989, a challenge was raised at the Saginaw (Michigan) Public Library, on the charge that the book was "too sexually graphic for a 12-year-old," but the challenge failed, and the book remained on the open shelves. The novel was also challenged but remained in Chattanooga, Tennessee, in 1989, when it appeared as a summer youth program reading assignment.

Challenges to *The Color Purple* continued into the 1990s. A parent in Ten Sleep, Wyoming, complained in 1990 about the inclusion of the book as an optional reading assignment for a sophomore English class. The superintendent of schools refused to remove the book and, instead, reminded parents that the students had numerous alternative readings from which to choose. That same year, parents in Tyrone, Pennsylvania, objected to the inclusion of the novel on a high school supplementary reading list. They found the language and the sexual activity embarrassing. The school board formed a committee to review guidelines for reading lists and to set standards for material that did not appear on approved curriculum lists. Parents of students in New Bern (North Carolina) High School raised objections to the novel, one of the 10th-grade reading assignments, after they read the passage in which Celie is raped by her stepfather. The high school principal appointed a review committee and allowed parents to select another book for their children. The review committee created restrictions that determined how the novel would be taught to future students. Also in 1992, the novel was banned from the Souderton (Pennsylvania) Area School District 10th-grade reading lists, when parents protested that the language and sexual situations of the novel made it more "smut" than literature.

The *Los Angeles Times* reported that many of the parents were believed to be members of religious organizations. Parents called for the resignation of Marion Dugan, director of curriculum, because she supported retention of the book, although after a long defense she retained her job.

In 2001, the *Atlanta Constitution* reported that *The Color Purple* had been removed from the Accelerated Reader Program in Cobb County in metropolitan Atlanta, Georgia. Until April 2001, the novel was recommended for reading by children as young as 11 in the reading program that encouraged younger students to read material with mature content aimed at teenage readers. Angry parents contacted Cobb County school officials and insisted on removal of the book because of the sexually explicit situations and the incidents of incest that occur. Pam McClure, the parent who led the challenge against the novel, told reporters, "The topic of incest was not appropriate . . . Sexually explicit situations—not appropriate."

FURTHER READING

American Library Association. *Censorship and Selection: Issues and Answers for Schools.* Chicago: American Library Association, 1993.
"Book Ban Includes *The Color Purple.*" *Chicago Tribune*, November 9, 1997, p. 11.
Christian, Barbara. *Black Feminist Criticism.* New York: Pergamon Press, 1985.
Gentry, Tony. *Alice Walker: Author.* New York: Chelsea House Publishers, 1993.
Kramer, Barbara. *Alice Walker: Author of "The Color Purple."* Springfield, N.J.: Enslow Publishers, 1995.
MacDonald, Mary. "Parents Say Preteens in Cobb Get Too Raunchy a Reading List." *Atlanta Constitution*, April 23, 2001, p. A-1.
People For the American Way. *Attacks on the Freedom to Learn: 1991–1992 Report.* Washington, D.C.: People For the American Way, 1992.
Shogren, Elizabeth, and Douglas Frantz. "Political, Religious Right Lead School Book Ban Efforts Censorship: A Survey by a Liberal-Leaning Group Finds 41% of 347 Attempts to Restrict Reading Material Succeeded. *The Color Purple* Is One Target." *Los Angeles Times*, September 2, 1993, p. 14.
Young Adult Services Division, Intellectual Freedom Committee. *Hit List: Frequently Challenged Young Adult Titles: References to Defend Them.* Chicago: YASD, American Library Association, 1989.

CUJO

Author: Stephen King
Original date and place of publication: 1981, United States
Original publisher: Viking Press
Literary form: Novel

SUMMARY

Cujo is the story of a 200-pound Saint Bernard, a placid and typical "good dog" who becomes a source of terror to the family that loves him and to the inhabitants of the small town of Castle Rock, Maine. The Camber family pet, Cujo is the best friend of 10-year-old Brett Camber. The dog is bitten by rabid bats when he bolts into a cave while chasing rabbits. As Cujo slowly and painfully succumbs to rabies, King introduces his readers to the inhabitants of Castle Rock, some of whom will be attacked violently by Cujo and die.

Joe Camber, an auto mechanic and an abusive husband, makes a strong effort to indoctrinate his son Brett in his brutal ways, an effort that his wife, Charity, tries to counteract. Vic Trenton, a New York advertising executive who has moved with his wife, Donna, and son, Tad, to enjoy the peaceful Maine surroundings, strives to keep his marriage together even as Donna has an affair with local poet Steve Kemp, who cannot resist writing to Vic, "I enjoyed fucking the shit out of her." After receiving the note, Vic imagines their sexual encounter in detail. Aunt Evie, at 93 the oldest inhabitant, fore-tells the weather and has been labeled "that old loudmouth bitch" by post-man George Meara, who is called "an old fart" by Aunt Evie. Gary Pervier, "meaner than a bull with a jackhandle up its ass," turned his Distinguished Service Cross into an ashtray in 1968. When hippies sought him out to tell him that he was "too fucking much," Gary threatened them with his rifle, for he considered them "a bunch of long-haired muff-diving crab-crawling asshole pinko fucksticks" and "told them he didn't give a shit if he blew their guts from Castle Rock to Fryeburg." The novel also contains "country club cunts" and several characters who routinely tell each other, "Fuck you."

Tad Trenton begins to see a monster in his closet each night soon after Cujo is bitten, and the two events are left for the reader to connect as rep-resentative of the evil that pervades ordinary life. The monster, "its eyes amber-glowing pits" that seem to follow him, frightens him and leaves "his scrotum crawling." He hears the monster's "purring growl" and smells "its sweet carrion breath." The monster disappears when Tad's parents enter the room but reappears after they leave and warns Tad that his name "was Frank Dodd once, and I killed the ladies and maybe I ate them, too." He also warns Tad that someday soon he will pounce on the little boy and eat him.

The narrative continues, lapsing occasionally into Cujo's consciousness as he relates his physical deterioration, notes his muscle aches and fester-ing muzzle, and puzzles over his growing desire to kill the humans around him. The suspense builds with each kill, until Cujo traps Donna and Tad in their car, which she has taken to Camber's garage for repairs. For nearly two days, Donna struggles to keep her son safe from Cujo until she is forced into a physical confrontation with the dog and eventually kills him, using a baseball bat as her defense. Donna survives, although her deep bites bleed profusely and she must be treated for rabies, but Tad dies of dehydration despite her efforts to save him. As the novel ends, Vic and Donna reconcile, and Charity and Brett Camber begin a new life, free of Joe's brutality.

CENSORSHIP HISTORY

Many works written by Stephen King have been challenged or removed from school and community libraries, including: *Carrie*, CHRISTINE, *The*

Dark Half, The Dead Zone, Different Seasons, The Drawing of the Three, The Eyes of the Dragon, Firestarter, Four Past Midnight, It, Night Shift, Pet Sematary, 'Salem's Lot, The Shining, The Skeleton Crew, The Stand, The Talisman, Thinner, and *The Tommyknockers.* The most frequently challenged of King's works is *Cujo,* which has been charged with "age inappropriateness," "unacceptable language," and being "violent."

In 1984, parents of students in the Rankin County (Mississippi) School District challenged the appearance of the novel in the school libraries, claiming that it is "profane and sexually objectionable." The school board voted to retain the book in the libraries. In 1985, the novel was removed from the high school library in Bradford, New York, after parents complained that it is "a bunch of garbage." Also in 1985, the school trustees in Hayward, California, refused to approve a purchase order for the book because of the "rough language" and "explicit sex scenes." That same year, the Washington County, Alabama, board of education made a unanimous decision to remove the novel from all school libraries in the county, based on their perception that the novel contains "unacceptable language" and is "pornographic." In 1987, school officials removed the novel from the high school library after parents in Durand, Wisconsin, objected to it because of "violence" and "inappropriate language." The school board appointed a nine-member panel composed of school personnel and community members to review the book, and the issue was not pursued further.

In 1992, parents complained to the school superintendent in Peru, Indiana, that the novel and two other King novels, *The Dead Zone* and *Christine,* contained "filthy language" and were "not suitable for high school students," and they asked for its removal. The superintendent recommended to the school board that the novels be kept in the school library and made available to students who have parental permission. The school board refused to consider the suggestion and voted 5-1 to ban the books entirely from the high school library. Also in 1992, parents of middle school students in South Portland, Maine, requested that the school board remove the novel from the middle school library because of its "profanity" and sexual references. A review committee appointed by the school board to consider the request recommended its retention in the library collection. That same year, parents of students in Sparta, Illinois, appeared before the board of education and requested the removal of all books by Stephen King from the school libraries, claiming they are "violent" and "contain sex and explicit language." The board honored the parents' request to bar their children from using the book but refused to ban the books.

In 1994, a local minister and a school board member in Bismarck, North Dakota, claimed that *Cujo* and eight other King novels (*Carrie, Christine, The Dead Zone, The Drawing of the Three, The Eyes of the Dragon, Pet Sematary, The Shining,* and *Thinner*) should be removed from the school libraries. They challenged the novel on grounds of "age appropriateness."

In October 1998, the West Hernando Middle School in Brooksville, Florida, removed the novel from general circulation and placed it into the restricted access area. The move came after several parents complained that the book contained vivid descriptions of sex and profanity.

FURTHER READING

Egan, James. "Sacral Parody in the Fiction of Stephen King." *Journal of Popular Culture* 23 (Winter 1989): 125–141.

Hohne, Karen A. "The Spoken Word in the Works of Stephen King." *Journal of Popular Culture* 28 (Fall 1994): 93–103.

King, Stephen. "Banned Books and Other Concerns: The Virginia Beach Lecture." In *The Stephen King Companion*, edited by George Beahm, 51–61. Kansas City, Mo.: Andrews & McMeel, 1989.

Newsletter on Intellectual Freedom (May 1984): 69; (January 1985): 8; (May 1985): 75, 77; (July 1985): 111; (January 1986): 7; (January 1987): 12; (March 1987): 54–55; (May 1987): 86; (July 1987): 125; (November 1987): 225, 226; (September 1988): 152; (January 1989): 11; (March 1989): 4; (May 1989): 75; (January 1990): 4–5; (January 1991): 12; (March 1992): 40; (May 1992): 79, 80; (July 1992): 105, 106; (March 1993): 41, 56; (July 1993): 124; (May 1994): 84–85; (September 1994): 166–167; (January 2002): 15.

DADDY'S ROOMMATE

Author: Michael Willhoite
Original date and place of publication: 1990, United States
Original publisher: Alyson Publications
Literary form: Children's book

SUMMARY

Daddy's Roommate is one of the first children's books to deal openly with the topic of homosexual male parents. Brightly illustrated with only one brief, straightforward sentence on each page, the book relates the story of a young boy whose parents divorce. The young narrator visits his father and meets his father's roommate. The reader learns that the little boy's father and roommate work, eat, sleep, shave, and sometimes even fight together but always make up. Both men act as fathers, and the three enjoy days at the zoo, baseball games, and the beach.

Near the end of the book, the narrator states to readers that "Mommy says Daddy and Frank are gay." Because he doesn't know what that means, his mother explains that "Being gay is just one more kind of love." Another illustration shows Frank and the father barefoot and curled up on the couch watching television, accompanied by the line, "Daddy and his roommate are very happy together." The book ends with the narrator stating, "And I'm happy too!" as he stands between Frank and his father in line at the movies.

CENSORSHIP HISTORY

Daddy's Roommate has been challenged repeatedly since its first appearance for reasons that range from a criticism of its language as "age inappropriate" to the charge that it is an indoctrination of children into the lesbian/gay lifestyle.

In 1992, nine incidents involving the book were recorded by the American Library Association. Bay Ridge School Board in Brooklyn, New York, removed this book and HEATHER HAS TWO MOMMIES, a book about lesbian parenting, from the district's grade-school curriculum. The books had been included in the optional reading list for first-grade students, but the school board president decided after reviewing the books that certain words in the work were "age inappropriate."

Patrons of Timberland Regional Libraries in Olympia, Washington, challenged the book, claiming that it was "offensive" and "promotes homosexuality," but it was retained. Despite challenges by patrons of Roswell (New Mexico) Public Library and the Dauphin County (Pennsylvania) Library System that the intent of the book was "indoctrination into a gay lifestyle," the book was retained in both library collections. Patrons of public libraries in Goldsboro, North Carolina; Grand Prairie, Texas; and Tillamook, Oregon, asserted in their separate challenges that the book "promotes a dangerous and ungodly lifestyle from which children must be protected," but the named libraries retained the book.

A well-organized and well-orchestrated challenge to the book occurred in Gwinnett County, Georgia, where objectors submitted increasingly numerous complaints to the Lake Lanier Regional Library System. The complaints were followed by two petitions, one with 150 names and another with 200. Despite the pressure to remove the book from the library collection, the library staff chose to retain it. The challengers then requested a review of the book by the library board, which voted to remove it from open shelves and to place it behind the circulation desk, where it would be available to patrons who requested it. In explaining the decision, the board president stated that "it might be damaging to a three- to seven-year-old who might get the wrong idea. . . . Homosexuality is something we have to deal with in our lifetime, and we don't want to be censors, but maybe a little restriction."

Three challenges to *Daddy's Roommate* in 1992 included objections to *Heather Has Two Mommies*. The challenge at Fayetteville (North Carolina) County Library was particularly risky to the future funding of the library. Six members of a Right-to-Life group submitted separate objections to the books and a petition. The library held a public hearing at which protesters, one of whom admitted that she had never seen the books, heatedly denounced the books and stated that "anything that promotes or teaches homosexuality is decaying the minds of children." Despite the vehement objections, the library board voted unanimously to keep the books in the children's section. One trustee observed that a ban of the books may have satisfied the objectors, but it would have "probably infuriated many and violated the rights of all." The decision was announced shortly before the city was to vote on a bond issue to finance the library system. The protesters retaliated by organizing a campaign to defeat the bond issue, claiming in their propaganda that the library system "encourages young children to affirm and endorse conduct or a 'life style' that leads to untimely death and serves no biological utility." Unlike the strong support shown for the library in earlier years, only a small majority passed the bond issue.

When the public library in Springfield, Oregon, received donations of *Daddy's Roommate* and *Heather Has Two Mommies,* the children's librarian was forced to decide if inclusion of the books in the library collection would violate a recently passed city charter amendment that prohibited the city from "promoting, encouraging or facilitating" homosexuality. The Oregon Citizens Alliance (OCA), the group that had spearheaded the amendment, warned the library that if either book were to be placed in the library, they would "do everything they can to get it out of there." A representative from the local chapter of the American Civil Liberties Union warned the library that if it rejected the books solely because they violated the city charter amendment, they would file suit. The librarian applied the standard library selection guidelines to the books, and they were eventually retained over the protests of the OCA.

Daddy's Roommate and *Heather Has Two Mommies* were also challenged in Elizabethtown, North Carolina, by members of the Bladen Coalition of Christians who approached the Bladen County Commission to prevent the librarian from placing the newly purchased books in the county library. Labeling the books as "wicked, seditious, and dangerous," the protesters demanded their elimination and the appointment of a committee that would include members of their coalition to create new library book selection guidelines. The books were placed in the adult section of the library.

The book faced an increased number of challenges in 1993, making it the most challenged book of the year. After objections from patrons, the book was moved from the children's section to the adult shelves in Manatee (Florida) Public Library and Mercer County Library System in Lawrence, New Jersey.

In Mesa, Arizona, a patron of the public library challenged the book because it "is vile, sick and goes against every law and constitution," but it was retained. It was challenged but retained at Alachua County Library in High Springs, Florida; Seekonk (Massachusetts) Public Library; North Brunswick (New Jersey) Public Library; Cumberland County (North Carolina) Public Library; Chattanooga-Hamilton County (Tennessee) Bicentennial Library; Wicomico County Free County Library in Salisbury, Maryland; Sussex (Wisconsin) Public Library; Dayton and Montgomery County (Ohio) Public Library; and Juneau, Alaska, school libraries. The book was also challenged but retained as a reading in the curriculum in Rosemount-Apple Valley-Eagen (Minnesota) School District.

In 1994, officials of the Lane County Head Start program in Cottage Grove, Oregon, removed *Daddy's Roommate* and *Heather Has Two Mommies* from its antibias curriculum after receiving complaints from parents. Challenged as being a "skillful presentation to the young child about lesbianism/homosexuality," the books were, nonetheless, retained by Chandler (Arizona) Public Library. In Fort Worth, Texas, however, the book was removed from the children's section and not relocated within the public library after critics charged that the book "legitimizes gay relationships."

FURTHER READING

"Daddy Is out of the Closet: *Daddy's Roommate* by Michael Willhoite / *Heather Has Two Mommies* by Leslea Newman." *Newsweek* 117 (January 7, 1991): 60.

Hardigg, Viva. "Censors at Work." *U.S. News & World Report* 117 (September 26, 1994): 29.

Hildebrand, Joan M. "Books for Children: *Daddy's Roommate.*" *Childhood Education* 70 (1994): 306.

Newsletter on Intellectual Freedom (May 1992): 83, 95; (September 1992): 162; (November 1992): 197–199; (January 1993): 7, 9–10, 28; (May 1993): 143–146; (November 1993): 179; (January 1994): 13, 34–36; (March 1994): 69; (July 1994): 115; (September 1994): 147–148, 166; (November 1994): 187; (January 1995): 4, 6, 8.

St. Lifer, Evan. "*Daddy's Roommate* Challenged in VT." *Library Journal* 120 (July 1995): 14–16.

Symons, Ann K. *Protecting the Right to Read: A How-to-Do Manual for School and Public Librarians.* New York: Neal-Schuman Publishers, 1996.

A DAY NO PIGS WOULD DIE

Author: Robert Newton Peck
Original date and place of publication: 1972, United States
Original publisher: Alfred A. Knopf
Literary form: Young adult novel

SUMMARY

A Day No Pigs Would Die is an autobiographical novel about a predominantly Shaker community in 1920s rural Vermont, during the year the author, as a young farm boy, is forced to grow from a 12-year-old child into a 13-year-old man. The novel opens with a bloody and graphic description of a cow giving birth. Rob, who has skipped school, sees her agony and goes to her aid. She nearly kills him, but the bull calves live, and he is rewarded with a piglet that he names Pinky.

Rob's father, Haven, is the community pig slaughterer, an uneducated farmer who wants more for his son. Although the Peck family doesn't follow the Shaker way, the Shakers respect Haven, who, in turn, inculcates strong values and a respect for all living creatures into Rob. This respect contains a tolerance for human error, for the community members are imperfect but decent people. Widow Bascom is said to be "carrying on" with her young hired man, Ira Long, whom she later marries. Sebring Hillman had a child with Haven's cousin Letty years earlier when she cared for his ill wife, and he is tormented with guilt over her murder of the infant and her suicide. One night, Hillman digs up the baby's grave and takes the small coffin to bury in his family plot, a move that seems just to Haven and Rob. Rob uses "damn" and "hell" occasionally, and his father reprimands him. Even Haven is fallible. When he captures a weasel that had been killing his chickens, he invites Ira Long to test the weasel-killing instincts of his "bitch terrier," Hussy, by placing the two in a barrel with the lid on. Hussy kills the weasel, but she is badly injured, and they must kill her. Haven decides never to allow that again, no matter how many chickens are killed.

Rob looks forward to breeding Pinky and marketing her offspring. She is mated several times with the neighbor's prize boar, beginning with one violent confrontation in which she fights but is unable to escape. "He was bigger and stronger and ten times meaner than Pinky. And so he had his way with her. All the time he was breeding into her, she squealed like her throat had been cut. Every breath. She just squealed like crying, and wouldn't stop." Afterward, Pinky's rump is bruised, blood runs down her leg and her body shakes violently. For all their efforts, Pinky is barren, and Rob must concede that they cannot afford to keep her and must slaughter her for food.

Haven dies after a winter of ill health, and Rob must run the farm for his mother and great-aunt Carrie. He makes the funeral arrangements, speaks the eulogy, and leads the mourners to the orchard to bury his father. He is keenly aware of his new responsibilities as the novel ends.

CENSORSHIP HISTORY

The novel had been in classrooms and libraries for more than a decade before the first objections to content and language appeared. The objections have ranged from concern about the language to objections to the "violence" and "cruelty" of the weasel killing and hog slaughtering to the "graphic sexuality" of the descriptive passage in which Rob's pet sow is mated with a neighbor's boar.

In 1988, parents of students in the Jefferson County, Colorado, school district challenged the book and asked for its removal from the school libraries. They claimed that it was "bigoted against Baptists and women and depicts violence, hatred, animal cruelty, and murder." The school board reviewed their request and voted to retain the book. In 1990, the book was challenged but retained in the Harwinton and Burlington, Connecticut, schools where parents had raised objections to the use of the book in the school curriculum because of its "inappropriate language and subject matter that set bad examples and give students negative views of life."

In Carbondale, Illinois, in 1991, the parent of a ninth-grade student challenged the use of the book in the classroom and its inclusion in the school library. The concern centered on the use of profanity in the book. The school board convened a review committee to consider the challenge, but the parent who complained did not appear at the hearing, so the board voided the complaint. The following year, several parents of students in a Califon, New Jersey, sixth-grade reading class demanded the removal of the book from the curriculum, asserting that it described violence to animals and "graphic depictions of animals mating." A review committee established by the school board recommended retention of the book, and the school board unanimously agreed.

In 1993, parents of students attending Sherwood Elementary School in Melbourne, Florida, challenged use of the book in the classroom, stating that it could give students the "impression that rape and violence are acceptable." Their concerns centered on the scene in which Pinky fights being mated. The book was retained. The novel was also challenged but retained in the school libraries in Waupaca, Wisconsin, in 1994, despite parents' objections to "graphic passages with sexuality in the book." That same year, the novel was removed from the seventh-grade classroom of Payson (Utah) Middle School after parents complained that they "had problems with language, with animal breeding, and with a scene that involves an infant grave exhumation."

FURTHER READING

Hartvigsen, M. Kip. "Haven Peck's Legacy in *A Day No Pigs Would Die.*" *English Journal* 74 (April 1985): 41–45.
Newsletter on Intellectual Freedom (May 1988): 85; (July 1988): 119–120, 139; (September 1988): 151, 177; (March 1991): 44; (May 1991): 90; (July 1993): 97–98; (May 1994): 98–99; (July 1994): 117, 129.

DELIVERANCE

Author: James Dickey
Original date and place of publication: 1970, United States
Original publisher: Houghton Mifflin Company
Literary form: Novel

SUMMARY

Deliverance is a stark novel that follows the adventures of four men from the city who embark on a three-day canoe trip into a wild and savage backwoods area of Georgia. Presented in journal form, the novel documents the self-awareness and reality that confront these men on September 14, 15, and 16 of an unidentified year, as well as their efforts to come to terms with the savage environment and find strengths to cope with the dangers that the environment poses.

The four men are individually introduced to the reader in the first section, "Before." Ed Gentry, part owner of a graphics studio, is the narrator and one of the two characters who prove themselves able to deal effectively with the brutal wilderness. The other survivor is Lewis Medlock, a champion archer who owns rental property in the city. The two weaker members of the party are Bobby Trippe, a mutual funds salesman, and Drew Ballinger, sales supervisor for a soft-drink company. The first third of the novel creates a lulling effect for the reader, who learns the reasons why each man feels the need to test his civilized self against the uncivilized environment. The second part of the novel begins abruptly as survival becomes an immediate concern. Events occur in quick succession, as one member of the group, Drew, is killed in an accident, another, Lewis, breaks his leg, and the two remaining members of the group, Bobby and Ed, are confronted by two brutal backwoodsmen who try to force them to commit homosexual acts. Ed succeeds in his struggle against his attacker, but Bobby is ineffective and is sodomized. The author makes this scene a confrontation between the civilized and the bestial and shows Bobby as a man so emasculated by society that he can only succumb when attacked.

In the final third of the novel, the reader learns the permanent effect of the trip on the surviving members. Ed has recognized his ability to deal with a hostile environment, so he can now accept his civilized life without further need to test himself. Lewis, whose broken leg had forced him to give up his leadership role to Ed, has learned to put aside his former proud and defiant attitude in favor of becoming more in touch with life. Bobby's new awareness is tragic, for he feels dehumanized and recognizes that he is unable to cope with elements outside the city.

CENSORSHIP HISTORY

Deliverance has been challenged by parents, teachers, school board members, and concerned citizens who have determined that it is an unsuitable text for several reasons, most prominently the homosexual rape scene. Complaints have been made against the language, claiming that it contained "unacceptable sexual references," "vulgar language," and "subject matter inappropriate for use in school." Parents have lodged stronger complaints against the rape scene, claiming that this made the book nothing more than "pornography and filth" and that it "promotes homosexuality." In several instances, questions have arisen regarding the brutality of the sodomy scene and the need to relegate use of the book to older high school students.

In 1974, parents in Montgomery County, Maryland, challenged the use of the novel as a required reading in the classroom and called for its immediate removal from both the classroom and the school library. In a presentation to the district board of education, challengers asserted that the novel employed "gutter language" and that it depicted "perverted acts." The decision was to offer an alternative reading to students, and the book was removed from the school library but later returned.

Similar complaints surfaced in 1993, voiced by parents of students at Hughes Junior High School in Bismarck, North Dakota. Basing their challenge on passages that they viewed as "obscene," "pornographic," and "filthy," parents protested that the novel was inappropriate for junior high school students. After consideration, the school board agreed and removed the novel both from classroom use and from the junior high school library. Copies of the book remained in use at the high school level.

The most extensive challenge to the novel occurred in 1973, in Drake, North Dakota, where the school board acted on parent complaints to remove *Deliverance*, Kurt Vonnegut's *SLAUGHTERHOUSE-FIVE*, and a collection of short stories by Hemingway, Faulkner, Steinbeck, Conrad, and other writers. The English teacher, who was later fired, assigned the books "to get the kids to think clearly about current problems." He defended his choices, noting that "a few four-letter words in a book is no big deal. These people have all heard these words before; none learned any new words. I've always thought the purpose of school is to prepare these people for the 'big, bad world,' but it evidently isn't so." None of the school board members had read the books, but based on parents' complaints, they decided that the books were "dirty."

The board ordered that the books be confiscated from students and burned, although only copies of *Slaughterhouse-Five* were destroyed. The school officials had planned to burn the other two books in equally public incidents but decided against doing so when their burning of the first book attracted nationwide attention, making people in Drake "sick and tired of all this publicity." The school superintendent defended the action of the board, claiming that he did not regret the action, only all of the publicity that it garnered. The English teacher was fired at the end of the school year, but the American Civil Liberties Union filed a suit on his behalf against the school district. The suit resulted in an out-of-court settlement in which the teacher was awarded $5,000 and the school board was ordered not to denigrate the teacher's performance either orally or in writing. Further, the settlement provided that teachers in the high school may use the three books in their junior- and senior-level classes.

FURTHER READING

Baughman, Ronald. *Understanding James Dickey*. Columbia: University of South Carolina Press, 1985.

"Book Burning in North Dakota." *Chicago Sun-Times*, November 14, 1973, p. 40.

Ebersole, Peter. "Dickey's *Deliverance*." *Explicator* 49 (Summer 1991): 249–251.

Moorhead, Michael. "Dickey's *Deliverance*." *Explicator* 51 (Summer 1993): 247–248.

Newsletter for Intellectual Freedom (July 1975): 118; (November 1975): 174; (September 1993): 145; (November 1993): 178–179; (January 1994): 38.

A DICTIONARY OF AMERICAN SLANG

Editors: Harold Wentworth and Stuart Berg Flexner
Original date and place of publication: 1960, United States
Original publisher: T. Y. Crowell
Literary form: Reference

DICTIONARY OF SLANG AND UNCONVENTIONAL ENGLISH

Editor: Eric Partridge
Original date and place of publication: 1970, United States
Original publisher: Macmillan
Literary form: Reference

NEW DICTIONARY OF AMERICAN SLANG

Editor: Robert L. Chapman
Original date and place of publication: 1986, United States
Original publisher: Harper and Row
Literary form: Reference

SUMMARY

These works are compilations of words and meanings that illuminate the colloquial underpinnings of the American language; many are not found in standard dictionaries. Included are slang terms created by members of a range of subcultures, such as the underworld, the military, industry, law enforcement, show business, sports, various occupational and age groups, as well as the slang of talk shows, technology, and different sexual orientations. Some terms have sexual associations, and others give offense because of the challenge they represent to traditional speech. Included are words that are commonly labeled as "vulgar," "obscene," or "dirty."

CENSORSHIP HISTORY

In 1963, Max Rafferty, the superintendent of public instruction in California, determined that among the approximately 8,000 entries contained in *A Dictionary of American Slang*, there were 150 "dirty" passages that made the book obscene. He suggested those passages necessitated "a little bit of censorship," removal of the book from libraries, and supporters in many communities agreed. The book was banned in Costa Mesa and Newport Beach and removed from library shelves in other communities throughout the state, but most libraries decided to keep the dictionary on a separate shelf for restricted use by "serious" students.

In 1979, a parent in Stuart (Florida) Middle School complained to school officials that the book was obscene. When other parents joined in the complaint, the school returned the book to the publisher. In 1981, the dictionary was removed from the Westminster County (Colorado) elementary and secondary school libraries after parents, members of the John Birch Society, and administrators labeled it obscene.

The *Dictionary of American Slang and Unconventional English* became the target of censors in 1973, when the Citizens Commission on Education challenged the Pinellas County (Florida) school board to explain the inclusion of the reference work in the high school libraries. The chair of the commission claimed that the book was responsible for encouraging students to use profanity and blamed the book for the 696 students suspended on that charge in recent years. School officials rebuffed the complaints and retained the book with the claim that to remove the book would be an infringement of students' right to read.

The *New Dictionary of American Slang*, an updated version of *A Dictionary of American Slang*, was challenged for use in Walled Lake School District in Commerce Township, Michigan, in 1994. Parents approached the school board and complained that the book contained profanity. School officials decided to restrict use of the reference work and labeled it with the following warning: "This book contains words which might be offensive to the reader."

FURTHER READING

Jenkinson, Edward. *Censors in the Classroom: The Mind Benders.* Carbondale: Southern Illinois University Press, 1979.
Newsletter on Intellectual Freedom (March 1974): 32; (July 1979): 75; (March 1982): 42–43; (September 1994): 146–147.

DOCTOR DOLITTLE (SERIES)

Author: Hugh John Lofting
Original date and place of publication: 1920, United States (first volume of series)
Original publisher: J. B. Lippincott Company
Literary form: Children's fiction

SUMMARY

"Doctor Dolittle" is a series of 12 volumes recounting the adventures of an English village doctor, John Dolittle, M.D., who loves animals so much that he gives up his human medical practice to devote himself to them. He is unique among men because he learns to understand and speak animal languages, and his compassion for animals takes him on adventures from his village of Puddleby-on-the-Marsh to strange continents and secret lakes, even to the moon on the back of a giant moth. His domestic menagerie of talking animals includes Dab-Dab, the duck who is his housekeeper; Jip, his loyal dog; Polynesia, the 182-year-old parrot known for her command of "the most dreadful seafaring swearwords you ever heard"; and Chee-Chee, Cheapside and the pushmipullyu.

Doctor Dolittle shows consistent enthusiasm for discovery, even to the point of staying up all night in order to learn the fish language of the silver fidgit. He shows concern for both animals and humans. In one adventure, he crosses the sea in a borrowed boat in order to save the monkeys of Africa from a mysterious, fatal disease. In another, he manages to persuade a judge in the British court to permit Bob, a dog, to testify at the murder trial of his master and thereby to save his master's life.

Throughout the series, Doctor Dolittle and the same animal characters appear and reappear in the selections and provide a sense of continuity to the works.

CENSORSHIP HISTORY

"Doctor Dolittle" was first expurgated in the 1960s by J. B. Lippincott Company in the effort to make the books conform to the changing sensibilities of a world that was beginning "to coalesce into one international, multiracial society." The society of the 1920s, when the books were first published, was significantly less concerned with minority issues, and unexamined feelings of racial superiority pervaded not only children's literature but also politics, religion, entertainment, and social ventures. African prince Bumpo, whom Doctor Dolittle and his animals meet when they sail to Africa on a mission of mercy, wants to be white, which produces a great deal of comedy as he sets about trying to achieve his desire. He appears ridiculous, but Lofting also makes the doctor appear ridiculous in many circumstances. In the 1960s, however, the growing pride in culture and multiculturalism made the desire of an African prince to be white offensive to many readers.

The language of the 182-year-old parrot, Polynesia, also a native of Africa, is similarly offensive when she uses the terms *darky* and *coon* in the first book in the series, *The Story of Doctor Dolittle*, then *nigger* in later books in the series. Lippincott purged the series of these terms in the 1960s, but more extensive changes were called for.

In an article in the bulletin of the Council on Interracial Books for Children in 1968, New York librarian Isabelle Suhl charged that "the 'real' Doctor Dolittle is in essence the personification of The Great White Father Nobly Bearing the White Man's Burden and his creator was a white racist and chauvinist, guilty of almost every prejudice known to modern white

Western Man." The stand taken by the council was that editing the language was not enough because the books were too racist to save. The recommendations of the council influenced librarians in schools and the public sector, and they simply stopped buying the Doctor Dolittle series after 1968. As a result, the 12 books went out of print in the early 1970s and did not reappear until 1988 in greatly altered form.

The 1988 version of the Dr. Dolittle books, published by Dell Publishing, was the result of radical censoring by two editors at Dell and by Christopher Lofting, the author's son. Prince Bumpo became neither black nor white, but colorless. All illustrations of the prince and of other African figures were omitted, and all of the characters were made racially neutral. The incident of the controversial desire of Prince Bumpo to become white so that Sleeping Beauty, his favorite fairy tale character, would marry him was removed. Changes were also made in the characters' responses to Doctor Dolittle. Representative of this change from the earlier version is a response given after Dr. Dolittle has saved the monkeys of Africa from a dread disease. In the original, they cheer him and shout gratefully, "Let us give him the finest present a White Man ever had!" This was changed to "Let us give him the finest present ever given." As a reviewer for the *New York Times* observed, "the present editors obviously hope to obliterate every emotionally tinted word."

FURTHER READING

French, Sean. "Diary." *New Statesman & Society*, February 4, 1994, p. 8.
Lanes, Selma G. "Doctor Dolittle, Innocent Again." *New York Times Book Review*, August 28, 1988, p. 20.
Perrin, Noel. *Dr. Bowdler's Legacy*. Boston: David R. Godine, 1992.

DOG DAY AFTERNOON

Author: Patrick Mann (pseudonym for Leslie Waller)
Original date and place of publication: 1974, United States
Original publisher: Delacorte Press
Literary form: Novel

SUMMARY

Dog Day Afternoon is based on the true story of a man who attempts to rob a bank to obtain money for his transsexual lover's operation. The first third of the novel describes the strange and tortured life of Joe Nowicki, half-Italian and half-Polish husband of the monstrously overweight Tina, "a religious guinea" with "immense breasts" whose "big soft lips" feel as if he "were biting ass" when he nibbles at them. His father never looks at him, but his mother can read his face so he avoids looking at her. He is sensitive about his slight build and wears four-inch clog heels to make himself appear taller, and he proudly flaunts the fact that he has a reputation in Greenwich Village as a tough guy known as Littlejoe.

Joe runs out on the weekly family dinner to meet his lover Lana, a pre-operative transsexual with whom he has gone through a mock wedding ceremony. When he later carries a stoned Lana to one of the several "welfare pads" that he maintains to receive multiple welfare checks, the two make love, and he tenderly strokes her face, noting that "she needed a shave again." As Lana comes to, she accuses Joe of not loving her enough because he hasn't come up with the $3,000 or $4,000 necessary for the complete operation. Lana then taunts Joe about the size of his penis, telling him that she has had sex with 13-year-old boys who were better endowed. Joe decides that he will prove his worth by obtaining the money needed.

The second part of the novel begins after Joe completes plans to rob a bank of a huge bakery payroll. The plan is carefully followed, and Joe enters the bank with his cohorts right on schedule, but the payroll delivery schedule has been changed so only a few thousand dollars are at the branch. The robbers decide to wait all night until the Wells Fargo delivery of $50,000 the following morning, and they also keep the hostages.

As the scheme begins to unravel, the police move in across the street, and Detective Sergeant Moretti begins a telephone dialogue with Joe. The two bargain while the television cameras move in. To keep the hostages alive, the police promise to meet Joe's demands, which include a million dollars, safe passage to Kennedy airport, a plane gassed and ready for transatlantic flight, and his "wife," Lana, to go with him. As they wait, a media circus forms outside the bank; ice cream, pizza, and beer vendors appear; and pizza is delivered to the bank for the hostages and the robbers. When the police finally locate Lana and bring her to the police barricades, the people realize that she is a man in drag and begin to chant: "Faggot! Faggot!" Lana faints, and inside the bank, Joe becomes defensive. Meanwhile, the police try to convince Lana to help them as they learn the real reason that Joe has tried to rob the bank.

When the ordeal appears about to end, the scene assumes an even more absurd tone. Joe's mother arrives, and in front of all of the onlookers and the police, they begin a disagreement about his wife, Tina, and what drove Joe into Lana's arms. Gay protesters appear with signs stating, "We Love You Joe." The limousine that appears to take the robbers to the airport bears a sign stating, "Total Relaxation Baths—Our Hostesses Make Life Worth Living," identifying it as transportation for an escort service. Before getting into the limousine, Joe mugs for the cameras and blows kisses into the crowd as the gay demonstrators chant, "Say it clear. Say it loud. I'm gay and I'm proud."

The novel ends with the FBI closing in and saving the hostages, but of the robbers only Joe survives.

CENSORSHIP HISTORY

Dog Day Afternoon has been quietly kept out of many school libraries over the two decades since its publication simply by librarians' failure to order the book. The language and the sexual situations have motivated much of this reticence and most of the challenges to the work. Both men and women in the novel respond without attention to social niceties. While flipping channels, Littlejoe's father pauses at a soap opera in which a character moans she will never be able to look her friend in the eyes ever again. Annoyed, he suggests, "Look 'er inna twat." When a news bulletin exposes Littlejoe as the robber in a bank robbery standoff, his mother cries for their son, and his father responds, "*Your* fucking son maybe." Littlejoe refers to his heritage from his father's side as being "Polack" while he is a "wop" on his mother's side of the family. His mother asks if he wants to taste something great, and he responds, "Four pounds of shit in a two-pound paper bag?" Although Littlejoe is married, he cruises Greenwich Village and has Lana, a preoperative transsexual, for his lover; his mother suspects, and she questions him regarding his "faggot" and "queer" friends. When he waits for Lana at the bar where she entertains, he confides to a friend, "Gonna ball Lana tonight, man, and that broad don't ball without I lay a few solid blasts on her." Numerous other phrases have been singled out as "offensive."

Concern has also been raised regarding the descriptions of the gay milieu in which Littlejoe functions and the street hustling in which a younger man named Sam and other teenagers at a safe house have sex to obtain money. Scenes of Littlejoe's sexual activities with Lana have also drawn criticism, as has the graphic description of Lana's striptease in a bar in which she exposes her breasts and strokes them to a hooting and yelping crowd, then turns away from the crowd for a moment "and stuck out her ass at the crowd . . . then she turned back and her penis, engorged, arose from between her legs like some primeval sea monster searching for its mate."

In 1978, the school board in Vergennes, Vermont, responded to parents' demands that the novel and *The Wanderers* be removed from the Union High School library. The librarian was also forbidden to buy additional works of fiction without having prior approval from both the district administration and the school board. Upset by the decision, a group of parents and students joined the school librarian, Elizabeth Phillips, to challenge the decision of the board.

When *Bicknell v. Vergennes Union High School Board*, 475 F. Supp. 615 (D. Vt. 1979) was decided, U.S. District Court judge Albert W. Coffin rejected the students' and parents' claims and decided in favor of the Vergennes school board. Basing his decision on *Presidents Council, District 25 v. Community School Board, No. 25* (New York City) (see DOWN THESE MEAN STREETS), the court determined that the policies and actions of the school board did not directly or sharply infringe upon the basic constitutional right of the students of Vergennes Union High School. The court acknowledged that other courts may have taken a benign view of library freedoms, but it also determined that "neither the board's failure to purchase a work nor its decision to remove or restrict access to a work in the school library violate the First Amendment rights of the student plaintiffs before this court" because the board removed the books for being vulgar and in bad taste.

Judge Coffin relied heavily on the *Presidents Council* decision in further denying that school librarians had the right to independent control over school library collections, rejecting their argument that denying such control amounted to denying their academic freedom. In 1980, the plaintiffs appealed to the U.S. Court of Appeals for the Second Circuit, but the court decision in *Bicknell v. Vergennes Union High School Board*, 638 F.2d 438 (2d Cir. 1980) affirmed that of the lower court.

FURTHER READING

Newsletter on Intellectual Freedom (January 1979): 6.
O'Neill, Robert M. *Classrooms in the Crossfire*. Bloomington: Indiana University Press, 1981.

DOWN THESE MEAN STREETS

Author: Piri Thomas
Original date and place of publication: 1967, United States
Original publisher: Alfred A. Knopf
Literary form: Autobiography

SUMMARY

Down These Mean Streets relates the author's life between the ages of 12 and 20 growing up in Spanish Harlem in the 1940s and 1950s. Born of a light-skinned, Puerto Rico–born mother and a mainland-born, African-American father, Thomas bluntly reveals his difficulties as a dark-skinned, Spanish-speaking male in an atmosphere in which to be "cool" means running with a gang, using drugs, committing robberies, using illegal weapons, and having indiscriminate sex. He relates his years on the streets, the temporary escape to suburbia, and the six years spent in prison before he turned his life around and began to work as a counselor.

As befits the setting, *Down These Mean Streets* is told in the crude and coarse language of the streets. The young Piri is a survivor, and he learns how to deal and to use drugs, how to steal, and how to make some quick money with a friend who occasionally acts as a male prostitute to obtain money from homosexuals in the neighborhood. The adult Piri graphically describes these adventures, providing detailed instructions for how to get the maximum high while smoking marijuana, how to prepare and to inject heroin, as well as specific aspects of the sexual acts performed. He uses ethnic and homophobic insults in describing those with whom he interacts and himself. Thus, "spics," "guineas," "faggots," and "niggers" frequently appear in the book, and "motherfucker" and "fuck" appear on almost every page. When Piri is sent to prison, the feeling of violence escalates and so does the daily physical threat. In unadorned language, he describes the threat of rape and the constant tensions of prison life that finally make him realize that he wants more in his life. He leaves prison rehabilitated, ready to begin a life of helping others to leave the streets and to make good lives for themselves.

CENSORSHIP HISTORY

Down These Mean Streets contains the raw street vernacular of life in Spanish Harlem and descriptions of experiences that accurately depict a young man's struggle to survive in that brutal environment. These elements of realism have made the work a target of censors who have complained that the language is immoral, obscene, and "just plain filthy." First challenged in 1971, the work was removed from the junior high school library by Community School Board 1250 in Queens, New York. The case that followed, *Presidents Council, District 25 v. Community School Board, No. 25* (New York City), 457 F.2d 289 (2d Cir. 1972), was the first to consider the issue of whether or not a school board had the authority to remove books from a school library. Parents were provoked by the language in the book, which they viewed as obscene, and requested the district board to order the book removed from school libraries. Responding to parent demands, the board held a public meeting where the book was described by 75 speakers, 73 of whom favored retention of the book on scholarly or educational grounds. Piri Thomas appeared at the meeting to speak: "I'm not here to defend the book. I'm here to defend the right of the truth to be said." Despite the support, the district board voted 5-3 to remove all copies of the book from the junior high school libraries in the district. Dissatisfied with this decision, a group of parents, students, teachers, and a school librarian joined with the New York Civil Liberties Union to bring suit against the board in the United States District Court, but the court refused to hear the case.

Six weeks after removing the book, the board conducted another public meeting, where the original decision was modified to allow the libraries that had bought the book to retain their copies, but only parents, not students, could take out the book. Nearly a year later, when the case was appealed, the Court of Appeals of the Second Circuit affirmed the dismissal of the suit, noting that a specific group must be authorized to determine the makeup of a library collection, and proclaimed that there was no reason to elevate an "intramural strife to First Amendment constitutional proportions." The court ignored the right of students to freedom of expression and their right to receive information and stated that "to suggest that the shelving or unshelving of books presents a constitutional issue, particularly where there is no showing of a curtailment of freedom of speech or thought, is a proposition we cannot accept." To do so, stated the decision, "would be a constant intrusion of the judiciary into the internal affairs of the school." Adamant in their fight, the group took the case to the United States Supreme Court, but the Supreme Court refused to review the case. Justice William O. Douglas stated in a dissenting opinion: "What else can the School Board now decide it does not like? How else will its sensibilities be offended? Are we sending children off to school to be educated by the norms of the School Board or are we educating our youth to shed the prejudices of the past, to explore all forms of thought, and to find solutions to our world's problems?"

In 1976, *Down These Mean Streets* was among nine books that school board members in Island Trees Union Free School District No. 26 in New York identified as being "objectionable." After a review committee examined the books, *Down These Mean Streets* was placed on a restricted list because it was judged by the committee to be "pornographic and filthy." Students needed parental permission to take out the book. The book was returned to the library on June 25, 1982, after the United States Supreme Court ruling in *Board of Education, Island Trees Union Free School District No. 26 v. Pico et al.* (See THE BEST SHORT STORIES BY NEGRO WRITERS for the full case.)

FURTHER READING

"Book Ban Is Eased by Queens Board." *New York Times*, June 3, 1971, p. 43.

Buder, Leonard. "Queens District Seeks Book Ban." *New York Times*, April 6, 1971, p. 47.

Maeroff, Gene I. "Book Ban Splits a Queens School District." *New York Times*, May 9, 1971, pp. BQ-71, 82.

Newsletter on Intellectual Freedom (July 1973): 115; (November 1982): 197.

Nolan, Kenneth P. "Book Ban Still Splits School Unit in Queens." *New York Times*, November 26, 1972, pp. BQ-11, 46.

O'Neil, Robert M. *Classrooms in the Crossfire: The Rights and Interests of Students, Parents, Teachers, Administrators, Librarians, and the Community.* Bloomington: Indiana University Press, 1981.

———. "Libraries, Liberty and the First Amendment." *University of Cincinnati Law Reviews* 42, no. 2 (1973): 209–252.

"Queens Book Ban Upheld by Judge." *New York Times*, August 5, 1971, p. 30.

DRACULA

Author: Bram Stoker
Original date and place of publication: 1897, England
Original publisher: Constable Publishers
Literary form: Novel

SUMMARY

Dracula is the story of the fiendish Count Dracula, whose activities are related in diary and journal entries written by principal characters. The novel begins and ends in Transylvania, the traditional site of vampire legends. At the outset, the count lures Jonathan Harker to his castle to explain the purchase of a London estate. Before leaving the inn in Bistritz, the young solicitor is puzzled by the behavior of the innkeeper's wife, who exhibits fear at the mention of the count's name and insists that he wear her crucifix around his neck. People in the crowd outside of the inn make the sign of the cross as Jonathan leaves for Dracula's castle. Once there, Harker becomes a prisoner of the count, who functions as his host, valet, driver, butler, and maid. Strange dreams and visions pursue Harker, who seeks to escape the intense danger that he senses in the castle.

Two young and beautiful women, Lucy and Mina, are the objects of Dracula's lust for blood. The count hypnotizes them before biting them, and even Jonathan falls under his spell as he must be awakened from "a stupor such as we know the Vampire can produce" after Mina's exchange of blood with Dracula. Once bitten by Dracula, the women become slaves to unlawful hunger for blood. The sweet and virginal Lucy Westenra is turned into a vampire, and former suitors see her returning to her grave after preying on a child, the blood dripping down her chin. Mina just barely escapes the same fate; her saving grace is that "she has a man's brain" and is more resistant than the ordinary woman. The young men who try to defend them are unable to do so alone. They must call in the assistance of Dr. Abraham Van Helsing, a Dutch professor whom Stoker describes as "a philosopher and a metaphysician, and one of the most advanced scientists of his day," and Dr. John Seward, a man of science and the head of "a large lunatic asylum."

The last third of the novel is rational and deliberately scientific in tone, as it documents the efforts of Van Helsing and Seward to use research and such technology as phonograph rolls and typewriters to locate Dracula and his followers and to destroy them.

CENSORSHIP HISTORY

Stoker professed to favor the censorship of fiction and wrote that "a close analysis will show that the only emotions which in the long run harm are those arising from sex impulses." He observed that "women are the worst offenders in this form of breach of moral law." This stance appears to exhibit a disparity between his prudery and the erotic and homoerotic undertones that readers have identified in *Dracula*. He ignored his own work when in 1908 he wrote a series of scathing articles for *Nineteenth Century* magazine in which he strongly advocated the censorship of eroticism in fiction.

Readers have long recognized the sexual overtones that pervade *Dracula*, from the first publication of the novel. Victorian readers professed to be scandalized by the intimacy of the count's act and the negative effect on Lucy's moral nature. Critics observed that the novel "is offensive to the sensibilities of the fair sex" and recommended that it be kept out of the hands of women. Booksellers in England were advised to keep the book out of view, so that the "fair sex will not be polluted" by the "devilish mockery of purity" of the work.

Several passages were identified as having motivated particular moral concerns. When Harker lies on a couch in the castle, pretending to be asleep, he is visited by three beautiful, ghostly ladies. As he waits in "languorous ecstasy," one of the women "went down on her knees and bent over me, . . . licked her lips like an animal. . . . I could feel her hot breath on my neck." After Lucy has become a vampire, she is observed sucking the blood from a child, whose body she then throws to the ground after seeing her fiancée, Arthur Holmwood. Having changed from "purity to voluptuous wantonness," she aggressively calls Arthur to her, provocatively telling him, "My arms are hungry for you." When Dr. Seward pries open Lucy's coffin to drive a stake into her heart, he sees "the bloodstained, voluptuous mouth . . . the whole carnal and unspiritual appearance."

Dracula has been largely eclipsed by the numerous film and stage adaptations of the work, and most people today have become familiar with the story of Count Dracula through these sources rather than by reading the original. The novel does not appear frequently on required reading lists in schools; thus school censorship has not been a significant facet of its history. Only one such instance has been reported. In 1994, school officials at Colony High School in Lewisville, Texas, banned the novel from the required reading lists for junior and senior advanced-placement English classes. Complaints centered on what critics viewed as "unacceptable descriptions in the introduction." The specific statement cited appears in an introduction written by George Stade: "Dracula is the symptom of a wish, largely sexual, that we wish we did not have."

FURTHER READING

Belford, Barbara. *Bram Stoker: A Biography of the Author of "Dracula."* New York: Alfred A. Knopf, 1996.

Croley, Laura Sagolla. "The Rhetoric of Reform in Stoker's *Dracula*: Depravity, Decline, and the Fin-de-siècle 'Residium.' " *Criticism* 37 (Winter 1995): 85–108.

Fowell, Frank, and Frank Palmer. *Censorship in England.* 1913. Reprint, New York: Burt Franklin, 1970.

Hendershot, Cyndy. "Vampire and Replicant: The One-Sex Body in a Two-Sex World." *Science-Fiction Studies* 22 (November 1995): 373–398.

Leatherdale, Clive. *Dracula: The Novel and the Legend.* Northamptonshire, U.K.: Aquarian Press, 1985.

Schaffer, Talia. " 'A Wilde Desire Took Me': The Homoerotic History of *Dracula.*" *ELH* 61 (Summer 1994): 381–425.

Senf, Carol A. "Dracula and the Victorian Male Sexual Imagination." *International Journal of Women's Studies* 3 (1980): 455.

Twitchell, James B. "Women and Vampires: *Dracula* as a Victorian Novel." *Midwest Quarterly* 18 (1977): 392–405.

THE DROWNING OF STEPHAN JONES

Author: Bette Greene
Original date and place of publication: 1991, United States
Original publisher: Delacorte Press
Literary form: Novel

SUMMARY

The Drowning of Stephan Jones takes place in Rachetville, Arkansas, a town that is not friendly toward people who are different, as Carla has learned by the reaction of the residents to her outspoken mother, the town librarian. When Carla goes to Harris's hardware store, determined to attract the attention of Andy Harris, who attends high school with her, she meets Frank and Stephan, two men who are new to the area. The two appear to be a couple, and their perceived relationship angers a woman customer who verbally attacks the two men after she hears Frank calling Stephan "my love." A shocked and speechless Carla watches as the Harris men join the woman in confronting Frank, who stands up to them while Stephan edges toward the door and looks poised to run. The next day at school, Andy stops Carla, who is thrilled at the attention until he begins to talk about Frank and Stephan and she realizes how deeply prejudiced he is against homosexuals. Even though she does not agree with his views, she remains quiet and does not defend Frank and Stephan because of her attraction to Andy.

Carla becomes increasingly infatuated with Andy and convinces her mother to attend Christmas services at the church Andy attends, where the Reverend Wheelwright delivers a sermon that condemns homosexuality, but Carla is concentrating too strongly on Andy to pay attention. Andy later makes a surprise visit to her home with an unexpected Christmas present, and the two become inseparable.

Andy and his friends Spider and Ironman begin a campaign of harassment against Frank and Stephan, who have opened an antiques store in a nearby town. They follow Stephan as he leaves his local pizza parlor and chase him into an alley, where they push his face into a steaming pizza, burning him. Their efforts escalate as they work to terrify the two men with the goal of driving them out of their store and town. They begin to make crank calls to the men and send threatening letters, which they claim are only pranks. Carla knows about their activities, but she refuses to become involved because she is more concerned with an upcoming prom.

Although frightened, Frank and Stephan are determined to stop the threats, but they feel that going to the police will be useless. Instead, they speak with Reverend Wheelwright, who offers them no assistance. The harassment continues. On the night of the prom, Carla and Andy and his friends unexpectedly meet Frank and Stephan, and the boys chase them, losing Frank and concentrating their chase on Stephan. They catch him and throw him into the river, where he drowns. When Andy is placed on trial for the murder of Stephan Jones, Carla is the key witness. Andy claims that Stephan had made sexual advances, and the court gives the three boys suspended sentences and probation. During the celebration that follows, Frank appears and shows all of the people present the letters Andy wrote to Stephan, which discredit him in the eyes of everyone. Disillusioned by events, Carla and her mother move out of Rachetville.

CENSORSHIP HISTORY

The Drowning of Stephan Jones has motivated strong negative reactions in many school districts where antigay and anti-lesbian sentiments have led parents to challenge the inclusion of the book in the curriculum or in the school library. In 1993, a school board member in Boling, Texas, objected to the use of the book in a cultural diversity curriculum, charging that the book promoted "anti-Christian beliefs" and contained "objectionable language." He also asserted that the book condones "illegal activity." The school board told the teacher that she would be fired if she did not stop using the book, but she defended the book as a "teaching tool that sets the foundation for our students to learn responsible behavior." The issue was referred to the district review committee, which recommended that the book be retained, but the school board voted to remove the book from the curriculum and from the library. With the assistance of the National Coalition Against Censorship (NCAC), the teacher retained an attorney and sued the school district; the book was returned to the curriculum and the library.

In 1995, in New Ipswich, New Hampshire, Penny Culliton, a respected English teacher at Mascenic Regional High School, was fired after she placed three books with gay or lesbian characters on the optional reading list for her English classes: *Maurice* by E. M. Forster, *The Education of Harriet Hatfield* by May Sarton, and *The Drowning of Stephan Jones* by Bette Greene. The books had been selected by a school review committee and were purchased with the approval of the superintendent of schools in the summer of 1994. Money for the purchase came from a grant given by the Respect for All Youth Fund, which supports efforts to counter negative stereotypes of gay and lesbian youth. School officials fired Culliton on a charge of "gross insubordination" and claimed that the books had not gone through the appropriate approval process. School board member Charles Saari moved to eliminate *The Drowning of Stephan Jones* entirely and to place the other two books into the school library, but other board members spoke up for including the books as readings in a proposed upper-level elective course, but not in required English classes. In the 4-3 vote, the board confirmed that decision and also voted to include the books in the school library. After voting to place the books in the proposed diversity course and in the school library, the board voted 5-1 with one abstention that none of the books would be used in any required course.

In 1998, *The Drowning of Stephan Jones*, Baby Be-Bop, *When Someone You Know Is Gay*, and *Two Teenagers in Twenty* were removed from the library shelves by school officials in Barron, Wisconsin.

In 2002, Eugene Carroll Craig, a resident of Socastee, South Carolina, filed a complaint with the Horry County School District Board, calling for removal of *The Drowning of Stephan Jones* from the school district. He claimed that he had examined a copy of the novel that the seventh-grade child of a friend had brought home from the Myrtle Beach Middle School and was shocked by the content. In an interview, Craig stated that the novel was "like a rattlesnake that needed to be killed right then and right there." After receiving letters from Craig, the school board removed copies of the book from six high school libraries and two middle school libraries until a review committee could determine whether or not to retain it. A panel composed of teachers, administrators, parents, and librarians determined that the book was suitable for high school students but that restrictions should be placed on its use with middle school students. In a presentation to the district school board on June 12, 2002, Craig asserted, "If the book's anti-Christian, anti-social agenda were anti-gay, anti-black, anti-Jewish, anti-Hispanic, it would have never been put in our schools in the first place." The board voted 7-3 the same night to keep the book off district middle school library shelves. Board member Bill Graham stated that he voted for the removal because the book is "educationally unsuitable and contains unacceptable language." School officials reported that this was the first time the district had voted to ban a book.

FURTHER READING

Associated Press. "Homosexual Themes in Schools." Available online. URL: http://www.angelfire.com/ga/page451/articles.html. Accessed December 12, 2009.

Craft, Mary Kathryn. "'Stephan Jones' Banned in Horry." *Sun News*, June 13, 2002.

Finnessy, Patrick K. "Drowning in Dichotomy: Interpreting *The Drowning of Stephan Jones*." *ALAN Review* 25, no. 3 (Spring 1998): 24–27.

Goldberg, Beverly. "Stephan Jones Submersed." *American Libraries* 33, no. 7 (August 2002): 25.

EAST OF EDEN

Author: John Steinbeck
Original date and place of publication: 1952, United States
Original publisher: Viking-Penguin Press
Literary form: Novel

SUMMARY

East of Eden is the story of the classic epic struggle between two brothers, Charles and Adam Trask, whose rivalry reflects that of the biblical Cain and Abel played out in modern times. In part a historical romance, the work relates the lives of several generations of two families, in Connecticut and California, covering significant incidents from the Civil War to World War I. The author incorporates historical events and actual historical figures into the narrative, and these act to mold lives and determine the destinies of the fictional characters. For the most part, Steinbeck does not permit his characters control over their lives. Instead, while they seem to have free will in their moral choices, external factors constantly place them into situations in which they must make choices to survive.

Cyrus Trask is the hard-nosed patriarch who makes his sons, each fathered by a different wife, live a military-like existence. He tolerates no weakness and determines that the gentle-natured Adam must become tougher, so he plans a military career for the boy. Fact blends with fantasy as Cyrus regales everyone with his purported military feats during the Civil War. Among these adventures is his oft-told story of contracting gonorrhea in 1862, when, as a young soldier, he paid ten cents to have sex with a prostitute whom he later hunted for revenge.

When Cyrus dies, he leaves the extensive land holdings in the Salinas Valley and a large amount of money, the source of which remains a mystery, to both sons to share equally. Charles, the stronger son, who has a propensity for evil, stays and farms, but gentle Adam wanders the world at first and returns uneasily to his home. Their lives are dominated by their sibling rivalry, which extends to women, the land, and life. After Adam settles down, his wife leaves him to own "a whorehouse, the most vicious and depraved in this whole end of the country," and he follows her to San Francisco, where she hurts him further by telling him that Charles fathered their twin sons. The novel details the drug use, attempt at self-induced abortion, and sadistic practices of the prostitutes, even as it shows Adam rising above the immorality.

As the lives of Charles and Adam near their end, the epic rivalry is exhibited clearly in the behavior of Adam's twin sons, who will continue the conflict between good and evil and the struggle of individuals to make the correct choices. In the end, Steinbeck shows that there is no Garden of Eden in this life.

CENSORSHIP HISTORY

The novel made readers uncomfortable when it was first published because it is a pessimistic look at man's ability to cope with fate. The language is vulgar in parts, and the novel contains explicit sex scenes that convey the sense of the characters' slow development throughout. These aspects motivated no legal challenges, but parents and school boards have been uncomfortable with the book.

In 1978, the novel was one of the numerous books removed from supplemental high school reading lists in Anaheim, California, despite their use for many years, after complaints by parents, who viewed the book as obscene. Teachers were instructed to simply store the book, along with others such as Richard Wright's BLACK BOY, and cautioned that they were not permitted to provide the books for supplemental reading nor were they to discuss the books with students. The local school board warned teachers that they risked dismissal if they taught any of the banned books. The president of the Anaheim board of education denied that the removal of these books constituted a restriction. Rather, he stated the need of the school district to emphasize the basics of grammar and noted that " 'the only effort to restrict comes from the content of basic grammar classes. . . . If they teach grammar properly, they will have no need for further books. Nor will they have time for them.' "

The novel was challenged or banned in other areas of the country. In 1982, school board officials ordered that the novel be removed from two Anniston, Alabama, high school libraries, because it was "obscene." They later reinstated the work on a restrictive basis. That same year, the novel was also removed from the Morris, Manitoba (Canada), school libraries due to its language. In 1991, parents in the Greenville, South Carolina, schools challenged the appropriateness of the book because of its profanity and because it contained "inappropriate sexual references." The school board made the decision to allow the book to be read with parental permission.

FURTHER READING

Newsletter on Intellectual Freedom (March 1983): 37; (July 1991): 130.
"Steinbeck Novel Creates Controversy." *Los Angeles Times*, June 3, 1978, p. 1.
"Steinbeck's *East of Eden*." *The Asterisk: An Occasional Journal of English Traditions*, October 1978, p. 2.

ELMER GANTRY

Author: Sinclair Lewis
Original date and place of publication: 1927, United States
Original publisher: Harcourt Brace & Company
Literary form: Novel

SUMMARY

Elmer Gantry is the story of a quintessential scoundrel, charlatan, and womanizer, an extravagant faker who also happens to be a minister. He is an opportunist with few scruples or morals, who knows nothing about theology but everything about greed and seduction. Before he is "saved," Gantry is known to his college classmates as "Hellcat," known to become "eloquently drunk, lovingly and pugnaciously drunk." A typical Gantry suggestion is, "Let's go over to Cato and see the girls and get drunk." After his conversion, he vows not to smoke, "to guzzle, to follow loose women, to blaspheme." Hours later, he decides that just one cigarette won't hurt and eventually returns to all of his vices. Gantry decides to preach even if it means losing his waitress girlfriend Juanita, for he can "find skirts like her any place." At Mizpah Seminary, however, his sexual needs lead him to moan, "If Juanita was just here!"

Ordained a Baptist minister, Gantry is appointed to a small church and meets Lulu Bains, a deacon's daughter. When they first meet, he determines, "God, I've *got* to have her!" Soon, "She was in his arms, on the couch . . . limp, unreasoning, at midnight." Lulu, whose babble soon bores him "and her lovemaking was equally unimaginative," expects marriage. He stalls for months and foists her on another man as soon as he can.

Reassigned, Gantry is sidetracked by one too many drinks. Three days late in reporting to his new post, Gantry calls the deacon, who knows all about his four days of drinking and carousing. He is fired but remains a Baptist minister and works as a salesman with the Pequot Farm Implement Company. For two years he makes a good living, buying himself fancy jewelry and clothing, but he misses the adulation of preaching. In Sauterville, Nebraska, he meets highly successful evangelist Sharon Falconer and decides at their first meeting "he was going to have Sharon Falconer." He follows her and becomes first her assistant, then her lover. Although he adores her, Gantry desires another woman, "feeling that it was sheer carelessness to let the pretty and anemic and virginal Lily be wasted."

Gantry next becomes the lover of a New Thought evangelist, but she ejects him from her circle for stealing. For a time, he preaches his own school of thought, then decides to "get in with a real big machine like the Methodists . . . with all their spondulix and big churches and big membership and everything to back me up." Assigned a church in Banjo Crossing, a town of 900, he feels that he is a failure at the age of 32 after the big-time evangelism with Sharon Falconer. Despite vows to the contrary, when he is led to his room by the Widow Clark's daughter, Jane, a girl of 14 or 15, his lechery surfaces and he thinks, "here was a girl he was going to pursue." Hours later, he meets Cleo, 27 years old and bosomy, and the daughter of a church trustee who is also the most successful man in town, worth at least $75,000. Gantry is soon married to Cleo, although on their honeymoon in Chicago "he concealed his distaste for her" and later discovers that "Cleo would never be a lively lover." His dislike of Cleo grows, and he finds "his whole body yearning toward" Jane Clark, but the promise of greater prominence in the Methodist hierarchy restrains him.

Six years and two churches later, Gantry is assigned to Sparta, a town of 129,000 people. Cleo and he sleep in separate bedrooms and, despite guilt, he does not refuse "whenever he found a woman parishioner who was willing to comfort him," nor does he desist from being "called on important but never explained affairs to Sparta." He becomes reacquainted with Lulu, now married, and resumes an affair with her until a good-looking woman becomes his secretary and his lover. His new secretary sets him up and tries to blackmail him using love letters that he wrote to her, but the clever intervention of lawyer T. J. Rigg clears him. In church the next Sunday, as the congregation crowds around to pray and to show their support, Gantry vows silently to never again become involved with a woman other than his wife. As he looks around, he sees a new choir singer, "a girl with charming ankles and lively eyes, with whom he would certainly have to become well acquainted."

CENSORSHIP HISTORY

Elmer Gantry has been singled out by censors because of the sexual adventures of its title character and for the language that frequently peppers his personal conversation. Completely oblivious to the standards that he is supposed to uphold, Gantry frequently yields when his libido is aroused, then deals with the ensuing problems later. He is also given to interjecting "damn" and "hell" into discussions with trusted friends.

Despite expectations, major efforts to ban the novel were not spearheaded by Baptist or Methodist groups, who might take offense that Gantry holds posts in both churches. Instead, it became the target of the Watch and Ward Society, an organization made up mostly of Catholics in Boston, still a largely Catholic city in the 1920s. The organization differed from the New York Society for the Suppression of Vice because it prosecuted the booksellers, not the publishers. Its usual method was to warn all booksellers that a particular book violated the Massachusetts obscenity statutes, then leave it to the retailers to withdraw the book from sale or risk being taken to court. This method appeared to be more effective in taking books out of circulation, because individual booksellers were less likely than publishers to have the resources or the energy to defend them.

The year 1927 was critical, as Massachusetts State District Attorney William J. Foley placed numerous books on the banned list, and *Elmer Gantry* was among the first whose sale he declared indictable. In his edict against the sale of the novel, the attorney general warned dealers of the severe penalties they would pay if they continued to sell it: "Evidence that this book is sold or offered for sale within the confines of Suffolk County will be followed by prompt action by this office."

Among the many books that appeared on the banned list, *Elmer Gantry* attracted the most attention. After Foley informed the Boston Booksellers' Committee that further sales of the novel would be prosecuted, the committee, which consisted of Richard F. Fuller of the Old Corner Bookstore, Charles E. Lauriat of the Charles E. Lauriat Co., and John Tracy of the New England News Co., brought to his office 57 other books that they believed were in danger if *Elmer Gantry* were suppressed. The booksellers claimed that they were in no position to fight the law.

A further repercussion of the ban was economic. Rather than fight the ban, the Old Corner Bookstore returned its unsold copies of the novel to the publisher, Harcourt Brace. When the publisher protested, Richard Fuller suggested that it should force legal action by publicly selling a copy of the book in Boston and, when the case came to court, obtain a decision applicable to Suffolk County that would supersede the threat of the attorney general. Harcourt Brace refused and chose to sue the Old Corner Bookstore for its loss on the returned copies in what they described as a "friendly suit" in civil court.

Sale of the novel was also banned in Camden, New Jersey, and Glasgow, Scotland, in 1927, and in Ireland in 1931, as "offensive to public morals." The ban in Ireland was upheld in 1953.

In another incident, a catalog named *Summer Reading, 1927*, published by R. R. Bowker Company, became the target of censorship by the United States Department of the Post Office because it contained announcements of *Elmer Gantry*, as well as John Gunther's *The Red Pavilion* and May Sinclair's *The Allinghams*, all of which had either been banned in Boston or publicly labeled as "immoral" books. A Fifth Avenue bookstore manager was summoned to the New York City Post Office to discuss the catalog after he had sent out 8,000 copies of it with his shop's imprint on them. A copy was submitted to Horace J. Donnelly, solicitor of the U.S. Post Office Department in Washington, and he advised New York officials that the catalog was unmailable. The first 8,000 were permitted to proceed through the mails, but the bookseller and all others were warned that no additional catalogs could be sent, and no further copies were printed or mailed. In 1931, the Post Office officially banned from the mails any catalog that listed this novel. The ban was lifted three years later.

FURTHER READING

"Boston Bans Sale of 'Elmer Gantry.' " *New York Times*, April 13, 1927, p. 16.
"Elmer Gantry' Banned in Boston." *Publishers Weekly*, April 16, 1927, p. 1,569.
Light, Martin. *The Quixotic Vision of Sinclair Lewis.* West Lafayette, Ind.: Purdue University Press, 1975.

END AS A MAN

Author: Calder Willingham
Original date and place of publication: 1947, United States
Original publisher: Vanguard Press
Literary form: Novel

SUMMARY

End as a Man is a satiric portrait of life in a southern military academy, an institution that is loosely based on The Citadel. The title of the work is taken from the speech of the commanding officer who claims that those who enter the academy undergo a training so thorough that they enter as boys but each will "end as a man." The reality conveyed by the characters is that the rigid academy code sadistically transforms each boy into a brute who learns to respect only what he fears. Thus, rather than become a man, each fully trained academy cadet must recognize that graduation from the academy marks his end as a man and his emergence as a fear-inducing brute.

The corruption inherent in the academy is personified by Robert Marquales, an unattractive character whose self-pitying and self-serving nature leads him to become an informer and henchman for Cadet Sergeant Jocko de Paris. Marquales ferrets out the secrets of vulnerable cadets, such as that of Perrin McKee, the homosexual cadet who, in bitterly sarcastic dialogue, vies with Marquales for the attention of de Paris. Marquales also fails to come to the aid of other cadets who are being treated sadistically, especially his roommate, the overweight Maurice Maynall "Sowbelly" Simmons, who prays all night and wets his bed repeatedly. Rather than help his roommate, Marquales disassociates himself from the pathetic cadet, who is later beaten so severely that blood coagulates on his boxer shorts. Simmons is found a few days after this incident lying on the floor of the latrine, exhausted from another beating and with his face and head smeared with human excrement.

While Marquales represents the corrupt aspects of the academy, de Paris represents the unrelenting cruelty as he leads the upperclassmen in their merciless behavior toward the cadets. In the opening chapter, de Paris bullies Simmons until he vomits at the dinner table, which establishes the cadet as the scapegoat, the "company crap-catcher," of the new first-year cadets. De Paris cheats in card games with fellow cadets, blackmails them, and lies to extricate himself from every situation without concern for what his lies will do to others.

The society of the academy turns even the first-year men against their own, and the less clever cadets often find themselves tortured by their quicker-witted brothers. Simmons's photograph of his dead 10-year-old sister disappears and is desecrated; when it reappears, "the child in the white dress had two breasts, a navel, and pubic hair from which a great penis emerged." Another unsuspecting first-year man lends his pen, engraved "From Myrtle to Bubber with oodles of love," to another cadet who learns that "Myrtle" is the pen owner's mother. The fact is soon made public, and humiliation follows.

The novel recounts one brutish action after another, slowly escalating until the commandant discovers the existence of a secret drinking and gambling club, after a public drinking brawl instigated by de Paris that results in disciplinary action against 28 cadets and the expulsion of four, including de Paris. Marquales saves himself from expulsion by becoming an informer and exposing the role that de Paris played in the scandal. As the novel ends, Marquales receives three crisp $10 bills and a letter from de Paris which states, "I hope your conscience doesn't torture you about what you did. There are worse things than cowardly selling out the best man you ever knew. I'm enclosing your reward." With a smile, Marquales pockets the money and later uses it to buy a portable radio.

CENSORSHIP HISTORY

John Sumner, appearing on behalf of the New York Society for the Suppression of Vice, issued a complaint against Vanguard Press in 1947 as soon as the novel was published. The unusually forthright language, which had been taboo before World War II, was cited as the chief cause of concern. In the novel, one cadet refers to a waitress as "table pussy," while another cadet speaks of his father finding "a rubber draped over the steering wheel" after he had borrowed the car. At various times, other cadets use such expressions as "Oh, piss," "Go shit in your hat," and "Kiss my butt." Admitting that he is homosexual, cadet Perrin McKee tells Marquales, "I had experiences at the age of 10 that would rot your prostate." In addition, throughout the novel, cadets speak repeatedly of "whores" and "whorehouses," and there are numerous references to masturbation.

The author and literary critics testified on behalf of *End as a Man* in *People v. Vanguard Press, Inc.*, 192 Misc. 127, 84 N.Y.S. 2d 427 (1947). In testimony, Willingham claimed that his purpose was "to show some of the spiritual and emotional consequences on the youths attending such a school" as well as the spiritual and emotional effects of the severe hazing and strict discipline at the academy. Magistrate Strong dismissed the case. In his decision, he acknowledged the large number of "so-called four-letter words, for the most part used as adjectives or expletives," but he determined that the most vital question is the effect of the book as a whole. After viewing the work in total, he concluded that "its effect on the reasonably normal reader would not be sexually demoralizing."

The following year *End as a Man* was again in court, this time in the Court of Quarter Sessions in Philadelphia County, Pennsylvania, as one of nine novels identified as obscene. Criminal proceedings were brought against five booksellers who were charged with possessing and intending to sell the following allegedly obscene novels: James Farrell's Studs Lonigan trilogy (*Young Lonigan*, *The Young Manhood of Studs Lonigan*, and *Judgment Day*), Farrell's A WORLD I NEVER MADE, William Faulkner's SANCTUARY and WILD PALMS, Erskine Caldwell's GOD'S LITTLE ACRE, Harold Robbins's NEVER LOVE A STRANGER, and Willingham's *End as a Man*. Judge Curtis Bok, who sat as trial judge in *Commonwealth v. Gordon et al.*, 66 D. & C. 101 (1949), read the books "with thoughtful care" and wrote the first really thoughtful judicial opinion about the limitations that the First Amendment's guarantees should be interpreted to exert upon obscenity proceedings. He determined that "obscenity" was an indeterminate term, "that different meanings given to it at different times are not constant, not historically or legally; and that it is not constitutionally indictable unless it takes the form of sexual impurity, i.e., 'dirt for dirt's sake' and can be traced to actual criminal behavior, either actual or demonstrably imminent." Judge Bok based his judgment on the books as a whole and upon their place in the arts. He discussed at length the concern whether in censoring obscenity the courts were contravening the principles of freedom of speech and of the press. Judge Bok concluded, "I hold that the books before me are not sexually impure and pornographic, and are therefore not obscene, lewd, lascivious, filthy, indecent, or disgusting." This judgment was later sustained in the Superior and Supreme Courts of Pennsylvania.

FURTHER READING

De Grazia, Edward. *Girls Lean Back Everywhere: The Law of Obscenity and the Assault on Genius.* New York: Random House, 1992.

Lewis, Felice Flanery. *Literature, Obscenity, and Law.* Carbondale: Southern Illinois University Press, 1976.

Parr, J. L. "Calder Willingham: The Forgotten Novelist." *Critique* 11 (1969): 57–65.

ESTHER WATERS

Author: George Moore
Original date and place of publication: 1894, England
Original publisher: J. M. Dent & Sons, Ltd.
Literary form: Novel

SUMMARY

Esther Waters relates the story of a servant girl who loses her job, her status, and her respectability when she becomes pregnant, then fights against her fate to survive and raise her son to manhood. The struggle is realistically presented, as are the temptations to give up, yet she perseveres in a life of unrelieved and uneventful toil. The theme of gambling and its toll on lives also runs through the novel.

The novel opens with 20-year-old Esther standing on the train platform, about to begin her work as a kitchen maid at the Barfields' elegant estate, Woodview. As she walks from the station, she meets William Latch, whose mother is the cook at Woodview and whose father's life had been ruined by betting on racehorses. She cannot return home because "her [step]father would curse her, and perhaps beat her mother and her too. . . . Her little brothers and sisters would cry if she came back. They had little enough to eat as it was."

The obsession with horse racing at Woodview is alien to Esther, who had "heard of racecourses as shameful places where men were led to their ruin, and betting she had always understood to be sinful." She is religious, but a friendly housemaid warns her to keep her religious views to herself because the others will call her a "Creeping Jesus." Fortunately for Esther, Mrs. Barfield is also a "Plymouth Sister" who senses a spiritual soulmate in Esther and tries to teach her to read.

One evening, after an important horse race is won by the Barfields, the servants celebrate with the rest of the household, and ale flows freely. Even Esther, formerly opposed to drink, has two pints of ale, which lower her defenses. When she walks out into the moonlight with her boyfriend William, "she could not put him away . . . though she knew her fate depended upon her resistance." She becomes pregnant after that one sexual experience, but William runs off with one of the wealthy Barfield daughters, deserting her without knowing that she carries his child.

With little money, Esther returns to her family, which she pays 10 shillings weekly for room and board. She soon leaves because her stepfather extorts increasing amounts of money from her, and she takes a room in a house near the hospital. When she goes into labor, she is treated with cold indifference by the nurses and doctors. Later, her only means of earning a living is to become a wet nurse for the baby of Mrs. Rivers, a fashionable lady. To do so, Esther must place her child into someone else's care, until she learns that the infants of two previous wet nurses have died while in such care. Frantic, Esther gives up the position, takes her child, and must again look for work.

In the seven years that follow, Esther works long hours to provide for Jackie, then finds a suitable position with a kindly mistress and meets a devout man who wants to marry her and become a father to Jackie. On an errand for her mistress, Esther meets William, her son's father, who expresses his remorse and desire to be a father to their son and a husband to Esther. He is now prosperous as the owner of the Kings' Head pub and a successful bookmaker for horse racing. Esther struggles to choose between the devout suitor and William and decides that Jackie would benefit from all that William could provide, so she becomes William's wife. They prosper, so much so that Esther now has servants, even though she worries as she views the numerous lives ruined by betting on the horses. When Jackie is 15, disaster befalls the family as William becomes fatally ill with consumption, the Kings' Head is raided because of the betting, and the license to operate is revoked. Esther struggles to keep Jackie in school and to keep life going as William wastes away in a hospital. When he dies, Jackie must leave school to work, and Esther must, once again, tolerate long, painful workdays and low pay.

At Jackie's urging, Esther contacts Mrs. Barfield, and the older woman welcomes Esther back to Woodview, now an impoverished estate, where the two live in seclusion and in anticipation of word from their sons. Mrs. Barfield worries because her son Arthur makes his living at the racetrack and rarely contacts her, and she helps Esther provide for Jackie, who works hard just to survive in London. Finally, unable to find suitable work, Jackie joins the military. The novel ends as the handsome adult son visits his mother before he must leave with his military unit. To Esther, all that she has gone through in "the long fight for his life" has been worthwhile, and she truly feels that "she had accomplished her woman's work—she had brought him up to man's estate."

CENSORSHIP HISTORY

Esther Waters is written in a stark and realistic style that both recounts the struggle of a servant girl to raise her illegitimate child alone and presents a bitter indictment of society. The novel was excluded from British circulating libraries in 1894, as both Mudie's Library and Smith's Library refused to stock it, viewing it as too risqué because the main character suffers as the result of her one sexual indiscretion, but she does not die, and because of the candid manner in which her situation is presented. For instance, when Esther returns to live with her family before her baby's birth, her stepfather tells her, "We wants no bastards 'ere." Her mother, like many poor women of the day, is severely abused and economically dependent, as she must bear child after child and eventually dies in childbirth. In a scene considered by censors of the time to be in poor taste simply due to its mention, the doctors and nurses at the maternity ward where Esther gives birth show little consideration for the needs of the financially destitute young woman. After the birth, the young mother learns that many young women of the lower classes allow their own babies to die and use their milk production to gain well-paid positions as wet nurses to babies of the rich.

By censoring the novel, the influential libraries greatly decreased potential sales because they held the power to set the tone for novels. Representatives of the libraries claimed that they sought to protect their subscribers from "certain blemishes of treatment." In essence, they were displeased by the factual, unsentimental account of the birth of Esther's illegitimate child, as well as by the manner in which a hypocritical and inhumane society shuns her, and by her strength and competence to raise her son and to achieve some degree of happiness regardless of public scorn. Despite the efforts to ban *Esther Waters*, the novel became Moore's first financial and artistic success.

The author had experienced a similar reception from the libraries to two earlier novels, *A Modern Lover* (1883) and *A Mummer's Wife* (1885). These attacks motivated Moore to take an aggressive stance against censorship, and he had responded with a scathing attack on the power of the circulating libraries in *Literature at Nurse, or Circulating Morals* in 1885. He denounced the manner in which the circulating libraries had reduced English fiction to formulaic plots, featuring either "a sentimental misunderstanding which is happily cleared up in the end, or . . . singular escapes over the edges of precipices, and miraculous recoveries of one or more of the senses of which the hero was deprived . . . ." Deploring the negative effects of the libraries, which had deprived modern publishing of the novel of analysis and observation, Moore wrote, "Let us renounce the effort to reconcile these two irreconcilable things—art and young girls." His attack failed to reverse the position of the libraries regarding his novels, and when *Esther Waters* came out in 1894, with its theme of unmarried motherhood and scenes of a maternity ward, both Smith's and Mudie's excluded it from their catalogs. When Moore later proved that the libraries had lost a minimum of £1,200 in profits because of their stance, they recanted and added the work to their catalogs.

FURTHER READING

Cirillo, Nancy R. "A Girl Need Never Go Wrong; or, the Female Servant as Ideological Image in Germinie Lacerteux and Esther Waters." *Comparative Literature Studies* 28 (1991): 68–88.

Morgan, Charles. *Epitaph on George Moore*. New York: Macmillan, 1935.

Schwab, A. T. "Irish Author and American Critic." *Nineteenth Century Fiction* 8 (March 1954): 256–277.

FAHRENHEIT 451

Author: Ray Bradbury
Original date and place of publication: 1953, United States
Original publisher: Ballantine Books
Literary form: Novel

SUMMARY

Fahrenheit 451 relates the story of an oppressive society in which books are forbidden objects and firemen are required to burn all books they encounter. The novel, an expanded version of a 1950 story entitled "The Fireman," takes its title from the temperature at which paper ignites: 451°F. One of a number of dystopic novels published after World War II, the work portrays humans as having lost touch with the natural world, with the world of the intellect, and with each other. As the fire captain observes, "the word 'intellectual' became the swear word it deserved to be."

People hurry from their homes to their workplaces and back, never speaking of what they feel or think but only spouting meaningless facts and figures. At home, they surround themselves with interactive picture walls, wall-size television screens on three walls (four walls if one can afford them) containing characters who become accepted as family in an otherwise unconnected life. The streets have become dangerous as *minimum* speed limits of 55 miles per hour must be maintained, and speeds well over 100 miles per hour are more common. Teenagers and daring adults race their cars through the streets without concern for human life. War with an unnamed enemy is imminent.

For one fireman, the realization that there is a better life comes in the form of a 17-year-old girl named Clarisse, whose appreciation of nature, desire to talk about feelings and thoughts, and appreciation for simply being alive mark her as an "odd duck." Guy Montag likes his job as a fireman, but he has clandestinely taken books from several sites where he and his fellow firemen have burned books and the houses in which they were hidden. Clarisse's questions as to why Montag became a fireman and her observations that the job does not seem right for him are disconcerting. A call to burn the books and house of a woman who refuses to leave the premises and, instead, ignites herself with the books increases Montag's discontent. He tries to speak with his wife, Mildred, but she blocks him out with her Seashell ear thimbles, tiny radios worn in the ear that play continuously, and her involvement with her "family" on the picture walls.

Montag learns that the major reason for the abolition of books was to keep everyone happy. His fire captain explains that without books there is no conflicting theory or thought, and no one learns anything more than anyone else. With books, "Who knows who might be the target of the well-read man?"

After his wife reports that Montag has books in the house and their home is destroyed by the firemen, he seeks the help of former English professor Faber, who is part of a broader movement to preserve the knowledge of the past. Following Faber's directions, Montag goes to the railroad yards, where he meets a group of old men, all former university professors who have each memorized specific literary works. They claim to be part of a network of thousands of individuals who will keep literature alive in their heads until the time when the oppression ceases and they can set the literature in type once more. Montag, who has memorized several books of the Old Testament, joins them, and the novel ends on a hopeful note.

CENSORSHIP HISTORY

Fahrenheit 451 is an indictment of censorship and expurgation, so the fact that this book was expurgated and marketed by the publisher that way for 13 years before the author became aware of the abuse is particularly ironic. In 1967, Ballantine Books published a special edition of the novel to be sold in high schools. Over 75 passages were modified to eliminate such words as *hell, damn,* and *abortion,* and two incidents were eliminated. The original first incident described a drunk man who was changed to a sick man in the expurgated edition. In the second incident, reference is made to cleaning fluff out of the human navel, but the expurgated edition changed the reference to cleaning ears. No one complained about the expurgation, mainly because few people were aware of the changes and many had not read the original. The copyright page made no mention of the changes, but thousands of people read only this version of *Fahrenheit 451* because the edition ran to 10 printings. At the same time, Ballantine Books continued to publish the "adult" version that was marketed to bookstores. After six years of the simultaneous editions, the publisher ceased publication of the adult version, leaving only the expurgated version for sale from 1973 through 1979, during which neither Bradbury nor anyone else suspected the truth.

In 1979, a friend alerted Bradbury to the expurgation, and he demanded that Ballantine Books withdraw completely the expurgated version and replace it with his original. The publisher agreed, and the complete version has been available since 1980.

This act of censorship had far-reaching effects for authors in regard to the school book clubs. The incident set in motion the American Library Association (ALA) Intellectual Freedom Committee, Young Adult Division. In 1981, the committee looked into expurgation by school book clubs, such as Scholastic, and found that all of them expurgated books to some extent. Using its clout, the ALA reminded the book clubs that it awards the Newbery and Caldecott medals for children's books, and the ALA also noted that buyers are attracted to books designated as "ALA Best Books." The organization warned that it would strip the award announcements from expurgated books. The ALA also alerted teacher groups to demand that an expurgated book in a school book club be clearly identified on the copyright page as an "edited school book edition."

In a coda that now appears in editions of *Fahrenheit 451*, Bradbury states, "I will not go gently onto a shelf, degutted, to become a non-book."

The "adult" version still has its critics. In 1992, students at Venado Middle School in Irvine, California, were issued copies of the novel with numerous words blacked out. School officials had ordered teachers to use black markers to obliterate all of the "hells," "damns," and other words deemed "obscene" in the books before giving them to students as required reading. Parents complained to the school and contacted local newspapers, who sent reporters to write stories about the irony of a book that condemns bookburning and censorship being expurgated. Faced with such an outcry, school officials announced that the censored copies would no longer be used.

FURTHER READING

Johnson, Wayne L. *Ray Bradbury*. New York: Frederick Ungar, 1980.
Moore, Everett T. "A Rationale for Bookburners: A Further Word from Ray Bradbury." *ALA Bulletin* 55 (May 1961): 403–404.
Newsletter on Intellectual Freedom (July 1992): 108–109.
Seed, David. "The Flight from the Good Life: 'Fahrenheit 451' in the Context of Postwar American Dystopias." *Journal of American Studies* 28, pt. 2 (August 1994): 225–240.

FALLEN ANGELS

Author: Walter Dean Myers
Original date and place of publication: 1988, United States
Original publisher: Scholastic Books
Literary form: Novel

SUMMARY

Walter Dean Myers dedicates this book to his late brother Thomas "Sonny" Myers, "whose dream of adding beauty to this world through his humanity and his art ended in Vietnam on May 7, 1968." He presents a realistic view of war by portraying his characters with believable dialogue and reactions to the horror and the brutality they experience. They curse, they doubt their involvement, and they must deal with the lost limbs and lost lives of their fellow soldiers, as did the men who served as soldiers in the Vietnam War.

Fallen Angels relates the experiences of Richie Perry, a 17-year-old African American and recent high school graduate who enlists in the U.S. Army and leaves his Harlem community to fight in Vietnam. While in basic training at Fort Devon, he learns that an old knee injury makes him unfit for combat, but his medical profile must be processed before his orders can be changed. Because of delays, he is forced to ship out to Vietnam. A captain assures him that it takes a long while to process a medical profile, but "Once it catches up with you, you'll be headed home." Eight months later, while wounded and in an army hospital, Richie learns that his medical file had been completed months earlier, but no one had notified him.

Once in Vietnam, Richie learns that many of the beliefs about war and about service in the military he had built up while in basic training are just illusions. The men periodically pass rumors that peace is about to be declared as they hear sporadic reports of proposed Paris peace talks. His images of brave U.S. soldiers confronting an evil, faceless enemy are destroyed as he realizes that he and other soldiers are frightened most of the time and sees that the Vietcong soldiers are much like him, serving in a war they have not created. His romantic view of war continues to erode as he sees the errors of judgment made by his commanding officers in situations they cannot control. Before being sent to their company, stationed near Chu Lai, Richie and two other new recruits, Harold "Peewee" Gates and Jenkins, are told by a sergeant that they are lucky to be sent to an area with little fighting. Only days after they arrive, however, Jenkins is killed during their first patrol when he steps on a land mine. Other realizations further disturb Richie, and he finds that he can no longer write letters home to his mother and his younger brother Kenny because the truth is too horrible to share with them.

Not long after his arrival in Vietnam, Richie begins to see that conventional morality cannot be applied in this atmosphere of brutality, fear, and devastation. His company commander, Captain Stewart, seems more concerned with earning a promotion to the rank of major than with keeping the soldiers under his command safe. The platoon leader, Lieutenant Carroll, dies during a combat mission, and Richie starts to question out loud why he and his fellow soldiers are even in Vietnam. Although other squad members caution Richie to just stop thinking, he struggles to find a way to justify everything he has seen. As much as he wishes to, he is unable to express to his family the horror and disillusionment he feels.

Richie's disillusionment with the war leads him to question why he enlisted in the army and to worry what he will do when he returns to civilian life. He originally said he had joined the army to earn money to keep his brother Kenny in school, because the family is poor. His father left years earlier and his mother is an alcoholic. Richie now wonders if he enlisted simply to escape one intolerable situation, only to enter another. He also wonders if he has any life to look forward to if he should survive combat.

Rumors fly through the camp that their squad leader, Sergeant Simpson, has been fighting with Captain Stewart, accusing the officer of sending his men all over the area to bolster his own career. As the combat activity increases, Richie is injured during a battle, suffering shrapnel wounds, a concussion, and a bullet wound to his wrist, and he is sent to a hospital to recuperate. While there, he thinks of ways to avoid returning to combat once he has healed. Although Richie considers deserting, he follows orders and rejoins his company but finds that the unit has changed. Sergeant Simpson has been sent home, and his replacement, Sergeant Dongan, is a racist who selects the African-American soldiers for the most dangerous missions. In reaction to his behavior, the squad members bond even more closely as they experience increasingly higher casualties. After the men engage in a particularly bloody battle during which many American lives are lost, including Dongan's, the men must hurry to burn the dead to prevent mutilation of the bodies by the Vietcong, and they are warned that the second North Vietnamese battalion is moving in their direction. Corporal Brunner takes command, and the men move on to track guerrilla forces along the river. A firefight occurs. Richie and Peewee are injured, and both are sent to the hospital, where they learn that their injuries are serious enough to send them home. While in the hospital, Richie learns that his medical profile had been processed eight months earlier and, had he been properly alerted, he would have avoided the terrors of combat.

While the two men wait for the plane that will take them and the silver caskets of dead soldiers back to the United States, Richie and Peewee attempt to hide their weariness and disillusionment from the new recruits.

CENSORSHIP HISTORY

Fallen Angels was awarded the Coretta Scott King Award in 1989, but parents in Michigan, Texas, Mississippi, Ohio, Georgia, and Pennsylvania have denounced the book for containing vulgar or profane language and called for its ban.

In 1999, *Fallen Angels* was removed from the curriculum in Livonia, Michigan, after a unanimous vote by the Livonia Public Schools trustees that banned the book from being taught in the classroom but allowed it to remain in the school library. The action was taken after a lengthy review of the book was initiated by a parent who complained that the book contains more than 300 "vulgarities." School board trustees reviewed *Fallen Angels* and, in an interview with the *Miami Times* on September 2, 1999, trustee Daniel Lessard stated, "I've read it. It's a filthy book. I think the language portrays what went on in Vietnam very accurately. But I don't think we should require a 14-year-old to read it."

In 2003, Franklin Central High School in Indianapolis, Indiana, principal Kevin Koers banned *Fallen Angels* from the curriculum because of concerns about the profanity in the book. In an interview with a local television station, Koers stated that two students drew attention to the profanity in the book when they told him that they would get into trouble if they used some of the language that appears in the book in school, and he agreed with them. The book was assigned reading for sophomore English classes, and Koers substituted another frequently banned book, To KILL A MOCKINGBIRD. Numerous parents agreed with the ban, many claiming that the use of such profanity was unnecessary in the literature students read. As a result of the controversy, school officials recognized that they needed to establish clear policies to deal with future controversies over literature. Franklin Township Community Schools official Scott Miley told a reporter for The Indy Channel that when future challenges to a book arise, "it will be assigned to a department chair, who will then evaluate whether the complaint is valid."

Also in 2003, the George County School Board in Pascagoula, Mississippi, voted to ban *Fallen Angels*, OF MICE AND MEN, and *THE THINGS THEY CARRIED* from the accelerated junior supplementary list because of "profanity" in the dialogue of the characters. The vote occurred on January 6, after the appointment of two new board members. Larry McDonald, one of the new board members, initiated the ban on the books. In an interview that appeared in the *Pascagoula Mississippi Press*, McDonald said that because the school has a policy that prevents students from using profanity in school, to have the three books containing so much profanity remain in the school library made him "uncomfortable." In taking this action, the board failed to follow the policy in place that should have been applied when a student or parent complains about the content of a book that appears on the approved supplemental list. According to policy, if a parent feels that a book the child has selected is inappropriate, then a teacher is asked to help the child select another. The action brought the attention of the American Library Association Committee for Intellectual Freedom and the National Council of Teachers of English, which were unsuccessful in their efforts to have the book restored to the reading list. As a result of the action, school superintendent Donnie Howell reported that he would suggest that the school board form a committee to review future objections by parents to school reading material.

Fallen Angels was also successfully challenged because of profanity in Bluffton, Ohio, in 1990 and in West Chester, Pennsylvania, in 1994; it was restricted as supplemental classroom reading material from the Jackson County Georgia High School in 1992 for "sensitive material" as well as "profanity." In Arlington, Texas, in April 2000, Donna Harkreader, the mother of a student attending Boles Junior High School, asked school librarian Sandra Cope to remove *Fallen Angels* from the library. She asserted that the "strong language" in the book and "graphic violence" made the book "too disturbing" for younger students. The school librarian refused her request, and Harkreader petitioned the board of education to consider the issue. After both school and administrative committees and the school superintendent, Mac Bernd, upheld the decision of the school librarian to retain the book, the issue was referred to the school trustees for final resolution. In a special meeting, called on September 28, 2000, which numerous residents attended, trustees of the Arlington Independent School District voted unanimously to keep the novel in the junior high school libraries. In explaining their decision, trustee Jim Ash stated, "There is no wiggle room . . . . We are created to uphold the law."

FURTHER READING

"*Fallen Angels* Resurrected in Arlington, Texas, Schools." *Newsletter for Intellectual Freedom*, October 2, 2000.

Nelson, Karen. "Book Ban Just Plain Silly, Say Some Students in George Co." *Sun Herald*, January 26, 2003.

"School Bans Book after Complaints about Profanity: Teachers to Replace One Controversial Story with Another." IndyChannel.com, November 10, 2003.

"Vietnam Books, Steinbeck Banned by Mississippi High School." *Newsletter for Intellectual Freedom*, January 13, 2003.

A FAREWELL TO ARMS

Author: Ernest Hemingway
Original date and place of publication: 1929, United States
Original publisher: Charles Scribner's Sons
Literary form: Novel

SUMMARY

A Farewell to Arms is both a powerful war novel and a love story. Told from the first-person point of view of American Frederic Henry, who becomes an ambulance driver for the Italian army in 1916, it chronicles fighting against the Austrian army along the Italian-Yugoslavian border. With the other officers, Henry first spends a lot of his time drinking and visiting the officers' brothel. On the battlefield, he is reckless in rescuing wounded soldiers and, after valorous conduct in his 11th battle, he is awarded a decoration. He also becomes involved with an English nurse named Catherine Barkley who serves in an Italian military hospital. He begins the relationship as a way to fill the time, after he learns that Catherine's fiancé was killed in the war and she is vulnerable.

After Henry is wounded and hospitalized, the affair intensifies, and he discovers that he really loves Catherine. He asks Catherine to marry him, but she refuses, knowing that she would then be sent back to England and away from him. However, the war imposes physical separations on them, when Henry is sent to the front just as Catherine learns that she is pregnant. His disillusionment with war escalates as he is involved in the retreat from Caporetto, which begins in an orderly, disciplined manner but eventually turns into a panicking mob as authority breaks down and self-preservation becomes paramount. Henry is captured with other officers and held for execution but manages to escape, thus completing his disillusionment with the war. He locates Catherine, and the two escape together to Switzerland, where they await the birth of their baby. They spend idyllic months, despite Catherine's worry that her narrow hips will make the birth difficult. When they seem about to achieve happiness together, their child is stillborn, and Catherine dies after suffering internal hemorrhaging, leaving Frederick Henry alone.

CENSORSHIP HISTORY

A Farewell to Arms has been censored both for its language and for sexual innuendo, as well as for the sexual relationship between Henry and Catherine and her unmarried pregnancy, although no graphic sexuality occurs in the novel. The soldiers frequent "bawdy houses" or the officers' "brothel." Henry has had "gonorrhea" and a military officer fears having "contracted syphilis from a prostitute." A dead sergeant who had attempted to desert the army is referred to as a "son of a bitch." Early in the novel, a boisterous officer teases a priest that he is often seen with the girls. When the priest protests, the officer jokingly accuses him of masturbating, saying, "Priest every night five against one." At one point, Catherine teases Henry, who says that he is lost without her and states that he at least had something to do at the front. She says, "Othello with his occupation gone." He replies, "Othello was a nigger."

In the few instances in which Hemingway seemed unable to substitute an innocuous word for what might be viewed as a vulgar term, he used dashes. When speaking about their chances against the Austrians, one of two Italian soldiers says, "They'll shell the———out of us." When the soldiers pass through a small Italian town, they pick up two girls and place them in a jeep, while they speculate about having sex. As they speak, the soldiers reassure the girls that there will be no sex, "using the vulgar word," but Hemingway places dashes in the four places where the "vulgar word" should appear. Then the soldiers bluntly ask the girls if they are sexually inexperienced: "Virgin? . . . Virgin too?"

An officer visits the wounded Henry in the hospital, and he tells Henry that the priest is making big preparations to visit. He teases Henry, "Sometimes I think you and he are a little that way. You know." Catherine visits Henry when he is moved to an American hospital in Milan, and they make love in his room, but the reader has to pay careful attention to the dialogue to know this has occurred. Their lines alternate between Catherine asking if Henry *really* loves her, and Henry reassuring her that he does. Afterward, as she sits in a chair by the bed, "the wildness was gone" for Henry, and Catherine asks, "Now do you believe I love you?" As the novel progresses, they discuss marrying, and the point is clearly made that Henry wants "to make an honest woman" out of Catherine. They are concerned about legitimizing her pregnancy.

The censorship of *A Farewell to Arms* began before the novel was published, leading to Hemingway's complaints to editor Maxwell Perkins that too many necessary "unsavory" words had been removed from the manuscript. In letters to Perkins, he stated that "if a word can be printed and is needed in the text it is a weakening to omit it." Perkins had warned Hemingway in 1926 in regard to the earlier novel THE SUN ALSO RISES that "papers now attack a book, not only on grounds of eroticism which could not hold here, but upon that of 'decency,' which means *words*." He had suggested that in that novel another word be substituted for the bull's "balls," as well as for other terms.

Two years later, Hemingway was faced with eliminating the natural speech of men at war. Thus, in the original manuscript in the section that detailed the retreat from Caporetto, Hemingway wrote the following: " 'Tomorrow maybe we'll sleep in *shit*,' Piani said. 'I'll sleep with the queen,' Bonello said. 'You'll sleep with *shit*,' Piani said sleepily." The italicized words appear as blanks or dashes in the final novel. Other passages in that same section of the novel have dashes to substitute for "the *fucking* cavalry" and in "So do you, *cocksucker*," as well as in other instances.

In 1929, *Scribner's Magazine* contracted to serialize the book with certain changes. As the editor Robert Bridges explained to the author in a letter:

we have in several places put in dashes instead of the realistic phrases which the soldiers of course used. This was not done from any particular squeamishness, but we have long been accepted in many schools as what is known, I believe, as "collateral reading," and have quite a clientage among those who teach mixed classics. Things which are perfectly natural and realistic in a book are not viewed with the same mind in a serial reading.

Bridges excised the following words from the manuscript that could not be used in a magazine: *balls, cocksucker, fuck, Jesus Christ, shit, son of a bitch, whore,* and *whorehound*. He also deleted a passage in which Henry fantasizes about his weekend in bed with Catherine, a passage that would later be returned to the novel when it was published. The second installment contained increased deletions of passages, including the sanitization of the seduction scene. Despite all of the changes, the June 1929 issue of *Scribner's Magazine* was banned from the bookstands in Boston, by order of the superintendent of police.

When Max Perkins edited the novel for publication, the following words deleted by Bridges were returned: *Jesus Christ, son of a bitch, whore,* and *whorehound*. However, Perkins suggested that Hemingway remove the following question: "Would you like to use a bedpan?" He also asked Hemingway to change " 'Miss Van Campen,' I said, 'did you ever know a man who tried to disable himself by kicking himself in the balls?' " to substitute the word *scrotum* for *balls*. Hemingway fought to retain use of the word *cocksucker* by the soldiers, and he claimed that eliminating it would completely emasculate the novel. His suggestion to use the term *c—s—r* was considered still too strong, so only dashes appear for that word.

In spite of the modifications to the text, the novel was considered too risqué. In a strongly negative review entitled "What Is Dirt?" in *Bookman*, Robert Herrick claimed that he was "adamantly opposed to censorship" but found that *A Farewell to Arms* presented one of those times when it was necessary. Other guardians of morality sent scathing letters to *Scribner's Magazine* threatening to cancel subscriptions because of the "vileness" of the novel, calling it "vulgar beyond express" and condemning the magazine for exploiting "such disgusting situations."

The novel was banned in Italy in 1929 because of its painfully accurate account of the Italian retreat from Caporetto during World War I. In 1930, the Watch and Ward Society in Boston, buoyed by the earlier successful outcry against the serialization in *Scribner's Magazine*, placed pressure on booksellers to remove the book from their store windows. In 1933, the novel was one of numerous books burned by the Nazis in Germany, allegedly for its "prurience." In 1938, the National Organization for Decent Literature (NODL) found the novel to be "objectionable" and placed it on their list of blacklisted books that was then sent to cooperating book dealers who agreed to remove the books from their racks. Such NODL blacklists resulted in elaborate collegial pressure among booksellers, although not legal enforcement against a work. The novel was also banned in Ireland in 1939 because of the "fornication" of Henry and Catherine and the pregnancy outside of marriage.

The novel has experienced more recent challenges. In 1974, parents of students in the Dallas (Texas) Independent School District demanded that it be removed from the high school libraries, along with Arthur Miller's *Death of a Salesman*, William Golding's LORD OF THE FLIES, and Robert Penn Warren's *All the King's Men*. They complained that the novel contained a depressing view of life and "immoral" situations. After reviewing the work, school officials retained the novel. The book was also challenged in the Vernon-Verona-Sherrill (New York) School District in 1980 for being a "sex novel," along with A SEPARATE PEACE, TO KILL A MOCKINGBIRD, *THE GRAPES OF WRATH*, OF MICE AND MEN, and THE RED PONY.

FURTHER READING

Benson, Jackson J. *Hemingway: The Writer's Art of Self-Defense*. Minneapolis: University of Minnesota Press, 1969.

Cohen, Peter F. " 'I Won't Kiss You. . . . I'll Send Your English Girl': Homoerotic Desire in 'A Farewell to Arms.' " *Hemingway Review* 15 (Fall 1995): 42–53.

Donaldson, Scott. "Censorship and 'A Farewell to Arms.' " *Studies in American Fiction* 19 (Spring 1991): 85–93.

Hemingway, Ernest. *Selected Letters: 1917–1961,* edited by Carlos Baker. New York: Charles Scribner's Sons, 1981.

Herrick, Robert. "What Is Dirt?" *Bookman* 70 (November 1929): 258–262.

Mandel, Miriam. "Ferguson and Lesbian Love: Unspoken Subplots in 'A Farewell to Arms.' " *Hemingway Review* 14 (Fall 1994): 18–24.

Meriweather, James B. "The Dashes in Hemingway's *A Farewell to Arms.*" *The Papers of the Bibliographical Society of America* 58 (Fourth Quarter 1964): 449–457.

Oldsey, Bernard. *Hemingway's Hidden Craft: The Writing of "A Farewell to Arms."* University Park: Pennsylvania State University Press, 1979.

Reynolds, Michael S. *Hemingway's First War: The Making of "A Farewell to Arms."* Princeton, N.J.: Princeton University Press, 1976.

Solotaroff, Robert. "Sexual Identity in 'A Farewell to Arms.' " *Hemingway Review* 9 (Fall 1989): 2–17.

FINAL EXIT: THE PRACTICALITIES OF SELF-DELIVERANCE AND ASSISTED SUICIDE FOR THE DYING

Author: Derek Humphry
Original date and place of publication: 1991, United States
Original publisher: Hemlock Society
Literary form: Nonfiction

SUMMARY

Final Exit is a handbook for assisted suicide that is meant for patients and the doctors and nurses who have to handle their requests for euthanasia. In clear, factual language, Humphry provides a set of instructions that anticipate questions of those considering suicide and provide a detailed process told in simple language. He makes clear that the book "is intended to be read by a mature adult who is suffering from a terminal illness and is considering the option of rational suicide if and when suffering becomes unbearable."

Part I of the book examines and assesses the various steps in committing suicide and suggests creative ways by which to obtain the means of assuring a painless death. Chapters instruct the individual on how to find the right doctor, how to avoid legal problems, how to select a means of death (with a special discussion of cyanide), how to store drugs, and how to obtain "magic pills," as well as discussing the dilemma of quadriplegics, the protocol of letters to be left, and whether to die solo or with someone. Humphry also provides chapters on determining the time to die, whether or not to make it a private affair, and the use of a plastic bag with rubber bands as a backup, should medications alone not be sufficient.

Part II is entitled "Euthanasia Involving Doctors and Nurses." Humphry examines the nature of "justifiable euthanasia" and discusses the roles that doctors and nurses can legally play in assisted suicide. The book also relates important information regarding having a living will and how to make certain that one's affairs are in order before taking the "final exit."

CENSORSHIP HISTORY

Final Exit has had relatively few problems with challenges in the United States, but censorship in varying degrees has occurred in Australia, New Zealand, France, and Great Britain.

In 1991, *Library Journal* announced that the book was making a "firm entrance into public libraries." That year, a challenge was raised in Libertyville, Illinois. Several patrons of the Cook Memorial Library in Libertyville submitted requests that the library remove *Final Exit* from library shelves because the book "diminishes the value of the elderly and encourages breaking the law by assisting homicide and drug abuse." The library rejected the challenge, and the book remained on the shelves.

In March 1992, the Australian censors ordered all copies of the book seized from bookstores and banned the sale of the book. After an appeal by book distributors, in June 1992, the Australian Film and Literature Board of Review reversed the decision of the censors and classified the book as Category 1—Restricted. Under this designation, the book must be sealed in plastic and cannot be sold to anyone under the age of 18. The book has remained banned in Queensland. That same year, New Zealand customs officers were ordered to seize all copies of the book coming into the country and to hold them until the Office of Indecent Publications could review the suitability of the work. After careful review, the censors determined that the book would be permitted unrestricted entry.

The official Web site for the book notes that *Final Exit* is banned in France. In Britain, because assisted suicide is against the law, publishers will not publish the work, but the editions imported from the United States may be sold freely.

FURTHER READING

"Euthanasia's Most Famous Textbook." *Final Exit*. Available online. URL: http://www.finalexit.org. Accessed December 12, 2009.
"'Final Exit' Author Decries Ban." *Washington Post*, March 11, 1992, p. B4.
"Final Exit." *The Economist* 320, no. 7724 (September 14, 1991): 104.
Giorgetti, Mario. "A Sober Guide to Ending It All." *Green Left Weekly*. Available online. URL: http://www.greenleft.org.au/back/1992/71/71p21b.htm. Accessed December 12, 2009.

Lands, David, and Darren Summers. "'Exit' Ban." *USA Today*, March 13, 1992, p. 9A.

Quinn, Judy, and Michael Rogers. "'Final Exit' Makes Firm Entrance into Public Libraries." *Library Journal* 116.15 (September 15, 1991): 15.

"Suicide Manual for Terminally Ill Stirs Heated Debate." *Wall Street Journal*, July 12, 1991, p. B1.

THE FIXER

Author: Bernard Malamud
Original date and place of publication: 1966, United States
Original publisher: Farrar, Straus & Giroux
Literary form: Novel

SUMMARY

The Fixer, winner of both the Pulitzer Prize and the National Book Award, is based on the 1913 trial of Mendel Beiliss, a Jew in Russia who was acquitted after being tried in Kiev. The novel takes place in turn-of-the-century Russia and opens with people hurriedly running away from town and toward a ravine that contains numerous caves. They are shouting excitedly that the dead body of a child has been found covered with stab wounds and the body has been bled white. Anti-Jewish propaganda leaflets are quickly circulated that accuse the Jews of the murder and claim that the boy's blood had been collected "for religious purposes . . . for the making of the Passover matzos." The ridiculous charge frightens many, including 30-year-old Yakov Bok, who passes for a Christian and lives in a sector of Kiev that is forbidden to Jews.

Yakov had only come to Kiev from the provinces five months earlier. He is a man whose life has been marred by tragedy. His mother died 10 minutes after his birth, his father was killed in an anti-Semitic incident a year later, and he spent a miserable childhood in an orphanage. When he married, his wife Raisl did not become pregnant after five years, so he shunned her, and she ran off with another man. In the shtetl, the Jewish ghetto area of Russia, he was known as a fixer, a man who would fix whatever was broken, but half the time he worked for nothing because inhabitants of the shtetl barely had enough to eat. He goes to Kiev hoping to change his luck and to become a financial success. To avoid the bias suffered by Jews, Yakov plans to pass as a Christian.

Passing as a Christian is difficult for Yakov, even after he is offered steady work by a man whose life he saves one bitter, snowy night. One time, for instance, the man's daughter attempts to seduce Yakov, who reluctantly allows himself to be led to her bedroom, but he nearly gives himself away when she stands naked by a washbowl and blood trickles down her leg. His immediate reaction is, "But you're unclean!" Despite her protests that "this is the safest time," he leaves. Already suspicious of Yakov, the woman identifies his reluctance to have sex with her while she is menstruating as a sign of his adherence to Jewish law. His supervisors have already expressed suspicion, and he is soon exposed.

When the murdered child is found, Yakov is made the scapegoat, possibly as punishment for his audacity in attempting to hide his Jewish heritage, and immediately placed in prison where he is subjected to physical and mental torment and spiritual degradation. Dealing with insects, pails of excrement, and beatings becomes secondary to enduring the humiliating body searches during which his body orifices are probed first twice daily then six times daily. After a few months of imprisonment, Yakov is offered a deal by the prosecutors to lessen his sentence if he will admit his guilt and sign a form stating that the Jewish Nation used him as its agent in the murder. He refuses, and they increase the pressure by offering a complete pardon and physical freedom if he will sign the confession, but Yakov insists on going to trial because an admission of guilt might motivate a pogrom.

After nearly two years, Yakov's wife visits him in prison and they recall his "curses and dirty names" directed against her because of her inability to conceive. Raisl tells him that she became pregnant after leaving him and that the boy is almost a year and a half old. She asks if Yakov will remove her stigma and her son's by claiming to be the child's father. Yakov agrees and signs a statement to that effect.

To the end, Yakov remains resolute and his case finally goes to trial, but the reader is denied knowledge of the outcome.

CENSORSHIP HISTORY

The Fixer has been challenged for several reasons, ranging from the "vivid grossness of scenes" to being "pornography and filth." The most surprising reason to Malamud has been the attack on the book for being "anti-Semitic" in its language and depiction of characters. Several instances of language use have been identified as "obscene." When his father-in-law suggests that Yakov blames him for Raisl's running off, Yakov responds, "You're blaming yourself for having brought up such a whore." In response to his father-in-law's caution that the horse that he has traded to Yakov is prone to gas if fed too much grass, Yakov replies, "If he's prone to gas let him fart." When a supervisor is accused by Yakov of dishonesty, "lifting his leg Proshko farted" in response. When Yakov is cautioned to not forget his God, he says angrily, "What do I get from him but a bang on the head and a stream of piss in my face?" When the fixer stops for lunch while on his journey, the horse "spattered a yellow stream on the road" and "Yakov urinated on some brown ferns."

Parents of students in Aurora (Colorado) High School English classes challenged the use of this book in the classroom because of "inappropriate" language, and the school board banned it from use in 1976. A Pennsylvania school district removed the book from classroom use and provided an alternate selection to students because of the "obscenities" in the novel.

The most extensive challenge to the novel occurred in 1982, in Island Trees Union Free School District No. 26 in New York (see THE BEST SHORT STORIES BY NEGRO WRITERS), where the school board ordered *The Fixer* and 10 other works removed from the junior and senior high school libraries. Special care was taken with *The Fixer*, one of the few books that was also used in English classes, and the principal removed all copies from the classroom and storage closet. In the court record, specific objectionable passages are cited as "filthy" or "anti-Semitic." As the brickyard overseer, Yakov's job is to watch that the men do not steal; when he challenges the supervisor, the man responds angrily, "What do you think goes on in the wagons at night? Are the drivers on their knees fucking their mothers?" After he is jailed, Yakov is harassed by his Russian cellmates: "So you're the bastard Jew who killed the Christian boy. . . . Who else would do anything like that but a motherfucking Zhid?" The investigating magistrate asks Proshko what Yakov did with the rubles he is accused of stealing, and the supervisor responds that he probably took the money to bed and gave "it a fuck once in a while." At another point in the novel, Yakov is threatened, "No more noise out of you or I'll shoot your Jew cock off."

Five students filed a suit against the school board, and the American Jewish Committee (AJC) and other organizations also became involved. In an amicus brief, filed by the AJC with the American Jewish Congress, Anti-Defamation League of B'nai B'rith, the American Orthopsychiatric Association, the Ethical Humanist Society of Long Island, Long Island Council of Churches, the National Council of Teachers of English, the Unitarian Universalist Association, and Writers in the Public Interest, submitted in the United States District Court for the Eastern District of New York against Island Trees School District, the groups declared their astonishment that *The Fixer* "was banned because it contained anti-Semitic references. That assertion can lead to one of two conclusions: that its author is either illiterate or dishonest. *The Fixer* clearly condemns anti-Semitism, as it does the authoritarian society which is the seed bed of anti-Semitism." The case was heard by the United States Supreme Court, which ruled against the school board on June 25, 1982, in *Board of Education, Island Trees Union Free School District No. 26 v. Pico*, and the books were returned to the libraries.

FURTHER READING

Avery, Evelyn Gross. *Rebels and Victims: The Fiction of Richard Wright and Bernard Malamud.* Port Washington, N.Y.: Kennikat Press, 1979.

Helterman, Jeffrey. *Understanding Bernard Malamud.* Columbia: University of South Carolina Press, 1985.

Newsletter on Intellectual Freedom (May 1977): 79; (November 1982): 197.

FREAKONOMICS: A ROGUE ECONOMIST EXPLORES THE HIDDEN SIDE OF EVERYTHING

Authors: Steven D. Levitt and Stephen J. Dubner
Original date and place of publication: 2005, United States
Original publisher: HarperCollins
Literary type: Nonfiction

SUMMARY

Freakonomics: A Rogue Economist Explores the Hidden Side of Everything, written by economist Steven D. Levitt and journalist Stephen J. Dubner, applies the conventional theories of economics in an unconventional manner to challenge modern assumptions about crime, parenting, teaching, drug dealing, and sumo wrestling, among many other topics. Rather than writing a book centered upon a unifying theme, the authors have chosen "a sort of treasure-hunt approach" that "allows us to follow whatever freakish curiosities may occur to us. Thus our invented field of study: Freakonomics." Despite this freewheeling description, the authors do acknowledge that the book "has been written from a very specific worldview, based on a few fundamental ideas: Incentives are the cornerstone of modern life. . . . The conventional wisdom is often wrong. . . . Dramatic effects often have distant, even subtle, causes. . . . 'Experts'—from criminologists to real-estate agents—use their informational advantage to serve their own agenda. . . . Knowing what to measure and how to measure it makes a complicated world much less so."

The authors' theories and discussions are neatly compartmentalized into six chapters: chapter 1—What Do Schoolteachers and Sumo Wrestlers Have in Common?; chapter 2—How Is the Ku Klux Klan Like a Group of Real-Estate Agents?; chapter 3—Why Do Drug Dealers Still Live with Their Moms?; chapter 4—Where Have All the Criminals Gone?; chapter 5—What Makes a Perfect Parent?; and chapter 6—Perfect Parenting, Part II; Or, Would a Roshanda by Any Other Name Smell as Sweet? In the introduction, the authors assert that "if morality represents how people would like the world to work, then economics shows how it actually does work," and they proceed to show in the six chapters that follow why conventional wisdom is often wrong.

In "What Do Schoolteachers and Sumo Wrestlers Have in Common?" the authors explore the important role that incentives play in motivating behavior and examine why they often fail to achieve the desired behavior. The chapter also discusses the reasons why teachers will change children's answers on standardized tests and why sumo wrestlers in Japan may deliberately lose certain high-stakes matches. In the second chapter, the authors identify the ways in which the Ku Klux Klan resembles a group of real estate agents. They examine the role that information asymmetry plays and argue "nothing is more powerful than information, especially when its power is abused." The third chapter questions the validity of experts and asserts that "the conventional wisdom is often found to be a web of fabrication, self-interest, and convenience." The chapter reveals the secret financial operations of a street drug-dealing operation and exhibits the close similarity between the numerous levels of the drug gang hierarchy and the organizational chart of the fast food giant McDonald's.

In "Where Have All the Criminals Gone?" the "facts of crime are sorted out from the fictions." This is the most controversial chapter in the book. Levitt and Dubner postulate a strong link between the legalization of abortion in the United States in 1973 and the dramatic drop in crime in the mid-1990s, the time when, had abortions not occurred, the children born unwanted and into crime-ridden areas would have reached their mid-to-late teens and begun active adult criminal careers. In the discussion of the impact of *Roe v. Wade* on the nation's crime rate, the book states: "Jane Roe, crime stopper: how the legalization of abortion changed everything."

Chapters 5 and 6 focus on the roles of parents and suggest that the parents' socioeconomic status has more to do with children's academic achievement than the advice commonly given by experts that parents should read to their children. The chapter also questions "from a variety of angles, a pressing question: Do parents really matter?" and assesses "the importance of a parent's first official act—naming the baby."

In the epilogue, the authors assert that the net effect of reading *Freakonomics* will probably be subtle: "You might become more skeptical of the conventional wisdom; you may begin looking for hints as to how things aren't quite what they seem; perhaps you will seek out some trove of data and sift through it, balancing your intelligence and your intuition to arrive at a glimmering new idea." At the very least, the authors express a simple hope: "You might find yourself asking a lot of questions."

CENSORSHIP HISTORY

In 2006, *Freakonomics* was among nine books on the required reading list that were challenged in the second-largest high school district in Illinois, an act that "triggered debate over whether works praised in literary circles are high art or smut." The controversy began when Leslie Pinney, a Township High School district 214 board member, identified books on the reading list that she considered to "contain vulgar language, brutal imagery or depictions of sexual situations inappropriate for students." The books Pinney identified as inappropriate reading material, in addition to FREAKONOMICS, are SLAUGHTERHOUSE-FIVE by Kurt Vonnegut, THE THINGS THEY CARRIED by Tim O'Brien, THE AWAKENING by Kate Chopin, HOW THE GARCIA GIRLS LOST THEIR ACCENTS by Julia Alvarez, THE BOTANY OF DESIRE: A PLANT'S EYE VIEW OF THE WORLD by Michael

Pollan, *THE PERKS OF BEING A WALLFLOWER* by Stephen Chbosky, FALLEN ANGELS by Walter Dean Myers, and BELOVED by Toni Morrison. The school board member admitted that she had not read most of the books she targeted and claimed that she did not want to ban the books from the district libraries, but in the classrooms she wanted "to replace them with books that address the same themes without explicit material." Her objection to *Freakonomics* was the discussion of abortion appearing in chapter 4 in which Levitt and Dunbar examine the extent to which crime decreased throughout the United States in the mid-1990s, nearly two decades after abortions were legalized in 1973. Pinney expressed dismay that the authors would postulate an abortion-crime link. In the book, the authors anticipate such reactions and assert, "This theory is bound to provoke a variety of reactions, ranging from disbelief to revulsion, and a variety of objections, ranging from the quotidian to the moral. . . . To discover that abortion was one of the greatest crime-lowering factors in American history is, needless to say, jarring." The challenges were the first in more than 20 years that someone had attempted to remove books from the reading lists in the Arlington Heights–based district, which employed an extensive review process based in established reading lists. In defense of the choices, English and fine arts department head Chuck Venegoni told a reporter for the *Chicago Tribune*, "This is not some serendipitous decision to allow someone to do what they felt like doing because they had something about talking about something kinky in front of kids. It's insulting to hardworking people who really do care about kids." He criticized Pinney's approach of taking a few passages out of context to condemn entire books and observed, "There is nothing in any of those books that even remotely approaches what an objective person would call pornography." Although the school district had an opt-out clause that allowed parents to request that their child read another book if they find the assigned material objectionable, Pinney found the current measures ineffectual "because unless you're digging around the student's backpack, looking at the books and reading them, how exactly will you know what your student is reading?"

Five hundred people attended the school board meeting on Thursday, May 25, 2006, to debate whether to keep *Freakonomics* and the other books on the school reading lists. Supporters of the ban asserted that their efforts were "to protect students from smut" and some people, such as Arlington Heights resident Brude Ticknell, claimed that "teachers promoting the books were motivated by their own progressive social agendas." Students took the debate to the social networking site MySpace.com, and sophomore Scott Leipprandt placed a petition against the ban on the Prospect High page, which nearly 500 students and alumni from the six high schools in the district signed. Leipprandt told a *Chicago Tribune* reporter that fighting the banning of books is important. "It's important because it shows us things. All these things happen in real life. By banning it, it doesn't give us the opportunity to talk about it before we encounter it in real life." After a long meeting during which hundreds of people spoke, the school board voted 6-1 in favor of approving the required reading list without change. The following year, the school board voted to provide parents with the reading lists for courses before voting on materials.

More recently, in 2009, the Texas Department of Criminal Justice (TDCJ) prevented an inmate from receiving the copy of *SuperFreakonomics*, the followup to *Freakonomics* that he ordered from Amazon, because it is "racially provocative." When author Steven Levitt heard about the incident, he contacted Texas officials who told him that they had made an error and that *Freakonomics* is the book that violates their censorship policies and the book that they had meant to ban. The incident began when Thomas Glesburg, a prisoner serving a 65-year sentence for murder, ordered a copy of *SuperFreakonomics*. The TDCJ confiscated the book, and Levitt wrote about the incident on his blog, after which Jason Clark, a spokesman for the TDCJ, contacted him and told him that the director's review committee had decided on May 25, 2005, to deny prisoners access to the book because it contained "racial material" on pages 50, 59, 67, and 90. Pages 50, 57, and 69 appear in chapter 2, "How Is the Ku Klux Klan Like a Group of Real-Estate Agents?" Writing in the *Statesman*, Dexheimer reports that page 57 contains a "rather tame and factual history of the Klan, with a single quote containing the use of the n word to describe blacks. Page 59 relates how a young reformer goes undercover and learns exactly how bigoted Klan members really are. It contains two uses of the n word, again both quotes. Page 60 adds details of the man's study, such as the Klan's hilarious secret handshake, which he describes as 'a left-handed, limp-wristed fish wiggle.' It, too, quotes a Klansman using the n word." The objection to page 97 is similar to the others and contains a single blue passage. In it, a drug dealer explains the hard life: "It's a war out here, man. I mean, every day people struggling to survive, so you know, we just do what we can. We ain't got no choice, and if that means getting killed, well shit, it's what niggers do around here to feed their family." Dexheimer observes that page 96 is not cited as part of the reason for the ban, yet it contains several uses of the N-word. He asked TDCJ officials about that omission and learned that the "detailed reason for originally denying the book in 2005 has been purged. All that remains is the ban."

FURTHER READING

Dexheimer, Eric. "Is SuperFreakonomics Inappropriate? No—but Freakonomics Is." *Statesman*. Available online. URL: http://www.statesman.com/blogs/content/shared-gen/blogs/austin/investigative/entries/2010/01/08/is_superfreakonomics_racist_no.html. Accessed July 29, 2010.

Francisco, Jamie. "Explicit Move Is Made to Ban Books from Reading List." *Chicago Tribune*, May 24, 2006.

FRUITS OF PHILOSOPHY: OR THE PRIVATE COMPANION OF YOUNG MARRIED PEOPLE

Author: Charles Knowlton
Original dates and places of publication: 1832, United States; 1833, England
Original publishers: Privately printed; James Watson
Literary form: Medical handbook

SUMMARY

Fruits of Philosophy: Or The Private Companion of Young Married People, the first popularly written English-language medical guide to preventing conception, was initially subtitled "The Private Companion of Married People." The book, written by a physician in simple and clear language so that the poorest members of society could understand and benefit from it, deals with reproductive physiology, coitus, and conception control. The book began as a slim pamphlet on the methods of preventing conception that Knowlton gave to patients who requested such knowledge.

The book opens with Knowlton's response to the arguments against birth control, then explains its many advantages, including the control of overpopulation, reduction of poverty and crime, prevention of hereditary diseases, preservation and improvement of the species, and reduction of abortions and the ill health suffered by women who are subjected to excessive childbearing. In brief, he first discusses the moral philosophy of contraception. He then provides an anatomical discussion of the reproductive organs and explains the processes of menstruation and conception, both promoting and preventing conception. Some of Knowlton's physiological descriptions are inaccurate and need updating, but his chemical methods of contraception were relatively effective, and "the tone and point of view are, on the whole, surprisingly modern."

CENSORSHIP HISTORY

The work gained little notice in the popular press, and the professional medical press waited 11 years after it appeared to publish a first review in the *Boston Medical and Surgical Journal*. In contrast, the legal authorities in Massachusetts gave it nearly immediate attention as they rushed to prevent the information from reaching readers. In early 1832, only months after publication of the work, a local lawyer circulated a pamphlet in which he accused Knowlton of making prostitution easy and inexpensive at 50 cents per copy, while removing from it the "inconvenience and dangers." The author was brought to trial in Taunton, Massachusetts, and charged with distributing "obscene material," then fined $50 and court costs. In December 1832, a rival physician signed a complaint in Cambridge, Massachusetts, charging that the book was "immoral" and that it "undermines chastity." Knowlton, who suffered from a heart condition, was found guilty of distributing his book and sentenced to three months of hard labor in the Cambridge House of Correction, from January through March 1833. Late in the following year, a clergyman from Ashfield, Massachusetts, registered a complaint that charged Knowlton with "undermining society" by distributing *Fruits of Philosophy*. From late 1834 through mid-1835, Knowlton appeared in court in Greenfield, Massachusetts, three different times to answer this charge, but the case was finally dismissed because the jury in all three trials could not come to a decision.

The notoriety of the trials made the book a best seller, which went through nine editions in Knowlton's lifetime. He died in 1850, but the book gained international fame after his death because of the epic 1877 Bradlaugh-Besant trial in England. The book had been published by British publisher James Watson; at his death in 1874, London publisher Charles Watts bought the plates from his widow and placed the book back into print. Two years later, Henry Cook published in Bristol, England, a pirated copy of the book with the addition of allegedly obscene illustrations to enliven the book. Cook was arrested, tried, and sentenced to two years at hard labor. At the advice of well-known freethinkers Charles Bradlaugh and Annie Besant, Watts sought an audience with the court to identify himself as the original publisher of the book in its original condition. His aim was to return the book to its original condition, minus illustrations, and original level of acceptance, for it had been published in England for 40 years without prosecution. Watts was arrested, taken to London, and arraigned. He pleaded guilty to publishing a book about the physiological details of sex and paid a fine in the amount of 500 pounds.

Bradlaugh and Besant were angered by the cowardliness of Watts in admitting to publishing an "obscene" book, and they were determined to test the court. Late in 1877, they published the book themselves, with a new introduction, through their Free Thought Publishing Society. To be certain that the police would arrest them, Bradlaugh and Besant sent the London police a copy of the book and informed the police exactly where and at what time they would sell the first copy. A few days later, a detective in plain clothes purchased a copy of the book for six pence, then arrested the two. They were tried before Lord Chief Justice, Sir Alexander Cockburn.

During the five days of the trial of *Charles Bradlaugh and Annie Besant v. The Queen*, large crowds gathered outside of Guildhall expressing their sympathy with the defendants. Sir Hardinge Gifford, the prosecutor, condemned the book as being "a dirty, filthy book. . . . The object of it is to enable a person to have sexual intercourse, and not to have that which in the order of providence is the natural result of that sexual intercourse." In contrast, Bradlaugh and Besant spoke of population problems and examined the meaning of the term "obscenity." They and their prominent witnesses, among them the consulting physician to Metropolitan Hospital, spoke of England's poor and the need to limit the population.

The jury returned an ambiguous verdict, stating: "We are unanimously of the opinion that the book in question is calculated to deprave public morals, but at the same time we entirely exonerate the defendants from any corrupt motives in publishing it." Although he interpreted the verdict to mean that the jury thought the defendants guilty, Cockburn let the defendants go without a sentence or a fine, but they were told that they had to surrender the book and vow never to publish it again. When Bradlaugh and Besant declared clearly to the judge that they planned to publish, the judge sentenced them to six months in prison, a fine of £200 each, and recognizances of £500 each for two years. The defendants were released on bail while they appealed the case on the grounds that the specific words upon which the prosecution based its charge of "obscene" had never been expressly identified. Thus, in writing the final opinion on the appeal decision, the judge made it clear that "we express no opinion whether this is a filthy and obscene, or an innocent book. We have not the materials before us for coming to a decision on this point. . . . the indictment simply averred that an offence had been committed, and did not shew how it had been committed." The defendants recovered their stock of books, stamped in red "Recovered from Police," and sold them.

FURTHER READING

Arnstein, Walter L. *The Bradlaugh Case*. Oxford: Clarendon Press, 1965.
Fryer, Peter. *The Birth Controllers*. London: Corgi Books, 1967.
Manvell, Roger. *The Trial of Annie Besant and Charles Bradlaugh*. New York: Horizon Press, 1976.
Nethercot, Arthur H. *The Last Four Lives of Annie Besant*. Chicago: University of Chicago Press, 1963.
Petersen, William. *The Politics of Population*. Garden City, N.Y.: Doubleday & Company, 1964.
Reed, James. *From Private Vice to Public Virtue: The Birth Control Movement and American Society*. New York: Basic Books, 1978.

GARGANTUA AND PANTAGRUEL

Author: François Rabelais
Original dates and places of publication: 1567, France; 1708, England; 1927, United States
Original publishers: Privately published (France and England); Boni & Liveright (United States)
Literary form: Satire

SUMMARY

Gargantua and Pantagruel, originally five separate volumes later combined under the one title, reflects the author's changing experiences, interests, and attitudes in Renaissance France. The five books were separately titled *Pantagruel* (1533), *Gargantua* (1535), the *Third Book* (1546), the *Fourth Book*

(1548–1552), and the *Fifth Book* (1562–1564). Although Rabelais had Cardinal Jean du Bellay as his longtime patron, and he was under the protection of François I of France for the publication of the *Fourth Book*, his bawdy and often obscene satires, joined with his lack of attention to social niceties, frequently put him into conflict with the authorities.

Written as a burlesque of the classical epic and chivalric romance, the work is an exuberant mock-heroic effort that purports to relate the lives, heroic deeds, and sayings of Gargantua and his son Pantagruel, two members of a pleasant race of giants who love to eat and drink heartily and who enjoy earthly pleasures and humor. The author claimed that the work "demonstrates the theme that the real purpose of life is to expand the soul by exploring the sources of varied experience." The unifying philosophy of the work is expressed by Pantagruel, "Do As Thou Wilt." Using puns, wordplay, synonyms, and flexible syntax, Rabelais creates a world in which restrictions on sensual or intellectual experience are not tolerated, and excessive discipline is considered inhuman and evil. Those who would restrict freedom are satirized throughout the five books: the militarists, abusers of justice, pedants, and medieval scholastics.

The five books are only loosely connected, and the work contains nothing resembling a plot, for to force an order on the events would be too restrictive for the author. Because his concern is freedom of the *mind*, anarchy is not an issue, but he avoids the unimaginative, conforming mind. In presenting the adventures, Rabelais used extremely frank language to carry out his purpose, to force readers to recognize the ludicrous preoccupations of mankind and to make them laugh at the incongruities and absurdities of society.

CENSORSHIP HISTORY

Gargantua and Pantagruel contains a large number of humorous references that have been labeled "obscene" for over four centuries. Rabelais frequently speaks of emetic subjects in an exaggerated manner to draw attention and laughter from readers. In one passage, he tells of Gargantua's horse who "pissed to ease her belly, but it was in such abundance, that it did overflow the country seven leagues, and all the piss of that urinal flood ran glib away towards the ford of Vede, wherewith the water was so swollen, that all the forces the enemy had there were with great horror drowned." In a second passage, he suggests that the city walls of Paris would be better fortified if female organs, "callibristis" or "contrapunctums," were used instead of stones, because they are cheaper and can more easily be arranged according to size. He states wryly that "no thunderbolt or lightning would fall upon it. For why? They are all either blest or consecrated." In still another passage, Rabelais relates the story of a miraculous codpiece that sexually arouses anyone near it. When its owner enters a theater in which a passion play is being performed, all on stage and in the audience are so sexually aroused that they immediately begin to copulate randomly with each other.

Although less frequently, deviance appears in some of the stories, as in the episode in which hermaphrodites appear and in another in which boys are maintained for sodomy. In an ode to wine, Rabelais speaks bluntly of oral sex: "If there came such liquor from my ballock, would you not willingly thereafter suck the udder whence it issued?"

The first two books were published under the pseudonym of Alcofribas Nasier without the author's knowledge in 1533 and were promptly suppressed by censors in the French Parliament in 1534 and placed on the Index of the Sorbonne for being obscene and sacrilegious. In 1535, a papal bull was issued to remove censure from the work, and the third book was published in France using the author's name with the endorsement of King François I. In 1552, while the king was out of the country, the Sorbonne censored the fourth book upon publication, but in 1554, Cardinal de Chatillon convinced Henri II to raise the ban on the work. In 1564, Rabelais was banned once again and listed in the Index Librorum Prohibitorum, and all of his works were banned.

The extreme frankness of Rabelais's language was preserved in a similarly frank English translation in the late 17th century by Sir Thomas Urquhat and Peter Motteux, in an edition that was not published until 1708 as a part of *The Complete Works of Doctor François Rabelais*. The translators used language that has been called "obscene," including such terms as *codpiece, bunghole, ballocks, teats, genitories*, and *spermatic vessels*. In 1894, the New York Society for the Suppression of Vice, under the zealous leadership of Anthony Comstock, brought civil proceedings against the bankrupt Worthington Book Publishing Company that sought the right to sell off assets. Among those assets were the complete works of Rabelais, Queen Margaret of Navarre's THE HEPTAMERON, Giovanni Boccaccio's THE DECAMERON, Henry Fielding's TOM JONES, Sir Richard Burton's THE ARABIAN NIGHTS, Jean-Jacques Rousseau's CONFESSIONS, and Ovid's ART OF LOVE. The receiver for the company asked the court to allow sale of the books, expensive volumes of world-renowned literary classics. Comstock appeared in the court record as opposing the sale. In stating the decision of the court in *In re Worthington Company*, 30 N.Y.S. 361 (1894), Judge Morgan J. O'Brien stated that "a seeker after the sensual and degrading parts of a narrative may find in all these works, as in those of other great authors, something to satisfy his pruriency," but he added that to simply condemn an entire literary work because of a few episodes "would compel the exclusion from circulation of a very large proportion of the works of fiction of the most famous writers of the English language." The court decision characterized the specific editions as being "choice editions, both as to the letter-press and the bindings . . . as to prevent their being generally sold or purchased, except by those who would desire them for their literary merit, or for their worth as specimens of fine book-making." In short, even though the text remained the same as that in cheaper editions, the "very artistic character, the high qualities of style, the absence of those glaring and crude pictures [set these books] entirely apart from such gross and obscene writings as it is the duty of the public authorities to suppress."

The United States Custom Office continued to ban the import of all of Rabelais's works until the 1930 Tariff Act ended the censorship of acknowledged literary works, including the Motteux translation of *Gargantua and Pantagruel* with Frank C. Pepe's illustrations.

In 1951, city and county law enforcement officers obtained a warrant and raided the Dubuque (Iowa) Public Library, where they seized books charged with being obscene. Among those works were *Gargantua and Pantagruel, The Decameron*, and *Tom Jones*. The works were later returned to library shelves, as "restricted" material.

FURTHER READING

Broun, Heywood, and Margaret Leech. *Anthony Comstock: Roundsman of the Lord.* New York: Literary Guild of America, 1927.
Kronhausen, Eberhard, and Phyllis Kronhausen. *Pornography and the Law.* New York: Ballantine Books, 1959.
Rigolet, François. "Rabelais, Misogyny, and Christian Charity. Biblical Intertextuality and the Renaissance Crisis of Exemplarity." *PMLA* 109 (March 1994): 225–237.

GENTLEMAN'S AGREEMENT

Author: Laura Z. Hobson
Original date and place of publication: 1947, United States
Original publisher: Simon & Schuster
Literary form: Novel

SUMMARY

In *Gentleman's Agreement*, Phil Green is portrayed as the man next door, the typical American, unaware of many of the problems in his society. Green is a middle-class man and a widowed father who earns his living as a reporter. In order to carry out a newspaper assignment about Jewish life in America, he pretends to be Jewish. As a result of his newly assumed identity, he realizes that discrimination is more far-reaching than he ever suspected.

Lonely after his wife's death, he becomes romantically linked with Kathy, a divorcée, whose resentment of his work surfaces when she has to adjust to his various aliases. While trying to convince Green that she is really not bigoted, she begins to display the characteristics of a latent bigot.

As he continues his research, Green discovers that a surprising number of the people around him, including his family and friends, harbor deep prejudices. As a result of this discovery, his newspaper story emerges even more powerfully than he anticipated.

Gentleman's Agreement delves into the imperfections of society, specifically the prejudices of the American mainstream in the 1940s. Keenly aware of subtle forms of discrimination, Hobson describes the latent anti-Semitism rampant in America at that time. She focuses on people who do not regard themselves as anti-Semites and who deny charges of bigotry with the familiar rationalization that "Some of my best friends are Jews." Hobson attempts to show that many of these people are as much enemies of the Jews as are the overt anti-Semites.

Social problems are highlighted as Green pursues his assignment posing as a Jew. He discovers that Jews are barred admission to various country clubs and hotel resorts, as well as prohibited from buying homes in some neighborhoods. He learns the extent to which there is a "gentlemen's agreement" existing in the United States concerning how to treat Jews.

The major theme in *Gentleman's Agreement* is the need to recognize dominant prejudices and to create a society where people are accepted for what they really are. The story appeals for mutual respect and tolerance for all people. Hobson emphasizes that prejudices are not natural but learned. As she writes, "We are born in innocence . . . in an unstained purity of heart."

The author provides her characters with lengthy speeches that expose the hidden biases of American society. At various points in the novel, Green's mother and Kathy refer to "those people" or "that kind" in shows of anti-Semitism that lead to lessons in tolerance delivered by Green. As Green gathers material for his exposé of anti-Semitism in the United States, his relationship with Kathy becomes strained. His growing identification with his subject and his increased awareness contrast with Kathy's indifference to the social injustice. Their relationship suffers. As Green perseveres in his crusade, and after he passionately lectures Kathy, she sees fully how ignorant she has been regarding the treatment of Jews in society. Her acceptance of this knowledge and her understanding of Green's determination bring them together.

CENSORSHIP HISTORY

Gentleman's Agreement was banned from reading lists at DeWitt Clinton High School, Bronx, New York, in February 1948, by high school principal Dr. John V. Walsh, who told a reporter for the *New York Times* that he "barred Mrs. Hobson's novel on the ground that it makes light of extra-marital relations." At the time, the high school was an all-boys' institution. A teacher had offered the novel as a gift to the high school library, but Dr. Walsh refused to accept the book because of its perceived "immoral passages." On February 15, 1948, the executive board of the Teachers Union, CIO, adopted a resolution to urge that the principal withdraw his orders to ban the novel from the library. In a letter addressed to both Walsh and the associate superintendent in charge of the academic high school division, Frederic Ernst, the resolution stated, "in the future, steps should be taken to insure there will be no repetition of indirect censorship of socially significant books." The resolution also accused the principal of banning the book on the "flimsiest of pretexts" and questioned "How long will we continue to pretend that our students know only what would be approved by the most unworldly of schoolmasters?"

The following month, the executive board of the Parent-Teacher Association also protested the ban. In a letter dated March 3, 1948, and addressed to Ernst, the president of the high school PTA, Mrs. Jean Subin, wrote that school libraries are filled with the works of Shakespeare, Tolstoy, Thackeray, Dumas, and Sinclair Lewis and noted that "these esteemed authors devote many passages to 'extra-marital relations.'" She asserted, "Your reason for the banning of 'Gentleman's Agreement' has, therefore, no foundation." As the *New York Times* reported, she ended her letter by reminding the school administration, "Censorship goes against the principle of democracy and has no place in our public schools."

On March 17, 1948, representatives of the United Parents Associations (UPA) contacted Dr. William Jansen, superintendent of schools, and urged him to create a new plan for reviewing books presented to the New York public school libraries as gifts to eliminate controversies similar to the one involving *Gentleman's Agreement*. The UPA suggested the formation of an advisory committee consisting of a member of the Board of Education, two members of the Board of Superintendents, "a representative of parent opinion to be selected by the UPA," and the chief librarian of the New York Public Library to study any gift book that a school principal believed should be rejected. The *New York Times* reported on March 18, 1948, that a committee of the Board of Education was currently studying *Gentleman's Agreement*. The board's committee was expected to make a recommendation regarding the novel within a short time, after which the Board of Superintendents would provide a final decision. In an interview, James Marshall, a Manhattan Board of Education member, told a reporter that he could not recall any time in which the Board of Education had overruled a decision of the superintendents on a book ban and declared that the superintendents "are the pedagogical experts and know whether a book should be banned or not."

The Board of Superintendents did not reverse the ban and approve the novel for public high school reading lists until October 21, 1948. Pressure was placed on the board by Maximilian Moss, vice president of the Board of Education, who submitted passages from 15 books currently on the approved reading list and asked the superintendents to compare them with the declared "immoral passage" in *Gentleman's Agreement*. In a statement given to the *New York Times*, the Board of Superintendents explained the following:

> The Board of Superintendents was aware of the very high purpose of "Gentleman's Agreement," but had reservations about authorizing its being in the high school libraries because of elements in the book that could be considered by many people as unsuitable for high school use.
>
> However, the Board of Superintendents listened to proponents of the book who advanced its fine purpose as against whatever limitations the book might have for purpose of high school listing. The Board of Superintendents, therefore, reconsidered all the aspects of the case and decided that the book should be authorized for use in high school libraries.

FURTHER READING

"Book Ban Is Lifted by School Board." *New York Times*, October 22, 1948, p. 23.
"Book Ban Protested." *New York Times*, February 16, 1948, p. 23.
"Book-Ban Review Urged by Parents." *New York Times*, March 18, 1948, p. 25.
"School Association Protests Book Ban." *New York Times*, March 4, 1948, p. 33.

THE GIVER

Author: Lois Lowry
Original date and place of publication: 1993, United States
Original publisher: Houghton Mifflin Company
Literary form: Science fiction novel

SUMMARY

Lois Lowry's *The Giver* is the story of Jonas, an exceptionally talented child in a utopian community who learns the price that humanity must pay to maintain a seemingly idyllic existence. The book is written in the third person, but the narrative viewpoint is always that of Jonas, as the reader sees what he sees and feels what he feels throughout. Until the age of 12, he leads a peaceful, albeit regulated, life with his sister, Lily, and parents; his mother is employed at the Department of Justice, and his father works as a Nurturer, keeping babies well. Jonas enjoys riding his bicycle, playing with his friends Asher and Fiona, and musing about his future. In Jonas's world, everything from individual desire, to the weather, to a person's career is regulated. The community rulers require that every member of this nameless, timeless community occupies a productive role in the society. At the age of three, all children begin the daily routine of "dreamtelling," which requires them to describe at their breakfast table the dreams they had the previous night. Three is also the age at which children are taught the correct use of language, regardless of individual development or speech skills. Children under the age of six wear jackets which fasten at the back, but when they turn seven they are given front-fastening clothing to signify their increased independence. At the age of eight their "comfort object" is taken away, and they are given another new jacket, which contains pockets to indicate that they must now look after small belongings. Eight-year-old children must also perform voluntary service outside of school hours. At the age of nine, girls remove their hair ribbons, and boys and girls receive their own bicycle, while at age 10 both boys and girls have their hair ceremoniously cut. When they reach the age of 11, boys are given long trousers and girls receive "new undergarments."

The members of the community receive a professional assignment at the Ceremony of Twelve, at which time the child becomes an adult. Jonas waits apprehensively for his assignment, while his friends receive desirable and appropriate assignments, such as "Fish Hatchery Attendant" and "Assistant Director of Recreation." After all of the other Twelves have received their assignments, Jonas continues to wait, then learns that he has been selected to become the next Receiver of Memory, because of his intelligence and courage, and because he has the "Capacity to See Beyond" (the ability to see colors). The assignment instantly changes his life, separating him even further from his friends than he has expected. The Chief Elder warns him that his training will involve pain. "Physical pain . . . of a magnitude that none of us here can comprehend because it is beyond our experience." While his friends find no surprises in their assignments, Jonas is "filled with fear"; he also knows that the last Twelve appointed to be Receiver of Memory failed. Not until Chapter 18 does he learn that 10 years earlier, the last Receiver of Memory, a girl named Rosemary, had found the memories of pain and sadness so unbearable after only five weeks of training that she had gone directly to the Chief Elder and asked to experience "Release" (to die). Because no rule existed at the time to prevent the fulfillment of her request, The Giver never saw her again, but he still grieves. He also reminds Jonas that the new rules Jonas has received prohibit him from doing the same.

The Ceremony of Twelve is the next to last ritual of the community because the children are now adults, and they are expected to spend the rest of their lives fulfilling their assignments. Two additional concerns remain for members of the community, aside from their functions in society: Sex and Death. Artificial insemination is the means by which members of the community procreate. A girl selected at the age of 12 to become a "Birthmother" spends three years at the Birthing Center and gives birth to three babies, who are not brought up by their natural mothers but allocated to volunteer parents who are permitted two children, one boy and one girl. All sexual longing is eliminated at puberty, aided by the process of "dream-telling," which is largely intended as a monitor of sexual desire, called "Stir-rings" in the novel. Jonas confesses one morning to an erotic dream, and he is immediately prescribed a daily pill to eliminate such stirrings, but he openly rebels later in the book and stops taking the pill.

Death is euphemistically named "Release" by the community, and it functions as the final ritual. Young children are encouraged to believe that those who undergo "Release" are simply choosing to leave the community. Immediately preceding the "Release," the community holds a ceremony, which includes a "telling of the life," a toast, an anthem, a good-bye speech from the individual to be released if an adult, some farewell speeches from those who know him or her, then a walk through the door to the Releasing Room. Infants that do not thrive are also sent there, as are persistent violators of the community codes.

Jonas becomes increasingly fearful in his new position when he learns in the first training instructions that he is no longer allowed to share his dreams with anyone and that he may lie, both of which contradict everything he has been taught. The only person who understands his fears is the current Receiver of Memories, a "bearded man with pale eyes," who tells Jonas to call him The Giver. His job, which will eventually fall on Jonas, is to consult his memories of "the whole world" and advise the Committee of Elders in their decisions. The Committee of Elders has no memories of the past, or of anywhere else, and they cannot imagine the world other than it is; therefore, they have trouble addressing new problems. Other than that, no other reason is given in the book for safekeeping by The Giver of the memories of how life used to be.

The Giver describes himself as not as old as he looks and says he has been made tired by the burden of knowledge and memories, which have consumed his life. He emphasizes to Jonas that it is not the memory of nostalgia—not the recollections of childhood normally indulged in by the old—that he must transmit. Rather, "It's the memories of the whole world," including the meaning of snow, rain, and other weather, because the community is climate-controlled. This involves a ritualistic laying on of hands and an extra-sensory simulation of the sensation of cold.

The Giver begins to transmit his memories to Jonas, first pleasant memories of snow, sledding, sun, and sailing, then gradually adding memories of injuries, of war, of hate, of horrors. As Jonas acquires a greater number of memories, he feels anger toward other community members, who are "satisfied with their lives which had none of the vibrance his own was taking on." None of them understand what Jonas is learning every day, and he begins to feel "desperately lonely" because his family cannot understand what he has experienced. He lies and describes his job as pleasant but grows more and more estranged from his community and feels increasingly distressed.

After continued transmissions of memories, both pleasurable and painful, The Giver concludes his education of Jonas by showing him a videotape recording of a "Release" of unwanted babies conducted by his father. Jonas had always assumed that babies who were released went "Elsewhere," and he had never imagined that his father gave a lethal injection to babies who were different because they were twins or because they, like his baby stepbrother, Gabriel, were difficult to care for. Jonas now feels a terrible responsibility to reform his community and decides to escape, believing that, when he leaves, his memories will be transmitted to others, and the community will regain its links to the past.

When Jonas learns that his temporarily adopted brother, Gabriel, is in danger of being released because the baby has not been thriving, he steals his father's bicycle and takes Gabriel with him on a ride toward "Elsewhere." During the cold, dark, and painful journey, Jonas twists an ankle and does his best to care for the weakening Gabriel. They reach a sled on a hilltop, and Jonas and Gabriel get onto the sled and sail toward "Elsewhere." "The runners sliced through the snow and the wind whipped at his face as they sped in a straight line through an incision that seemed to lead to the final destination, the place that he had always felt was waiting, the 'Elsewhere' that held their future and their past."

The novel's ending is ambiguous, and the reader is left to question if the vision of lights at the bottom of the hill and the sound of voices singing are actual or if they are a sign that Jonas is sinking into unconsciousness.

CENSORSHIP HISTORY

The Giver has been a critical success, receiving numerous prestigious literary awards, including the Newbery Medal in 1994, an award for the best book published in the United States for children or young adults in the preceding year. Many critics compare it favorably to adult classics such as BRAVE NEW WORLD (1933), FAHRENHEIT 451 (1953), and *1984* (1948), and to children's classics such as *White Mountains* (1967) and *A Wrinkle in Time* (1962). Despite critical acclaim and the enthusiastic support of librarians, educators, and students, the novel has been the source of controversy across the United States. According to a report by the organization People For the American Way, *The Giver* was the second most frequently challenged book in 1996.

Parents have protested use of the novel in public schools because it contains the themes of infanticide and euthanasia, as well as suicide. In one particularly controversial scene, the protagonist watches his father sticking a needle filled with lethal liquid into the skull of an infant, "puncturing the place where the fragile skin pulsed." His father says cheerfully, "I know, I know. It hurts, little guy. But I have to use a vein, and the veins in your arms are still too teeny-weeny." Jonas's father pushes in the plunger, then says, "All done," and sends the small corpse down a chute. Challengers object to the scene because it is so graphic and transforms Jonas's once beloved father into a cold-blooded murderer.

Most people who have fought to censor *The Giver* confess that they have never read the novel in its entirety, and they sometimes misquote events. For example, parent Anna Cerbasi of Port Saint Lucie, Florida, who asked school board members in 1999 to remove the novel from middle-school shelves, objected to the book because "Nobody is a family. They kill the baby who cries at night. I read it and thought—no way. Not for sixth grade. Maybe high school, maybe." Ms. Cerbasi's concerns about the novel raise legitimate questions about who should decide which books are appropriate for which children, and whether or not disturbing stories are appropriate for youth even if they teach a valuable lesson. The incident she specifies, however, does not occur in the novel; the authorities plan to "release" Gabriel, the baby who cries constantly, but he is rescued by Jonas.

The outcry against *The Giver* is often fueled by taking issues in the book out of context. In 2003, former Oregon Republican Party activist Betty Freauf posted the article "Is *The Giver* on Your Horizon?" on her Web site, NewsWithViews.com. The article opens with her claim that a 1963 issue of the *Congressional Record* states that the 17th of the 45 Communist Party goals was "to get control of the schools and use them as transmission belts for socialism and current Communist propaganda. They also wanted to get control of the teachers associations and put the Communist party line into textbooks." From that opening, Freauf interprets various education measures passed in recent years by Oregon lawmakers and proclaims their goals similar to the planned community of *The Giver*.

The Giver, which received the 1994 Newbery Award, told about a special community where every child felt safe, ate plenty of food, took pills to stop any pain and lived in a family no larger than four. Overpopulation was not a problem since new babies were limited to 50 a year and non-productive people such as the severally [sic] handicapped or the elderly were simply expected to voluntarily check out! Today, animals are placed on a higher pedestal than humans!!

Can you image the trauma that book might cause in a young child if they had a handicapped sibling or an elderly grandparent with a stroke? (Oregon voters passed the first euthanasia law in the U.S. in 1994. On the [sic] 5/31/2003 there was a story on T.V. about the Australian who has built a suicide machine which will cost $100 in America). Read my article "Are We Destined for Selective Reduction?"

Why would such a book, which glamorizes death and the occult, be read to children as young as third graders? Book selection committees, perhaps without even reading *The Giver*, may have erroneously assumed because it received the prestigious Newbery Award, it would be safe. . . . Schools teach death education classes, take children to mortuaries and then wring their hands when teenagers commit suicide.

The Giver faced a challenge in 1999, in South Carolina, when the parent of a Pickens County student complained to the school board that references to death in the novel are inappropriate for children in elementary school classrooms. After additional parents joined the complaint, the school board voted to ban the novel from elementary school libraries and classrooms, but they agreed to allow the book to remain in high school classrooms and libraries. That same year, the superintendent of schools, Eugene Dukes, ordered the temporary removal of the novel from seventh-grade classrooms in the Union County (Florida) school district. Sandy Lane Avery, the mother of a seventh-grade student, began the drive to remove the book from classrooms, stating at a school board meeting that she objected to many of the explicit details in the book, especially the manner in which the babies receive a lethal injection. She asked the board, "Why do we need a fictional book to teach our children things we are trying not to get them to get involved in?" Brenda Burgin, mother of another student, also spoke out and told the board that 12-year-old children are too young emotionally to deal with concepts presented in the book: "This book opens a child's mind to experiences and thoughts that are not appropriate." Among opponents of the proposed ban was Reverend Bo Hammock, pastor of the Providence Village Baptist Church, who told the board that he is in favor of censorship, but he had recommended the book to his 12-year-old daughter. He voiced the opinion, "This book does not paint a picture of encouragement for murder. If you hold this stuff to its context, you will have no problem with this book." After hearing both opponents and supporters of *The Giver*, school board chairman Richard Cason stated that the district had not followed the board's policy for challenged books. In October 1999, the five-member committee composed of librarians, educators, and a community member reviewed the book and determined that it was appropriate for classroom use. On October 26, 1999, the matter came before the Union County school board, which overturned the superintendent's decision to pull the novel from middle schools, after hearing from parents and students who supported the book.

In 2001, parents in the Colorado school district in which Columbine High School is located complained to the school board that it was inappropriate for teachers to read *The Giver* aloud in the classroom because "it portrays suicide, euthanasia, and infanticide in a neutral to positive light." Mark S. Hanson, father of an 11-year-old daughter, told the board that the book is particularly inappropriate "in a state with the nation's fifth-highest suicide rate and in the same state school district as Columbine High School . . . A lot has changed in our community and some things should be re-evaluated." The school board voted to keep the book in the elementary school library and to allow teachers to read the book in the classroom and to openly discuss the disturbing issues.

On January 10, 2005, WDAF-TV4 in Missouri interviewed representatives of a parents' group that had approached the Blue Springs School District board of education in the attempt to have *The Giver* removed from the eighth-grade curriculum at Delta Wood Junior High School in Blue Springs. Led by parent Eileen Casper, the 20-member group claimed that the book is "celebrating euthanasia and teen suicide." The group wrote letters to the district, sought entry to closed-door board meetings, and asked the school board to read the book. The book remains on the eighth-grade required reading list, but students who object to the content may select an alternative title. In another broadcast, KCRG-TV9, a television station in Cedar Rapids, Iowa, reported on April 21, 2005, that Shaun and Lorrie Holcomb, the parents of a fourth-grade student, complained to a school district review committee that passages in *The Giver* containing sex and death made their son feel uncomfortable. Numerous teachers and parents defended the book, but the review committee recommended that elementary school teachers not teach the book and that it should be removed from classrooms and the school library.

FURTHER READING

"Award-winning Book Frequent Target in Schools." Associated Press (July 8, 2001).
"Book Controversy in Blue Springs School District." WDAF-TV4. Broadcast January 10, 2005. Available online. URL: http://www.wdaftv4.com/PrintNews.asp?id=7195. Accessed December 11, 2009.

"Censorship Roundup." *School Library Journal*, October 2001, p. 24.

Cooper, Ilene. "Giving and Receiving." *Booklist* 89 (April 15, 1993): 1,506.

Freauf, Betty. "Is *The Giver* on Your Horizon?" Available online. URL: http://www. newswithviews.com/BettyFreauf27.htm. Accessed December 12, 2009.

Geary, Mark. "Committee Says *The Giver* Isn't for Young Children." KCRG-TV9 (April 21, 2005).

"*The Giver* Goes Back to Middle School Classrooms." Associated Press. October 13, 1999. Available online. URL: http://www.freedomforum.org/templates/ document.asp?documentID=10135&printerfriend. Accessed December 12, 2009.

Kester, Seymour. *Utopian Episodes: Daily Life in Experimental Colonies Dedicated to Changing the World*. Syracuse, N.Y.: Syracuse University Press, 1996.

Lorraine, Walter. "Lois Lowry." *Horn Book Magazine* 70 (July–August, 1994): 423–426.

Malone, Jann. "Some Want Us All to Read Book; Others Want to Keep It from Us." *Richmond Times-Dispatch*, March 13, 2005.

Ray, Karen. "*The Giver* [Book Review]." *New York Times Book Review*, October 31, 1993, p. 26.

"Suicide Book Challenged in Schools." *USA Today*. July 20, 2001. Available online. URL: http://www.usatoday.com/life/books/2001-07-20-the-giver.htm. Accessed December 12, 2009.

GO ASK ALICE

Author: Anonymous
Original date and place of publication: 1971, United States
Original publisher: Prentice Hall
Literary form: Novel

SUMMARY

Go Ask Alice is a fictionalized account said to be based on the actual diary of a middle-class 15-year-old drug user, the daughter of a college professor. The publisher only identifies "Anonymous" as the author. At the outset, the author has very low self-esteem and expresses dissatisfaction with her appearance. She dislikes her hair, hates the condition of her skin, and feels fat, and she has just broken up with her boyfriend. She learns that her family will soon move because her father has received an appointment as dean of political science at another university, and she is excited at the prospect. When school is out for the summer in her new place of residence, the author returns to her old friends while spending the summer with her grandparents.

Bored with her summer, the author jumps at the chance to attend a party given by one of the "top echelon," a girl who ignored her before but who wants to attend the university where the author's father is a dean. The partygoers play a variation on the children's game, "Button, Button, Who's Got the Button?" but the author is not aware that 10 of the 14 colas are spiked with LSD and the "lucky" winners are those who unwittingly select the acid-laced soda. This is her first experience, and she is both fearful and pleased afterward. In her entry a few days later, she writes, "I simply can't wait to try pot." She has also decided that LSD is not so bad and that "all the things I've heard about LSD were obviously written by uninformed, ignorant people like my parents who obviously don't know what they are talking about." Her drug experiences escalate to taking "speed" and to stealing her grandmother's sleeping pills and tranquilizers. During her second acid trip, the author has sex, then worries afterward that she might become pregnant. She vows to stop using drugs, but she keeps her grandmother's sleeping pills.

The author returns home and becomes caught up in a vicious cycle of "Bennies," "Dexies," and hashish. She takes pills to give her bursts of energy during the day and pills to calm her down and let her sleep at night. She and a female friend become involved with two male college students who convince the girls to sell pot, which the girls do gladly, because the boys do not have time to sell and fewer girls than boys are "busted" for selling. Further, the author views herself as "Rich's chick all the way" so she has to do what she can to help him. That includes selling marijuana, LSD, and barbiturates not only to high school students but also to junior high and grade school students as well. Rich allows her to visit the apartment that he shares with Ted only when he restocks her supply of drugs. She finds that she has been used when she and Chris arrive unexpectedly at the apartment and find the two young men having sex. The author berates herself for all that she did for Rich, and she and her friend decide that they will "stay clean," which means running away to San Francisco. Introduced to heroin, she and Chris are sexually and sadistically abused. They return to their parents and high school, but the drug use does not stop. The author is eventually sent to a psychiatrist to deal with the drug use, but she runs away to Denver. She shares a hovel with several others who remain constantly stoned, and the dirt and depressing surroundings convince her to return home again.

Once home, the author decides to finally stop her drug use, but her former friends refuse to allow that. When she has remained drug-free for a time, others begin to threaten her. While babysitting, she unknowingly consumes a batch of homemade candy that has been laced with LSD, which results in a placement in the state mental hospital. Upon her release, the author seems determined to remain free of drugs, and her diary entries are all upbeat. In the final entry, she decides not to keep another diary because she now feels strong enough not to need that crutch. An afterword reveals that only three weeks later she is found dead of a drug overdose that may or may not have been accidental.

CENSORSHIP HISTORY

Go Ask Alice has been the target of numerous challenges and attempts to ban it because of its language, drug use, and sexual violence and promiscuity.

In the 1970s, schools cited the "objectionable" language and explicit sexual scenes as their reasons for removing it from their libraries in Kalamazoo, Michigan (1974); Saginaw, Michigan (1975); Eagle Pass, Texas (1977); and Trenton, New Jersey (1977). Written parental permission was required to take the book out of the library in Marcellus (New York) School District (1975), Ogden (Utah) School District (1979), and Safety Harbor Middle School Library in Safety Harbor, Florida (1982).

The work was one of 11 books banned by the school board in Island Trees Free School District No. 26 in New York in 1982. The court record specified the following passage as "objectionable" and representative of the reason for the ban: "shitty, goddamned, pissing, ass, goddamned be Jesus, screwing life's, ass, shit. Doris was ten and had humped with who knows how many men in between but now when I face a girl it's like facing a boy. I get all excited and turned on. I want to screw with the girl." The novel was returned to the library after the U.S. Supreme Court ruled in *Board of Education, Island Trees Union Free School District No. 26 et al. v. Pico et al.*, 457 U.S. 853 (1982) that the First Amendment rights of students had been violated in the banning.

In 1983, the book was removed from the school libraries because a school board member in Osseo School District in Brooklyn Park, Minnesota, found the language in the book to be "personally offensive," and the same occurred in the Pagosa Springs, Colorado, schools when a parent objected to the "graphic language, subject matter, immoral tone, and lack of literary quality found in the book." The book was challenged in 1984 in Rankin County (Mississippi) School District because it was "profane and sexually objectionable" and at the Central Gwinnett (Georgia) High School library in 1986 because "it encourages students to steal and take drugs."

Go Ask Alice was removed from the school library bookshelves in Kalkaska, Michigan, in 1986 because of "objectionable language," and that same year, the Gainesville (Georgia) Public Library prohibited young readers from checking out the book by keeping it in a locked room with other books on the topics of drug use, sexual dysfunction, hypnosis, and breast-feeding.

In 1993, the superintendent of schools of Wall Township, New Jersey, ordered the book removed from the intermediate school library because of "inappropriate" language and claims that it "borders on pornography." He expressed shock that the book was still available, because he had ordered the book removed from all reading lists and classroom book collections five years previously after receiving an anonymous letter that condemned the work. Also in 1993, the work was removed because of "graphic" language from an English class at Buckhannon-Upshur (West Virginia) High School and challenged as a required reading assignment at Johnstown (New York) High School because of "numerous obscenities." In 1994, Shepherd Hill High School in Dudley, Massachusetts, banned the book from its ninth-grade reading list due to "gross and vulgar language and graphic description of drug use and sexual conduct."

In 1998, eighth-grade students in Tiverton, Rhode Island, were asked by their teacher to return the copies of the book, which they had been reading as a class assignment. The middle school principal had received complaints from a mother who objected to the language and images of drug use in the book. Without advisement, the principal, who had not read the book, also ordered the book removed from the middle school library. The actions of the principal were in violation of the district's complaint policies and procedures; a review committee had to determine the outcome. In summer 1998, the review committee decided to return *Go Ask Alice* to the library but delayed a decision of whether to return the book to the classroom.

Obscene language, drug, use, and references to sex were also charges leveled against the book in 2008 in Berkeley County, South Carolina, where the complaints by one parent led to the abrupt removal of the book from the school curriculum. The book was assigned reading at Hanahan Middle School, attended by the 13-year-old daughter of Jill Hunt, who "found blatant, explicit language using street terms for sex, talk of worms eating body parts, and lots of curse words taking God's name in vain." After her daughter read aloud several passages, on February 21, 2008, Hunt went to the school principal Robin Rogers and complained. The next day, Berkeley County School District superintendent Chester Floyd removed the book from the curriculum, not having read it but after having excerpts from the book read to him by the administrative supervisor for secondary schools in the county. In an interview with the Charleston *Post and Courier*, Floyd stated his reasons for removing the book, "I think it's totally inappropriate for us to have inappropriate language to teach our lessons." Hanahan Middle School principal Rogers sent a letter home to parents and explained that the teachers obtained an instructional unit for the book at a Southern Regional Education Board conference, an organization that sponsors the "Making Middle Grades Work" program. He further explained that "the book contains some controversial issues that our district administration has decided is [sic] inappropriate for our eighth-graders" and noted that teachers "would not be reprimanded for using the book because it was approved as instructional material by an administrator at the school." Hunt, whose complaint resulted in the removal of *Go Ask Alice* from the curriculum, told a reporter for the Charleston *Post and Courier* that she hoped that other superintendents in the state would follow Floyd's lead. "We will not stop until the state of South Carolina has banned this book. No child in middle or high school should be reading this book."

FURTHER READING

"*Go Ask Alice* Snatched from Students." *Censorship News* no. 70 (Summer 1998).
Hurwitz, Leon. *Historical Dictionary of Censorship in the United States*. Westport, Conn.: Greenwood Press, 1985.

Massie, Dorothy C. "Censorship in the Schools Something Old and Something New." *Today's Education* 69 (November/December 1980): 56–60.

Newsletter on Intellectual Freedom (January 1975): 6; (March 1975): 41; (May 1975): 76; (May 1977): 73; (July 1977): 100; (May 1979): 49; (March 1980): 32; (July 1982): 142; (March 1983): 52; (March 1984): 53; (May 1984): 69; (July 1986): 117; (September 1986): 151–152; (November 1986): 207; (January 1987): 32; (March 1989): 39; (May 1993): 71; (July 1993): 109–110; (March 1994): 54; (September 1994): 150; (May 2008): 97–99.

Wise, Warren. "Controversial Book Pulled Out of Schools." *Post and Courier*, February 22, 2008. Available online. URL: http://www.postandcourier.com/news/2008/feb/22/controversial_book_pulled_out_schools/. Accessed December 12, 2009.

GONE WITH THE WIND

Author: Margaret Mitchell
Original date and place of publication: 1936, United States
Original publisher: Macmillan Company
Literary form: Novel

SUMMARY

Gone with the Wind was one of the two best-selling novels of the 1930s in the United States, with Hervey Allen's *Anthony Adverse*, a story set in the Napoleonic era. One million copies of the novel were sold in the first six months, and 1.5 million in the first two years. In 1937, Mitchell won the Pulitzer Prize and the American Booksellers' Association award for the novel.

Set in the American South from about 1861 through 1873, *Gone with the Wind* is a historical novel that portrays the struggle for survival by people whose secure lives were changed forever by the death and destruction of the Civil War. The daughter of a cultured French mother and a temperamental, hard-scrabble Irish father, Scarlett O'Hara is the spoiled center of life at the expansive plantation, Tara. Her obsession with the weak-willed Ashley Wilkes dominates her life, but he marries his cousin Melanie, a reticent and caring woman who understands his honorable yet ineffectual nature and accepts it. Scarlett spitefully marries Charles Hamilton, who dies in the war and leaves her with a child. After Atlanta is burned by Sherman's troops, Scarlett returns to Tara, where her mother dies and her father goes mad, leaving the sheltered Scarlett to assume responsibility for Melanie, her sisters, her child, Melanie's child, and the remaining faithful servants. Worked to exhaustion and suffering from lack of food, she struggles to keep Tara and vows that she "will never be hungry again."

After the war ends, the carpetbaggers appear ready to take through taxes what the Union Army did not take in battle, so Scarlett marries her sister's fiancé to obtain the needed money to keep Tara. Her second husband, Frank Kennedy, is a modestly successful businessman, and Scarlett dominates his mill enterprise and store to emerge from the poverty and struggle in which the war has left her. After Kennedy is killed when he and area men stage a midnight raid to avenge a physical attack on Scarlett, she makes a third marriage with Rhett Butler, even as she pines for Ashley Wilkes.

Scarlett and Rhett are similar in their lack of scruples, their tenacity, and their fierce passions. He has no illusion about Scarlett, and he willingly allows her to enjoy the immense wealth that he acquired as a blockade runner during the war, as he waits for her to forget Ashley and to truly love him. After their daughter, Eugenia Victoria "Bonnie Blue" Butler, is born, Rhett works to attain respectability among the Old Guard of Atlanta society for his daughter's sake. He realizes what Scarlett does not, that money alone will not bring acceptance. As Rhett guarantees their daughter's social future, Scarlett continues her unscrupulous business practices, and she continues to associate with what Rhett and her beloved Mammy refer to as "white trash Northerners" and "scalawags."

The indulged Bonnie Blue dies in a riding accident, placing Rhett and Scarlett at even greater emotional distance. Rhett turns with greater frequency to drink and to spending nights at Belle Watling's brothel. When Melanie Wilkes dies, Scarlett recognizes that Ashley is a weak, unstable character and that she really loves Rhett, who is unmoved by her revelation. Faced with the challenge of rekindling Rhett's love, Scarlett decides to return to Tara, the one constant in her life, where she will think about it tomorrow.

CENSORSHIP HISTORY

Gone with the Wind captured the attention of both the public and the censors before it was even published, but a strong advertising campaign by the Macmillan Company produced 100,000 in advance sales that obscured any threat posed by John Sumner and the New York Society for the Suppression of Vice upon its release in 1936. The society had objections to Scarlett O'Hara's serial marriages and her unscrupulous behavior, as well as to the marital rape of Scarlett, but public opinion was clearly on the side of the novel. In Boston, the Watch and Ward Society hoped to arouse some concern about the prominence that brothel madam Belle Watling holds in one part of the novel, as well as the use of "damn" and "whore," but Boston booksellers were unwilling to forgo the huge profits that the massive advertising campaign waged by the Macmillan Company promised. The hint of scandal actually fueled sales of the novel.

Direct challenges to the book did not appear until it entered schools as supplemental reading. In 1963, Lee Burress conducted a survey of high school English department chairpersons and school administrators regarding school censorship in Wisconsin. In an unnamed district in the state, a clergyman and a parent had challenged the appearance of the novel on a recommended reading list. They objected to Scarlett's "immorality." The district retained the book on the list. In a 1966 national sample of school librarians and high school English chairpersons, Burress reported that a teacher in an unnamed state challenged the availability of the book in the high school library, claiming that it could be "misunderstood." The novel was placed on a closed shelf and made unavailable to students.

In 1978, school officials in Anaheim (California) Union High School District banned the book from all English classrooms, at the same time that George Eliot's *Silas Marner* was banned, according to the Anaheim Secondary Teachers' Association. Parents condemned the "ruthless" and "immoral" behavior of Scarlett O'Hara and expressed concern about the negative depiction of freed slaves.

In 1984, an alderman in Waukegan, Illinois, challenged the appearance of the book on the recommended reading list in the Waukegan School District on grounds of "racism" and "unacceptable language." The main complaint was that the word *nigger* appears repeatedly in the novel. Joseph Conrad's *The Nigger of the "Narcissus"*, Harper Lee's To KILL A MOCKINGBIRD, Harriet Beecher Stowe's UNCLE TOM'S CABIN, and Mark Twain's ADVENTURES OF HUCKLEBERRY FINN were named in the same complaint and also removed from the list.

FURTHER READING

Burgess-Jackson, Keith. "Rape and Persuasive Definition." *Canadian Journal of Philosophy* 25 (September 1995): 415–454.

Burress, Lee. *Battle of the Books: Literary Censorship in the Public Schools, 1950–1985.* Metuchen, N.J.: Scarecrow Press, 1989.

Harwell, Richard, ed. *Margaret Mitchell's "Gone with the Wind" Letters, 1936–1949.* New York: Macmillan, 1976.

Newsletter on Intellectual Freedom (January 1979): 6; (July 1984): 105.

Taylor, Helen. *Scarlett's Women: "Gone with the Wind" and Its Female Fans.* New Brunswick, N.J.: Rutgers University Press, 1989.

GORILLAS IN THE MIST

Author: Dian Fossey
Original date and place of publication: 1983, United States
Original publisher: Houghton Mifflin
Literary form: Zoological study

SUMMARY

Gorillas in the Mist, written by the world authority on the endangered mountain gorilla, relates Dian Fossey's experiences over the 14 years in which she conducted field studies among four gorilla families in the Virunga Mountains shared by Zaire, Rwanda, and Uganda. The scientist became well known to villagers, who signaled her approach by shouting, *"Nyiramacha-belli!"* meaning, "The old lady who lives in the forest without a man."

To gain the acceptance of the gorillas, Fossey imitated their feeding and contentment sounds, as well as other behavior such as self-grooming and averting her eyes from their glances. After gaining their trust, she tracked the various groups and identified the adult animals with names, then gave names to the offspring that were born during the course of the study. Fossey viewed the gorillas as individuals, and she relates their unique characteristics in the book. She was eventually fully accepted by one gorilla group and made history when a fully mature male gorilla reached out to touch her.

As she studied the gorillas, Fossey meticulously documented male-female interactions, parent-child interactions, mating behavior, parenting skills, and both intragroup and intergroup behavior. Fossey's report of the sexual behavior and mating patterns of the gorillas is equally detailed. In one instance, the scientist reports that a young gorilla named Puck goes off alone and Fossey sees him "actively masturbating."

The author also documents mating behavior in careful detail, as well as other behavior of the young, sexually immature but curious gorillas. The book includes a photograph of a female being mounted by a male in her group. Fossey also tells of three-year-old Pablo, who is so obsessively interested in sexual activities that "he often tried to examine the penises of the older males but was usually shoved away." He also engages frequently in sex play with Poppy, a female gorilla 20 months his junior.

In addition to studying the lives of the gorillas, Fossey informs readers of the devastation that poachers have wreaked in the gorilla population and calls for a stop to their actions. She also relates instances in which she stood up to poachers and reported them, thus placing her life in danger.

CENSORSHIP HISTORY

The work was acclaimed by scientists as a breakthrough study, and Fossey was later thrust into the international spotlight after one of the gorillas was killed by poachers. She spoke to groups to focus attention on the rain forest and the plight of the gorillas, and she was brutally murdered in 1985. The passages regarding masturbation and mating behavior in her book are integral to the study and were accepted as such by scientists, but the same passages raised objections when the books appeared in schools and school libraries.

The book was kept out of many classrooms and not ordered for school libraries to avoid controversy over the details of the gorillas' sexual behavior. Many school administrators viewed the study as suitable for older students but unsuitable for or of less interest to middle school or younger students.

In 1993, teachers in Westlake Middle School in Erie, Pennsylvania, were instructed by school administrators to use felt-tip pens to black out "objectionable" passages in the book. Parents had challenged the use of the book in the classroom, claiming that the passages about gorilla sexual behavior and mating habits were "filthy," "unnecessary," and "inappropriate." The following passage regarding the masturbating gorilla was one of the "objectionable" passages blacked out:

> His head was flexed backward, his eyes were closed, and he wore a semismile expression while using his right forefinger to manipulate his genital area. For about two minutes, Puck appeared to be obtaining great pleasure from his actions. . . . It was the only time I have ever seen a gorilla in the wild actively masturbate.

The teachers were also required to block out lines detailing the sex play of three-year-old Pablo and one-year-old Poppy which "could result in an erection for Pablo, who with a puzzled smile, lay back and twiddled his penis" while Poppy watched with interest "or, occasionally even sucked his penis."

Farley Mowat's WOMAN IN THE MISTS (Warner Books, 1987), which recounted Dian Fossey's dedication to her cause and her brutal death, was also subject to censorship. In 1991, the work was removed from a required reading list in the Omaha, Nebraska, school district. Parents who objected to the book claimed that it contained racial slurs, as well as "profanity" and passages that degraded women. They also objected to Mowat's long discussion of the aftermath of Fossey's abortion.

FURTHER READING

Montgomery, Sy. *Walking with the Great Apes*. Boston: Houghton Mifflin, 1991.
Morrell, Virginia. "Called 'Trimates,' Three Bold Women Shaped Their Field." *Science* 260 (April 16, 1993): 420–425.
Newsletter on Intellectual Freedom (March 1992): 44; (July 1993): 109.
Webb, C. Anne. "The Battle Continues." *English Journal* 48 (September 1995): 123–124.

GO TELL IT ON THE MOUNTAIN

Author: James Baldwin
Original date and place of publication: 1953, United States
Original publisher: Alfred A. Knopf
Literary form: Novel

SUMMARY

Go Tell It on the Mountain chronicles the struggles of a black evangelist and his family as they fight to live a moral life and to save others in the Harlem ghetto. The opening pages of the novel are highly autobiographical, as they show John Grimes, cruelly called "frog eyes" by his stepfather, living in poverty with his parents, Gabriel and Elizabeth, his brother, Roy, and his sisters Ruth and Sarah. People always said that John would be a preacher when he grew older, just like his stepfather, Gabriel, who has imposed a puritanical lifestyle on the boy. Despite John's obedience to Gabriel, the preacher favors his natural son, Roy, and views John as "a stranger, living unalterable testimony to his mother's days in sin."

The novel, which covers 24 hours in actual time, is divided into three parts. Part I, entitled "The Seventh Day," consists of one unbroken narrative that is set in Harlem. It relates the family's experiences as they move from their home to their storefront church, the Temple of the Fire Baptized. The family is an anomaly in the area; dressed in their Sunday best, on their way to church they pass men and women on the streets who "had spent the night in bars, or in cat houses, or on the streets, or on rooftops, or under the stairs." Sex is a fact of life where they live. John and Roy, the preacher's expected successor who would rather be like the people on the streets, have watched a man and woman in the basement of a condemned house who "did it standing up." Roy also claims to have watched others many times, and "he had done it with some girls down the block." Moreover, the family lives in a tenement above "the harlot's house downstairs."

Part II, entitled "The Prayers of the Saints," is more than twice the length of the other two parts. It takes place in the Temple of the Fire Baptized, as each character's prayer is framed into a separate chapter. Through "Florence's Prayer," "Gabriel's Prayer," and "Elizabeth's Prayer," each beginning with their Southern roots, the reader learns brief histories of John's mother, stepfather, and aunt. Their mistakes, joys, and pains are revealed, and all are shown to have flawed pasts. Gabriel has fathered a child by a "harlot," while married to his first wife. Elizabeth bore John while unmarried. Florence loved her first husband hopelessly and lost him to war. This part ends in the church, with 14-year-old John lying on the floor before the altar, struggling with salvation.

Part III relates John's long night in church, praying and crying as he eventually becomes "saved."

CENSORSHIP HISTORY

Go Tell It on the Mountain was not known as a mainstream novel for many years after it was first published in the United States. Part of the opposition was to its antiwhite rhetoric, expressed most forcefully by Gabriel when Roy is slashed in a fight with a white street gang; other objections were made against the discussions of "bastard" children, extramarital sex, and frank sensuality. For the most part, before 1960, Baldwin had "a very touch-and-go relationship with censorship" both in the United States and in England. Libraries might purchase the book, but more often than not, it would be kept on the public library "poison shelves," only available to the patron who asked specifically for the book. As with many such books, the novel was only available in an expensive hardcover for nearly 10 years before it was published in inexpensive paperback by Signet Books in 1963. In England, the novel was published in hardcover in 1954 by Michael Joseph, but it did not emerge in paperback until Corgi published it in 1963.

The novel was challenged for many of the same reasons once it entered the school libraries and classrooms, and most of the challenges took place in the 1970s. The lack of extensive challenges should not be taken as a sign of acceptance. Rather, the relatively small number of challenges simply reflects the lack of widespread adoption of the novel by schools, who refrained from adding the book to required or supplemental reading lists. In a 1973 national survey of English department chairpersons, Burress found one challenge in an unnamed school district in the North. A student and his parent objected to the required reading as being "nigger" literature. The school board agreed to allow the student to substitute another book for the novel. In 1975, in a survey of book challenges in Tennessee, Weathersby reported that the book was challenged by a parent in an unidentified school district for providing "a trashy idea of sex" and "filling a child's mind with ideas that cause him to lose confidence in the authorities." The book was removed from the classroom. In a 1977 national survey of English chairpersons, Burress reported that a clergyman in Illinois had challenged the book as "immoral" and demanded its removal from the high school classroom. The book was retained as a required reading.

In 1994, parents of students in the Hudson Falls, New York, school district objected to the inclusion of the book as a required reading in the high school English curriculum. Objectors claimed that the book contained "obscene language" and recurring themes of rape, masturbation, violence, and the degrading treatment of women. The book was retained, but students could substitute another book from an approved list.

FURTHER READING

Baldwin, James. *Conversations with James Baldwin*, edited by Fred L. Standley and Louis H. Pratt. Jackson: University Press of Mississippi, 1989.

Burress, Lee. *Battle of the Books: Literary Censorship in the Public Schools, 1950–1985.* Metuchen, N.J.: Scarecrow Press, 1989.

Harris, Trudier. *Black Women in the Fiction of James Baldwin.* Knoxville: University of Tennessee Press, 1985.

Newsletter on Intellectual Freedom (November 1994): 190; (January 1995): 13; (March 1995): 55.

Porter, Horace A. *Stealing the Fire: The Art and Protest of James Baldwin.* Middletown, Conn.: Wesleyan University Press, 1989.

Sutherland, John. *Offensive Literature: Decensorship in Britain, 1960–1982.* London: Junction Books, 1982.

Weathersby, Dorothy T. *Censorship of Literature Textbooks in Tennessee: A Study of the Commission, Publishers, Teachers, and Textbooks.* Ed.D. diss., University of Tennessee, 1975.

THE GREAT GATSBY

Author: F. Scott Fitzgerald
Original date and place of publication: 1925, United States
Original publisher: Charles Scribner's Sons
Literary form: Novel

SUMMARY

The story of *The Great Gatsby* is well known, and the name continues to suggest an age of opulence, decadence, and wild abandon. Hidden by the facade of the large, overdecorated mansions, wild parties fueled by illegal liquor, flashy big cars, and mistresses is a world of lonely individuals all unable to find a sort peace in the post–World War I world. Rather than a celebration of such decadence, the novel functions as a cautionary tale in which an unhappy fate is inevitable for the poor and striving individual, and the rich are allowed to continue without penalty their careless treatment of others' lives. Narrated from the perspective of Nick Carraway, a veteran of World War I, Yale graduate, and would-be Wall Street bond seller, the novel relates the downfall of a socially ambitious man who rises from an obscure and impoverished Midwestern childhood to become a wealthy and sought-after center of Long Island society. Nick is a second cousin once removed of Daisy Buchanan, whom Gatsby met nearly a decade earlier when he was a young and poor army officer. His love for her, and his desire to become socially and financially acceptable to her, seems to have driven him to obtain wealth and property through unscrupulous means. Rumors about Gatsby and about the source of his wealth abound, and people who attend his lavish parties speculate where his money was made. Later in the novel, readers learn that Gatsby is a bootlegger who has built his wealth upon the illegal production and sale of liquor and associates with shady characters such as Meyer Wolfsheim.

Nick Carraway stands outside the action of the novel for the most part and relates and comments upon the simultaneous activities of the characters. His cousin Daisy Buchanan is bright, attractive, and flighty, careless in her parenting of her three-year-old daughter Pammy and indifferent to the intense obsession that Jay Gatsby has held for her for nearly a decade. He describes Daisy's husband, the arrogant and extremely wealthy Tom Buchanan, in unflattering terms but has little interaction with him, aside from characterizing him as a former athlete now long past his glory days.

For a time Nick becomes romantically involved with Jordan Baker, Daisy's friend and a professional golfer with a tarnished reputation, but the affair begins with the clear knowledge that it will not last long. He expresses his most sympathetic perceptions when relating the character and activities of George Wilson, a mechanic and the owner of the garage located near the homes of the wealthy, and his wife, Myrtle, who is Tom Buchanan's mistress.

The novel portrays the wealthy in an unsympathetic light and exhibits the manner in which they exploit the feelings of others. Tom Buchanan may enjoy Myrtle Wilson physically as his mistress, but his behavior toward her and attitude of superiority show that he views her as only a temporary amusement. Daisy had once before rejected Gatsby when he was a poor army officer and, although she engages in an affair with him while married to Tom, she remains socially aloof and emotionally beyond his reach. Myrtle Wilson exists only to be used by the rich Tom Buchanan, as does her husband. However friendly Tom may appear when he brings his big car into the station for gas or service, he treats George as someone who exists only to serve him. Even James/Jimmy/Jay Gatsby, once a nobody from North Dakota and now in possession of wealth and a huge mansion on Long Island Sound, remains forever inferior to the old wealth represented by the Buchanans. He may have money, but he is not able to elevate his social value nor does he share the elite privileges of the wealthy.

While at the Plaza Hotel in Manhattan, Tom and Daisy quarrel and Daisy leaves, driving Gatsby's car in an effort to relax. The tragedy that occurs is threefold. While racing through the village of West Egg on her way home, Daisy runs down Myrtle with the car, which belongs to Gatsby. The next day, the grief-stricken George Wilson tracks down Gatsby and, believing that he was driving the car that killed Myrtle, he shoots Gatsby and leaves him floating dead in the pool, then commits suicide. Despite all of the people that attended Gatsby's parties, drank his liquor, and ate his food, only three show up at his funeral: Nick, Jay's estranged father, and a man identified only as "Owl eyes," whom Nick once met admiring books in Gatsby's library. After the funeral, disreputable individuals appear at the mansion and take art and other of Gatsby's belongings in payment for debts.

The tragedies do not touch Tom and Daisy Buchanan, and they are left to continue their lives, indifferent to the destruction that they have left behind them. Nick Carroway expresses one of the most revealing sentiments in the book after Tom rationalizes having falsely implicated Gatsby in the death of Myrtle: "They were careless people, Tom and Daisy—they smashed up things and creatures and then retreated back into their money or their vast carelessness, or whatever is was that kept them together and let other people clean up the mess they had made. . . ." The novel ends as Nick has sold his car and packed his possessions, ready to return to the Midwest, because after Gatsby's death, "the East was haunted for me like that, distorted beyond my eyes' power of correction. So when the blue smoke of brittle leaves was in the air and the wind blew the wet laundry stiff on the line I decided to come back home."

CENSORSHIP HISTORY

The Great Gatsby excited controversy even before the book was published for its daring expose of the wild decadence of the wealthy. In 1923, as Fitzgerald edited and revised the proofs, he explored serialization of the book in various magazines. The 1923 option contract had provided Hearst magazines with the right of first refusal for the serial rights, and the author's expectations of earning from $15,000 to $20,000 were destroyed when editor Ray Long declined the novel. In *Some Sort of Epic Grandeur, The Life of F. Scott Fitzgerald,* Matthew J. Bruccoli relates, "Inoffensive as the material now seems, it was regarded as too strong for magazines whose readership was largely female." Fitzgerald's literary agent Harold Ober attempted to sell the rights to editor John Wheeler for *Liberty* magazine, a weekly magazine. Wheeler also turned down the offer and told Ober, "It is too ripe for us. Running only one serial as we do, we could not publish this story with as many mistresses and as much adultery as there is in it."

In more recent decades, as *The Great Gatsby* has become a perennial selection on high school and college reading lists, challenges have emerged in various areas of the United States, although many receive little publicity because they remain unreported to the American Library Association. Every Web site dedicated to celebrating the freedom to read identifies the novel as having been "challenged at the Baptist College in Charleston, SC (1987) because of 'language and sexual references in the book,'" but the details of the challenge as well as all actual news accounts are not available.

In the same year, however, the Bay County School Board, in Panama City, Florida, and superintendent of schools Leonard Hall created a censorship controversy when they announced a "three-tier book classification system" to evaluate and to eliminate books on the current high school reading list. Superintendent Hall, who claimed that he was "elected to restore Christian values to the schools," developed the categories. The first category consisted of works that contained "no vulgarity or explicit sex," and the second category or tier contains books that the board and superintendent assessed as containing "a sprinkling of vulgarity." The third tier, made of books that were removed from classroom discussion, were those the school officials characterized as having "a lot of vulgarity" and the curse "goddamn." Among the works in this third tier were *The Great Gatsby,* FAHRENHEIT 451, *THE RED BADGE OF COURAGE,* and THE OLD MAN AND THE SEA. Students, teachers, and parents brought suit against the school district to challenge the school board policy banning the classroom use of these classics. In May 1987, 44 residents filed a class action lawsuit in federal district court in Pensacola, Florida, in which they contended that their constitutional rights had been violated by the book policy instituted by the Bay County School Board and superintendent Hall. A day after residents filed the lawsuit, the school board and superintendent retracted their earlier actions, a move influenced both by the lawsuit and by the lengthy school board meeting attended by hundreds of area residents, which was also broadcast on local radio and television stations. Students arrived at the school board meeting wearing black armbands and asking to be allowed to speak. A member of the Bay County School Board, Deane Bozeman told reporters that the censorship attempt actually had an effect opposite from what had been intended: "The only thing we succeeded in doing is making sure every child in Bay County reads the books we banned." After meeting for eight hours and listening to hundreds of residents speak, the board moved to change its policy and to approve all books that were currently being used in the county of 110,000 people.

In 2008, the Coeur d'Alene, Idaho, school board developed an approval system to assess and remove books from the school reading lists after some parents complained that teachers had selected and were discussing books that "contained vulgar, profane language and dealt with subjects inappropriate for students." The books were removed from classrooms before the school year began and teachers were instructed to refrain from making reference to the novels until the appropriate approval process had been completed. The school district created a committee of parents, educators, district officials, and community members to review the 26 books that had raised objections. Included on the list were BRAVE NEW WORLD, ALICE'S ADVENTURES IN WONDERLAND, *THE GRAPES OF WRATH*, *THE SCARLET LETTER*, *1984*, THE CATCHER IN THE RYE, and *The Great Gatsby*. Nearly 100 people attended the December 15, 2008, meeting. The board listened to public comments for more than an hour, then voted unanimously to return the books to lists of novels from which teachers can select for required assignments for students in sixth through 12th grades.

FURTHER READING

Bruccoli, Matthew J. *Some Sort of Epic Grandeur: The Life of F. Scott Fitzgerald*. New York: Harcourt Brace Jovanovich, 1981.

"Florida Officials Yield on Book Ban." *New York Times*, May 15, 1987, p. D18.

"Idaho City's School Board Drops Book Ban." Associated Press. Available online. URL: http://www.firstamendmentcenter.org/news.aspx?id21029. Accessed January 12, 2010.

LeVot, Andre. *F. Scott Fitzgerald: A Biography*. New York: Doubleday & Company, 1983.

Rimer, Sara. "Gatsby's Green Light Beckons a New Generation of Strivers." *New York Times*, February 17, 2008, p. A1.

"Suit Challenges School Book Ban." *New York Times*, May 14, 1987, p. A18.

Yardley, Jonathan. "'Gatsby': The Greatest of Them All." *Washington Post*, January 2, 2007, p. C1.

GRENDEL

Author: John Gardner
Original date and place of publication: 1971, United States
Original publisher: Alfred A. Knopf
Literary form: Novel

SUMMARY

Grendel is a novel derived from the classic Anglo-Saxon epic *Beowulf,* in which the monster Grendel is presented as the embodiment of evil, whose vicious attacks serve to test the hero, Beowulf. Gardner modifies the epic to tell the story from Grendel's point of view, creating a sympathetic creature whose actions in *Beowulf* seem justified when the monster explains them. An unlikely hero, Grendel professes to have a highly idealized view of humankind, but he admits that humankind's actions continually tarnish that image and disappoint him. He exhibits a strong sense of conscience for his rages and ravaging of the Danes and claims that he was blinded by brute rage when he attacked the Danes' mead hall, Heorot, killed the drunken and celebrating men, and destroyed the hall. He also wonders at the human propensity for war and the often petty excuses for it. As he cries out in one instance, " 'Why can't these creatures discover a little dignity?' . . . I make a face, uplift a defiant middle finger, and give an obscene little kick."

Before his final battle, Grendel makes astute observations regarding human affairs, as well as the nature of animals. In viewing a very old ruler, Hrothgar, with the young woman Wealtheow, whose brother had offered her as a sacrifice so that Hrothgar's forces would not attack, Grendel muses that she could have given herself to a man whom she could have loved, a more vigorous man. He relates her unhappiness and her courage in fulfilling the role for which she had been sacrificed. When he warns away a mountain goat that will soon be within his dangerous reach, Grendel watches as the goat continues its mindless and mechanical climb, "because it is the business of goats to climb." Similarly, when he later comes across children playing in the deepening twilight, those who choose to feign deafness when their mothers call them in from play "are gone forever. So it goes."

The end of the novel reflects the ending of the epic, as Beowulf kills Grendel in a bloody, violent battle. The difference is that Grendel maintains that Beowulf wins "by mindless chance. . . . Accident." Skill, right and good are not the basis for Beowulf's victory. He only wins because "Poor Grendel's had an accident."

CENSORSHIP HISTORY

The novel has been challenged, banned, and restricted from use in the classroom because of "obscene" language, as well as the violent and graphic nature of the action. Characters go out to "piss," and the word "shit" is freely used throughout. In contemplating various deaths, the monster ponders roasting first the genital area of one character in front of the multitudes. The physical damage and amount of blood spilled in confrontations are graphically presented.

In 1978, the Frederick County, Maryland, school system declared the novel to be "full of vulgarity" and banned it from use in the classroom. In 1986, after the high school principal objected to the "profane" nature of *Grendel*, the novel became the only work placed on the restricted list at Wasco (California) High School. A "restricted list policy" was developed, and use of the novel was prohibited until every student in the classroom brought in written parental permission. A teacher brought suit against the school district, and a settlement was reached in 1991. Under terms agreed upon, the book could remain in the library and on display in the classroom, but teachers were not permitted to assign reading of the book. Also in 1986, the novel was challenged for use as an assignment in an accelerated English class in the Indianapolis, Indiana, school system.

In 1991, the parent of a student in Viewmont High School in Farmington, Utah, challenged use of the book as a required reading. She complained that her daughter had been asked to read sexist and sexual passages in the book and noted further that it "is obscene and should not be a required reading." The district review committee considered the request and voted to retain the book for use only in the 12th-grade classroom and only in connection with the study of *Beowulf*. The student was given the option of an alternative assignment.

The book was also challenged as part of the English curriculum at Pinelands Regional High School in Bass River Township, New Jersey, in 1992. Parents complained that the book contained "numerous obscenities," but the school board voted to retain the book. The parents then appealed to the mayor, who criticized the book but supported the right for it to remain in the library or for students to buy it, though he added that "it shouldn't be given to children in the school." Complaints about the "violence" and the "graphic nature" of the book were the basis of a 1993 challenge to the placement of the book on the supplemental reading list for advanced English students in Clayton County School District in Jonesboro, Georgia. The book remained on the list.

FURTHER READING

Baldwin, Deborah. "John Gardner: The Serious Optimist." *Common Cause* 15 (September 1989): 34–38.

Fawcett, Barry. "The Twelve Traps in John Gardner's *Grendel*." *American Literature* 62 (December 1990): 634–647.

Gardner, John. *On Moral Fiction*. New York: Basic Books, 1978.

Henderson, Jeff. *Thor's Hammer: Essays on John Gardner*. Conway: University of Central Arkansas Press, 1985.

Howell, John Michael. *Understanding John Gardner.* Columbia: University of South Carolina Press, 1993.

Newsletter on Intellectual Freedom (March 1978): 39; (May 1978): 58; (May 1986): 81–82; (July 1986): 119; (January 1987): 32; (May 1989): 87; (May 1991): 92; (January 1993): 11; (March 1993): 56; (May 1993): 87.

People For the American Way. *Attacks on the Freedom to Learn: 1991–1992 Report.* Washington, D.C.: People For the American Way, 1992.

HEATHER HAS TWO MOMMIES

Author: Leslea Newman
Original date and place of publication: 1989, United States
Original publisher: Alyson Publications
Literary form: Children's book

SUMMARY

Heather Has Two Mommies is the story of a three-year-old girl being raised by a lesbian couple. For her, having two mothers feels perfectly normal, until she becomes part of a play group. Heather listens to the other children and realizes for the first time that many of them have one mother and a father, and she becomes upset. The leader of the play group encourages the children to talk about the different types of families that exist. As the children learn more about families, they realize that many children are growing up in non-traditional families. They also realize that the most important part of any type of family is love.

In the first part of the book, the events leading to Heather's conception through artificial insemination and her birth are dealt with in a matter-of-fact manner. The choices being made by the two "mommies" are discussed, as are their reasons for those choices. The second half of the book focuses on the family structure and shows that Heather's family is similar to those of other children, except for the "two mommies."

CENSORSHIP HISTORY

Heather Has Two Mommies has been challenged repeatedly since it was first published. In 1992, this book and DADDY'S ROOMMATE were removed from the first-grade reading list in the Bay Ridge School District in Brooklyn, New York; challenged but retained in Fayetteville (North Carolina) County Library and Springfield (Oregon) Public Library; and placed in the adult section of the Bladen County Library in Elizabethtown, North Carolina.

In 1993, *Heather Has Two Mommies* and *Daddy's Roommate* were moved from the children's room to the adult section in Mercer County Library System in Lawrence, New Jersey. They were also challenged but retained in the public library in Mesa, Arizona; North Brunswick (New Jersey) Public Library; Cumberland County (North Carolina) Public Library; Wicomico County Free County Library in Salisbury, Maryland; and Dayton and Montgomery County (Ohio) Public Library. In 1994, the two books were taken out of the Lane County Head Start program in Cottage Grove, Oregon, and challenged but retained by Chandler (Arizona) Public Library.

Heather Has Two Mommies was also challenged in 1993 by patrons of Chestatee Regional Library System in Gainesville, Georgia, who believed that the book was "not suitable" to be shelved in the children's section. Librarians moved the book to the young adult section, but three state legislators who became involved in the case wanted it removed. The legislators stated, "We could put together a resolution to amend the Georgia state constitution to say that tax dollars cannot be used to promote homosexuality, pedophilia or sado-masochism." The book remained in the young adult section, and the controversy faded away.

In 1994, parents challenged the inclusion of the book in an Oak Bluffs, Massachusetts, elementary school library. The parent who led the protest spoke out at a public meeting and stated that the subject matter of the book "is obscene and vulgar and the message is that homosexuality is okay." The school board created a review committee to examine the book and voted unanimously to keep the book in the library.

FURTHER READING

Buttenweiser, Susan. "A Child's Garden of . . . Diversity." *Ms.*, January 1993, pp. 61–62.
"Heather's Two Moms, Three Censors." *The Atlanta Journal* and *The Atlanta Constitution*, July 27, 1993, p. H4.
Hildebrand, Joan M. "Books for Children: *Heather Has Two Mommies*." *Childhood Education* 70 (1994), p. 305.

A HERO AIN'T NOTHIN' BUT A SANDWICH

Author: Alice Childress
Original date and place of publication: 1973, United States
Original publisher: Coward, McCann & Geoghegan
Literary form: Novel

SUMMARY

A Hero Ain't Nothin' but a Sandwich is a young adult novel made up of 23 short chapters, each told from a different character's point of view. The number of chapters related by each character provides an indication of the importance of the character to the novel. Thirteen-year-old Benjie Johnson relates seven chapters, his stepfather, Butler Craig, relates four, and other characters relate only one or two of the remaining chapters.

The story focuses on Benjie, whose drug habit worries his family, his close friend Jimmy, and two teachers who care very much for him, but Benjie contends that the others are worrying needlessly for he has no habit. He misses his former closeness with his mother and blames Butler Craig for moving in with them and taking his mother's affections. Bored at home and at school, he begins to distrust everyone around him, including a black teacher named Nigeria Greene who joins another teacher in convincing the principal to sign necessary papers to hospitalize Benjie in a detoxification facility. After the treatment period ends and Benjie returns home, he decides to try drugs one more time, because he wants to remember what he is giving up forever. He steals Butler's best suit and overcoat; then he is caught stealing a toaster from a neighboring apartment. As Butler chases him to their building rooftop, Benjie slips and nearly dives over the edge to his death, but Butler catches him with one hand. Benjie yells out, "Let me die," but Butler holds on and saves him. This leads them to a new level of trust, and Benjie even calls Butler Dad. Butler's action has made him a hero, as has his tenaciousness in regularly meeting the responsibilities that are thrust upon him, despite the difficulties that must be overcome.

At the end of the novel, Butler, his arm in a sling, waits outside the drug rehabilitation center where Benjie has promised to continue treatment. He insists that Benjie is just late, because he has been looking in store windows or otherwise dawdling, and believes that the boy will appear.

CENSORSHIP HISTORY

A Hero Ain't Nothin' but a Sandwich depicts urban ghetto life and people who are fragmented and alienated because of race and class barriers. The language in the novel is a variety of Black English that violates the rules of standard grammar and pronunciation. Drugs pervade the work, and street terms are used with profanity throughout the novel. The setting is ugly, as is the devastation created by drugs, and the language is consistent with this devastation. The novel has been challenged for being "objectionable" and for containing "street language" and "abusive language," as well as because of the sexual descriptions.

The novel was one of 11 books banned by the school board in Island Trees Free School District No. 26 in New York (see THE BEST SHORT STORIES BY NEGRO WRITERS) in 1982. It was charged with being "immoral" and "just plain filthy," and the following passage is specified in the court record as representative of passages determined to be "objectionable": "Hell, no! Fuck the society. They can have back the spread and curtains, I'm too old for them fuckin' bunnies anyway." The novel was returned to the library after the U.S. Supreme Court ruled in *Board of Education, Island Trees Union Free School*

District No. 26 et al. v. Pico et al., 457 U.S. 853 (1982) that the First Amendment rights of students had been violated in the banning.

In 1978, school officials removed the novel from the high school libraries in San Antonio, Texas, after complaints from parents that the novel contained "objectionable" passages. Teachers filed a grievance to protest the banning, and the book was reinstated. That same year, the school board in Savannah, Georgia, ordered that all copies of the novel be removed from all school libraries in the district because of "objectionable language." Calling the book "garbage," the president of the school board stated, "We don't need people going around and calling other people 'jive-asses' and 'Fuck the society'."

Language was also the reason that parents of students attending Lamar Elementary School in Darlington, South Carolina, demanded that the book be removed from the school library in 1994. Citing examples from the book, parents stated in their complaint that "offensive language in the book makes it unsuitable for any children." That same year, the novel was challenged in Aberdeen High School in Bel Air, Maryland, for being "racist and vulgar."

FURTHER READING

Gebhard, Ann O. "The Emerging Self: Young Adult and Classic Novels of the Black Experience." *English Journal* 82 (September 1993): 50–54.

Kirk, Ersye. *The Black Experience in Books for Children and Young Adults.* Ardmore, Okla.: Positive Impact, 1993.

Newsletter on Intellectual Freedom (July 1978): 87; (September 1978): 123; (November 1982): 197; (May 1994): 85; (January 1995): 12.

Sullivan, Charles, ed. *Children of Promise: African-American Literature and Art for Young People.* New York: Harry N. Abrams, 1991.

HOWL AND OTHER POEMS

Author: Allen Ginsberg
Original date and place of publication: 1956, United States
Original publisher: City Lights Books
Literary form: Poetry collection

SUMMARY

Howl and Other Poems contains 11 poems that explore what poet William Carlos Williams called "a howl of defeat." Dedicated to fellow Beat writers Jack Kerouac, William Seward Burroughs, and Neal Cassady, of whose works Ginsberg claims "all these books are published in Heaven," the work contains the poet's passionate expressions on numerous taboos of the time.

The title poem opens with the following lines: "I saw the best minds of my generation destroyed by madness, starving hysterical naked, / dragging themselves through the negro streets at dawn looking for an angry fix." He continues to speak of similarly unsavory topics, including "angelheaded hipsters . . . holloweyed and high sat up smoking in the supernatural darkness of cold-water flats . . . staggering on tenement roofs illuminated . . . publishing obscene odes on the windows of the skull." The veiled, symbolic references in these lines kept the poems relatively safe from prosecution, but his distinct references to homosexuality and to anal and oral sex in such lines as "Who let themselves be fucked in the ass by saintly motorcyclists, / and screamed with joy, / who blew and were blown by those human seraphim, the sailors" have been more easily singled out by censors as obscene. References to drug use abound in the poems, as do Ginsberg's private sexual fantasies and excretory images.

Although the title poem has been most heavily criticized for its obscene imagery and language, other poems in the collection celebrate Ginsberg's loss of virginity ("Transcription of Organ Music"), his disillusionment with America and the declaration that "I smoke marijuana every chance I get," ("America") and reference to the "fairy Sam" ("In the Baggage Room at Greyhound"). Taken in total, *Howl and Other Poems* explores the horrors of the poet's life and, as William Carlos Williams states in the final lines of his introduction to the collection, "Hold back the edges of your gowns, Ladies, we are going through hell."

CENSORSHIP HISTORY

Howl and Other Poems was first printed in England by Villiers and passed through Customs without incident to be published by City Lights Bookstore in fall 1956. On March 5, 1957, a second printing was seized in San Francisco by U.S. Customs officials, who confiscated 520 copies with the excuse that "the words and the sense of the writing is obscene . . . . You wouldn't want your children to come across it." Lawrence Ferlinghetti, owner of the City Lights Bookstore, had the forethought to contact the American Civil Liberties Union (ACLU) before sending the work to England to be printed and had received assurance that the ACLU would defend him if the book were challenged. Thus, when the local U.S. attorney's office requested permission from a federal judge to destroy the book, the ACLU notified the collector of Customs and the U.S. attorney that it would defend the book. The U.S. attorney decided to drop proceedings.

Despite clearance from U.S. Customs, copies of the book were later seized by the San Francisco police, who claimed that the material was not suitable for children, even though the City Lights Bookstore did not carry books for children. Ferlinghetti was booked and fingerprinted in the San Francisco Hall of Justice, after being arrested by two juvenile-squad police officers.

The case went to trial and nine literary experts were called to defend the "social importance" of Ginsberg's poem: Mark Schorer, Leo Lowenthal, Walter Van Tilburg Clark, Herbert Blau, Arthur Foff, Mark Linenthal, Kenneth Rexroth, Vincent McHugh, and Luther Nichols. The experts identified the work as "social criticism . . . a literary work that hurled *ideological* accusation after accusation against American society." Prosecuting attorney Ralph McIntosh repeatedly attempted to coerce the witnesses into translating the poetry into prose, reading aloud passages from *Howl* that contained what he classified as "dirty" words and sexual images. He also baited the experts by asking if the terms that he deemed to be obscene could have been worded differently by Ginsberg, but presiding Judge Horn stopped him, saying "'it is obvious that the author could have used another term'" but that it was "'up to the author'" to decide.

In handing down his decision on *Howl and Other Poems*, the judge cited the decision of Justice William J. Brennan only four months earlier in *Roth v. the United States*, 354 U.S. 476 (1957), stating that "unless the book is entirely lacking in 'social importance' it cannot be held 'obscene.'" He added further that, while the poem contained "unorthodox and controversial ideas" that were expressed at times through "coarse and vulgar" words, including *cock, fuck, ass, cunt, gyzym,* and *asshole,* the work was protected by the constitutional freedoms of speech and press. Horn stated, "An author should be real in treating his subject and be allowed to express his thoughts and ideas in his own words."

Although Judge Horn's decision freed *Howl and Other Poems* in 1957, the poem has remained controversial. In 1988, the listener-supported Pacifica Radio Network did not carry a broadcast of the poem that was set to be read on radio stations nationwide on the evening of January 6, 1988, as part of a weeklong series about censorship called "Open Ears/Open Minds." The network made the decision after being threatened with possible obscenity prosecution by the Justice Department a few months before for broadcasting a play about homosexuality. The decision was also made based on an April 1987 ruling by the Federal Communications Commission stating that stations faced possible penalties for broadcasting "material that depicts or describes, in terms patently offensive as measured by contemporary community standards for the broadcast medium, sexual or excretory activities or organs." In response to Pacifica's decision, the author said, "The Government now has set out rules which have had an intimidating and chilling effect on broadcasters. . . . it's the last desperate gasp of the Reagan neo-conservatives."

FURTHER READING

D'Emilio, John, and Estelle B. Freedman. *Intimate Matters: A History of Sexuality in America.* New York: Harper & Row, 1988.

Robins, Natalie. *Alien Ink: The FBI's War on Freedom of Expression.* New York: William Morrow, 1992.

Yarrow, Andrew L. "Allen Ginsberg's 'Howl' in a New Controversy." *New York Times,* January 6, 1988, p. C2.

I KNOW WHY THE CAGED BIRD SINGS

Author: Maya Angelou (Marguerite Johnson)
Original date and place of publication: 1969, United States
Original publisher: Random House
Literary form: Autobiography

SUMMARY

I Know Why the Caged Bird Sings is the first of five autobiographical books written by the author. The others are *Gather Together in My Name* (1974), *Singin' and Swingin' and Gettin' Merry Like Christmas* (1976), *The Heart of a Woman* (1981), and *All God's Children Need Traveling Shoes* (1986). The first book chronicles Angelou's life from age three to age 16 and the birth of her only child, Guy, to whom she dedicates this book.

The book describes the divorce of her parents and her own difficulties as she is sent with her brother from Long Beach, California, to live with her grandmother and uncle in Stamps, Arkansas, spends a year in St. Louis with her mother, then returns to Stamps and eventually moves to California to be with her mother. The years in Stamps are largely happy years as her grandmother, "Momma," protects and shields the young girl. There are, however, some social realities from which she cannot be protected. The book recalls the despair often felt by the black cotton pickers as they filed into Momma's general store, returning from the fields on bad days. The rampant racism is evident in incidents such as the one in which her uncle must be hidden after a former sheriff warns the family that "Some of the boys'll be coming over here later" because Willie had "messed with a white lady today." When Maya is in need of a dentist, she overhears her grandmother being told by a white dentist to whom she had lent money during the Depression, "my policy is I'd rather stick my hand in a dog's mouth than in a nigger's."

Maya also suffers personal indignities as a child. When she moves to St. Louis to live with her mother, she is raped by her mother's live-in lover, who is later murdered. When she travels to Los Angeles to spend a summer with her father, the woman with whom he lives stabs Maya with a knife. Maya is nearly six feet tall, flat-chested, and unsure of sexuality at 15 when she decides to have sex with a handsome neighborhood boy. He forgets her name the next day, but she becomes pregnant and later gives birth to her only child, her son. The autobiography ends with 16-year-old Maya holding her child protectively and going peacefully to sleep.

CENSORSHIP HISTORY

The majority of the challenges to *I Know Why the Caged Bird Sings* have resulted from parents' complaints about the rape scene and Maya's pregnancy out of wedlock. In 1983, the Alabama State Textbook Committee rejected the book because they believed that it "preaches bitterness and hatred against whites." The book was challenged at Mount Abram Regional High School in Strong, Maine, in 1988, because parents objected to the rape scene. In 1990, a parent in Bremerton, Washington, objected to the book as a required reading for the gifted ninth-grade class because of the "graphic" description of the molestation. The parent also complained that the book "raised sexual issues without giving them a moral resolution." Despite the teacher's defense that the molestation passages were only a small part of the book and that the main focus was the fulfillment that Angelou reached in spite of adversity, the school board removed the book from the classroom. The board president justified the action by explaining that his constituents expected him to uphold a higher level of moral standard than is evidenced by the book.

In 1991, several parents in Benning, California, complained about the explicit passages involving child molestation and requested that the book be removed from the eighth-grade curriculum. One parent complained that her son did not want to go back to class to read that "gross" book, and another characterized the work as "morally and religiously offensive smut." The book was removed from the curriculum. In 1992, the work was retained after the parent of a student in Amador Valley High School, in Pleasanton, California, complained of the sexually explicit language.

The work was challenged but retained in several 1993 incidents, all of which objected to the passage in which the rape of the seven-year-old Maya is discussed. The book was temporarily banned from Caledonia Middle School, in Columbus, Mississippi, on the grounds that it was too sexually explicit. In Haines City, Florida, parents objected to the same passage and challenged inclusion of the book in both the English curriculum and the high school library. The same challenge occurred in Hooks (Texas) High School, where the book was assigned in a freshman honors history class.

In 1994, the work was challenged but retained as required reading for Dowling High School sophomores in Des Moines, Iowa, and the book became an issue at Ponderosa High School in Castle Rock, Colorado, when parents charged that it was "a lurid tale of sexual perversion." In their 1994 challenge to the book, parents at Westwood High School in Austin, Texas, claimed that the book was "pornographic, contains profanity, and encourages premarital sex and homosexuality." The challenge motivated a new policy at the school for the reading of potentially controversial literature. The superintendent decreed that children would have to obtain their parents' permission in writing before they would be taught controversial literature.

In 2002, parents of students in freshman English classes in Hamilton, Montana, took issue with the references to rape and premarital sexual intercourse in the book, as well as the author's description of her molestation as an eight-year-old child. The parents also criticized the book for its suggestions of homosexuality. The same year, a group named the Parents Against Bad Books in Schools (PABBIS), represented by parents Richard and Alice Ess, complained to the school officials in Fairfax County, Virginia, that this book, along with 17 others, should be removed from elementary and secondary school libraries. They asserted that the book "contains profanity and descriptions of drug abuse, sexually explicit conduct, and torture."

FURTHER READING

Elliot, Jeffrey, ed. *Conversations with Maya Angelou*. Jackson: University of Mississippi Press, 1989.

Fox-Genovese, Elizabeth. "Myth and History: Discourse of Origins in Zora Neale Hurston and Maya Angelou." *Black American Literature Forum* 42 (Summer 1990): 221–235.

Newsletter on Intellectual Freedom (March 1983): 39; (January 1989): 8; (March 1989): 38; (November 1990): 211; (March 1992): 42; (July 1992): 109; (July 1993): 107; (January 1994): 34; (July 1994): 130; (January 1995): 11; (May 1995): 56; (November 2002): 258; (January 2003): 10.

Pettit, Jayne. *Maya Angelou: Journey of the Heart*. New York: Lodestar Books, 1996.

Shuker, Nancy. *Maya Angelou*. Englewood Cliffs, N.J.: Silver Burdett Press, 1990.

IN THE NIGHT KITCHEN

Author: Maurice Sendak
Original date and place of publication: 1970, United States
Original publisher: Harper & Row
Literary form: Children's picture book

SUMMARY

In the Night Kitchen, a winner of the Caldecott Medal, is a dream fantasy in which a child named Mickey awakens in bed and believes that he hears talking downstairs in the kitchen. He leaps out of bed and falls through the night darkness, and out of his clothes, into the night kitchen, which is brightly lighted. Three plump bakers dump him into cake batter; but he emerges, then jumps into the bread dough. Mickey then kneads and shapes the bread dough into an airplane in which he flies to the Milky Way to obtain milk for the bakers. He provides the bakers with milk, then stands proudly, still nude, while he crows, "Cock-a-doodle-doo!" He then slides straight into his bed and into his clothes and goes to sleep.

CENSORSHIP HISTORY

The book was removed from many public and school libraries that had bought it because parents complained that showing a fully naked child with some semblance of the genitals sketched in the appropriate place was "pornography." In many other libraries where the book had been purchased, the offending organ was either carefully whited out or equipped with a diaper or a pair of shorts drawn on with marker.

In 1974, a mother in Camden, New York, complained to school authorities that the book should be removed from elementary school libraries because it contained nudity and "children are already exposed to enough profanity in the media." The school superintendent reviewed the book and determined that it did not have "sufficient merit" to keep in the libraries. In announcing his decision to remove the book, the superintendent stated that schools had "a real obligation to represent what is moral, what is honest, what is decent."

In 1977, the book was removed from the elementary school library in Northridge, Illinois, because of parent complaints that it contained "nudity for no purpose." That same year, copies of the book sent to 40 kindergarten classes were expurgated in Springfield, Missouri, by Wanda Gray, the director of elementary education, who drew shorts on the nude boy with a black felt pen. No one had complained, but the director said that she thought "it should be covered."

In 1985, parents of students attending Cunningham Elementary School in Beloit, Wisconsin, challenged the book as part of the school library collection, claiming that it "desensitizes children to nudity." One of the parents who issued the challenge insisted on parents' right to dictate book selection and stated, "You don't have to have a degree to know that teaching low morals and disrespect is wrong." The school board voted to retain the book in the library. In 1988, the book was challenged but retained after parents of students at Robeson Elementary School in Champaign, Illinois, complained that the book contained "gratuitous" nudity.

In 1990, parents of students in the Morrisonville, New York, elementary school requested that the book be removed from the school library because "it promotes nudity and child abuse." The school board appointed a review committee to consider the request and later accepted the recommendation of the review committee to retain the book in the elementary school library collection.

In 1991, a parent in Jacksonville, Florida, asked that the book be removed from the elementary school classroom because it contained "illustrations of a boy without his clothes." The parent appeared before the school board, calling the nudity "disgraceful and appalling." A review committee appointed by the school board voted to retain the book without restriction, and the board concurred.

That same year, parents in Cornish, Maine, requested that the school board remove the book from the elementary school library because the illustrations of a naked boy "encourage child molestation." In their official complaint, the parents stated that the book would cause the following harm: "Child abuse. Children are taught that their private parts are private. This book is contrary to this teaching." A review committee appointed by the school board voted to retain the book, calling it "a masterpiece example of the timeless theme of childhood fantasy."

In 1992, parents of students attending the Elk River, Minnesota, schools challenged the use of the book in the classroom because the nudity found within it "could lay the foundation for future use of pornography." The school board failed to agree and retained the book. In El Paso, Texas, in 1994, parents challenged the inclusion of the book in the children's section because "the little boy pictured did not have any clothes on and it pictured his private area." The challenge was considered by the library board, but the book was retained.

FURTHER READING

Cech, John. *Angels and Wild Things*. University Park: Pennsylvania State University Press, 1993.

Huck, Charlotte S., Susan Hepler, and Janet Hickman. *Children's Literature in Elementary School*. New York: Holt, Rinehart & Winston, 1987.

Newsletter on Intellectual Freedom (May 1977): 71; (September 1977): 134; (July 1985): 134; (March 1989): 43; (November 1989): 217; (March 1993): 41; (September 1994): 148.

People For the American Way. *Attacks on the Freedom to Learn, 1991–1992 Report*. Washington, D.C.: People For the American Way, 1992.

Sutherland, Zena, and May Hill Arbuthnot. *Children's Books*. New York: HarperCollins Publishers, 1991.

INVISIBLE MAN

Author: Ralph Ellison
Original date and place of publication: 1952, United States
Original publisher: Random House
Literary form: Novel

SUMMARY

Invisible Man is related by an unnamed narrator who reveals that he is an African-American man who is invisible because of an impersonal and indifferent world. While portions of the narration are realistic, a surreal quality pervades much of the novel as events occur chaotically and in rapid succession. The narrator lives in an underground cellar; after introducing his current situation, he explains his experiences moving from the South to the North that led to his present state.

"Battle Royal," the first chapter, tells of the narrator's experience when he is invited by the town's leading white citizens to give his high school graduation speech at a local hotel. He is made part of a "battle royal" with other blindfolded African-American students, who fight each other as entertainment for the white businessmen. Their reward is the money that they obtain by crawling on an electrified carpet to pick up coins. A well-endowed, blonde-haired stripper with an American flag tattooed between her thighs appears, but she is only for the whites to ogle. During the evening, the narrator makes his speech and receives as his reward a leather briefcase and a scholarship to a state college for blacks.

At college, the narrator is a good student who is entrusted with driving white visitors around campus. In his junior year, he drives a trustee named Mr. Norton out into the country, accidentally meeting the "fieldnigger" family, the Truebloods, who relate their family incest scandal. Norton becomes nauseous and unsteady on his feet because the story reawakens his own desires for his recently deceased daughter. Unsure of where they might find medical help, the narrator decides that a drink of strong liquor might revive Norton, so they stop at a nearby bar and brothel. A brawl breaks out, during which Norton passes out and must be carried upstairs into the prostitutes' quarters, where he is revived.

After the narrator returns the trustee to the college, he is expelled. Dr. Bedsoe, the college president, gives him what appear to be letters of recommendation to potential employers in New York, but the letters are actually warnings not to trust the narrator or to help him. He takes a job at the Liberty Paint Company, then is knocked out in an explosion when he fails to follow instructions. After a period of hospitalization, he walks back to Harlem and inadvertently becomes part of a protest against the eviction of an old black couple. This brings him to the attention of The Brotherhood, who ask him to be their speaker in Harlem and to organize black residents. He also becomes the object of the lust of a married white woman who views him as a sexual "stud" and insists on being "taken" by him.

In rapid succession, the narrator is held responsible for the disappearance of another activist, tried by The Brotherhood for conspiracy, and mistaken for Bliss Proteus Rinehart, a numbers runner, prolific lover, clergyman, and politician. Harlem erupts into violence and, as he strives to head for the safety of his home, he runs into a pillaging crowd that pushes him to the ground and into a coal cellar, where he decides to stay in order to understand what has happened in his life. At the end of the novel, the narrator has burned all of the false promises of his past, including his high school diploma, the recommendation letters, and the slip of paper with his Brotherhood name. He has made himself visible by lighting his cellar with 1,369 lightbulbs that run illegally on electricity from the "Monopolated Light & Power" company. The "Epilogue" explains that the narrator's story has also been that of the African-American community and ends by asking: "Who knows but that, on the lower frequencies, I speak for you?"

CENSORSHIP HISTORY

The novel was well received when it was first published in 1952. Ellison won the National Book Award in 1953, the same year that he won the Russwurm Award and the National Newspaper Publishers' Award. Critics viewed it as signaling a black literary renaissance by its decided difference from the earlier "Negro protest fiction" of Richard Wright, Ann Petry, and Chester Himes. Protests against its content did not occur until the work entered the school curriculum. In a 1973 national sample of English department chairpersons, Lee Burress reported that a parent and a student in an unnamed midwestern city had objected to the assignment of the novel as a required reading for a high school English class. The challenge was based upon three aspects of the novel: 1) the fight staged by the black youths for the white businessmen, 2) the story of the black sharecropper raping his daughter and 3) the "vulgarity" of language. The school board retained the book but offered students the right to substitute another book for their assignment.

In 1975, several parents of students in the Butler, Pennsylvania, school district raised objections to *Contemporary American Short Stories*, the reading anthology being used in a high school English class, because it contained the selection "The Battle Royal," the first chapter of *Invisible Man*. They protested against the "vulgar language" of several sentences in the work and requested that the entire anthology be banned from use. The school board complied with their request and removed the anthology from the classroom.

In 1994, two parents challenged this novel, as well as Carlos Fuentes's *The Death of Artemio Cruz*, Nadine Gordimer's *July's People*, and Richard Wright's *Native Son*, as required readings for advanced English classes in the Yakima, Washington, high school. They charged that the books contained "profanity," "images of violence," and "unacceptable" sexuality and requested that the books be removed from the required reading list. A school review committee was convened and voted to retain the books, a move with which the school board concurred.

FURTHER READING

Burress, Lee. *Battle of the Books: Literary Censorship in the Public Schools, 1950–1985.* Metuchen, N.J.: Scarecrow Press, 1989.

Kostelanetz, Richard. *Politics in the African-American Novel: James Weldon Johnson, W.E.B. DuBois, Richard Wright, and Ralph Ellison.* New York: Greenwood Press, 1991.

Lisack, Thomas. "Books Worth Teaching Even Though They Have Proven Controversial: *Invisible Man* by Ralph Ellison." *English Journal* 82 (April 1993): 88.

Newsletter on Intellectual Freedom (July 1975): 105; (November 1994): 202–203.

Overmyer, Janet. "The Invisible Man and White Women." *Notes on Contemporary Literature* 6 (May 1976): 13–15.

JAKE AND HONEYBUNCH GO TO HEAVEN

Author: Margot Zemach
Original date and place of publication: 1982, United States
Original publisher: Farrar, Straus & Giroux
Literary form: Children's picture book

SUMMARY

Jake and Honeybunch Go to Heaven is a 34-page children's picture book that contains bright, pastel, impressionist-style illustrations of a Depression-era African-American man and his "crazy mule," Honeybunch, and their experiences in Heaven, after a collision with a locomotive.

Jake is one of many poor people in the United States made even poorer by the economic depression of the 1930s. He lives in a dilapidated old house near a town named Hard Times. His only companion is Honeybunch, who some people believe he acquired from a witch. "Other folks said the Devil put a curse on Honeybunch when she ran under a clothesline between Christmas and New Year's." Whatever her origins, Honeybunch does her best to be unmanageable. Illustrations show her deliberately leaping onto the hood of a new car and upsetting her cart so that Jake topples into it. Folks often hear Jake mutter, "This misbegotten mule will be the death of me someday!"

His prediction is fulfilled one summer evening when Jake and Honeybunch are crossing the railroad tracks as a slow-moving train is heading toward them. Although he tries his best to make Honeybunch move forward, she refuses to leave the tracks, and they are struck by the train. The impact sends Jake and Honeybunch flying through the sky. For 15 minutes, Jake shoots upward until he reaches "the top of the sky," and he takes "another ten minutes to flip-flop his way along the Glory Road," which takes him in sight of the Pearly Gates. Illustrations of the Pearly Gates depict African-American men and women dressed in their Sunday best and wearing wings, with some clapping in heavenly rapture.

Standing outside the gates, Jake shouts "Hallelujah" and announces "Here's old Jake come from Hard Times, just been hit by the slow freight." He rings the bell repeatedly, "but God's angels were singing and making a powerful sound," and he concludes, "Maybe St. Peter can't hear me." Undaunted, Jake shakes the gates a bit, and they open slightly, so he squeezes through the opening and walks into Heaven.

The Heaven he encounters is filled with African-American angels, young and old, all wearing golden wings. Some are singing and dancing, others are playing in a jazz band, while others are lounging in the grass. In additional illustrations, groups of angels are seen cooking massive amounts of chicken, what appear to be pork spareribs, and pots of sauce. Jake sees wings hanging to dry on a clothesline and takes two of the shiniest. "As it happened, they were left wings, but they felt just fine." He begins to fly in erratic movements over the other angels, who shout for him to be careful and to stop, but Jake tells them, "I can't stop now. I'm just a flying fool." His wild flight, which upsets picnic tables where angels have been eating fried chicken, ribs, pies, and cakes, ends with Jake landing "in a Heavenly tree, his wings all bent and broken."

Several of the angels take Jake before God, also African-American, who demands to know why Jake did not wait for St. Peter to let him into Heaven in an orderly fashion. He then tells Jake to leave and warns him not to hang around the top step. Disappointed, Jake is led by St. Peter to the Pearly Gates, which are slammed shut once Jake is outside. As he sits and bemoans his bad luck, he hears the familiar clip-clop sound of Honeybunch and, looking up, sees her "coming along the Glory Road." He tells her to stop, but she ignores him and goes up to the Pearly Gates and bangs on them. When St. Peter opens them slightly, Honeybunch sees the Great Green Pastures of Heaven and charges through the gates, where she rampages all over Heaven. "She was so excited that she rolled in the clouds, kicking and carrying on, scattering angels in every direction."

Angels try repeatedly to capture Honeybunch, but they are unable to, so God tells St. Peter to find Jake, "Tell him to come and catch his crazy mule." Jake runs in and grabs Honeybunch, who continues to charge around until Jake whispers a warning in her ear, telling her that if she continues to create a ruckus, she will never "get a chance to graze in those Green Pastures." The warning works, and Honeybunch immediately calms down.

God and the angels are favorably impressed by Jake's quick action, and they decide to offer him another chance. God tells Jake that he "needs a Moon Regulator to hang the moon out at night and put all the stars in their places." If Jake does well, he will receive a pair of wings. Shouting, "Lord, I'm your man," Jake hurriedly hitches Honeybunch to the Moon Regulator wagon, which is already loaded with stars, and "they set off across Heaven, with Jake rolling the moon along." Jake and Honeybunch faithfully perform their task, and Jake eventually earns a beautiful pair of wings.

The book ends with an illustration of Honeybunch grazing peacefully in a flower-filled pasture, while Jake flies above. Readers are told that if the Moon and stars are not shining some nights, that is because Jake and Honeybunch are taking some time off. "Honeybunch is grazing in those Great Green Pastures and Jake is loop-the-looping all over Heaven, just like a flying fool."

CENSORSHIP HISTORY

Jake and Honeybunch Go to Heaven was written by Margot Zemach, a Caucasian prize-winning author and illustrator of more than 40 children's books
who won the American Library Association's 1974 Caldecott Medal for
most distinguished American picture book for children and who spent eight
months researching black folklore before writing the book. When the book
was first published in 1982, the *New York Times Book Review* praised the
book for its literary merit. In 1987, when the paperback version of the book
appeared, the *Washington Post* complimented Zemach for "her exuberant
watercolors to an hilarious adaptation of black Depression-era folklore"
and called Zemach's Heaven "a lively enough place already, with its cast of
'30s-style angels and other denizens busy barbecuing, playing jazz, and just
shooting the breeze under the stars."

Critics Beryle Banfield and Geraldine Wilson identified and criticized
symbolic representations and distortions in the book, writing, "Significantly
the book misrepresents the unique, culturally distinctive view of spiritual
life held by people of African descent. . . . Zemach has not used one culturally authentic clue about heaven as understood by generations of black
people." Denise Wilms wrote about potential controversy surrounding the
book in the January 1, 1983, issue of *Booklist*, "While the book's art and story
are sound, its depiction of a certain segment of black culture will stir controversy. . . . In addition, its lighthearted view of heaven may be an affront to
some groups who see heaven in a more somber light."

The library systems of Chicago, San Francisco, and Milwaukee alleged,
after surveying librarians employed in the public libraries in their systems,
that the book is "racially offensive" and refused to acquire it. In a letter to
the publisher in November 1982, Elizabeth Huntoon, coordinator of children's services for the Chicago library system, explained that the book had
been submitted to 14 librarians within the system for review. The librarians
had all recommended against acquisition of the book because they believed
that "the depiction of a black heaven would offend many people and that it
reinforced many stereotypes which are not offset by a wealth of children's
literature portraying the black experience." In their letter, the Chicago
public library system did admit that one of their librarians, "a black woman
who works in a predominantly black neighborhood, at first wanted to buy
the book. She took it to her minister, who felt the book was positive and
a good story." The remaining librarians ruled against that decision. The
librarians also wrote a letter to Margot Zemach on November 3, 1982, stating that they rejected the book because it contains racial stereotyping. They
acknowledged that the book jacket for *Jake and Honeybunch Go to Heaven*
claimed that the author "has drawn freely on themes from black American
folklore," but they asserted they could "not determine any such themes
other than a jazz cabaret. The 'celestial fish fry and barbecue,' complete
with copious amounts of ribs and chicken drumsticks, appears to us not so

much as one of the pleasures of heaven, but as a sadly obvious racial stereotype." Instead, they compared the book to the racially biased "*Cabin in the Sky* mentality," from a movie in which African Americans endure their lot on Earth for a promise of joy and plenty in heaven, and concluded that the book "does not strive to present an entirely dignified view of an otherwise rich, black cultural heritage."

The publisher charged that the library system was engaging in censorship, and a company spokesman quoted in the *New York Times* stated, "In this case, librarians are deliberately keeping a widely acclaimed book by a major author-artist off their shelves in the name of morality."

The San Francisco library system also refused to order *Jake and Honeybunch Go to Heaven* for its collections, and representatives refused at first to respond to an inquiry sent by Stephen Roxburgh, editor in chief of Farrar, Straus & Giroux, requesting an explanation. City librarian John C. Frantz wrote to Roger W. Straus, president of Farrar, Straus & Giroux, and accused Roxburgh of attempting to intimidate the library and of "feigning ignorance." In his letter, Frantz wrote, "If he really doesn't know why we are not going to buy 'Jake and Honeybunch,' he is in the wrong line of work and should be selling banjos to minstrel troupes." Straus responded to the accusations and repeated the earlier request for an explanation. Frantz spoke, instead, to a reporter for the *New York Times* and told him that "the book perpetuates overt and covert racism." He stated that children's librarians in the San Francisco library system reviewed the book and "gave it an unfavorable reception," and one staff member specified that it was "offensive and degrading, wholly inappropriate for children whether they be black or white."

In a parting shot to the publisher, Frantz told the reporter, "Flaps over books are very temporary, and 50 years from now this will be only a historical footnote. Meanwhile, there are too many good children's books around to mess with this." In response, Straus said, "Fifty years from now, when Mr. Frantz is only a footnote, this book will still be enjoying a long, fruitful life in most of the libraries of America."

FURTHER READING

Banfield, Beryle, and Geraldine L. Wilson. "The Black Experience through White Eyes—The Same Old Story Again." In *The Black American in Books for Children: Readings in Racism*, edited by Donnarae MacCann and Gloria Woodard, 192–207. Metuchen, N.J.: Scarecrow Press, 1985.

Brandehoff, Susan E. "*Jake and Honeybunch Go to Heaven*: Children's Book Fans Smoldering Debate." *American Libraries* 14 (March 1983): 130–132.

Ciolli, Rita. *APF Reporter* 6, no. 6. Available online. URL: http://www.aliciapatterson. org/APF0606/Ciolli/Ciolli.html. Accessed December 12, 2009.

McDowell, Edwin. "Publishing: When Book Is Ruled out by Library." *New York Times*, January 21, 1983, p. C-28.

"New in Paperback." *Washington Post*, August 16, 1987, p. X-12.

JAMES AND THE GIANT PEACH

Author: Roald Dahl
Original date and place of publication: 1961, United States
Original publisher: Penguin Books
Literary form: Children's novel

SUMMARY

James and the Giant Peach is the story of a four-year-old boy whose happy and secure life changes when his parents go shopping in London and are eaten by "an enormous angry rhinoceros which had escaped from the London Zoo." He must live with his cruel and lazy Aunts Sponge and Spiker, who mistreat him, and he becomes a sad and lonely young boy with no friends. He endures this life for three years, then meets an old man who gives him magic crystals that, if ingested, will make "*marvelous* things" start happening to James, "*fabulous, unbelievable* things—and you will never be miserable again in your life." James runs back to the house but trips and falls. The bag bursts open, and the magic crystals scatter and immediately sink into the ground.

The aunts see him lying on the ground and shout at him, then notice a peach growing to giant size high on their tree. Greedily hoping to make money with the peach, they hire carpenters to build a fence around it and charge people to view the peach. A hungry James climbs into the giant peach and nibbles bits of it as he walks through to the stone. There, he finds large and talkative insects who want to leave the tree and James's horrible aunts, so the centipede with his "pair of jaws as sharp as razors" gnaws at the stem that binds the peach to the tree. The peach rolls, crushes the aunts to death, and carries its passengers to various adventures. They first roll into the sea, where they encounter sharks that thrash around them. James saves them by convincing the silkworm to produce threads by which sea gulls lift them away from danger. In the air, they become victims of the Cloud Men, who pelt the peach with buckets of paint, frying pans, and bottle of hair oil, but they escape.

The peach hovers over New York City, and the centipede bites the strings attaching the peach to the seagulls, so it falls on the Empire State Building. Their appearance first creates pandemonium in the city; then the group is given a ticker tape parade. City workers place the peach on a large truck in the procession, where thousands of children take bites from it.

James and his insect friends decide to stay in America, where "Everyone of them became rich and successful" and where James makes many new friends. The huge peach stone is placed in Central Park and becomes a famous monument as well as James's home, where "hundreds and hundreds of children from far and near" visit the once lonely boy.

CENSORSHIP HISTORY

James and the Giant Peach is only one of several Dahl books that has evoked challenges because of "unsavory activities" or because adult readers believe that the works are "unhealthy for children." Despite challenges in schools, the novel has done well commercially and continues to appear in the children's section of most bookstores and libraries, and it is frequently referred to as a "classic in children's literature."

The novel was challenged in 1991 by the parent of a fourth-grade student in Deep Creek Elementary School in Charlotte Harbor, Florida, who claimed that the book is "not appropriate reading material for young children." When the student took the book home for a reading assignment, the parent, after examining the text, wrote a letter to the local newspaper. Noting that "The whole book is strange if you ask me," the mother urged other parents to complain to the school. The child told her teacher that she was not allowed to read the book, so an alternative assignment was given. The school principal and the director of special projects in the district identified the work as a classic and retained the book.

That same year, the mother of a nine-year-old boy at Pederson Elementary School in Altoona, Wisconsin, demanded that the book he removed from the school library because the word "ass" appears in it. The parent expressed further concern that the book promotes an "unhealthy" lifestyle, because wine, tobacco and snuff appear in it. She requested that the book be removed from the school library to spare other children. The district reconsideration committee reviewed the parent's request and voted unanimously to retain the book, a decision that the school board upheld. In reporting the decision, the school superintendent stated, "According to board policy no parent has the right to exclude material from other students in the district and I think that's a very fair standard."

In 1992, parents of students at Morton Elementary School in Brooksville, Florida, demanded that the book be removed from the school library because it contained "a foul word" and "promotes drugs and whiskey." Two review committees considered the book, and both voted unanimously to retain it, a decision with which the county school board concurred. In reporting the decision, the county school superintendent stated that the book was "merely a fantasy about good triumphing over evil."

FURTHER READING

Hitchens, Christopher. "The Grimmest Tales." *Vanity Fair*, January 1994, pp. 26–30.

Meeks, Christopher. *Roald Dahl: Kids Love His Stories*. Vero Beach, Fla.: Rourke Publishing, 1993.

Newsletter on Intellectual Freedom (July 1991): 108; (March 1992): 65; (January 1993): 27.

Powling, Chris. *Roald Dahl*. London: Evans Bros., 1993.

Treglown, Jeremy. *Roald Dahl: A Biography*. New York: Farrar, Straus & Giroux, 1994.

JAWS

Author: Peter Benchley
Original date and place of publication: 1974, United States
Original publisher: Doubleday & Company
Literary form: Novel

SUMMARY

Jaws relates the story of an ocean resort community terrified by the appearance of a great white shark. The year-round residents of Amity, Long Island, depend upon summer crowds for their living, and the biggest holiday is the Fourth of July. The shark appears shortly before that date, violently chopping a woman in two and leaving pieces of her body at the water's edge. The businessmen seek to cover up the death, placing Police Chief Martin Brody in a moral dilemma. Leaving the beaches open will expose swimmers to danger, but closing the beaches will ruin summer business. As the town leaders forbid Brody to close the beaches, the shark strikes again, killing a six-year-old boy and a 65-year-old man and leading one witness to describe it as "the biggest fuckin' fish I ever saw in my whole life, big as a fuckin' station wagon." Unwilling to risk more lives, Brody closes the beaches, angering property and business owners.

The appearance of the shark initiates a private crisis on shore for Brody. The town calls upon the services of ichthyologist Matt Hooper, whose older brother once dated Brody's wife Ellen. Learning this makes the police chief's insecurities surface. He recalls his wife's early life, as part of the "country club set" that summered at Southampton and Amity, playing tennis and generally remaining idle. He and other year-round residents were largely working class. Hooper's appearance also evokes memories for Ellen, who aches for the old days. She examines her naked body in a mirror, assessing her breasts, belly, hips, and legs to determine if the "goods were good enough." In an effort to "resuscitate" herself, she calls Hooper, 10 years her junior, to meet her for lunch, during which they drink too much and discuss sexual fantasies, penis size, and "threesies." At a motel afterward, their intense sexual encounter, with Hooper's "obvious violent climax" when he "continued to pump madly," disturbs Ellen.

Brody and Hooper go out into the ocean with Quint, a charter boat captain, to kill the shark. The men tempt it to come near to the boat with buckets of chum, and Quint stands ready with a harpoon. Hooper asks to be lowered into the water in a cage so that he can take pictures, but the shark butts the cage repeatedly, separating the bars until the huge jaws reach in to grasp Hooper and devour him. When Brody and Quint go out the next day, the shark chases the boat, leading Quint to refer to it repeatedly as a "cocksucker," "an uppity fuck," and a "prick" as he thrusts harpoons into the shark's underbelly. The men believe that the shark is dead, but it rears up in the water, landing its jaw on the deck as the boat sinks. Quint is pulled into the water, leaving only Brody to survive as the shark finally dies.

CENSORSHIP HISTORY

The novel has been removed from school classrooms and school libraries for complaints ranging from "objectionable" language to explicit sex. In 1977, a parent with the support of a minister in Montgomery, Alabama, challenged the book for containing explicit details about sex and requested the book be removed from the recommended reading list. The school board granted the request. The following year in Gardner-Edgerton-Antioch School District in Gardner, Kansas, several parents of students complained that the book contained an "explicit sex act" and requested its removal from the school library. The school board voted unanimously to take the book out of circulation, and all copies of *Jaws* were removed from all of the school libraries in the district. In 1979, parents challenged the availability of the book in the Ogden (Utah) High School library. The school board voted to place the book in a "restricted circulation" category, requiring students to have written parental permission to take the book out.

In 1980, parents of elementary and middle school students in Clinton, North Carolina, challenged the book for its "objectionable language" and asked for its removal from the school libraries. The school board voted to remove all copies of the book from the elementary and middle school libraries. In 1986, "obscene language" was the basis for a challenge by parents of students in the Gwinnett County, Georgia, public schools. The book was removed from the recommended reading list.

FURTHER READING

Newsletter on Intellectual Freedom (May 1978): 56; (May 1979): 49; (September 1980): 99; (March 1987): 65.

JUNKY (ORIGINALLY, JUNKY: CONFESSIONS OF AN UNREDEEMED DRUG ADDICT)

Author: William S. Burroughs
Original date and place of publication: 1953, United States
Original publisher: Ace Books
Literary form: Novel

SUMMARY

Junky is a graphic rendering of heroin addiction that chronicles the addict's life in full detail. Contained within are the hallucinations, the ghostly nocturnal wanderings, the strange and changing sexuality, and the continuous hunger for the needle. The "hero" of the novel, a barely disguised persona of the author, is a young midwesterner whose quest for the continuous high takes him to New York City, New Orleans, and Mexico City, as he experiences on his journey any substance that promises an escape. In often graphic, sometimes surreal, detail, the book identifies and discusses frankly the use and the effects of heroin, marijuana ("tea" or "weed"), "goof balls," "bennies," morphine, codeine, and peyote. The author also expresses his "junk equation": "Junk is not, like alcohol or weed, a means to increased enjoyment of life. Junk is not a kick. It is a way of life."

Burroughs also writes of the unscrupulous doctors who give numerous prescriptions ("scripts") for narcotics to addicts and of his efforts to have these prescriptions filled as he travels from one pharmacy to another. Along the way, he reveals the drug laws of the 1930s, providing details about the Narcotics Bureau inspectors who close down both doctors who write too many prescriptions and the pharmacies that fill too many. Burroughs deals bluntly with the fears of the addicts, who give fake names to obtain numerous prescriptions, and he identifies the tricks used to obtain these prescriptions—complaining of kidney stones, gallstones, or migraine headaches to obtain prescriptions for morphine or codeine.

Burroughs also discusses his homosexual cruising paired with his addiction, and the nature of his relationships while addicted. Such relationships are rendered in a surreal manner, with violent, nightmare-like details. As the novel draws to a close, the author speaks of his and others' efforts to kick the habit and of the false hope provided by the incarceration of friends on Riker's Island, for what they and law-enforcement officials refer to as the "thirty-day cure," after which they return to drugs as soon as they are again on the streets. The work ends with a glossary of terms used in the book, to enlighten the reader regarding the "junk lingo."

CENSORSHIP HISTORY

Burroughs first published the novel under the pseudonym William Lee because of what Allen Ginsberg called his "police state paranoia cultivated by Narcotics Bureaus . . . that if you talked about 'tea' (much less Junk) on the bus or subway, you might be arrested—even if you were only discussing a change in the law."

His first publisher, Ace Books, was even more nervous "lest the publisher be implicated criminally with the author." As protection, the publisher required that the pseudonymous Burroughs write a preface that explained his "distinguished family background" and to exhibit the social significance of the work by giving "some hint how some supposedly normal citizen could arrive at being a dope fiend, to soften the blow for readers, censors, reviewers, police, critical eyes in walls & publishers' row, god [sic] knows who." Carl Solomon, the editor at Ace Books who handled *Junky*, also wrote an introduction that emphasized the serious nature of the book and its social importance. As further protection, the publisher excised a description of "Texas agricultural society" that might have opened the company to a lawsuit and included disclaimers throughout the text at "crucial medico-political statements of fact or opinion by Wm. Lee." As a final attempt to avoid prosecution, the publisher justified the existence of the book by binding it back to back with the title *Narcotic Agent*, written by Maurice Helbront. The first printing of 100,000 copies sold out the first year, and more than a million copies were sold over the next decade.

The first complete and unexpurgated edition was not published until 1977, when Penguin Books, in New York, issued the work alone, with an introduction by Allen Ginsberg. The book has remained out of schools because the title is sufficiently blunt to convey the content of the book, and many public libraries have avoided challenges by simply not ordering it.

FURTHER READING

Burroughs, William S. *Letters to Allen Ginsberg, 1953–1957*. Introduction by Allen Ginsberg. New York: Full Court Press, 1982.
Ginsberg, Allen. "Introduction." In *Junky*, by William S. Burroughs, v–ix. New York: Penguin Books, 1977.
Morgan, Ted. *Literary Outlaw: The Life and Times of William S. Burroughs*. New York: Henry Holt & Company, 1988.

KING & KING

Authors: Linda de Haan and Stern Nijland
Original date and place of publication: 2002, United States
Original publisher: Tricycle Press
Literary form: Children's picture book

SUMMARY

King & King presents a royal love story with a twist. Rather than a handsome prince searching for and finding a beautiful princess to marry and to live with "happily ever after," this brightly illustrated large-format children's book ends with the wedding of two princes.

Prince Bertie's mother, the queen, has ruled the kingdom for a very long time and has become tired of the responsibilities. She wants the freedom to live her life, so she makes up her mind that her son must marry and become King Bertie by the end of the summer. A direct woman, the queen marches into her son's room, wakes him up and announces, "I've had enough. You're getting married and that's all there is to it."

While the prince sits across the table from her, unable to eat his breakfast, the queen insists that Bertie is the only prince she knows who has not been married and reminds him, "When I was your age, I'd been married twice already." As the queen talks on and on, the prince pushes aside his food and claims that he cannot eat a bite. To appease his mother, whose talking has made him dizzy, Prince Bertie acquiesces to marry but cautions, "I must say, though, I've never cared much for princesses." The queen ignores her son's comment regarding his lack of interest in princesses and, after toasting the upcoming marriage with wine, locates her list of eligible princesses and methodically calls "every castle, alcazar, and palazzo from afar."

The following morning, a crowd of princesses waits at the palace gates, and they are led to Prince Bertie one at a time to show off their talents. The first is Princess Aria from Austria, a very full-figured woman with several chins who sings "a thunderous opera" for the prince. After she is shown to the door, Princess Dolly, who has flown all the way from Texas, performs a magic act, aided by "the crown kitty," but neither the queen nor Prince Bertie is amused. The unattractive, comical-looking princess from Greenland also fails to impress the prince, but he approves fully when his page falls in love with her.

The fourth choice is the elegant Princess Rahjmashputtin from Mumbai, who ignites an interest from the prince, though not the one she had hoped, when he proclaims, "Boy, those long arms will certainly come in handy when waving to the people."

After meeting all of the princesses and declaring them unsatisfactory, the queen and the prince sit sadly, thinking that none of this was what they had expected. As they brood, a palace page appears and announces that one more princess has arrived, Princess Madeleine, with her brother, Prince Lee. When Prince Bertie sees them, "At last, the prince felt a stir in his heart. It was love at sight." As the two princes stare deeply into each other's eyes, both exclaim, "What a wonderful prince!" The illustration emphasizes their sudden realization of love, and a profusion of hearts cover two facing pages of the book.

With the queen's blessings, Prince Bertie and Prince Lee marry in a wedding that "was very special. The queen even shed a tear or two." The pews in the church are filled with the rejected princesses and members of the court. After the ceremony, the two princes hold their wedding cake between them, and atop the cake are figures of the two princes. The illustration shows streamers containing "Congratulations" in huge letters above them.

The book ends with the two princes now known as "King and King," and a happy queen who now has some time for herself. "And everyone lives happily ever after." The final page shows the two kings kissing, but a large heart covers their joined lips.

CENSORSHIP HISTORY

King & King has brought out strong emotions among parents and community members who have labeled the book "pro–homosexual marriage," equated it with *Playboy* and "other dirty books," and led them to question "Are public schools the next battleground over homosexuality?" In contrast, the book was viewed favorably by reputable reviewers for the *School Library Journal, Kirkus Reviews, Horn Book Magazine,* and *Publishers Weekly,* and in 2002, *King & King* received honorable mention from *Publishers Weekly*'s 2002 "Off the Cuff Awards" in the "most unusual book of the year" category. Controversy has been good for sales. On March 19, 2004, the day after the book received national media attention when parents in North Carolina called for its ban from their public school library, Amazon.com reported a surge in sales of the book, making it number 38 on the site's list of best sellers.

The parents who initiated the call for a ban in North Carolina were Michael and Tonya Hartsell, parents of seven-year-old daughter Olivia, who brought the book home from the Rachel Freeman Elementary School library. Michael Hartsell told a reporter for the Associated Press that his daughter "is not old enough to understand something like that, especially when it's not in our beliefs." The Hartsells said that they first became suspicious about the content of the book as their daughter read it to them, especially "when the queen in the story tells her unmarried son that she had already been married twice by the time she was his age," but they were "stunned" as they took the book from their daughter and read further. Tonya Hartsell told a reporter for the North Carolina Family Policy Council newsletter, "All I could think about was how long has this book been on the shelves at the library, and how many other innocent children have gotten hold of it?"

The Hartsells contacted the school librarian and media coordinator, Barbara Hawley, who told them that the book had been on the library shelves since early 2003. When asked by reporters about the book, Hawley stated that she "couldn't comment on the book" because she hadn't seen it, and she declined to answer when asked if she "had knowingly selected a book on gay marriage." The Hartsells then approached the school principal, Elizabeth Miars, who supported inclusion of the book in the school library and told an Associated Press reporter, "What might be inappropriate for one family, in another family is a totally acceptable thing." Dissatisfied with the responses, the Hartsells refused to return the book to the library because they wanted to prevent other children from being exposed to it and because they wanted to submit the book, along with their formal complaint, to the New Hanover County School District Media Advisory Committee, a group that reviews books after their appropriateness has been challenged. D. John Morris, Jr., school district superintendent, told a reporter for the *Washington Times* the complaint by the Hartsells was the first complaint he had received about the book and that a decision would be made after the Media

Advisory Committee completed the appeals process. Two school board members expressed sympathy for the viewpoint of the Hartsells. Janice Cavenaugh agreed that the book is not appropriate for elementary school children, and Maryann Nunnally expressed discomfort with censorship but said that she would prefer "to put such controversial books out of children's reach and circulate them only with parental permission."

Several groups in North Carolina joined the Hartsells in the opposition to the book. Robert Knight, director of the Culture and Family Institute, which is affiliated with Concerned Women for America, told a reporter for the *Washington Times*, "You can't make children feel valuable by validating immoral behavior." He also said that he was "appalled" by the message sent by the book, "What a message to send a little girl: that a mommy isn't necessary." The North Carolina Family Policy Council also supported the stand taken by the Hartsells and expressed the following in their newsletter: "What happened to the Hartsells in Wilmington, NC, is just one example of how homosexual activists are seeking to infiltrate public schools and libraries with the message that homosexuality is 'normal'. It also highlights how important it is for parents to investigate what is on the shelves of their public schools and libraries and raise concerns with public officials when they find objectionable materials." Knight also warned parents that homosexual activists embed books such as *King & King* in school libraries, and they "are serious about taking over schools and indoctrinating children so they believe homosexuality is normal and healthy." He also accused publishers of such books of "pursuing a political agenda."

The New Hanover County School District Media Advisory Committee determined in an 8-3 vote that *King & King* was inappropriate for young children. Although the book remains in the Rachel Freeman Elementary School library, it has been moved to the "parenting collection," where only adults are permitted to take it out. In response to the controversy in his state, Republican congressman Walter Jones wrote a letter to the North Carolina superintendent of public instruction, Michael Ward, and requested the removal of *King & King* from school libraries throughout the state. In the letter, which he made public, Jones wrote, "Either the State Board of Education has inadequate policies surrounding the selection and procurement of library books, or it is inadequately enforcing whatever rules it does have." In May 2005, Jones introduced legislation named the Parental Empowerment Act of 2005 (H.R. 2295), which would restrict federal funds for states that fail to adopt guidelines for elementary school book purchases. The legislation would create parent-based advisory boards at the school district level to review material for school libraries and classrooms. As Jones told a reporter for the *Kinston Free Press*, "It would let parents, in blocks of five to 15, decide whether the country's youngest children are ready for themes of homosexuality and gay marriage." As of September 2005, the bill had five cosponsors from other states and was in the Subcommittee on Education Reform, with an anticipated hearing in 2006.

In Oklahoma on March 24, 2005, 75 members of the state legislature signed a petition calling for *King & King* to be removed from the children's section of libraries and placed in the adult section. The move came after parents of an elementary school child living in Oklahoma City, the district represented by Republican state legislator Sally Kern, contacted her and expressed surprise to learn that a book their child checked out was about homosexual marriage. Republican legislator Michael Jackson of Enid, Oklahoma, told reporters that he did not want to restrict free speech, but he was concerned that "parents don't even know a lot of times that these kinds of materials are available for children to check out." Curt Roggow, also a Republican legislator from Enid, stated, "I just found it offensive that it was a children's book with a homosexual theme." The state legislators submitted their petition to Oklahoma City's Metropolitan Library Commission, which oversees libraries in Oklahoma County. The move sparked heavy attendance at the May 2005 meeting of the Public Services Committee. The group met to review the library system's policies on selecting books and responding to customer complaints, issues sparked by the petition. The books receiving specific focus were *King & King*, HEATHER HAS TWO MOMMIES, DADDY'S ROOMMATE, and *The Duke Who Outlawed Jelly Beans.* Many of the speakers agreed that "children's books showing family situations different from traditional marriage are pornography" and called for libraries to place such books "in a special category or on a special shelf." Chairman Jose Jimenez questioned speakers, "But how are we going to decide which books to put there? Is that going to be my responsibility? Or yours? Or someone else's?"

The executive director of the Metropolitan Library System, Donna Morris, told speakers, "None of the material in question is illegal or pornographic." After the committee members voted to retain the current system policies for book selection, Morris told the crowd that the existing policies serve to "facilitate the free flow of information and ideas by providing access to materials, services and programs to Oklahoma County's diverse community." Despite support for the book by both the Public Services Committee and the director of the Metropolitan Library System, the commission voted 10-7 in May 2005 to place *King & King* in the adult section of system libraries.

In early May 2005, the Oklahoma House of Representatives also passed, in a vote of 81-3, House resolution 1039, introduced by Representative Sally Kern, that called upon Oklahoma libraries to "confine homosexually themed books and other age-inappropriate material to areas exclusively for adult access and distribution." Although the resolution does not have the power of law, some members of the Oklahoma legislature threatened to decrease new funding for the Department of Libraries "unless libraries across the state remove homosexual-themed books from children's shelves." Lynn McIntosh, president of the Oklahoma Library Association responded that libraries are a reflection of their communities and questioned if the legislature should control what appears in libraries across the state. Kern refuted that view and said that "community standards are state standards."

Libraries in other states have also received challenges to *King & King*, but most have handled the issue with little fanfare, as did the Shelbyville-Shelby County Public Library in Indiana. In April 2004, library patron Dustin McCullough wrote a formal letter to the library board telling him that his young son had "stumbled across the book" and brought it home, then asked questions that forced him to explain why two men were kissing in it and talk about two men being gay, "which is something we disagree with." He suggested that the book is "inappropriate for the library" and requested its removal. The board disagreed but did acquiesce to move the book to the section for children ages eight to 12. The library director, Janet Wallace, reported that the book had been checked out regularly since it had been acquired the year before.

FURTHER READING

"Brave New Schools: Homosexual Book for 1st Graders—Parents Outraged over Story Where Prince Finds Love with Another Prince." *World Net Daily*. March 18, 2004. Available online. URL: http://www.wnd.com/news/article.asp?ARTICLE_ID=37643. Accessed December 12, 2009.

Brown, Jim. "School Shelves Pro-Homosexual Children's Book; Now Restricted to Adults." *Agape Press*. April 1, 2004.

Foust, Michael. "Are Public Schools the Next Battleground over Homosexuality?" *Baptist Press*. June 7, 2005. Available online. URL: http://www.bpnews.net/bpnews.asp?Id=20922. Accessed December 12, 2009.

Gammill, Andy. "Gay-Themed Book Sparks Objection." *Indianapolis Star*. April 9, 2004.

de Grandpre, Andrew, and Diane Mouskourie. "Jones Introduces Bill Allowing Parents to Censor School Material." *Kinston Free Press*. May 18, 2005.

de Haan, Linda, and Stern Nijland. *King & King*. Berkeley, Calif.: Tricycle Press, 2002.

Holder, Nelda. "When Princes Kiss." *Mountain Express*. September 7, 2005.

"Homosexual Kids' Book Now Best Seller." *World Net Daily*. March 20, 2004. Available online. URL: http://www.wnd.com/news/article.asp?ARTICLE_ID=37664. Accessed December 12, 2009.

Jackson, Fred, and Jenni Parker. "Parents Want Pro-Homosexual Children's Book Taken off School Shelf; Father Flabbergasted by Same-Sex Marriage 'Fairy Tale.' " *Agape Press*. March 18, 2004.

Klinka, Karen. "Children's Books Come under Fire at Library." *Oklahoman*. May 5, 2005. Available online. URL: http://www.lisnews.com/articles/05/05/07/1914217.shtml?tid=78. Accessed December 12, 2009.

"Lawmakers Vote to Restrict Access to Homosexual-Themed Children's Books." Oklahoma House of Representatives Media Division press release. May 9, 2005.

Meltzer, Eartha. "Federal Bill Restricts Access to Gay Books." *Washington Blade*, May 27, 2005. Available online. URL: http://www.washblade.com/2005/5-27/new/national/bookban.cfm. Accessed December 12, 2009.

Miller, Joe. "Jones Sees Morality, Deficit as Key Issues." *Jacksonville Daily News*. August 4, 2005.

"Parents Object to Pro–Homosexual 'Marriage' Book." North Family Policy Council. Special Report. March 18, 2004.

Previch, Chad, and Carrie Coppernoll. "Libraries Haven't Pulled Gay-Themed Kids' Books." *Oklahoman*, March 24, 2005.

Price, Joyce Howard. "Gay Princes Book Irks Girl's Parents." *Washington Times*, March 19, 2004.

Robinson, Judy Gibbs. "Library Funds Threatened." *Oklahoman*, May 21, 2005.

Trice, Dawn Turner. "'Banned Books' Event Highlights Need for Liberty." *Chicago Tribune*, October 4, 2004, p. 1.

KINGSBLOOD ROYAL

Author: Sinclair Lewis
Original date and place of publication: 1947, United States
Original publisher: Random House
Literary form: Novel

SUMMARY

Kingsblood Royal examines the consequences of a previously racist white man discovering that his maternal great-great-great-grandfather was black. Set in the town of Grand Republic, Minnesota, the novel is the story of Neil Kingsblood, an unassuming bank assistant who learns the truth when tracing his family lines. Given the prejudice of the times during which most southern states and a few northern ones determined that by law "a 'Negro' is defined by having even 'one drop of Negro blood,' " Neil is understandably upset by what he learns.

Thirty-one-year-old Neil, who served as an army captain during World War II, is married to Vestal and has a golden-haired daughter named Biddy. He has a promising future at the bank, where he is developing a new account system. He has also established a Veterans' Advisory Center and hopes to lure new business to the bank in the form of mortgages and new accounts.

Before making his discovery, Neil is a well-liked success, and he is also racist in ways that he does not recognize. He and his wife own a black cocker spaniel named "Nigger," and they fail to understand why their black maid feels insulted. He has also internalized the negative beliefs regarding the intellect, industry, and sexuality of blacks.

Neil's self-confidence is shattered after he reads a letter written by his great-great-great-grandfather, which states, "I am to all intent a full-blooded negro born in Martinique. . . . please [do] not say anything about my color and how black it is." Neil is fearful of having to live under the limitations placed on blacks by society, and he begins to feel that he will now have to "live in a decaying shanty," "work in kitchens," "have unpleasant manners," "be an animal physically," and be unable "to grasp any science beyond addition and plain cooking and driving of a car."

His maternal grandmother and grandfather vehemently deny the ancestry, to the point that his grandfather rages, "Are you trying to make me out to be the father of part-nigger kids—make your Uncle Emery and your own mother into niggers?"

Plagued with guilt that he is "passing," Neil tries to find a way to actually "be Negro," but the more that he tries to experience the "Negro culture" and find "special Negro things to be," the more he becomes aware of the similarities rather than the differences between the two races. When white neighbors, coworkers, and other townspeople learn his secret, Neil loses his job, and his family is shunned. The novel ends as he and Vestal are taken to jail, charged with violence after they defend their home against an angry white mob that attacks them and tries to force them out of the neighborhood.

CENSORSHIP HISTORY

The novel was a daring effort to explore the issue of racial prejudice in 1940s America, and it won Sinclair Lewis an award from *Ebony* magazine for his attempts to promote racial understanding. In contrast, when the novel was first published in 1947, this effort also cost him and his publisher, Random House, sales in many small and moderately sized cities in the South, where the company's salesmen were forewarned to not even attempt to market the book. Several objections to the book were raised. One objection was to the intelligence and educational levels of many of the blacks portrayed in the novel. One man holds a Ph.D. in chemistry, another holds a doctorate from Columbia University, and all seem to converse about issues of importance. Another objection to the book centered on the negative way in which white characters were portrayed in their reactions to a man who, when thought to be white, was accepted and liked.

Lewis noted in one of his letters that he may have struck a chord with many white southerners who had doubts about their own ancestry being revealed. In several large cities, notably Atlanta and New Orleans, booksellers kept copies of the novel on closed shelves, only selling them if someone specifically asked to buy the book. Random House received numerous letters denouncing Lewis and threatening to stop buying any of his books.

In New York City, the Society for the Suppression of Vice sought to prevent sales of the book after complaints arose about the suggested sexual content of the novel. When Neil first learns of his ancestry and seeks out black friends, he meets an attractive black nurse to whose one-room tenement apartment he goes one evening. There, he rests his cheek "on the smoothness of her [clothed] breast" and kisses her "with quietness and propriety." The efforts by the society to bring charges against the book were fruitless, and only a few booksellers agreed to remove the novel from their stock.

In 1953, the novel was removed from an Illinois library after a mother complained that her daughter had borrowed the book and that it was offensive. The novel was also banned in Ireland in 1953 for the use of the term *nigger* and the "suggestive sexuality."

The novel also aroused interest by the Federal Bureau of Investigation after, in 1947, "the FBI was flooded with letters denouncing Lewis's *Kingsblood Royal.*" The FBI report in Lewis's file states that the book was of concern for it seemed "to be propaganda for the white man's acceptance of the negro as a social equal."

FURTHER READING

Conroy, Stephen S. "Sinclair Lewis's Sociological Imagination." *American Literature* 42 (November 1970): 348–362.

Light, Martin. *The Quixotic Vision of Sinclair Lewis.* West Lafayette, Ind.: Purdue University Press, 1975.

Manfred, Frederick. "Sinclair Lewis: A Portrait." *American Scholar* 23 (Spring 1954): 162–184.

Robins, Natalie. *Alien Ink: The FBI's War on Freedom of Expressionism.* New York: William Morrow and Company, 1992.

THE KITE RUNNER

Author: Khaled Hosseini
Original date and place of publication: 2003, United States
Original publisher: Riverhead Books (A Penguin Books Imprint)
Literary form: Novel

SUMMARY

The Kite Runner, which derives its name from the Afghan custom of kite fighting, focuses on the relationship between two boys of different social classes and religious backgrounds and the lasting effect that one boy's moment of cowardice has on their lives. A large portion of the novel is told in flashback, opening in December 2001 in San Francisco and moving back to 1975 and relating events through 1981 in Afghanistan and subsequent years in the United States. The story is as much an account of the trials faced by the nation of Afghanistan in those years as it is the story of one man's efforts to achieve redemption and to make peace with his past. The "kite runner" of the title refers to the friend he betrayed when a boy.

Amir and Hassan have grown up in the same household, one the acknowledged son of Baba, a wealthy businessman in Kabul, and the other the putative son of Ali, a servant in the same household. Amir, the narrator, is a Pashtun and a Sunni Muslim, and Hassan, one year younger, is a Hazara and a Shi'a. Their ethnic and religious differences create tensions between the two boys who, nonetheless, become constant companions and share a deep bond from infancy. Both have lost their mothers early in life and are raised by their fathers. Amir's mother died giving birth to him, thus depriving his rigid, successful father of his "beautiful princess," and Hassan's mother left his much-older, impoverished father five days after giving birth, disgusted by both her husband's physical disfigurement and her baby's cleft palate. The boys were also breast-fed by the same woman, whom Baba hired first for Amir, then for Hassan a year later. He

> would remind us that there was a brotherhood between people who had fed from the same breast, a kinship that not even time could break.
> Hassan and I fed from the same breasts. We took our first steps on the same lawn in the same yard. And, under the same roof, we spoke our first words.
> Mine was *Baba*.
> His was *Amir*. My name.
> Looking back on it now, I think the foundation for what happened in the winter of 1975—and all that followed—was already laid in those first words.

Baba's father, a judge, had brought an orphaned, five-year-old Ali into his household years earlier, and Baba had grown up with Ali in the same manner as Amir and Hassan. Baba's father had provided for the young Ali's physical wants, but he did not educate the child nor did he move him above his presumed station in life as a Hazara. Ali became a servant, a role he would continue to play in Baba's household, and a role in which his son Hassan would follow, each knowing his place in Afghan society. "When the sun dropped low behind the hills and we were done playing for the day, Hassan and I parted ways. I went past the rosebushes to Baba's mansion, Hassan to the mud shack where he had been born, where he'd lived his entire life." Each morning, Hassan enters the mansion to make Amir's breakfast, to iron his clothes, to gather and to pack his school supplies, and to help him get dressed, before attending to other duties around the house with Ali while Amir goes to school. Hassan is illiterate, but he is an eager learner who asks Amir the meanings of words and who enjoys Amir's reading to him. His illiteracy sometimes tempts Amir to "tease him, expose his ignorance," as when Hassan asks the meaning of "imbecile," a word he hears in a story Amir reads aloud. To Hassan's question, Amir responds in a condescending manner, "But it's such a common word!" At the other boy's persistence, he replies, "Well, everyone in my school knows what it means. Let's see. 'Imbecile.' It means smart, intelligent. I'll use it in a sentence for you. When it comes to words, Hassan is an imbecile."

Baba maintains a social distance from Ali and Hassan, but he is kind and generous toward them. He remembers Hassan's birthday with especially selected gifts, and he arranges for a renowned Indian surgeon to correct the boy's cleft palate. Baba also recognizes that, although a year younger than his son, Hassan is fiercely loyal to Amir and defends him against physical attacks on many occasions. One such instance creates an enemy who later retaliates, changing forever the lives of Amir and Hassan.

Amir has no interest in sports or other physical activity, nor does he exhibit the courage and bluster for which the demanding Baba is known. Instead, he is a dreamer who enjoys reading rather than roughhousing and who acknowledges that he "aspired to be a coward." He is jealous of Baba's approval of and kindness toward Hassan. In a desperate move to win his father's love and approval, Amir becomes involved in the sport of kite fighting and, at age 12, wins the annual tournament in Kabul, a victory he owes largely to Hassan who trains with him and shows an exceptional skill as a kite runner. The kites are made of tissue paper with glass-coated cutting lines that are used to sever the lines of the other kites. The tournament ends when only one winning kite remains in the sky. Kites that have been cut loose are pursued by "kite runners," children who chase the spiraling and drifting kites, shoving each other aside as they grasp for the falling kites.

> For kite runners, the most coveted prize was the last fallen kite of a winter tournament. It was a trophy of honor, something to be displayed on a mantle for guests to admire. When the sky cleared of kites and only the two final remained, every kite runner readied himself for the chance to land his prize. He positioned himself at a spot that he thought would give him a head start. Tense muscles readied themselves to uncoil. Necks craned. Eyes crinkled. Fights broke out. And when the last kite was cut, all hell broke loose.
>
> Over the years, I had seen a lot of guys run kites. But Hassan was by far the greatest kite runner I'd ever seen. It was downright eerie the way he always got to the spot the kite would *before* the kite did, as if he had some sort of inner compass.

After the kite-fighting tournament, Hassan runs through the streets of Kabul and retrieves the final kite Amir cut down to win the tournament. Months earlier, three older boys had trapped Amir and Hassan and threatened to beat them, but the boys were frightened away when Hassan aimed his slingshot at Assef, the most aggressive of the boys, and threatened to knock out his eye. Assef, the son of an Afghan airline pilot father and German mother, has known Amir's family for years, and Baba greatly admires him for his aggression, sports ability, and swagger, but he is not aware of Assef's propensity for violence and his intense admiration for Adolf Hitler. More than a year later, on the night of the kite-fighting tournament, Assef exacts his revenge. As Baba stands on a rooftop and cheers loudly for his son, following Amir's victory at the kite-fighting tournament, Hassan races away to run down the blue kite, the last one cut down and a trophy that Amir will present to his father. Hours pass, and Amir searches for Hassan, eager to obtain the blue kite, and finds him in an alley trapped by the three older boys who had threatened him earlier. Without revealing himself, Amir watches and listens as Assef berates Hassan and tries to wrest the blue kite from him. Loyal to Amir, and knowing how much the blue kite means to him, Hassan steadfastly refuses to hand it over, despite Assef's insults and threats. Amir also watches as Assef decides to let Hassan keep the kite, "I'll let you keep it so it will always remind you of what I am about to do." Amir sees Hassan's corduroy pants thrown carelessly on a pile of rubble and listens as Assef attempts to coerce his friends Wali and Kamal into "teaching a lesson to a disrespectful donkey." When they refuse, he calls them weaklings and orders them to hold Hassan down.

> Assef knelt behind Hassan, put his hands on Hassan's hips and lifted his bare buttocks. He kept one hand on Hassan's back and undid his own belt buckle with his free hand. He unzipped his jeans. Dropped his underwear. He positioned himself behind Hassan. Hassan didn't struggle. Didn't even whimper. He moved his head slightly and I caught a glimpse of his face. Saw the resignation in it. It was a look I had seen before. It was the look of a lamb.

Amir hesitates for a moment and thinks that he had one last chance to make a decision, one "final opportunity to decide who I was going to be. I could step into that alley, stand up for Hassan—the way he'd stood up for me all those times in the past. . . . Or I could run." He ran. As Amir runs away, he tells himself that he does so because he is a coward, "I actually *aspired* to cowardice," but he knows that his real reasons is more sinister. "Maybe Hassan was the price I had to pay, the lamb I had to slay to win Baba. . . . He was just a Hazara, wasn't he?" When the boys finally meet later in the evening, Hassan is carrying the blue kite, fulfilling his promise to Amir, who lies and says that he has been searching for the other boy. Hassan's voice cracks, but all he says is "Agha sahib [Baba] will worry," as he turns and limps away. Amir pretends he does not hear, and he pretends that he does not see "the dark stain in the seat of his pants. Or those tiny drops that fell from between his legs and stained the snow black."

After his moment of cowardice, Amir avoids Hassan, too ashamed to look the younger boy in the eye. A confused and hurt Hassan tries to reestablish their relationship, but Amir rebuffs his attempts and continues to suffer the guilt of his actions, surrounded as he is by the numerous signs of Hassan's presence in the breakfast each morning, the freshly ironed clothes, the warm slippers left outside his door. Hassan's continuing loyalty tortures Amir to the point that he can no longer stand to see Ali and his son and feels compelled to ask Baba about getting new servants. Baba's response is swift and definite as he refuses and warns Amir to never ask that question again. The pain of Amir's shame intensifies at his 13th birthday party, where Assef appears with his friends and gives a biography of Hitler. Between flashes of fireworks, Amir watches as Hassan serves drinks to Assef and Wali on a silver platter, then sees Assef "grinning, kneading Hassan in the chest with a knuckle."

The discomfort of seeing Hassan continue to carry out his duties without complaining and to remain loyal without question is too much for Amir to bear. He decides to frame Hassan as a thief and hides his birthday watch and some Afghani money under Hassan's mattress, then lies to his father, calling Hassan a thief and hoping the incident will finally drive Hassan out of his life and end his guilt. Baba confronts Ali and Hassan about the presumed theft, and neither fights the accusation, but Amir knows from the way they look at him that Hassan has told Ali about the sexual attack and that they will leave without a fight.

In 1981, after the Russians invade Afghanistan, Amir and his father take a long and dangerous journey through their country and go to the United States. They settle in San Francisco, where the formerly wealthy and powerful Baba finds adjusting difficult. He barely speaks English and responds with disdain when Amir suggests that he take English-as-a-second-language classes. Rather than managing employees, he joins his son in gathering old and discarded objects to sell in the flea market that hosts the booths and tables of many Afghan immigrants. Amir graduates from high school and junior college and continues to write stories, as he had as a boy. And he falls in love with Soraya Taheri, the daughter of a former Afghan general and ministry member. In the United States, Baba and Amir have grown emotionally closer, and Amir turns to his father to ask General Taheri for his daughter's hand in marriage. Once they are married and Baba is stricken by cancer, Soraya nurses the old man in his last months of life. After 15 years, Amir receives a telephone call from his father's close friend Rahim Khan, who is dying, and who asks to see him. Khan has left the chaos and escaped to Pakistan, where Amir meets with him and learns that Hassan is actually his half brother, fathered by Baba months after the death of Amir's mother in childbirth. He learns that Khan had lived in Baba's mansion in Kabul with Hassan and his family, including a son Sohrab, named after Hassan's favorite hero from a book Amir used to read to him. Khan tells him that soon after he left Kabul, the Taliban accused Hassan and his wife of illegally occupying the mansion and executed them in the street, but they took Sohrab away. Khan begs Amir to find the little boy.

Amir protests that he has a wife and a good life in the United States, and he has a novel to finish, but Khan reminds him of the debts he owes to the past and reawakens the guilt he has carried for a quarter of a century. Frightened and with great reluctance, Amir travels to Kabul and searches for Sohrab, whom he finds has been sent to an orphanage. At the orphanage, he learns that a local Taliban commander stops by regularly to give the director money to help the orphanage and routinely leaves with a little girl or a little boy, some of whom are later returned to the orphanage bearing signs of abuse. Amir is horrified to learn that Sohrab is one such child, but he has not been returned. Despite the great difficulty and danger, he approaches a guard after two public executions that take place during halftime of a soccer game and requests an appointment with the Taliban commander who has carried out the stonings and who matches the description provided by the orphanage director. He is granted the appointment, and at the meeting learns that Sohrab has become a sexual victim of the commander who reveals himself to be Assef, the bully who had raped Hassan in the alley years before when Amir failed to act. The little boy has eyes "darkened with mascara, and his cheeks glowed with an unnatural red"; jingling bells encircle his ankles. Enraged by the victimization of his childhood friend's son, Amir demands to be given the boy, but Assef tells him that he must fight to the death for that right. Assef uses brass knuckles and viciously attacks Amir, breaking bones and slashing at his face, stopping only when Sohrab calls for him to stop. The little boy, like his late father, is a great marksman with his slingshot, which he is holding poised to shoot with a brass ball from the table decorations firmly in the pouch. Assef lunges, and Sohrab releases the sling, catapulting the ball firmly into one eye socket and knocking Assef to the ground. The little boy half drags and half carries Amir to the waiting car, and Amir is taken to a hospital where he endures many surgical procedures and begins a lengthy recuperation process.

As soon as Amir is able to move, he removes Sohrab from Afghanistan to the United States, where he and Soraya will adopt the boy. For months after Sohrab reaches the United States, he remains silent and unapproachable, until Amir gives him a kite and shows him how he and Hassan used to fly kites in Kabul. As Sohrab relaxes his guard and flies the kite, Amir tells him that Hassan was the best kite runner he had ever known, and he offers to be Sohrab's kite runner, telling him he would do so, as Hassan had once told him, "For you, a thousand times over."

CENSORSHIP HISTORY

The Kite Runner earned the praise of *Publishers Weekly* upon publication as being "an incisive, perceptive examination of recent Afghan history . . . a complete work of literature that succeeds in exploring the culture of a previously obscure nation that has become a pivot point in the global politics of the new millennium." The novel was on the *New York Times* list of best-selling books, and reviewers of the novel have echoed this praise and lauded the author for creating a sensitive portrayal of the devastating effects that the political turbulence in Afghanistan has had upon its citizens. Parents across the United States have not been as admiring, and their protests against the novel made *The Kite Runner* one of the top books challenged in 2008. Although the book was published in 2003, little attention appears to have been given to formal challenges until after the filmed version of the movie was released in 2007.

In January 2008, Burke County, North Carolina, school board member Tracy Norman criticized the use of the book in the Freedom High School honors class because of the scene of male rape and the use of "profanities" throughout the novel. She charged that the book contains content that is "inappropriate for high schoolers" and recommended removing it from the county public school system curriculum. In an interview with the *Charlotte Observer*, Norman stated, "I don't think it's the public schools' place to be the one exposing them to this." Buddy Armour, another school board member, contradicted Norman's view and defended the novel, "It's not about vulgarity or the rape scene that's depicted. It's a look into the culture, and there's value there. Our kids need to know a little bit about the world, and it's not all pretty and lovely." Other parents defended the book, including Tony Matthews, pastor at the North Morganton United Methodist Church and a parent of a 10th-grade daughter. Matthews observed that "The point of the book was to show the horrors of living under an oppressive regime such as the Taliban. Getting a set of facts on a piece of paper is a way to sterilize the problem. A character in a book becomes someone you're familiar with and you bond with. By telling the story in a piece of fiction . . . it makes the horrors more real."

The novel was taught in the fall semester 2007 to a 10th-grade world literature class at Freedom High School and intended as a text to teach honors students about other parts of the world. The school board refused to act on Norman's attempt to remove the book and, instead, decided to rely on the challenge procedure, begun in 2006 in the school system, which allows parents and community members the right to file formal complaints with the school system for materials they believe are not appropriate for students. The challenge is then reviewed by a media advisory committee made up of teachers, students, and parents who review the complaint and content at issue and decide whether the materials should be removed from the system. School superintendent David Burleson stated that such a decision cannot be made by just one person. "Where do you draw the line? That's a fair and valid question. You draw the line based on your community make-up and what the community expects. That's why we have the advisory committee." Board member Norman asserted that teenagers were being forced into reading content that is too mature for a high school setting and said there must be other ways "to teach students about other cultures without depending on scenes of sexual abuse and books with foul language." She expressed her concern with not only *The Kite Runner* but with "all books that use profane language and include graphic sex scenes and other potentially offensive material." Her comments caused fellow school board member Armour to observe that "what Norman proposes borders on censorship. If *The Kite Runner* is banned from Burke schools, other material will likely also be forced from the curriculum." No media reports have been located to determine the outcome of the committee review.

In May 2008, David McGowan, the parent of a Marianna High School student in Jackson County (Florida) School District, protested to staff and administration at the high school that *The Kite Runner* was disturbing and should not be required reading. In response, the high school principal Randy Ward removed the book from the required reading list but ordered that the book remain in the school library. The action did not go far enough for McGowan who sent a letter in July 2008 to the district director of middle and secondary education and requested that the district form a committee to consider removing the book entirely from the school district. He wrote, "I do not wish to stand in the way of any educational advantage that literature provides. I am simply asking for your help in shielding my children from this particular book." McGowan also appeared before the school board in early August 2008 and read aloud excerpts from the book that contained "profane language and sexual situations" and asked them to remove the book. The school board formed a district review committee of seven consisting of parents, a media specialist, a teacher, members of the community, and a student. The committee voted five to two in favor of keeping the book in the school district. The decision went before the school board members, who had mixed reactions to the report of the committee. In the discussion the school board's final vote, board president Dr. Terry Nichols, who cast the sole opposing vote, stated, "I think it's a good book. But in looking at this I think it's a book that's good for the adult population. There are vivid scenes that don't promote evil, but are a little bit too vivid for our younger students in high school." Chris Johnson, another board member, voted in favor of keeping the book and said that he would not want his child reading the book but feared that banning *The Kite Runner* "could lead to the issue of banning other books, such as Huck Finn and Macbeth." Johnson expressed concern that the book is available for students in the sixth grade or higher: "When the librarian told me that was a sixth grade book I almost fainted. But what I ban today might be something that hurts me tomorrow." School board member Kenneth Griffin asserted that the passages were offensive and made a motion for the board to consider making the book available only to juniors and seniors, but the school board attorney Frank Bondurant stated that "legal complications might occur in trying to enforce such a rule," so Griffin withdrew the motion.

In November 2008, Laura Stovall, a parent in the Okaloosa County (Florida) School District, expressed concern about the "mature content" of the novel and filed a "Request for Reconsideration of Educational Materials" with the school district after learning that the novel would be taught in the Choctawhatchee High School English classes in the International Baccalaureate (IB) program. The novel was also taught in the Fort Walton Beach High School. Stovall's son was only a ninth-grade student at the time, but she told a reporter for the *Northwest Florida Daily News* that "the book's obscene and profane content should not be a part of the curriculum at any level." The district routinely sent a letter to parents of Choctawhatchee High School students to inform them about the IB program, which noted that students "may encounter literature with mature content." Stovall obtained both of the books mentioned—*To Kill a Mockingbird* and *The Kite Runner*—and read them both. "I thought 'To Kill a Mockingbird' was one of the most pleasant and intriguing books I had read and I hoped to be as pleasantly surprised by 'Kite Runner.' I wasn't." Stovall told school officials she was "mortified" by the book's content and stated that it was "unacceptable to present such R-rated material to high school students who cannot even get into R-rated movies." To support her concerns, Stovall compiled five pages containing passages from the book that she found offensive. In the "Request for Reconsideration," she wrote "The level of profanity and 'R-rated' content of the book is altogether inappropriate in our high schools."

In response to Stovall's challenge, Fort Walton Beach High School and Choctawhatchee High School formed committees to review the novel and to make recommendations to the school district officials based on the novel's instructional and educational merits. Both committees quickly and unanimously recommended that the school district keep *The Kite Runner* as part of the curriculum and on the school district reading list. Their decisions were then reviewed by a district-level committee, which also recommended to the Okaloosa County School Board to retain the book. On January 12, 2009, the school board voted unanimously to keep the novel on the reading lists of both high schools in the Advanced Placement and International Baccalaureate curricula, as well as on the recommended readings lists and in media centers.

FURTHER READING

"BOOKS Library Group Finds *Kite Runner* Problematic." *Houston Chronicle*, April 16, 2009, p. 4.

"Censorship Dateline: Schools." *Newsletter for Intellectual Freedom* 57, no. 3 (May 2008): 97–99.

Hernandez, Kelli. "Choctaw Committee: Keep *Kite Runner*." *Northwest Florida Daily News* (Fort Walton Beach), November 21, 2008. Available online. URL: http://www.nwfdailynews.com/news/school-12902-committee-district.html. Accessed December 26, 2009.

———. "District Committee Recommends 'The Kite Runner' Stay on Reading Lists." *Northwest Florida Daily News* (Fort Walton Beach), December 14, 2008. Available online. URL: http://www.nwfdailynews.com/news/book-13508-district-school. html. Accessed December 27, 2009.

———. "Parents Object to 'Kite Runner.' " *Northwest Florida Daily News* (Fort Walton Beach), November 15, 2008. Available online. URL: http://www.nwfdailynews. com/news/book-12772-school-stovall.html. Accessed December 27, 2009.

———. "School Board Approves 'Kite Runner.' " *Northwest Florida Daily News* (Fort Walton Beach), January 13, 2009. Available online. URL: http://www.nwfdaily-news.com/news/board-14162-school-schools.html. Accessed December 26, 2009.

Kern, Kate McCardell. "'Kite' Still Flies: School Board Rejects Book Ban." Available online. URL: http://www2.jcfloridan.com/jcf/news/local/article/kite_still_flies_school_board_rejects_book_ban/32549. Accessed October 25, 2010.

"Kite Runner, The." *Publishers Weekly* (May 12, 2003): 43.

"Kite Runner Joins Gay Penguins on Top 10 Books Americans Want Banned." *Europe Intelligence Wire*, April 16, 2009. *General Business File ASAP*. Gale Research. Available online. URL: http://find.galegroup.com/gps/start.do?prodId=IPS&user GroupName=bergen_main. Accessed December 27, 2009.

Young, Marcie. "Book Too Raw for School?" *Charlotte Observer*, February 24, 2008. *General Business File ASAP*. Gale Research. Available online. URL: http://find.gale group.com/gps/infomark.do?&contentSet=IAC-Documents&type=retrieve&tab ID=T004&prodId=IPS&docId=CJ175296057&source=gale&userGroupName= bergen_main&version=1.0>. Accessed on December 28, 2009.

LAST EXIT TO BROOKLYN

Author: Hubert Selby, Jr.
Original date and place of publication: 1964, United States
Original publisher: Grove Press
Literary form: Novel

SUMMARY

Last Exit to Brooklyn consists of six linked episodes, each preceded by a quotation from the Old Testament, that form a novel detailing the brutal and violent lives of a group of lower economic class Brooklyn, New York, youths in the late 1940s through the 1950s. The squalor of the environment and the hopelessness of their drug- and violence-dominated lives leave them devoid of human compassion and lacking in conventional morality. Married and single, gay and straight, the men are portrayed as relentlessly brutal, opportunistic and cruel to other men, to women, and to the children whom they conceive. Women, powerless for the most part, accept their limited roles, exacting revenge on those weaker than they whenever possible. Children are conditioned to live life as a daily struggle and to accept abusive behavior as normal. For everyone in this novel, crime is an everyday fact of existence.

The novel takes its title from the sign "Last Exit to Brooklyn" that once appeared on the Gowanus Expressway, just before the entrance to the Brooklyn-Battery Tunnel. The exit is depicted as an entrance into a hell composed of waterfront docks, dirty factory buildings, slum housing, cheap bars, and subsidized city apartment projects for the poor, with empty, bottle-strewn lots and concrete playgrounds. The language throughout the novel is in the vernacular, and the author omits the use of apostrophes in contractions or to indicate the possessive form of nouns, and he often runs words together to reflect the characters' states of mind. Four young criminals, each of whom boasts of his prison record, spend their lives "hanging out" at "the Greeks" diner, mocking the prostitutes such as Tralala and boasting of recent "scores," having "lushed a drunk" or "pulled a job." Opportunistic, they claim to be completely heterosexual but become involved with a crowd of male transvestites whom they pretend to view as women in order to take advantage of the free gin, abundant benzedrine tablets, and cheap thrills. The young hoodlums pretend to care about the transvestites but are brutal, leading one to overdose on benzedrine tablets.

Tralala descends into a nightmare of alcoholism and drug addiction, trading her body for drinks and even giving it away for free just to feel wanted.

She dies after being taken to a vacant lot filled with broken bottles and rusty cans and raped by 50 or more men from several area barrooms. Afterward, as Selby writes in a stream-of-consciousness tone,

> the kids who were watching and waiting to take a turn took out their disappointment on Tralala and tore her clothes to small scraps put out a few cigarettes on her nipples pissed on her jerkedoff on her jammed a broomstick up her snatch then bored they left her lying amongst the broken bottles rusty cans and rubble of the lot and Jack and Fred and Ruthy and Annie stumbled into a cab still laughing and they leaned toward the window as they passed the lot and got a good look at Tralala lying naked covered with blood urine and semen and a small blot forming on the seat between her legs as blood seeped from her crotch and Ruth and Annie happy and completely relaxed now that they were on their way downtown.

Later sections explore the brutality of Harry Black, now a union organizer, who repeatedly blames and physically abuses his wife to compensate for his disgust with all women. A braggart and bully who drinks heavily, he has frequent violent dreams in which he sees himself torn to shreds. The dreams end, and he achieves temporary happiness and even softens toward all but his wife once he begins a passionate affair with a male transvestite upon whom he lavishes money taken from his union strike expense account. Black believes that he has found true love, but his lover leaves when the strike account closes and the flow of money stops. In a confused state, Black attempts to perform oral sex on a 10-year-old boy in his neighborhood, and neighborhood toughs brutally beat him as punishment.

Two other sections, "And Baby Makes Three" and "Landsend," continue the pervasive theme of despair. None of the characters are happy, and all of the husbands and some of the wives appear to remain eager for extramarital sex. Husbands who work are physically abusive and grudgingly give their stay-at-home wives money to buy food for their children; husbands who do not work but who depend on their wives' paychecks are also abusive and refuse to assume any household or child-care responsibilities. Capital letters dominate the conversations as Selby indicates the continued arguments that pass for marital communication. Children are neglected and subjected to the constant fighting of their parents. The novel portrays a hellish existence that appears to continue as the characters age.

CENSORSHIP HISTORY

Last Exit to Brooklyn has been censored on both sides of the Atlantic. Several of the chapters have appeared separately in *Black Mountain Review*, *New Directions #17*, *Provincetown Review*, and *Swank*. The section entitled "Tralala" first appeared as a play that was banned from off-Broadway production in 1957. In 1965, in Boston, Massachusetts, a local city attorney sought an injunction against the book, but the complaint was dismissed. The following year, a circuit court in Connecticut issued a temporary injunction against sale of the book, now published by both Grove Press and Dell Publishing, charging that it was "obscene and pornographic." The injunction was overturned and sales were again permitted. The novel has also been banned in Italy and Ireland and placed on a restricted list in Russia.

The most extensive censorship case occurred in England, where the novel was published by Calder and Boyars. In late 1966, a Conservative Member of Parliament, Sir Charles Taylor, received a copy of the novel, sent to him by Sir Basil Blackwell, member of an Oxford bookselling family and a man in his seventies who claimed that his few remaining years had been "defiled" by reading *Last Exit to Brooklyn*. Disgusted by the book, Taylor alerted the attorney general in June 1967 to register a complaint with the Office of the Director of Public Prosecutions (DPP). That office replied that Taylor was too late to make an effective complaint because over 11,000 copies of the book had already been sold, and sales were slowing. Attorney General Sir Elwyn Jones stated further that "Literary Criticism was almost unanimous that it had literary merit." The publisher taunted Taylor by including his name in an advertisement in the *Sunday Times*, stating: "Sir Charles Taylor, MP has described *Last Exit* as filthy, disgusting, degrading. It is one of the most important novels to come out of America."

The audacity of the publisher angered another Member of Parliament, Sir Cyril Black (Conservative), who used the private prosecutions feature of Section 3 of the *Obscene Publications Act of 1959* to challenge the publishers. He brought a formal complaint against the book in July 1966, calling upon the publisher to prove that the book had value and to establish why it should not be banned. The magistrate who granted the application was Sir Robert Blundell, a chief opponent of *FANNY HILL*, who issued a search warrant for members of law enforcement to seize all copies from area bookshops. The trial was held at Marlborough Street Magistrates Court in November 1966, and the numerous prosecution witnesses were consistent in expressing their disgust with the scenes depicted in the novel, especially with the brutal rape and humiliation of Tralala. This section has drawn the greatest objection in proceedings against the book because of the horrifying picture that Selby creates of the humiliation and death of Tralala and the cold indifference of onlookers. The presiding magistrate rejected the book, observing that "this book in its descriptions goes beyond any book of a merely pornographic kind that we have seen in this court [and] . . . is more likely to deprave and corrupt than any of those cyclostyled horrors."

Buoyed by the published opinion of several critics that Britain "had made herself the laughing stock of the civilized world," Calder and Boyars announced that they would continue publication. In response, the DPP announced that it would prosecute, using section 2 of the 1959 act that prohibited "possessing an obscene article for gain." The trial was set for November 1967, and an all-male jury was selected to spare women the embarrassment of reading the material. The trial lasted nine days and brought together numerous prominent witnesses. The prosecution spotlighted David

Shepherd, a former cricket star who had taken religious orders and would later become a bishop, who claimed that he had emerged "not unscathed" by reading the novel, although as a social worker in the East End of London he could identify many of the character types among his clients. To counter this testimony, Calder and Boyars assembled a list of nearly 30 writers, critics, professors, and members of the media who praised Selby's work and his expression of theme. The effort was fruitless for, after deliberating five and a half hours, the jury declared the book guilty of being obscene and that "the effect of reading the book was to horrify, shock, disgust, and nauseate." Although the judge determined that the book had been published in good faith by a respectable publishing house, he fined Calder and Boyars £100 and ordered them to pay £500 in court costs.

The publishers once again appealed the decision, represented this time by John Mortimer, who convinced the appeal judges that the judge in the earlier trial had not sufficiently explained the complexities of the 1959 act to the jury and had left too much to "commonsense" and not enough to law. As a result, the conviction was overturned and *Last Exit to Brooklyn* was free to appear in a complete and unexpurgated edition. To avoid further embarrassing litigation based on private prosecution, Section 3 of the *Obscene Publications Act of 1959* was changed. *Last Exit to Brooklyn* holds the distinction of being the last serious novel, poem, or play prosecuted under the 1959 act.

FURTHER READING

Kermode, Frank. "'Obscenity' and the 'Public Interest.'" *New American Review* 3 (April 1968): 229–241.
Lane, James B. "Violence and Sex in the Post-War Popular Urban Novel: With a Consideration of Harold Robbins's *A Stone for Danny Fisher* and Hubert Selby, Jr.'s, *Last Exit to Brooklyn*." *Journal of Popular Culture* 8 (Fall 1974): 295–308.
Sutherland, John. *Offensive Literature: Decensorship in Britain, 1960–1982*. Totowa, N.J.: Barnes & Noble Books, 1983.
Wertime, Richard A. "Psychic Vengeance in *Last Exit to Brooklyn*." *Literature and Psychology* 24 (November 1974): 153–166.

LEAVES OF GRASS

Author: Walt Whitman
Original date and place of publication: 1855, United States
Original publisher: Self-published
Literary form: Poetry collection

SUMMARY

Leaves of Grass appeared in 1855 as a quarto of 95 pages that had been typeset by Whitman in the Brooklyn print shop of Andrew and James Rome. Whitman's name did not appear on the title page, nor did the name of a publisher or printer appear. He did not hide his authorship, however, for the copyright notice was credited to "Walter Whitman" and his portrait faced the title page. The 12 poems in the 1855 edition had no titles, but Whitman created titles for them, with which we are now familiar, in later editions: "Song of Myself," "A Song for Occupations," "To Think of Time," "The Sleepers," "I Sing the Body Electric," "Faces," "Song of the Answerer," "Europe the 72d and 73d Years of These States," "A Boston Ballad," "There Was a Child Went Forth," "Who Learns My Lesson Complete," and "Great Are the Myths." The collection went through five more editions in Whitman's lifetime. The third edition of the collection, published in 1860, contained more than 100 additional poems, many of them with homosexual overtones that brought more notoriety to the work.

The first edition fulfilled Walt Whitman's goal to write a serious work in a clearly sensuous manner. His subject is the common man, unlike other writers of his time who wrote about and for an educated elite. He chose to draw attention to the ordinary people who made up American society. He also had another purpose to his poetry. Whitman stated in the preface to the 1855 edition of *Leaves of Grass* his purpose of uniting the physical aspect of the human with the spiritual, and this purpose appears in the poetry, as in "Song of Myself," which contains the line "I am the poet of the body, / And I am the poet of the soul."

In developing his theme of accepting everything in life equally, excluding nothing, Whitman included blunt anatomical references that offended many of his readers for whom such references remained taboos for many decades into the future. In accepting all of nature, he wrote of "the litter of the grunting sow as they tug at her teats" and "where the bull advances to do his masculine work, and the stud to the mare, and the cock is treading the hen." He similarly accepted people in all stations and situations of life, as he wrote that "the keptwoman [sic] and sponger and thief are hereby invited—the heavy-lipped slave is invited—the veneralee is invited." He offered friendship and brotherhood "to a drudge of the cottonfields or emptier of privies . . . on his right cheek I place the family kiss."

Throughout the poems, Whitman speaks of the physical actions and realities that his contemporaries strained to keep hidden as not being "nice" or "appropriate" to speak of:

> Copulation is no more rank to me than death is.
> I believe in the flesh and the appetites,
> Seeing hearing and feeling are miracles, and
> each part and tag of me is a miracle.
> . . . .
> The scent of these arm-pits is aroma finer than prayer, . . .
> . . . .
> I turn the bridegroom out of bed and stay
> with the bride myself,

And tighten her all night to my thighs and lips.

. . . .

Darkness you are gentler than my lover—
his flesh was sweaty and panting,
I feel the hot moisture yet that he left me.

In numerous lines throughout the collection, Whitman celebrated sensuality and reminded people of their most primitive desires.

CENSORSHIP HISTORY

Leaves of Grass was declared obscene from its first publication. The first bookseller to whom Whitman took his book refused to sell it, claiming that it was "too sensual." Whitman met Lorenzo and Orson Fowler, who agreed to distribute the book, but sales were low and Whitman gave away many copies of the first edition. As cries of "immorality" were raised against the work, the Fowler brothers became frightened and gave existing copies of the second edition of the work to Whitman and resigned the whole edition. Libraries refused to buy the book; the Library Company of Philadelphia is the only one on record in America to have bought a copy when it was first published. Thus, other libraries effectively censored the book by their refusal to buy it.

Critic R. W. Griswold, writing on November 10, 1855, in the *New Criterion*, observed, "Thus, then we leave this gathering of muck to the laws which, certainly, if they fulfill their intent, must have power to suppress such obscenity." A review in the English magazine *Saturday Review* also condemned the collection and stated in March 1856: "After every five or six pages . . . Mr. Whitman suddenly becomes very intelligible, but exceedingly obscene. If the *Leaves of Grass* should come into anybody's possession, our advice is to throw them immediately behind the fire." In 1865, Walt Whitman lost his job with the U.S. Department of the Interior because Chief Secretary James Harlan found an annotated copy of the poetry collection in Whitman's desk drawer and determined that he was "the author of an indecent book." In 1870, Noah Porter, president of Yale University, wrote in *Books and Reading* that "a generation cannot be entirely pure which tolerates writers who, like Walt Whitman, commit, in writing, an offense like that indictable at common law of walking naked through the streets."

Many people, among them Ralph Waldo Emerson, who had praised the book in a letter that Whitman arranged to have published in the *New York Times*, urged Whitman to permit an expurgated version of the collection. He remained staunchly opposed to expurgation, and American copyright law protected him unless he consented to it. From the time that the collection appeared in 1855, his editors suggested that a bowdlerized version for the general public would be good for sales. Whitman violently opposed expurgation, viewing such books as "the dirtiest book in all the world." Not until 1892, not long before his death, did he finally agree to an expurgated version as a gesture of friendship for Arthur Stedman, whose father, Edward Clarence Stedman, had done many favors for Whitman.

Leaves of Grass was not expurgated in the United States until 1892, but it was banned entirely, if informally, in New York and Philadelphia bookstores in the 1870s and legally in Boston in the 1880s. As per their usual practice, the Watch and Ward Society in Boston and the New York Society for the Suppression of Vice placed pressure on booksellers to suppress the sale of the book in their shops. Booksellers agreed not to advertise the book nor to suggest its sale to customers.

In 1881, the Society for the Suppression of Vice sought to obtain a legal ban of a proposed new edition of *Leaves of Grass* in Boston. At the urging of the society, the district attorney threatened criminal action against a publisher who had planned a new edition of the work unless it were expurgated. The edition was withdrawn.

In 1883, author, publisher, and free-love advocate Ezra Heywood was arrested by Anthony Comstock, the head of the New York Society for the Suppression of Vice, on the charge of sending obscene matter through the mail. The material consisted of *Cupid's Yokes*, a pamphlet that contained "unconventional social and sexual views," and an anthology entitled *The Word Extra* that contained two poems from *Leaves of Grass*, "To a Common Prostitute" and "A Woman Waits for Me." When the case went to trial, the grand jury declared the Whitman poems "too grossly obscene and lewd to be placed on the records of the court." This meant that members of the jury would decide Heywood's fate without being permitted to review copies of the poem nor to hear lines from the poem read before making their decision; they were expected to accept the decision of the prosecution that the works were obscene. Judge T. L. Nelson, presiding in the U.S. Circuit Court in Boston, threw out the case, "on the grounds that the allegation in the indictment was untrue."

The English bowdlerized the collection from its first appearance in England in 1868. Pre-Raphaelite ex-bohemian William Michael Rossetti, the editor of the expurgated collection, explained in the preface that he had omitted about half the poems of the 1860s edition because he and Whitman lived in "this peculiarly nervous age." He also proudly proclaimed that he was not bowdlerizing the work, because "I have not in a single instance excised *parts* of poems." Noel Perrin observed, "it is the sort of preface a liberal poet might write if he happened to get involved in bowdlerism." Although Rossetti did not excise parts of any poems, he did make numerous changes in Whitman's preface to the original 1855 edition of the collection, excising even the term *prostitute*. The expurgated version of *Leaves of Grass* became part of the Everyman Library in 1886 and existed well into the twentieth century. Ernest de Selincourt used that version for Oxford's "World Classics" series in 1920, removing several more poems. Late in life, Whitman considered his work and expressed his dissatisfaction with the English editions, noting that "I now feel somehow as if none of the changes should have been made: that I should have assumed that position: that's the only possible, final, logical position."

FURTHER READING

Blodgett, Harold. *Walt Whitman in England.* Ithaca, N.Y.: Cornell University Press, 1934.

Broun, Heywood, and Margaret Leech. *Anthony Comstock.* New York: Albert & Charles Boni, 1927.

Cavitch, David. *My Soul and I: The Inner Life of Walt Whitman.* Boston: Beacon Press, 1985.

Cowley, Malcolm, ed. *Walt Whitman's Leaves of Grass: The First (1855) Edition.* New York: Viking Press, 1959.

Everson, William. *American Bard: The Original Preface to "Leaves of Grass."* New York: Viking Press, 1982.

McCoy, Ralph E. *Banned in Boston: The Development of Literary Censorship in Massachusetts.* Urbana: University of Illinois Press, 1956.

Mordell, Albert. *Notorious Literary Attacks.* New York: Boni & Liveright, 1926.

Perrin, Noel. *Dr. Bowdler's Legacy.* Boston: David R. Godine, 1969.

A LIGHT IN THE ATTIC

Author: Shel Silverstein
Original date and place of publication: 1981, United States
Original publisher: HarperCollins
Literary form: Collection of poems and drawings

SUMMARY

A Light in the Attic is a collection of funny and irreverent poems and drawings that mix nonsense and philosophy in a way that has delighted children for three decades. Some of the poems have rhymed lines and a consistent meter, while many more of them are free-form and appear to be random collections of words simply gathered around a central thought. The title poem, "A Light in the Attic," is illustrated by the sketch of a moon-faced boy with round eyes and hair feathering out from each side of his face. His forehead contains the peak of a roof with a chimney and an unshuttered open window about which Silverstein writes:

> There's a light on in the attic.
> Though the house is dark and shuttered.
> I can see a flickerin' flutter,
> And I know what it's about.

There's a light on in the attic.
I can see it from the outside,
And I know you're on the inside . . . lookin' out.

The poems contain such memorable characters as Backward Bill, who "puts his underwear over his clothes," and the "Polar Bear / In our Frigidaire," as well as silly situations as in "Crowded Tub" in which the speaker is in a tub with too many others and laments, "I just washed a behind / That I'm sure wasn't mine." Silverstein adds a twist to well-known stories, in poems like "The Man in the Iron Pail Mask," "He's the Brave and the Fearless / The usually Tearless / Man in the iron pail mask," and "Captain Blackbeard Did What?" in which the captain shaves his signature beard. In "Rockabye," he provides a new perspective to a well-known lullaby:

Rockabye baby, in the treetop.
Don't you know a treetop
Is no safe place to rock?
And who put you up there,
And your cradle too?
Baby, I think someone down here's
Got it in for you.

Some of the poems contain grotesque situations that deal with death and dismemberment. In "Ticklish Tom," Tom is "tickled by his mom," as well as by his friends, a toad, the falling rain, the brown grass, the clouds and everything else he passes, until: "He rolled on the railroad track. / Rumble, rumble, whistle, roar— / Tom ain't ticklish anymore." In "It's Hot!" the speaker complains that the heat is so intense that he cannot become cool, despite having "drunk a quart of lemonade," using an electric fan, and taking off his shoes. He concludes that the only way to cool off: "I think I'll take my skin off / And sit around in my bones." In "Strange Wind," the speaker tells about the wind "Whistlin' and whirlin' and scurlin' away" that it blows his head away but leaves his hat on. In "Who Ordered a Broiled Face?"—"Broiled face with butter sauce, / Mashed potatoes on the side" the speaker asks, "What do you mean you wanted me fried?" Readers also meet Pamela Purse who always shouts "Ladies First" as she pushes herself through crowds to be first in the ice cream line and at dinner. On a jungle trip, she and her friends become the captives of "A cannibal known as Fry-'Em-Up Dan, / Who sat on his throne in a bib so grand / With a lick on his lips and a fork in his hand, / As he tried to decide who'd be first in the pan—." True to form, "From the back of the line, in that shrill voice of hers, / Pamela Purse yelled, 'Ladies first.'" In "Little Abigail and the Beautiful Pony," the little girl named Abigail whose parents refuse to buy her a pony cries and tells that she will die if she does not get her wish. They refuse to give in to her demands, so she goes to bed when they return home and refuses to eat or sleep "And she DID die—/ all because of a pony / That her parents wouldn't buy." In the final lines of the poem, Silverstein counsels children: "(This is a good story / To read to your folks / Whey they won't buy / You something you want.)"

Silverstein's irreverence extends to encouraging children to trade in their parents when they become tiresome and to respond in extreme ways when they do not receive what they want. In "Clarence," Clarence Lee is a young boy who watches television commercials and "bought everything they advertised." One day, he orders a new mother and father who arrive in the morning mail.

> The old one he sold at a garage sale.
> And now they all are doing fine:
> His new folks treat him sweet and kind,
> His old ones work in an old coal mine.
> So if your Maw and Paw are mean
> And make you eat your lima beans
> And make you wash and make you wait
> And never let you stay up late
> And scream and scold and preach and pout,
> That simply means they're wearing out.
> So send off for two brand-new parents
> And you'll be as happy as little Clarence.

The collection also contains poems that verge on the risqué, although the language remains sing-songy and nonsense-filled. In "They've Put a Brassiere on the Camel," accompanied by the sketch of a camel with a huge lacy undergarment covering its humps and a bewildered expression on its face, the reader learns "They claim she's more decent this way." The illustrations that accompany seemingly innocent poems often add a risqué twist. In "Something Missing," the speaker relates that he remembered to put on his socks, shoes, tie, and coat, "Yet I feel there is something / I may have forgot—What is it? What is it? . . ." The illustration to the poem is a man sketched in side view, wearing a hat, jacket and tie, and socks and shoes, with naked legs and buttocks. In "Spelling Bee," the speaker relates, "I got stung by a bee. / I won't tell you where." The accompanying illustration is of a naked woman standing with her back exposed and the following message on her buttocks: "HELLO YOU'VE BEEN STUNG BY A BEE."

Among all of the silliness and the grotesque images are several poems that do teach a very important lesson to children. One of the most touching is "The Little Boy and the Old Man."

> Said the little boy, "Sometimes I drop my spoon."
> Said the little old man, "I do that too."
> The little boy whispered, "I wet my pants."
> "I do that too," laughed the little old man.
> Said the little boy, "I often cry."
> The old man nodded, "So do I."
> "But worst of all," said the boy, "it seems

Grown-ups don't pay attention to me."
And he felt the warmth of a wrinkled old hand.
"I know what you mean," said the little old man.

CENSORSHIP HISTORY

A Light in the Attic has received several prestigious awards, including the 1983 Garden State Children's Book Award, given by the New Jersey Library Association; the 1984 William Allen White Children's Book Award; the 1987 Children's Book Award given by the Claremont, California, Center for Children's Books; the American Library Association Notable Book Award; the Buckeye Shoestring Award; and the American Best Graphic Illustration Award.

The collection has also been challenged in many school districts because of the subject matter of the poems and the illustrations that accompany both the poems to which parents object and those which accompany poems containing seemingly innocuous material.

In 1985, parents of students attending the Cunningham Elementary School in Beloit, Wisconsin, asked school administrators to remove the book from the school library because such poems as "How Not to Have to Dry Dishes" teach children how to avoid chores and encourage them "to break dishes so they won't have to dry them." The following year was a year of multiple challenges to *A Light in the Attic*. The book was removed from the public school libraries in Minot, North Dakota, when the superintendent of schools discovered what he found to be "suggestive illustrations" on several pages, especially those accompanying the poems "Spelling Bee" and "Something Missing." In the same year, parents of students attending the Big Bend Elementary School in Mukwonago, Wisconsin, asserted that the collection "glorified Satan, suicide, and cannibalism, and also encouraged children to be disobedient." In West Allis West Milwaukee, Wisconsin, parents of children in the school district asked school administrators to remove the book from the school libraries because it "suggests drug use, the occult, suicide, death, violence, disrespect for truth, disrespect for legitimate authority, rebellion against parents," as well as inspiring adolescents to "commit acts of violence, disbelief and disrespect." In Omaha, Nebraska, parents of students attending the elementary schools in the Papillon-La Vista School District submitted a formal request to remove the book from the school libraries, asserting that it "promotes behavior abusive to women and children, suicide as a way to manipulate parents, mockery of God, and selfish and disrespectful behavior."

In 1987, the collection was the target of challenges in school districts on both the East and West Coasts. Parents of students enrolled in the Appoquinimink schools in Middletown, Delaware, contacted school officials and protested the inclusion of *A Light in the Attic* in the school libraries due to what they believed to be a preoccupation with violence and death and their concern that it "makes light of manipulative behavior." In the Moreno Valley Unified School District in California, parents asked to have the book removed from the school libraries because it "contains profanity, sexual situations, and themes that allegedly encourage disrespectful behavior."

The poem "Little Abigail and the Beautiful Pony" was the focus in 1989 of the attempted ban of the book by the mother of a second-grade student in an elementary school in Huffman, Texas, who charged that the poem "exposes children to the horrors of suicide." That same year, parents of students attending the Hot Springs, North Dakota, elementary school challenged the use of the book as suitable classroom material because of "its objectionable nature," and it was challenged for use in the South Adams, Indiana, school libraries.

The caricature of a person whose buttocks have been stung by a bee, which accompanies the poem "Spelling Bee," raised concerns in 1992 among parents in Duval County, Florida, where school administrators chose to restrict access to the book to students who had permission from their parents to check it out of the library. In 1993, the poem "Little Abigail and the Beautiful Pony" was the catalyst for the move to ban the book from the Fruitland Park Elementary School library in Lake County, Florida, where parents charged that the book "promotes disrespect, horror, and violence." The same poem motivated a similar attack by parents in 1996 in Webb City, Missouri, where the book was challenged but retained in the school library after several parents singled out "Little Abigail . . ." as being "morbid" and asserted that the illustrations are "suggestive" and the book "imparts a dreary and negative message."

FURTHER READING

Becker, Beverley C., Susan Stan, and Donna Reidly Pistolis. *Hit List 2 for Children: Frequently Challenged Books.* Chicago: American Library Association, 2002.
Livingston, Myra Cohn. "The Light in His Attic." *New York Times Book Review* 91 (March 9, 1986): 36–37.
Rogak, Lisa. *A Boy Named Shel: The Life and Times of Shel Silverstein.* New York: St. Martin's Press, 2007.

LITTLE BLACK SAMBO

Author: Helen Bannerman
Original dates and places of publication: 1898, England; 1923, United States
Original publishers: Platt & Munk, Inc.; J. B. Lippincott Company
Literary form: Children's book

SUMMARY

Little Black Sambo, one of many stories created by the author to amuse her daughters, was made up while on a long railway journey, and it "was the favourite." The "Preface" establishes the setting and states: "Once upon a time there was an English lady in India, where black children abound and tigers are everyday affairs, who had two little girls." Bannerman also "drew and coloured the pictures" that became so embroiled in controversy a half-century after publication.

The story is simple. Sambo is "a little black boy" whose father is Black Jumbo and mother is Black Mumbo. His mother makes him "a beautiful Red Coat, and a pair of beautiful little Blue Trousers." His father buys him "a beautiful Green Umbrella, and a lovely little Pair of Purple Shoes with Crimson soles and Crimson Linings" at the bazaar. Feeling very grand, Sambo takes a long walk in the forest and meets four dangerous tigers, one at a time. To prevent them from eating him, Sambo bargains with them, giving each a piece of his finery until he is left with what in the illustrations looks to be a towel around his waist. He walks home, crying, but hears the tigers and believes that they are coming as a group to eat him, so he hides behind a palm tree. As he watches, they remove the clothes and begin to claw each other. Finally, each grabs another's tail as they form a circle around a tree, running around it and "trying to eat each other up," while Sambo retrieves his clothes and goes home. The tigers run so quickly that they melt into a pool of butter, which Black Jumbo finds on his way home from work; he places it into a big brass pot and takes it home for Black Mumbo to use in cooking. The story ends as the family enjoys "a huge big plate of most lovely pancakes" that have been fried "in the melted butter which the Tigers had made."

The book was first published in England nearly a century ago, and it has appeared in nearly 50 different editions and collections over the years, the text or the illustrations varying according to the whims of the publisher. In the first American edition, published in 1923 by the J. B. Lippincott Company in Philadelphia, the title page bears the statement "The Only Authorized American Edition," as do all Lippincott reprintings of the book. In the "Preface," the reader learns that in the Lippincott version, "the pictures [are] copied as exactly as possible" from Bannerman's original illustrations. This point is significant because the illustrations have frequently been subject to heavier criticism than the text. Also significant is the realization that the Lippincott edition has been "most often in the line of fire and least often on library shelves" in the past three decades.

CENSORSHIP HISTORY

Little Black Sambo first attracted public criticism in the late 1950s, as the momentum of the civil rights movement in the United States increased. This public criticism intensified in the 1960s as greater attention was paid to the ways in which African Americans were treated and represented in all media. Critics viewed the story as "a dangerous and cruel book" that depicted African Americans in an extremely unfavorable light, dehumanizing them and perpetuating negative stereotypes. The name "Sambo" is itself rooted in controversy. The 1966 edition of *The Oxford Dictionary of English Etymology* defined the word as being "a colloquial term for any Negro," but various popular dictionaries of the time, including the 1964 Webster's *New World Dictionary*, defined "sambo" as a noun of Spanish derivation meaning "Negro, mulatto, monkey." The term does not even appear in the 1991 edition of Webster's *New World Dictionary*.

In 1956, the Toronto Board of Education ordered *Little Black Sambo* removed from classrooms and school library shelves after the board received complaints from several groups that "the popular book was a cause of mental suffering to Negroes in particular and children in general." Canadian librarians protested the move and pointed out that the setting is India, not Africa: "Everything in it pertains to India, even the clothing and the house where Black Sambo lives." A children's librarian asserted that "all the boys and girls who have read *Little Black Sambo* have done so without any suggestion of harboring derogatory feelings."

In 1959, the book was removed from a school library in New York City after a black resident challenged the book as racially derogatory. The school board convened a committee to review the charge. The committee determined that the charge was "unfounded" and voted to restore the book to library shelves.

In 1965, Lincoln (Nebraska) School Superintendent Steven N. Watkins ordered the book removed from the open shelves of the school libraries. The move was made following Watkins' receipt of a letter from the local Human Relations Council, which explained the "inherent racism" of the work. He concluded that the book was "not worth making an issue over . . . There are plenty of good stories left." A few weeks later, Watkins ordered copies of the book taken from storage and placed on the "Reserved" shelves, accompanied by a note stating that even though the book was "not a part of the instructional program, it will be available to those who want to read it as optional material."

A well-publicized banning of the work occurred in Montgomery, Alabama, in 1971. After receiving parent complaints, the county school superintendent in conjunction with a committee of principals, librarians, teachers, and a county staff member voted to remove all copies of the book, as well as filmstrips and records featuring the story, from the county school libraries. Committee members labeled the book "inappropriate" and "not in keeping with good human relations." In a memo to principals and librarians announcing the removal, the county director of educational media and technology stated that "the decision is not to be construed as book burning, but rather as book selection."

In January 1972, the Montreal-based Canadian National Black Coalition mobilized efforts to remove the book from school and library shelves. In

Hamilton, Ontario, teachers ordered students to tear from school readers the pages that contained the story. The book was banned entirely in New Brunswick.

Later that spring in the United States, a multiethnic committee in Dallas, Texas, lodged a formal complaint against the book and demanded its removal from the city school libraries because it "distorts a child's view of black people." The school district conducted an investigation of the complaint and determined that the book had been informally removed from the school libraries in 1965, but it was later returned because officials questioned if they were depriving children of their literary freedom. The book was formally removed again.

Little Black Sambo was also attacked in England in 1972, where a coalition of educators campaigned against retaining the book in libraries and schools because it symbolized "the kind of dangerous and obsolete books that must go." A member of the group noted that the story unfairly "depicts the Negro as an almost unclothed, illiterate and inferior savage from whose antics great humor can be derived."

The banning and removal of *Little Black Sambo* sparked considerable debate regarding the conditions that justify censorship. Howard N. Meyer, an attorney writing in 1980 in the bulletin published by the Council on Interracial Books for Children, took the position of many who demanded the removal of *Little Black Sambo* and other books such as ADVENTURES OF HUCKLEBERRY FINN or *Nicodemus and Sally* on the grounds that they were "racist." He stated that "censorship" is an act of "official agencies" and asserted that "citizens who urged that *Little Black Sambo* and *Adventures of Huckleberry Finn* be removed from school libraries as racial books should not be called censors since they are not state officials." The following year, Michael Farris, president of the Moral Majority in the state of Washington, appeared as a speaker at the American Library Association conference in San Francisco. After claiming that he had searched several libraries and not found a copy of *Little Black Sambo*, Farris labeled as "intellectual hypocrisy" the move to ban presumably "racist" and "sexist" books but to contest the efforts of the Moral Majority to remove what they view as "sexually offensive materials."

FURTHER READING

Baker, Augusta. "The Black Experience in Children's Literature—An Introductory Essay." *New York Public Library Bulletin* 75 (March 1971): 143–145.

Broderick, Dorothy M. *Image of the Black in Children's Fiction.* New York: R. R. Bowker Company, 1973.

Cohen, David. "Selection and Racism." *Library Journal,* October 15, 1969, p. 3,585.

Davis, Mavis Wormley. "Black Images in Children's Literature: Revised Editions Needed." *Library Journal,* January 15, 1972, pp. 261–263.

"Librarians Decry Toronto Book Ban." *New York Times*, February 5, 1956, p. 19.

Messiano, Lindalee. "Even When It Offends." *Library Journal*, May 15, 1969, p. 2,031.

Meyer, Howard N. "Neutralism Isn't Neutral." *CIBC Bulletin* 11 (1980): 13.

Newsletter on Intellectual Freedom (April 1956): 3–4; (July 1963): 51; (January 1965): 12.

"Sambo Banned by Montgomery County Schools." *Library Journal*, September 15, 1971, pp. 2,813–2,814.

"Sambo Removal Sought by National Black Coalition." *Library Journal*, January 15, 1972, pp. 237–238.

LITTLE HOUSE ON THE PRAIRIE

Author: Laura Ingalls Wilder
Original date and place of publication: 1935, United States
Original publisher: Harper & Row
Literary form: Young adult novel

SUMMARY

Little House on the Prairie continues the adventures of the Ingalls family, which the author had begun in *Little House in the Big Woods*, published in 1932. The earlier novel told of the hardships suffered by Pa and Ma Ingalls and their daughters, Laura, Mary, and later baby Carrie, who lived on the edge of the Big Woods of Wisconsin and faced the difficulties of pioneer life. *Little House on the Prairie* relates their move to Kansas, an area of the country that was still heavily populated by Native Americans. They travel numerous days until they find a location that is suitable for building a log cabin.

The family soon reestablishes a home and begins to plow and to plant, as well as to hunt wild ducks and turkeys and to raise their livestock. They must also function without close neighbors or family for security and block out the howling of the wolves at night. The Ingalls also live in constant fear of "Indians" without having had any previous contact with them. When Laura yells out to her mother, she is admonished, "you yell like an Indian." Ma Ingalls also cautions her girls that they are "getting to look like Indians."

Numerous tribes gather several miles from the Ingalls' cabin, shouting and yelling in the night and terrifying the girls. Various Native American males visit the cabin, but their presence is upsetting, as they frighten Ma Ingalls into preparing food and giving them her husband's tobacco. After several months of worrying about their fate, the Ingalls learn that the tribes dispersed after the Osage tribe threatened to fight the other tribes who want to kill all of the white settlers. The settlers also learn that they will have to move because the government has declared the area to be Indian Territory.

The novel ends as the family accepts its fate, loads the covered wagon, and moves on to find another place to settle.

CENSORSHIP HISTORY

Objections to *Little House on the Prairie* emerged only in the 1990s. Before this decade, the novel and others in the series were highly praised; in 1954, the Laura Ingalls Wilder Award was established by the American Library Association and was first presented to Wilder for her series. The award is now presented every three years to an author who has produced a body of work that has made a substantial and lasting contribution to children's literature.

In 1993, the novel was challenged by parents of students in the Lafourche Parish elementary schools in Thibodaux, Louisiana, who requested its removal from the school libraries because it was "offensive to Indians." Among their objections, the parents cited the repeated description of the Native Americans as "naked wild men" or "terrible men" with "glittering black eyes." The phrase "The only good Indian is a dead Indian" is repeated several times by the Ingalls' neighbor, Mrs. Scott. Further, the objectors cited the appearance of two Native American males who appear at the house when Charles is out hunting: "Those Indians were dirty and scowling and mean. They acted as if the house belonged to them." The two men look through all of the cupboards and take food and tobacco; then one goes to take the bundle of furs that are supposed to be traded for a plow and seeds, but he is stopped by his companion. The school board denied the request, and the book was retained.

In contrast, the novel was banned that same year from elementary school classrooms in Sturgis, South Dakota, because objectors asserted that "it contains statements that are considered derogatory to Native Americans." The objections presented to the Sturgis School Board were mainly those cited in the Lafourche Parish challenge, and Sturgis evidenced significantly greater public support for the ban.

FURTHER READING

McCullough, Debbie. "Idealism and Reality in the Works of Laura Ingalls Wilder." *English in Education* 26 (Spring 1992): 33–37.

Mills, Claudia. "From Obedience to Autonomy: Moral Growth in the 'Little House' Books." *Children's Literature: An International Journal* 24 (1996): 127–140.

Segel, Elizabeth. "Laura Ingalls Wilder's America: An Unflinching Assessment." *Children's Literature in Education* 8 (February 1978): 63–70.

Wolf, Virginia L. "The Symbolic Center: *Little House in the Big Woods*." *Children's Literature in Education* 13 (Fall 1982): 107–114.

LITTLE RED RIDING HOOD

Author: Charles Perrault
Original dates and places of publication: 1697, Paris; 1729, London
(first English translation)
Original publishers: Privately printed
Literary form: Children's story

SUMMARY

Little Red Riding Hood was part of the collection "Histoires ou Contes du temps passé, avec des Moralités," stories created out of folktales by Charles Perrault, that was intended to be used in the nurseries at Versailles in the court of Louis XIV. Perrault's tales were first translated into English in 1729 by Robert Samber in *Histories or Tales of Past Times*. The story, now often published alone, has undergone numerous transformations. The popular contemporary version found in children's books in the United States is based upon the rewriting of the folktale by Jacob and Wilhelm Grimm that appeared as "Little Red Cap" in their *Nursery and Household Tales*, published in Germany in 1812. The first accurate U.S. translation of this collection appeared in 1944 as *Grimm's Fairy Tales*.

Little Red Riding Hood is the story of a sweet young girl who visits her grandmother and takes with her a basket of food and wine. As she travels through the woods on her way to her grandmother's house, she meets a wolf who asks where she is going. After she tells him, the wolf takes a shortcut and arrives at grandmother's house long before Little Red Riding Hood. He eats grandmother, dresses in her clothing, and waits for the little girl to arrive. Puzzled by her grandmother's appearance, the little girl states a series of observations regarding the large size of the wolf's eyes, ears, and other parts. The final observation is "Oh, Grandmother, what a terribly big mouth you have." The wolf responds by leaping forward and shouting "The better to eat you with, my dear." He then eats Little Red Riding Hood. After the wolf falls asleep, a hunter appears, cuts open the wolf's stomach, and frees the little girl and her grandmother. They gather large rocks and place them in the wolf's stomach. Then the hunter joins them in celebrating by eating the food and drinking the wine.

CENSORSHIP HISTORY

Perrault's *Little Red Riding Hood* ended with both the little girl and her grandmother dead and no hunter to save them. The fairytales were written for the court of Louis XIV as a means of teaching children about the dangers lurking in the world surrounding them. Perrault's moral is not stated, but his tale may have been intended as a warning against strangers and traveling alone. Contemporary writers, such as Maria Tatar and Jack Zipes, suggest that a specific warning appears to be directed toward women, reminding them of their need for male protectors.

The Grimm brothers softened the ending to suit their intention of entertainment rather than the moralizing of Perrault's tales. They included a fierce woodsman with an axe to rescue and resuscitate the two female characters and retained the violent appearance and behavior of the wolf. Versions published in the United States have maintained the ending, but they have varied in regard to the violence contained within the story, sometimes making the woodsman into a kind hunter who saves Little Red Riding Hood and her grandmother.

Challenges to the story in the United States have involved the 1989 version published by Houghton Mifflin that won the Caldecott Honor Book Award. In 1990, the Empire, California, school district banned the book from the district because the bottle of wine appeared to "condone the use of alcohol" to district decision makers. The district curriculum director expressed further concern that the descriptions of the hunter's rescue of Little Red Riding Hood and her grandmother were too violent and inappropriate for young students. That same year, the book was also banned from elementary schools in Culver City, California, because the story "gives the wrong impression about alcohol" to children. Assistant Superintendent Vera Jashni expressed specific concern about the final paragraph of the story, which tells that, after the hunter has killed the wolf, the grandmother drinks some of the wine. She then feels strong and healthy enough to clean up that mess left by the wolf.

The presence of the wine bottle in illustrations of *Little Red Riding Hood* motivated challenges by parents of students in the fifth and sixth grades in the Clay County, Florida, elementary schools in 1990. The school board established a review committee to consider the objections and to examine the books, and the books were removed from the classrooms during the three weeks that the committee deliberated. The books were later returned to the classrooms after the review committee voted to retain the books and the school board concurred with their decision.

In 1991, a teacher in Bradford County, Florida, initiated a complaint that the book was violent because of the actions of the wolf. The teacher also questioned the appropriateness of the little girl taking wine to her grandmother and her grandmother later drinking the wine. The book was placed on the "restricted" shelf, where it was available only to students who specifically requested the book by title and author, while the school sought to locate a "nonalcoholic" version. In the same year, two teachers in Levy County, Florida, challenged the storybook for the same reason, but a review committee of educators and parents voted to retain the book in the schools.

FURTHER READING

Bettelheim, Bruno. *The Uses of Enchantment: The Meaning and Importance of Fairy Tales.* New York: Random House, 1977.

Chase, Richard, Jr. "Little Red Riding Hood: Werewolf and Prostitute." *Journal of History* 57 (Summer 1995): 769–776.

Moore, Robert B. "From Rags to Witches: Stereotypes, Distortions and Anti-Humanism in Fairy Tales." *CIBC Bulletin* 8 (1975): 1.

Newsletter on Intellectual Freedom (July 1990): 128.

Tatar, Maria. *The Hard Facts of the Grimm's Fairy Tales.* Princeton, N.J.: Princeton University Press, 1987.

Zipes, Jack. *Fairy Tales and the Art of Subversion: The Classical Genre for Children and the Process of Civilization.* New York: Wildman Press, 1983.

LORD OF THE FLIES

Author: William Golding
Original dates and places of publication: 1954, England; 1955, United States
Original publishers: Faber and Faber; Coward-McCann
Literary form: Novel

SUMMARY

Lord of the Flies is an allegorical novel that relates the adventures of a group of English schoolboys whose plane crashes on a deserted island, killing all adults aboard. Using their instincts, early social training, and education, the boys attempt to form an organized society. Their efforts result in some of the boys' emerging as leaders or bullies, while others remain destined to follow or to be bullied. Rather than develop a caring and harmonious society free of the corrupting influences of adults, the boys revert to savage behavior and primitive rites.

The novel seems at first to be a simple adventure story of survival, but the growing brutality of the boys toward each other reveals the second level of meaning that questions the nature of civilization and the effect of instinct versus society on behavior. Told from the third-person point of view, the novel opens with a conversation between Ralph and Piggy, who are walking through a tangled jungle on their way back to the beach. The reader learns that they and a large number of other boys, ranging in age from five to 12, were being transported out of a besieged England in the midst of an atomic war when their plane crashed.

The boys emerge in different, seemingly natural roles as the novel progresses. Ralph takes the initiative of calling the boys together, and he emerges as leader of the group, much to the disappointment of Jack, one of the older boys who had hoped to become sole leader. The two boys attract followers. Ralph becomes the builder and organizer who takes a careful and rational look at their needs, while Jack hunts with his followers and becomes increasing brutal and primitive in behavior. The two groups take turns at maintaining a signal fire on the beach in the hope of attracting passing ships, but Jack's group irresponsibly allows the fire to go out while they hunt and kill a pig. Aroused by their success, Jack's followers urge the others to join them in hunting, and the boys seems nearly overcome by a blood lust that almost leads to the death of one of the boys.

The island paradise soon becomes filled with fear. The younger boys cry out that they see beasts in the darkness despite the contention of Simon that it is only the beast inside themselves. As Jack fights more strongly for a leadership role, he gathers around him a majority of the boys, and they form their own "tribe." They kill a mother pig whom they have surprised while she is nursing her young, and the feast draws all of the boys. As if to worship the dead animal, Jack's followers place the pig's head on a stake as their offering to the beast on the mountain. As flies cover the head, Simon realizes that it represents the potent emergence of the boys' wickedness.

The boys soon begin to direct their brutal behavior at each other. One of the younger boys burns to death when the signal fire rages out of control. Then Simon, the poetic, level-headed member of the group, is beaten to death by the boys in a frenzied ritualistic dance. The last to die is Piggy, one of the remaining boys to continue to act with civilized restraint, killed by the sadistic Roger, who crushes him by deliberately rolling a boulder down the mountain. After Piggy's death, Jack hurls a spear at Ralph in a failed attempt to kill him. Forced into hiding, Ralph collapses in exhaustion on the beach and is found by naval officers who have arrived to rescue the boys.

CENSORSHIP HISTORY

The novel has raised objections regarding its use in the classroom because of its pessimistic view of human society as well as for the scenes of brutality. The novel was challenged in Dallas (Texas) Independent School District high school libraries in 1974 and at Sully Buttes (South Dakota) High School in 1981. Critics at Owen (North Carolina) High School challenged the book in 1981 for being "demoralizing" by implying that man is little more than an animal, and the appropriateness of the novel as a reading assignment was challenged at Marana (Arizona) High School in 1983. The school district in Olney, Texas, challenged the use of the book in the classroom for containing "excessive violence and bad language." The Toronto (Ontario, Canada) board of education ruled on June 23, 1988 that the novel is "racist and recommended that it be removed from all schools," after parents and members of the black community complained that it degraded blacks because the boys paint themselves and savagely hunt and kill both wild boars and later several of their group, while they refer to themselves as a "tribe."

The novel was challenged by parents who demanded that it be removed from the junior high school reading list in Rocklin, California, in 1990. The parents claimed that the book did not provide a good model of "the social standards" and "good citizenship" that are expected of students. The school board rejected the complaint and retained the novel on its lists. The same year, the Gloucester County, New Jersey, school district quietly acquiesced to the protests of parents who claimed that the author's notes to the novel were not appropriate reading for the eighth-grade honors English class. With no formal fanfare, the school simply removed the novel from use until new copies of the novel, minus the author's notes, were obtained.

In 1992, the novel was challenged as indecent by protesters in the Waterloo, Iowa, schools. The challenge was based on perceived profanity, lurid passages, and statements viewed as being derogatory to minorities, women, and the disabled. The protesters pointed out that Piggy, who suffers from asthma and cannot see without his glasses, is ridiculed by the others and deprived of his glasses. They also identified as offensive a passage in which the boys trap a sow, who is feeding her piglets, pursue her and stab her repeatedly until she falls; then, one boy proudly proclaims that he has stuck a spear "Right up her ass!" In several instances when the boys act in a manner that is out of step with expected masculine behavior, they are criticized as acting "just like a girl." Despite the opposition, only one of the seven school board members voted against purchasing the book for use in the classroom.

FURTHER READING

Barr, Donald. "Should Holden Caulfield Read These Books?" *New York Times Book Review* 91, May 4, 1986, pp. 1, 50–51.

Egan, John M. "Golding's View of Man." *America* 108 (January 26, 1963): 140–141.

Newsletter on Intellectual Freedom (January 1975): 6; (July 1981): 103; (January 1982): 17; (January 1984): 25–26; (July 1984): 122; (September 1988): 152; (July 1992): 126.

Slayton, Paul. "Teaching Rationale for William Golding's *Lord of the Flies*." In *Censored Books: Critical Viewpoints*, edited by Nicholas J. Karolides, Lee Burress, and John M. Kean, 351–357. Metuchen, N.J.: Scarecrow Press, 1993.

MANCHILD IN THE PROMISED LAND

Author: Claude Brown
Original date and place of publication: 1965, United States
Original publisher: Macmillan
Literary form: Autobiographical novel

SUMMARY

Manchild in the Promised Land is a fictionalized account of Claude Brown's maturation from drug-dealing gang member to one of America's most powerful writers about the African-American experience. The work bears the following dedication: "To Eleanor Roosevelt, who founded the Wiltwyck School for Boys. And to the Wiltwyck School, which is still finding Claude Browns." Throughout the work, Brown uses the vernacular of the Harlem streets in recounting the drug addiction, prostitution, and murders that threatened to destroy the generation of young black boys and girls struggling in the 1940s and 1950s to survive in a hostile environment.

The book is narrated by "Sonny," Claude Brown's persona, who tells his story of growth and endurance in Harlem, where survival depends upon an individual's ability to outfight and outmaneuver everyone and everything. He is unhappy at home, disdainful of his complacent mother and angry with his abusive father, and he makes the streets his home. Just 13 when the book opens, he has been shot while stealing bedsheets from a clothesline and is about to be sent away. Already experienced with heroin use, like many of his friends he is headed for a life of poverty, addiction, and early death.

After recovering from his wound, Sonny is sent to the Wiltwyck School for socially maladjusted boys, founded by Eleanor Roosevelt, whom he meets when he sees "this rich old lady hanging around Wiltwyck . . . she used to be married to a cat who was President of the United States." At the school, Sonny is impressed by the school administrator, Mr. Papanek, who commands respect through his knowledge and authoritative personality and who recognizes Sonny's potential to overcome his environment. For the first time, the young boy realizes that a man does not have to use a gun, a knife, or a fist to exert power over others; education and intelligence are far more powerful weapons. That awareness stays with him throughout the years ahead.

Once he is back in Harlem, the abuse at home sends him back onto the street, where he continues to deal drugs and to steal. At 14, he is arrested again and sent to a reformatory. This cycle of crime and arrests lasts through most of his teenage years, but the brief experience at Wiltwyck gives him the power to realize that he is going to be just another Harlem statistic who will die of heroin addiction or a gunshot wound unless he makes some changes. The only course is to get a college education. He begins by leaving Harlem to work and to earn a high school diploma.

Once out of Harlem, Sonny takes any job available to pay for his classes. He explores African-American culture as he becomes involved in the Beat movement in art and literature, and new opportunities to grow and learn appear as he becomes friends with musicians who are proud and passionate in exploring their African heritage. He also learns that drugs become unnecessary when life has purpose, as he experiments with spiritual movements. For a time, he is drawn to the Coptic faith, more for its African roots than for the religious aspect; then he becomes deeply involved in the Muslim faith. His belief in formal education also strengthens, and he makes plans to leave New York to attend college. Before making this move, he returns to Harlem, walks the streets, and assesses what has happened to the people whom he has known. One of his best friends has just died of a drug overdose, his younger brother is in jail for armed robbery, and many of his acquaintances are heroin addicts. Only one has had the will to rise above the situation, one of his oldest friends, Danny, who survived heroin addiction and now has a stable marriage and family life and religious convictions. Sonny recognizes that his only hope of escaping the human misery of Harlem is to leave New York behind.

CENSORSHIP HISTORY

Manchild in the Promised Land has been the target of criticism as well as of numerous attempts to remove it from school libraries and the school curriculum since its publication in 1965. Criticized upon its first appearance for what one reviewer called its limited vocabulary that was "not a language at all but an impoverished patois," the work has since been condemned for containing a host of other evils.

Lee Burress reported that *Manchild in the Promised Land* was among the 10 most frequently challenged books in schools between 1965 and 1975. In a 1973 national survey of English department chairpersons, Burress, who does not identify the cities or states in which the bans occurred, only the geographical region of the United States, found that the book was banned across the nation. In the Northeast, a combined group consisting of a parent, clergyman, student, and member of the board of education complained that "Trash like this does not belong in the classroom . . . . That hippie English teacher is perverted." The result was that students would not be required to fulfill any reading assignments if a book was judged "graphically realistic." The book was also placed on a closed shelf in the library to which students had no access.

In a case in the West, a parent complained of the "language and content," and the book was again placed on a closed shelf of the library to which students had no access. In a case in the Midwest, a teacher complained that the book was "obscene," and the book was removed from classroom use. In the Southwest, a group calling itself the Committee of Concerned Parents complained to school officials that the book should be removed from the high school library because of "profanity" and sex scenes that are "too explicit." School officials ordered the book placed on a closed shelf to which students had no access.

In 1974, after one parent of a student in the Waukesha, Wisconsin, school system complained about the language in the work as "filth and obscenity," school administrators removed the work from the high school library. Similar charges were leveled by parents in Plant City, Florida, in 1976 and in North Jackson, Ohio, in 1980; school officials in both these school systems also removed the work from their high school libraries.

A national survey of high school English department chairpersons conducted by Burress in 1977 found that the work had been removed from classroom use in two New York schools because of parents' complaints that the work was "obscene," and it had been removed from the library in a Massachusetts school after the book was brought to the attention of a teacher who found that the book was "not suitable for some grade level students." That same survey reported that a parent's request that the book be removed from classroom use because of objections to the "obscene" language and the masturbation scene was denied in Massachusetts.

In 1977, Concerned Citizens and Taxpayers for Decent Books in Baton Rouge, Louisiana, listed the work with 64 other "offensive" works. Characterizing the book as "pornography and filth," the group called for its removal from the classrooms and the school libraries. The work was removed from classroom use and placed on the restricted shelf in the school library.

In 1987, different complaints were voiced when parents and "concerned citizens" challenged the appearance of the book on reading lists for English classes at Parkrose (Oregon) High School. They protested that the content was "violent, the language offensive, and women are degraded." They further questioned the relevance of the work to the lives of students in Parkrose and claimed that their students "have no need to understand life in a black ghetto."

FURTHER READING

Brown, Claude. "Manchild in Harlem." *New York Times Magazine*, April 14, 1996, p. 111.

Burress, Lee. *Battle of the Books: Literary Censorship in the Public School, 1950–1985.* Metuchen, N.J.: Scarecrow Press, 1989.

Hartshorne, Thomas L. "Horatio Alger in Harlem: Manchild in the Promised Land." *Journal of American Studies* 24 (August 1990): 243–248.

Miller, Warren. "One Score in Harlem—Review of *Manchild in the Promised Land*, by Claude Brown." *Saturday Review*, August 28, 1965, p. 49.

Newsletter on Intellectual Freedom (September 1974): 111; (May 1980): 51; (September 1987): 176; (November 1987): 240.

MARRIED LOVE

Author: Marie Stopes
Original dates and places of publication: 1918, England; 1919, United States
Original publishers: Fifield & Co.; The Critic and Guide Co.
Literary form: Marriage manual

SUMMARY

Married Love was an attempt to explain to married men and women how their mutual sex lives could be made happier, and the chapter titles indicate a blend of the clinical and the romantic: "The Heart's Desire," "The Broken Joy," "Woman's Contrariness," "The Fundamental Pulse," "Marital Adjustment," "Sleep, Modesty and Romance," "Abstinence," "Children," "Society," and "The Glorious Unfolding." Although much of what Stopes says about married sexuality had already been covered in writings by Havelock Ellis, she brought a new perspective by emphasizing "the woman's side of sex questions." Rather than being merely a clinical "how-to," the work includes efforts at counseling couples and pleading with husbands to make greater efforts at understanding the emotional and physical sides of their wives' sexual natures. She also criticizes those men who demand their "conjugal rights" without concern for their spouses' mental and physical comfort.

When it first appeared, *Married Love* was described as a "strange amalgam of purple prose, suffragist philosophy, and sage advice on lovemaking." The book became a vital sex guide because it offered frank discussions of the difficulties that may occur for both men and women in sexual intimacy.

CENSORSHIP HISTORY

In 1919, American feminist activist Margaret Sanger bore "the brunt of insults from publishers because I tried to get 'Married Love' published" before finding an American publisher, but Stopes was completely unhappy with the arrangement. Dr. W. J. Robinson of The Critic and Guide Co. expurgated the manuscript, editing it extensively, toning down the author's enthusiasm and making her specific language more vague. The intent and effect of the book were subverted by the expurgation.

In 1930, the Tariff Act provided the United States Customs Bureau of the Treasury Department with a new procedure for censoring books that permitted officials to judge books before they were permitted to enter American shores and exclude them if they were "below standard." Under the *in rem* ("against the thing") provision, a local Customs official would refuse to deliver the offending book and advise in a letter that "this volume will be destroyed unless you claim it and are willing to test the issue in a court." Jail sentences and fines were not meted out to publishers or distributors, but the books were destroyed.

In 1930, *Married Love* was declared "not obscene or immoral" in Philadelphia after Fanny and Ida Teller, two social workers, imported copies of *Married Love* to use in their work. The volumes were seized by Customs, and the case went before Judge Kirkpatrick, United States District Judge for the Eastern District of Pennsylvania, who made the ruling. The copies were returned to the Tellers. Despite the judge's decision, the book was again seized later that year and again went to court.

In 1930, before the Philadelphia case had gone to trial, American publisher G. P. Putnam imported *Married Love* and notified Customs officials in advance in an effort to test the new Customs law. Lawyers for the publisher argued in *United States v. One Obscene Book Entitled "Married Love,"* 48 F. 2d 821 (1931), that the law was unconstitutional. Judge John M. Woolsey heard the case of obscenity brought by Customs against the work in New York City and decided that the book was not obscene. Woolsey declared that the Philadelphia decision should have been a bar to another similar proceeding. In a decision handed down on April 6, 1931, he stated: "I hold that Judge Kirkpatrick's decision established the book 'Married Love' as having an admissible status at any point around the Customs' barriers of the United States." To forestall critics who might charge that he was merely concurring with a previous decision, Judge Woolsey stated: "I cannot imagine a normal mind to which this book would seem to be obscene or immoral within the proper definition of the words, or whose sex impulses would be stirred by reading it." Instead of banning the book, the judge asserted that it should "be welcomed within our borders."

In 1931, the work was banned by the Irish Censorship Board for its discussion of contraception, despite the praise of many such as George Bernard Shaw, who called Dr. Marie Stopes "an expert instructress" on technique and claimed that "numbers of unhappy marriages have been set right by her instruction."

FURTHER READING

Beckett, Samuel. "Censorship in the Saorstat." In *Disjecta: Miscellaneous Writings and a Dramatic Fragment by Samuel Beckett*, edited by Ruby Cohn, 84–88. London: John Calder, 1983.

Rose, June. *Marie Stopes and the Sexual Revolution.* Boston: Faber & Faber, 1992.

Shaw, George Bernard. "The Censorship." *Irish Statesman* 11 (1928): 206–208. Reprinted in *Banned in Ireland: Censorship and the Irish Writer*, edited by Julia Carlson, 133–141. Athens: University of Georgia Press, 1990.

MOTHER GOOSE'S NURSERY RHYMES AND FAIRY TALES

Author: Unknown
Original date and place of publication: 1895, United States
Original publisher: Privately published
Literary form: Nursery rhyme collection

SUMMARY

The name "Mother Goose" has been associated with rhymes, songs, and stories for children from the mid-18th century when a marketplace for children's books first appeared. In England, John Carnan published the first collection of nursery rhymes in 1780, under the title *Mother Goose's*

Melody; or Sonnets for the Cradle. Publishers in the United States soon followed, and in 1786, Isaiah Thomas published the first American edition of the book. Numerous collections have followed, and the popularity of such collections has made Mother Goose a symbol of childhood. Generations of children have grown up reciting "Hey diddle diddle / The cat and the fiddle / The cow jumped over the moon; The little dog laughed to see such a sport / And the dish ran away with the spoon." Standards such as "Little Jack Horner," "Mary, Mary, Quite Contrary," and "Ring around the Rosie" have appeared in most editions. Scholars have pored over hundreds of nursery rhymes and their thousands of variations, sorting through the different renditions to determine which rhymes began as simply songs, which were meant to teach, and which had a deeper political meaning. The rhyme "Mary, Mary, Quite Contrary" has been associated with Bloody Queen Mary and the garden imagery, rather than pastoral, identified as detailing her torture and executions of political enemies. Scholars identify "Ring around the Rosie" as a rhyme associated with the plague and the rash that appeared on the bodies of those who eventually died, i.e., "we all fall down."

Delving into the origins of the more than 200 nursery rhymes that are commonly collected into books identified with the title "Mother Goose" can consume a lifetime of scholarly study and more space than is available in one entry. More interesting is the censorship of various collected rhymes in the modern period.

CENSORSHIP HISTORY

In 1969, the Xerox Corporation in partnership with Arno Press published a facsimile edition of the 1895 *Mother Goose's Nursery Rhymes and Fairy Tales* as part of their Legendary Library series. The edition contained 217 nursery rhymes, but two of them contained offensive words and images that brought outcries from African-American groups and Jewish organizations, and Xerox was forced to take the book off the market. The nursery rhyme "Ten Little Niggers" (a popular English rhyme and also the original title of a novel by Agatha Christie) brought protests from African Americans, and the rhyme was renamed "Ten Little Indians" in later editions. The opening rhyme offended members of the Jewish faith in its accusation of the "rogue of a Jew" who is "cheating" the seller of a golden egg "out of his due." Although Xerox published the book as legendary, the company must have experienced some prepublication concerns because they included the following disclaimer in the foreword: "Some of its statements are deplorable when they are not confusing." The book was publicly condemned by the American Jewish Congress, which issued the original complaint against the book. In response, a representative of the Xerox Corporation wrote, "I share your concern and unfortunately can offer no justification for the printing of this edition" shortly before the book was withdrawn from publication.

Criticism from other publishers was quick. In an article published in *Library Journal* on May 15, 1969, the withdrawal was characterized as "silly and not a very wise precedent." Civil rights groups played down the danger of the work, and one agency stated, "We've stopped worrying about the classics years ago. There are more pressing issues these days."

In 1983, another edition of Mother Goose rhymes was challenged. The Miami metro commissioner called for the removal of *Mother Goose: Old Nursery Rhymes*, illustrated by Arthur Rackham and published in London by Heinemann in 1913, because of its "anti-Semitism." Judith Krug, the late head of the American Library Association Intellectual Freedom Committee, observed in a 1983 article that this edition of Mother Goose rhymes is the version most often challenged and it is "this challenge that is referred to when Mother Goose is included in Banned Book lists and displays."

FURTHER READING

Carter, B. "A Second Look: The Inner City Mother Goose." *Horn Book Magazine* 72 (6): 707–712.

Darling, R. L. "Goose Feathers." *IFC ALA Newsletter on Intellectual Freedom* (May 1972): 69, 97–98.

Doyle, Robert P. *Caution! Some People Consider These Books Dangerous. IFC ALA Newsletter on Intellectual Freedom*. Chicago: ALA, 1996.

Krug, Judith. "Mother Goose: Old Nursery Rhymes." *IFC ALA Newsletter on Intellectual Freedom* (May 1983): 107.

Mesiano, L. "Even When It Offends." *Library Journal* 94 (May 15, 1969): 2,031.

"Xerox Withdraws 'Mother Goose.'" *Library Journal* 94 (May 15, 1969): 2,034.

MY HOUSE

Author: Nikki Giovanni
Original date and place of publication: 1972, United States
Original publisher: William Morrow Publishers
Literary form: Poetry collection

SUMMARY

My House is a collection of 36 personal and autobiographical poems that deal with thoughts of home, family, and humanness as written from the perspective of a black woman who is trying to verbalize the experience of other black women in balancing the desire to assert oneself and to help others. Grouped into two parts, 23 poems under the heading of "The Rooms Inside" and 13 poems under the heading of "The Rooms Outside," the poems continue the expressions of black pride that characterized her earlier work. The first section contains poems that reflect the warmth, pleasures, and comforts of home and family, as well as the intimate relations, personal thoughts, and love that are integral to family life. In "The Only Song I'm Singing," she asks "baby please / please somehow show me what i need / to know so i can love you right / now" as the persona struggles to determine her relationship to others.

The second section, "The Rooms Outside," deals with people who are outside of the home environment and focuses on the struggles that they must face. In "Categories," the persona considers occasions when she has seen "an old white woman" and wants to relate to her as a person but finds that impossible. She states, "if she weren't such an aggressive bitch she would see / that if you weren't such a Black one / there would be a relationship but anyway—it doesn't matter / much—except that you started out to kill her and now find/ you just don't give a damn . . . ."

The collection is largely a monologue that uses rich, descriptive, rhythmical language to reveal the mood and thoughts of the changing personae of the poems, the African-American woman who is trying "to put her house in order to keep outside atrocities from tearing down her house."

CENSORSHIP HISTORY

The collection was banned from the public school libraries in Waukesha, Wisconsin, in 1975 for "vulgarity" and for use of the word *nigger*. In 1990, parents of students at West Genesee High School in Syracuse, New York, called for a ban of the book from the classroom, charging that it contained "obscenities." In 1992, school officials in Duval County, Florida, challenged the inclusion of the book in the public school libraries because it contained the word *nigger* and because of numerous identified instances of "vulgarity," racism, and sex. That same year, a middle school librarian in Jacksonville, Florida, received complaints that *My House* was vulgar and racist. Questioned by school officials about the book, the librarian asked that it be moved from the middle school library to the high school or that it be restricted to students who have parental permission to read the book. She concurred with the parental objections that the book contained "explicit sexual connotations" and racial bias. The district review committee voted that the book should remain in the middle school library but on the restricted-access shelf available only to students with parental permission.

FURTHER READING

Giovanni, Nikki. *Conversations with Nikki Giovanni.* Jackson: University Press of Mississippi, 1992.

Newsletter on Intellectual Freedom (July 1975): 104; (July 1990): 127; (July 1992): 105.

Webb, C. Anne. "Censorship in the Pennsylvania Schools." *English Journal* 84 (April 1995): 84.

THE NAKED APE

Author: Desmond Morris
Original date and place of publication: 1967, United States
Original publisher: McGraw-Hill Book Company
Literary form: Anthropology textbook

SUMMARY

The Naked Ape created a sensation among academics and the public alike when it was first published, because zoologist Desmond Morris treated his subject, the human species, as he might an animal and analyzed humans in much the same way. The irreverent tone is evident from the first lines of the introduction, in which Morris notes that there are 193 living species of monkeys and apes, 192 of which are covered with hair. The one exception is the "naked ape," the human who "is proud that he has the biggest brain of all the primates, but attempts to conceal the fact that he also has the biggest penis, preferring to accord this honour falsely to the mighty gorilla." He observes that humans may have acquired "lofty new motives," but they have "lost none of the earthy old ones." It is to these earthy impulses that Morris directs most of his attention in the study.

The study contains chapters that examine humans in much the same terms and contexts that other mammals had been studied by zoologists for many decades. Chapter titles include "Origins," "Sex," "Rearing," "Exploration," "Fighting," "Feeding," "Comfort," and "Animals." The first seven chapters examine the interactions of humans with each other, and the final chapter examines human activities in relation to other animals. The most controversial chapter was Chapter 2, "Sex," which provides detailed discussion of sexual development, sexual practices, and sexual aberrations. Using a clinical tone and an analytical approach that has been applied to countless studies of a diverse number of animal species, Morris painstakingly dissects the environmental and nurturing practices that help and hinder human sexual development and details its physical signs. He identifies sexual practices that humans have in common with other animals and the signs of physical arousal and sexual response that appear at each stage of "copulatory behaviour."

In his discussion of sexual "aberrations," Morris explains that he cannot discuss them in "the usual moralistic way." Instead, the zoologist approaches these sexual differences, such as celibacy and homosexuality, as "biological morality in terms of population success and failure." Morris is emphatic in his defense of all sexual practices and asserts that none, "no matter how disgusting and obscene it may appear to the members of a particular culture, can be criticized biologically providing it does not hinder general reproductive success." He makes an exception in regard to the threat of overpopulation and suggests that birth control is sometimes a needed precaution to preserve the human race at its best.

CENSORSHIP HISTORY

The work was used as a college text for several years after publication without negative repercussions, but challenges arose when it entered high school classrooms and libraries. In 1975, a group in Baton Rouge, Louisiana, called the Concerned Citizens and Taxpayers for Decent Books challenged the inclusion of the book in the local school libraries. They complained that the book was "pornography and filth" and demanded its removal. The school board complied with the demand.

The most extensive challenge to *The Naked Ape* began in 1976, when school board members removed this book, along with 10 others, from the Island Trees (New York) Union Free School District High School library (see THE BEST SHORT STORIES BY NEGRO WRITERS), claiming that it was "just plain filthy." The court record of the case that was eventually heard before the United States Supreme Court, *Board of Education, Island Trees Union Free School District No. 26 v. Pico et al.*, 457 U.S. 853 (1982), identified the following objectionable passage from the book:

> If either males or females cannot for some reason obtain sexual access to their opposite numbers, they will find sexual outlets in other ways. They may use other members of their own sex, or they may even use members of other species, or they may masturbate.

The book was returned to the school library after the Supreme Court ruled in favor of the book.

In 1989, parents of students in Mifflinburg (Pennsylvania) High School challenged the use of the book as a required reading in the English curriculum. They charged that it contained "explicit, almost manual descriptions of what some would refer to as deviant sexual relations." The book, temporarily removed from the classroom while a review committee considered the complaint, was later reinstated upon the recommendation of the committee.

FURTHER READING

Newsletter on Intellectual Freedom (September 1975): 148; (November 1976): 183; (November 1982): 197; (May 1989): 93.

NAKED LUNCH

Author: William S. Burroughs
Original dates and places of publication: 1959, France; 1962, United
States
Original publishers: Olympia Press; Grove Press
Literary form: Novel

SUMMARY

Begun in Tangier in 1955, *Naked Lunch* is a montage of shocking scenes that
combine surreal fantasy and hallucination to create a nightmarish blend of
drug addiction, pederasty, and cannibalism. The unconventional narrative
patterns of shifting point of view and stream-of-consciousness rambling
make it less a unified novel than it is a series of images that are linked by
their theme of the destructive effects of man's addictions. The lack of a
consistent narrative and the frequently changing point of view reflect the
nightmare world in which William Lee, the main character, fights himself as
often as he must fight with others. Burroughs claimed in his "Introduction"
to have illuminated his technique through the title that "means exactly what
the words say: NAKED Lunch—a frozen moment when everyone sees what
is on the end of every fork."

Three sections make up the work: the account of drug withdrawal in the
Introduction, which is subtitled "Deposition: Testimony Concerning a Sickness"; the paranoid-sexual fantasy of the body of the novel with erratically
placed subheadings; and the scholarly examination of drug addiction in the
Appendix.

The Introduction offers Burroughs' explanation of "The Sickness," his
15-year addiction to opium and opium derivatives. The author scrupulously
distinguishes between drugs that create physical dependence and hallucino-
gens, which he claims are wrongly condemned. Using a sometimes jarring
word order, he also describes in painstaking detail the economics of drug dealing and the victimization of the addict. The Introduction ends with his apocalyptic warning: "Look down LOOK DOWN along that junk road before you
travel there and get in with the Wrong Mob . . . A word to the wise guy."

The body of the novel is the story of William Lee, a junkie who struggles
to free himself of the strictures imposed by drugs, sex, language, and bureau-
cracy. He roams from New York to Mexico to Tangier and beyond, searching
for escape from "the heat," which at first is slang reference for the police, but
which eventually comes to refer to the pressures of life that have driven him to
drug addiction. Space and time fluctuate wildly, and Lee lives in a nightmarish
world in which time stretches or constricts according to the amount and type
of drug consumed. Locations become interchangeable as Lee travels through
a world of sadistic sex, extensive drug use, and squalid surroundings. Heterosexual and homosexual acts that emphasize pain and degradation are described

in lurid detail, and mutilation imagery abounds in the novel. The names and specific effects of various drugs are detailed, as are the most and least effective means of administering the drugs in order to achieve their maximum effects.

Burroughs juxtaposes seemingly realistic scenes with brutal nightmarish acts that exhibit the degradation of his characters through the violent, bestial acts of others and of themselves. He uses colloquial language to refer to the human body, especially to genitalia, and strives for maximum shock effect in the extended descriptions of drug paraphernalia and use and the forced sexual encounters suffered by men, women, and boys.

In the Appendix, an essay entitled "Letter from a Master Addict to Dangerous Drugs" that was published in the *British Journal of Addiction* (53:2), Burroughs discusses the relative merits and dangers of opiates, cannabis indica, peyote, cocaine, and synthetic drugs. He interpolates his own experiences with each substance into an examination of sources and precautions, thus providing a guide to the unwary.

CENSORSHIP HISTORY

The novel has the distinction of being the last literary work to be declared obscene and brought to trial in America. From the 1959 publication of the book until January 1963, Customs agents seized copies of the work entering the United States, justifying their actions under the Tariff Act (1930), which provided for the seizure of allegedly obscene materials. The work was later involved in two legal actions. Although cleared in Los Angeles in 1965 before the case went to trial, it was declared obscene the same year in Boston, where the attorney general argued that the work was "trash." Writers Norman Mailer, Allen Ginsberg, and John Ciardi were called as expert witnesses, along with psychiatrists and academics, to testify regarding the literary merit of the work, but Judge Eugene Hudson remained unconvinced. In delivering his verdict, the judge declared the book to be "obscene, indecent and impure . . . and taken as a whole . . . predominantly prurient, hardcore pornography and utterly without redeeming social importance." In response to the claim by the defense that the work held significant social and scientific value, Hudson declared *Naked Lunch* to be trash written by a "mentally sick" individual.

An appeal was made to the Massachusetts Supreme Judicial Court, and *Attorney General v. A Book Named "Naked Lunch,"* 351 Mass. 298, 218 N.E.2d 571 (1966) was heard on October 8, 1965. The Supreme Judicial Court acknowledged that the book was "grossly offensive" and reminded those present that the author had himself described the book as "brutal, obscene and disgusting." They also applied the test of redeeming social value to the work and could find no reason to declare the novel as "not utterly without redeeming social value." Their determination that the work was not lacking in social importance resulted from the many reviews and articles in literary and other publications that discussed seriously the controversial book and showed that a "substantial and intelligent group" within the community believed the book to be of literary significance. On July 7, 1966, the Massachusetts Supreme Judicial Court declared the book not obscene. The four members of the court who delivered the favorable decision and the two dissenting members declared further that the book could be sold in the state but that people would be subject to prosecution if they "have been or are advertising or distributing this book in this Commonwealth in a manner to exploit it for the sake of its possible prurient appeal."

FURTHER READING

De Grazia, Edward. *Censorship Landmarks*. New York: R. R. Bowker, 1969.
Goodman, Michael B. *Contemporary Literary Censorship: The Case History of Burroughs' Naked Lunch*. Metuchen, N.J.: Scarecrow Press, 1981.
Miles, Barry. *William Burroughs: El Hombre Invisible*. New York: Hyperion, 1983.
Morgan, Ted. *Literary Outlaw: The Life and Times of William S. Burroughs*. New York: Henry Holt, 1988.
Sutherland, John. *Offensive Literature: Decensorship in Britain, 1960–1982*. Totowa, N.J.: Barnes and Noble Books, 1981.

NANA

Author: Émile Zola
Original dates and places of publication: 1880, France; 1888, England
Original publishers: Charpentier; Henry Vizetelly & Co.
Literary form: Novel

SUMMARY

Nana is the ninth novel in a 20-novel series entitled *Les Rougon-Macquart*, which traces the fortunes of two families, the Rougons and the Macquarts, their entry into the modern world and into all social classes. Not merely the work of imagination, the novels were based on documented evidence obtained through books, newspaper clippings, and first-person investigations to ensure historical, social, and political accuracy. *Nana* presents a picture of French life and society from 1852 through 1870 as it follows the career of a vulgar, greedy, and cruel courtesan named Nana.

The novel opens at the theater premiere of *The Blonde Venus*, a mediocre play with amateur singer Nana, whose daring appearance in the last act clothed only in her long, golden hair and a transparent gauze veil mesmerizes the audience. The audience is fascinated by Nana's marble-like body, and the former street urchin recognizes the power that her flesh exerts on others.

She is soon a sought-after courtesan, captivating wealthy men who provide the money that she needs for her sickly son, who is living with her aunt, and for her own extravagant nature. With little regard for their feelings, and no delicacy of manner, Nana flaunts her multiple relationships. She is verbally abusive and physically destructive and demands money from her lovers according to her whims. Her sensuality captivates a coterie of adoring admirers, but the attraction wears thin: Some men return to their more compassionate and accommodating wives and mistresses while others are bankrupted.

Oblivious to anyone's feelings but her own, Nana becomes infatuated with the physically ugly comic actor Fontan and begins to live with him. He soon dominates the relationship, slapping her, bullying her, repeatedly calling her a "whore," and using all of her money while hoarding his own. Once her money is gone, he tells her that they must share costs. Nana loves him, so she plans to support them both, hoping to please him. She returns to streetwalking and meets Satin, a street "slut" who opens her eyes to the world of "perversion." They dine at Laure, "in which faded dresses and tattered hats were to be seen side by side with elegant costumes, in the fraternity of the same perversions." Nana is surprised to find successful courtesans in the restaurant, all flirting with younger women.

Nana becomes jaded, coming to believe that "there was no virtue left in the world. . . . everyone was wallowing in sensuality." She even imagines that if she could look into all of the bedrooms in Paris between nine in the evening and three in the morning, "she could see some funny sights: poor people going at it for all they were worth, and quite a few rich people sticking their noses into filth more deeply than the others." One evening, after running from police rounding up prostitutes, she races home to find the door bolted and Fontan with another woman. He tells Nana that he will kill her if she ever returns. Despondent, she goes to Satin, and the two commiserate at a hotel, then go to bed, where they kiss and Nana "began returning Satin's caresses . . . uttering words of love." The romantic interlude is cut short by police raiding the hotel for prostitutes. Nana goes to her aunt's house, and she finds her son sickly and anemic.

Nana returns to being a courtesan, recapturing one of her former lovers, Count Muffat, who buys her a mansion and furnishes it elegantly. He looks the other way as she brings home numerous male and female lovers but finally leaves when he catches her in bed with his elderly father-in-law. She visits her son and finds him dying of smallpox, a death that Nana could have prevented by paying for medical care rather than lavish frivolity. Nana becomes ill with smallpox and dies. The final page of the novel emphasizes the destruction that the pustules had wreaked on her beautiful face. "It was as though the virus she had brought from the gutter . . . had risen to her face and rotted it."

CENSORSHIP HISTORY

Nana was censored before it even appeared in book form. In 1879, Zola sold serialization rights to the newspaper *Le Voltaire*, published by Jules Lafitte. Eager to make money on the venture, Lafitte sent sandwich-board men throughout Paris carrying signs stating *"LISEZ NANA! LISEZ NANA!"*

("READ NANA! READ NANA!"), and he inundated the city with large colored posters to announce the forthcoming serialization. Zola felt that the prepublication publicity made his work appear "cheap, nasty and frivolous." Although Lafitte promised not to change a word, he did delete what he considered to be controversial parts to avoid government censorship. Léon Gambetta, the famous Republican leader and opponent of Napoleon III, warned Lafitte that *Nana* was "too strong" and would have to be further sanitized to avoid the risks of a fine, a shutdown of the paper, and even jail. Lafitte increased the expurgations with each new installment in the serial, at the end of which Charpentier produced the unexpurgated novel that sold 55,000 copies within a few weeks and required additional printings. People bought eagerly to read what "evil" and "decadence" Lafitte had removed.

In 1885, the United States Customs Department seized the imported French edition of the novel, as well as invoices for an English translation. The department commissioned an official literal translation of the work from the original for the Customs officers to read, after which they ordered all copies of the book burned.

In 1888, Zola's English publisher, Vizetelly, came under attack by the National Vigilance Association (NVA), a group composed mainly of clergymen, to continue the work of the Society for the Suppression of Vice, which had ceased operation a few years before. All of Zola's works, translated from French into English by the publisher's son, were specifically cited, as were works by Flaubert, Goncourt, Maupassant, Daudet, and Bourget. The NVA gained the attention of House of Commons member Samuel Smith, M.P., who spoke in May 1888 against Vizetelly, "the chief culprit in the spread of pernicious literature." Citing Zola's works as an example of "obscene publications," Smith asserted that "nothing more diabolical had ever been written by the pen of man; they are only fit for swine, and those who read them must turn their minds into cesspools." The House passed a motion that "the law against obscene publications and indecent pictures and prints should be vigorously enforced and, if necessary, strengthened." The government would leave the initiation of proceedings to private individuals.

Other politicians and the newspapers joined the campaign against pornography, widening the scope of the battle to include other works, but Zola remained the focus. The Roman Catholic newspaper *Tablet* attacked him as "a pornographer," the *Globe* charged that Zola "sapped the foundations of manhood and womanhood," and the *Whitehall Review* demanded immediate action against his books. The law firm Collette & Collette, retained by the NVA, obtained a summons on August 10, 1888, against Henry Vizetelly for publishing three "obscene" novels by Zola: *The Soil* (*La Terre*), *Piping Hot* (*Pot-bouille*), and *Nana*. Henry Asquith, prosecutor for the Crown, referred to these novels as "the three most immoral books ever published." The defense argued that Vizetelly had carefully expurgated the books while translating them into English and pointed out that the unexpurgated French versions were being freely circulated and sold in England at the same time.

The prosecution declared the fact irrelevant, and the publisher went to trial at the Old Bailey in October 1888. Vizetelly was sentenced to four months in Holloway Prison and ordered not to publish any more of Zola's works. The court further agreed that all of Zola's works must be withdrawn from circulation in England, making Zola the only writer to have his works outlawed in England in the 19th century.

All of Zola's novels were banned at once in 1894, when they were placed on the Index librorum prohibitorum in Rome; in 1929, when Yugoslavia banned all of his works; and in 1953, when Ireland did the same. The major complaints centered on the perception that Zola had made a heroine of a prostitute and had discussed "debased man's nature" by uncovering the often sordid sexuality of the period.

FURTHER READING

Brooks, Peter. "Storied Bodies, or Nana at Last Unveil'd." *Critical Inquiry* 16 (Autumn 1989): 1–32.

Brown, Frederick. "Zola and the Making of Nana." *Hudson Review* 45 (Summer 1992): 191–217.

Brownlie, Siobhan. "Examining Self-Censorship, Zola's Nana in English Translation." In *Modes of Censorship and Translation: Contents*, edited by Francesca Billiani, 205–234. Manchester, U.K.: St. Jerome Publishing, 2007.

Hemmings, F. W. J. *The Life and Times of Emile Zola*. New York: Charles Scribner's Sons, 1977.

Josephson, Matthew. *Zola and His Time*. Garden City, N.Y.: Garden City Publishing Company, 1928.

Kendrick, Walter. *The Secret Museum*. New York: Viking Press, 1987.

Schom, Alan. *Emile Zola: A Biography*. New York: Henry Holt & Company, 1987.

NEVER LOVE A STRANGER

Author: Harold Robbins
Original date and place of publication: 1948, United States
Original publisher: Alfred A. Knopf
Literary form: Novel

SUMMARY

Never Love a Stranger is a carefully structured rags-to-riches story of a Depression-era hero who starts life in a Catholic orphanage and later becomes an important figure in the New York City crime world. The early chapters of the novel are largely autobiographical. Francis Kane is the name that Harold Robbins was given by the Paulist fathers in whose New York orphanage he was left as an infant. At the age of 10, he was adopted by a Jewish family and lived the early life of his fictionalized persona of this book.

The novel opens at the home of an Italian midwife who answers her door to find a pregnant young woman in the early stages of labor. After a difficult labor, she gives birth to a male infant, then dies. The midwife gives the baby the mother's name, Francis Kane. It is all that his mother leaves him.

Frankie Kane grows up in St. Therese's Catholic orphanage, eventually working part time as a numbers runner for a local criminal and, at 15, becoming sexually involved with an older French-Canadian housemaid. Frankie is adopted by his maternal uncle and learns that he is Jewish, but he finds himself unable to attend synagogue after years of daily Mass attendance and instruction in Roman Catholic doctrine. Instead of making a choice, he leaves organized religion entirely.

Happy to have a home, Frankie attends high school, hoping to enter a profession and leave numbers running far behind. His uncle contracts tuberculosis and the family makes plans to move, but state law requires that Frankie must return to the orphanage. The distraught boy runs away and loses touch with his family. After a tour of duty with the navy, he returns to New York and works his way up to become head of New York City's gambling rackets. His language is coarse and his sexual experiences are frequent, but he leaves this behind when he marries childhood friend Ruth. After she dies in childbirth, he enlists in the army, eventually dying in the war. The novel ends as childhood friends read a letter in which Frankie reveals that his son with Ruth survived and was placed in the Orphanage of St. Therese. He begs his friends to care for his son, "to give him roots in the earth, in society, to teach him the true values in the world."

CENSORSHIP HISTORY

A trend emerged in the years after World War II among writers toward an increased use of frank language and more detailed description of sexual relationships. In many cases, both tendencies were classified as "obscenity" when litigation occurred. In addition, many novels in this period also depicted a greater social acceptance of extramarital sex. Reviewers criticized the language and the behavior of Frankie Kane, whose tough-spirited attitude and ability to survive read "almost like a handbook on how to be a gangster." Isabelle Mallet observed in a *New York Times* review that Kane's story would have had "more direct appeal" had he been "more introspective." In an article in the *Saturday Review of Literature*, Nathan L. Rothman condemned the use of "obscenities" in the novel and claimed that it "isn't realistic or important."

In 1948, *Never Love a Stranger* was one of nine novels identified as obscene in criminal proceedings in the Court of Quarter sessions in Philadelphia County, Pennsylvania. (See END AS A MAN for complete discussion of the case.) Indictments were brought by the state district attorney, John H. Maurer, against five booksellers who were charged with possessing and intending to sell the books. The other allegedly obscene novels were James

Farrell's Studs Lonigan trilogy (*Young Lonigan, The Young Manhood of Studs Lonigan,* and *Judgment Day*), Farrell's A WORLD I NEVER MADE, William Faulkner's SANCTUARY and WILD PALMS, Erskine Caldwell's GOD'S LITTLE ACRE, and Calder Willingham's *End as a Man.*

In his March 18, 1949, decision in *Commonwealth v. Gordon,* 66 D. & C. 101 (1949) that *Never Love a Stranger* is not obscene, Judge Curtis Bok stated:

> It is a swift story that covers a great deal of ground, its point being to portray a hard and lonely man who could not fully trust or give himself to anyone. Its last and least convincing part is also the least open to attack for obscenity; the rest, particularly the section dealing with New York City during the depression of the early 1930's, is very moving, not because there are sexual incidents but because the lines of the story are deep and authentic.

Bok refused to declare *Never Love a Stranger* "obscene" because the definition in cases that he cited in his decision restricted the meaning of obscenity "to that of sexual impurity, and with those cases that have made erotic allurement the test of its effect." The work also failed to meet Bok's definition of sexual impurity in literature, which he defined "as any writing whose dominant purpose and effect is erotic allurement—that is to say, a calculated and effective incitement to sexual desire." In Robbins's novel, references to sexual activity are brief and general, and Kane's language is important to developing the character.

FURTHER READING

De Grazia, Edward. *Girls Lean Back Everywhere.* New York: Random House, 1992.
Mallet, Isabelle. "Unruly Local Color." *New York Times Book Review,* March 7, 1948, p. 26.
Parker, Ian. "Making Advances." *New Yorker,* April 1, 1996, pp. 72–80.
Rothman, Nathan L. "A Slick Toughie." *Saturday Review of Literature,* May 22, 1948, p. 27.

OF MICE AND MEN

Author: John Steinbeck
Original date and place of publication: 1937, United States
Original publisher: Viking Penguin
Literary form: Novel

SUMMARY

Of Mice and Men is the story of two men, big and simpleminded Lennie and small and cunning George, who drift from one ranchhand job to another as they pursue their dream of owning their own place. Despite their mismatched intellectual capabilities, the two men are good friends who share the same dream, the simple desire to have their own farm where Lennie will be able to raise rabbits. As they travel from job to job, George becomes frustrated with Lennie's limitations and often loses patience, but he does not desert the childlike giant. George knows that Lennie will inadvertently become involved in a situation from which he will be unable to extricate himself, so vigilance is necessary.

Although the two men are thrilled to be given a ranch job, George must, as usual, cover for Lennie and make him appear to be more capable and intelligent that he really is. The boss's son Curley bullies the childlike Lennie, who finds himself drawn to the bully's lovely young wife. Curley's wife, however, does not treat Lennie fairly and she teases him playfully, unaware of how seriously he perceives her actions. He sees her as being similar to the soft and cuddly puppy that he once had, and he wants only to stroke her soft hair as he had stroked the puppy's soft fur. When Lennie approaches Curley's wife to stroke her hair, she becomes frightened and struggles and starts to scream. He places his hand on her mouth to quiet her, but he is not capable of judging his strength and breaks her neck. When George finds them, Lennie apologizes and cries that he has hurt her just like he had hurt the puppy. George is aware that the ranchhands led by Curley will not have pity for Lennie, so he tells Lennie to pack up so that they can leave. A short time later, as the two sit on a riverbank, George shoots Lennie to death to save him from the more terrifying tortures of a mob.

CENSORSHIP HISTORY

Of Mice and Men earned the dubious prestige of being the second most frequently banned book in the public school curriculum of the 1990s, second only to the reading anthology *IMPRESSIONS*, and challenges were frequent in earlier decades and continue today. Censors claim that the novel contains crude heroes who speak vulgar language and whose experiences exhibit a sadly deficient social system in the United States.

The novel was placed on the banned list in Ireland in 1953 because of "obscenities" and "vulgar" language. It was banned for similar reasons in Syracuse, Indiana, in 1974; Oil City, Pennsylvania, in 1977; Grand Blanc, Michigan, in 1979; and Continental, Ohio, in 1980. In 1977, in Greenville, North Carolina, the Fourth Province of the Knights of the Ku Klux Klan challenged the use of the book in the local school district, for containing "profanities and using God's name in vain." The same reason was given by parents who challenged the book in Vernon-Verona-Sherill (New York) School District in 1980 and in school districts in St. David, Arizona, in 1981 and Tell City, Indiana, in 1982. The school board of Scottsboro, Alabama, banned the novel from Skyline High School in 1983 because of "profanity," and the chair of the Knoxville, Tennessee, school board vowed to remove all "filthy books" from the local school system, beginning with *Of Mice and Men* because of "its vulgar language."

The novel was challenged as "vulgar" and "offensive" by parents in the Christian County, Kentucky, school district in 1987, but it was later reinstated in the school libraries and English classes. "Profanity" was also the reason for the 1988 challenges in Marion County, West Virginia, schools; Wheaton-Warrenville (Illinois) Middle School; and Berrien Springs (Michigan) High School. In 1989, the school board ordered the novel removed from Northside High School in Tuscaloosa, Alabama, because of "profanity," and it was challenged as a reading assignment at a summer youth program in Chattanooga, Tennessee, because "Steinbeck is known to have had an anti-business attitude." That same year, the novel was also removed from all reading lists and all copies were stored away in White Chapel High School in Pine Bluff, Arkansas, because parents objected to the language. "Offensive language" was the reason that parents in the Shelby County, Tennessee, school system challenged the appropriateness of including the novel on the high school reading list.

The 1990s brought an increase in the number of challenges to *Of Mice and Men*. In 1990, a parent in Salinas, Kansas, challenged the use of the book in a 10th-grade English class because it contained "profanity" and "takes the Lord's name in vain." The school board review committee considered the complaint and recommended that the work be retained as a required reading but cautioned that no excerpts from the book should be read aloud in the classroom. That same year, a parent in Riviera, Texas, complained that the novel contained profanities and requested that it be removed from the 11th-grade English classes. At an open school board meeting to consider the request, 50 teachers and administrators and 10 high school students appeared to support continued use of the book. The only person who spoke against the novel was the parent who raised the original challenge. After the parent went through two more levels of appeal, the school board voted to continue assigning the novel.

In 1991, a Fresno, California, parent demanded that the book be removed from the 10th-grade English college preparatory curriculum, citing "profanity" and "racial slurs." The book was retained, and the child of the objecting parent was provided with an alternative reading assignment. In Iowa City, Iowa, a parent complained of the use of *Of Mice and Men* in the seventh-grade literature courses because of the profanity in the book, such as the word "Goddamn." She claimed that her daughter was subjected to "psychological and emotional abuse" when the book was read aloud and expressed the hope that her daughter would "not talk like a migrant worker" when she completed school. The district review committee retained the book. "Profanity," "excessive cursing," and "sexual overtones" were behind challenges to reading of the novel in high schools in Suwanee, Florida; Jacksboro, Tennessee; Buckingham, Virginia; and Branford, Florida.

A large number of challenges arose in 1992. A coalition of community members and clergy in Mobile, Alabama, requested that local school officials form a special textbook screening committee to "weed out objectionable things." Their first target was to be *Of Mice and Men*, which they claimed contained "profanity" and "morbid and depressing themes." No formal complaint was lodged, so school officials rejected the request. Challenges in Waterloo, Iowa, and Duval County, Florida, were made because of "profanity," "lurid passages about sex," and "statements defamatory to minorities." A parent in Modesto, California, challenged the novel on the basis of profanity for the use of the word *nigger*, and the NAACP joined in demanding that the novel be removed from the reading list. "Profanity" prompted the challenge at Oak Hill High School in Alexandria, Louisiana, where it was retained.

One of the more detailed complaints emerged in 1992 in Hamilton, Ohio, where the book was temporarily removed from the high school reading list after a parent complained that it contained "vulgarity" and "racial slurs." The parent, vice president of the Parents' Coalition in Hamilton, stated that the novel contained 108 profanities and 12 racial slurs. The school board suggested the use of alternative reading assignments, which the coalition refused, and the novel was temporarily removed from the optional reading list. At the meeting of the board-appointed review committee, 150 parents, students, and teachers appeared and enthusiastically supported the book. One student submitted a petition bearing 333 signatures of people who favored retaining the book. A local minister who opposed the book told the board, "Anybody that's got a child shouldn't want them to read this book. It should be burned up, put in a fire." The board of education voted unanimously to retain the book.

The novel was challenged in 1993 as an appropriate English curriculum assignment by parents of students at Mingus (Arizona) Union High School who were concerned about the "profane language, moral statement, treatment of the retarded, and the violent ending." In 1994, the school superintendent of Putnam County, Tennessee, removed the novel from the classroom "due to the language in it, we just can't have this kind of book being taught." That same year, parents of students at Loganville (Georgia) High School called for a ban of the book because of "its vulgar language throughout."

In spring 1997, after 13 years of teaching *Of Mice and Men*, eighth-grade teacher Dan Brooks, in Peru, Illinois, was told to stop teaching the book. The school had received three anonymous letters complaining that the language of the book was "inappropriate." Although Peru school superintendent John Jacobson stated that he viewed the novel as a "quality piece of literature," he supported the ban. The National Coalition Against Censorship (NCAC) stepped in to point out the lack of clear policies for responding to challenges, and the Peru, Illinois, school board lifted the ban while the board developed formal curriculum selection policies. In 1998, Brooks told NCAC that since the incident he has been observed more often and reprimanded frequently.

In 2002, the novel was challenged by parents in Grandville, Michigan, who wanted the book removed from high school classes as required reading, because it "is full of racism, profanity, and foul language." School officials considered the complaint but decided to retain the novel as required reading. That same year, after parents in George County, Mississippi, complained to school officials about "profanity" in the novel, the school board voted to ban *Of Mice and Men* from the school system.

In Lucedale, Mississippi, in January 2003, the school board voted to ban the novel. *School Library Journal* reported that a grandparent complained *Of Mice and Men* contains excessive profanity and violence. The book was removed from all classrooms and libraries in the district.

Also in 2003, parents of a student attending Community High School in Normal, Illinois, challenged the use of the novel in the classroom because it contains "racial slurs, profanity, violence, and does not represent traditional values." After a school district review committee considered the challenge and voted to retain the novel, the school district provided the student with the option of reading *The Pearl*, another Steinbeck work, as an alternative, but the family challenging the novel rejected the offer. The committee reconsidered, then recommended two other alternatives, *The House on Mango Street* and *The Way to Rainy Mountain*, which the family accepted.

In 2007, parents of students attending high school in Newton, Iowa, submitted a formal complaint to the local board of education to remove *Of Mice and Men* from the curriculum, charging that it contained "profanity" and expressing concerns about its portrayal of Jesus Christ. The novel had been part of the high school curriculum since the early 1980s, and the nearby city of Des Moines included it in both the required reading list for ninth-grade English students and the 11th-grade special education classes. Despite repeated attempts by several parents to have the board remove the novel, it was retained in the curriculum. That same year, parents in Olathe, Kansas, also sought to remove the novel from the school curriculum and in their complaint characterized the novel as "a worthless, and profanity-ridden book," that is, "derogatory to women, African Americans, and the developmentally disabled." Their request was denied, and the school board voted to retain the book in the curriculum.

In 2008, the parents of a 14-year-old student attending Washington High School in Kansas City, Missouri, filed a complaint with school officials to have the novel removed from the school district reading list. Dana Washington said in a television interview that she did not feel that her request was radical: "I'm not asking for the book to be banned, but for it to be removed from the list of required reading in the USD 500 school list." The parent said that her son had been "uncomfortable" when the teacher asked students to read aloud from the text and the N-word occurred repeatedly throughout the text. School officials responded to Washington and another parent who joined her in the complaint by offering students an alternative reading choice if they were uncomfortable with the language in *Of Mice and Men*. Washington rejected the offer by the school district and told a reporter for the local television station KMBC: "I want them to find another book that doesn't use the word so violently and profusely." She promised to continue her fight to remove the novel from the required reading list.

FURTHER READING

Carrington, Ildiko de Papp. "Talking Dirty: Alice Munro's 'Open Secrets' and John Steinbeck's 'Of Mice and Men.'" *Studies in Short Fiction* 31 (Fall 1994): 595–606.

"Censorship Round Up." *School Library Journal*, February 2003.

Johnson, Claudia. *Stifled Laughter: Woman's Story about Fighting Censorship*. Golden, Colo.: Fulcrum Publishing, 1994.

"The Long and Short of It." *Censorship News* 69 (Spring 1998). Available online. URL: http://www.ncac.org/censorship_news/20030305~cn069~The_Long_And_The_Short_Of_It.cfm. Accessed August 10, 2010.

Newsletter on Intellectual Freedom (March 1975): 41; (November 1977): 155; (January 1978): 7; (March 1979): 27; (May 1980): 62; (July 1980): 77; (May 1982): 84–85; (July 1983): 198; (July 1984): 104; (May 1988): 90; (July 1988): 140; (September 1988): 154, 179; (November 1988): 201; (January 1989): 28; (November 1989): 162; (January 1990): 10–12; (March 1990): 45; (March 1991): 62; (July 1991): 110; (January 1992): 25; (March 1992): 64; (July 1992): 111–112; (September 1992): 140, 163–164; (January 1993): 29; (March 1994): 53; (March 1995): 46, 53; (November 2002): 280; (March 2003): 55; (January 2004): 11; (September 2004): 177–178; (July 2007): 146–147; (January 2008): 27–28.

Noble, Donald R. *The Steinbeck Question*. Troy, N.Y.: Whinston Publishing, 1993.

"*Of Mice and Men* 'Inappropriate in Illinois.'" *Censorship News* 65 (Spring 1997). Available online. URL: http://www.ncac.org/censorship_news/20030305~en065~Of_Mice_and_Men_Inappropriate_in_Illinois.cfm. Accessed August 10, 2010.

"Woman: School Should Drop Steinbeck Book." Available online. URL: http://kmbc.com/education/17530918/detail.html. Accessed August 10, 2010.

OF TIME AND THE RIVER

Author: Thomas Wolfe
Original date and place of publication: 1935, United States
Original publisher: Charles Scribner's Sons
Literary form: Novel

SUMMARY

Of Time and the River is an autobiographical novel in which Wolfe, in the persona of Eugene Gant, relates his experiences as a southern man who leaves home to pursue his education in the North. As the book opens, Gant thinks of the distance, in both time and space, between the little town of Altamount in North Carolina that he is leaving and the city of Boston, where he will attend Harvard. While on the train moving northward, he recalls his unhappy childhood and the hunger for experience that he could never quite satisfy.

At Harvard, Gant takes a drama class, then wanders the streets to gain experience to use in his own plays. He hungrily reads everything that he can. He also becomes closer with another man from his town, Robert Weaver, who has insanity in his family. After graduating, Gant briefly goes home, where Robert and he get drunk and are jailed. Gant eventually decides to return north to live in New York City and work as an English instructor. Weaver reappears and takes a room at the apartment hotel where Gant lives. Weaver drinks heavily, destroys property, takes a mistress, and makes Gant's life miserable. Through another friend, Joel Pierce, Gant is introduced to the wealthy people of New York in their palatial homes. He is at first entranced by the opulence but eventually realizes that the wealth and luxury that he craves result from the misery of others.

On vacation in England, Gant meets old friend Francis Starwick, touring Europe with two women who are paying all of his bills. Gant becomes disgusted with them and travels alone to France. He visits Chartres, Orleans, and Tours, which remind him of Altamount, and he thinks of America and of his family and childhood. The thoughts make him homesick, and he makes reservations to return home. While on the ocean liner, Gant sees a woman whose face glows with great excitement. A woman companion calls her Esther, and Gant feels that she will be his destiny. The novel ends at that point.

CENSORSHIP HISTORY

Of Time and the River was a lumbering collection of half a million words when famed editor Max Perkins of Charles Scribner's Sons began the task of giving it form in 1933. After reading it, Perkins told Wolfe that the pile of papers contained two complete novels, one which told of "the period of unrest, wandering, search, and hunger in a man's youth" and a second that "was dominated by a unity of a single passion," the fictional account of Wolfe's affair with Aline Bernstein. The publishing house convinced Wolfe that the first part was the superior literary product and that his inability to be fully objective about the affair interfered with the quality of his writing in the second part. The real reason was that Scribner's "could not overlook the grave possibility that Aline Bernstein, or some member of her family, might well sue for libel if Wolfe's account of their love affair was published." Aline had already made Wolfe promise not to write anything about her or her family without approval, and he had given his word. Yet none of what Perkins read in the lumbering manuscript had been approved, and it was not likely to gain her approval. Thus, Perkins and Scribner's censored the author's original work before publication by removing the second half of the work because they "had every reason to think that Aline Bernstein might explode if Charles Scribner's Sons published a major book, half of which was devoted to her love life."

Once published, the novel became the object of criticism and of a call for its suppression by groups who perceived it as being both racist and anti-Semitic. Critics objected to his treatment of African Americans, pointing out that these minor characters are treated more like "frantic children." The growing activism of the New Deal era and the increasing awareness of individual human rights led critics to feel that Wolfe was contemptuous of blacks and that black characters in his books "hardly qualify as human beings." More troubling to Wolfe was the charge of anti-Semitism. He saw nothing wrong in writing in *Of Time and the River* that the main character, Eugene Gant, feels when he begins teaching in New York City that he is in a world "overrun by Jews" and that his students with their "Yiddish" faces are "beak-nosed" and engage in "Kike" laughter. Cognizant of the growing threats to Jews in Germany, a Jewish leader wrote to Scribner's from Philadelphia objecting to Wolfe's "hymn of hate directed against an oppressed minority," while another critic wrote that the novel "fairly reeks of the narrow-mindedness engendered in anti-Semitism." Such criticism angered Wolfe, who had taken pains to create a view that "was so much more flattering than his own personal assessment of the Jews." Aside from isolated individual refusals to buy the novel, no formal banning occurred.

In 1963, the novel was removed from four high school libraries in the Amarillo, Texas, area after parents of students attending the high schools raised charges of obscenity against the book. They protested the depiction of the relationship of Reverend Pentland with the "widder" as "pornographic" because one character teases him with "a lewd smile" that "she's let him have a little of it." The objectors also cited the "profanities" that were "inappropriate for a school" and identified "damn," "hell," "son of a bitch," and the "lovely bastard of a train" used early in the book. Parents also protested references to sex and noted one character's identification of a woman in a play as a "society whore. . . . you can find plenty of her kind for three dollars a throw," as well as the open references to Weaver's mistress.

In 1983, the Alabama State Textbook Committee removed Wolfe's novel from use in the Alabama public schools. At the same time, the committee also removed Maya Angelou's I Know Why the Caged Bird Sings and Henrik Ibsen's *A Doll's House*. The committee claimed that they took the action in response to parent complaints about the "obscenities" and "inappropriate situations" in the works.

FURTHER READING

Donald, David Herbert. *Look Homeward: A Life of Thomas Wolfe*. Boston: Little, Brown & Company, 1987.

Holman, C. Hugh. *The Letters of Thomas Wolfe to His Mother*. Chapel Hill: University of North Carolina Press, 1968.

Newsletter on Intellectual Freedom (March 1983): 39.

Roberts, Terry. "Irreconcilable Talents: Thomas Wolfe's Struggle to Compose *Of Time and the River*." *Mississippi Quarterly* 43 (Winter 1989): 22–32.

Stutman, Suzanne, ed. *My Other Loneliness: Letters of Thomas Wolfe and Aline Bernstein*. Chapel Hill: University of North Carolina Press, 1983.

THE OLD MAN AND THE SEA

Author: Ernest Hemingway
Original date and place of publication: 1952, United States
Original publisher: Charles Scribner's Sons
Literary form: Novella

SUMMARY

Ernest Hemingway's *The Old Man and the Sea*, originally subtitled "The Story of a Common Man," is a novella that relates the story of the fisherman Santiago and his epic struggle near the end of his long life to capture a large and legendary marlin in the waters surrounding Cuba. Although the plot is simple, the philosophical implications of the story are complex as Santiago recognizes that his former fame and prowess as a fisherman have waned and the end of his life is drawing closer. Even his dreams have changed: "He no longer dreamed of storms, nor of women, nor of great occurrences, nor of great fish, nor fights, nor contests of strength, nor of his wife. He only dreamed of places now and of the lions on the beach. They played like young cats in the dusk and he loved them like he loved the boy."

Known once as a great fisherman, Santiago is now the object of ridicule by the younger and more successful fishermen and the focus of the pity of the older fishermen. Many view him as "*salao*, which is the worst form of unlucky." The novel opens on the 84th day of a period during which he has not caught a fish. When he was younger, he had experienced a stretch of 87 days without catching a fish, and he comforts himself with remembering that this streak of bad luck can also end, as the earlier had. He comforts himself, as well, by talking to the boy Manolin about his beloved Yankees and his hero "the great DiMaggio," who had similarly experienced a lengthy losing streak that he eventually overcame. Manolin had fished alongside Santiago for the first 40 days of the dry period, but his parents forced him to leave the old man and to join another boat that was bringing fish every day. Although Manolin is forbidden to fish with Santiago, he does continue to look after the old man. He brings food that he claims the owner of Terrace café has provided, he places a blanket around Santiago's shoulders as the old man dozes in the cool evening breeze, and he worries about obtaining clothing and blankets to keep Santiago warm the next winter.

Santiago goes out alone on the 85th day, carrying with him the bait of sardines, tuna, and albacore that Manolin has prepared. As the boat moves further into the ocean, Santiago speaks aloud to himself, noticing the movements of birds and identifying the signs that a large fish is somewhere nearby. He feels the fish gnaw at one of the baited hooks, then move to another as he softy murmurs, "Eat it a little more . . . Eat it well." He misjudges the size of the fish that begins to tow the boat after Santiago gives a mighty pull on the line, and he attempts to bring the fish to the surface, but the fish begins to swim forward, pulling the boat along. As the old man stands solidly on the deck with the line braced across his back, the fish swims steadily out to sea and tows the skiff with it. The struggle with the huge fish continues from late afternoon through the next morning, an epic struggle as Santiago holds the line tightly and thinks repeatedly, "I wish I had the boy here." He imagines that the fish is an old warrior of the sea, as he is, and he expresses a deep respect for his catch as the hours pass and their struggles continue: "Fish, I love you and respect you very much. But I will kill you dead before this day ends." During the ordeal, Santiago's thoughts wander as he thinks about American baseball and his heroes the Yankees. He tells himself that he "must have confidence and I must be worthy of the great DiMaggio, who does all things perfectly even with the pain of the bone spur in his heel," then wonders "What is a bone spur?

Santiago manages to bring the fish to the surface and to kill it with his harpoon. He recognizes that he has killed the fish for reasons other than to provide food for himself and a small income from the sale of its flesh. "You did not kill the fish only to keep alive and to sell for food, he thought. You killed him for pride and because you are a fisherman. You loved him when he was alive and you loved him after. If you love him, it is not a sin to kill him. Or is it more?" The blood from the kill trails in the water behind the skiff as Santiago steers for home, and the scent attracts sharks that surround the boat. In pain and with cramped and bleeding hands, he struggles to defend himself and creates a crude harpoon by lashing his knife to an oar and strikes out at the sharks, stabbing one repeatedly in the head. The sharks continue to attack the trailing fish and tear off huge chunks of meat, while Santiago experiences great regret for having captured and killed the fish, which has now become shark bait.

> He could not talk to the fish anymore because the fish had been ruined too badly. Then something came into his head.
> "Half fish," he said. "Fish that you were. I am sorry that I went out too far. I ruined us both. But we have killed many sharks, you and I, and ruined many others. How many did you ever kill, old fish? You do not have that spear on your head for nothing."

As Santiago nears home after three days without sleep and in near delirium, a final pack of sharks attack his fish, and he realizes that he has lost his great trophy to them. When he pulls into the little harbor near his home, only the great tail of the formerly massive marlin remains, and he sees only "the white naked line of his backbone and the dark mass of the head with the projecting bill and all the nakedness between." The old man docks his boat and returns to his shack without fanfare, too exhausted to do anything other than to simply collapse into bed. Manolin finds him lying there in an exhausted sleep, his hands badly cut, and he cries. The other fishermen marvel at the size of the fish that Santiago caught and call out in wonder that "he was eighteen feet from nose to tail." While the others reevaluate their perceptions of the old man, Manolin worries about his physical health and takes hot coffee "with plenty of milk and sugar in it" to the shack. He is determined to help Santiago heal, and he wants to join the old man and fish with him once again: "You must get well fast for there is much that I can learn and you can teach me everything." As Santiago sleeps and dreams of his youth in Africa and of the lions, the remnants of his prize catch floats "in the water among the empty beer cans. . . . the great fish that was not just garbage waiting to go out with the tide."

CENSORSHIP HISTORY

The Old Man and the Sea has a long history of critical acclaim, and many critics assert that the publication of this work both revived Ernest Hemingway's career and prepared the way for his receiving the Nobel Prize in literature in 1954. The brief novel has been a reading list staple for decades, selected by students for its brevity and accepted by teachers as being a book that students will likely read because it is brief. Aside from its genesis in the years that Hemingway spent traveling to Cuba and the friendships he made during that time, critics have found little controversy in the work.

In 1987, the novel was one of 64 books that the superintendent of schools in Bay County, Florida, proposed to remove from the classrooms in the school district. In early May 1987, Superintendent Leonard Hall, who claimed that he had been appointed "to restore Christian values to the schools," created a three-tier book classification system into which he categorized all of the books then in use in the school system. Only those books that fit the requirements of the first category, "works considered to contain no vulgarity or explicit sex," would be taught in the classroom. Books in the second tier, those having "a 'sprinkling' of vulgarity," would be allowed in the district but they would be subject to periodic review and limited mostly to the school library. The third tier, books that Superintendent Hall identified as having "a lot of vulgarity" and the "curse goddamn" were removed from the schools. *The Old Man and the Sea* was placed in the third tier and banned from the classrooms. The superintendent identified as objectionable a passage early in the novella when Santiago awakens after dreaming about the lions on the beach in Africa, where he lived as boy: "He urinated outside the shack and then went up the road to wake the boy." He also cited several instances in which "inappropriate language" appears. When Santiago goes out to sea on the 85th day of not catching any fish, he encounters a Portuguese man-of-war floating close beside the boat. As it turns on its side, then rights itself, trailing "its long deadly purple filaments" he addresses it, "*Agua mala* . . . You whore." Hall also identified as inappropriate the old man's musings about the "the huge, stupid loggerheads, yellow in their armour-plating, strange in their lovemaking, and happily eating the Portuguese men-of-war with their eyes shut" and the old man's dreams of "a vast school of porpoises that stretched for eight or 10 miles and it was in the time of their mating." The Bay County School Board initially supported the actions of Superintendent Hall and agreed to ban the 64 books on the list. The board ordered teachers to remove the 64 books from the classrooms and adopted a screening policy to use before books are introduced into the classroom, the book three-tier book classification system.

In response to the actions of the school board and the school superintendent, a group of 44 parents, teachers, and students countered the move by filing a class action lawsuit in federal district court in Pensacola in which they contended that their "constitutional rights have been violated by the book policy of the Bay County School Board and the Superintendent of Schools, Leonard Hall." The following day, at a school board meeting that lasted eight hours, the board voted to change its policy and to tear up the list of books the superintendent wanted banned from the classrooms. Members also voted to approve "all books that are currently in use in all public high schools in the county of 110,000 people."

FURTHER READING

Bruccoli, Matthew J. *Fitzgerald & Hemingway: A Dangerous Friendship*. New York: Carroll & Graf, 1994.
"Florida Officials Yield on Book Ban." *New York Times*, May 15, 1987, p. D18.
Hotchner, A. E. *Papa Hemingway: A Personal Memoir*. New York: Carroll & Graf, 1999.
Myers, Jeffrey. *Hemingway: Life into Art*. New York: Cooper Square Press, 2000.
Reynolds, Michael S. *Hemingway: The Final Years*. New York: W. W. Norton, 1999.
"Suit Challenges School Book Ban." *New York Times*, May 14, 1987, p. A16.
Zwingle, Erla. "The Importance of Being Ernest." *Chicago Tribune*, December 3, 2006, p. 16.

ONE FLEW OVER THE CUCKOO'S NEST

Author: Ken Kesey
Original date and place of publication: 1962, United States
Original publisher: Viking Press
Literary form: Novel

SUMMARY

One Flew over the Cuckoo's Nest is told from the point of view of Bromden, a tall and heavyset schizophrenic Native American called the Chief, who is an inmate of a mental hospital ward. He pretends to be mute as a defense against his surroundings, but the arrival of Randle Patrick McMurphy, a fast-talking con artist who has feigned insanity to enter the mental hospital rather than a prison work farm, gives Bromden confidence and helps him to rebel against the sterile, domineering Miss Ratched. Known to the inmates as Big Nurse, she runs a tightly controlled, efficient ward in which the heavily medicated patients mechanically follow her orders without question and even the orderlies stand at attention, "ready to quell even the feeblest insurrection." McMurphy disrupts her efficiency with his irrepressible high spirits and his goal to create havoc on her well-run ward. The chilling authority of Nurse Ratched appalls McMurphy, who provides a direct contrast to the other patients. They "long ago gave up the struggle to assert themselves. Cowed, docile, they have surrendered completely to her unbridled authority."

The boisterous, fun-loving, rebellious McMurphy is a lusty and profane fighter whose brawling and gambling challenge the rigidly structured world over which Nurse Ratched presides. Against all hospital rules, he initiates gambling among the inmates and smuggles women and wine into the ward. As he openly defies Big Nurse, the other men gradually emerge from their fear-induced inactivity and learn to express happiness, anger, and other emotions that have long been repressed. Such behavior becomes dangerous for McMurphy because he has been committed by the state, not voluntarily as have most of the men, and his behavior will determine the length of his stay. The greater his rebellion against the repressive atmosphere created by Big Nurse, the greater the danger that he will be forced to remain in the hospital for a longer period of commitment.

From taking forbidden cigarettes left at the nurses' station to stealing a fishing boat for an inmates' fishing expedition, McMurphy shows a disregard for the rules that have long dominated the lives of the other inmates, as his vitality and enthusiasm radically change them. His escapades have sometimes tragic consequences that result from the clash of authority with the inmates' newfound freedom. One man drowns in the therapeutic swimming pool when his fingers become stuck in the grate at the bottom of the pool, while young Billy Bibbit takes his own life after Nurse Ratched threatens to tell his mother that he has had sex with a prostitute whom McMurphy sneaked onto the ward. Even McMurphy must eventually yield to the misguided technology of the mental hospital after he attacks Big Nurse, blaming her brutal treatment and threats for young Billy's death. A few weeks after the attack, McMurphy disappears from the ward for a week. When he returns, the other inmates refuse to accept the changed man and claim that he is an impostor who looks "like one of those department store dummies . . . a crummy sideshow fake lying there on the Gurney." A lobotomy destroys all that has made McMurphy human and makes him the perfect example of what happens to a man who bucks the system. Unable to bear seeing their friend deprived of his vitality, the remaining inmates decide to provide him with a dignified end. The Chief smothers him with a pillow, then escapes from the hospital to freedom.

CENSORSHIP HISTORY

The novel has been frequently censored and challenged as being racist, obscene, and immoral because of its raw language and for its emphasis upon the defiance of authority. The white inmates repeatedly refer to the black orderlies with such racial slurs as "coons," "boys," and "niggers," while the Japanese nurse from the Disturbed ward is spoken of as the "Jap." Numerous obscenities pepper McMurphy's speech, and he appears to purposely taunt the doctors and nurses, as when he challenges their question regarding his psychopathic tendencies: "'Is it my fightin' tendencies or my fuckin' tendencies? Must be fuckin', mustn't it? All that wham-bam-thank-you-ma'am . . . '" He further describes Nurse Ratched as having "the too big boobs" and as "a bitch and a buzzard and a ballcutter."

Identified as containing "obscene, filthy language," the novel was challenged in 1971 in Greeley, Colorado, where parents in the public school district demanded that it be removed from the nonrequired American Culture reading list along with *I Never Promised You a Rose Garden* and *Love Story.* In 1974, five residents of Strongsville, Ohio, sued the board of education to remove *One Flew over the Cuckoo's Nest* and MANCHILD IN THE PROMISED LAND from the classroom. Labeling both books "pornographic materials," they charged that the works "glorify criminal activity, have a tendency to corrupt juveniles, and contain descriptions of bestiality, bizarre violence, and torture, dismemberment, death, and human elimination." In 1975, the book was removed from public school libraries in Randolph, New York, and Alton, Oklahoma, and school officials in Westport, Massachusetts, removed the novel from the required reading list in 1977.

In 1978, the novel was banned from St. Anthony Freemont (Idaho) High School classrooms, and the contract of the instructor was not renewed after parents complained about the language in the book. The school superintendent did not read the book, but he collected all copies from students without attempting to determine its literary or scholastic value. The teacher claimed to have sent home a list of books to be read with the condition that alternative titles would be provided for students who chose not to read a specific assigned book, and no one had objected. The teacher worked with the American Civil Liberties Union to file a complaint in the United States District Court for the District of Idaho, claiming that his rights and the rights of his students under the First and Fourteenth Amendments had been violated. *Fogarty v. Atchley* was filed but not decided. The novel was also challenged in 1982 by parents of students in

Merrimack (New Hampshire) High School, where it was removed, but in a 1986 challenge to the novel as part of the honors English curriculum at Aberdeen (Washington) High School, the school board voted to retain the novel.

In 2000, parents of students attending Esperanza High School in the Placentia-Yorba Linda Unified School District complained to school officials that *One Flew over the Cuckoo's Nest* provides a "glorification of prostitution, murder and obscenity," and asked the school district to remove the novel from the schools. The California Department of Education had recommended the inclusion of the novel in the curriculum, and educators and other academic experts categorized the novel as "a valuable teaching tool," but the protesting parents described it as "dangerous." Anna Marie Buckner, the parent of three children ages seven, eight, and 17, told a newspaper reporter that the novel "teaches how very easy it is to smother somebody. I don't want to put these kinds of images in children's minds. They're going to think that when they get mad at their parents, they can just ax them out." After learning that her son would be required to read the novel in spring 2001, Buckner filed a two-page complaint in November 2000 with school officials. She was joined by the mother of four children Jenelle Cox in gathering 150 signatures on a petition that requested the removal of the novel from the classroom. Cox told a reporter for the *Los Angeles Times* that the situation was "frustrating. They can choose the best books, but they keep choosing this garbage over and over again." Both parents said that their children would read alternative choices, "books with good morals and heroes with values." School district officials turned the issue over to the district "book challenge review committee," 12 teachers, administrators, and parents who were asked to "establish criteria and resolve the issue." The novel had been used for seven years in the district core 11th-grade reading list before the complaint occurred, and the high school principal David Flynn supported retaining the novel in the curriculum. After months of debate, the board of education voted to keep *One Flew over the Cuckoo's Nest* in the curriculum.

FURTHER READING

Newsletter on Intellectual Freedom (May 1971): 59; (November 1974): 152; (May 1975): 41; (July 1975): 108; (May 1978): 57; (July 1978): 96, 100; (May 1980): 52; (September 1982): 170; (November 1986): 225.

O'Neil, Robert M. *Classrooms in the Crossfire: The Rights and Interests of Students, Parents, Teachers, Administrators, Librarians, and the Community.* Bloomington: Indiana University Press, 1981.

Tebbel, John. *A History of Book Publishing in the United States.* Vol. 4. New York: R. R. Bowker, 1981.

Tran, Mai. "Parents Ask School District to Ban 'Cuckoo's Nest.'" *Los Angles Times*, December 3, 2000. Avilable online. URL: http://articles.latimes.com/2000/dec/03/local/me–60611. Accessed August 10, 2010.

ORDINARY PEOPLE

Author: Judith Guest
Original date and place of publication: 1976, United States
Original publisher: Viking Press
Literary form: Novel

SUMMARY

Ordinary People is the story of a family attempting to come to terms with the death of one son and the attempted suicide of another son who blames himself for his older brother's drowning death. The novel begins a month after 17-year-old Conrad Jarrett has been released from the mental institution where he had spent eight months after using a razor blade to cut the vein in his wrist. The suicide attempt came one year after Conrad and his brother Buck had capsized while sailing on unexpectedly rough waters. For hours, they had held onto the overturned hull, one on each side for balance, but Buck drowned while Conrad was rescued despite Buck's greater endurance and greater strength as a swimmer. Conrad's inability to forgive himself for living, coupled with his mother's innately cold nature that deprives her of the ability to cry even at her son's funeral, created a feeling of helplessness for Conrad.

The novel traces the difficulties that Conrad faces in returning to school and family life. He had always been the "perfect child," while Buck had been the daredevil. Whatever danger signals Conrad sent out before the suicide attempt were missed because no one was watching. After he returns from the hospital, his father watches him constantly for changes in behavior or emotional responses.

Tortured with guilt, Conrad quits the swimming team and isolates himself from his former friends because they were also Buck's friends and the associations are too painful. Describing himself as "Conrad Jarrett, outcast, quitter, *fuck-up*," he is nearly successful in turning everyone away from him, but his salvation comes when he obeys his father and keeps his promise to meet with a psychiatrist to continue the work begun in the hospital. Dr. Berger manages to lead Conrad to recognize that he is punishing himself because of his brother's death. He encourages Conrad to elude the control of others and to say, "Fuck off. . . . Go to hell," if he feels like doing so. He also listens without judging when Conrad admits, "I jack off a lot." Conrad allows himself to become close to Jeanine, a young woman who has her own guilty secret, and his intense physical response to her makes him feel human.

Meanwhile, there appears to be no solution to the marital problems of Conrad's parents, Cal and Beth Jarrett. Beth accuses Cal of allowing himself to be manipulated by Conrad when he refuses to spend Christmas in London. Cal reminds her that they were in Miami the previous Christmas when

Conrad attempted suicide. The closer that Cal attempts to become with his wife, the further she pushes him away, until she finally decides to take an indefinitely long vacation in Europe. As the novel closes, Conrad appears to have overcome his past. He has come to terms with Buck's death and seems ready to resume old friendships.

CENSORSHIP HISTORY

In 1981, the novel was temporarily banned from junior and senior high school English classrooms in Enon, Ohio, because of the language used by the character Conrad and because he refers to masturbation at several points in the novel. After consideration by a districtwide committee, the book was reinstated as an optional reading choice but not a required reading. In 1982, a parent in Merrimack, New Hampshire, challenged the use of the novel in the classroom as being "obscene and depressing." The parent objected to the topic of suicide and noted that there "is enough tragedy in the world" to not have to subject students to it in their reading. The objection to the language related to the use of "damn," "Goddamn," and the desperate cry at several points in the novel of " . . . who the fuck needs anybody?" Thomas Tryon's *The Other* and Kenneth Kesey's ONE FLEW OVER THE CUCKOO NEST were challenged in the same incident.

In 1985, several parents challenged the novel as an optional summer reading book for 10th-grade students in North Salem, New York, because they believed that the topic of teenage suicide was "too intense," as well as because of "profanity" and "graphic sex scenes." One scene presented as an example occurs between Conrad's parents:

> She reaches up to put her arms around him, all tawny, smooth skin, those gray eyes with thick lashes, silent and insistent. She leads tonight, and he follows, moving swiftly down that dark river, everything floating, melting, perfect, and complete. Afterward, she slides away from him, and her hair, soft and furry against his shoulder, smells sweet and fresh, like wood fern.

A second specified scene is more graphic and occurs between Conrad and Jeanine:

> Her tongue in his mouth, exploring. He cannot concentrate any more, gathers her against him tightly as his groin hardens, spreads warmth through his whole body. His face in the hollow of her neck, he rocks her slowly, gently in his arms.
>
> They lie drugged and submerged, facing each other on the bed. Conrad's head is on his arm, one hand curved around her breast, eyes closed, shielding himself from the shining look of her. . . . his skin feels branded everywhere that she has touched him . . .

In 1993, parents of students at Anaheim (California) Union High School District challenged the book because it was "degrading to Christians." Cited in the complaint were Conrad's uses of the words *damn* and *Goddamn* and his admission to Jeanine that he did not believe in God. After consideration by a district-appointed review committee, the book was retained with another book that had been challenged for being "obscene and pornographic," Pat Conroy's *The Great Santini*.

In 1994, the book was removed from the required reading list for students at Delta High School in Delaware, Indiana, after parents and students complained of "profanity" and descriptions of "sexual situations," citing those already identified. That same year, the novel was also removed from use in all classrooms throughout the district in Faulkton, South Dakota, because of "profanity."

FURTHER READING

Newsletter on Intellectual Freedom (January 1982): 77; (September 1982): 170; (September 1985): 168; (May 1993): 86–87; (November 1993): 192–193; (January 1994): 14; (September 1994): 150, 152.

THE OX-BOW INCIDENT

Author: Walter Van Tilburg Clark
Original date and place of publication: 1940, United States
Original publisher: Random House
Literary form: Novel

SUMMARY

The Ox-Bow Incident, a tale of mob justice set in the Old West, warns of the danger that results when people take the law into their own hands. The novel begins much like most western tales, with two young cowboys entering a small town in the spring after spending months cooped up in a shack on the winter range with a herd. Art Croft, one of the two, is the first-person narrator.

Gil and Art, who are well known by the bartender Canby, go through a familiar routine of criticizing the bar service, commenting on a large, grimy painting above the bar and becoming used to some semblance of civilization. Gil calls the painting, which depicts a full-fleshed naked woman lying on a couch with a man in the background, "The Bitching Hour," and Clark refers to it as the Bitch in the narrative. As they drink heavily, they play poker and bemoan the lack of unmarried women in Bridger's Wells. The players' tempers flare, one calls another "bastard," and the poker game erupts into a fight shortly before a boy runs into the saloon and announces that a ranch foreman named Kinkaid has been killed and that 50 head of cattle have been stolen. The group of men begin to call for justice, and a mob forms to track down the killers and lynch them.

Twenty men join the vigilante group, but only two enthusiastically call for revenge. The rest are indecisive, and most are simply too morally weak to refuse to participate or to oppose the action. The men ride out blindly in the middle of the night, with no specific suspects in mind, and they come across three men sleeping soundly in a valley that contains a mountain stream with a course that looks like an ox-bow. They find 50 head of cattle bearing the brand of the reportedly stolen cattle and refuse to listen to the protests of one of the men, who claims to have bought the cattle that morning from the rancher Drew. The mob leaders, Tetley, and the boisterous and belligerent Ma Grier taunt those members of the group who seem hesitant. When the decision to lynch is put to a vote, only three vote against the action.

The hanging occurs at sunrise. On the ride back to town, the lynching party meets the sheriff, the judge, and a much alive Kinkaid, whose head is bandaged. What caused the head wound is never revealed. The mob also learns that the cattle had been bought and not stolen by the hanged men. The realization that they are murderers affects several of the mob deeply, leading a few men to seek affirmation that they did try to stop the act. Two others commit suicide: Young Gerald Tetley hangs himself when they return home, and his father jumps on his cavalry sword to die. The story ends with no legal punishment for any of the participants.

CENSORSHIP HISTORY

The novel has been challenged in several incidents by parents of students because of "vulgar" and "objectionable" language. In a 1963 survey of school administrators and high school English department chairpersons on censorship in Wisconsin, Burress reported one incident in which a parent complained about the language in the book and asked that it be removed from classroom use. The words objected to were *bitch*, *bastard*, *shit*, and *nigger*. The school board voted to grant the request. In 1966, in a national survey of high school librarians and high school English department chairpersons, Burress reported one incident in an unidentified state in which a local parent group called for a ban of the novel from the high school English curriculum. They based their objection on the presence of "too many obscene descriptions" and "swear words." The school board voted to retain the book in the curriculum.

In a 1967 investigation of censorship in Arizona, Burress reported two challenges to the novel. In one incident, parents complained of the "vulgar" language in the novel, citing the term *bastard*, which appears throughout. The school board voted to remove the book from classroom use. In a second incident in the same state, parents challenged the work because of the language, but the school board voted to retain the work.

In 1980, several parents of students in the Johnson City, Illinois, school district requested the removal of the book from the high school English curriculum, citing the same words as in earlier challenges. The school board voted to retain the book.

FURTHER READING

Budd, John M. "Law and Morality in *Billy Budd* and *The Ox-Bow Incident*." *CLA Journal* 35 (December 1991): 185–197.
Burress, Lee. *Battle of the Books: Literary Censorship in the Public Schools, 1950–1985.* Metuchen, N.J.: Scarecrow Press, 1989.
Newsletter on Intellectual Freedom (September 1980): 107.

THE RED PONY

Author: John Steinbeck
Original date and place of publication: 1933, United States
Original publisher: Viking Press
Literary form: Novel

SUMMARY

The Red Pony relates the story of 10-year-old Jody Triflin, who learns very important truths about life and death on his father's ranch. The brief novel is divided into four chapters: "The Gift," "The Great Mountains," "The Promise," and "The Leader of the People." Jody is thrilled when his father presents him with his first horse, a red pony that he names Gabilan. Ranch hand and horse-taming expert Billy Buck promises to teach Jody to ride the feisty Gabilan as soon as the pony is fully grown, but until then he shows Jody how to care for the animal. While Jody is at school, Billy leaves Gabilan in the corral during an unexpected rainstorm, and the pony becomes fatally ill.

Still grieving for his pony, Jody meets an old man named Gitano who has come to the Triflin ranch to die. He had lived in an adobe hut on the land years earlier, and he now wants to die at the place that he considers home. Jody's father, Carl Triflin, reluctantly lets Gitano stay the night, but he insists that the old man must go to relatives and not "die with strangers." Early the following morning, Jody sees Gitano riding Carl's old horse toward the mountains, with a rapier glittering in his hand. The reader is left to wonder about Gitano's fate.

In the third chapter, Carl tells Jody that he will get another horse because Billy Buck has praised Jody's hard work in training Gabilan. Carl tells the boy to take their mare to the neighbor's range "and get her bred." The book graphically describes Nellie's struggle to free herself from the rope, her high-pitched scream and that of the stallion whose "eyes glittered feverishly" and whose "stiff, erect nostrils were as red as flame." After the violence in their initial encounter, Nellie's mood changes, and she becomes "coquettishly feminine. She nibbled his arched neck with her lips. She edged around and rubbed her shoulder against his shoulder." In the months that follow, Jody learns about the birth process from Billy. The discussion is detailed regarding what constitutes "a good right birth." As Nellie's time to "throw her colt" comes near, Jody becomes increasingly anxious. Nellie has difficulty, and Billy reaches inside her to try to turn the colt, but he can't. He kills Nellie and slits her belly open to save the colt, desperate to recapture Jody's trust and respect that he had lost when Gabilan died.

In the final chapter, Jody's maternal grandfather arrives unexpectedly and tells his worn-out stories about leading a wagon train and fighting Indians as a young man. Carl is tired of the stories and says that "nobody wants to hear it over and over," hurting the old man's feelings but drawing Jody closer to him.

CENSORSHIP HISTORY

In a 1966 survey of a national sample of high school librarians and English department chairpersons concerning school censorship, Lee Burress recorded only one challenge in an unidentified locale. A parent objected to the "profanity" in the book and requested its removal from the high school library. The request was denied. In 1980, parents of students in Vernon-Verona-Sherill (New York) School District objected to the novel as being a "filthy, trashy, sex novel" in a challenge that also called for the removal of A FAREWELL TO ARMS, THE GRAPES OF WRATH, OF MICE AND MEN, A SEPARATE PEACE, and TO KILL A MOCKINGBIRD from a district recommended reading list. Among their objections is one instance in the book in which 10-year-old Jody "could smell the delicious smell of brandy" on his father's breath, and the boy later speaks of the "damn mice." The parents also condemned Billy Buck's explicit description of the birth process and of his efforts to turn the colt inside Nellie as she struggles to give birth. After reviewing the work, the school board voted to retain the book.

In 1994, parents of students attending schools in Oconee County, Georgia challenged the inclusion of the novel in the school libraries and charged that it contained profanity. Also challenged at that time "due to the filthiness of the material" were 10 books by V. C. Andrews: *Dark Angel, Darkest Hour, Dawn, Flowers in the Attic, Garden of Shadows, If There Be Thorns, My Sweet Audrina, Petals on the Wind, Seeds of Yesterday,* and *Twilight.* The Oconee school board voted to remove *The Red Pony* and the books by Andrews from the school libraries. Those who challenged *The Red Pony* objected to Jody's use of the word *damn* and viewed the breeding scene between the mare and the stallion as "filthy." Parents stated that the details regarding the birth of the colt were unnecessary to the story. A review committee recommended removal of the books from the school district, a move with which the district school board concurred. They further decided to evaluate all 40,000 volumes used in the classrooms and existing in the school libraries and to remove from the district public schools any books and teaching materials that contained "explicit sex and pornography."

FURTHER READING

Burress, Lee. *Battle of the Books: Literary Censorship in the Public Schools, 1950–1985.* Metuchen, N.J.: Scarecrow Press, 1989.
Ferrell, Keith. *John Steinbeck: The Voice of the Land.* New York: M. Evans, 1986.
Newsletter on Intellectual Freedom (May 1980): 62; (September 1994): 145.
Steinbeck, Elaine, and Robert Wallsten, eds. *Steinbeck: A Life in Letters.* New York: Viking Press, 1975.
Timmerman, John. *John Steinbeck's Fiction: The Aesthetics of the Road Taken.* Norman: University of Oklahoma Press, 1986.

THE SCARLET LETTER

Author: Nathaniel Hawthorne
Original date and place of publication: 1850, United States
Original publisher: Ticknor and Fields
Literary form: Novel

SUMMARY

The Scarlet Letter opens with a long, detailed preface entitled "The Custom House: Introductory to *The Scarlet Letter*" in which Hawthorne creates the illusion that the novel is based on fact. He claims that, while working as a customhouse agent, he found a manuscript and a faded and worn red letter "A" in one of the upper rooms. The manuscript, written by Jonathan Pue, a predecessor of his in the Custom House in Salem, Massachusetts, detailed the story of a Mistress Hester Prynne, who had been found guilty of adultery in Boston two centuries earlier and punished. In addition to creating the premise for the novel, the section also makes reference to Hawthorne's ancestors and provides insight into his daily work as a civil servant.

The story of *The Scarlet Letter* is that of a romantic triangle. Hester Prynne, the beautiful young wife of an old and introverted scholar, is separated from her husband for two years after being taken from her home in England to the wildlands of the New World. Lonely and without friends, she falls in love with Arthur Dimmesdale, an attractive young minister, and bears his child, whom she names Pearl, for she "was purchased at great price." Condemned by the townspeople, especially the women, who feel that jailing Hester, forcing her to stand on a scaffold in the middle of town, and making her wear the scarlet letter "A," for adultery, for life are not severe enough, Hester carries herself with dignity.

True to her strong character, Hester bears the shame and punishment alone and never reveals her child's father, although to do so would alleviate a great part of her punishment. Instead, Hester creates her own world for Pearl and supports herself by her excellent needlework skills. Her husband appears as a physician just returned from the frontier, but they agree to keep his identity a secret as the bitter and physically misshapen man takes the name Roger Chillingworth. He treats the physical ailments of Dimmesdale and eventually uncovers the identity of Pearl's father. The evil Chillingworth, feigning friendship, slowly destroys the minister. As Dimmesdale sinks into physical decay and Chillingworth decays morally, Hester wins the respect of the townspeople, who begin to view the "A" as representing "angel" for the many kind deeds she performs.

At the end of the novel, the dying Dimmesdale confesses publicly that he is Pearl's father as he stands holding hands with Hester and Pearl, on the same scaffold on which Hester alone stood soon after Pearl's birth to display her shame to the townspeople. Dimmesdale dies, and Hester takes Pearl to Europe, then returns years later to her small cottage. After she dies, Hester is buried under the same grave marker as Dimmesdale.

CENSORSHIP HISTORY

The novel was a success when it was first published, selling out a first printing within a few days. Although critics and literary figures praised the novel, religious journals and clergymen denounced it as "a dirty story" that belonged only in "a Brothel Library." A review in *Brownson's Quarterly* declared that neither Dimmesdale nor Hester exhibited "remorse" or "really repents of the criminal deed" and that "it is a story that should not have been told." In *Church Review*, Rev. Arthur C. Coxe also condemned the two main characters as not being sufficiently repentant and stated that "the nauseous amour" was not appropriate subject matter for fiction. In 1852, Coxe called for the banning of *The Scarlet Letter* as he launched a savage attack, proclaiming that he was against "any toleration to a popular and gifted writer when he perpetrates bad morals—let his brokerage of lust be put down at the very beginning." He stated that he could not tolerate a novel that dealt with an "illicit relationship."

The main complaint of those who wanted to ban the novel at the outset was that Hawthorne sided with Hester and condemned her husband's revenge. Strict morality required that Hester suffer in more painful and obvious ways than Hawthorne provided. The citizens of Salem were so incensed by Hawthorne's novel that he moved his family out of the city to a farmhouse in the Berkshires. In 1852, the novel was banned in Russia by Czar Nicholas I in a "censorship terror," but the ban was lifted four years later when Czar Alexander II came into power.

Little attention was paid to the novel for nearly a century. In 1949, in stating the deciding opinion in *Commonwealth of Massachusetts v. Gordon*, 66 D. & C. 101 (1949), Judge Curtis Bok used the novel as an example of the manner in which public morals change, when he noted that when first published, "Hawthorne's *Scarlet Letter* was referred to as 'a brokerage of lust,'" but it had become fully accepted by 1949.

In 1961, parents of students in Michigan objected to the assignment of the novel in high school English classes, claiming that it was "pornographic and obscene." They demanded that the book be taken out of the curriculum, but the request was denied. In a 1966 national sample of school librarians and English department chairpersons conducted by Lee Burress, four challenges were raised in locales unidentified by the investigator. In one, a student challenged the assignment of the book to freshman high school students, but no action was taken on the complaint. In a second challenge, a parent complained that the book was "immoral" because it dealt with a "misbegotten" child. The school board denied the request for removal of the book from the curriculum. In a third request to have the book removed from a reading list because it dealt with adultery, the request was also denied. The only successful challenge reported in the survey occurred when a high school principal declared the book too "frank" and "revealing" and removed it from the recommended reading list. A 1967 survey of high school censorship in Arizona conducted by Kenneth Donelson and Retha K. Foster reported one challenge by a parent who demanded the book be removed as a required reading because it discussed adultery. The request was denied.

In 1977, a parent and a principal in Michigan objected to the inclusion of the novel in the high school English curriculum because it dealt with a clergyman's "involvement in fornication." The book was removed from classroom use and from the recommended reading list. That same year, a parent in Missouri condemned the book for its use of "4-letter words" and "other undesirable content" and demanded its removal from the high school library. The school librarian recognized that the parent had not read the book because no obscenities appeared in the novel, and she convinced the parent of his error. The book was retained.

In a 1982 survey of English department chairpersons in Ohio, James Davis reported one challenge to the novel in which a parent claimed that the book was about "adultery," a "womanizing preacher," and "prostitution" and requested its removal as an assigned reading in a high school English class. The school board denied the request.

FURTHER READING

Burress, Lee. *Battle of the Books: Literary Censorship in the Public Schools, 1950–1985.* Metuchen, N.J.: Scarecrow Press, 1989.

Crowley, J. Donald, ed. *Hawthorne: The Critical Heritage.* New York: Barnes and Noble Books, 1970.

Davis, James E., ed. *Dealing with Censorship.* Urbana, Ill.: National Council of Teachers of English, 1983.

Donelson, Kenneth, ed. *The Student's Right to Read.* Urbana, Ill.: National Council of Teachers of English, 1972.

McClure, Robert C. "Literature, the Law of Obscenity, and the Constitution." *Minnesota Law Review* 38 (March 1954): 325.

Miller, Edwin Haviland. *Salem Is My Dwelling Place: A Life of Nathaniel Hawthorne.* Iowa City: University of Iowa Press, 1991.

Tebbel, John. *A History of Book Publishing in the United States, 1630–1865.* Vol. 1. New York: R. R. Bowker, 1972.

Wood, James Playsted. *The Unpardonable Sin.* New York: Pantheon Books, 1970.

A SEPARATE PEACE

Author: John Knowles
Original date and place of publication: 1960, United States
Original publisher: Macmillan Company
Literary form: Novel

SUMMARY

A Separate Peace takes place at a small New England preparatory school named Devon, where the narrator, Gene Forrester, has returned 15 years after graduation. He visits the tree from which his close friend Finny fell and broke his leg the first time and the First Academy Building, where the second break occurred. These locations stimulate a flashback to the summer of 1942, between his junior and senior years, when the novel really begins.

The main character is Gene's friend Phineas, "Finny," who forms the Super Suicide Society of the Summer Session. Seemingly fearless, his foolhardy behavior, athletic prowess, and quirky sense of humor make him a leader of the boys, whom he repeatedly challenges to jump from a tree on the riverbank into the cold water below. As the summer progresses, all except Finny speak of the threat of enlistment after graduation.

Despite their friendship, a rivalry exists between Gene and Finny. Gene tries to do well academically, but Finny's games interfere with his studies. When Gene fails a math test after Finny convinces him to go to the beach rather than study, he believes that his friend wants him to fail. Finny again distracts Gene on the evening before an important French examination by leading him to a jumping session at the riverbank, and Gene becomes vengeful. As the two boys crawl out onto a tree limb, Gene moves on the branch and causes Finny to fall and break his leg. This incident drastically changes Finny's life because he can no longer participate in sports, so he returns home.

As fall term begins, Gene decides that he might as well enlist in the army, but when Finny returns with his leg in a cast, Gene changes his mind and serves as the injured boy's guide and helper. As the year progresses, the two boys make their peace with each other, and Finny's leg heals imperfectly. Other students who are jealous of Gene's attention to Finny decide to hold a mock trial to determine what really happened. One student testifies that Gene shook the tree limb, a statement that upsets Finny and sends him racing out of the room toward a flight of marble stairs, where his cane slips and he falls, breaking the same leg. Finny dies when the doctor sets the bone a few days later; the official diagnosis is that some of the bone marrow must have escaped into his bloodstream and stopped his heart.

After graduation, Gene and many other Devon graduates enlist, but for Gene the war is of little consequence compared with the enemy he has overcome in trying to achieve a separate peace with Finny's death. He observes at the end of the novel, "my war ended before I ever put on the uniform; I was on active duty all my time at the school; I killed my enemy there."

CENSORSHIP HISTORY

The novel was challenged in 1980 by parents in Vernon-Verona-Sherrill (New York) School District for being a "filthy, trashy sex novel." In their challenge, the parents claimed that the novel contained homosexuality as an underlying theme, which "encourages homosexuality." They also complained of "swear words" to which their children should not be subjected, including "bastard," the barely disguised "f———ing," and "damn." The school board voted to offer students another selection and to remove the book from classroom use. In 1985, parents of students at Fannett-Metal High School in Shippensburg, Pennsylvania, challenged the book because of "offensive language." They claimed that the book was "too adult," for high school students and asked that it be removed from the required reading list. The request was denied, but students whose parents objected to the book were given an alternative assignment. In 1989, the novel was challenged by parents of students in the Shelby County, Tennessee, school system who felt that the "offensive language" in the novel made it inappropriate for the high school reading list. The school board replaced the novel with another book, and the issue ended.

After 22 years of being assigned in the local schools in Champaign, Illinois, without complaints, the novel was challenged by three parents who claimed that "unsuitable language" in the novel made it inappropriate for assignment in high school English classes. The parents specified the use of "damn" and "goddamn" in their complaint. The school board appointed a curriculum review committee to respond to the complaint and agreed with the decision of the committee to retain the novel. In a 1991 challenge to the novel issued by the parent of a high school student in Troy, Illinois, profanity and negative attitudes were cited in the request that the novel be removed from the classroom. The parent identified 34 "profane references" in the book, including "God damn," "Shut up," and "I swear to God." Students were offered alternative assignments while the school board took the matter under advisement, but no further action was taken on the complaint.

A more extensive challenge emerged in 1992, when a parent in Jacksonville, Florida, learned that the high school library contained a copy of *A Separate Peace* and challenged it as being "unsuitable for youth" and "encouraging rebellion against authority." The challenge cited "vulgar language" and characters who skip classes, break school rules, and trespass on school property as offering inappropriate models for students. The "objectionable language" identified includes "for God's sake," "damn," "hell," "Christ," and "Oh God." The district review committee considered the challenge and voted to retain the work that it characterized as "truly a well-written piece of art." In the report of the decision to retain the novel in the high school library, the committee wrote: "To ban or restrict this book reflects the paranoia existing in today's society. Reasons conjured for the banning of the book are unjustifiable."

FURTHER READING

Newsletter on Intellectual Freedom (May 1980): 62; (November 1985): 204; (January 1990): 11–12.
People For the American Way. *Attacks on the Freedom to Learn: 1991–1992 Report.* Washington, D.C.: People For the American Way, 1992.
Rice, Anne M. "Still Good Reading: Adolescent Novels Written before 1967— *A Separate Peace* by John Knowles." *English Journal*, April 1992, p. 88.

SISTER CARRIE

Author: Theodore Dreiser
Original date and place of publication: 1900, United States
Original publisher: Doubleday Page
Literary form: Novel

SUMMARY

Sister Carrie relates the story of a young Wisconsin girl who leaves her smalltown home and travels to Chicago, where she hopes to make her fortune. Eighteen-year-old Caroline Meeber, the naive "Sister Carrie" of the title, desires the fine clothes and financial success that she sees in the fast-paced city, and she views with scorn the impoverished life of her sister Minnie and laborer brother-in-law Hanson, with whom she lives. When she meets again the flashy and seemingly affluent Charles Drouet, a salesman whom she had first met on her train journey to Chicago, she realizes that her rise in society can only occur through her associations with men.

Life in Chicago depresses Carrie at first, as she attempts to find work but learns that her lack of training and inexperience in business make the sweatshop her only job option. Desperate to escape her misery, Carrie eagerly becomes Drouet's mistress, grateful for the modest apartment and equally modest allowance that accompany her new role. Her comfort and contentment soon turn to dissatisfaction as she views the grand homes that line Chicago's Lake Shore and her desire for material items increases. Introduced by Drouet to George Hurstwood, the polished and well-dressed manager of a fashionable restaurant-bar, Carrie leaves Drouet to become the mistress of the married Hurstwood, who risks his family and reputation for her. With money stolen from his employers, Hurstwood runs off with Carrie, first to Montreal and then to New York, where he invests in a bar. As Carrie's dreams become increasingly expensive, Hurstwood experiences economic reversals that drive Carrie to find her own success. She becomes a member of the chorus line in a dance review and, through clever use of her associations with successful men, achieves a stage career. Carrie leaves the now-impoverished Hurstwood, who survives by eating in soup kitchens and sleeping in flophouses before taking his own life.

As she enjoys her success, Carrie becomes close to yet one more man, an electrical engineer named Robert Ames, who reveals to her the emptiness of her life despite her material success. Immune to her desire to forge a physical relationship, Ames exerts the greatest influence over her life of all her relationships by making her see that she has achieved a hollow success. As the novel ends, the materially successful and calculating Carrie realizes that her life remains as empty and unfulfilled as when she first arrived in Chicago.

CENSORSHIP HISTORY

The novel became an object of censorship before it was even published. Dreiser first sent it to Harper & Brothers, which praised the work but said that they could not publish *Sister Carrie* because of its subject. The returned manuscript contained praise for the work as a "superior piece of reportorial realism," even as the company rejected it. The reader's report noted that the author's touch was "neither firm enough nor sufficiently delicate to depict without offense to the reader the continued illicit relations of the heroine." In response, the author asked his friend Arthur Henry to excise "offensive" passages; in other words, to cut those that alluded in even an indirect way to sexuality.

Dreiser next sent the manuscript to Doubleday Page, which offered the author a contract because of the enthusiasm shown toward the novel by the publisher's reader, author Frank Norris. Despite having signed a contract with Dreiser, firm owner Frank Doubleday tried to stop publication of the novel and contended that the story should not be published by anybody "because it is immoral." Rumors emerged that Mrs. Frank Doubleday had read the manuscript and "was horrified by its frankness." A social worker and moral reformer, she insisted that her husband withdraw the novel from publication, but the legal contract was binding. The firm published the novel, according to contract, but did not make an effort to distribute the book, and no copies were sold by Doubleday Page. In 1901, Heinemann in London published an abridged version of the novel, but the uncut version was not published until 1907, when Dreiser persuaded the newly formed publisher B. W. Dodge Company to take a chance. In 1908, Grosset and Dunlap created public outrage when it published the novel, but no legal restraints emerged, and the controversy was good for sales. By the time that Harper & Brothers reissued the novel in 1911, public outrage had turned to other subjects.

FURTHER READING

Dreiser, Theodore. "The Early Adventures of Sister Carrie." Foreword to *Sister Carrie*. New York: The Modern Library, 1927.
Lingeman, Richard. *Theodore Dreiser: At the Gates of the City, 1871–1907*. Vol. 1. New York: G. P. Putnam's Sons, 1986.

SOUL ON ICE

Author: Eldridge Cleaver
Original date and place of publication: 1968, United States
Original publisher: McGraw-Hill
Literary form: Collection of autobiographical essays

SUMMARY

Soul on Ice conveys Cleaver's experience of what it meant to be a black man in the ghetto, in prison, and in the society of the 1950s and the 1960s. Written while he was in prison, the book is divided into four parts: "Letters from Prison," "Blood of the Beast," "Prelude to Love—Three Letters," and "White Woman, Black Woman." Contained within each part are essays that focus on Cleaver's specific concerns and experiences, from his days as a street hoodlum in East Los Angeles through his long prison career to the emergence of a man who has shaken off his own feelings of bigotry and writes love letters to a white woman, a San Francisco lawyer who assisted in his appeals and in respect for whom he stopped calling women "bitches."

The essays contain a raw edge that reflects the reality of Cleaver's life. The first essay, "On Becoming," relates his experience in 1954 as an 18-year-old who had just begun to serve a sentence in Folsom Prison for a marijuana charge, one month after the Supreme Court decision outlawing segregation. He becomes aware of the sharp divisions of society and makes the connection between race and the burdens of poverty and powerlessness. Released from prison, Cleaver relates that he became a rapist, for whom "rape was an insurrectionary act." Back in prison, he reads voraciously from the Greek classics, American history, the psychology of Freud and Jung, and the works of African-American writers. Cleaver also refines his own views of the Civil Rights movement, Black Muslims teachings, and the Black Power movement in a way that exhibits his own mental evolution regarding the black struggle.

The final section deals with Cleaver's perceptions of the relationships that black men establish with black women and with white women. He explores the myth of "the walking phallus symbol" of the "Supermasculine Menial" black male with "the fiery steel of his rod," who "wets the juices" of the "Ultrafeminine Doll," the pure white southern woman. Cleaver perceives them as the embodiments of a racial caste system as he condemns the "Amazon" black women for viewing the black man as only "half a man." In the final essay, Cleaver rants that he is a "Black Eunuch, divested of my balls," but he makes peace with the African-American woman whom he calls "my Queen" and urges her to join him in building a new civilization "on these ruins."

CENSORSHIP HISTORY

Soul on Ice provoked controversy from its first publication, earning rave views from social critics who hailed Cleaver as a man who "throws light on the dark areas we wish he would leave alone" and calling his work "an exceptional volume both in what it says and how the author came to say it." Reviewers also acknowledged that the book "makes you twist and flinch because he is no damned gentleman." The discomfort that the book caused led some groups, such as Save Our Children, to label it "trash" and to call for its removal.

In 1969, California Superintendent of Instruction Max Rafferty, with the backing of the state board of education, barred Cleaver's book and *Dutchman* by Imamu Amiri Baraka from elective courses in black studies. The board claimed that the works contained "obscene" language and images that made them unsuitable for use in the school curriculum.

In 1973, Ridgefield, Connecticut, school board member Leo Carroll, retired after 33 years on the state police force, started a movement to ban *Soul on Ice* and a report on police relations entitled *Police, Courts and the Ghetto* by Marjorie Kilbane and Patricia Claire from the school curriculum. The first book was being read in a senior high school ethnic studies class, while the second book was being read by eighth-grade students in a social studies course. Carroll asserted to reporters that he found "nothing of redeeming social or educational value in the books. I find nothing in Cleaver's book but a horrible hatred of the white man and the law-abiding black man." After a two-hour meeting in the East Ridge Junior High Auditorium, attended on February 6, 1973, by 500 residents of the town, the school board decided in a vote of 5-4 against banning the two controversial books from the classroom. Moments later, however, the board decided in a vote of 5-3 to eliminate the courses in which the books are being used, effective with the end of the school year in June.

In 1975, parents of students at Greenwich (Connecticut) High School asked for the removal of the book from the school library, charging that it was "crime provoking and anti-American as well as obscene and pornographic." That same year, a group called the Concerned Citizens and Taxpayers for Decent Books in Baton Rouge, Louisiana, called for the removal from libraries and schools of 65 books, including *Soul on Ice*, which they viewed as being "pornography and filth." The books were retained in both incidents.

In a survey of a national sample of English department chairpersons conducted in 1977, Lee Burress recorded one instance in which parent complaints had resulted in the restriction of the work to only the upper grades. In a similar survey of librarians in 1982, Burress reported that a high school principal of an Ohio school district had ordered the book placed on a closed shelf in the high school library because of complaints that the "obscene language and criticism of whites stirs up trouble." Parents of students in Omak, Washington, challenged the use of the book in the classroom in 1979 because of "profane language," but it was retained.

The most extensive challenge to *Soul on Ice* began in 1976, when two school board members in Island Trees Free School District No. 26 in New York ordered librarians to remove the title and 10 others from the school library (see THE BEST SHORT STORIES BY NEGRO WRITERS) in 1982. With the others, *Soul on Ice* was charged with being "immoral" and "just plain filthy," and the following passage was specified in the court record as representative of "objectionable" passages:

> There are white men who will pay you to fuck their wives. They approach you and say, "How would you like to fuck a white woman?" "What is this?" you ask. "On the up-and-up," he assures you. "It's all right. She's my wife. She needs a black rod, is all. She has to have it. It's like a medicine or drug to her. She has to have it. I'll pay you. It's all on the level, no trick involved. Interested?"

The work was returned to the library after the United States Supreme Court ruled in *Board of Education, Island Trees Union Free School District No. 26 et al. v. Pico et al.*, 457 U.S. 853 (1982) that the First Amendment rights of students had been violated in the banning.

FURTHER READING

"Book Ban Beaten in Connecticut—But Ridgefield Board Votes to Discontinue Classes." *New York Times*, February 6, 1973, p. 17.

Burress, Lee. *Battle of the Books: Literary Censorship in the Public Schools, 1950–1985.* Metuchen, N.J.: Scarecrow Press, 1989.

Cummins, Eric. *The Rise and Fall of the California Radical Prison Movement.* New York: Oxford University Press, 1995.

Haskins, James. *Profiles in Black Power.* Garden City, N.Y.: Doubleday & Company, 1972.

Lockwood, Lee. *Conversation with Eldridge Cleaver: Algiers.* New York: McGraw-Hill, 1970.

Newsletter on Intellectual Freedom (May 1975): 87; (July 1979): 75; (November 1982): 197.

Waldrep, Shelton. "Being Bridges: Cleaver, Baldwin and Lorde and African-American Sexism and Sexuality." *Journal of Homosexuality* 26 (1993): 167–180.

STEPPENWOLF

Author: Hermann Hesse
Original dates and places of publication: 1927, Germany; 1929, England; 1929, United States
Original publishers: S. Fischer Verlag; Secker; Holt
Literary form: Novel

SUMMARY

Steppenwolf begins with a preface narrated by a young businessman who claims to have edited a sheaf of notes left several years before by a lodger in the attic room of his aunt's home. The notes relate the strange adventures of Harry Haller, the eccentric lodger, who refers to himself as a wolf of the steppes, or the Steppenwolf. The preface recounts the narrator's few meetings with Haller—on the stairs in the house, at a concert, in a tavern, or at a lecture. He decides to publish the manuscript, subtitled "For Madmen Only," even though he does not know if Haller's account is fact or fiction.

"For Madmen Only" begins as Haller takes a walk at dusk. He follows a flickering sign to a door in a church wall; the door leads into an imaginary world and a peddler who carries a placard that advertises "Magic Theater—Entrance Not for Everybody." Before vanishing, the peddler hands Harry a pamphlet entitled "Treatise on the Steppenwolf." Back in his room, Harry reads the pamphlet and learns that it contains a psychological portrait of men like him, analyzing them as two selves in conflict—half man and half wolf. The pamphlet explains the role in middle-class society of the Steppenwolves, the artists and intellectuals, as well as the role of the geniuses who break free and become the Immortals, those above ordinary social rules. Harry recognizes that he has hundreds of selves, and the pamphlet assures him that he may one day see himself in the magic mirrors of the Immortals or learn in one of their magic theaters what he needs to free his soul.

After reading the treatise, Harry realizes his loneliness. He begins a nightly search, eventually finding again the peddler who leads him to a seedy tavern where he meets a sensuous bar girl named Hermine, the prostitute Maria, and the androgynous jazz musician Pablo. Through Hermine, Harry learns to dance and to enjoy sex and the nightlife of the city. He also enjoys the pleasures of various drugs, including cocaine and opium, supplied by Pablo, who "was a master in mixing and prescribing them." Hermine, who "cast the spell of the hermaphrodite," also hints of sensuous nights spent with Maria and tells Harry of having seduced a woman at the masked ball "with the spell of Lesbos." Pablo invites Harry into the Magic Theater, where he experiences a series of surreal adventures and learns that he is condemned to continue living. As the manuscript ends, Harry resolves to go on confronting his inner self and to work toward becoming one of the Immortals.

CENSORSHIP HISTORY

Steppenwolf, the most autobiographical of all Hesse's novels, was severely criticized by critics and readers for its jazz, drugs, and sexual practices, including lesbianism and androgyny. Mileck writes that German critics called the book "pornographic" upon its first publication and Hesse "a man without morals." No formal attempts to suppress the book occurred at its publication in Germany nor when it first appeared in England and in the United States, although the novel appeared on a list of books condemned by the Boston Watch and Ward Society in 1930. In 1932, an increasingly conservative populace focused attention on Hesse, who was openly accused of "wallowing in filth."

Freedman notes that in 1932 Hesee wrote to a friend, H. Zwissler, that "A young adherent of Hitler from Swabia wrote that [the book] was merely an expression of the lewd lustfulness of an aging man and that he hoped I would soon kick the bucket." In 1943 and 1944, Hitler's dictatorship made all of Hesse's books forbidden reading in Nazi Germany; some, like *Steppenwolf,* for their "lewd lustfulness," and others because he did not take a stand and publish pro-Nazi propaganda nor did he speak out against the Nazis.

The novel was accepted again in Germany after World War II ended and became a counterculture favorite in the late 1950s and the 1960s in the United States. The Beat Generation made it an urban underground classic, "a bible for all." Drug proponent Dr. Timothy Leary wrote that *Steppenwolf* was "a psychedelic journey" and offered a "heightened sensibility" that was a response to "a corrupt and menacing external 'reality.' " No formal efforts to suppress the book in the United States occurred until 1982, when the parents of several students attending Glenwood Springs (Colorado) High School demanded that the novel be removed from the high school library. In their complaint to the school board, the parents cited as the reasons references in the book to "lesbianism," "hermaphroditism," "sexual perversion," "drugs," "murder," and "insanity." A committee created by the school board reviewed the novel and voted to retain it.

FURTHER READING

Freedman, Ralph. *Hermann Hesse: Pilgrim of Crisis.* New York: Pantheon Books, 1978.

Leary, Timothy, and Ralph Metzner. "Hermann Hesse: Poet of the Interior Journey." *Psychedelic Review* 1 (1963): 167–182.

Mileck, Joseph. *Hermann Hesse: Life and Art.* Berkeley: University of California Press, 1978.

Newsletter on Intellectual Freedom (September 1982): 169.

STRANGE FRUIT

Author: Lillian Smith
Original date and place of publication: 1944, United States
Original publisher: Harcourt, Brace & World
Literary form: Novel

SUMMARY

Strange Fruit deals with the topic of miscegenation and details a relationship between a young, white college dropout, Tracy Deen, and his college-educated black girlfriend, Nonnie Anderson, who works as a servant and is carrying his child. The setting is Maxwell, Georgia, a town divided into "White Town" and "Colored Town," where marriage between the races is still against the law. The other black citizens of the town look upon the "Anderson niggers" as odd because they are all college educated, but the Andersons are tolerated because they "work hard and know their place." The white women envy Mrs. Brown for having a college-educated servant, and the white men in town desire the physically attractive young woman.

As the novel opens, the reader learns that Nonnie and Tracy have been sexually intimate since she was 14 and he was 20 and had recently dropped out of college. Nonnie's sister Bess had hoped that the doomed relationship would end when Nonnie went to Spelman College and Tracy left Maxwell to serve in the army during the war, but it continued once they were together in Maxwell. Tracy served in France and saw racially mixed couples there, but he realized that the same was impossible in his hometown. Nonnie clings to the hope that she and Tracy will be able to marry, but the weight of family opinion and his mother's dominance of his life are too strong for him. His minister counsels Tracy to give up Nonnie, as many white men before him have given up their "colored women," and tells Tracy that Nonnie, like other "colored women," will manage all right. He states that "most of them sooner or later gets a man their color, maybe marry them. Live a fairly decent, respectable life—that is, if a nigger woman can live a decent, respectable life. . . . You have to keep pushing them back across that nigger line." Told that Nonnie is pregnant, the minister urges Tracy to "find some good nigger you can count on to marry her" and suggests that Tracy sweeten the deal with money.

Nonnie's family is not any happier with the situation. Her sister Bess wants her to have an abortion. Her brother Ed, now a government employee in Washington, returns for a vacation week and questions Nonnie's willingness to remain subservient when she has a college education and wonders why she remains in Maxwell.

Despite protestations of love, Tracy takes the minister's advice. He arranges a marriage for Nonnie with Henry McIntosh, a man who had exposed himself to her when she was 11 years old and asked her, "How about fuckin' with me?" Henry works for Tracy's parents, Dr. Tutweiler and Mrs. Alma Deen, and used to be Tracy's playmate. One night, Nonnie's brother flies into a rage and shoots Tracy to death. "White Town" blames Henry, who had flashed money only days before and bragged about a "deal" with Tracy. They lynch and burn Henry, despite the efforts of several white men to save him. The novel ends the day after the tragedy, with everything returning to its old routine, appearing on the surface that nothing had happened. One marked difference is that the black citizens of Maxwell are now more deferential than before.

CENSORSHIP HISTORY

The novel was strongly criticized soon after publication for its references to sexual intercourse, the sexual assault of a young girl, a murder, a lynching, and physical descriptions that were perceived as too frequent and designed to titillate. Moreover, the unconventional behavior of the couple unable to marry because of their racial differences and the sexually related language, including the use of the word *fuck* in two instances, also motivated significant complaint. Words like *bitch* and *whore* are common in the novel, *tail* and *teat* are each used once in reference to a woman, and one description of "nice little rumps, hard from chopping cotton" is given. Also identified as obscene were the references to urination, the discussion of a rich white man's penchant for deflowering young schoolteachers because he is afraid of syphilis, and the use of the words *coition* and *orgasm* in discussing the frigidity of white women.

On May 16, 1944, the U.S. Department of the Post Office declared that *Strange Fruit* could not be sent through the mails without risk of prosecution under Section 598 of the Postal Laws and Regulations, 1940, which prohibited "the mailing of lewd books, pictures, advertisements and other matter." Magazine and newspaper companies were also warned in a letter from Postmaster Arthur Goldman that they could not continue to print advertisements for the banned book without risk. Curtice Hitchcock, president of the publisher Reynal & Hitchcock, consulted with his attorneys and learned that the company had 15 days until the ban took full effect and decided to continue to advertise and to sell the book until a formal charge emerged. A *New York Times* article published on May 16, 1944, states that "Mrs. Franklin D. Roosevelt was quoted in advertisements on March 12 as describing *Strange Fruit* as 'a very moving book and a very extraordinary one.' " The editor of the *Saturday Review* held an equally high opinion of the book—and of the right of the publisher to advertise the work—and wrote to the U.S. Department of the Post Office:

> We feel obliged and privileged to state that it is our intention to continue advertising for "Strange Fruit" should the publishers request space. In the event the publishers do not request space we will seek permission to publish such advertisements without charge to them. Censorship is no trivial matter, Mr. Goldman. So far as Americans are concerned it involves their very traditions. Who in the post office is charged with the responsibility for seeing that these traditions are not easily and ignorantly brushed aside. We not only protest your order, we refuse to follow it without due process of law. If, after a properly constituted hearing or trial, it is decided that "Strange Fruit" is "obscene" we will of course abide by the decision of the court. Until that time we hope our readers will not blame us for seeing it through.

The post office lawyer who assessed the book acknowledged that it was a plea for social equality, noting that "the book aspires to fill the role of 'Uncle Tom's Cabin' in the life of the modern negro problem." Despite the social intent, the book was labeled "obscene" because "it deals with the sexual relations of a ne'er-do-well son of a respected white southern family with a mestee [sic]. Some incidents are too much detailed but the worst part is the filthy language. . . . It is obscene in that it is disgusting, repulsive, nauseating." In the report, the post office lawyer admitted that, under the standards set by the Supreme Court in the 1933 *Ulysses* case, "this book would not be held to be obscene in that the sexual scenes are merely incidental to the principal theme of the book—the social degradation of the negro in the South." Despite this acknowledgment, he found that the book was simply too strongly obscene by his own standard, so he recommended that it be excluded from the mails, even though it was sold in many states in the United States. The solicitor general of the postal department accepted the recommendation.

Strange Fruit was also declared obscene in 1945 in a Supreme Judicial Court of Massachusetts decision rendered by Judges Field, Qua, Ronan, and Wilkins. In *Commonwealth of Massachusetts v. Isenstadt*, 318 Mass. 543 (1945), a bookseller named Abraham A. Isenstadt was charged with the possession and sale of a book that was "obscene, indecent, or impure, or manifestly tends to corrupt the morals of youth," under Massachusetts statutes. The case came about because a noted literary critic of the time, Bernard DeVoto, sought to test the statute and the concept of extralegal censorship, after *Strange Fruit* was informally banned in Massachusetts. The critic purchased the book, and the bookseller was arrested and convicted by a Massachusetts

Superior Court judge without a jury. In an appeal to the Supreme Judicial Court of Massachusetts, the book was again declared "obscene" by four of the five judges presiding. Judge Qua delivered the majority opinion and accepted the work as possessing literary merit, but he noted that "obscenity may sometimes be made even more alluring and suggestive by the zeal which comes from sincerity and by the added force of artistic presentation." Rather, "a book that adversely affects a substantial proportion of its readers may well be found to lower appreciably the average moral tone of the mass."

Judge Lummus, the dissenting judge in the case, acknowledged that the book "is blemished by coarse words and scenes, none of which appear irrelevant to the plot." He stated that, rather than providing erotic allurement, "their coarseness is repellent." He declared further that the book was a serious study of race relations, "a grim tragedy" in which "virtue is not derided, neither is vice made attractive." Judge Lummus ended the dissent by observing that rather than being titillated by the book, "the reader is depressed, unable to solve a tragic problem."

FURTHER READING

"Book Ban Put to Test." *New York Times*, April 7, 1944, p. 21.

Grant, S. S., and S. E. Angoff. "Massachusetts Censorship." *Boston University Law Review* 10 (1946): 147.

Paul, James C. N., and Murray L. Schwartz. *Federal Censorship: Obscenity in the Mail.* Glencoe, Ill.: Free Press, 1961.

"*Strange Fruit* Barred by Mails, Then Admitted at Sender's Risk." *New York Times*, May 16, 1944, p. 1.

STRANGER IN A STRANGE LAND

Author: Robert A. Heinlein
Original date and place of publication: 1961, United States
Original publisher: G. P. Putnam's Sons
Literary form: Science fiction novel

SUMMARY

Stranger in a Strange Land relates the story of Valentine Michael Smith, conceived by adulterous lovers on the first human expedition to Mars, a three-year journey. The novel consists of five parts: His Maculate Origin, His Preposterous Heritage, His Eccentric Education, His Scandalous Career, and His Happy Destiny. Orphaned soon after birth, the main character is raised by Martians in their culture and returns 25 years later to his home planet as an alien being who becomes the messiah of a new religion. The novel, which became an underground classic and campus cult favorite in the 1960s, attacks human folly under several guises, especially in the person or persons of the

Establishment. The government, the military, and organized religion are skewered as the author advances a religion of love aimed at revolutionizing human affairs and bringing about an apocalyptic change for the better.

The original *Envoy* expedition of four married couples makes a successful entry into the orbit of Mars, then is never again heard from. World War III prevents an immediate search of space, and 25 years pass before another manned expedition is sent to Mars. When it arrives, the crew finds that Mars is inhabited and that only one survivor of the *Envoy* remains, Valentine Michael Smith. The government views the survivor as "a treasure trove of information" and hopes to study him, but the young man's body must first become acclimated to the increased pull of gravity and changed air pressure. The doctors soon learn that Smith is able to slow his respiration, heartbeat, and blood pressure to the point where he appears in shock. This and other observations lead the captain of the expedition to observe that "Smith is not a *man*. He is an intelligent creature with the genes and ancestry of a man, but he is not a man. He's more a Martian than a man. . . . He thinks like a Martian, he feels like a Martian." The differing influences of his human ancestry and his Martian environment form the basis for social criticism in the novel.

Dubbed "Mike," the reclaimed Earthling receives training in human social life from wealthy eccentric Jubal Harshaw and his brain trust in the Pocono Mountains in Pennsylvania. In contrast to the more usual wise adviser in literature, who guides the mythic hero in learning the good of civilization, Harshaw focuses on revealing what is wrong with the world. Mike comes to understand American culture, but from his Martian viewpoint human religion, fear of death, and sexual inhibitions seem absurd.

Conversely, other humans view his Martian heritage as absurd, as he reveals his capabilities of suspended animation, astral projection, telekinesis, and the ability to will objects and people out of existence. He also exhibits a capability that is even more frightening, "grokking," the total and immediate understanding of people, situations, and love. A central term of the Martian language, "to grok" signifies the ability to know in a holistic way that includes intellect and intuition, a knowledge that is as absolute, unambiguous, and instant as a god's or an angel's knowledge. Mike can also read minds and change his body shape, but many are more disturbed by his revelation that Martians practice ritual cannibalism.

As Mike becomes comfortable in his new home, he discovers money as an idea, a symbolic structure. He also gains a following as the leader of a new cult, the Church of All Worlds. Water-sharing rituals and guilt-free sexuality characterize the new religion, as does instruction in the psycholinguistic powers and perceptions of Martians. The importance of water sharing and the concept of the "water brothers," both male and female, emerge from the importance of water on a dry planet where its sharing is an intimate ritual between those who seek to grow so intimate that their "eggs share the same nest."

Sexual promiscuity is the norm, marriage is irrelevant, and promiscuous group sex is among the religion's ceremonies. Mike fathers several children

who requested that the novel be removed from the recommended reading list. The parent claimed that the characters were "too flagrant" in behavior and that their language was "too explicit." After a review committee considered the parent's complaint, the book was removed from the recommended reading list. Burress also reported in a 1982 national survey of librarians that a parent in Indiana challenged the assignment of the book in the classroom because of the "obscene" language. The school board reviewed the book and removed the material from the classroom.

FURTHER READING

Baker, Carlos. *Hemingway: A Life Story*. New York: Charles Scribner's Sons, 1969.

Burress, Lee. *Battle of the Books: Literary Censorship in the Public Schools, 1950–1985*. Metuchen, N.J.: Scarecrow Press, 1989.

Djos, Matt. "Alcoholism in Ernest Hemingway's *The Sun Also Rises:* A Wine and Roses Perspective on the Lost Generation." *Hemingway Review* 14 (Spring 1995): 64–78.

Elliott, Ira. "Performance Art: Jake Barnes and 'Masculine' Signification in *The Sun Also Rises*." *American Literature* 67 (March 1995): 77–94.

Meyers, Jeffrey. *Hemingway: A Biography*. New York: Harper & Row, 1985.

Pinsker, Sanford. "Individual Authors: A Rotten Way to Be Wounded." *Journal of Modern Literature* 18 (Spring 1993): 277–278.

Reynolds, Michael. *Hemingway: The American Homecoming*. Cambridge, Mass.: Blackwell Publishers, 1992.

Rudat, Wolfgang. "Sexual Dilemma in *The Sun Also Rises:* Hemingway's Count and the Education of Jacob Barnes." *Hemingway Review* 8 (Spring 1989): 2–13.

Strychacz, Thomas. "Dramatizations of Manhood in Hemingway's *In Our Time* and *The Sun Also Rises*." *American Literature* 61 (May 1989): 245–260.

Wylder, Delbert E. *Hemingway's Heroes*. Albuquerque: University of New Mexico Press, 1969.

TO HAVE AND HAVE NOT

Author: Ernest Hemingway
Original date and place of publication: 1937, United States
Original publisher: Charles Scribner's Sons
Literary form: Novel

SUMMARY

To Have and Have Not is Ernest Hemingway's most experimental novel and his financially least successful. The work began as two short stories about former Miami police officer Harry Morgan, who runs a charter boat business between Florida and Cuba during the Depression. Hemingway added a third section to create a novel in three parts: "Harry Morgan—

Spring," "Harry Morgan—Fall," and "Harry Morgan—Winter." He sought to examine economic and social status and to contrast the "haves" with the "have nots."

Harry Morgan is a tough and resourceful figure who struggles to make a living. Desperate for money, he accepts a dangerous mission to transport Chinese refugees from Cuba to Florida. With alcoholic Eddy Marshall as crew, Harry locks the refugees below deck and kills the smuggling organizer after receiving payment. He then forces the 12 men onto the beach and returns home.

The second part opens with Harry Morgan and a black crew member named Wesley suffering gunshot wounds—Harry in the arm and Wesley in the leg—while illegally transporting rum. Fearing that Customs will spot them, they pull close to shore and dump the liquor bottles. Seen by a government official on another boat, they escape temporarily. Harry loses his boat to Customs, but they cannot identify who was piloting the craft.

In part three, Harry has lost his arm after being wounded, and his boat has been taken from him. He agrees to use a borrowed boat to transport Cuban revolutionaries from Florida to Cuba after they rob a bank. The night before he leaves, he and his wife make love, and she later thinks, "I could do that all night if a man was built that way." On the boat, Harry considers the Cubans' ideals and thinks "F——— the revolution" as he plans to take the money, but one shoots him. As he lies dying, he worries that his wife is "too old to peddle her hips now."

Contrasted with Harry's desperate efforts to scratch a living are the problems of other characters—a playboy writer and his adulterous wife, a Hollywood director's frustrated wife who masturbates in the night, a grain broker who cheats on his tax returns, and a homosexual couple ending their relationship—tourists in Key West who are financially well off but morally and emotionally empty. Helen, the embittered wife of writer Richard Gordon, conveys their cynicism: "Love is that dirty aborting horror that you took me to. Love is my insides all messed up. It's half catheters and half whirling douches. I know about love. Love hangs up behind the bathroom door. It smells like lysol [sic]. To hell with love." Hemingway contrasts their continued survival with the defeat of the relentless individualist Harry Morgan, who is no match for a hostile social and economic environment.

CENSORSHIP HISTORY

The first submitted draft of the novel contained material that publisher Charles Scribner's Sons told Hemingway to excise before the work could be published. In an extended section, the author had used character Tommy Bradley, husband of the sexually promiscuous Helene Bradley, as a vehicle for savaging writers that he had known. In that initial version, Hemingway spoke of Hart Crane as "an unfortunate bugger, always propositioning the wrong sailors and getting beaten up." Harry Crosby was "a silly ass," and F. Scott Fitzgerald had "jumped from youth to senility. . . . Might pull out of it yet if he wasn't so sorry for himself." Hemingway said of James Joyce that he "wrote two fine books and a very great book and went blind. You cant [sic] blame a man for going blind." The publisher was uncomfortable with the criticism of other writers and asked Hemingway to eliminate the passages or to heavily disguise the individuals. As a result of the revision, the character of Tommy Bradley does not appear and is only referred to in the novel. Another change involves the masturbation scene of Dorothy Hollis. More straightforward in the initial version, it was changed to include an awkward and convoluted soliloquy that suggests rather than states her actions.

Even with the revisions, the language and the sexual suggestiveness of the novel raised cries for censorship after publication. Labeled "obscene" is the frequent reference among the monied tourists to the promiscuous Helene Bradley as a "bitch" or a "whore." Other words that have drawn criticism are *fuck* or *fucking*. Midway through the novel, Hemingway uses dashes when Harry thinks "F—— the revolution," yet in Harry's dying thoughts the word is fully spelled out: "No matter how a man alone ain't got no bloody fucking chance." In 1938, the novel was banned in Detroit, Michigan, by the local prosecutor, who first ordered it removed from the Detroit Public Library. Booksellers in Detroit were also prevented from selling the book under the ban, an order that they contested. The Wayne County prosecutor had acted after receiving complaints from Catholic organizations that it was "obscene" and contained "sexual situations" that were "corruptive." Harry Schuman, a rare book dealer, and Alvin C. Hamer, a well-known Detroit bookseller, contested the order, and two years later the book was available for sale in Wayne County. The public libraries, however, placed the book on shelves containing works by "writers of standing," meant for the request of adults alone.

That same year, law-enforcement authorities in Queens, New York, forbade the sale and distribution of the novel after receiving complaints from local Catholic organizations. Concerns raised over the "obscene" language and the sexual promiscuity (mostly implied) of the characters were the basis for the ban. The American Civil Liberties Union reported that *To Have and Have Not* was the only novel suppressed in the United States in 1938.

FURTHER READING

Mellow, James R. *Hemingway: A Life without Consequences.* New York: Houghton Mifflin, 1992.

Meyers, Jeffrey. *Hemingway: A Biography.* New York: Harper & Row, 1985.

Wylder, Delbert E. *Hemingway's Heroes.* Albuquerque: University of New Mexico Press, 1969.

TO KILL A MOCKINGBIRD

Author: (Nelle) Harper Lee
Original date and place of publication: 1960, United States
Original publisher: J. B. Lippincott
Literary form: Novel

SUMMARY

Harper Lee's only novel touched a nerve in American society when it was first published, becoming a best seller as well as a critical success that won the Pulitzer Prize in 1961. The author claimed that her story of racial bias in the sleepy fictional Alabama town of Maycomb was pure imagination, but reporters who visited her hometown of Monroeville, Alabama, on the 30th anniversary of the book's publication found remarkable similarities to the novel in both setting and character. In essence, the racial ills chronicled in the novel appear to have been realistically drawn from the author's life.

The novel is told from the point of view of the adult Jean Louise Finch, known as Scout to her friends, who relates the events of three years, beginning with her sixth summer. With her brother Jem, four years her senior, and summer visitor Dill, modeled after a real-life summer playmate who grew up to be the writer Truman Capote, Scout devises a series of projects to make their mysterious next-door neighbor, Arthur "Boo" Radley, emerge from his house. The early chapters of the novel detail the comfortable cocoon of childhood that Scout enjoys, as she enters school, engages in fistfights with boys, and shares confidences with her father, lawyer Atticus Finch.

Scout's comfortable world is shattered when her father agrees to take the unpopular defense of black laborer Tom Robinson, accused of raping white Mayella Ewell. The townspeople want Tom to die, but Atticus believes that Tom is innocent and establishes that Tom's withered left arm could not have made the bruises on the right side of Mayella's face.

As bitterness engulfs the town, Atticus must defend his client not only in court but also from a lynch mob. Atticus manages to prove that Tom is physically incapable of committing the crime, yet the jury brings in a verdict of guilty despite the revelation that Mayella had made sexual advances to Tom that he had refused out of fear for his life. In addition, townspeople are angered because Tom expresses pity for a white woman.

Atticus plans to appeal the decision, but Tom is fatally shot while trying to escape during a jail exercise period. The final chapters of the novel contain Bob Ewell's attempted revenge against Atticus for having defended Tom and the emergence of Boo Radley from his house to save Jem and Scout from Ewell's knife.

CENSORSHIP HISTORY

Despite its strong annual sales and appearance on required reading lists in numerous high schools throughout the United States, *To Kill a Mockingbird* has frequently been challenged by parents and groups who object to either the language or the way in which race is represented. The Committee on Intellectual Freedom of the American Library Association listed the novel as being among the 10 most frequently challenged books. In 1977, Eden Valley (Minnesota) School District temporarily banned the book because the words *damn* and *whore lady* appeared in the text, and parents in Vernon-Verona-Sherill (New York) School District challenged the book in 1980 as being a "filthy, trashy novel." Black parents in Warren Township (Indiana) schools charged in 1981 that passages in the book that portrayed the submissive behavior of Tom Robinson, Calpurnia, and other blacks and the frequent use of the word *nigger* advocated institutionalized racism and were harmful to the integration process. Despite their vehement efforts, the attempt to censor the book was unsuccessful. As a result, three black parents resigned in protest from the town's human relations advisory council.

The novel was also challenged in 1984 in the Waukegan, Illinois, schools for inclusion of the word *nigger,* and in 1985, Park Hill (Missouri) Junior High School parents challenged the novel because it contained racial slurs and offensive language. In 1985 in Casa Grande (Arizona) Elementary School District, black parents and the National Association for the Advancement of Colored People protested that the book was unfit for use in the junior high school. School officials there changed the status of the book from required reading to retention on a supplemental reading list.

In 2001, a school board member in Glynn County, Georgia, challenged the use of the novel in the classroom because it contains profanity, but no action was taken, and the book was retained.

In August 2002, Terry Saul, the principal of Muskogee High School in Oklahoma, removed the novel from the high school reading list after African-American parents and students complained about racial slurs in the novel. The Muskogee Public Library created a program in response to the action, including showing the movie in two screenings and sponsoring two read-and-discuss programs led by local black educators. The library also adapted the One City–One Book program from the Chicago Public Library and staged a musical and reading program with reminiscences by the child stars of the movie after raising $7,000 in donations. The resulting coalition of participation by community leaders led the school board to vote in October 9, 2002, to reverse the ban.

In 2003, parents of students enrolled in the sophomore literature class in Community High School in Normal, Illinois, challenged the use of the novel and claimed that it is degrading to African Americans. After review by a school district committee, the school board voted in 2004 to retain the novel.

In 2004, Garvey Jackson, an African-American eighth-grade student attending Stanford Middle School in Durham, South Carolina, protested being required to read *To Kill a Mockingbird* because it forced him to repeatedly hear and to read the most offensive word he knew, "nigger." His family joined him in protesting the required reading. Andrew Jackson, his father, stated that the family did not want the book in the school system: "We do want to kill the mockingbird, if it takes until the end of the school year." With the help of his family, the student created a T-shirt that they emblazoned with offensive phrases: "nigger rape," "nigger lover," "nigger snowman," and others. Although the family was aware that the boy might be suspended from school for the action, they thought that making the point during Black History Month was especially important. Jackson's English teacher sent him to the principal's office where, after his parents arrived, Principal David Ebert explained that wearing the shirt was against the school dress code. He also explained to Jackson's parents the formal procedure for challenging a book in the school district. He also told Jackson that he did not have to speak the word "nigger" aloud if it made him uncomfortable. Although Jackson complied with the dress code and removed the shirt, he attempted the following week to protest the screening of the movie version of *To Kill a Mockingbird* and made armbands to pass out to other students. His fellow students refused: "They didn't want to wear them. They said they made them look ugly." Jackson wore his anyway, and his family planned a mock funeral for the book to which they would invite the community. The novel was retained in the curriculum.

In 2007, a resident of Cherry Hill, New Jersey, submitted a request to the school board to remove the novel from the school curriculum because she was concerned that African-American children would become upset by reading about the racism among white members of the community in 1930s Alabama.

In August 2009, the Dufferin-Peel Catholic School Board in Brampton, Ontario, chose not to interfere when the principal of the St. Edmund Campion High School removed *To Kill a Mockingbird* from the 10th-grade English curriculum after one parent complained about the use of the word "nigger" throughout the book. Principal Kevin McGuire stated that he did not ban the book, nor did he remove it from the district, because it was still available in the school library. Rather, he simply made a decision to replace the book at the same time that a parent protested its use in the classroom.

FURTHER READING

"Another Furor over Books." *Ohio State University Monthly* 55 (December 1963): 8–12.

Bruell, Edwin. "Keen Scalpel on Racial Ills." *English Journal* 53 (December 1964): 658–661.

Dave, R. A. "*To Kill a Mockingbird:* Harper Lee's Tragic Vision." In *Indian Studies in American Literature,* edited by M. K. Naik, S. K. Desai, and S. Mokashi, 311–323. Dharwar, India: Karnatak University, 1974.

Doyle, Robert P. *Books Challenged and Banned in 2008–2009.* Chicago: American Library Association, 2009.

May, Jill. "In Defense of *To Kill a Mockingbird.*" In *Censored Books: Critical Viewpoints,* edited by Nicholas J. Karolides, Lee Burress, and John M. Kean, 476–484. Metuchen, N.J.: Scarecrow Press, 1993.

"Mockingbird Returns to Oklahoma High School's Reading List." Associated Press. October 15, 2001. Available online. URL: http://www.freedomforum.org/templates/document.asp?documentID=15150. Accessed August 10, 2010.

Newsletter on Intellectual Freedom (March 1966): 16; (March 1968): 22; (March 1978): 31; (May 1980): 62; (March 1982): 47; (July 1984): 105; (March 1986): 57–58; (November 2001): 277–278; (January 2002): 50; (January 2004): 11; (May 2004): 98–99; (September 2004): 175–176; (November 2009): 202–204.

Skaggs, Merrill. *The Folk of Southern Fiction.* Athens: University of Georgia Press, 1972.

UNCLE REMUS

Author: Joel Chandler Harris
Original date and place of publication: 1880, United States
Original publisher: D. Appleton and Company
Literary form: Short story collection

SUMMARY

The stories told by Uncle Remus first appeared as newspaper columns in the Atlanta *Constitution* before they were collected into a series of books that made Joel Chandler Harris famous and a favorite author among such prominent Americans as President Theodore Roosevelt and wealthy industrialist Andrew Carnegie. The books of tales also appeared regularly on lists of suggested reading for young men and women in the late 19th and early 20th centuries and among favorite childhood books cited by prominent individuals. Nine books in a series contain the 185 tales: *Uncle Remus: His Songs and Sayings* (New York: D. Appleton & Company, 1880); *Nights with Uncle Remus: Myths and Legends of the Old Plantation* (Boston: James R. Osgood & Company, 1883), *Daddy Jake, the Runaway: And Short Stories Told after Dark* (New York: The Century Company, 1889), *Uncle Remus and His Friends: Old Plantation Stories, Songs, and Ballads with Sketches of Negro Character* (Boston: Houghton Mifflin & Company, 1892), *Told by Uncle Remus: New Stories of the Old Plantation* (New York: McClure, Phillips & Company, 1905), *Uncle Remus and Brer Rabbit* (New York: Frederick A. Stokes Company 1907), *Uncle Remus and the Little Boy* (Boston: Small, Maynard & Company, 1910), *Uncle Remus Returns* (Boston: Houghton Mifflin Company, 1918), and *Seven Tales of Uncle Remus* (Atlanta: Emory University, 1948).

The first stories appeared in the *Constitution*, and Harris developed an immediate following. The premise of the stories is simple and remains consistent throughout the tales. The seven-year-old white son of the plantation's owner is troubled by the tensions between his parents, and he escapes the house to sit with Uncle Remus, a former slave, and to listen to the tales of the trickster rabbit (Brer Rabbit), the wicked fox (Brer Fox), the lethargic Brer B'ar, and numerous other animals whom Harris anthropomorphizes, as well as to other stories that occasionally include humans such as Mr. Man and Blacksmiff. The stories contain the folklore of the slaves and are told in a dialect that is sometimes difficult to understand and frequently criticized by African Americans. Uncle Remus introduces the most famous of the stories, "The Wonderful Tar-Baby Story," by answering the child's question if the fox ever did catch the rabbit as follows:

> "He come mighty nigh it, honey, sho's you born—Brer Fox did. One day atter Brer Rabbit fool 'im wid dat calamus root Brer Fox went ter wuk en got 'im some tar,en mix it wid some turkentime, en fix up a contrapshun w'at he call a Tar-Baby, en he tuck dish yer Tar-Baby en he sot 'er inde big road, en den he lay off in de bushes fer to see what de news wuz gwine ter be. En he didn't hatter wait long, nudder, kaze bimeby here come Brer Rabbit pacin' down the road—lippity-clippity, clippity-lippity—dez ez sassy ez a jay-bird. Brer Rabbit come prancin' 'long twel he spy de Tar-Baby, en den he fotch up on his behime legs like he wuz 'stonished. De Tar-Baby, she sot dar, she did, en Brer Fox, he lay low."

Harris wrote in the introduction to the tales from *Daddy Jack, the Runaway* that using the dialect was critical to the expression in his tales because "it would be impossible to separate these stories from the idiom in which they have been recited for generations. The dialect is part of the legends themselves, and to present them in any other way would rob them of everything that gives them vitality."

The tales have also lost favor over the years because they portray a former slave as content in his role of living in a cabin on the plantation and of playing a seemingly avuncular role for the son of his former owner. Johnson writes

> Besides his use of dialect spellings and humor, Harris's glorification of plantation society and his attempt to portray the slavery that supported it as benign, perhaps even pleasant, negatively influence the modern reader's perception of his work. In the stories' frame, an old slave, Uncle Remus, tells stories to a little white boy, the master's child. Many critics agree that the Uncle Remus character causes more reaction against Harris than his use of dialect does. In his loyalty to his white master, he has become an Uncle Tom figure, a sentimental "old darky" in the eyes of whites who would romanticize the Old South, a figure despised by blacks who know how important it is to remember the horrors of slavery.

Scholars point out that such a simplistic reading of the stories misses the depth and meaning in the stories that are largely modifications of slave tales in which the sly and seemingly weak and powerless Brer Rabbit consistently manages to get the best of those who are stronger and more powerful. "Brer Rabbit is supposedly weaker than those around him, just as the slaves were, but in hundreds of tales based on African lore he manages not just to escape but also to outwit and embarrass his persecutors."

The scholarship regarding Harris's contribution to literature and his place in the literary canon is mixed. In *Down Home: A History of Afro-American Short Fiction from Its Beginnings to the End of the Harlem Renaissance*, Richard Bone's review of the scholarship from the 1950s through 1975 shows that Harris's "work had already been devalued by charges of racism." In the January–February 2003 issue of *Oxford American*, Schone labels the tales "raceporn" and describes Harris as "a dead white Confederate who spouts Ebonics" and someone who has earned "eternal black anger." In contrast, Keith Cartwright asserts in *Reading Africa into American Literature* that Harris's Uncle Remus tales are "born of an expansive, truly multicultural American vision" and that Harris's respect for Africa-American folk narratives and his genius in developing [them] should not be underestimated."

CENSORSHIP HISTORY

President Theodore Roosevelt was one of the biggest fans of the Uncle Remus tales and has been quoted as saying, "Presidents may come and presidents may go, but Uncle Remus stays put." The stories were once a staple in classrooms, but they no longer appear in textbooks and are not included on reading lists.

In his lifetime, Harris was ranked just behind Mark Twain as America's second most popular writer. After Harris's death, Andrew Carnegie and Theodore Roosevelt raised money to buy Harris's house and to turn it into a museum in 1913. Auchmutey reports that "In the 1920s, a survey of English teachers ranked the Uncle Remus tales as one of the five greatest achievements of American literature, ahead of *Moby-Dick*. Many blacks embraced the stories too. James Weldon Johnson, the Harlem Renaissance writer, called them 'the greatest body of folklore that America has produced.'"

Today, the tales are out of the classroom and, in some cases, not available in libraries. Beyond the changes in social perception, scholars blame the Walt Disney film *Song of the South*, which the film company pulled from distribution in 1970, for distorting Harris's work and for "romanticizing the Old South." Auchmutey relates that the National Association for the Advancement of Colored People (NAACP) planned to boycott the movie at its release, then decided against doing so and, instead, issued a statement that accused Disney of using "the beautiful Uncle Remus folklore" to present "a glorified picture of slavery." Harris scholars assert that the film is distinctly separate from the folklore that Harris presented. They contend that in making a family-friendly film, "Disney oversimplified the characters and lost the layers of irony that had made them more complicated in print."

In addition to the banishment of Uncle Remus from the classrooms, public acknowledgments that formerly honored the author or his creation have been changed. In 1982, the Board of Trustees of the Atlanta Public Library renamed the Uncle Remus Branch of the library the West End Branch and told reporters that using the original name is "offensive." Michael Lomax, a member of the Atlanta Library Board and also the chairman of Georgia's Fulton County Commission asserted that Uncle Remus is "a stereotyped character from the old plantation school of southern literature [and] calling a library the 'Uncle Remus Branch' in a black community is equivalent to calling a library the 'Shylock Branch' in the Jewish community." In December 1986, school officials in the Savannah-Chatham County school district canceled all performances of a play named *Br'er Rabbit's Big Secret* that Ken Watkins and the Savannah Theatre Company were going to present. Watkins stated that "They felt there were things children wouldn't understand—the tar baby would be taken as a racial slur. Other than that, I think they were bothered by poor grammatical language." A spokesman for the school system denied that censorship occurred and said that the school district canceled the performances because study guides were not provided. "This is not an attempt at censorship. The main concern is to prepare teachers and children for something that is very different. They needed to be coached on dialect and language not considered acceptable. The children needed to be taught a historical perspective."

FURTHER READING

Auchmutey, Jim. "In Search of 'Uncle Remus': Sixty Years Ago, Walt Disney Turned Joel Chandler Harris's Creations into a Hit Movie. But Times Have Changed. Now the Film Is Locked Away, and the Author's Reputation Has Dimmed." *Atlanta Journal-Constitution*, November 12, 2006, p. K1.

Bone, Robert. *Down Home: A History of Afro-American Short Fiction from Its Beginnings to the End of the Harlem Renaissance*. New York: G. P. Putnam's Sons, 1975.

Brasch, Walter. *Brer Rabbit, Uncle Remus and the 'Cornfield Journalist': The Tale of Joel Chandler Harris*. Macon, Ga.: Mercer University Press, 2000.

Bumgardner, Stan. "Rehabilitating *Uncle Remus*." *American History* 42 (December 2007): 12.

"Carnegie Embraces 'Uncle Remus' Harris. Makes Special Stop at Atlanta in Order to Meet Him." *New York Times*, April 7, 1906, p. 9.

Cartwright, Keith. *Reading Africa into American Literature*. Lexington: University Press of Kentucky, 2002.

Johnson, Ellen. "Geographic Context and Ethnic Context: Joel Chandler Harris and Alice Walker." *Mississippi Quarterly* 60 (Spring 2007): 235–255.

"Play on Br'er Rabbit Banned in Savannah." *New York Times*, December 11, 1986, p. A24.

Schone, Mark. "Uncle Remus Is Dead, Long Live Uncle Remus." *Oxford American* (January/February 2003): 86–92.

Starnes, Joe Samuel. "Georgia: We Are Finally Coming to Claim Our Writers." *Washington Post*, November 11, 2007, p. 1.

"Uncle Remus Told Stories and Roosevelt, His Host, Told Stories." *New York Times*, November 19, 1907, p. 1.

UNLIVED AFFECTIONS

Author: George Shannon
Original date and place of publication: 1989, United States
Original publisher: Harper & Row
Literary form: Young adult novel

SUMMARY

Unlived Affections is a novel about secrets and about the people who are hurt by these secrets and by their refusal to love others as they are and not as they wish them to be.

Willie Ramsey has never known his father, and his mother died when he was two, leaving his maternal grandmother ("Grom") to raise him. A rigid woman who works as a school nurse while he is young, Grom has created a museum of her house, in which everything is neatly ordered and nothing is thrown away, and the subject of Willie's father is never raised. Despite his love for Grom, Willie cannot wait to escape the smothering atmosphere of her house and attend college in Nebraska. "He just meant to leave his grandmother, Ottawa and everything else like his parents had left him."

The novel opens with a bereft Willie preparing to empty the contents of the house for a yard sale of his grandmother's belongings. Only weeks before he was supposed to leave for college, Grom had a heart attack and died, leaving him the house, money for college, and many unanswered questions. Throughout the novel, as Willie sorts through the many items that fill every closet and corner of the house, he learns the truth about his parents and achieves a level of peace with himself. In numerous flashbacks, the reader also learns of Willie's intense desire to love and to be loved and of the fear of being hurt by love that has made him avoid Libby, a young woman from school whom he likes and whose patient understanding eventually breaks through his shell. "He was so frightened of being left that he truly believed if he left Libby, she couldn't leave him. She meant too much to him."

Willie methodically sorts items for the yard sale, hoping that he will find some clues about his father and his mother. He finds stacks of carefully arranged issues of magazines dating back to 1967, boxes of letters and cards arranged alphabetically in shoeboxes, and photographs in a box marked "Grateful Patients." "Pictures of every friggin' kid who ever skinned a knee at school, but no pictures of my father. Nothing."

As Willie works, memories of his grandmother sitting in the living room, watching television, smoking, and crocheting come to mind, and he remembers the softer side that came out when she would touch the old cigar box in which she kept her crocheting supplies. The box had been her husband's, his grandfather's, as well as the source of her rigidity and rules for shutting off lights, saving water by taking short showers, and warnings against running in the house. He also thinks of her passion for the multitude of flowers in her garden and her celebrations when the gladiolas bloomed and the poppies produced their profusion of color. The memories make Willie wish that he could have learned more about the secrets that his grandmother kept.

One of those secrets is his late mother's bedroom, which Grom kept locked and which she warned him never to enter. She entered it one Saturday each month for one hour in order to clean the room, then carefully locked it as she left. Willie recalls picking the lock when he was in fourth grade and entering the room, which he found in the same condition as it was the day his mother died. Her clothes were in the closet, letters and postcards were tucked around her mirror, and a smell that he imagined was hers lingered. As he left the room, Grom caught him and warned him to never enter it again.

Grom told him that his father was dead and that his mother had died of a heart attack, but he overhears her telling a teacher in school: "It's the saddest story you'll ever hear. . . . His father ran off and died before he was born; then my daughter and the fool she was dating were killed when a truck crashed into their car. I'm all he's got in the world." Whenever Willie asked about his father, his grandmother simply told him that he was dead and better off that way. When Willie asked about his mother, Grom only talked about the perfect little girl she was and praised her beauty and talents, but she refused to speak about the adult Kate Davenport Ramsey.

The yard sale is imminent, so Willie completes the inventory of the entire house and saves the locked room—his mother's room—for last. Willie searches for some clue to his origin, to the father whom he has never known and the mother who was only presented to him in an idealized light. He looks through his mother's address book, but finds no evidence of any relatives: "Willie thumbed to the R's. No Ramseys. Then the D's. No Davenports either." That leaves him feeling even more alone.

Willie unloads the drawers of the desk and finds a shoebox wedged tightly in the back that contains a six-inch stack of letters, all with the return name of "Bill Ramsey," sent from Kentucky and addressed to his mother's married name, Kate Ramsey. The realization that these letters are from his father to his mother frighten him, even as he understands that they will probably provide the answers to his many questions.

The letters begin before Willie was born and are written by a man who was obviously very much in love with his wife and who left her in Kansas to become an apprentice to a fine furniture maker in Kentucky. Willie reads the first few letters, and periodically questions what could have happened to make his grandmother hate a man who had so loved her daughter. As he reads later letters, he learns that his father became infatuated with another man, Larry, whose picture is in one of the envelopes. He learns that Kate did not condemn Bill but loved him so much that she tried to wait out the infatuation. In one of her visits to Bill, Willie is conceived, but Kate keeps her pregnancy a secret and, instead, paints a happy picture that she is dating several men and even considering marrying again. Willie also learns in the letters that the rocking chair in his room, in which Grom would never sit, was made by his father for his mother. The letters reveal that his mother did not tell Grom that his father was leaving her for a man; Kate lied that he was leaving her for another woman, as Grom's husband had "run off to Kansas City" with another woman.

The realization of the many lost opportunities for love makes Willie angry, first at his grandmother, then at his mother, and, finally, at his father. He rereads his father's letter reassuring his mother that the choice had nothing to do with her: "I'm doing what I'm doing because I do love you. And because I finally like me. You can't really believe that this has anything to do with your looks or brains. You're wonderful!" His father urges Kate to divorce him and to find a man who can fully love her. "Tell the lawyer I'll sign anything he wants me to. Tell him whatever you want to. Tell anything that makes it easier on you. People will talk no matter what. Tell them the truth about me like you finally did to your mother." As he reads a later letter in which Bill tells Kate that he has found the love of his life, a dentist named Evan, Willie realizes that the dates of the letters are coming closer to his mother's date of death and mutters "Damn queers" and becomes deeply sad. He has received answers to questions that have plagued him for most of his life, but he is no longer certain that the lies may not have been better.

On the day of the yard sale, Willie places the letters and the rocking chair aside, the only two items that link him to his mother and his father, and prepares to deal with the crowds. He is surprised to find Libby at the door when the sale begins, and he reluctantly tells her what he learned from the letters. Rather than expressing shock, Libby offers sympathy and tells him that his father did not abandon him because Kate never told Bill that she was pregnant. As they speak, Willie also realizes how much his grandmother really loved him and how much pain she experienced in being abandoned by her husband, then watching her daughter have the same experience before dying very young. In a final gesture, Willie visits his mother's and Grom's graves, to cry and to bury the shoebox of letters in one and the cigar box of crochet threads in the other.

CENSORSHIP HISTORY

Unlived Affections is a coming-of-age novel that does not contain an active gay character, has no mention of homosexual activity, offers no approval of homosexual relationships, and does not proselytize about the homosexual lifestyle. However, controversy has ensued over Willie's recognition through letters two decades old that his father realized his own homosexuality after having married and fathered a child (albeit a child he did not know existed).

In 1993, the mother of a sixth-grade girl attending Lundahl Junior High School in Crystal Lake, Illinois, discovered that her daughter's teacher was reading *Unlived Affections* aloud in class. She became upset when she learned that it contained references to homosexuality. The mother wrote a formal letter of complaint to the school district and charged that the references to homosexuality in the book made it unsuitable for students in junior high school. The matter was referred to a book review committee at Lundahl Junior High School, which voted to remove the book from library shelves. The Crystal Lake District School 47, which includes Lundahl Junior High School, had a committee composed of teachers, administrators, and librarians also review the book. The committee voted to ban the book because they believed it "was unfit for junior high students."

School Superintendent Richard Bemotas spoke to reporters for the committee members, who declined to comment, and concluded, "The building-level committee said it was not age-appropriate. Something that is appropriate for one age level may not be appropriate for another." Supporters of the book, including the school librarian who was one of two dissenters on the book review committee, planned to take the decision before a district-wide committee, then, if necessary, to the school board. The ban of *Unlived Affections* initiated a debate over the issue of freedom of speech versus parental rights to decide what is best for children, and it also raised questions as to how library materials are selected.

George Shannon, author of the novel, told a reporter for the *Chicago Tribune* that despite the criticism of his book, he believes that "a parent has the responsibility or right to know what their own child is reading or viewing or listening to. Every family has different religious views on what is right and what is wrong." Although he acknowledges that standards do vary from family to family, Shannon asserts, "I am against any individual deciding what another group can or can't do, or know or believe." At the same time, the author expressed surprise that the book created debate, and he decided to simply stay out of the fray. He told a reporter that his part was writing the book and "in general supporting intellectual freedom in my daily life. I can't decide if it's right or wrong for the school; that's for the community to decide."

FURTHER READING

Hawkins, H. "Opening the Closet Door: Services for Gay, Lesbian, and Bisexual Teens." *Colorado Libraries* 20 (1994): 28–31.

Haynes, V. Dion. "Book Ban at School Stirs Debate." *Chicago Tribune*, March 5, 1992, p. 1.

Jenkins, C. "From Queer to Gay and Back Again: Young Adult Novels with Gay/Lesbian/Queer Content, 1969–1997." *Library Quarterly* 68, no. 3: 298–334.

Rothbauer, Paulette M., and Lynne E. F. McKechnie. "Gay and Lesbian Fiction for Young Adults: A Survey of Holdings in Canadian Public Libraries." *Collection Building* 18, no. 1 (1999): 32–39.

Wolf, V. "The Gay Family in Literature for Young People." *Children's Literature in Education* 20 (1989): 275–288.

WE ALL FALL DOWN

Author: Robert Cormier
Original date and place of publication: 1991, United States
Original publisher: Delacorte Press
Literary form: Young adult novel

SUMMARY

In *We All Fall Down*, Robert Cormier examines the issue of vandalism and violence in an upper-middle-class neighborhood. In a suspenseful plot that contains numerous unexpected twists and turns, the novel leads readers to question why somebody would commit such acts of random violence and explains the motivation that might lead people to act in unexpected ways.

The setting of the novel is the small suburb of Burnside, a well-kept, upper-middle-class residential area at Cape Cod, with "neat houses, with shutters and rose arbors, birdbaths on front lawns, and the lawns carefully manicured." This area, especially Arbor Lane, the street on which the Jerome family lives, has a quiet atmosphere of friendly neighbors and a feeling of safety: "People waving hello to each other, evening barbecues in the backyards and the aroma of burning charcoal or wood smoke from chimneys. A neighborhood of station wagons and vans, family cars." This is not a neighborhood where violence, vandalism, and terror usually occur. Yet it is precisely in this idyllic setting that the Jerome family and their daughter Karen become victims of a random act of violence committed by four high school seniors. The novel examines the consequences that the act of violence has for both the perpetrators and the victims.

The novel begins in a matter-of-fact tone, detailing the horror that sets the events of the novel into motion:

They entered the house at 9:02 p.m. on the evening of April Fools' Day. In the next forty-five minutes, they shit on the floor and pissed on the walls and trashed their way through the seven-room Cape Cod cottage. They overturned the furniture, smashed the picture tubes in three television sets, tore two VCRs from their sockets and crashed them to the floor. They spray-painted the wall orange. They flooded the bathrooms, both upstairs and down, and flushed face towels down the toilet bowls. They broke every mirror in the place and toppled a magnificent hutch to the floor, sending china cups and saucers and plates and assorted crystal through the air. In the second-floor

WE ALL FALL DOWN

bedrooms, they pulled out dresser drawers, spilled their contents on the floor, yanked clothing from the closets and slashed the mattresses. In the downstairs den, they performed a special job on the spinet, smashing the keys with a hammer, the noise like a crazy soundtrack to the scenes of plunder.

As four high school seniors vandalize the home of the Jerome family, the youngest daughter, 14-year-old Karen, arrives home unexpectedly, and three of the boys attempt to rape her while the fourth stands by drunk and stunned. When Karen struggles to get away and pulls open the door to the cellar, one of the boys pushes her with both hands, causing her to fall down the stairs and go into a coma. An unidentified watcher called only the Avenger watches the boys trash the home and vows to hunt them down and punish them, but he fails to see Karen being dragged across the hallway by the boys. In the months that follow, as Karen lies in a coma and the Jeromes cope with the violation of their home, the mentally unbalanced Avenger lurks and waits to carry out his own form of justice. The novel explores the moral responsibilities of people toward others and analyzes the motivation of teenagers to commit such acts of brutal violence against people and their property.

The four young men who break into the Jerome house are Harry Flowers, Marty Sanders, Randy Pierce, and Buddy Walker, four middle-class seniors in high school in the neighboring town of Wickburg. Harry Flowers is the spoiled son of an architect who is too busy to deal with his son and his problems. Harry's parents have no idea what their son is doing after school and only seem to care about his report cards from school. They try to compensate their own lack of time and interest in him by giving him money. Harry acts as the leader of the group of boys who vandalize the Jerome house; he is constantly looking for excitement, which includes harassing other people, driving around town in his car, and drinking alcohol.

Marty Sanders and Randy Pierce try very hard to imitate Harry and attempt to impress him, but they are simply his lackeys, willing to follow him just to gain his approval. Buddy Walker is different. He is vulnerable because he is still dealing with the shock of learning that his parents are going to divorce, and although he is very much under the influence of Harry, he feels uncomfortable with the behavior of the four boys during their "Funtimes." Buddy is the only one of the four who has scruples about their actions.

The families of these four perpetrators evidence a lack of communication and an unwillingness to address and solve family problems. In contrast, the victimized Jeromes are a warm and close-knit family. Fourteen-year-old Karen, 16-year-old Jane, and their younger brother Artie, as well as their parents, seem to really care about each other, and they share common interests and values. A business manager of the Wickburg telephone company, Mr. Jerome spends every minute he can after work with his family.

A neighbor returning from a monthlong business trip recalls writing down the license plate of a suspicious car parked outside the Jerome home.

He provides the police with their only clue as to the identity of the vandals. The car belongs to the Flowers family, and Harry Flowers admits to vandalizing the house but claims that he did it alone and that he had a key to enter the house given to him by Jane. The authorities cannot charge him with breaking and entering, and his father pays for the damage to the house. Jane is devastated by the claim, and her parents realize that she had dropped her house key at the mall months before. After watching her drop the key and retrieving it, Flowers had gained as much information as he could about her and her family, then targeted them, but he did not tell his friends that he had the key.

Remorseful for what he has done, Buddy calls Jane and apologizes but does not give his name. Her voice makes him want to know her better, and he arranges to meet her accidentally at different public places. In a short while, they become friends. Without knowing Buddy's involvement in the trashing of her family's house, Jane falls in love with him. For the first time, Buddy experiences an important relationship, and he works to improve his life. Jane means so much to him that he tries very hard to quit drinking.

Although this relationship is based on a lie, Buddy's character is developed with compassion, and the growing trust makes readers believe that their romance will work out. However, after Jane learns that Buddy was one of the four vandals who had destroyed her family home, placed her sister in a coma, and wreaked havoc with her family's life, she ends the relationship.

Cormier uses the character of the Avenger to provide a second perspective on the issue of moral responsibility. Only at the end does the reader learn that the Avenger is not an 11-year-old boy but the mentally disturbed, 41-year-old Michael Stallings, nicknamed "Mickey Looney" by Jane because he looks like actor Mickey Rooney and acts strange. He observes what happened in the Jerome home and sets out to avenge that act. Although the Avenger's plans to carry out his vengeance remain unclear, the actions would probably be as brutal and violent as his killing of a bully when he was 11 years old and of his grandfather, a retired police sergeant who suspected the crime. He had stolen his grandfather's service revolver and shot the bully to death, then later killed his grandfather to avoid exposure. At the end of the novel, the Avenger lures Jane to a shed, ties her up, and frantically threatens to kill her and himself. She manages to calm him and keep them both alive until Buddy and the police arrive.

CENSORSHIP HISTORY

We All Fall Down has been challenged in school districts and libraries for its profanity, violence, and the attempted rape at the beginning of the book, as well as the violent suicide attempt near the end of the novel. The American Library Association lists the novel as 35th among the 100 most challenged books from 1990 to 2000.

In 1997, members of Oklahomans for Children and Families (OCAF), an Oklahoma City–based group, charged that some of the materials found in the Oklahoma County Metropolitan Library System were pornographic and obscene. With the support of the Virginia-based Family Friendly Libraries (FFL), OCAF protested at Metropolitan Library System (MLS) meetings over four months and asked library officials to remove the books from the general collection and to place them in a restricted area behind the circulation desk. The groups objected to three works by Robert Cormier—*We All Fall Down*, *Beyond the Chocolate War*, and *Fade*—as well as *Boys and Sex* by Wardell B. Pomeroy and *IT'S PERFECTLY NORMAL* by Robie H. Harris. Lee Brawner, MLS director, said that in his 38 years of library work, he had heard many complaints but never received the complaints in so organized a manner as those submitted by OCAF and FFL. The MLS efforts to keep the materials in the general collection were defended by American Civil Liberties Union lawyers, who called efforts to change the library policy "clear-cut censorship."

In March 14, 2000, *We All Fall Down* was placed on the restricted list in the Arlington (Texas) Independent School District. During the fall of 1999, Donna Harkreader, the parent of a student in the school district, filed a complaint with district administrators, objecting to the violence in the book. The matter was referred to a panel of school librarians. On March 14, 2000, the panel submitted its recommendation to retain the book in the middle and high school libraries. On March 17, 2000, school superintendent Mac Bernd ordered the book removed from the general shelves in the school library and restricted it to students who had their parents' written permission to borrow the book.

We All Fall Down was pulled from classrooms in Baldwin City High School by the school superintendent in Baldwin, Kansas, in September 2003, after Lois Krysztof, the mother of a Baldwin freshman, sent a list of excerpts and complaints that the book was not appropriate reading material for a freshman orientation class. School Superintendent James White received the request, in which Krysztof cited more than 50 objectionable paragraphs she had found in the book, and removed the book from the class curriculum. He told a reporter for the *Baldwin City Signal*, "It doesn't look to me like something the kids should be reading at the freshman level." Krysztof had spoken with Baldwin High School principal Allen Poplin about the book in spring 2003 and afterward filled out a "request for consideration of instructional materials" and sent the request and book excerpts to all members of the board of education, as well as to the superintendent. School board member Stacy Cohen, voiced strong objections to the superintendent's action and expressed the view that the book should remain in the classroom until the school board had the opportunity to consider the matter; White wanted the book removed until a review would take place. At a special meeting on September 22, 2003, the school board determined that although a policy existed in the district to review challenges to books in the school libraries, no policy existed regarding books in the classroom curriculum. The board voted 5-2 against returning copies of the book to the ninth-grade orientation class until a review committee could decide if the book should remain part of the curriculum. On September 26, 2003, at an emergency meeting of the school board, members voted 6-1 to dissolve the review committee because the district policy only covered books in the school libraries and the recommendations of the panel would have no bearing on a decision regarding classroom curriculum. On October 27, 2003, the school board then reversed its decision and reinstated the review committee but voted 4-3 to keep the book out of the classroom until the evaluation process was completed. Three days later, on October 30, 2003, four Baldwin High School students who attended a football game between Baldwin and Perry-Lecompton High School brought further attention to the banning by passing out a large number of copies of *We All Fall Down* to spectators.

The issue was finally resolved in November 2003, after the district committee reviewing the book recommended that it be returned to the curriculum and that use of the book should be left to the classroom teacher, school principal, and district curriculum director. The school board voted 5-2 to make the book available to students of the high school's freshman orientation class, not as required reading but as supplemental curricular material.

At a meeting of the Cherry Hill Public Library board of directors on July 27, 2005, Ellen Schwartz, the mother of a 13-year-old girl, asked through representation by the mayor's deputy chief of staff for the library to move *We All Fall Down* out of the young adult section. She had appealed to Mayor Bernie Platt, who sent his deputy Anthony Bucchi to represent him at the meeting. Schwartz claimed that the content was "deplorable" and that it was "unfit for young minds." Bucchi told a reporter for a local newspaper that "The mayor wanted the board to make sure we're doing everything on the same level with regard to the accepted book selection policies." The library director Barbara Shapiro stated that the challenge to *We All Fall Down* was the only official challenge to a book at the Cherry Hill Public Library in a decade. At the meeting, the mother who protested admitted that she had not read the book and said that, if she had, she "might not have objected so strenuously." Her concern was that, although written for teenagers, the book "deals with mature subject matters such as alcoholism and divorce." In anticipation of a large crowd, the board moved the meeting from the boardroom into a larger meeting room, but few people turned out. Instead, the library board president Stephen Barbell explained how the book selection procedure worked, but none of the board members indicated support of Schwartz's attempt to move the novel out of the young adult section. The matter was dismissed.

FURTHER READING

American Civil Liberties Union. "The People v. Robert Cormier?" *American Civil Liberties Union Freedom Network News*, January 10, 1997.

Carpenter, Tim. "Banned Book Reinstated." *Lawrence Journal-World*, November 19, 2003.

———. "Book Ban Ignites Censorship Debate." *Lawrence Journal-World*, September 14, 2003.

"Censorship Dateline: Schools: Lawrence, Kansas." *Newsletter on Intellectual Freedom* 53 (January 2004): 12.

Dymacek, Kristen. "Board Requests Review of Ninth-Grade Book." *Baldwin City Signal*, September 24, 2003.

———. "Book's Appropriateness in Class Questioned." *Baldwin City Signal*, September 17, 2003.

Estes, Sally. "Cormier, Robert. *We All Fall Down*." *Booklist* 15 (September 1991): 137.

Goldberg, Beverly. "*We All Fall Down* Restricted." *American Libraries* 31 (May 2000): 23.

Newsletter on Intellectual Freedom (November 2005): 207–208.

Petterson, John L. "School Board to Discuss Superintendent's Decision to Pull Book." *Kansas City Star*, September 21, 2003. Available online. URL: http://www.kansascity. com/mld/kansascity/news/6821149.htm?1c. Accessed August 10, 2010.

"School Board Dissolves Book Review Panel." KCTV5. Broadcast September 30, 2003. Available online. URL: http://www.kctv5.com/global/story.asp?s=1463539&Client Type=Printable. Accessed August 10, 2010.

WELCOME TO THE MONKEY HOUSE

Author: Kurt Vonnegut, Jr.
Original date and place of publication: 1968, United States
Original publisher: Delacorte Press
Literary form: Short story collection

SUMMARY

Welcome to the Monkey House consists of 25 short stories, 11 reprinted from Vonnegut's 1961 short story collection *Canary in a Cat House*. All of the stories originally appeared in such diverse publications as the *Atlantic Monthly, Colliers, Cosmopolitan, Ladies' Home Journal,* and *Fantasy and Science Fiction Magazine* from 1950 through 1964, but the title story appeared in *Playboy* magazine the same year that the collection was released.

Many of the 25 stories have as their setting Hyannis Port, Massachusetts, where the Kennedy family has long had its compound, and Vonnegut weaves the Kennedy name throughout many of the stories. The settings vary from the present to hundreds of years into the future, but all offer perceptive criticism of contemporary ills. "Welcome to the Monkey House" is the only story singled out for criticism regarding language and sexual situations, but the entire collection has been removed where such cases have occurred.

The story is set in Cape Cod, Massachusetts, and its environs, in an unspecified future in which antiaging shots make everyone appear no older than 22 and the Earth is overpopulated with 17 billion people. The World Government has launched a two-pronged attack on the problem by encouraging "compulsory ethical birth control" and "ethical suicide." Everyone must take the "ethical birth control pill" three times daily. It is the only legal form of birth control and does not interfere with a person's ability to reproduce, "which would have been unnatural and immoral," but it does "take every bit of pleasure out of the sex act." The pills make people numb from the waist down, and they are so effective that you could "blindfold a man who had taken one, tell him to recite the Gettysburg Address, kick him in the balls while he was doing it, and he wouldn't miss a syllable."

The pills were invented by J. Edgar Nation, a pharmacist from Grand Rapids, Michigan, who created them to "introduce morality into the monkey house at the Grand Rapids Zoo." After he and his 11 children went to the zoo one Easter day and saw a monkey "playing with his private parts," he rushed home "to make a pill that would make monkeys in the springtime fit things for a Christian to see." The World Government adopted his discovery after the United Nations announced a population crisis and scientists stated that people had to stop reproducing while moralists declared that society would collapse if people used sex for nothing but pleasure. The pill was the solution. "Thus did science and morals go hand in hand."

The Federal Ethical Suicide Parlors are run by Ethical Suicide Service (ESS) hostesses, all of whom are six feet tall or more, seductively made up and dressed, "plump and rosy," skilled in judo and karate, and virgins. They prepare their clients for death by providing pleasant conversation and a last meal before administering the fatal shot with a hypodermic needle.

"Nothingheads," rebels who refuse to take the ethical birth control pills, threaten society. They are "bombed out of their skulls with the sex madness that came from taking nothing." The most notorious nothinghead is Billy the Poet, who specializes in deflowering the hostesses of suicide parlors. He usually sends his potential victims "dirty poems" far in advance, then abducts them, forces them to wait the eight hours until their pills wear off, and "deflowers them with a clinical skill." Afterward, they are "grateful" and join the growing nothingheads movement. After raping Nancy, a 63-year-old virgin ESS hostess, Billy reads a passage from Elizabeth Barrett Browning's *Sonnets from the Portuguese* to her, tells her that lawmakers throughout history "have been absolutely disgusted and terrified by the natural sexuality of common men and women," and gives her a bottle of pills to be taken monthly to prevent pregnancy. The label on the bottle states: "WELCOME TO THE MONKEY HOUSE."

CENSORSHIP HISTORY

In 1970, Marilyn Parducci, a teacher in Montgomery, Alabama, was dismissed for assigning the title story of the collection to her 11th-grade English class. Three high school juniors of the teacher's 90 students asked to be excused from reading the story, and their parents complained about "vulgarities" and a reference to rape in the story. Objectors stated that the references to the monkey "playing with his private parts" and the phrase "kick him in the balls" were "vulgar." They also objected to lines in two of Billy's poems: "A-goosing statues in the dark," "And when I peed, I peed turquoise" and "Mourn my pecker, purple daughter." The high school principal and the associate school superintendent called the book "literary garbage" and chastised Parducci for teaching a book that promoted "the killing off of elderly people and free sex." Parducci brought suit against the school district in *Parducci v. Rutland*, 316 F. Supp. 352 (M.D. Ala 1970), asking reinstatement and financial remuneration. In rendering his decision, Judge Frank Johnson observed that, despite the "vulgar terms," the story could be considered an appropriate assignment when judged in the larger literary context. He noted that the words objected to were

> less ribald than those found in many of Shakespeare's plays. The reference in the story to an act of sexual intercourse is no more descriptive than the rape scene in Pope's "Rape of the Lock." . . . It appears to the Court, moreover, that the author, rather than advocating the "killing off of old people," satirizes the practice to symbolize the increasing depersonalization of man in society.

The presiding judge stated further, "that teachers are entitled to first amendment freedom is an issue no longer in dispute" and such freedoms of expression should only be restricted if evidence exists that school activities would be disrupted. Because only three students had requested to be excused from the assignment, the judge determined that no disruption of the school schedule had occurred and ruled in favor of the teacher, who was reinstated in her teaching position.

In 1977, a parent in Bloomington, Minnesota, perused the books in the junior high school library and discovered three that contained "sexually explicit language." The parent complained to the school board, indicating that he had been concerned for a while about the materials used in the school "but when this came out, I really became uncoiled." The offending books were *Welcome to the Monkey House* and the two-volume science fiction story collection *Again, Dangerous Vision*, edited by Harlan Ellison. The parent raised objections to use of the words *balls*, *peed*, and *pecker* and noted that the word *fucking* was used in two instances as an adjective. The school superintendent stated his own dissatisfaction over "the fact that the obscene books were purchased and made available to students." He explained that the books were supplementary and had not been ordered through the normal purchase authorization channels, so he had not had the power of veto in advance. Although the superintendent promised that steps would be taken to prevent a reoccurrence, the parent removed his seven children from the Bloomington schools.

FURTHER READING

Allen, William Rodney. *Understanding Kurt Vonnegut.* Columbia: University of South Carolina Press, 1990.

Hipkiss, Robert A. *The American Absurd: Pynchon, Vonnegut, and Barth.* Port Washington, N.Y.: Associated Faculty Press, 1984.

Newsletter on Intellectual Freedom (January 1970): 28; (March 1977): 37.

O'Neil, Robert M. *Classrooms in the Crossfire.* Bloomington: Indiana University Press, 1981.

Vonnegut, Kurt, Jr. *Welcome to the Monkey House.* New York: Delacorte Press, 1968.

THE WELL OF LONELINESS

Author: Radclyffe Hall (Marguerite Radclyffe-Hall)
Original date and place of publication: 1928, England
Original publisher: Jonathan Cape
Literary form: Novel

SUMMARY

The Well of Loneliness was the first novel to openly portray a lesbian relationship and, despite an introduction by Havelock Ellis, who characterized the work as possessing "a notable psychological and sociological significance," it shocked readers. The main character of the novel is Stephen Gordon, a young woman of wealthy parents who strongly desire a son and raise their daughter to become the son that they lack. She mimics her father in every aspect of her life, from mannerisms, abilities, and tastes through possessing a boyish figure that fails to develop significantly as she grows older. At the age of eight, she develops an intense crush on the housemaid. As she grows older, Stephen refuses to wear stereotyped feminine clothing or to take part in feminine activities. She also refuses to become romantically involved with male suitors.

When she turns 20, Stephen's infatuation with the American wife of a new neighbor leads to her downfall. Although the other woman, a former chorus girl, flirts, teases, and accepts several expensive gifts and passionate letters, she stops short at physical involvement beyond kisses with Stephen, who becomes furious that she has been led on. To avoid accusations, the former chorus girl tells her husband about Stephen's infatuation and shows him the letters that he, in turn, hands over to Stephen's mother. The mother's reaction is swift, and Stephen is driven out of her home.

Stephen travels to London and Paris, where she meets other lesbians whose company she avoids because she is eager to be taken for "normal." The start of World War I provides her with the chance to enjoy the excitement of driving for the ambulance unit, and she also finds romance with a female coworker. Their feelings remain sublimated for a long while, during which Stephen dashingly protects her love, Mary Llewellyn, as the two drive their assigned ambulance through the battlefields. The valorous Stephen leaves the war with a scar on her right cheek, where a shell splinter had cut it open.

After the war ends, Stephen and Mary set up a household in Paris, and the two vow to remain together, but neither is comfortable with her existence. They shun the bohemian lifestyle of the homosexual community, and they are in turn shunned by conventional society. More sensitive to social criticism, Mary has difficulty living life as an outsider. When an old suitor of Stephen appears and Mary seems to reciprocate the man's show of love, Stephen decides to release her from all promises. Knowing that Mary will remain true to her earlier vow, Stephen decides to force Mary to leave to give her the chance for a normal life, and she pretends to have an affair with the notorious lesbian party hostess, Valerie Seymour. Disillusioned, Mary leaves with her male love to start a new life, and Stephen is left alone and suffering with only her dog David for company.

CENSORSHIP HISTORY

The novel achieved notoriety soon after publication when James Douglas, the book reviewer for the *London Sunday Express*, condemned strongly the theme of a lesbian emotional relationship. Douglas railed against the "hideous and loathsome vices" that he felt existed in this story of "female inverts" and claimed that he "would rather place a vial of prussic acid into the hands of a healthy boy or girl than to place the vile and hateful book into a child's hand."

The passages that so disturbed the reviewer and others are those that recount Stephen's physical affection with other women, although none of these passages contains graphic sexual activity. Early in the novel, Stephen greets with a kiss the married woman with whom she has become infatuated and to whom she gives an expensive pearl ring. In a room in which they stand lighted only by the fireplace, Stephen's "strong but unhappy arms went round her . . . and Stephen spoke such words as a lover will speak when his heart is burdened to breaking. . . . she spoke such words as lovers have spoken ever since the divine, sweet madness of God flung the thought of love into Creation." Later in the novel, when Stephen returns from war to begin her life with Mary, several passages describe their passionate kisses and expressions of love, but only one line in the novel suggests sexual activity. After Mary declares that she belongs entirely to Stephen, the reader learns ". . . and that night they were not divided." These passages outraged censors and fueled discussion regarding the immorality of the novel.

Faced with growing controversy, the publishers first printed an expurgated version of the book, then offered to withdraw it entirely at the urging of the home secretary Sir William Joynson-Hicks, despite protests by the author and her supporters. In late 1928, Pegasus Press in Paris prepared an unexpurgated version of the novel, but the first shipment of books was seized by British Customs and, using the Obscene Publications Act of 1857, the home secretary ordered that the books be destroyed.

At the trial held on November 9, 1929, the presiding magistrate, Sir Charles Biron, refused to hear the testimony of numerous expert witnesses who asked to speak on behalf of Hall and her book. In rendering his decision that the book be destroyed, Biron condemned the novel for glorifying "unnatural tendencies" rather than condemning lesbianism. He voiced particular displeasure that the relationship between the women in the novel was marked by "extraordinary rest, contentment and pleasure." Hall's defense counsel, Lord Birkett of Ulverston, claimed that the judge refused to let the author testify in her own defense. In defending the book Birkett stated that he could find little of concern in the novel and "I may add that I had to read that book several times before I could discover the alleged obscenity." Despite support from many doctors, psychiatrists, and authors, an appeal heard in Quarter Sessions the following year upheld the decision, and copies of the novel were burned. The book was banned in England until 1949.

The novel was originally supposed to be published in 1928 by Knopf in New York at the same time as its English publication. The furor in England convinced Knopf to end their plans, but Covici-Friede published it instead. Based on the counsel of attorney Morris Ernst, Donald Friede decided to take the offensive regarding the possible controversy. He called John Sumner, the head of the New York Society for the Suppression of Vice, told him that the book would be distributed, and invited him to buy an advance copy from the publisher rather than to arrest a bookstore clerk later. Sumner did so, then returned a month later with his aides, confiscated the publisher's entire stock of the novel, and arrested Friede. *The Well of Loneliness* promptly became the subject of a court case in *People v. Friede*, 233 N.Y.S. 565 (1929), under which the defendants were charged with the possession and sale of an obscene book. The New York Society for the Suppression of Vice spearheaded the effort to ban publication of the book.

Magistrate Bushell declared in his decision that the novel portrayed the story of a "female invert" whose "sex experiences are set forth in some detail and also her visits to various resorts frequented by male and female inverts. . . . The unnatural and depraved relationships portrayed are sought to be idealized and extolled." He characterized the novel as "antisocial and offensive to public morals and decency" and noted that it sought to justify and idealize these ideas in a way that "is strongly calculated to corrupt and debase those members of the community who would be susceptible to its immoral influence."

Numerous well-known authors condemned the censorship and wrote or sent telegrams to the court. Sinclair Lewis wired that he viewed the novel as being "almost lugubriously moral," while Edna St. Vincent Millay's husband, Eugene Boissevain, wired the following: "Will not some Christian teach Mr. Sumner to abuse himself instead of us and thus get rid of all this public nuisance?" Calling upon the power of the Hicklin Statute, which allowed that if certain passages are judged obscene the work might also be judged obscene, Bushell determined that the novel "tends to debauch public morals" and "that it is calculated to deprave and corrupt minds open to its immoral influences and who might come into contact with it." He concluded that *The Well of Loneliness* was in violation of the statute.

FURTHER READING

Brittain, Vera. *Radclyffe Hall: A Case of Obscenity?* New York: A. S. Barnes, 1969.

Dickson, Lovat. *Radclyffe Hall at the Well of Loneliness: A Sapphic Chronicle.* New York: Charles Scribner's Sons, 1975.

Faderman, Lillian. *Surpassing the Love of Men.* New York: William Morrow and Company, 1981.

Foster, Jeannette H. *Sex Variant Women in Literature.* Tallahassee, Fla.: Naiad Press, 1985.

Hyde, H. Montgomery. *Lord Justice: The Life and Times of Lord Birkett of Ulverston.* New York: Random House, 1964.

Katz, Jonathan Ned. *Gay American History: Lesbians and Gay Men in the U.S.A.* Rev. ed. New York: Penguin Books, 1992.

Kendrick, Walter. *The Secret Museum.* New York: Viking Press, 1987.

WHALE TALK

Author: Chris Crutcher
Original date and place of publication: 2001, United States
Original publisher: HarperCollins
Literary form: Young adult novel

SUMMARY

Whale Talk is the story of Tao Jones, better known as T. J., and a group of high school misfits who are brought together to form an unusual swim team for Cutter High School, where earning a sports jacket is the most prestigious of all symbols. Sports jackets create caste levels and symbolize the discriminatory attitudes and close-mindedness by which T. J. has been victimized and which he despises. With a goal of lessening the power that the letter athletes hold in Cutter High and to get revenge for the abuses he has suffered in life, T. J. intends to help every member of the swim team, a group of emotionally and physically handicapped teenagers, earn a jacket.

At the All Night Gym, T. J. meets Icko, a man who lives in the gym, whom T. J. asks to be their swim coach. At the gym, the team acquires a new freedom to simply practice swimming without having to experience the prejudice and verbal abuse that they experience at Cutter High School. As the team members increase their self-confidence, they also experience a sense of belonging that they have never felt in school. Not only do they attain the revered Cutter letter jacket, but they also gain personal dignity and respect.

Whale Talk is related in the first person by T. J., who is "black. And Japanese. And white." He lives happily with his adoptive parents, "two white, upwardly mobile ex-children of the sixties." He explains that only his mother, Abby Jones, is really upwardly mobile. She is a lawyer who works on child-abuse cases for the attorney general's office. "Dad likes motorcycles; he's just mobile."

The main characters in this novel, members of the Cutter swim team, are students who are marginalized in high school because of mental or physical handicaps or as the result of the prejudice and intolerance of others. As the self-appointed leader of the group, T. J. becomes the defender of the downtrodden, including a mentally handicapped young man named Chris Coughlin. His compassion for fellow victims of prejudice is most evident when Chris is harassed by Mike Barbour, the worst bully at Cutter High. Mike slams Chris against a locker for daring to wear his dead brother's Cutter letter jacket. T. J. quickly comes to Chris's rescue, using his sharp wit and defiant attitude to save Chris, even though he makes an enemy of Mike.

When Coach Simet approaches T. J. about forming a swim team for Cutter High, T. J. chooses to recruit an unlikely group of misfits to challenge the letter jacket elitists. His first recruit is Chris Coughlin, whom T. J. sees helping a little girl with shriveled arms paddle a kickboard across the pool. He realizes that Chris is capable of great compassion toward the less fortunate. The rest of the team is composed of Daniel Hole, a "geek"; Simon DeLong, a 300-pound young man whose weight makes him the object of ridicule; Jackie Craig, a quiet and totally nondescript young man who never speaks; Andy Mott, a swimmer with only one leg; and Tay Roy, the massive bench presser who is burned-out on wrestling. With this unlikely group, T. J. intends to show up Mike and other Cutter High bullies by earning a letter jacket for every member of the swim team.

Whale Talk takes place in three important settings. The primary setting is Cutter High School in Spokane, Washington, which the author vividly re-creates with descriptions of locker-lined hallways and gyms and the feeling of adolescents struggling to establish an identity and often showing intolerance to those who are different. The second setting of the novel, the All Night Gym, offers members of the swim team both a practice space and a private retreat. The third setting of the novel is the swim team bus, which provides a sheltered environment where the boys can reveal their inner fears and share the tragedies of their lives. T. J. learns that he is not the only victim of intolerance and close-mindedness. In one instance, when the bus is stranded in a snowstorm, the boys share their experiences and talk about the abuse, deaths, and family difficulties which have so tragically marred their lives. Chris talks of the pain he feels over the loss of his older brother, a great Cutter athlete. Andy Mott reveals that he lost his leg at the hands of his

mother's abusive boyfriend. T. J. questions what sort of world allows innocent young children, like a little girl named Heidi, to suffer physical abuse at
the hands of a racist stepfather. Although they vent their anger and frustration on one another, they also support each other and find the acceptance
each needs to face life.

The themes of the novel are developed through the tragic stories and
relationships the characters build with one another. As the team begins
practicing in the privacy of the All Night Gym, they find the freedom to be
who they really are, and they develop a sense of belonging. Each young man
pushes the limits of his physical endurance, and each finds he has a great deal
to offer. They are bound both by their common goal and by their need for
understanding and acceptance. By the time they reach the end of the season,
each member of the team is transformed. Chris is greeting the cheering
crowd with waves and confidence. Simon is swimming well and earning the
respect of his school, and Jackie Craig stands unembarrassed before a crowd
and actually speaks. A self-confident Tay Roy reaches out to form a relationship with a girl, and T. J. feels the pride of accomplishing his goal to earn a
letter jacket for each member of his team.

The title of the story represents what the team really learns, although
the specific incident from which the title derives involves T. J.'s father. As a
young man, he was a truck driver who had a brief relationship with a widow
who had a toddler son. After spending one loving night with her, he left in
his truck and did not discover until later that the boy had crawled onto the
axle of the truck while the lovers were together and was killed when T. J.'s
father drove away. Unaware of the tragedy until hours later, his father has
never been able to forgive himself for his part in the death of the child, and
he is, at times, completely overwhelmed by remorse.

One day, T. J. finds his father, depressed and alone in the dark with a videotape of a group of humpback whales swimming across the screen, "emit-
ting faint whale songs." His father explains that whales, unlike humans, send
messages that are not edited. Whales do not attempt to protect other whales
from the realities of life; rather, "whale talk" is transmitted as it is felt to all
whales for miles around. Consequently, whales know what it means to be
a whale, unlike many humans who never discover what it is to be human.
By the end of the story, when T. J.'s father is killed accidentally by Heidi's
vicious and abusive stepfather, who had been aiming his gun at Heidi, T. J.
has learned from his father and his own experiences with the Cutter swim
team what it means to be human. His sorrow and the events leading to his
father's death transmit a bit of that lesson to Mike Barbour, as well, who
approaches him as a friend at the end of the novel.

CENSORSHIP HISTORY

Whale Talk presents a realistic portrayal of such serious issues as child
abuse, racism, prejudice, and intolerance. Critics have complained that the

language of the book is "vulgar" and "obscene." They point to such scenes as the one in which, due to pent-up anger, Daniel Hole gives the crowd "a double middle digit salute," and they condemn the boys' conversations, which are filled with sarcasm, sexual references, slang, and profanity. In an interview for *Voices from the Middle*, Chris Crutcher observes that his books are often censored for "bad" language.

> Censors love to take language out of context, purposely. On three different occasions, would-be censors have gone through *Whale Talk* and listed what they considered to be offensive words. One counted 128 words. I hope they were counting each usage. I don't know 128 offensive words. The point is, language out of context can be made to look pretty disgusting, when, in fact, most kids don't even notice, or when they do, say it makes the story more authentic.

Readers have also objected to the graphic depictions of Heidi's abuse, as well as to the realistic use of abusive language and profanity in the scene emphasizing the horror of Heidi's everyday existence and the irrational prejudice some individuals harbor. Concerns have been raised regarding the appropriateness of the private discussions in which the characters examine the real-life questions adolescents have regarding sex, love and relationships, religion, personal values, and the developing sense of self. Each character's personal story raises serious moral and ethical concerns, including the inadequacy of the justice system, the unpredictability of life, the hypocrisy of adults, and the inequalities which persist in today's world. Such disturbing questions have led some to challenge the use of this book in schools and to request its ban from school libraries.

In December 2004, parents of students attending the Carvers Bay High School appeared before the South Carolina Board of Education to protest three books that they found to contain "objectionable material." In a handwritten letter to the school district superintendent Randy Dozier, the parents called for the removal of *Whale Talk*, A SEPARATE PEACE by John Knowles, and *Lay That Trumpet in Our Hands* by Susan McCarthy from the school curriculum. Derick Marsh, spokesman for the group, had a daughter in elementary school, but he led the group because, although he did not have a child in high school, he felt "it's important to get such books out of the school" before his daughter reached high school. When the group met with District Superintendent Dozier, they learned that the books were placed in the school as part of a state-supplied supplementary book list. Therefore, he advised the parents to take the matter before the state board. Marsh told a reporter for the *Georgetown Times*, "We're Christians, and it's time that Christians take a stand." He also said that if the state did not remove the book, he might possibly file a lawsuit against the district. The group told both local and state boards that the books "are full of profanity" and gave both boards handwritten lists of the words and page numbers on which the words could be found. After the first complaints were made, *Whale Talk* was taken out of the classroom as a required reading assignment, but it remains available in the high school library.

In February 2005, Christi Brooks, the parent of a student attending Ardmore High School in the Limestone County (Alabama) School District, submitted a complaint to the superintendent of schools Barry Carroll, stating that *Whale Talk* contains "questionable content" and inappropriate language. The woman expressed concern that T. J.—an adopted, mixed-race boy—refers to his conception as resulting when his white mother had a one-night stand with a sperm donor of black-Japanese descent. Other parents were disturbed by the manner in which Heidi is mistreated by her stepfather, who calls her a "stupid black bitch" and makes her feel so unclean for being biracial that she "vigorously scrubs her brown arms with a bristle brush at the kitchen sink" in the attempt to become white so her stepfather will love her. The superintendent referred the complaint to a school materials review committee, which recommended that the book be retained and which stated in a written report that the message of the book "is more important than the language used." The report also recommended keeping *Whale Talk* in the school libraries because it presents "a realistic view of life, including the consequences of prejudice, outspoken and malicious people. It highlights the importance of forgiveness over revenge."

Based on the recommendation of the review committee, Superintendent Carroll recommended that the novel remain in the Ardmore High School library, but his recommendation was rejected by the Limestone County board of education. On March 7, 2005, the board voted 4-3 to remove the book from all five high school libraries in the school system. Members who voted to remove the book cited the use of profanity in the book as their reason. Board member James Shannon told a writer for the *Decatur Daily*, "We can't allow students to go down our halls and say those words, and we shouldn't let them read it. That book's got a lot of bad, bad words in it."

Whale Talk also came under fire in February 2005 in the Grand Ledge High School in Eaton County, Michigan. The local television station WOOD-TV in Grand Rapids reported on February 14, 2005, that the 1,800 students in the high school were to start the day reading the book and spend the first 20 minutes of each day during two weeks reading. Bad weather on the first day forced a late start to school, so the book was put on hold, giving parents time to rethink the decision. Before beginning the program, school administrators sent home letters, "warning them about the profanity" and offering students the opportunity to read another book if they chose. One parent, Ken Himebaugh, described by WOOD-TV as "a reverend and a parent," protested use of the book. He asserted, "I've chosen not to have this in my home" and claimed that he could not believe that "the staff chose a book with words we're not allowed to say on TV . . . words kids would get in trouble for using at school." The principal of Grand Ledge High School told reporters that "taking part in the program will outweigh any language drawbacks" and noted that fewer than a dozen parents had asked that their children read a different book.

In 2007, the Missouri Valley School District in western Iowa removed *Whale Talk* from the sophomore English classes at the Missouri Valley High School, after receiving complaints that the novel contains profanity and racial slurs. The complaints came from a local church pastor who said the novel contained "explicit language." Reverend Nathan Slaughter asserted that "the book looks innocuous enough when you look at the jacket cover. It's about teaching tolerance. But it's filled with obscenities and tries to use negative things to teach the lesson." The Missouri Valley school superintendent Tom Micek told reporters that a specially appointed committee would review the novel to determine if it should remain permanently out of the district classrooms. The committee assigned to review the book included the school superintendent, as well as other school officials and members of the community. The superintendent instructed committee members to read the book and to "recommend to the school board whether to ban it."

FURTHER READING

"Another Book from the Same Author Is under Fire in Another Michigan School." WOOD-TV, Grand Rapids, Michigan. Broadcast February 14, 2005.

Bushman, John H., and Kay P. Bushman. "Coping with the Harsh Realities: The Novels of Chris Crutcher." *English Journal*, March 1992, pp. 82–84.

Davis, Terry. *Presenting Chris Crutcher.* New York: Twayne Publishers, 1997.

Greenway, Betty. "Chris Crutcher—Hero or Villain?" *ALAN Review*, Fall 1994, pp. 19–22.

Harper, Scott. "Censored in SC." *Georgetown Times*, December 1, 2004.

Hollman, Holly. "Forbidden Reading: Limestone County, Like Nation, Seeing Trend of Book Challenges." *Decatur Daily News*, April 17, 2005.

———. "Parent Challenges *Whale Talk;* Limestone Board Examining Issue." *Decatur Daily News*, February 8, 2005.

Hughes, Bayne. "Limestone Bans Book for Curses." *Decatur Daily News*, March 8, 2005.

Lesesne, Teri S. "Censorship: The Mind You Close May Be Your Own." *Voices from the Middle* 13 (September 2005): 72–77.

McDonnell, Christine. "New Voices, New Visions: Chris Crutcher." *Horn Book Magazine*, May–June 1988, pp. 332–334.

Nash, Tanjie. "Librarians Challenge Book Ban." *News-Courier*, May 2, 2005.

"Pastor's Complaint Prompts District & Pull Book from Classroom." Available online. URL: http://www.firstamendmentcenter.org/news.aspx?id=18198. Accessed August 10, 2010.

Pearse, Emma. "U.S.: Younger Readers Face New Adventures in Censorship." *WOMENSENEWS*, April 13, 2005, p. 1.

Stancil, Clyde L. "Banned Author Coming Here to Defend His Book." *Decatur Daily News,* September 22, 2005.

"*Whale Talk* Beached for Bad Words." *American Libraries* 36 (May 2005): 15.

WORKING: PEOPLE TALK ABOUT WHAT THEY DO ALL DAY AND HOW THEY FEEL ABOUT WHAT THEY DO

Author: Studs Terkel
Original date and place of publication: 1974, United States
Original publisher: Pantheon Books
Literary form: Collection of interviews

SUMMARY

Working is a collection of interviews with people in a wide variety of occupations who reveal not only what they do but how they feel about their jobs and their lives. Terkel draws his subjects out and leads them to tell him what they hate and what they like about their jobs, their bosses, and their coworkers. He interviewed such disparate individuals as a hooker, a priest, a farmer, a corporate executive, a writer, a producer, a baseball player, a hockey player, a waitress, a dentist, a supermarket box boy, a steelworker, a nun, and 120 others.

In their sometimes blunt language, the workers reveal their daily humiliations and the violence of their work "to the spirit as well as to the body. In the introduction, Terkel speaks of the ulcers, accidents, nervous breakdowns, and physical fights detailed by many of the people interviewed. He found that "to survive the day is triumph enough for the walking wounded among the great many of us." Although some are content with their jobs, a great number question the "work ethic" that rewards "the careless worker who turns out more that is bad rather than the careful craftsman who turns out less that is good." They complain of feeling indistinguishable from their fellow workers and unappreciated.

There are also those who find value in their work, such as Tom Patrick, the fireman who knows that he has the right job for him:

> The fuckin' world's so fucked up, the country's fucked up. But the firemen, you actually see them produce. You see them put out a fire. You see them come out with babies in their hands. You see them give mouth-to-mouth when a guy's dying. You can't get around that shit. That's real. To me, that's what I want to be.

Terkel allows the interviews to reveal the feelings of the workers, without modifying them to serve his own purposes.

CENSORSHIP HISTORY

Working has been challenged for reasons ranging from "obscene language" to the perception that it is too depressing for students, despite the fact that the book contains interviews with real workers. In a 1977 survey of a nationwide sample of English department chairpersons, Lee Burress recorded one challenge to the work by a California parent who wanted the book removed from the school library because it was "too negative" and contained "objectionable language." The request was denied. In 1978, 200 parents of students in Kettle Moraine High School in Wales, Wisconsin, signed a petition that called for the banning of *Working* because of the "obscene language" used by many of the workers and because an interview with a prostitute appeared in the book. The challenge was carefully orchestrated by a local group, but, as with many efforts to ban books, the group took great pains to disguise their organization. Teachers were aware that the parents shared an affiliation, although members of the group sat in different parts of the meeting room at board meetings called to deal with the issue. Claiming that "it takes only one paragraph to make a book obscene," parents blamed the "filth of the book" for the "drug problem" and for the words written on students' desks. A review committee appointed by the school board recommended use of the book as a supplemental reading, but alternatives were made available to students whose parents objected to the book.

In a 1982 survey of a national sample of librarians, Burress recorded one challenge by a Michigan parent who asked that the book be removed from the classroom because it contained "obscenities," but no action occurred because the parent did not follow through. That same year, parents challenged the assignment of the work in the senior vocational-technical English class in Girard, Pennsylvania. They complained that the book was "obscene" and "crude," but the school retained the book in the curriculum. In 1983, *Working* was removed from the optional reading list at South Kitsap (Washington) High School after parents complained that the interview with a prostitute demeaned marriage and "degraded the sex act." That same year, parents of seventh- and eighth-grade students in Washington (Arizona) School District demanded removal of the book from the curriculum due to its "profane language." They claimed that the book required "idealistic and sensitive youth to be burdened with despair, ugliness and hopelessness." The school board removed *Working* from the curriculum.

FURTHER READING

Burress, Lee. *Battle of the Books: Literary Censorship in the Public Schools, 1950–1985.* Metuchen, N.J.: Scarecrow Press, 1989.
Newsletter on Intellectual Freedom (July 1978): 89; (September 1978): 123; (July 1982): 143; (November 1983): 187; (January 1984): 10–11.

A WORLD I NEVER MADE

Author: James T. Farrell
Original date and place of publication: 1936, United States
Original publisher: Vanguard Press
Literary form: Novel

SUMMARY

A World I Never Made is the first entry and the only financially success-ful book in the O'Neill-O'Flaherty pentalogy, which followed Farrell's highly successful Studs Lonigan trilogy. The series is centered around a minor character from the earlier trilogy, Danny O'Neill, an intelligent, thoughtful, and sensitive Irish-American youth who serves as Farrell's autobiographical persona. Set in Chicago in 1911, the novel relates the trauma suffered by the very young Danny when his working-class par-ents experience financial difficulty and send him to live with his widowed grandmother, Mary O'Flaherty. The move creates a conflict in the young boy, whose thoughts, values, attitudes, and outlook are shaped by the differing perspectives of his working-class parents and his middle-class grandmother. For Danny, these class differences are personified by his shoe salesman uncle, Al O'Flaherty, and his teamster father, Jim O'Neill. Uncle Al places great stock in the acquisition of education and culture, but Danny's father is afraid that Al's ideas of education and culture will turn Danny into a soft "dude."

The novel deals realistically with Danny's Chicago milieu, citing Chi-cago landmarks and portraying Danny and a friend discussing whether the Chicago White Sox will win the pennant in 1911. Farrell also allows his char-acters, both the children and the adults, to freely use such terms as *shit, fuck, piss, balls, prick, pecker,* and *hard on.* Unlike the earlier Studs Lonigan trilogy, this novel also contains substantial reference to emetic matter. Danny's brother, Bill, described as "farting," states "I got to go and crap." Danny is aware of "the noise from the movement of Bill's bowels." In another scene, Danny's father listens to his wife "urinating into a pot."

The book also includes frankly sexual discussions between six-year-old Danny and his older brother, 11-year-old Bill. Such passages as the one that follows have been cited as "obscene":

> When Pa and Ma want a baby, they go to bed. And there is a hole in all women where they pee, and Pa puts his dick into Ma's hole.
>
> And does he pee into her, and does that make a baby? That's funny, I don't believe it. You're teasing me. God makes babies.

The family works hard and, as the novel ends, the O'Neills and the O'Flahertys enjoy temporary prosperity. Danny's uncle talks optimistically about sending him to military school after graduation from Catholic elementary school.

CENSORSHIP HISTORY

A World I Never Made contains expressions and situations that Farrell's earlier novels had avoided, a difference noted by critics and readers alike. In 1936, the *New York Times* refused to sell Vanguard Press advertising space for *A World I Never Made.* The newspaper made its position clear to readers by stating that it did not object to the advertising copy that would appear. Rather, the paper refused the advertising because the publisher believed that the novel was itself "too frank."

In 1937, John Sumner and the Society for the Suppression of Vice took Vanguard Press to court, claiming that the novel was "obscene" and "pornographic," after sending a confederate named Bamberger to purchase a copy. The tone of the trial was more lighthearted than those occurring in other parts of the nation and those that had occurred in New York City in earlier decades. Before the trial began, a reporter passed a copy of the book around the courtroom to be autographed. Sumner wrote, "I thoroughly disapprove of this book" after his name. Literary scholar Carl Van Doren wrote his name beneath Sumner's and the following: "I thoroughly disapprove of John S. Sumner and his works." Van Doren joined writer Heywood Broun and literary critic Bernard DeVoto as witnesses for Farrell.

The court seemed to join in the lightheartedness. Ruling in *Bamberger v. The Vanguard Press, Inc.*, docket no. 329, as to whether or not the novel was pornography, Magistrate Henry Curran related the judgment to comparing contemporary swim apparel with what had been acceptable in an earlier age:

> I don't think this book is pornographic. I think it is photographic . . . consider the young ladies in their bathing suits nowadays, how they toil not neither do they spin, but the Gibson girl in all her glory was not arrayed like one of these. If one of those lovely creatures of the far away nineties had really appeared in one of the little forget-me-not suits of today, I fancy there would have been a commotion on the beach—and the rockers on the summer hotel piazzas would have rocked hard and long.

The case was dismissed.

In 1948, the novel was one of nine novels identified as obscene in criminal proceedings in the Court of Quarter Sessions in Philadelphia County, Pennsylvania. Indictments were brought by the state district attorney, John H. Maurer, against five booksellers who were charged with possessing and intending to sell them. The other allegedly obscene novels were James Farrell's Studs Lonigan trilogy (*Young Lonigan, The Young Manhood of Studs Lonigan,* and *Judgment Day*), William Faulkner's SANCTUARY and WILD PALMS, Erskine Caldwell's GOD'S LITTLE ACRE, Arnold Robbins's NEVER

LOVE A STRANGER, and Calder Willingham's END AS A MAN. In his determination that the novels were not obscene, Judge Curtis Bok said of *A World I Never Made*:

> . . . this book is plastered with the short Saxon words of common vulgarity; they are consistent with the characters who use them and with the quality of their lives and actions that are the subject of the author's scrutiny.
>
> I am not of a mind, nor do I have the authority, to require an author to write about one kind of people and not about another, nor do I object to his effort to paint a complete picture of those whom he has chosen.

Although the book once again had been declared "not obscene" by a court, the Select Committee on Current Pornographic Materials, usually called the Gathings Committee, condemned the novel in 1953 as pornographic. Authorized by the House of Representatives to hold hearings, the committee established special commissions or licensing bureaus in some communities that informally pressured dealers to withdraw books on their blacklist. *A World I Never Made* was banned in Milwaukee, Wisconsin, and St. Cloud, Minnesota, as a result of the committee's efforts. In 1957, the U.S. Information Agency banned all of Farrell's novels from overseas libraries under its control.

FURTHER READING

Blanshard, Paul. *The Right to Read*. Boston: Beacon Press, 1955.

Ernst, Morris, and Ernest Lindley. *The Censor Marches On*. New York: Doubleday, Doran, 1940.

Frohock, William M. *The Novel of Violence in America, 1920–1950*. Dallas, Tex.: Southern Methodist University Press, 1958.

Rideout, Walter. *The Radical Novel in the U.S.* New York: Hill & Wang, 1966.

Biographical Profiles

ALEXIE, SHERMAN (1966–   )

Sherman Alexie is of Spokane-Coeur d'Alene Native American heritage and grew up on the Spokane Indian Reservation in Wellpinit, Washington. His poetry and fiction have earned him numerous awards, including the 2007 National Book Award in Young People's Literature for his first young adult novel, *The Absolutely True Adventures of a Part-Time Indian*, a 2008 Scandiuzzi Children's Book Award for middle grades and young adult literature, a 2008 Stranger Genius Award, the 2009 Mason Award, and the 2010 PEN/ Faulkner Award for his short story collection *War Dances*. His first short story collection, *The Lone Ranger and Tonto Fistfight in Heaven*, published in 1993, won the PEN/Hemingway Award for Best First Book of Fiction and the Lila Wallace Reader's Digest Award. Alexie has also written screenplays and performed stand-up comedy routines based on his experiences. He was a frail child who was born with hydroencephalitis and who was not expected to live beyond infancy. When he survived, doctors were wrongly concerned that the young Alexie would be mentally disabled; rather, he suffered severe side effects throughout his childhood, including seizures. He has told interviewers that, despite his medically difficult beginning in life, he learned to read by the age of three and that by the age of five he had read John Steinbeck's *Grapes of Wrath*, an accomplishment that made him the object of ridicule among the reservation children. Similar to his character in *The Absolutely True Adventures of a Part-Time Indian*, his first young adult novel, he decided that he had to leave the reservation and obtain a better education after he found his mother's name written in one of his textbooks, which proved to him the outdated nature of his education. He has been involved in numerous efforts to encourage young Native Americans to seek higher education and to be proud of their heritage.

ANGELOU, MAYA (1928–   )

Born in St. Louis, Missouri, the author is an African-American writer, stage performer, and composer best known for her widely acclaimed autobiography, *I Know Why the Caged Bird Sings* (1970), an account of her childhood in segregated Arkansas. She has written several sequels and produced plays, screenplays, songs, musical scores, and books of poetry, including *And Still I Rise* (1978), as well as a collection of meditative essays, *Wouldn't Take Nothing for My Journey Now* (1993). Critics have challenged use in the classroom of *I Know Why the Caged Bird Sings* because it describes Angelou's rape as a child, and the imagery of poems in *And Still I Rise* has led to calls for its removal from school libraries.

BALDWIN, JAMES (1924–1987)

Born in Harlem in New York City, the author was a highly acclaimed African-American writer who made his home primarily in France, although he returned to the United States to teach and lecture. Baldwin's writing, which conveys the attitudes of blacks living in a white-dominated society, made him a vital literary voice in the 1950s and 1960s. His first novel, *Go Tell It on the Mountain* (1953), is a partially autobiographical account of his youth. This work, with *Giovanni's Room* (1956) and *Another Country* (1962), has been most frequently challenged as being "obscene" and "vulgar," although other works, including essay collections, a play, and other novels that provide bitter, incisive views of American racism, have also come under attack.

BANNERMAN, HELEN (1862–1946)

Born in Edinburgh, Scotland, Bannerman was a children's book author and illustrator who is best known for her first book, *Little Black Sambo* (1898), one of the most beloved as well as one of the most controversial books in children's literature. She wrote and illustrated 12 other books based on her experiences living in India, but the bright, unrefined illustrations, suspenseful narrative, and rhythmic, repetitive sentences of the first book made it the most popular. The growth of racial consciousness in the 20th century made the book an object of harsh criticism, and critics have charged that it presents a patronizing and stereotypical view of blacks.

BAUER, MARION DANE (1938–)

Born in Ogleby, Illinois, Bauer is the author of many books that deal with the sometimes harsh realities of growing up. Although some of Bauer's novels feature extreme situations and themes, most of her works, such as *Rain of Fire* (1983) and *On My Honor* (1986), focus on young people who must learn to cope with traumatic events in everyday life and make serious moral choices. Bauer has told interviewers that she draws the plots for her fiction from personal experiences, and her books feature places she has lived in or visited often. In 1994, Bauer edited and contributed to a collection of short stories on gay and lesbian themes, *Am I Blue? Coming out from the Silence*, containing stories by 15 popular young adult writers. Bauer has been the recipient of numerous awards, including the American Library Association Notable Book Award in 1976 for *Shelter from the Wind*, the Newbery Honor Book in 1987 for *On My Honor*, and the Gay-Lesbian-Bisexual Book Award for Literature.

BENCHLEY, PETER (1940–2006)

Born in New York City, Benchley became the most successful first novelist in literary history when *Jaws* stayed on the *New York Times* best-seller list for over 40 weeks. None of the author's succeeding novels achieved the same success or notoriety as *Jaws*. The sexual situations and language have made the novel a target of school censors.

BLOCK, FRANCESCA LIA (1962–)

Born in Hollywood, California, Block created a new direction in young adult literature, beginning with *Weetzie Bat* (1989), which contained stories of 1990s Los Angeles subculture complete with sex, drugs, and rock and roll. The book caused a minor uproar among reviewers and some librarians. In 1995, Block provided a prequel to *Weetzie Bat* with the novel *Baby Be-Bop* (1995). Block's next two books *Girl Goddess #9* (1996), a collection of short stories, and *I Was a Teenage Fairy* (1998) also deal with young people fighting to come to grips with a rapidly changing world and their place in it. In addition to her books for teenagers, Block has published two adult titles, *Ecstasia* (1993) and *Primavera* (1994), which are influenced by Greek mythology and explore much the same ground as the young adult novels. Awards for her books have included the American Library Association Recommended Books for Reluctant Young Adult Readers citations for *Weetzie Bat* (in 1989), *Witch Baby* (in 1990), *Cherokee Bat and the Goat Guys* (1991), and *Missing Angel Juan* (1993), as well as the 2005 Margaret A. Edwards Award for lifetime contribution in writing for young adults.

BLUME, JUDY (1938–)

Born in Elizabeth, New Jersey, the author writes romantic books for young people and has earned a reputation for dealing candidly with problems of early adolescence that traditional children's literature ignores. Most of her 22 books have ignited challenges as to their appropriateness for school libraries and classrooms due to their language, religious references, and sexual content. *Then Again, Maybe I Won't* (1971), *Blubber* (1974), and *Forever* (1975) have been the most frequent objects of challenges.

BRADBURY, RAY (1920–)

Born in Waukegan, Illinois, the author writes science fiction and fantasy and began his career by submitting stories to pulp magazines in the 1940s. Bradbury's works, several of which have been adapted for motion pictures, often comment on the dehumanizing influence of a machine-dominated society, and he is recognized as an innovator in that genre. He has also written stage and screen plays, verse, and children's literature. His principal theme is the disruptive nature of imagination, and his most frequently challenged book, *Fahrenheit 451* (1953), is ironically a condemnation of censorship.

BROWN, CLAUDE (1937–2002)

Born in New York City, this African-American writer and lecturer presents a realistic portrayal of ghetto life and searing social criticism in his work. The autobiographical *Manchild in the Promised Land* (1965) is candid in its descriptions of the physical and psychological brutalities suffered by Brown in his Harlem boyhood, characteristics that have led many parents to demand removal of the novel from school libraries and classrooms. *The Children of Ham* (1976) is even grimmer, but it has received less attention.

BURGESS, ANTHONY (1917–1993)

Born John Anthony Burgess Wilson in Manchester, England, the versatile English author, who also published under his birth name and the name Joseph Kell, was an essayist, linguist, translator, musician, and comic novelist who wrote contemporary fiction as well as critical studies and several important works in the field of linguistics. He is perhaps best known for his futuristic novel *A Clockwork Orange* (1962), a terrifying view of a violence-ridden world that has motivated parent and school board challenges.

BURROUGHS, WILLIAM S. (1914–1997)

Born in St. Louis, Missouri, into affluence as the grandson of the founder of the Burroughs Adding Machine Company, the novelist achieved distinction for his irreverent themes, related in a multiple-perspective, prismatic, stream-of-consciousness style. Both his first novel, *Junky* (1953), published under the pseudonym William Lee, and his second novel, *The Naked Lunch* (1959), are based on his experiences as a drug addict, and they alone among his works have received sufficient popular attention to motivate legal challenges for their content.

CARROLL, JIM (JAMES DENNIS) (1950–2009)

Born in New York City, Carroll had already gained a reputation as one of the most prominent poets in the New York–based arts community by the time he was 18 years old, and his "pure" poetry received the praise of Beat Movement founders William S. Burroughs, Allen Ginsberg, and Jack Kerouac. Most of his work is autobiographical and describes his life, friends, and acquaintances in New York, as well as the 10-year heroin addiction he eventually overcame. As his reputation as a poet grew throughout the 1960s and the 1970s, Carroll began publishing prose in journals and poetry magazines, describing in harsh detail the beginnings of his 10-year heroin addiction. These were later published in a collection as *The Basketball Diaries* (1973). Carroll later published *Forced Entries: The Downtown Diaries, 1971–1973* (1987), which continues where *The Basketball Diaries* ended. In the late '80s and early '90s, Carroll began to combine music and poetry, appearing on the New York City rock-and-roll nightclub scene, and he was among the first poets to perform spoken-word on MTV and VH1. In 1995, a film version of *The Basketball Diaries* that starred Leonardo DiCaprio was released by East Side Films. In 1970, Carroll received the Random House Young Writers Award for an excerpt from *The Basketball Diaries* published in *Paris Review.*

CARROLL, LEWIS (1832–1898)

Born Charles Lutwidge Dodgson in Daresbury, Cheshire, England, the mathematician, logician, and author is best known for his creation of the fantasy *Alice's Adventures in Wonderland.* He also published several mathematical treatises under his real name, in addition to works for children written under his pseudonym. Although widely accepted as a classic, *Alice* has had detractors who object to Alice's freedom and to the fantasy of the work.

CHAPMAN, ROBERT L. (1920–2002)

Born in Huntington, West Virginia, the author was a college English professor and served as the supervising editor on *Funk & Wagnall's Standard College Dictionary* (1963) and *The Hold Intermediate Dictionary of American English* (1966). He was also the editor of *The New Dictionary of Slang* (1986) and the *New Dictionary of American Slang* (1987), which has been challenged in numerous schools due to the "obscene" nature of many of its entries.

CHAUCER, GEOFFREY (1363?–1400)

Born the son of a prosperous wine merchant in London, England, the author is believed to have been a courtier and civil servant to the courts of Edward III and Richard II, as well as to have studied law at the Inns of Court. Best known for *The Canterbury Tales,* Chaucer is also credited with translations and adaptations of religious, political and philosophical works, and poetry. The *Tales* contain bawdy language and imagery, and "The Miller's Tale" has been declared "obscene" by contemporary standards and has been the subject of challenges.

CHILDRESS, ALICE (1920–1994)

Born in South Carolina and raised in Harlem, Childress was first a playwright whose plays were saturated with alienated poor people. Her first novel, *A Hero Ain't Nothin' but a Sandwich,* also portrays African Americans who struggle to survive in a basically insensitive and unfriendly world. Unlike her later novels, which include *A Short Walk* (1979), *Rainbow Jordan* (1981), and *These Other People* (1990), *A Hero . . .* warned that black youth were threatened by drugs. The discussion of drugs and the street language have made this novel a target of censors.

CLARK, WALTER VAN TILBURG (1909–1971)

Born in East Orlando, Maine, but raised in Nevada cattle country, the author was a college English professor and writer of prose fiction. His best-known work, *The Ox-Bow Incident* (1940), is set in 1885 in Nevada and presents a perceptive analysis of mob violence. The psychological realism of the novel and the brutality of the men's language and actions have led to removal of the novel from school curricula.

CLEAVER, ELDRIDGE (1935–1998)

Born Leroy Eldridge Cleaver near Little Rock, Arkansas, the author is an African-American activist who presented a vivid, personal view of black experience in a white society in *Soul on Ice* (1968), a collection of essays and letters written in California's Folsom Prison. His later work, *Soul on Fire* (1978), describes disillusionment with radical politics and governments and his spiritual rebirth as a Christian, a topic upon which he lectured. *Soul on Ice* has been challenged because of its raw language and graphic descriptions of violence, including rape.

CORMIER, ROBERT (1925–2000)

Born in Leominster, Massachusetts, the author wrote three novels for adults before turning his talents to fiction for adolescents. Focusing in his novels on the relationship between good and evil and the abuse of authority, Cormier wrote novels, such as *The Chocolate War* (1974), that are disturbing in their realism. Reviewers, educators, and parents have challenged the suitability of *The Chocolate War* for adolescents and have made numerous attempts to ban it from high school and public libraries.

CRUTCHER, CHRIS(TOPHER) (1946–)

Born in Cascade, Idaho, Crutcher taught in tough, inner-city schools and ran an alternative school for inner-city kids in Oakland, California, before becoming a child and family therapist. He used his experiences to write young adult novels that contain serious problems with which adolescents are confronted daily in modern American culture. Critics have described such novels as *Running Loose* (1986), *Stotan!* (1989), *Ironman* (1995), and *The Crazy Horse Electric Game* (1988) as giving readers a clear view of young men, sports, and growing up. The main characters are sensitive and reflective, but they are often forced to confront ugly and painful situations. In *Whale Talk* (2001), Crutcher positions his main character to fight elitism, racism, and arrogance to help a swim team build emotional strength and win. In 2003, Crutcher changed his writing direction with *King of the Mild Frontier: An Ill-Advised Autobiography* (2003). Crutcher has won the Michigan Library Association Best Young Adult Book of 1992 for *Athletic Shorts* (2002), the National Council of Teachers of English in 1998, the American Library

Association Margaret A. Edwards for lifetime achievement in writing for teachers in 2000. For *Whale Talk*, he received the Pacific Northwest Booksellers Association and Washington State Book Award in 2002.

DAHL, ROALD (1916–1990)

Born in Llandaff, Wales, the author was widely known for both his children's books and his short stories for adults, which he wrote almost exclusively during the 1940s and 1950s, winning three Edgar Allan Poe Awards (1954, 1959, 1980). Dahl's success in children's literature began in 1961 with *James and the Giant Peach*, followed, most notably, by *Charlie and the Chocolate Factory* (1964). Dahl's fiction for children is fast-paced and usually contains a theme of harsh punishment, often death, for adult characters who meddle in the lives of his young protagonists, a factor that has led to challenges.

DICKEY, JAMES (LAFAYETTE) (1923–1997)

Born in Atlanta, Georgia, the author was a major American poet who is probably best known for his novel *Deliverance* (1970), the story of four city-bred men who take a raft trip down a wild southern river only to encounter savagery and death. Dickey used his experiences as a bomber pilot in World War II and Korea to inform some of his best poems, and the themes that are prominent in his poetry—the war, family, nature—appear in his novels. From 1966 to 1968, Dickey was consultant in poetry to the Library of Congress.

DOYLE, SIR ARTHUR CONAN (1859–1930)

Born in Edinburgh, Scotland, the British novelist and physician introduced the world's most famous fictional detective, Sherlock Holmes, in *A Study in Scarlet* (1887), later followed by four novels and 56 stories. Doyle had an inquiring mind that took an interest in history, science, and technology; one of his tales foresaw the use of the submarine in World War I. He later became deeply involved in the study of spiritualism. Doyle did not want to be remembered for his detective stories but for what he viewed as his more notable work, the historical novels. He also wrote other tales of mystery and adventure, including science fiction novels and *History of Spiritualism*.

DREISER, THEODORE (1871–1945)

Born in Terre Haute, Indiana, the American journalist, magazine editor, playwright, and prolific novelist pioneered the literary movement known as naturalism. Dreiser depicted the lives of common people in such novels as *Sister Carrie* (1900) and *An American Tragedy* (1925). *Sister Carrie* was attacked and heavily censored as an immoral treatment of a scandalous woman's rise to success. He also endured failure due to censorship of *The Genius* (1915), an autobiographical novel about power and sex that was labeled "pornography" and attacked by moralists. In 1925, Dreiser published *An American Tragedy*, widely regarded as his finest achievement. Critics labeled it "immoral," and the novel became the subject of a notorious trial.

DUBNER, STEPHEN J. (1963–)

Stephen J. Dubner is a professional journalist who was an editor and writer at *New York* magazine from 1990 to 1994 and the *New York Times Magazine* from 1994 until 1999. He has published many articles in such publications as the *New Yorker* and the *Washington Post* and is the coauthor of the highly popular award-winning book *Freakonomics* and its sequel, *SuperFreakonomics*. He is also the author of *Turbulent Souls: (Choosing My Religion), Confessions of a Hero-Worshipper*, and *The Boy with Two Belly Buttons*.

DUMAS, ALEXANDRE, JR. (1824–1895)

Born in Paris, France, and known as Dumas *fils* (Jr.), the author wrote numerous novels and plays and refined a genre known as the problem, or thesis, play. His most famous work is *La Dame aux camélias*, known in English as *Camille* (1848), the story of a Parisian courtesan who becomes morally regenerated by the power of true love. The 1852 theatrical version inspired Verdi's opera *La Traviata*. Dumas attempted to analyze the social ills of his times, but this subject for study in *Camille* made the work a target of censors. He was admitted to the Académie française in 1875.

ELLISON, RALPH (1914–1994)

Born in Oklahoma City, Oklahoma, this African-American essayist and novelist received international literary recognition with his first and most important novel, *The Invisible Man* (1952), which won the National Book Award in 1953. Its theme is a black man's search for identity in a society where black individuality is "invisible," and blacks are recognized only in the roles they have been assigned by whites. Challenges to oust the novel from schools have arisen because of the "vulgar" language and "inappropriate situations" in the novel. Because Ellison did not take militant public positions on the condition of black Americans, his influence upon the younger generation of black writers has not been widespread.

FARRELL, JAMES T. (1904–1979)

Born in Chicago, the poet, critic, journalist, and novelist often depicted in his fiction the lives of Irish Americans in Chicago from 1990 through the Depression of the 1930s. His best-known novels make up the *Studs Lonigan* trilogy, which, with *A World I Never Made* (1936), were repeatedly subjected to attempts to ban them for their language and sexual situations. Farrell's fiction is a part of the tradition of naturalistic writing.

FAULKNER, WILLIAM (1897–1962)

Born in Oxford, Mississippi, this major figure of contemporary American literature wrote 19 novels, 80 short stories, two books of poems, and numerous essays. One of America's most innovative novelists, he depicted ordinary society in terms of ageless human dramas. In 1949, Faulkner won the Nobel Prize for literature. He repeatedly explored the question of human freedom and the obstacles to it—racism, regimentation, shame, fear, pride, and overly abstract principles—infusing his novels with this honesty. Such works as *I Lay Dying* (1930), *Sanctuary* (1931), and *The Wild Palms* (1939) have been attacked as being "vulgar" and "immoral" precisely because they depict realistically how people think, speak, and feel.

FITZGERALD, F. SCOTT (FRANCIS SCOTT KEY) (1896–1940)

Considered the foremost chronicler of the American Jazz Age of the 1920s, F. Scott Fitzgerald was a member of the Lost Generation who became known as much for his heavy drinking and society associations as for his literary output. His novels are filled with lively stories of the rich and privileged and of expensive parties that mirrored the lives of Fitzgerald and his wife, Zelda Sayre. He was born in St. Paul, Minnesota, to a transplanted Southern gentleman who was a failed furniture business owner and a mother whose father was a successful wholesale grocer. After St. Paul's Academy, Fitzgerald attended Princeton University, but left in 1917 after a year because his grades were low. He received a commission into the U.S. Army. His military service was unremarkable and, after leaving the army in 1919, he began to write in earnest. In 1920, he married Zelda Sayre and published his first novel, *This Side of Paradise*. Meeting Zelda was the turning point in his life, and his slight propensity for alcohol increased as the two attended parties and Zelda danced on tables while the convivial Fitzgerald held court at or near the bar. When Zelda became pregnant, Fitzgerald began to submit and publish a larger number of stories in *Scribner's* and *Saturday Review* to make money to support his family. In 1921, after the birth of his daughter, he published *The Beautiful and the Damned*, but the book was not received well. He moved to Paris to join other expatriates in pursuing his literary dreams. The publication of *The Great Gatsby* brought him a measure of literary praise, but the book was not as successful as Fitzgerald wished and his drinking became heavier. For five years, the family traveled throughout Europe, and Zelda had repeated mental breakdowns; each breakdown took her further from recovery. In 1939, Fitzgerald began *The Last Tycoon*, a novel about Hollywood that remained unfinished at his death. Zelda died in 1948 in a fire at the mental hospital in which she was living.

FOSSEY, DIAN (1932–1985)

Born in San Francisco, the author was a zoologist known for her field studies of rare mountain gorillas in their natural habitat in east central Africa. *Gorillas in the Mist* (1983) chronicles her observations of three generations of mountain gorillas and includes detailed information of the gorillas' sexual habits, a factor that has resulted in challenges to the book in classrooms and school libraries. Fossey was murdered on December 27, 1985, at the Karisoke Research Center in Rwanda, which she established in 1967.

FRANK, ANNE (1929–1945)

Born in Frankfurt am Main, Germany, this young Jewish diarist hid with her family from the Nazi persecution in Amsterdam during World War II. She wrote *Anne Frank: The Diary of a Young Girl*, producing the major testament of the Holocaust. She and her family lived in a secret apartment in Amsterdam for two years before being discovered. Anne died in a German concentration camp. An abridgment of her poignant diary was published in 1947, a complete English edition appeared in 1995. The work has been challenged in schools because Anne writes frankly of her adolescent longings and because parents view the book as a "downer."

FRANKLIN, BENJAMIN (1706–1790)

Born in Boston, Massachusetts, the scientist, inventor, statesman, printer, and writer figured prominently in the governmental organization of the emerging American nation. Franklin helped to start the first public lending library, the first fire department, a college (later the University of Pennsylvania), an insurance company, and a hospital. Franklin's writings include numerous treatises and essays and *Poor Richard's Almanack* (1732), a collection of aphorisms. His *Autobiography* is among the most frequently expurgated books published in the United States and has been censored from its first publication.

GAINES, ERNEST J. (1933–)

Born in Oscar, Louisiana, the African-American author is best known for his 1971 novel *The Autobiography of Miss Jane Pittman*, a realistic account of the life of southern blacks from the time of slavery to the civil rights movement, as told by its centenarian heroine, Jane Pittman. Objections have been raised against the "obscene" language of the book, as well as the stereotyping of both African-American and white characters. Gaines wrote four other novels, none of which garnered significant attention.

GARDEN, NANCY (1938–)

Born in Boston, Massachusetts, the author has published many books for young people, including the highly acclaimed *Annie on My Mind*, which was selected for the 1982 *Booklist* Reviewer's Choice, the 1982 American Library Association (ALA) Best Books, and the 1970–83 ALA Best of the Best lists. The novel has also been the target of numerous censors, who object to the theme of two romantically involved high school girls.

GARDNER, JOHN (1933–1982)

Born in Batavia, New York, the author, critic, and educator was a professor of medieval literature as well as a novelist. His fiction ranges from fairy tales for children to his imaginative fantasies and contemporary stories for adults, books in which he characteristically poses metaphysical problems. Of his four novels and one short story collection, only the novel *Grendel* (1971), which retells the Beowulf legend from the monster's point of view, gained notoriety. Challenges to its use in the classroom and in school libraries charge that the novel contains "obscene" language and "sexist" passages.

GINSBERG, ALLEN (1926–1997)

Born in Newark, New Jersey, the poet and cultural rebel became a prophet of the Beat generation with his first published work, *Howl and Other Poems* (1956), which sparked the San Francisco Renaissance and defined the generation of the 1950s. In the 1960s, while vigorously participating in the anti-Vietnam War movement, he published several poetic works, including *Reality Sandwiches* (1963) and *Planet News* (1969), then won the National Book Award in 1974 for *The Fall of America*. Ginsberg's works have quietly been omitted from school anthologies and libraries, but *Howl and Other Poems* became the subject of a major trial as well as the object of a decision rendered by the Federal Communications Commission.

GIOVANNI, NIKKI (1943–)

Born Yolande Cornelia Giovanni in Knoxville, Tennessee, the poet has infused her work with the unifying themes of the black struggle and her political activism. As one of the most noted poets of the new black renaissance that began in the 1960s, Giovanni has combined the raw language of the streets with sensitive imagery in her 15 poetry collections, including *My House* (1972), leading to challenges to their use in classrooms.

GLASSER, RONALD J. (1940–)

A physician, nephrologist, and rheumatologist living in Minnesota, Glasser uses his own experiences as a physician to accurately depict in his works the often complicated relationship between doctor and patient. Glasser also examines the social and ethical problems that influence the decisions doctors make in treating their patients as medicine advances in the age of technology. The author served as an officer in the U.S. Army Medical Corps in the 1960s, stationed at U.S. Evacuation Hospital, Camp Zama, Japan, where he witnessed horrors firsthand. His experiences were detailed on his first and best-known book, *365 Days*. In *Ward 402* (1973), Glasser tackled the issue of health care in a story that centers on a young girl dying from leukemia. The author retained his focus on medicine and war in *The Greatest Battle* (1976),

Another War, Another Place: A Novel (1985), and *The Light in the Skull: An Odyssey of Medical Discovery* (1997).

GOLDING, WILLIAM (GERALD) (1911–1993)

Born in Cornwall, England, the prominent novelist, essayist, and poet was one of the most original post–World War II British writers. Winner of the 1983 Nobel Prize for literature and knighted in 1988, he is best known for *Lord of the Flies* (1954), a bleak examination of human nature that is among the 10 most frequently banned books in the United States. The book has been challenged in numerous instances for "obscene" language, violence, and racism. Golding's later novels did not win the critical praise his earlier works achieved.

GREENE, BETTE (1934–   )

Born in Memphis, Tennessee, Bette Greene is a popular and respected author of young adult books that are notable for their sympathetic depictions of young people who are alienated from society. Greene's best-known novel is *The Summer of My German Soldier* (1973), followed by the sequel *Morning Is a Long Time Coming*, then *Them That Glitter and Them That Don't* (1978), all featuring young women who must make difficult decisions that conflict with their families' beliefs. *The Drowning of Stephan Jones* (1991) is based on an actual event and explores the death of a young gay man at the hands of three youths. Lighter in tone than Greene's other novels, *Philip Hall Likes Me. I Reckon Maybe.* (1989) focused on the rivalry between two successful black sixth-graders, Beth and Philip. In its sequel, *Get on out of Here, Philip Hall!* (1981), Beth learns to cope with failure and forms a friendship with Philip. In 1973, *The Summer of My German Soldier* was nominated for a National Book Award and received the *New York Times* Outstanding Book Award, the Golden Kite Society Children's Book Writer's Award, and the American Library Association Notable Book Award. In 1974, *Philip Hall Likes Me. I Reckon Maybe.* received the *New York Times* Outstanding Book and Outstanding Title Awards, the American Library Association Notable Children's Book Award, the Child Study Association Children's Book Award, and Kirkus Choice Award and in 1975 the Newbery Honor Book Award.

GRIFFIN, JOHN HOWARD (1920–1980)

Born in Dallas, Texas, the author worked as a photographer, lecturer, and journalist before publishing nine books, including *The Devil Rides Outside* (1952), banned for its frank sexuality, and *Black Like Me* (1961), for which Griffin is best known. The Caucasian author used chemicals and ultraviolet light to darken his skin, then traveled throughout the south as a black man. The resulting realism was disturbing to society.

GUEST, JUDITH (ANN) (1936–   )

Born in Detroit, Michigan, the author is a former grade-school teacher and housewife who achieved success with her first novel, *Ordinary People* (1976). The work reflects the story of a teenage boy who returns to his suburban home from a stay in a mental hospital after attempting suicide. Challenges to the book in the classroom or in school libraries criticize the "vulgar" language of the novel and the theme of suicide as being "unsuitable." Guest's later novels include *Second Heaven* (1982), *Killing Time in St. Cloud* (1989), *Errands* (1997), and *The Tarnished Eye* (2004).

HAAN, LINDA DE (1965–   )

De Haan and Stern Nijland wrote and illustrated the controversial *King & King* (2002), which was originally published as *Koning & Koning* in the Netherlands by Gottmer and Becht, who provided Tricycle Books with a rough English translation of the story. De Haan met Nijland when the two were in art school in the Netherlands. When their book first came out in the Netherlands in 2000, parents told them they were glad that there was a book that reflected their lifestyle. De Haan and Nijland published a second book, *King & King & Family* (2004), in which the married kings adopt a little girl. *King & King* was a Lambda Literary Award finalist in 2002.

HALL, RADCLYFFE (1880–1943)

Born Marguerite Radclyffe-Hall in Lancashire, England, the author preferred to be known in her private life as "John." Openly lesbian, Hall identified herself with "the third sex" and was instantly recognizable by her close-cropped hair, tailored jackets, wide-brimmed hats, and ties. The author of five volumes of poetry, one short story collection, and six novels, she is best known as the author of *The Well of Loneliness*, a novel that dealt explicitly with a lesbian theme and was considered by critics to be the most important lesbian novel of the 20th century.

HARRIS, JOEL CHANDLER (1845–1908)

Acclaimed in his time as a brilliant folklorist and popular journalist, Harris has lost literary favor since the mid-20th century. Although, with Mark Twain, he was named a charter member of the American Folklore Society, those people who still know his name tend to view with disfavor the main source of his fame, the tales of Uncle Remus. He was praised by Mark Twain, and both the industrialist Andrew Carnegie and President Theodore Roosevelt proclaimed him as their favorite author, although he preferred to refer to himself as a "cornfield journalist." His accounts of African-American trickster stories, most popularly that of Brer Rabbit and the Tar Baby, and his tales of life on the plantation told in the slave dialect of his alter ego Uncle Remus elicit the opposite reaction among modern critics, some of whom have characterized his use of slave dialect as racist. As a journalist, Harris worked at the Atlanta (Georgia) *Constitution*, where he first invented the character of Uncle Remus, through whom he related stories he had heard from the plantation field hands and other workers as a child and as a young man. His first series of newspaper stories about Uncle Remus were collected and published in *Uncle Remus: His Songs and Sayings*, and he gained an immediate following that guaranteed the success of the later five books of Uncle Remus stories. In the beginning of the 21st century, literary critics have taken a new look at the stories Harris wrote, and folklorists have begun to reevaluate his literary legacy and to reconsider the role his work played in keeping early African-American storytelling traditions alive.

HAWTHORNE, NATHANIEL (1804–1864)

Born in Salem, Massachusetts, Hawthorne was the first American writer to apply artistic judgment to Puritan society. He exhibited profound moral and psychological insight into human motivation in *The Scarlet Letter* (1850), written while he worked in the Boston Custom House and for which he was roundly criticized for the theme of adultery. *Twice-Told Tales* (1837) was a model for Edgar Allan Poe in his critical analysis of the art of the short story. In 1841, Hawthorne joined the utopian community at Brooke Farm for a time and later became friendly with Ralph Waldo Emerson, Henry David Thoreau, and their circle of transcendentalists. Following quickly upon the success of *The Scarlet Letter* came *The House of the Seven Gables* (1851) and *The Blithedale Romance* (1852).

HEINLEIN, ROBERT A. (1907–1988)

Born in Butler, Missouri, Heinlein did much to popularize science fiction, beginning with a series of stories, first published in the *Saturday Evening Post* and later collected in *The Green Hills of Earth* (1951). Heinlein won science fiction's Hugo Award four times—for *Double Star* (1956), *Starship Troopers* (1959), *Stranger in a Strange Land* (1961), and *The Moon Is a Harsh Mistress* (1966). The last two novels became cult favorites in the late 1960s and the early 1970s among college students in the United States, and substantial criticism was heaped upon *Stranger in a Strange Land* for its views of marriage and family life that ran counter to those of traditional society.

HELLER, JOSEPH (1923–1999)

Born in Brooklyn, New York, the novelist and dramatist's works are satiric and often criticize the propensity of the military-industrial complex and similar forces to manipulate individuals in the name of reason or morality. His best-known novel, *Catch-22* (1961), uses protest and a sense of the absurd to explore the human condition and underscore the horrors of war and the power of modern society to destroy the human spirit. It has been the object of numerous challenges because of its language and pessimistic view of society. Its sequel, *Closing Time* (1994), takes the now-aged characters through the absurdities of the century's end and, with other of Heller's novels, continues the author's attack on society's values and conventions.

HEMINGWAY, ERNEST (1899–1961)

Born in Oak Park, Illinois, the novelist, journalist, and short story writer is considered one of the most influential authors of the first half of the 20th century. He was awarded the Nobel Prize for literature in 1954 and created a large and distinguished body of literature, much of it based on his adventurous life. His most memorable novel, *The Sun Also Rises* (1926), became an immediate success and made him a leader of the so-called lost generation, but its references to impotence and perceived undertones of homosexuality motivated efforts to censor the novel. *A Farewell to Arms* (1929) was his most successful novel, but the sexual relationship between the unmarried main characters and hints at abortion made it the target of censors. *To Have and Have Not* (1937) was challenged and barred from sale for its language. *Across the River and Into the Trees* (1950), a novel that used a Venetian locale, was widely attacked for its sexual content.

HESSE, HERMANN (1877–1962)

Born in Calw, Germany, the novelist and poet explored the conflicts of human nature through the application of Eastern and Western philosophy in his writings, which emphasized the human quest for spiritual enlightenment. *Demian* (1919), *Siddhartha* (1922), and *Steppenwolf* (1927) incorporate Jungian psychology and Buddhist mysticism with the influence of Nietzsche, Spengler, and Dostoyevsky. He received the 1946 Nobel Prize for literature. Although Hesse wrote no novels after 1943, his works gained immense popularity during the 1950s and 1960s in the English-speaking world, echoing the growing rebellion of the younger generation in their criticism of middle-class values and their interest in Eastern religious philosophy. The themes of Hesse's most popular novels, such as *Steppenwolf,* are often at odds with the aims of authority, thus making them targets of challenges in schools.

HOBSON, LAURA Z. (1900–1986)

Born in New York City, Laura Z. Hobson was best known for the novel *Gentleman's Agreement* (1947), which sold more than 2 million copies in the United States, was made into a successful movie, and was translated into at least a dozen foreign languages. The book was filmed by 20th Century Fox, with a screenplay written by Moss Hart. It received the New York Film Critics Award and the Academy Award for best motion picture of 1947. Most of Hobson's other books came about because of her concern with social issues, and she claimed that most of the subject matter reflected her life. She used her background as an outspoken political activist and foe of fascism to write *The Trespassers* (1943), as a crusader for civil rights to write *Gentleman's Agreement* (1947), as the daughter of radical Socialists to write *First Papers* (1964), as an unwed mother to write *The Tenth Month* (1971), as the parent of a homosexual son to write *Consenting Adult* (1975), and she fictionalized her experience as a topnotch advertising copywriter to write *Untold Millions* (2002).

HOSSEINI, KHALED (1966–)

Khaled Hosseini was born in Kabul, Afghanistan, the son of a Afghan foreig diplomat father and high school teacher mother. In 1976, the Foreign Ministry temporarily relocated the family to Paris. They sought to return to Afghanistan in 1980, but a bloody coup made that return impossible, so the family sought and were granted political asylum in the United States. Hosseini attended schools in the United States and graduated in 1993 with a degee in medicine from the University of California, San Diego, and served his residency at Cedars Sinai Hospital in Los Angeles. While in medical practice, Hosseini wrote his first novel, *The Kite Runner*, published in 2001 and since published in 48 countries. His second novel, *A Thousand Splendid Suns*, appeared in 2007. Hosseini has been named a goodwill ambassador for UNHCR, the United Nations Refugee Agency, and he has worked to provide humanitarian assistance in Afghanistan.

HUGHES, LANGSTON (1902–1967)

Born James Mercer Langston Hughes in Joplin, Missouri, the African-American poet, dramatist, and prose writer was prominent in the Harlem Renaissance movement. From his first published poem, "The Negro Speaks of Rivers" (1921), through his later critical essay, "The Negro Artist and the Racial Movement" (1925), and his autobiography, *The Big Sea* (1940), Hughes conveys his belief in the commonality of all cultures and the universality of human suffering, which he dramatically projected in *Lament for Dark People and Other Suffering* (1944). Despite his body of work, he experienced censorship for his work as an editor for *The Best Short Stories by Negro Writers*, rather than as a writer.

HUMPHRY, DEREK (1930–)

Born in Bath, Somerset, England, euthanasia rights advocate Derek Humphry is the author of the controversial book *Final Exit* (1991). As a former journalist, he examined race relations in the 1970s in such books as *Because They're Black* (1971) and *Police Power and Black People* (1972). He joined the euthanasia movement after his wife, Jean, contracted incurable cancer; he assisted with her suicide by administering a drink laced with bar-biturates in 1975. He then wrote *Jean's Way* (1978), which made Humphry a major figure in the right-to-die campaign. In 1980, Humphry founded the Hemlock Society, whose motto is "Good Life, Good Death," which claims tens of thousands of dues-paying members. *The Right to Die: Understanding Euthanasia* (1986) asks the question: Should human life be prolonged at all costs? Since the publication of *Final Exit*, Humphry has continued fighting for the rights of the terminally ill and has also worked in California, Oregon, Washington, Michigan, and Maine for the passage of laws that would protect doctors from liability when they assist a suicide. Humphry's next two books, *Dying with Dignity: Understanding Euthanasia* and *Lawful Exit: The Limits of Freedom for Help in Dying* (1992), again attempted to raise public awareness about his cause. In 1992, Humphry retired after 12 years as the Hemlock Society's national director, and in 1993, he started a euthanasia think tank named Euthanasia Research and Guidance Organization. Humphry won the Martin Luther King Memorial Prize in 1972 for *Because They're Black*. In 1997, he won the Socrates Award for right-to-die activism, and in 2000, he was given the Saba Medal for world euthanasia activism.

HUXLEY, ALDOUS LEONARD (1894–1963)

Born in Goldaming, Surrey, England, the novelist, essayist, and critic is best known for his witty and humorous satiric portraits of early-20th-century upper-class British society in *Antic Hay* (1923) and POINT COUNTER POINT (1928), as well as for his scathing indictment of oppressive government and the dangers of technology in BRAVE NEW WORLD (1932). All three works have been subject to censorship attempts. His disillusionment led him toward mysticism and the use of hallucinatory drugs and to write such works as *Eyeless in Gaza* (1936), *The Doors of Perception* (1954), and *Heaven and Hell* (1956), in which he describes the use of mescaline to induce visionary states.

KESEY, KEN (1935–2001)

Born in La Junta, Colorado, the novelist and screenwriter was a member of the Beat generation and best known for his first novel, *One Flew over the Cuckoo's Nest* (1962). The novel, based on his experiences as a ward attendant at a mental institution, has been the target of censors for its raw language and violent action. Kesey also achieved notoriety as an LSD advocate and a member of the Merry Pranksters, an LSD-fueled group that toured the country in a school bus, a trip that Kesey later condemned in *The Further Inquiry* (1990).

KING, STEPHEN (1947–)

Born in Portland, Maine, the writer of suspense and horror novels and stories is one of America's best-selling authors, under his own name and the pseudonym Richard Bachman, whose works have gained both critical acclaim and popular success. At the same time, many of his better-known works, among them *Carrie* (1974), *The Shining* (1977), *Cujo* (1981), *Christine* (1983), *Pet Sematary* (1983), and *The Stand* (1990), have been singled out by censors who have sought to remove these novels and, in some cases, all of King's works from their school and public libraries.

KNOWLES, JOHN (1926–2001)

Born in rural West Virginia, the author is best known for *A Separate Peace* (1960) and its sequel, *Peace Breaks Out* (1981), among his seven novels, a collection of short stories, and a travel book. Challenges to *A Separate Peace* have cited "obscene" and "vulgar" language, as well as concerns that the novel contains an underlying theme of homosexuality.

KNOWLTON, CHARLES (1800-1850)

Born in Massachusetts, the physician and writer is best-known for his guide to birth control, *Fruits of Philosphy: Or the Private Companion of Young Married People*. Knowlton's first book, *Elements of Modern Materialism* (1829), is considered an early Freethinker tract.

KOSINSKI, JERZY (NIKODEM) (1933–1991)

Born in Lodz, Poland, the novelist wrote in English and used sardonic humor in grimly pessimistic novels published under his own name, as well as two nonfiction works under the pseudonym Joseph Novak. His bitter first novel, *The Painted Bird* (1965), relates the dehumanizing childhood years he spent hiding from the Nazis in Poland during World War II. The pessimistic view of this novel is also evident in six later novels, among them *Being There* (1970), which was banned from high school reading lists for its masturbation scene and homosexual near-experience.

LEE, HARPER (1926–)

Born in Monroeville, Alabama, the novelist is known solely for her Pulitzer Prize-winning novel *To Kill a Mockingbird* (1960), which relates the impact of a rape trial on a small southern town. The novel remains among the most frequently banned in the United States, and challengers cite the "vulgar" language, discussion of the rape, and racial relationships among their complaints.

LEVITT, STEVEN D. (1967–)

One of the best-known contemporary American economists because of the popularity of *Freakonomics*, Levitt has made a career of studying controversial relationships, such as the effect of the abortion rate on crime or the similarity of sumo wrestlers and schoolteachers. Although his conclusions have been hotly debated and the sources of his statistics have sometimes been called into question, the logic of his arguments has received grudging admiration in the public sphere. Levitt was awarded the John Bates Clark Medal in 2003, and he is presently the Alvin H. Baum Professor of Economics at the University of Chicago, as well as the director of the Becker Center on Chicago Price Theory at the University of Chicago Graduate School of Business. In 2006, *Time* named him as one of the "100 People Who Shape Our World."

LEWIS, SINCLAIR (1885–1951)

Born in Sauk Centre, Minnesota, the novelist was the first American writer to win the Nobel Prize in literature as well as the first American to be awarded both the Nobel and Pulitzer Prizes. He created satirical portraits of middle-class life in the United States during the 1920s in a succession of best-selling novels, including *Main Street* (1920), *Babbitt* (1922), and *Arrowsmith* (1925), which won the Pulitzer Prize in 1926. In 1930, he was awarded the Nobel Prize in literature, after publishing *Elmer Gantry* (1927) and *Dodsworth* (1929). *Elmer Gantry* and *Kingsblood Royal* (1947), a savage attack on racial discrimination in both the south and north, have been targets of censors who have labeled both books "immoral" because of their language and "suggested" sexual scenes.

LOFTING, HUGH JOHN (1886–1947)

Born in Maidenhead, Berkshire, England, the author entered the United States in 1912 and became a naturalized citizen. He became a surveyor and civil engineer, traveling to Canada, Africa, and the West Indies. He served with the British army in World War I, during which he conceived of the Dolittle story, which he wrote in letters home to his children. The first of the 13 books that eventually made up the Dolittle series was published in 1920 and maintained strong popularity until the 1960s, when growing racial awareness caused the books to be labeled racist and demeaning to African Americans.

LOUŸS, PIERRE (1875–1925)

Born Pierre Louis in Paris, the author lived his entire life in that city, leaving it only to travel around the Mediterranean coast, where so many of his works of art were set. He had many close friends among the writers of his day but preferred to remain apart from literary cliques. Louÿs's evocations of Hellenistic society brought him fame as a writer in both France and England, as much for his skill in recreating the ancient world as for the risqué subjects of such works as *Aphrodite* (1886) and *Les Chansons de Bilitis* (1894).

LOWRY, LOIS (1937–   )

Born in Honolulu, Hawaii, Lois Lowry is an award-winning author of young adult novels that cover topics ranging from the death of a sibling and the Nazi occupation of Denmark, to the humorous antics of the rebellious Anastasia Krupnik, to futuristic dystopian societies. In her first novel, *A Summer to Die* (1977), Lowry portrayed an adolescent's struggle with her older sister's illness and eventual death. In *Find a Stranger, Say Goodbye* (1978), she documented an adopted child's search for her biological mother. Memories of her childhood as well as her experiences as a parent led Lowry to her most popular character: Anastasia Krupnik, the spunky, rebellious, and irreverent adolescent who stars in a series of books that began in 1979. In 1990, Lowry received the Newbery Medal for her distinguished contribution to children's literature with *Number the Stars* (1989), a novel based on a factual story set against the backdrop of Nazi-occupied Denmark. Lowry received the prestigious Newbery Medal a second time for her 1993 novel, *The Giver* (1993). *Gathering Blue* (2000) is a companion piece to *The Giver,* which depicts a technologically primitive world in which "disorder, savagery, and self-interest" rule. Lowry recounted her lifetime of remembrances in *Looking Back: A Book of Memories* (1998).

MALAMUD, BERNARD (1914–1986)

Born in Brooklyn, New York, the novelist and short story writer was best known for his stories of ordinary people whose survival makes them universal symbols of the triumph of the human spirit. *The Assistant* (1957), the author's most highly praised novel, is characteristic in both style and theme, as are *The Tenants* (1971) and *Dubin's Lives* (1979). *The Fixer* (1966), for which Malamud received both a National Book Award and a Pulitzer Prize, is his only work to be challenged by censors, who have labeled the novel anti-Semitic and complained of its language.

MALCOLM X (1925–1965)

Born Malcolm Little in Omaha, Nebraska, he was for a time the leading spokesperson for the Black Muslims in the outside world. After a split developed between Malcolm and the more conservative Elijah Muhammad in 1963, Malcolm founded the rival Organization for Afro-American Unity, and he no longer preached racial separation but rather a socialist revolution. He was assassinated in 1965. *The Autobiography of Malcolm X,* which relates his life, has been attacked by censors who claim that the language and situations depicted are "obscene" and do not belong on high school reading lists.

MANN, PATRICK (1923–2007)

Born in Chicago, Illinois, as Leslie Waller, the author wrote 28 books for adults under his real name and two pseudonyms, Patrick Mann and C. S. Cody, as well as 16 books for juveniles. *Dog Day Afternoon* (1974), the most notorious of his works and the most successful, has motivated challenges in both school and public libraries for its language, transsexual character, and sexual references.

MITCHELL, MARGARET (1900–1949)

Born in Atlanta, Georgia, the novelist and journalist produced one of the most successful novels ever written in *Gone with the Wind*, which also won the Pulitzer Prize and the National Book Award. The novel, which made publishing history by setting a sales record of 50,000 copies in one day and 1.5 million copies in its first year of release, has been the target of censors who object to its language, the prominence of a female brothel owner, and the marital rape of the protagonist.

MOORE, GEORGE (1852–1933)

Born in County Mayo, Ireland, the novelist and playwright was active in the Irish Literary Renaissance of the early 1900s. His best-known novel, *Esther Waters* (1894), relates the story of a religious young woman with an illegitimate son. The novel was attacked for its subject matter and banned from Mudie's Circulating Library, as were the author's earlier novels, *A Modern Lover* (1883) and *A Mummer's Wife* (1885). A collection of short stories, *A Story Teller's Holiday* (1918), was banned by Customs for its perceived sexual content.

MORRIS, DESMOND J. (1928–)

Born in Purton, Wiltshire, England, the author is a zoologist whose writings have detailed both animal and human behavior. Of his 26 books for adults, including the highly popular *Catwatching* (1986) and *Dogwatching* (1987), and four books for children, only *The Naked Ape* (1967) has generated significant controversy. Critics charge that Morris devotes one-fourth of the book to human sexual habits and ignores language and learning, but the omission did not prevent the book from selling over 8 million copies in 23 countries.

MORRISON, TONI (1931–)

Born in Lorain, Ohio, the editor, novelist, educator, playwright, and Nobel laureate proudly embraces her designation as "a black woman writer." Her novels focus on the struggles of female characters faced with the difficulties of growing up in a predominantly white society. BELOVED (1987) was the target of censors for its sexual violence.

MOWAT, FARLEY (1921–)

Born in Belleville, Ontario, the author is best known for his books about northern Canada. He has published works on other topics, including *My Discovery of America* (1985), which tells of his experience being barred from the United States as an "undesirable," and *Woman in the Mists* (1987), an account of zoologist Dian Fossey's dedication to saving mountain gorillas, which was banned because of its "profanity" and discussion of Fossey's abortion.

MYERS, WALTER DEAN (1938–)

Born Walter Milton Myers in Martinsburg, West Virginia, Walter Dean Myers is considered among the premier authors of fiction for young adults, and his books have won dozens of awards, including the prestigious Coretta Scott King Award for multiple books. While Myers is perhaps best known for his novels that explore the lives of young Harlem blacks, he is equally adept at producing modern fairy tales, ghost stories, and adventure sagas. *Where Does the Day Go?* (1969), his first book, won a contest sponsored by the Council on Interracial Books for Children. Myers turned his attention to producing more picture books, including *The Dancers* (1972), *The Dragon Takes a Wife* (1972), and *Fly, Jimmy, Fly!* (1974). After publishing numerous juvenile fiction, Myers established a reputation as an able author of fiction geared for African-American children. *Fast Sam, Cool Clyde, and Stuff* (1975) and *Mojo and the Russians* (1977) depicted the learning experiences of most youths growing up in a big city where negative influences abound, and they were followed by *It Ain't All for Nothin'* (1978), as well as Myers's first Coretta Scott King Award–winner, *The Young Landlords* (1979). Myers has continued to write and win awards through the present with *Fallen Angels* (1988), *The Journal of Biddy Owens, the Negro Leagues* (2001), and *The Dream Bearer* (2003).

NEWMAN, LESLEA (1955–)

Born in Brooklyn, New York, the author published a novel, *Good Enough to Eat* (1986), a poetry collection, *Love Me Like You Mean It* (1987), and a short story collection, *A Letter to Harvey Milk and Other Stories* (1988), before the taboo-shattering *Heather Has Two Mommies* in 1989. The latter children's book has been the source of vehement community outcry and efforts to ban it from both school and public libraries. Newman has also written *Gloria Goes to Gay Pride* (1991), *Too Far Away to Touch* (1996), and *Felicia's Favorite Story* (2003), among other books.

NIJLAND, STERN (1976–)

Nijland and Linda De Haan wrote and illustrated the controversial *King & King* (2002), which was originally published as *Koning & Koning* in the Netherlands by Gottmer and Becht, who provided Tricycle Books with a rough English translation of the story. Nijland met De Haan when the two were in art school in the Netherlands. De Haan and Nijland published a second book, *King & King & Family* (2004), in which the married kings adopt a little girl. *King & King* was a Lambda Literary Award finalist in 2002.

O'HARA, JOHN (1905–1970)

Born in Pottsville, Pennsylvania, the novelist and short story writer was one of the most popular writers of the 20th century. His ear for irony and acute powers of observation made his first novel, *Appointment in Samarra* (1934), a great success, and many later novels, including *Butterfield 8* (1935), *A Rage to Live* (1955), *Ten North Frederick* (1955), and *From the Terrace* (1958), became popular films. He set most of his novels in the fictitious community of Gibbsville, Pennsylvania, and infused the works with realistic portrayals of the American upper middle class, including its sex and drinking patterns. *Appointment in Samarra* and *Ten North Frederick* both shocked reviewers and motivated censors, who complained of the "vulgarity" in the novels and their sexual suggestiveness.

PARNELL, PETER (1953–)

Best known as a playwright or adapter for such works as *The Cider House Rules*, *Flaubert's Latest*, *Hyde in Hollywood*, and other works, Parnell has also written for television. Although he has received good reviews for his plays, he has received the greatest amount of attention for the children's book *And Tango Makes Three*, a true story he cowrote with Justin Richardson about two male penguins in Central Park who hatch their own chick and coparent a baby female penguin.

PARTRIDGE, ERIC (1894–1979)

Born in New Zealand, Partridge served in the Australian infantry in World War I but spent much of his life teaching and writing in Great Britain. His best-known work is his *Dictionary of Slang and Unconventional English* (1937). His interest in slang is said to date from his time as a soldier.

PATERSON, KATHERINE (1932–)

Born in Qing Jiang, China, to missionary parents, the author has earned numerous children's book awards for her many books written for juveniles. *Bridge to Terabithia* (1977), winner of four awards, is her most frequently challenged novel because of its language and depressing subject, death.

PECK, ROBERT NEWTON (1928–)

Born in rural Vermont, the author has set many of his more than 50 young adult novels in the 1930s of his boyhood and focuses on the honest simplicity of the time. *A Day No Pigs Would Die* is his first novel, ranked by critics as among the most notable of his works. It is also the most severely criticized and challenged of Peck's works for its honest depiction of the brutality of farm life and the realistic portrayal of the life cycle.

PERRAULT, CHARLES (1628–1703)

Born in Paris, France, the poet and literary critic is better known today for his *Tales of Past Times* (1697) than for his role during the 17th century as the leading champion of contemporary French writers in the "quarrel between the ancients and the moderns." The fairy tales collected by Perrault are frequently violent, and his version of "Little Red Riding Hood" has experienced several challenges in school districts.

PILKEY, DAV (1966–)

Born in Cleveland, Ohio, Pilkey writes with a humorous irreverence that often teaches a moral. His popular books include those in the "Dragon," "Captain Underpants," and "Big Dog and Little Dog" series, all self-illustrated, and the "Ricky Ricotta" series, illustrated by Martin Ontiveros. In his "Dragon" series, Pilkey tells of a lovable but zany dragon and his many adventures. His popular "Captain Underpants" series features a hero who sports underpants while having various adventures. The series capitalizes on the kind of bathroom humor that appeals to young readers. Teachers and parents have expressed concern over the contents of the books. In the "Ricotta" series, Ricky Ricotta is a timid mouse who teams up with a robot to battle various forces of evil, such as vultures from the planet Venus who use a voodoo ray to hypnotize people through their televisions. Pilkey's individual creation, *The Paperboy* (1996), was named a Caldecott Medal Honor Book. Pilkey claimed that many of his characters are an extension of the humor he made up in grade school and for which teachers repeatedly punished him.

PLATH, SYLVIA (1932–1963)

Born in Boston, Massachusetts, the poet and novelist is best known for her semiautobiographical novel, *The Bell Jar* (1963), the account of a young woman's mental breakdown, which was published soon after her death. The novel has generated challenges in schools for containing "filthy" material. She published one collection of poetry, *Colossus* (1960), before committing suicide in 1963, but her fame rests on works that appeared after her death. The posthumous publication of *Ariel* (1965) made her a cult hero. Her status was reinforced by two other posthumous collections, *Crossing the Water* (1971) and *Winter Trees* (1971).

RABELAIS, FRANÇOIS (1532–1564)

Born in Chinon, Touraine, France, the scholar and cleric remains best known for *Gargantua and Pantagruel* (1533–1564), his satiric portrait of 16th-century French society. Rabelais began his clerical career at a Franciscan monastery and later transferred to a Benedictine order, where he qualified as a physician. He practiced medicine in Lyon and was credited with performing the first public dissection in France. The first two books of the five-volume *Gargantua and Pantagruel* were condemned by the Sorbonne as "obscene," and the grotesque adventures of his giants and his comic and often obscene anecdotes made the work the target of censors in the United States.

RICHARDSON, JUSTIN (NO DATES AVAILABLE)

A medical doctor as well as a clinical and academic psychiatrist, Richardson teaches psychoanalytic theory at Columbia University and has a thriving private practice. With Dr. Mark Schuster, he is the author of *Everything You Never Wanted Your Kids to Know About Sex (But Were Afraid They'd Ask)*, published in 2003, and he lectures about child and teen sexuality throughout the United States. He also served as the psychiatric adviser to the HBO television series *In Treatment*. He is the recipient of numerous awards for his research in psychiatry, including the Columbia Psychoanalytic Center's Lionel Ovesey Award for Research and awards from the American Medical Association. Despite his prestige, Richardon's most visible work and the work that has gained him the most attention is the book for children he coauthored with Peter Parnell, *And Tango Makes Three*, the 2005 picture book that is based on the true story of two male penguins at the Central Park Zoo who hatch an egg and raise a female baby penguin.

ROBBINS, HAROLD (1916–1997)

Born in New York City, the novelist produced a large number of financially successful novels that were derided by critics for being sensationalist and poorly constructed. His autobiographical first novel, *Never Love a Stranger* (1948), was the target of censors for its frank language and references to sexuality. *The Carpetbaggers* (1961) suffered attempts at suppression for its blatant portrayal of sexual activity. Changing mores have prevented further censorship of Robbins's increasingly explicit novels.

SALINGER, J. D. (JEROME DAVID) (1919–2010)

Born in New York City, the reputation of the reclusive novelist and short story writer is based largely on *The Catcher in the Rye* (1951), a novel that is frequently banned by schools on the request of parents who are made uncomfortable by the main character's "vulgar" language and sexuality-oriented thoughts. The novel gained a large readership among high school and college students who could relate fully to the principal character, Holden Caulfield. The resulting public attention that came with the success of the book led Salinger to move from New York to the remote hills of Cornish, New Hampshire, to avoid admirers.

SELBY, HUBERT, JR. (1928–2004)

Born in Brooklyn, New York, the author spent two years as a deckhand in the United States Merchant Marine and 14 years as an insurance analyst before publication of his first and best-known work, *Last Exit to Brooklyn*. An amoral exploration of the world of prostitutes, drug abusers, and criminals, the work became the subject of an obscenity trial and other attempts to ban it.

SENDAK, MAURICE (BERNARD) (1928–   )

Born in Brooklyn, New York, the illustrator and writer has been a major influence in children's literature for over three decades, beginning with the publication of *Where the Wild Things Are* (1963), which won the 1964 Caldecott Medal. Sendak has also written and illustrated *Higglety Pigglety Pop!* (1967), *In the Night Kitchen* (1970), and *Outside over There* (1981), in addition to illustrating many books for others. His drawings, described by critics as bizarre, display a nightmarish quality, but only *In the Night Kitchen* has generated controversy, in this case for its illustration of a naked boy that challengers labeled "pornography" and "obscene."

SHANNON, GEORGE (1952–   )

Born in Caldwell, Kansas, and also known as George William Bones Shannon, the author is a professional storyteller who combines his interest in folklore and the oral storytelling tradition with his love of literature for children in a series of picture books, including *Lizard's Home* (1981), *Frog Legs: A Picture Book of Action Verse* (2000), and *Tippy-Toe Chick, Go!* (2004). He produced the well-received work *The Piney Woods Peddler* (1980), which won the American Library Association Notable Book Designation in 1981 and became the Children's Choice Book in 1982. Other works include *Dancing the Breeze* (1981) and *Climbing Kansas Mountains* (1993), as well as an award-winning and controversial young adult novel, *Unlived Affections* (1989), which won the Friends of American Writers Award in 1990.

SHULMAN, IRVING (1913–1995)

Born in Brooklyn, New York, the author was a college English professor, novelist, biographer, and screenwriter who adapted his own novel *Children of the Dark* into the 1955 screenplay for *Rebel Without a Cause*. Of his 10 novels, *The Amboy Dukes* (1947) achieved notoriety as a result of efforts to ban it. Its popularity among high school students caused educators and parents to fear that its scenes of criminal activity and sexuality would promote "delinquency."

SILVERSTEIN, SHEL (SHELDON) (1932–1999)

Once a lead cartoonist for *Playboy* magazine, 'Shel' Silverstein created cartoons that appeared in every issue from 1957 through 1970. He was also an award-winning composer of country and contemporary music, and his songs were recorded by Johnny Cash, Marianne Faithfull, Loretta Lynn, Dr. Hook, and Bobby Bare. Silverstein's sketches and songs were also featured on radio shows throughout the United States. Silverstein's early cartoons in the 1950s appeared in *Sports Illustrated* and *Look*. In this period he produced his most famous cartoon, which depicted two scruffy-looking men shackled to a wall, seemingly prisoners in a dungeon, with the caption "Now here's my plan." Among his more than 20 published collections of cartoons and poetry, none have generated more controversy than his books for children, particularly *The Giving Tree* (1964), *Where the Sidewalk Ends* (1974), and *A Light in the Attic* (1981), which represent in sometimes ridiculous forms the dark side of human nature that many parents and educators have characterized as inappropriate for young minds. The many now-grown readers of his works have disagreed and, in his defense, have pointed out that children know that a dark side of life exists, and that Shel Silverstein simply respected young people enough to deal with it honestly.

SMITH, LILLIAN (1897–1966)

Born near Atlanta, Georgia, the author was referred to by contemporary critics as "the Negro's White Joan of Arc" for her founding of *Pseudopodia* (later *North Georgia Review* and *South Today*), the only southern literary journal to showcase African-American writers in the 1930s and 1940s. As with her nonfiction, Smith protested stereotyped gender and racial roles in *Strange Fruit*, a novel that was branded "obscene" and banned by the United States Department of the Post Office.

STEINBECK, JOHN (1902–1968)

Born in Salinas, California, the novelist and short story writer was awarded the Nobel Prize for literature in 1962. Much of his work focuses on the American poor and the social injustices that the poor and dispossessed face. His first popular success was *Tortilla Flat* (1935), a semihumorous work that was quickly followed by grim, tragic novels and stories, such as *In Dubious Battle* (1936), *Of Mice and Men* (1937), *The Red Pony* (1938), and *The Grapes of Wrath* (1939), which won both the Pulitzer Prize and the National Book Award. In the 1940s and later, Steinbeck wrote numerous screenplays, some from his novels and stories, and moved his focus to the dispossessed in other areas of society. Among his successes are *The Wayward Bus* (1947) and *East of Eden* (1952), which with *The Red Pony* and *Of Mice and Men*, have been challenged for what critics view as "filthy" language, "vulgarity," and "bad grammar."

STOKER, BRAM (1847–1912)

Born Abraham Stoker in Dublin, the civil servant, novelist, and drama critic is best known for creating *Dracula* (1897), one of the most powerful Gothic figures in literary history. Other stories of horror written by Stoker have faded from existence, but his Transylvanian Count Dracula has become the subject of numerous films and books, as well as the prototype for most later vampire creations. The sexual overtones of the novel have been recognized from its first publication and underlie attempts to suppress it.

STOPES, MARIE (1880–1958)

Born in Edinburgh, Scotland, Marie Stopes won international acclaim for her work in promoting birth control and opened the first free birth control clinic in the British Empire. Admired by George Bernard Shaw and the Duke of Windsor, she also gained detractors through her crusades that brought violent opposition from the Roman Catholic Church. *Married Love*, which she characterized as "a book about the plain facts of marriage," sold over a million copies and was translated into 13 languages, but it was strongly attacked for being immoral.

SWARTHOUT, GLENDON (1918–1992)

Born in Pinckney, Michigan, the author wrote short stories, mysteries, film scripts, plays, and children's books, many of them set in the American West. Although Swarthout's novels *Where the Boys Are* (1961) and *The Shootist* (1975) achieved success in print and on the movie screen, *Bless the Beasts and the Children* (1970) brought him greater acclaim and was also the source of numerous challenges and attempts at censorship.

TERKEL, STUDS (1912–2008)

Born Louis Terkel in New York City, the oral historian, radio broadcaster, journalist, sports columnist, lecturer, and playwright has conducted interviews all over the world with people from all walks of life. He won the Pulitzer Prize in 1985 for *The Good War: An Oral History of World War II* (1984), and he has also dealt with urban unrest in *Division Street, America* (1966), the Depression in *Hard Times: An Oral History of the Great Depression* (1970), the dwindling American dream in *The Great Divide* (1988), and the 20th century in *Coming of Age* (1995). Only *Working: People Talk about What They Do All Day and How They Feel about What They Do* (1974) has motivated challenges for its "vulgar" and "offensive" language.

THOMAS, PIRI (1928–)

Born in Spanish Harlem in New York City, the author is a former drug addict and street gang member who served six years of a 15-year prison sentence for an attempted armed robbery in 1950. His memoir, *Down These Mean Streets* (1972), portrays the brutal life of his past in candid language and with vivid descriptions that have led critics to label the book "obscene" and to condemn it.

TROCCHI, ALEXANDER (1925–1984)

Born in Glasgow, Scotland, the author was cofounder of *Merlin*, the first publisher of Romanian dramatist Eugene Ionesco and among the first to publish the work of French dramatist Jean Genet in English. He also wrote erotic novels on a work-for-hire basis for Olympia Press (Paris) while exploring his talents as a serious novelist. *Cain's Book* (1960) features a drug-addicted narrator who is neither remorseful for his addiction nor condemnatory of drugs, factors that led to seizures of the book and a lengthy trial in England.

TWAIN, MARK (1835–1910)

Born Samuel Langhorne Clemens in Florida, Missouri, the humorist, novelist, journalist, lecturer, and travel writer took his pseudonym from a phrase meaning "two fathoms deep" used by Mississippi river boatmen. Although largely associated with life on the Mississippi River because of the literary success of *The Adventures of Tom Sawyer* (1876), *Life on the Mississippi* (1883), and *Adventures of Huckleberry Finn* (1884–1885), Twain also chronicled his journeys to the West and experiences in California, as well as adventures abroad in *Innocents Abroad* (1869), *Roughing It* (1872), and others. Two of Twain's most popular works are also among the most frequently banned or censored in the United States: *The Adventures of Tom Sawyer* and *Adventures of Huckleberry Finn*. Both books have been criticized as being "racist" and for containing "vulgar" and "profane" language.

VONNEGUT, KURT, JR. (1922–2007)

Born in Indianapolis, Indiana, the novelist and short story writer combines science fiction, social satire, and black comedy to expose the dehumanizing effects of 20th-century society and the technology and powerful institutions that perpetuate the dehumanization. Vonnegut's colloquial style and rebellious tone made him a campus favorite in the 1960s and the early 1970s, through such works as *Player Piano* (1952), *Cat's Cradle* (1963), *Welcome to the Monkey House* (1968), and *Slaughterhouse-Five* (1969). While several of Vonnegut's works have been challenged for their political or religious references, challenges to *Welcome to the Monkey House* have included complaints of "sexuality explicit language" and "vulgarities."

WALKER, ALICE (1944–   )

Born in Eatonton, Georgia, the poet, novelist, and short story writer grew up in a sharecropper family and participated in the 1960s civil rights movement, later using those events in *The Third Life of George Copeland* (1970) and *Meridian* (1976). In 1982, Walker won both the Pulitzer Prize and the American Book Award for *The Color Purple* (1982), followed by other successful novels, *The Temple of My Familiar* (1989) and *Possessing the Secret of Joy* (1992). Her most popular novel, *The Color Purple*, has also been frequently challenged for "explicit sexual language," "insulting" portraits of African-American males, and "vulgarities."

WENTWORTH, HAROLD (1904–1973)

Born in Homer, New York, Wentworth is a college English professor who has edited or served as consulting editor for various dictionaries, including *Webster's New International Dictionary*, second edition, and others, in addition to the *Dictionary of American Slang*, which has been banned by school districts for its inclusion of "unacceptable" and "vulgar" words.

WHITMAN, WALT (1819–1892)

Born in West Hill, Long Island, New York, the poet, journalist, newspaper editor, and printer vowed to create a distinctly new form of poetry that would reflect the democratic nature and vastness of the United States. His first book of poetry, *Leaves of Grass* (1855), offended many of his contemporaries with its anatomical references. Whitman served as a hospital volunteer in the Civil War, then published *Drum-Taps* (1865). Two of his most famous works, "When Lilacs Last in the Dooryard Bloom'd" and "O Captain! My Captain!" that commemorated the death of Lincoln, appeared in *Sequel to Drum-Taps* (1865–66).

WILDER, LAURA INGALLS (1867–1957)

Born in Pepin, Wisconsin, the novelist's *Little House* series of autobiographical novels, recounting her childhood growing up on the American frontier, have become classics of childhood literature. The series began with *Little House in the Big Woods* (1932) and includes *Little House on the Prairie* (1935), the inspiration for a successful television series in the 1970s. The novels have been challenged for being "derogatory to Native Americans."

WILLHOITE, MICHAEL (1946–   )

Born in Hobart, Oklahoma, the writer and illustrator began his career by publishing cartoons and caricatures in a weekly gay newspaper, the *Washington Blade*. In *Daddy's Roommate* (1990), Willhoite depicts a divorce in which the father begins cohabitation with another man while the mother explains to their child that his father is gay. Numerous challenges have emerged to the book because it "legitimizes" gay relationships. Willhoite's most recent book, *Daddy's Wedding* (1996), is a sequel that shows the father marrying his male roommate.

WILLINGHAM, CALDER (1922–1995)

Born in Atlanta, Georgia, novelist and screenwriter Willingham became an instant literary star at 24 with the publication of *End as a Man*, the best known of his 10 novels and the one that generated both critical praise and controversy. The publicity surrounding the obscenity trial involving that novel cast a shadow on the author that he was never able to escape. From 1955 onward, Willingham also wrote screenplays for films, including those for *The Graduate* (1967), *Little Big Men* (1970), and *Rambling Rose* (1991).

WOLFE, THOMAS (1900–1938)

Born Thomas Clayton Wolfe in Asheville, North Carolina, the novelist and playwright has been acclaimed as one of the great American novelists of the 20th century. After completing a master's degree in English in 1924 at Harvard University, where he wrote plays, Wolfe began the autobiographical novel *Look Homeward, Angel* (1929) when he found that he could not get his plays produced. His two major autobiographical novels, *Look Homeward, Angel* and *You Can't Go Home Again* (1940), established Wolfe as a major figure in American literature, and *Of Time and the River* (1935), a fictional account of his experience at Harvard, affirmed that reputation. The latter novel has been accused of being "racist," "anti-Semitic," and "pornographic."

ZEMACH, MARGOT (1931–1989)

Born in Los Angeles, Margot Zemach was a renowned children's author and illustrator who specialized in adapting folktales for children. Her books included retellings of such classic tales as *The Little Red Hen* (1983) and *The Three Little Pigs* (1986), as well as stories drawn from Yiddish folklore. Zemach was the U.S. nominee for the Hans Christian Anderson Medal for illustration in 1980, and she collaborated on numerous distinguished picture books with her husband, Harve Zemach, including *Duffy and the Devil* (1973), which won the Caldecott Medal in 1974; *The Judge* (1969), which was a Caldecott Honor book in 1970; *Salt* (1965); *A Penny a Look* (1971); and *Mommy, Buy Me a Doll* (1966). Zemach also wrote and illustrated *It Could Always Be Worse* (1977), a Caldecott Honor Book, in 1978 and *Jake and Honeybunch go to Heaven* (1981), which won the Commonwealth Club Silver Medal for literature in 1982.

ZOLA, ÉMILE (1840–1902)

Born in Aix-en-Provence, France, the journalist and novelist used his fiction to campaign for social reform and justice. He became the major proponent of literary naturalism. Zola created a cycle of 20 novels called, collectively, *Les Rougon Macquart*, which were published between 1871 and 1893 and criticized for their gratuitous brutality and obscenity. Today they are valued as fictionalized sociology. Of particular interest are *Nana* (1880) and *La Terre*, translated variously as *The Earth* and *The Soil* (1887). In later years, Zola gained further notoriety for his celebrated campaign and notorious "J'accuse" letter in defense of Captain Alfred Dreyfus.

BIBLIOGRAPHY

BOOKS

Aggeler, Geoffrey. *Anthony Burgess: The Artist as Novelist*. Birmingham: University of Alabama Press, 1979.

Aldiss, Brian W. *Billion Year Spree: The True History of Science Fiction*. Garden City, N.Y.: Doubleday & Company, 1973.

Alexander, Paul. *Rough Magic: A Biography of Sylvia Plath*. New York: Viking Press, 1991.

Alexie, Sherman. *The Absolutely True Diary of a Part-Time Indian*. New York: Little, Brown and Company, 2007.

Allen, William Rodney. *Understanding Kurt Vonnegut*. Columbia: University of South Carolina Press, 1990.

American Library Association. *Censorship and Selection: Issues and Answers for Schools*. Chicago: American Library Association, 1993.

Arnstein, Walter L. *The Bradlaugh Case*. Oxford: Clarendon Press, 1965.

Avery, Evelyn Gross. *Rebels and Victims: The Fiction of Richard Wright and Bernard Malamud*. Port Washington, N.Y.: Kennikat Press, 1979.

Babb, Valerie Melissa. *Ernest Gaines*. Boston: Twayne, 1991.

Baker, Carlos. *Hemingway: A Life Story*. New York: Charles Scribner's Sons, 1969.

Baldwin, James. *Conversations with James Baldwin*. Edited by Fred L. Standley and Louis H. Pratt. Jackson: University Press of Mississippi, 1989.

Banfield, Beryle, and Geraldine L. Wilson. "The Black Experience through White Eyes—The Same Old Story Again." In *The Black American in Books for Children: Readings in Racism*, edited by Donnarae MacCann and Gloria Woodard, 192–207. Metuchen, N.J.: Scarecrow Press, 1985.

Baughman, Ronald. *Understanding James Dickey*. Columbia: University of South Carolina Press, 1985.

Becker, Beverley C., Susan Stan, and Donna Reidly Pistolis. *Hit List 2 for Children: Frequently Challenged Books*. Chicago: American Library Association, 2002.

Beckett, Samuel. "Censorship in the Saorstat." In *Disjecta: Miscellaneous Writings and a Dramatic Fragment by Samuel Beckett*, edited by Ruby Cohn, 84–88. London: John Calder, 1983.

Bedford, Sybille. *Aldous Huxley: A Biography*. 2 vols. London: Chatto and Windus Collins, 1973–1974.

Belford, Barbara. *Bram Stoker: A Biography of the Author of "Dracula."* New York: Alfred A. Knopf, 1996.

Benson, Jackson J. *Hemingway: The Writer's Art of Self-Defense*. Minneapolis: University of Minnesota Press, 1969.

Bettelheim, Bruno. *The Uses of Enchantment: The Meaning and Importance of Fairy Tales*. New York: Random House, 1977.

Bjork, Christina. *The Other Alice: The Story of Alice Liddell and Alice in Wonderland*. New York: R&S Books, 1993.

Blanshard, Paul. *The Right to Read*. Boston: Beacon Press, 1955.

Blodgett, Harold. *Walt Whitman in England*. Ithaca, N.Y.: Cornell University Press, 1934.

Bone, Robert. *Down Home: A History of Afro-American Short Fiction from Its Beginnings to the End of the Harlem Renaissance.* New York: G. P. Putnam's Sons, 1975.

Brasch, Walter. *Brer Rabbit, Uncle Remus and the 'Cornfield Journalist': The Tale of Joel Chandler Harris.* Macon, Ga.: Mercer University Press, 2000.

Brittain, Vera. *Radclyffe Hall: A Case of Obscenity?* New York: A. S. Barnes, 1969.

Broderick, Dorothy M. *Image of the Black in Children's Fiction.* New York: R. R. Bowker Company, 1973.

Broun, Heywood, and Margaret Leech. *Anthony Comstock: Roundsman of the Lord.* New York: Literary Guild of America, 1927.

Bruccoli, Matthew J. *Fitzgerald & Hemingway: A Dangerous Friendship.* New York: Carroll & Graf, 1994.

———. *The O'Hara Concern: A Biography of John O'Hara.* New York: Random House, 1975.

———. *Some Sort of Epic Grandeur: The Life of F. Scott Fitzgerald.* New York: Harcourt Brace Jovanovich, 1981.

Burke, Redmond A. *What Is the Index?* Milwaukee, Wis.: Bruce Publishing Company, 1952.

Burress, Lee. *Battle of the Books: Literary Censorship in the Public Schools, 1950–1985.* Metuchen, N.J.: Scarecrow Press, 1989.

Burroughs, William S. *Letters to Allen Ginsberg, 1953–1957.* Introduction by Allen Ginsberg. New York: Full Court Press, 1982.

Butscher, Edward. *Sylvia Plath: Method and Madness.* New York: Seabury Press, 1975.

Campbell, James. *Talking at the Gates: A Life of James Baldwin.* New York: Penguin Books, 1991.

Carson, Clayborne. *Malcolm X: The FBI File.* New York: Carroll & Graf, 1991.

Carter, B. "A Second Look: The Inner City Mother Goose." *Horn Book Magazine* 72, no. 6: 707–712.

Cartwright, Keith. *Reading Africa into American Literature.* Lexington: University Press of Kentucky, 2002.

Cavitch, David. *My Soul and I: The Inner Life of Walt Whitman.* Boston: Beacon Press, 1985.

Cech, John. *Angels and Wild Things.* University Park: Pennsylvania State University Press, 1993.

Christian, Barbara. *Black Feminist Criticism.* New York: Pergamon Press, 1985.

Coale, Samuel. *Anthony Burgess.* New York: Frederick Ungar, 1981.

Cohen, Morton N. *Lewis Carroll: A Biography.* New York: Alfred A. Knopf, 1995.

Cowley, Malcolm, ed. *Walt Whitman's Leaves of Grass: The First (1855) Edition.* New York: Viking Press, 1959.

Cox, Don Richard. *Arthur Conan Doyle.* New York: Frederick Ungar, 1985.

Crowley, J. Donald, ed. *Hawthorne: The Critical Heritage.* New York: Barnes & Noble, 1970.

Cummins, Eric. *The Rise and Fall of California's Radical Prison Movement.* New York: Oxford University Press, 1995.

Darling, R. L. "Goose Feathers." *IFC ALA Newsletter on Intellectual Freedom* (May 1972): 69, 97–98.

Dave, R. A. "*To Kill a Mockingbird:* Harper Lee's Tragic Vision." In *Indian Studies in American Literature,* edited by M. K. Naik, S. K. Desai, and S. Mokashi, 311–323. Dharwar, India: Karnatak University, 1974.

Davis, James E., ed. *Dealing with Censorship.* Urbana, Ill.: National Council of Teachers of English, 1983.

Davis, Terry. *Presenting Chris Crutcher.* New York: Twayne, 1997.

De Grazia, Edward. *Censorship Landmarks.* New York: R. R. Bowker Company, 1969.

———. *Girls Lean Back Everywhere: The Law of Obscenity and the Assault on Genius.* New York: Random House, 1992.

D'Emilio, John, and Estelle B. Freedman. *Intimate Matters: A History of Sexuality in America.* New York: Harper & Row, 1988.

Dickson, Lovat. *Radclyffe Hall at the Well of Loneliness: A Sapphic Chronicle.* New York: Charles Scribner's Sons, 1975.

Donald, David Herbert. *Look Homeward: A Life of Thomas Wolfe.* Boston: Little, Brown & Company, 1987.

Donelson, Kenneth, ed. *The Student's Right to Read.* Urbana, Ill.: National Council of Teachers of English, 1972.

Donelson, Kenneth L., and Alleen Pace Nilsen. *Literature for Today's Young Adults.* Glenview, Ill.: Scott Foresman, 1989.

Doyle, Robert P. *Caution! Some People Consider These Books Dangerous. IFC ALA Newsletter on Intellectual Freedom.* Chicago: ALA, 1996.

Dreiser, Theodore. "The Early Adventures of Sister Carrie." Foreword to *Sister Carrie.* New York: Modern Library, 1927.

Dyson, Michael Eric. *Making Malcolm: The Myth and Meaning of Malcolm X.* New York: Oxford University Press, 1994.

Elliot, Jeffrey, ed. *Conversations with Maya Angelou.* Jackson: University of Mississippi Press, 1989.

Ernst, Morris, and Ernest Lindley. *The Censor Marches On.* New York: Doubleday, Doran, 1940.

Everson, William. *American Bard: The Original Preface to "Leaves of Grass."* New York: Viking Press, 1982.

Faderman, Lillian. *Surpassing the Love of Men.* New York: William Morrow & Company, 1981.

Farrell, Walter C., Jr. "*Black Like Me:* In Defense of a Racial Reality." In *Censored Books: Critical Viewpoints,* edited by Nicholas Karolides, Lee Burress, and John M. Kean: 117–124. Metuchen, N.J.: Scarecrow Press, 1993.

Ferrell, Keith. *John Steinbeck: The Voice of the Land.* New York: M. Evans, 1986.

Fitzgerald, F. Scott. *The Great Gatsby.* New York: Charles Scribner's Sons, 1925.

Foster, Jeannette H. *Sex Variant Women in Literature.* Tallahassee, Fla.: Naiad Press, 1985.

Fowell, Frank, and Frank Palmer. *Censorship in England.* 1913. Reprint, New York: Burt Franklin, 1970.

Frank, Otto. "Introduction." In *Anne Frank, The Diary of a Young Girl: The Definitive Edition,* edited by Otto Frank and Mirjam Pressler. New York: Doubleday & Company, 1995.

Franklin, Howard Bruce. *Robert A. Heinlein: America as Science Fiction.* New York: Oxford University Press, 1980.

Freedman, Ralph. *Hermann Hesse: Pilgrim of Crisis.* New York: Pantheon Books, 1978.

Frohock, William M. *The Novel of Violence in America, 1920–1950.* Dallas, Tex.: Southern Methodist University Press, 1958.

Fryer, Peter. *The Birth Controllers.* London: Corgi Books, 1967.

Gaines, Ernest. *Porch Talk with Ernest Gaines: Conversations on the Writer's Craft.* Baton Rouge: Louisiana State University Press, 1990.

Gardner, John. *On Moral Fiction.* New York: Basic Books, 1978.

Geller, Evelyn. *Forbidden Books in American Public Libraries, 1876–1939: A Study in Cultural Change.* Westport, Conn.: Greenwood Press, 1984.

Gentry, Tony. *Alice Walker.* New York: Chelsea House Publishers, 1993.

Ginsberg, Allen. "Introduction." In *Junky,* written by William S. Burroughs, v–ix. New York: Penguin Books, 1977.

Giovanni, Nikki. *Conversations with Nikki Giovanni.* Jackson: University Press of Mississippi, 1992.

Goodman, Michael B. *Contemporary Literary Censorship: The Case History of Burroughs' Naked Lunch.* Metuchen, N.J.: Scarecrow Press, 1981.

Greenblatt, Stephen Jay. *Three Modern Satirists: Waugh, Orwell, and Huxley.* New Haven, Conn.: Yale University Press, 1965.

Griffin, John Howard. *Racial Equality: The Myth and the Reality.* ERIC Education Document Reprint Series, No. 26 (March 1971).

Gutman, Stanley T. *Mankind in Barbary: The Individual and Society in the Novels of Norman Mailer.* Hanover, N.H.: University Press of New England, 1975.

Haney, Robert W. *Comstockery in America: Patterns of Censorship and Control.* Boston: Beacon Press, 1960.

Harris, Trudier. *Black Women in the Fiction of James Baldwin.* Knoxville: University of Tennessee Press, 1985.

Harwell, Richard, ed. *Margaret Mitchell's "Gone with the Wind" Letters, 1936–1949.* New York: Macmillan, 1976.

Haskins, James. *Profiles in Black Power.* Garden City, N.Y.: Doubleday & Company, 1972.

Hawthorn, Jeremy. *Multiple Personality and the Disintegration of Literary Character: From Oliver Goldsmith to Sylvia Plath.* New York: Ballantine Books, 1983.

Helterman, Jeffrey. *Understanding Bernard Malamud.* Columbia: University of South Carolina Press, 1985.

Hemingway, Ernest. *Selected Letters: 1917–1961.* Edited by Carlos Baker. New York: Charles Scribner's Sons, 1981.

Hemmings, F. W. J. *The Life and Times of Emile Zola.* New York: Charles Scribner's Sons, 1977.

Henderson, Jeff. *Thor's Hammer: Essays on John Gardner.* Conway: University of Central Arkansas Press, 1985.

Hipkiss, Robert A. *The American Absurd: Pynchon, Vonnegut, and Barth.* Port Washington, N.Y.: Associated Faculty Press, 1984.

Holman, C. Hugh. *The Letters of Thomas Wolfe to His Mother.* Chapel Hill: University of North Carolina Press, 1968.

Hotchner, A. E. *Papa Hemingway: A Personal Memoir.* New York: Carroll & Graf, 1999.

Howell, John Michael. *Understanding John Gardner.* Columbia: University of South Carolina Press, 1993.

Huck, Charlotte S., Susan Hepler, and Janet Hickman. *Children's Literature in Elementary School.* New York: Holt, Rinehart & Winston, 1987.

Hurwitz, Leon. *Historical Dictionary of Censorship in the United States.* Westport, Conn.: Greenwood Press, 1985.

Hyde, H. Montgomery. *Lord Justice: The Life and Times of Lord Birkett of Ulverston.* New York: Random House, 1964.

Index of Prohibited Books. Revised and published by the order of His Holiness Pope Pius XII. Vatican: Polyglot Press, 1948.

Jenkinson, Edward B. *Censors in the Classroom: The Mind Benders.* Carbondale: Southern Illinois University Press, 1979.

Johnson, Claudia. *Stifled Laughter: A Woman's Story about Fighting Censorship.* Golden, Colo.: Fulcrum Publishing, 1994.

Johnson, Wayne L. *Ray Bradbury.* New York: Frederick Ungar, 1980.

Josephson, Matthew. *Zola and His Time.* Garden City, N.Y.: Garden City Publishing Company, 1928.

Kallen, Stuart A. *Maya Angelou: Woman of Words, Deeds, and Dreams.* Minneapolis, Minn.: Abdo and Daughters, 1993.

Karolides, Nicholas J., Lee Burress, and John M. Kean, eds. *Censored Books: Critical Viewpoints.* Metuchen, N.J.: Scarecrow Press, 1993.

Katz, Jonathan Ned. *Gay American History: Lesbians and Gay Men in the U.S.A.* Rev. ed. New York: Penguin Books, 1992.

Kendrick, Walter. *The Secret Museum.* New York: Viking Press, 1987.

Kester, Seymour. *Utopian Episodes: Daily Life in Experimental Colonies Dedicated to Changing the World.* Syracuse, N.Y.: Syracuse University Press, 1996.

King, Stephen. "Banned Books and Other Concerns: The Virginia Beach Lecture." In *The Stephen King Companion,* edited by George Beahm, 51–61. Kansas City, Mo.: Andrews and McMeel, 1989.

Kirk, Ersye. *The Black Experience in Books for Children and Young Adults.* Ardmore, Okla.: Positive Impact, 1993.

Knowles, Sebastian. *British and Irish—A Purgatorial Flame: Seven British Writers in the Second World War.* London: Routledge Paul, 1991.

Kostelanetz, Richard. *Politics in the African-American Novel: James Weldon Johnson, W. E. B. DuBois, Richard Wright, and Ralph Ellison.* New York: Greenwood Press, 1991.

Kramer, Barbara. *Alice Walker: Author of "The Color Purple."* Springfield, N.J.: Enslow Publishers, 1995.

Kronhausen, Eberhard, and Phyllis Kronhausen. *Pornography and the Law.* New York: Ballantine Books, 1959.

Lamond, John. *Arthur Conan Doyle: A Memoir.* Port Washington, N.Y.: Kennikat Press, 1972.

Larabee, Leonard W., ed. *The Autobiography of Benjamin Franklin.* New Haven, Conn.: Yale University Press, 1964.

Leatherdale, Clive. *Dracula: The Novel and the Legend.* Northamptonshire, U.K.: Aquarian Press, 1985.

Lennon, Florence Becker. *The Life of Lewis Carroll.* New York: Dover Publications, 1972.

Lennon, J. Michael, ed. *Conversations with Norman Mailer.* Jackson: University Press of Mississippi, 1988.

Levitt, Steven D., and Stephen J. Dubner. *Freakonomics: A Rogue Economist Explores the Hidden Side of Everything.* New York: HarperCollins, 2005.

LeVot, Andre. *F. Scott Fitzgerald: A Biography.* New York: Doubleday & Company, 1983.

Lewis, Felice Flanery. *Literature, Obscenity, and Law.* Carbondale: Southern Illinois University Press, 1976.

Light, Martin. *The Quixotic Vision of Sinclair Lewis.* West Lafayette, Ind.: Purdue University Press, 1975.

Lingeman, Richard. *Theodore Dreiser: At the Gates of the City, 1871–1907*. Vol. 1. New York: G. P. Putnam's Sons, 1986.

Lockwood, Lee. *Conversation with Eldridge Cleaver: Algiers*. New York: McGraw-Hill, 1970.

Loth, David. *The Erotic in Literature*. New York: Dorset Press, 1961.

Louÿs, Pierre. "Preface." *Aphrodite*. Translated by Lewis Galantiere. New York: Modern Library, 1933.

MacPherson, Pat. *Reflecting in the Bell Jar*. New York: Routledge Kegan Paul, 1991.

Manso, Peter. *Mailer: His Life and Times*. New York: Simon & Schuster, 1985.

Manvell, Roger. *The Trial of Annie Besant and Charles Bradlaugh*. New York: Horizon Press, 1976.

May, Jill. "In Defense of *To Kill a Mockingbird*." In *Censored Books: Critical Viewpoints*, edited by Nicholas J. Karolides, Lee Burress, and John M. Kean, 476–484. Metuchen, N.J.: Scarecrow Press, 1993.

McCoy, Ralph E. *Banned in Boston: The Development of Literary Censorship in Massachusetts*. Urbana: University of Illinois Press, 1956.

Meeks, Christopher. *Roald Dahl: Kids Love His Stories*. Vero Beach, Fla.: Rourke Publishing, 1993.

Mellow, James R. *Hemingway: A Life without Consequences*. New York: Houghton Mifflin, 1992.

Meyers, Jeffrey. *Hemingway: A Biography*. New York: Harper & Row, 1985.

Mileck, Joseph. *Hermann Hesse: Life and Art*. Berkeley: University of California Press, 1978.

Miles, Barry. *William Burroughs: El Hombre Invisible*. New York: Hyperion, 1983.

Miller, Edwin Haviland. *Salem Is My Dwelling Place: A Life of Nathaniel Hawthorne*. Iowa City: University of Iowa Press, 1991.

Montgomery, Sy. *Walking with the Great Apes*. Boston: Houghton Mifflin, 1991.

Mordell, Albert. *Notorious Literary Attacks*. New York: Boni & Liveright, 1926.

Morgan, Charles. *Epitaph on George Moore*. New York: Macmillan, 1935.

Morgan, Ted. *Literary Outlaw: The Life and Times of William S. Burroughs*. New York: Henry Holt, 1988.

Morrison, Toni. *Beloved*. New York: Alfred A. Knopf, 1987.

Myers, Jeffrey. *Hemingway: Life into Art*. New York: Cooper Square Press, 2000.

Nethercot, Arthur H. *The Last Four Lives of Annie Besant*. Chicago: University of Chicago Press, 1963.

Noble, Donald R. *The Steinbeck Question*. Troy, N.Y.: Whitston Publishing, 1993.

Noble, William. *Bookbanning in America: Who Bans Books?—And Why*. Middlebury, Vt.: Paul S. Eriksson, 1990.

O'Higgins, Paul. *Censorship in England*. London: Nelson, 1972.

Olander, Joseph D., and Martin Harry Greenberg. *Robert A. Heinlein*. New York: Taplinger Publishing, 1978.

Oldsey, Bernard. *Hemingway's Hidden Craft: The Writing of "A Farewell to Arms."* University Park: Pennsylvania State University Press, 1979.

O'Neil, Robert M. *Classrooms in the Crossfire: The Rights and Interests of Students, Parents, Teachers, Administrators, Librarians, and the Community*. Bloomington: Indiana University Press, 1981.

Orel, Harold, ed. *Critical Essays on Sir Arthur Conan Doyle*. New York: G. K. Hall, 1992.

Padover, Saul Kussiel. *The Complete Jefferson*. New York: Duell, Sloan & Pearce, 1943.

————. *The Complete Madison.* New York: Harper & Brothers, 1953.

Paul, James C. N., and Murray L. Schwartz. *Federal Censorship: Obscenity in the Mail.* New York: Free Press of Glencoe, 1961.

People For the American Way. *Attacks on the Freedom to Learn, 1990–1991 Report.* Washington, D.C.: People For the American Way, 1991.

Perrin, Noel. *Dr. Bowdler's Legacy: A History of Expurgated Books in England and America.* Boston: David R. Godine, 1992.

Petersen, William. *The Politics of Population.* Garden City, N.Y.: Doubleday & Company, 1964.

Pettit, Jayne. *Maya Angelou: Journey of the Heart.* New York: Lodester Books, 1996.

Pinsker, Sanford. *Understanding Joseph Heller.* Columbia: University of South Carolina Press, 1991.

Popkin, Michael. *Modern Black Writers.* New York: Frederick Ungar, 1978.

Porter, Horace A. *Stealing the Fire: The Art and Protest of James Baldwin.* Middletown, Conn.: Wesleyan University Press, 1989.

Potts, Stephen. *Catch-22: Antiheroic Antinovel.* Boston: Twayne, 1989.

————. *From Here to Absurdity: The Moral Battlefields of Joseph Heller.* San Bernardino, Calif.: Borgo Press, 1982.

Powling, Chris. *Roald Dahl.* London: Evans Bros., 1993.

Reed, James. *From Private Vice to Public Virtue: The Birth Control Movement and American Society.* New York: Basic Books, 1978.

Reichman, Henry. *Censorship and Selection: Issues and Answers for Schools.* Chicago and Arlington, Va.: American Library Association and American Association of School Administrators, 1993. A joint publication.

Reynolds, Michael. *Hemingway: The American Homecoming.* Cambridge, Mass.: Blackwell, 1992.

————. *Hemingway: The Final Years.* New York: W. W. Norton, 1999.

————. *Hemingway's First War: The Making of "A Farewell to Arms."* Princeton, N.J.: Princeton University Press, 1976.

Rideout, Walter. *The Radical Novel in the U.S.* New York: Hill & Wang, 1966.

Robertson, Geoffrey. *Obscenity: An Account of the Censorship Laws and Their Enforcement in England and Wales.* London: Weidenfeld & Nicolson, 1979.

Robins, Natalie. *Alien Ink: The FBI's War on Freedom of Expression.* New York: William Morrow & Company, 1992.

Rogak, Lisa. *A Boy Named Shel: The Life and Times of Shel Silverstein.* New York: St. Martin's Press, 2007.

Rollyson, Carl. *The Lives of Norman Mailer.* New York: Paragon House, 1991.

Rose, June. *Marie Stopes and the Sexual Revolution.* Boston: Faber & Faber, 1992.

Samuelson, David W. "Stranger in the Mirror: Model or Mirror?" In *Critical Encounters: Writers and Themes in Science Fiction,* edited by Dick Riley, 144–175. New York: Frederick Ungar, 1978.

Sanders, Ed. *The Family: The Story of Charles Manson's Dune Buggy Attack Battalion.* New York: Berkeley Books, 1971.

Saunders, Edith. *The Prodigal Father.* New York: Longmans, Green & Company, 1951.

Schom, Alan. *Emile Zola: A Biography.* New York: Henry Holt, 1987.

Select Committee on Pornographic Materials, House of Representatives, 82nd Congress. *Report of the Committee on Pornographic Materials.* House Report No. 2510. 1952. (Known as the Gathings Committee Report because E. C. Gathings headed the committee.)

Shaw, George Bernard. "The Censorship." *Irish Statesman* 11 (1928): 206–208. Reprinted in *Banned in Ireland: Censorship and the Irish Writer*, edited by Julia Carlson, 133–141. Athens: University of Georgia Press, 1990.

Shuker, Nancy. *Maya Angelou.* Englewood Cliffs, N.J.: Silver Burdett Press, 1990.

Silverstein, Shel. *A Light in the Attic.* New York: HarperCollins, 1981.

Skaggs, Merrill. *The Folk of Southern Fiction.* Athens: University of Georgia Press, 1972.

Slayton, Paul. "Teaching Rationale for William Golding's *Lord of the Flies.*" In *Censored Books: Critical Viewpoints,* edited by Nicholas J. Karolides, Lee Burress, and John M. Kean, 351–357. Metuchen, N.J.: Scarecrow Press, 1993.

Sloan, James Park. *Jerzy Kosinski: A Biography.* New York: E. P. Dutton & Company, 1996.

Slusser, George Edgar. *Robert A. Heinlein: Stranger in His Own Land.* San Bernardino, Calif.: Borgo Press, 1976.

Smith, Grover, ed. *Letters of Aldous Huxley.* London: Chatto & Windus, 1969.

Spain, Valerie. *Meet Maya Angelou.* New York: Random House, 1995.

Steinbeck, Elaine, and Robert Wallsten, eds. *Steinbeck: A Life in Letters.* New York: Viking Press, 1975.

Stutman, Suzanne, ed. *My Other Loneliness: Letters of Thomas Wolfe and Aline Bernstein.* Chapel Hill: University of North Carolina Press, 1983.

Sullivan, Charles, ed. *Children of Promise: African-American Literature and Art for Young People.* New York: Harry N. Abrams, 1991.

Sutherland, John. *Offensive Literature: Decensorship in Britain, 1960–1982.* London: Junction Books, 1982.

Symons, Ann K. *Protecting the Right to Read: A How-to-Do Manual for School and Public Librarians.* New York: Neal-Schuman Publishers, 1996.

Tatar, Maria. *The Hard Facts of the Grimm's Fairy Tales.* Princeton, N.J.: Princeton University Press, 1987.

Taylor, Helen. *Scarlett's Women: "Gone with the Wind" and Its Female Fans.* New Brunswick, N.J.: Rutgers University Press, 1989.

Tebbel, John. *A History of Book Publishing in the United States, 1630–1865.* Vol. 1. New York: R. R. Bowker Company, 1972.

———. *A History of Book Publishing in the United States.* Vol. 4. New York: R. R. Bowker & Company, 1981.

Timmerman, John. *John Steinbeck's Fiction: The Aesthetics of the Road Taken.* Norman: University of Oklahoma Press, 1986.

Treglown, Jeremy. *Roald Dahl: A Biography.* New York: Farrar, Straus & Giroux, 1994.

Van Doren, Carl. *Ben Franklin.* New York: Bramhall House, 1987.

Weathersby, Dorothy T. *Censorship of Literature Textbooks in Tennessee: A Study of the Commission, Publishers, Teachers, and Textbooks.* Ed.D. diss., University of Tennessee, 1975.

Weil-Norden, P. *Sir Arthur Conan Doyle.* Centenary edition. Garden City, N.Y.: Doubleday & Company, 1959.

Wenke, Joseph. *Mailer's America.* Hanover, N.H.: University Press of New England, 1987.

Williams, John A. "Blackballing." In *Censored Books: Critical Viewpoints,* edited by Nicholas J. Karolides, Lee Burress, and Jon M. Kean: 11–18. Metuchen, N.J.: Scarecrow Press, 1992.

Wood, James Playsted. *The Unpardonable Sin.* New York: Pantheon Books, 1970.

Wullschlager, Jackie. *Inventing Wonderland: The Lives and Fantasies of Lewis Carroll, Edward Lear, J. M. Barrie, Kenneth Grahame and A. A. Milne.* New York: Free Press, 1995.

Wylder, Delbert E. *Hemingway's Heroes.* Albuquerque: University of New Mexico Press, 1969.

Young Adult Services Division, Intellectual Freedom Committee. *Hit List: Frequently Challenged Young Adult Titles: References to Defend Them.* Chicago: YASD, American Library Association, 1989.

Zipes, Jack. *Fairy Tales and the Art of Subversion: The Classical Genre for Children and the Process of Civilization.* New York: Wildman Press, 1983.

PERIODICALS

Alvino, James. "Is It Book Burning Time Again?" *New York Times,* December 28, 1980, pp. 11–18.

"Annie Goes Back to School." *School Library Journal* 42 (January 1996): 13.

"Another Furor over Books." *Ohio State University Monthly* 55 (December 1963): 8–12.

"*Aphrodite* Brings Fine." *New York Times,* June 24, 1930, p. 8.

Auchmutey, Jim. "In Search of 'Uncle Remus': Sixty Years Ago, Walt Disney Turned Joel Chandler Harris's Creations into a Hit Movie. But Times Have Changed. Now the Film Is Locked Away, and the Author's Reputation Has Dimmed." *Atlanta Journal-Constitution,* November 12, 2006, p. K1.

Bach, Deborah. "'Huck Finn' Back in Renton: School District Now Provides More Guidance to Teachers." *Seattle Post-Intelligencer,* March 17, 2000, p. B2.

Baker, Augusta. "The Black Experience in Children's Literature—An Introductory Essay." *New York Public Library Bulletin* 75 (March 1971): 143–145.

Baldwin, Deborah. "John Gardner: The Serious Optimist." *Common Cause* 15 (September 1989): 34–38.

"Banned Book to Be Restored to Maine Library." *Boston Globe,* August 22, 1982.

Barr, Donald. "Should Holden Caulfield Read These Books?" *New York Times Book Review* 91, May 4, 1986, pp. 1, 50–51.

Black, Lisa. "Antioch School Won't Ban Book: District Calls It a Valuable Read but Offers Alternative." *Chicago Tribune,* June 23, 2009, p. 1.8.

Blaine, Diana York. "The Abjection of Addie and Other Myths of the Maternal in *As I Lay Dying.*" *Mississippi Quarterly* 47 (Summer 1994): 418–419.

Blythe, Will. "Heroin Is Habit-Forming . . . Rabbit-Forming, Babbitt-Forming." *Esquire* 118, no. 5 (November 1992): 51–52.

"Book Ban Beaten in Connecticut—But Ridgefield Board Votes to Discontinue Classes." *New York Times,* February 6, 1973, p. 17.

"Book Ban Includes *The Color Purple.*" *Chicago Tribune,* November 9, 1997, p. 11.

"Book Ban Is Eased by Queens Board." *New York Times,* June 3, 1971, p. 43.

"Book Ban Is Lifted by School Board." *New York Times,* October 22, 1948, p. 23.

"Book Ban Protested." *New York Times,* February 16, 1948, p. 23.

"Book Ban Put to Test." *New York Times,* April 7, 1944, p. 21.

"Book-Ban Review Urged by Parents." *New York Times,* March 18, 1948, p. 25.

"Book Ban Stopped." *Advocate,* December 21, 2004, p. 14.

"Book Burning in North Dakota." *Chicago Sun-Times,* November 14, 1973, p. 40.

"Book Scored, Seller Held." *New York Times,* March 5, 1930, p. 25.

"BOOKS Library Group Finds *Kite Runner* Problematic." *Houston Chronicle*, April 16, 2009, p. 4.

"Books Published Today." *New York Times*, March 22, 1934, p. 10.

Booth, Wayne C. "Censorship and the Values of Fiction." *English Journal* 53 (March 1964): 155–164.

"Boston Bans Sale of 'Elmer Gantry.'" *New York Times*, April 13, 1927, p. 16.

Bradley, Julia T. "Censoring the School Library: Do Students Have the Right to Read?" *Connecticut Law Review* 10 (Spring 1978): 747–771.

Brandehoff, Susan E. "*Jake and Honeybunch Go to Heaven:* Children's Book Fans Smoldering Debate." *American Libraries* 14 (March 1983): 130–132.

"Britain Bans U.S. Book—Novel by Wallace Smith Is Called Indecent—Publisher Fined." *New York Times*, April 11, 1935, p. 19.

Brooks, Peter. "Storied Bodies, or *Nana* at Last Unveil'd." *Critical Inquiry* 16 (Autumn 1989): 1–32.

Brown, Claude. "Manchild in Harlem." *New York Times Magazine*, April 14, 1996, p. 111.

Brown, Frederick. "Zola and the Making of *Nana.*" *Hudson Review* 45 (Summer 1992): 191–217.

Broz, William J. "Defending *Am I Blue?*" *Journal of Adolescent & Adult Literacy* 45 (February 2002): 340–350.

Bruell, Edwin. "Keen Scalpel on Racial Ills." *English Journal* 53 (December 1964): 658–661.

Budd, John M. "Law and Morality in *Billy Budd* and *The Ox-Bow Incident.*" *CLA Journal* 35 (December 1991): 185–197.

Buder, Leonard. "Queens District Seeks Book Ban." *New York Times*, April 6, 1971, p. 47.

Bumgardner, Stan. "Rehabilitating *Uncle Remus.*" *American History* 42 (December 2007): 12.

Burgess-Jackson, Keith. "Rape and Persuasive Definition." *Canadian Journal of Philosophy* 25 (September 1995): 415–454.

Bushman, John H., and Kay P. Bushman. "Coping with the Harsh Realities: The Novels of Chris Crutcher." *English Journal*, March 1992, pp. 82–84.

Buttenwieser, Susan. "A Child's Garden of . . . Diversity." *Ms.* 3 (January 1993): 61–62.

Campbell, James. "Alexander Trocchi: The Biggest Fiend of All." *Antioch Review* 50, no. 3 (Summer 1992): 458.

"Carnegie Embraces 'Uncle Remus' Harris. Makes Special Stop at Atlanta in Order to Meet Him." *New York Times*, April 7, 1906, p. 9.

Carrington, Ildiko de Papp. "Talking Dirty: Alice Munro's 'Open Secrets' and John Steinbeck's 'Of Mice and Men.'" *Studies in Short Fiction* 31 (Fall 1994): 595–606.

Cart, Michael. "Carte Blanche: Winning One for the First Amendment." *Booklist* 92 (April 15, 1996): 1,431.

Carter, B. "A Second Look: The Inner City Mother Goose." *Horn Book Magazine* 72, no. 6: 707–712.

Carter, Cassie. "'A Sickness That Takes Years to Perfect': Jim Carroll's Alchemical Vision." *Dionysos: Literature and Addiction Quarterly* 6 (Winter 1996): 6–19.

Cartwright, Keith. *Reading Africa into American Literature.* Lexington: University Press of Kentucky, 2002.

"Censorship Dateline: Schools." *Newsletter for Intellectual Freedom* 57, no. 3 (May 2008): 3, 97–99.

"Censorship Roundup." *School Library Journal*, October 2001, p. 24.

Chase, Richard, Jr. "Little Red Riding Hood: Werewolf and Prostitute." *Journal of History* 57 (Summer 1995): 769–776.

Cirillo, Nancy R. "A Girl Need Never Go Wrong; or, the Female Servant as Ideological Image in Germinie Lacerteux and Esther Waters." *Comparative Literature Studies* 28 (1991): 68–88.

Clarke, Elyse. "A Slow, Subtle Exercise in Censorship." *School Library Journal* 32 (March 1986): 93–96.

"Class *Aphrodite* as Indecent Book." *New York Times*, June 14, 1930, p. 12.

Cloonan, Michele. "The Censorship of the Adventures of Huckleberry Finn." *Top of the News*, Winter 1984, pp. 191–194.

Cohen, David. "Selection and Racism." *Library Journal*, October 15, 1969, p. 3,585.

Cohen, Peter F. "'I Won't Kiss You . . . I'll Send Your English Girl': Homoerotic Desire in 'A Farewell to Arms.'" *Hemingway Review* 15 (Fall 1995): 42–53.

Conroy, Stephen S. "Sinclair Lewis's Sociological Imagination." *American Literature* 42 (November 1970): 348–362.

Cooper, Ilene. "Giving and Receiving." *Booklist* 89 (April 15, 1993): 1,506.

Corbett, Edward P. J. "Raise High the Barriers, Censors." *America* 54 (January 7, 1961): 441–444.

Croley, Laura Sagolla. "The Rhetoric of Reform in Stoker's *Dracula*: Depravity, Decline, and the Fin-de-siecle 'Residium.'" *Criticism* 37 (Winter 1995): 85–108.

"Daddy Is out of the Closet: *Daddy's Roommate* by Michael Willhoite/*Heather Has Two Mommies* by Leslea Newman." *Newsweek* 117 (January 7, 1991): 60.

Darling, R. L. "Goose Feathers." *IFC ALA Newsletter on Intellectual Freedom* 69 (May 1972): 97–98.

Davis, Mavis Wormley. "Black Images in Children's Literature: Revised Editions Needed." *Library Journal*, January 15, 1972, pp. 261–263.

Djos, Matt. "Alcoholism in Ernest Hemingway's *The Sun Also Rises*: A Wine and Roses Perspective on the Lost Generation." *Hemingway Review* 14 (Spring 1995): 64–78.

Donaldson, Scott. "Censorship and 'A Farewell to Arms.'" *Studies in American Fiction* 19 (Spring 1991): 85–93.

Doyle, Robert P. *Caution! Some People Consider These Books Dangerous. IFC ALA Newsletter on Intellectual Freedom.* Chicago: ALA, 1996.

Early, Gerald. "Their Malcolm, My Problem." *Harper's* 285 (December 1992): 62–74.

Ebersole, Peter. "Dickey's *Deliverance*." *Explicator* 49 (Summer 1991): 249–251.

Egan, James. "Sacral Parody in the Fiction of Stephen King." *Journal of Popular Culture* 23 (Winter 1989): 125–141.

Egan, John M. "Golding's View of Man." *America* 108 (January 26, 1963): 140–141.

Elliott, Ira. "Performance Art: Jake Barnes and 'Masculine' Signification in *The Sun Also Rises*." *American Literature* 67 (March 1995): 77–94.

"'Elmer Gantry' Banned in Boston." *Publishers Weekly*, April 16, 1927, p. 1,569.

Estes, Sally. "Cormier, Robert. *We All Fall Down*." *Booklist* 15 (September 1991): 137.

"Final Exit." *Economist* 320, no. 7724 (September 14, 1991): 104.

"*Final Exit* Author Decries Ban." *Washington Post*, March 11, 1992, p. B4.

Finnessy, Patrick K. "Drowning in Dichotomy: Interpreting *The Drowning of Stephan Jones*." *ALAN Review* 24, no. 3 (Spring 1998): 24–27.

"Florida Officials Yield on Book Ban." *New York Times*, May 15, 1987, p. D18.

Fox-Genovese, Elizabeth. "Myth and History: Discourse of Origins in Zora Neale Hurston and Maya Angelou." *Black American Literature Forum* 42 (Summer 1990): 221–235.

Francisco, Jamie. "Book-Ban Debate Is Long, Impassioned: More Than 350 Sign Up to Speak to School Board." *Chicago Tribune*, May 26, 2006, p. 2NW.1.

———. "Explicit Move Is Made to Ban Books from Reading List." *Chicago Tribune*, May 24, 2006, p. 2NS.8.

Fuller, Ruth. "Some Parents Urge Board to Ban Book: School Official Says Book Is Relevant to Incoming Freshmen." *Chicago Tribune*, June 22, 2009, p. 1.8.

Gebhard, Ann O. "The Emerging Self: Young Adult and Classic Novels of the Black Experience." *English Journal* 82 (September 1993): 50–54.

Glasser, Ronald. "Dan Quayle's Parents Were Right: Having a Son in the Guard Was Better than Having Him Maimed." *Washington Post*, August 28, 1988. p. B-2.

Goldberg, Beverly. "Captain Underpants Yanked Again." *American Libraries* 33, issue 5 (May 2005): 23.

———. "Stephan Jones Submersed." *American Libraries* 33, issue 7 (August 2002): 25.

———. "*We All Fall Down* Restricted." *American Libraries* 31 (May 2000): 23.

Goldman, Ari L. "After 14 Months, a Vote on 'the Books.'" *New York Times*, May 22, 1977, p. 50.

Grant, S. S., and S. E. Angoff. "Massachusetts Censorship." *Boston University Law Review* 10 (1946): 147.

Green Daniel. "A World Worth Laughing At: *Catch-22* and the Humor of Black Humor." *Studies in the Novel* 27 (Summer 1995): 186–196.

Greenway, Betty. "Chris Crutcher—Hero or Villain?" *ALAN Review*, Fall 1994, pp. 19–22.

Hale, Dorothy J. "*As I Lay Dying*'s Heterogeneous Discourse." *Novel: A Forum on Fiction* 23 (Fall 1989): 5–23.

Hardigg, Viva. "Censors at Work." *U.S. News & World Report* 117 (September 26, 1994): 29.

Hartshorne, Thomas L. "Horatio Alger in Harlem: Manchild in the Promised Land." *Journal of American Studies* 24 (August 1990): 243–248.

Hartvigsen, M. Kip. "Haven Peck's Legacy in *A Day No Pigs Would Die*." *English Journal* 74 (April 1985): 41–45.

Hawkins, H. "Opening the Closet Door: Services for Gay, Lesbian, and Bisexual Teens." *Colorado Libraries* 20 (1994): 28–31.

Hayes, Elizabeth. "Tension between Darl and Jewel." *Southern Literary Journal* 24 (Spring 1992): 49–61.

Haynes, V. Dion. "Book Ban at School Stirs Debate." *Chicago Tribune*, March 5, 1992, p. 1.

"Hearings Held on Ban of Vietnam War Book." *New York Times*, December 22, 1981, p. A-9.

"Heather's Two Mommies, Three Censors." *Atlanta Journal-Constitution*, July 27, 1993, p. H-4.

Hechivger, Fred M. "Censorship Rises in the Nation's Public Schools." *New York Times*, January 3, 1984, p. C-7.

Hendershot, Cyndy. "Vampire and Replicant: The One-Sex Body in a Two-Sex World." *Science-Fiction Studies* 22 (November 1995): 373–398.

Herrick, Robert. "What Is Dirt?" *Bookman* 70 (November 1929): 258–262.

Hildebrand, Joan M. "Books for Children: *Daddy's Roommate*." *Childhood Education* 70 (1994): 306.

———. "Books for Children: *Heather Has Two Mommies*." *Childhood Education* 70 (1994): 305.

Hitchens, Christopher. "The Grimmest Tales." *Vanity Fair*, January 1994, pp. 26–30.

Hohne, Karen A. "The Spoken Word in the Works of Stephen King." *Journal of Popular Culture* 28 (Fall 1994): 93–103.

Ippolito, Milo. "Board Members Expect Book to Remain on Shelves." *Atlanta Journal-Constitution*, August 3, 1998, p. JJ-03.

———. "Book-Banning Vote Not Likely until August." *Atlanta Journal-Constitution*, July 14, 1998, p. JJ-02.

———. "Library Board Wants Book Out: Removal to Rest on Legal Call." *Atlanta Journal-Constitution*, June 9, 1998, p. JJ-01.

———. "Library Votes Rare Wins for Conservatives." *Atlanta Journal-Constitution*, June 14, 1998, p. JJ-01.

James, Jamie. "Review of *The Basketball Diaries*." *American Book Review* 2 (February 1980): 9.

Jenkins, C. "From Queer to Gay and Back Again: Young Adult Novels with Gay/Lesbian/Queer Content, 1969–1997." *Library Quarterly* 68, no. 3: 298–334.

Johnson, Ellen. "Geographic Context and Ethnic Context: Joel Chandler Harris and Alice Walker." *Mississippi Quarterly* 60 (Spring 2007): 235–255.

Kakutani, Michiko. "The Famed Will Gather to Read the Forbidden." *New York Times*, April 5, 1982, p. C-11.

Keilman, John, and Jamie Francisco. "Book-Ban Fights Are Far from Over: Reading Lists Face Scrutiny across the State." *Chicago Tribune*, May 28, 2006, p. 4C.1.

Kermode, Frank. "'Obscenity' and the 'Public Interest.'" *New American Review* 3 (April 1968): 229–244.

Kincaid, Nanci. "As Me and Addie Lay Dying." *Southern Review* 30 (Summer 1994): 582–595.

Kirschenbaum, Gayle. "*The Basketball Diaries* Gets Bounced around in a Georgia Public Library." *School Library Journal* 44 (October 1998): 18.

"Kite Runner, The." *Publishers Weekly* (May 12, 2003): 43.

Klein, Norma. "Some Thoughts on Censorship: An Author Symposium." *Top of the News* 39 (Winter 1983): 137–153.

Krug, Judith. "Mother Goose: Old Nursery Rhymes." *IFC ALA Newsletter on Intellectual Freedom* (May 1983): 107.

Lands, David, and Darren Summers. "'Exit' Ban." *USA Today*, March 13, 1992, p. 9-A.

Lane, James B. "Violence and Sex in the Post-War Popular Urban Novel: With a Consideration of Harold Robbins's *A Stone for Danny Fisher* and Hubert Selby, Jr.'s, *Last Exit to Brooklyn*." *Journal of Popular Culture* 8 (Fall 1974): 295–308.

Lanes, Selma G. "Doctor Dolittle, Innocent Again." *New York Times Book Review*, August 28, 1988, p. 20.

Leary, Timothy, and Ralph Metzner. "Hermann Hesse: Poet of the Interior Journey." *Psychedelic Review* 1 (1963): 167–182.

Leider, Paula. "Does Huck Finn Belong in My Classroom? Reflections of Cultural Choice, Multicultural Education, and Diversity." *Multicultural Education* 13, no. 4 (Summer 2006): 49–50.

Lesesne, Teri S. "Censorship: The Mind You Close May Be Your Own." *Voices from the Middle* 13 (September 2005): 72–77.

Levantis, Angie, and *St. Louis Post Dispatch*. "Children's Book on Gay Penguins Has Parents Concerned." *The Record* (Bergen County, N.J.), December 8, 2006, p. A27.

Lewis-House, Nancy. "Books Worth Teaching Even Though They Have Proven Controversial: *The Chocolate War* by Robert Cormier." *English Journal* 82 (April 1993): 88.

"L.I. Parents Draft Protest to Nyquist on School Book Ban." *New York Times*, March 24, 1976, p. 41.

Lisack, Thomas. "Books Worth Teaching Even Though They Have Proven Controversial: *Invisible Man* by Ralph Ellison." *English Journal* 82 (April 1993): 88.

"L.I. Schools Press Effort to Avert Book Ban Trial." *New York Times*, March 8, 1981, p. 40.

"L.I. Students File Suit to Overturn School Book Ban." *New York Times*, January 5, 1977, p. 23.

Livingston, Myra Cohn. "The Light in His Attic." *New York Times Book Review* 91 (March 9, 1986): 36–7.

Lorraine, Walter. "Lois Lowry." *Horn Book Magazine* 70 (July–August 1994): 423–426.

MacDonald, Mary. "Parents Say Preteens in Cobb Get Too Raunchy a Reading List." *Atlanta Journal-Constitution*, April 23, 2001, p. A-1.

Maeroff, Gene I. "Book Ban Splits a Queens School District." *New York Times*, May 9, 1971, pp. BQ-71, 82.

Mallet, Isabelle. "Unruly Local Color." *New York Times Book Review*, March 7, 1948, p. 26.

Mandel, Miriam. "Ferguson and Lesbian Love: Unspoken Subplots in 'A Farewell to Arms.'" *Hemingway Review* 14 (Fall 1994): 18–24.

Manfred, Frederick. "Sinclair Lewis: A Portrait." *American Scholar* 23 (Spring 1954): 162–184.

Massie, Dorothy C. "Censorship in the Schools: Something Old and Something New." *Today's Education* 69 (November/December 1980): 56–62.

Matter, William W. "The Utopian Tradition and Aldous Huxley." *Science Fiction Studies* 2 (1975): 146–151.

McClure, Robert C. "Literature, the Law of Obscenity, and the Constitution." *Minnesota Law Review* 38 (March 1954): 325.

McCullough, Debbie. "Idealism and Reality in the Works of Laura Ingalls Wilder." *English in Education* 26 (Spring 1992): 33–37.

McDonnell, Christine. "New Voices, New Visions: Chris Crutcher." *Horn Book Magazine*, May–June 1988, pp. 332–334.

McDowell, Edwin. "Publishing: When Book Is Ruled out by Library." *New York Times*, January 21, 1983, p. C28.

McGee, Tim. "The Adolescent Novel in AP English." *English Journal*, April 1992, pp. 57–58.

Meriwether, James B. "The Dashes in Hemingway's *A Farewell to Arms*." *The Papers of the Bibliographical Society of America* 58 (Fourth Quarter 1964): 449–457.

Messiano, Lindalee. "Even When It Offends." *Library Journal*, May 15, 1969, p. 2,031.

Meyer, Howard N. "Neutralism Isn't Neutral." *CIBC Bulletin* 11 (1980): 13.

Miller, Warren. "One Score in Harlem—Review of *Manchild in the Promised Land*, by Claude Brown." *Saturday Review*, August 28, 1965, p. 49.

Mills, Claudia. "From Obedience to Autonomy: Moral Growth in the 'Little House' Books." *Children's Literature: An International Journal* 24 (1996): 127–140.

"'Miss Jane Pittman' Is Removed from a Class at Blacks' Behest." *New York Times*, January 22, 1995, sec. 1, 19.

Modern Fiction Studies (special Burgess issue) 27 (Autumn 1981).

Moore, Everett T. "A Rationale for Bookburners: A Further Word from Ray Bradbury." *ALA Bulletin* 55 (May 1961): 403–404.

Moore, Michael. "Pathological Communication Patterns in Heller's *Catch-22*." *Et Cetera* 52 (Winter 1995): 431–459.

Moore, Robert B. "From Rags to Witches: Stereotypes, Distortions and Anti-Humanism in Fairy Tales." *CIBC Bulletin* 8 (1975): 1.

Moorhead, Michael. "Dickey's *Deliverance*." *Explicator* 51 (Summer 1993): 247–248.

Morrell, Virginia. "Called 'Trimates,' Three Bold Women Shaped Their Field." *Science* 260 (April 16, 1993): 420–425.

Nahmod, Sheldon H. "Controversy in the Classroom: The High School Teacher and Freedom of Expression." *George Washington University Law Review* 39 (July 1974): 1,031.

Nelms, Elizabeth D. "Books, Films, and Culture: Reading in the Classroom: *The Chocolate War*/'The Chocolate War.'" *English Journal*, January 1991, p. 85.

Nelson, Emmanuel. "Critical Deviance: Homophobia and the Reception of James Baldwin's Fiction." *Journal of American Culture* 14 (Fall 1991): 91–96.

Nelson, Randy F. "Banned in Boston and Elsewhere." *The Almanac of American Letters.* Los Altos, Calif.: William Kaufman, 1981.

"New in Paperback." *Washington Post*, August 16, 1987, p. X12.

Newsletter on Intellectual Freedom. Judith F. Krug, ed. Chicago: American Library Association, Intellectual Freedom Committee. Numerous issues from April 1956 through March 2005.

Nolan, Kenneth P. "Book Ban Still Splits School Unit in Queens." *New York Times*, November 26, 1971, pp. BQ-11, 46.

Oboler, Eli M. "Idaho School Librarians and Salinger's *Catcher in the Rye:* A Candid Report." *Idaho Librarian* 15 (October 1963): 137–139.

Olson, Renee. "Battles over Books Usher in New School Year." *School Library Journal* 41 (October 1995): 10–11.

O'Neil, Robert M. "Libraries, Liberty and the First Amendment." *University of Cincinnati Law Review* 42:2 (1973): 209–252.

Overmyer, Janet. "The Invisible Man and White Women." *Notes on Contemporary Literature* 6 (May 1976): 13–15.

Pace, Eric. "Fears of Local Censorship Haunt the Book Trade." *New York Times*, January 8, 1974, p. 26.

Parker, Ian. "Making Advances." *New Yorker*, April 1, 1996, pp. 72–80.

Parr, J. L. "Calder Willingham: The Forgotten Novelist." *Critique* 11 (1969): 57–65.

Pearse, Emma. "U.S.: Younger Readers Face New Adventures in Censorship." *WOMENSENEWS*, April 13, 2005, p. 1.

Pinsker, Sanford. "Individual Authors: A Rotten Way to Be Wounded." *Journal of Modern Literature* 18 (Spring 1993): 277–278.

"Play on Br'er Rabbit Banned in Savannah." *New York Times*, December 11, 1986, p. A24.

Podhoretz, Norman. "Gibbsville and New Leeds: The America of John O'Hara and Mary McCarthy." *Commentary* 1 (March 1956): 493–499.

"Queens Book Ban Upheld by Judge." *New York Times*, August 5, 1971, p. 30.

Quinn, Judy, and Michael Rogers. "*Final Exit* Makes Firm Entrance into Public Libraries." *Library Journal* 116, no. 15 (September 15, 1991): 15.

Ray, Karen. "Review of *The Giver.*" *New York Times Book Review*, October 31, 1993, p. 26.

"Recorded Book Wins 2009 Odyssey Award for *The Absolutely True Diary of a Part-Time Indian*." *Young Adult Library Services* 7, no. 3 (Spring 2009): 18–19.

Rice, Anne M. "Still Good Reading: Adolescent Novels Written before 1967–*A Separate Peace* by John Knowles." *English Journal*, April 1992, p. 88.

Richards, David. "Theater for Soldier Survivors." *Washington Post*, October 12, 1988. p. D-01.

Rigolet, François. "Rabelais, Misogyny, and Christian Charity: Biblical Intertextuality and the Renaissance Crisis of Exemplarity." *PMLA* 109 (March 1994): 225–237.

Rimer, Sara. "Gatsby's Green Light Beckons a New Generation of Strivers." *New York Times*, February 17, 2008, p. A1.

Roberts, Terry. "Irreconcilable Talents: Thomas Wolfe's Struggle to Compose *Of Time and the River.*" *Mississippi Quarterly* 43 (Winter 1989): 22–32.

Rothbauer, Paulette M., and Lynne E. F. McKechnie. "Gay and Lesbian Fiction for Young Adults: A Survey of Holdings in Canadian Public Libraries." *Collection Building* 18, no. 1 (1999): 32–39.

Rothman, Nathan L. "A Slick Toughie." *Saturday Review of Literature*, May 22, 1948, p. 27.

Rowden, Terry. "A Play of Abstractions: Race, Sexuality, and Community in James Baldwin's *Another Country.*" *Southern Review* 29 (Winter 1993): 41–50.

Rudat, Wolfgang. "Sexual Dilemma in *The Sun Also Rises:* Hemingway's Count and the Education of Jacob Barnes." *Hemingway Review* 8 (Spring 1989): 2–13.

St. Lifer, Evan. "*Daddy's Roommate* Challenged in VT." *Library Journal* 120 (July 1995): 14–16.

"Sambo Banned by Montgomery County Schools." *Library Journal*, September 15, 1971, pp. 2,813–2,814.

"Sambo Removal Sought by National Black Coalition." *Library Journal*, January 15, 1972, pp. 237–238.

Sauerwein, Kristina. "Irate Grandma Fights 'Captain Underpants.'" *Los Angeles Times*, June 4, 2003, p. 21.

———. "Super Diaper Baby Survives: A Riverside Schools Committee Rejects a Request to Ban the Toilet-Humor Tone." *Los Angeles Times*, June 13, 2003, p. B-1.

Scala, Elizabeth. "Canace and the Chaucer Canon." *Chaucer Review* 30 (1995): 15–39.

Schaffer, Talia. "A Wilde Desire Took Me: The Homoerotic History of 'Dracula.'" *ELH* 61 (Summer 1994): 381–425.

Schone, Mark. "Uncle Remus Is Dead, Long Live Uncle Remus." *Oxford American* (January/February 2003): 86–92.

"School Association Protests Book Ban." *New York Times*, March 4, 1948, p. 33.

"School Board Bans Morrison's 'Beloved.'" *Chicago Tribune*, May 17, 1998, p. 8.

Schwab, A. T. "Irish Author and American Critic." *Nineteenth Century Fiction* 8 (March 1954): 256–277.

Seed, David. "The Flight from the Good Life: 'Fahrenheit 451' in the Context of Postwar American Dystopias." *Journal of American Studies* 28, pt. 2 (August 1994): 225–240.

Segel, Elizabeth. "Laura Ingalls Wilder's America: An Unflinching Assessment." *Children's Literature in Education* 8 (February 1978): 63–70.

Senf, Carol A. "Dracula and the Victorian Male Sexual Imagination." *International Journal of Women's Studies* 3 (1980): 455.

Sharpe, Ernest, Jr. "The Man Who Changed His Skin." *American Heritage* 40 (February 1989): 44–55.

"Sherman Alexie Gets National Book Award." *Seattle Post-Intelligencer*, November 15, 2007, p. C1.

Shogren, Elizabeth, and Douglas Frantz. "Political, Religious Right Lead School Book Ban Efforts Censorship: A Survey by a Liberal-Leaning Group Finds 41% of 347 Attempts to Restrict Reading Material Succeeded. *The Color Purple* Is One Target." *Los Angeles Times*, September 2, 1993, p. 14.

Silver, Roy R. "High Court Appeal Likely on Book Ban." *New York Times*, August 5, 1979, p. 17.

———. "L.I. School Board Bans Nine Books." *New York Times*, July 29, 1976, p. 37.

Sloan, James Park. "Kosinski's War." *New Yorker*, October 10, 1994, pp. 46–53.

Solotaroff, Robert. "Sexual Identity in 'A Farewell to Arms.'" *Hemingway Review* 9 (Fall 1989): 2–17.

Starnes, Joe Samuel. "Georgia: We Are Finally Coming to Claim Our Writers." *Washington Post*, November 11, 2007, p. 1.

"Steinbeck Novel Creates Controversy." *Los Angeles Times*, June 3, 1978, p. 1.

"Steinbeck's *East of Eden*." *The Asterisk: An Occasional Journal of English Traditions*, October 1978, p. 2.

"*Strange Fruit* Barred by Mails, Then Admitted at Sender's Risk." *New York Times*, May 16, 1944, p. 1.

Straus, Dorothea. "Remembering Jerzy Kosinski." *Partisan Review* 60 (Winter 1993): 138–142.

Strychacz, Thomas. "Dramatizations of Manhood in Hemingway's *In Our Time* and *The Sun Also Rises*." *American Literature* 61 (May 1989): 245–260.

"Success Stories: Libraries." *Newsletter on Intellectual Freedom* 56, no. 2 (March 2007)): 71–72. First reported in the *Bradenton Herald*, January 2007.

"Success Stories: Libraries." *Newsletter on Intellectual Freedom* 56, no. 4 (July 2007): 163–164. First reported in the *Stockton Record*, May 5, 2007.

"Success Stories: Libraries." *Newsletter on Intellectual Freedom* 57, no. 3 (May 2008): 115–117. First reported in American *Libraries online, March 7, 2008; Loudoun Times-Mirror*, February 27, 2008.

"Success Stories: Libraries." *Newsletter on Intellectual Freedom* 58, no. 1 (January 2009): 21–22. First reported in the *Washington Post*, October 23, 2008.

"Success Stories: Libraries." *Newsletter on Intellectual Freedom* 58, no. 2 (March 2009): 55–56. First reported in the *Des Moines Register*, December 14 and 15, 2009.

"Suicide Manual for Terminally Ill Stirs Heated Debate." *Wall Street Journal*, July 12, 1991, p. B-1.

"Suit Challenges School Book Ban." *New York Times*, May 14, 1987, p. A18.

Swanson, Stevenson. "Penguin Papas Lead a List of Literary Controversies." *Los Angeles Times*, October 7, 2007, p. A20.

Trice, Dawn Turner. "'Banned Books' Event Highlights Need for Liberty." *Chicago Tribune*, October 4, 2004, p. 1.

Trilling, Lionel. "John O'Hara Observes Our Mores." *New York Times Book Review*, March 18, 1945, pp. 1, 9. Reprinted as the introduction to *Selected Short Stories of John O'Hara*. New York: Random House, 1956.

Twitchell, James B. "Women and Vampires: *Dracula* as a Victorian Novel." *Midwest Quarterly* 18 (1977): 392–405.

Ulin, David L. "Book Reviews—*Cain's Book* by Alexander Trocchi, with an Introduction by Richard Seaver and a Foreword by Greil Marcus." *Review of Contemporary Fiction* 12, no. 3 (Fall 1992): 209.

"Uncle Remus Told Stories and Roosevelt, His Host, Told Stories." *New York Times*, November 19, 1907, p. 1.

"Using Adolescent Novels as Transitions to Literary Classics: *Bless the Beasts and Children.*" *English Journal* 78 (March 1989): 83–84.

"Veterans Protest Book Ban." *New York Times*, December 22, 1981, p. A-9.

Vincent, Ted. "The Garveyite Parents of Malcolm X." *Black Scholar* 20 (March 1989): 10–13.

Waldrep, Shelton. "Being Bridges: Cleaver, Baldwin and Lorde and African-American Sexism and Sexuality." *Journal of Homosexuality* 26 (1993): 167–180.

Wascoe, Dan, and *Minneapolis Star Tribune*. "'N-word' Fight Over Classic: Couple Want 'Huck Finn' Off Reading List." *The Record* (Bergen County, N.J.), March 23, 2007, p. A20.

Webb, C. Anne. "The Battle Continues." *English Journal* 84 (September 1995): 123–124.

———. "Censorship in the Pennsylvania Schools." *English Journal* 84 (April 1995): 84.

Wertime, Richard A. "Psychic Vengeance in *Last Exit to Brooklyn.*" *Literature and Psychology* 24 (November 1974): 153–166.

"*Whale Talk* Beached for Bad Words." *American Libraries* 36 (May 2005): 15.

Wisse, Ruth. "A Romance of the Secret Annex." *New York Times Book Review*, July 2, 1989, p. 2.

Wolf, V. "The Gay Family in Literature for Young People." *Children's Literature in Education* 20 (1989): 275–288.

Wolf, Virginia L. "The Symbolic Center: *Little House in the Big Woods.*" *Children's Literature in Education* 13 (Fall 1982): 107–114.

"Xerox Withdraws 'Mother Goose.'" *Library Journal* 94 (May 15, 1969): 2,034.

Yardley, Jonathan. "'Gatsby': The Greatest of Them All." *Washington Post*, January 2, 2007, p. C1.

Yarrow, Andrew L. "Allen Ginsberg's 'Howl' in a New Controversy." *New York Times*, January 6, 1988, p. C2.

Zwingle, Erla. "The Importance of Being Ernest." *Chicago Tribune*, December 3, 2006, p. 16.

ONLINE RESOURCES

American Civil Liberties Union of Wisconsin. "ACLU of Wisconsin Fights School Censorship of Gay-Themed Books." Press Release. October 6, 1998. Available online. URL: www.qrd.org/qrd/education/1998/misc.news-10.08.98. Accessed December 10, 2009.

———. "ACLU to Sue WI School District for Censoring Gay-Themed Books." Press Release. December 22, 1998. Available online. URL: www.theroc.org/roc-news.school.html. Accessed December 1, 2009.

American Library Association. "Banned Barron Books Are Back for Now." Available online. URL: www.ala/org/ala/alonline/currentnews/newsarchive/1999/march1999/bannedbarron.cfm. Accessed December 10, 2009.

"'And Tango Makes Three' Prompts Serious Challenge in Massachusetts School." *School Library Journal*. Available online. URL: http://www.schoollibraryjournal.com/index.asp?layout=articlePrint&articleID=CA6440187. Accessed January 6, 2010.

Associated Press. "Homosexual Themes in Schools." 1996. Available online. URL: http://www.angelfire.com/ga/page451/articles.html. Accessed December 1, 2009.

"Award-winning Book Frequent Target in Schools." Associated Press. July 8, 2001. Available online. URL: http://www.freedomforum.org/templates/document.asp?documentID=14344&printerfriend. Accessed July 29, 2010.

"Brave New Schools: Homosexual Book for 1st Graders—Parents Outraged over Story Where Prince Finds Love with Another Prince." *World Net Daily*. March 18, 2004. Available online. URL: http://www.wnd.com/news/article.asp?ARTICLE_ID=37643. Accessed July 29, 2010.

Dexheimer, Eric. "Is SuperFreakonomics Inappropriate? No—but Freakonomics Is." *The Statesman*. Available online. URL: http://www.statesman.com/blogs/content/shared-gen/blogs/austin/investigative/entries/2010/01/08/is_superfreakonomics_racist_no.html. Accessed July 29, 2010.

Dorning, Anne-Marie. "Library Book Riles Small Wisconson Town: 'Baby Be-Bop' and Its Gay Teen Angst Too Much for Christian Civil Liberties Union" *ABC News* (June 19, 2009). Available online. URL: http://abcnews.go.com/us/story?id=7874866. Accessed December 12, 2009.

"Euthanasia's Most Famous Textbook." Final Exit Web site. Available online. URL: http://www.finalexit.org. Accessed July 29, 2010.

"*Fallen Angels* Resurrected in Arlington, Texas, Schools." *Newsletter for Intellectual Freedom*. October 2, 2000. Available online. URL: http://www.ala.org/ala/alonline/currentnews/newsarchive/2000/october2000/fallenangels.htm. Accessed July 29, 2010.

Foust, Michael. "Are Public Schools the Next Battleground over Homosexuality?" *Baptist Press*. June 7, 2005. Available online. URL: http://www.bpnews.net/bpnews.asp?Id=20922. Accessed July 29, 2010.

Giorgetti, Mario. "A Sober Guide to Ending It All." *Green Left Weekly*. Available online. URL: http://www.greenleft.org.au/back/1992/71/71p21b.htm. Accessed July 29, 2010.

"*The Giver* Goes Back to Middle School Classrooms." Associated Press. October 13, 1999. Available online. URL: http://www.freedomforum.org/templates/document.asp?documentID=10135&printerfriend. Accessed July 29, 2010.

Goldberg, Beverly. "Milwaukee Group Seeks Fiery Alternative to Materials Challenge." *American Library Online*. Available online. URL: http://www.alaorg/ala/alonline/currentnews/newsarchive/2009/june2009/westendbabybebop060309.cfm. Accessed December 12, 2009.

Hernandez, Kelli. "Choctaw Committee: Keep *Kite Runner*." *Northwest Florida Daily News* (Fort Walton Beach), November 21, 2008. Available online. URL: http://www.nwfdailynews.com/news/school-12902-committee-district.html. Accessed December 26, 2009.

———. "District Committee Recommends 'The Kite Runner' Stay on Reading Lists." *Northwest Florida Daily News* (Fort Walton Beach), December 14, 2008. Available online. URL: http://www.nwfdailynews.com/news/book-13508-district-school.html. Accessed December 27, 2009.

———. "Parents Object to 'Kite Runner.'" *Northwest Florida Daily News* (Fort Walton Beach), November 15, 2008. Available online. URL: http://www.nwfdailynews.com/news/book-12772-school-stovall.html. Accessed December 27, 2009.

———. "School Board Approves 'Kite Runner.'" *Northwest Florida Daily News* (Fort Walton Beach), January 13, 2009. Available online. URL: http://www.nwfdailynews.com/news/ board-14162-school-schools.html. Accessed December 26, 2009.

"Homosexual Kids' Book Now Best Seller." *World Net Daily.* March 20, 2004. Available online. URL: http://www.wnd.com/news/article.asp?ARTICLE_ID=37664. Accessed December 26, 2009.

"Idaho City's School Board Drops Book Ban." Associated Press. Available online. URL: http://www.firstamendmentcenter.org/news.aspx?id21029. Accessed January 12, 2010.

Kern, Kate McCardell. "'Kite' Still Flies: School Board Rejects Book Ban." *JCFloridian.com.* Available online. URL: http://www2.jcfloridan.com/jcf/news/local/article/kite_still_flies_school_board_rejects_book_ban/32549. Accessed December 12, 2009.

Kirch, Claire. "Chicago School Keeps Alexie Novel on Summer Reading List." *Publishers Weekly* (June 25, 2009). Available online. URL: http://www.publishersweekly.com/article/CA6666906.html?nid=2788&source=title&rid=630002055 Accessed December 15, 2009.

"Kite Runner Joins Gay Penguins on Top 10 Books Americans Want Banned." *Europe Intelligence Wire.* April 16, 2009. *General Business File ASAP.* Gale Research. Available online. URL: http://find.galegroup.com/gps/start.do?prodId=IPS&userGroupName=bergen_main. Accessed December 27, 2009.

Klinka, Karen. "Children's Books Come under Fire at Library." *Oklahoman.* May 5, 2005. Available online. URL: http://www.lisnews.com/articles/05/05/07/1914217.shtml?tid=78. Accessed December 27, 2009.

Martinez, Al. "Life Support: A Home for 'Captain Underpants'—Where Do the Scatological Children's Books Belong? Not in the School Library, Says Captain Grandma." *Post-Gazette Lifestyle.* July 14, 2003. Available online. URL: http://www.post-gazette.com/lifestyle/20030714life6.asp. Accessed December 27, 2009.

McClatchy Newspapers. "Schools Chief Bans Book on Penguins." Available online. URL: http://www.boston.com/news/nation/articles/2006/12/20/schools_chief_bans_book_on_penguins?mode=PF. Accessed January 15, 2010.

"Mockingbird Returns to Oklahoma High School's Reading List." Associated Press (October 15, 2001). Available online. URL: http://www.freedomforum.org/templates/document.asp?ID=15150. Accessed August 5, 2010.

"Pastor's Complaint Prompts District to Pull Book from Classroom." Available online. URL: http://www.firstamendmentcenter.org/news.aspx?id=18198. Accessed December 16, 2009.

Pierri, Vincent. "Books Stirring Controversy at Antioch High School." *Daily Herald,* June 19, 2009. Available online. URL: www.dailyherald.com/story/?id=302477. Accessed December 16, 2009.

"Suicide Book Challenged in Schools." *USA Today,* July 20, 2001. Available online. URL: http://www.usatoday.com/life/books/2001-07-20-the-giver.htm. Accessed December 16, 2009.

Tran, Mai. "Parents Ask School District to Ban 'Cuckoo's Nest.'" *Los Angeles Times,* December 3, 2000. Available online. URL: http://articles.latimes.com/2000/dec/03/local/me-60611. Accessed December 16, 2009.

"Vietnam Books, Steinbeck Banned by Mississippi High School." *Newsletter for Intellectual Freedom.* January 13, 2003. Available online. URL: http://www.ala.org/ala/alonline/currentnews/newsarchive/2003/january2003/vietnambooks.htm. Accessed December 16, 2009.

Wise, Warren. "Controversial Book Pulled Out of Schools." *Post and Courier,* February 22, 2008. Available online. URL: http://www.postandcourier.com/

news/2008/feb22/controversal_book_pulled_out_schools. Accessed December 12, 2009.

"Woman: School Should Drop Steinbeck Book." Available online. URL: http://kmbc. com/education/17530918/detail.html. Accessed August 10, 2010.

Young, Marcie. "Book Too Raw for School?" *Charlotte Observer*, February 24, 2008. Available online. URL: http://find.galegroup.com/gps/infomark.do?&contentSet= IAC-Documents&type=retrieve&tabID=T004&prodId=IPS&docId=CJ1752 96057&source=gale&userGroupName=bergen_main&version=1.0>.Accessed December 28, 2009.

WORKS DISCUSSED IN OTHER VOLUMES OF THIS SERIES

BANNED BOOKS ON POLITICAL GROUNDS

THE AFFLUENT SOCIETY
John Kenneth Galbraith

AFTER SUCH KNOWLEDGE, WHAT FORGIVENESS?—
  MY ENCOUNTERS WITH KURDISTAN
Jonathan C. Randal

THE AGE OF KEYNES
Robert Lekachman

ALL QUIET ON THE WESTERN FRONT
Erich Maria Remarque

AMERICA IN LEGEND
Richard M. Dorson

AMERICAN CIVICS
William H. Hartley and William S. Vincent

THE AMERICAN PAGEANT: A HISTORY OF THE REPUBLIC
Thomas A. Bailey

ANDERSONVILLE
MacKinlay Kantor

ANIMAL FARM
George Orwell

THE APPOINTMENT
Herta Müller

AREOPAGITICA
John Milton

THE BASTARD OF ISTANBUL
Elif Shafak

BLACK BOY
Richard Wright

*BLOODS: AN ORAL HISTORY OF THE VIETNAM WAR BY
    BLACK VETERANS*
Wallace Terry

BORN ON THE FOURTH OF JULY
Ron Kovic

BOSS: RICHARD J. DALEY OF CHICAGO
Mike Royko

BURGER'S DAUGHTER
Nadine Gordimer

BURY MY HEART AT WOUNDED KNEE
Dee Brown

BUS STOP (CHEZHAN)
Gao Xingjian

*BY WAY OF DECEPTION: THE MAKING AND UNMAKING
    OF A MOSSAD OFFICER*
Victor Ostrovsky and Claire Hoy

CANCER WARD
Aleksandr Solzhenitsyn

CAT'S CRADLE
Kurt Vonnegut, Jr.

THE CHINA LOBBY IN AMERICAN POLITICS
Ross Y. Koen

THE CIA AND THE CULT OF INTELLIGENCE
Victor Marchetti and John D. Marks

CITIES OF SALT
Abdul Rahman Munif

CITIZEN TOM PAINE
Howard Fast

THE FRAGILE FLAG
Jane Langton

THE FUGITIVE (PERBURUAN)
Pramoedya Ananta Toer

FUGITIVES (TAOWANG)
Gao Xingjian

GIRLS OF RIYADH
Rajaa Alsanea

THE GRAPES OF WRATH
John Steinbeck

THE GULAG ARCHIPELAGO 1918–1956
Aleksandr Solzhenitsyn

GULLIVER'S TRAVELS
Jonathan Swift

HANDBOOK FOR CONSCIENTIOUS OBJECTORS
Robert A. Seeley, editor

THE HOAX OF THE TWENTIETH CENTURY
Arthur R. Butz

I AM THE CHEESE
Robert Cormier

INSIDE RUSSIA TODAY
John Gunther

INSIDE THE COMPANY: CIA DIARY
Philip Agee

IN THE SPIRIT OF CRAZY HORSE
Peter Matthiessen

AN INTRODUCTION TO PROBLEMS OF AMERICAN CULTURE
Harold O. Rugg

THE INVISIBLE GOVERNMENT
David Wise and Thomas B. Ross

IT CAN'T HAPPEN HERE
Sinclair Lewis

JOHNNY GOT HIS GUN
Dalton Trumbo

THE JOKE (ŽERT)
Milan Kundera

A JOURNEY FROM ST. PETERSBURG TO MOSCOW
Aleksandr Nikolaevich Radishchev

JULIE OF THE WOLVES
Jean Craighead George

THE JUNGLE
Upton Sinclair

KEEPING FAITH: MEMOIRS OF A PRESIDENT
Jimmy Carter

KISS OF THE SPIDER WOMAN
Manuel Puig

THE LAND AND PEOPLE OF CUBA
Victoria Ortiz

LAND OF THE FREE: A HISTORY OF THE UNITED STATES
John W. Caughey, John Hope Franklin, and Ernest R. May

LAUGHING BOY
Oliver La Farge

EL LIBRO NEGRO DE LA JUSTICIA CHILENA
  (THE BLACK BOOK OF CHILEAN JUSTICE)
Alejandra Matus

THE MAN DIED: PRISON NOTES OF WOLE SOYINKA
Wole Soyinka

THE MANIFESTO OF THE COMMUNIST PARTY
Karl Marx and Friedrich Engels

MARXISM VERSUS SOCIALISM
Vladimir G. Simkhovitch

MEIN KAMPF
Adolf Hitler

LES MISÉRABLES
Victor Hugo

A MONTH AND A DAY: A DETENTION DIARY
Ken Saro-Wiwa

MY BROTHER SAM IS DEAD
James Lincoln Collier and Christopher Collier

MY NAME IS ASHER LEV
Chaim Potok

MY PEOPLE: THE STORY OF THE JEWS
Abba Eban

NELSON AND WINNIE MANDELA
Dorothy Hoobler and Thomas Hoobler

1984
George Orwell

NOVEL WITHOUT A NAME
Duong Thu Huong

OIL!
Upton Sinclair

ONE DAY IN THE LIFE OF IVAN DENISOVICH
Aleksandr Solzhenitsyn

*ONE PEOPLE, ONE DESTINY: THE CARIBBEAN AND
  CENTRAL AMERICA TODAY*
Don Rojas

*THE OPEN SORE OF A CONTINENT: A PERSONAL NARRATIVE
  OF THE NIGERIAN CRISIS*
Wole Soyinka

OUR LAND, OUR TIME: A HISTORY OF THE UNITED STATES
Joseph Robert Conlin

PARADISE OF THE BLIND
Duong Thu Huong

THE PATRIOT (HA PATRIOT)
THE QUEEN OF THE BATHTUB (MALKAT AMBATYA)
Hanoch Levin

THE POLITICS OF DISPOSSESSION
Edward W. Said

THE PRINCE
Niccolò Machiavelli

PRINCIPLES OF NATURE
Elihu Palmer

PROMISE OF AMERICA
Larry Cuban and Philip Roden

REPORT OF THE SIBERIAN DELEGATION
Leon Trotsky

THE RIGHTS OF MAN
Thomas Paine

RUSSIA
Vernon Ives

SECRECY AND DEMOCRACY: THE CIA IN TRANSITION
Stansfield Turner

EL SEÑOR PRESIDENTE (THE PRESIDENT)
Miguel Angel Asturias

SLAUGHTERHOUSE-FIVE, OR THE CHILDREN'S CRUSADE
Kurt Vonnegut, Jr.

SNOW
Orhan Pamuk

SPYCATCHER
Peter Wright

THE STATE AND REVOLUTION
Vladimir I. Lenin

STRONG WIND (VIENTO FUERTE)
THE GREEN POPE (EL PAPA VERDE)
Miguel Angel Asturias

THE STRUGGLE IS MY LIFE
Nelson Mandela

A SUMMARY VIEW OF THE RIGHTS OF BRITISH AMERICA
Thomas Jefferson

SYLVESTER AND THE MAGIC PEBBLE
William Steig

TEN DAYS THAT SHOOK THE WORLD
John Reed

THE THINGS THEY CARRIED
Tim O'Brien

THIS EARTH OF MANKIND
CHILD OF ALL NATIONS
Pramoedya Ananta Toer

365 DAYS
Ronald J. Glasser

TODAY'S ISMS: COMMUNISM, FASCISM, CAPITALISM, SOCIALISM
William Ebenstein

THE UGLY AMERICAN
William J. Lederer and Eugene Burdick

UNCLE TOM'S CABIN
Harriet Beecher Stowe

UNITED STATES–VIETNAM RELATIONS, 1945–1967
(THE PENTAGON PAPERS)
U.S. Department of Defense

THE VANĚK PLAYS
Václav Havel

WAITING
Ha Jin

WHY ARE WE IN VIETNAM?
Norman Mailer

*A WOMAN IN BERLIN: EIGHT WEEKS IN
  THE CONQUERED CITY*
Anonymous

*WORDS OF CONSCIENCE: RELIGIOUS STATEMENTS
  ON CONSCIENTIOUS OBJECTION*
A. Stauffer Curry, editor (first edition)
Shawn Perry, editor (ninth edition)

YANGTZE! YANGTZE!
Dai Qing

BANNED BOOKS ON RELIGIOUS GROUNDS
*ADDRESS TO THE CHRISTIAN NOBILITY OF THE GERMAN
  NATION*
Martin Luther

THE ADVANCEMENT OF LEARNING
Francis Bacon

THE AGE OF REASON
Thomas Paine

ALCIPHRON, OR THE MINUTE PHILOSOPHER
George Berkeley

THE ANALECTS
Confucius

ARCANA COELESTIA
Emanuel Swedenborg

THE BABYLONIAN CAPTIVITY OF THE CHURCH
Martin Luther

THE BATTLE FOR GOD
Karen Armstrong

THE BIBLE

THE BLIND OWL
Sadegh Hedayat

THE BLOUDY TENENT OF PERSECUTION
Roger Williams

THE BOOK OF COMMON PRAYER
Thomas Cranmer and others

THE CARTOONS THAT SHOOK THE WORLD
Jytte Klausen

CHILDREN OF THE ALLEY
Naguib Mahfouz

THE CHRISTIAN COMMONWEALTH
John Eliot

CHRISTIANITY NOT MYSTERIOUS
John Toland

CHRISTIANITY RESTORED
Michael Servetus

*CHURCH: CHARISM AND POWER: LIBERATION THEOLOGY
AND THE INSTITUTIONAL CHURCH*
Leonardo Boff

COLLOQUIES
Desiderius Erasmus

COMMENTARIES
Averroës

COMPENDIUM REVELATIONUM
Girolamo Savonarola

CONCERNING HERETICS
Sebastian Castellio

THE COURSE OF POSITIVE PHILOSOPHY
Auguste Comte

CREATIVE EVOLUTION
Henri Bergson

THE CRITIQUE OF PURE REASON
Immanuel Kant

THE DA VINCI CODE
Dan Brown

DE ECCLESIA
Jan Hus

DE INVENTORIBUS RERUM
Polydore Vergil

DE L'ESPRIT
Claude-Adrien Helvétius

DIALOGUE CONCERNING THE TWO CHIEF WORLD SYSTEMS
Galileo Galilei

DIALOGUES CONCERNING NATURAL RELIGION
David Hume

DISCOURSE ON METHOD
René Descartes

DON QUIXOTE
Miguel de Cervantes Saavedra

DRAGONWINGS
Laurence Yep

ÉMILE
Jean-Jacques Rousseau

ENCYCLOPÉDIE
Denis Diderot and Jean Le Rond d'Alembert, eds.

AN ESSAY CONCERNING HUMAN UNDERSTANDING
John Locke

ESSAYS
Michel de Montaigne

ETHICS
Baruch Spinoza

THE FABLE OF THE BEES
Bernard Mandeville

THE GUIDE OF THE PERPLEXED
Maimonides

HARRY POTTER AND THE SORCERER'S STONE
J. K. Rowling

HARRY POTTER AND THE CHAMBER OF SECRETS
J. K. Rowling

HARRY POTTER AND THE PRISONER OF AZKABAN
J. K. Rowling

HARRY POTTER AND THE GOBLET OF FIRE
J. K. Rowling

HARRY POTTER AND THE ORDER OF THE PHOENIX
J. K. Rowling

HARRY POTTER AND THE HALF-BLOOD PRINCE
J. K. Rowling

HARRY POTTER AND THE DEATHLY HALLOWS
J. K. Rowling

THE HIDDEN FACE OF EVE: WOMEN IN THE ARAB WORLD
Nawal El Saadawi

HIS DARK MATERIALS TRILOGY, BOOK I: *THE GOLDEN
    COMPASS*
Philip Pullman

HIS DARK MATERIALS TRILOGY, BOOK II: *THE SUBTLE KNIFE*
Philip Pullman

HIS DARK MATERIALS TRILOGY, BOOK III: *THE AMBER
    SPYGLASS*
Philip Pullman

HISTORICAL AND CRITICAL DICTIONARY
Pierre Bayle

HISTORY OF THE CONFLICT BETWEEN RELIGION AND SCIENCE
John William Draper

*THE HISTORY OF THE DECLINE AND FALL OF THE ROMAN
    EMPIRE*
Edward Gibbon

HOLT BASIC READING SERIES
Bernard J. Weiss, sr. ed.

IMPRESSIONS READING SERIES
Jack Booth, gen. ed.

INFALLIBLE? AN INQUIRY
Hans Küng

AN INQUIRY CONCERNING HUMAN UNDERSTANDING
David Hume

INSTITUTES OF THE CHRISTIAN RELIGION
John Calvin

INTRODUCTION TO THEOLOGY
Peter Abelard

*AN INTRODUCTION TO THE PRINCIPLES OF MORALS AND
    LEGISLATION*
Jeremy Bentham

INTRODUCTORY LECTURES ON PSYCHOANALYSIS
Sigmund Freud

THE JEWEL OF MEDINA
Sherry Jones

THE KORAN (QUR'AN)

LAJJA (SHAME)
Taslima Nasrin

THE LAST TEMPTATION OF CHRIST
Nikos Kazantzakis

LETTER ON THE BLIND
Denis Diderot

LETTERS CONCERNING THE ENGLISH NATION
Voltaire

LEVIATHAN
Thomas Hobbes

THE LIFE OF JESUS
Ernest Renan

MARY AND HUMAN LIBERATION
Tissa Balasuriya

MEDITATIONS ON FIRST PHILOSOPHY
René Descartes

THE MERITORIOUS PRICE OF OUR REDEMPTION
William Pynchon

THE METAPHYSICS
Aristotle

MEYEBELA: MY BENGALI GIRLHOOD
Taslima Nasrin

THE NEW ASTRONOMY
Johannes Kepler

THE NEW TESTAMENT
William Tyndale, trans.

NINETY-FIVE THESES
Martin Luther

OF THE VANITIE AND UNCERTAINTIE OF ARTES AND SCIENCES
Henricus Cornelius Agrippa

OLIVER TWIST
Charles Dickens

ON CIVIL LORDSHIP
John Wycliffe

ON JUSTICE IN THE REVOLUTION AND IN THE CHURCH
Pierre-Joseph Proudhon

ON MONARCHY
Dante Alighieri

ON THE INFINITE UNIVERSE AND WORLDS
Giordano Bruno

ON THE LAW OF WAR AND PEACE
Hugo Grotius

ON THE ORIGIN OF SPECIES
Charles Darwin

ON THE REVOLUTION OF HEAVENLY SPHERES
Nicolaus Copernicus

OPUS MAJUS
Roger Bacon

PENGUIN ISLAND
Anatole France

THE PERSIAN LETTERS
Charles-Louis de Secondat, baron de La Brède et de Montesquieu

PHILOSOPHICAL DICTIONARY
Voltaire

THE POLITICAL HISTORY OF THE DEVIL
Daniel Defoe

POPOL VUH

THE POWER AND THE GLORY
Graham Greene

THE PRAISE OF FOLLY
Desiderius Erasmus

PRINCIPLES OF POLITICAL ECONOMY
John Stuart Mill

THE PROVINCIAL LETTERS
Blaise Pascal

THE RAPE OF SITA
Lindsey Collen

THE RED AND THE BLACK
Stendhal

RELIGIO MEDICI
Sir Thomas Browne

RELIGION WITHIN THE LIMITS OF REASON ALONE
Immanuel Kant

THE RIGHTS OF THE CHRISTIAN CHURCH ASSERTED
Matthew Tindal

THE SANDY FOUNDATION SHAKEN
William Penn

THE SATANIC VERSES
Salman Rushdie

SHIVAJI: HINDU KING IN ISLAMIC INDIA
James W. Laine

A SHORT DECLARATION OF THE MISTERY OF INIQUITY
Thomas Helwys

THE SHORTEST WAY WITH THE DISSENTERS
Daniel Defoe

THE SOCIAL CONTRACT
Jean-Jacques Rousseau

THE SORROWS OF YOUNG WERTHER
Johann Wolfgang von Goethe

THE SPIRIT OF LAWS
Charles-Louis de Secondat, baron de La Brède et de Montesquieu

SPIRITS REBELLIOUS
Kahlil Gibran

THE STORY OF ZAHRA
Hanan al-Shaykh

A TALE OF A TUB
Jonathan Swift

THE TALMUD

THEOLOGICAL-POLITICAL TREATISE
Baruch Spinoza

THREE-PART WORK
Meister Eckhart

TOUBA AND THE MEANING OF NIGHT
Shahrnush Parsipur

THE VEIL AND THE MALE ELITE: A FEMINIST INTERPRETATION OF WOMEN'S RIGHTS IN ISLAM
Fatima Mernissi

VOODOO & HOODOO: THEIR TRADITIONAL CRAFTS AS REVEALED BY ACTUAL PRACTITIONERS
Jim Haskins

VOYAGES TO THE MOON AND THE SUN
Savinien Cyrano de Bergerac

THE WITCHES
Roald Dahl

WOMEN WITHOUT MEN: A NOVEL OF MODERN IRAN
Shahrnush Parsipur

ZHUAN FALUN: THE COMPLETE TEACHINGS OF FALUN GONG
Li Hongzhi

ZOONOMIA
Erasmus Darwin

BANNED BOOKS ON SEXUAL GROUNDS
ALICE SERIES
Phyllis Reynolds Naylor

ALWAYS RUNNING—LA VIDA LOCA: GANG DAYS IN L.A.
Luis T. Rodriguez

AMERICA (THE BOOK): A CITIZEN'S GUIDE TO DEMOCRACY INACTION
Jon Stewart, Ben Karlin, David Javerbaum

AN AMERICAN TRAGEDY
Theodore Dreiser

THE ARABIAN NIGHTS, OR THE THOUSAND AND ONE NIGHTS
Sir Richard Burton, trans.

THE ART OF LOVE (ARS AMATORIA)
Ovid (Publius Ovidius Naso)

THE AWAKENING
Kate Chopin

BESSIE COTTER
Wallace Smith

BLESS ME, ULTIMA
Rudolfo Anaya

THE BLUEST EYE
Toni Morrison

BOY
James Hanley

THE BUFFALO TREE
Adam Rapp

CANDIDE
Voltaire (François Marie Arouet Voltaire)

CANDY
Maxwell Kenton

THE CARPETBAGGERS
Harold Robbins

CASANOVA'S HOMECOMING (CASANOVA'S HEIMFAHRT)
Arthur Schnitzler

THE CHINESE ROOM
Vivian Connell

CHRISTINE
Stephen King

THE CLAN OF THE CAVE BEAR
Jean Auel

CONFESSIONS
Jean-Jacques Rousseau

THE DECAMERON
Giovanni Boccaccio

THE DEER PARK
Norman Mailer

THE DEVIL RIDES OUTSIDE
John Howard Griffin

THE DIARY OF SAMUEL PEPYS
Samuel Pepys

DROLL STORIES
Honoré de Balzac

DUBLINERS
James Joyce

EAT ME
Linda Jaivin

THE EPIC OF GILGAMESH
Unknown

FANNY HILL, OR MEMOIRS OF A WOMAN OF PLEASURE
John Cleland

THE FIFTEEN PLAGUES OF A MAIDENHEAD
Anonymous

FLOWERS FOR ALGERNON
Daniel Keyes

THE FLOWERS OF EVIL (LES FLEURS DU MAL)
Charles Baudelaire

FOREVER
Judy Blume

FOREVER AMBER
Kathleen Winsor

FROM HERE TO ETERNITY
James Jones

THE GENIUS
Theodore Dreiser

THE GILDED HEARSE
Charles O. Gorham

THE GINGER MAN
J. P. Donleavy

THE GOATS
Brock Cole

GOD'S LITTLE ACRE
Erskine Caldwell

GOSSIP GIRL SERIES
Cecily von Ziegesar

THE GROUP
Mary McCarthy

HAGAR REVELLY
Daniel Carson Goodman

THE HANDMAID'S TALE
Margaret Atwood

THE HEPTAMERON (L'HEPTAMERON OU HISTOIRES DES AMANS FORTUNEZ)
Marguerite d'Angoulême, Queen of Navarre

THE HISTORY OF TOM JONES, A FOUNDLING
Henry Fielding

HOMO SAPIENS
Stanley Przybyskzewski

HOW THE GARCÍA GIRLS LOST THEIR ACCENTS
Julia Alvarez

HOW TO MAKE LOVE LIKE A PORN STAR
Jenna Jameson

IF IT DIE
André Gide

ISLE OF PINES
Henry Neville

*IT'S PERFECTLY NORMAL: CHANGING BODIES,
   GROWING UP, SEX, AND SEXUAL HEALTH*
Robie H. Harris

JANET MARCH
Floyd Dell

JUDE THE OBSCURE
Thomas Hardy

JURGEN: A COMEDY OF JUSTICE
James Branch Cabell

*JUSTINE, OR THE MISFORTUNES OF VIRTUE;
JULIETTE, HER SISTER, OR THE PROSPERITIES OF VICE*
Marquis de Sade

THE KAMA SUTRA OF VATSAYANA
Sir Richard Burton, F. F. Arbuthnot, translators

THE KREUTZER SONATA
Leo Tolstoy

LADIES IN THE PARLOR
Jim Tully

LADY CHATTERLEY'S LOVER
D. H. Lawrence

LA TERRE (THE EARTH)
Émile Zola

LOLITA
Vladimir Nabokov

THE LUSTFUL TURK
Anonymous

MADAME BOVARY
Gustave Flaubert

MADELEINE
Anonymous

MADEMOISELLE DE MAUPIN
Théophile Gautier

THE MAID OF ORLEANS (LA PUCELLE)
François-Marie Arouet Voltaire

MEMOIRES
Giovanni Casanova de Seingalt

MEMOIRS OF A YOUNG RAKEHELL
Guillaume Apollinaire

MEMOIRS OF HECATE COUNTY
Edmund Wilson

THE MERRY MUSES OF CALEDONIA
Robert Burns

MOLL FLANDERS
Daniel Defoe

MY LIFE AND LOVES
Frank Harris

NATIVE SON
Richard Wright

A NIGHT IN A MOORISH HAREM
Anonymous

NOVEMBER (NOVEMBRE)
Gustave Flaubert

THE 120 DAYS OF SODOM (LES 120 JOURNÉES DE SODOME)
Marquis de Sade

OUR LADY OF THE FLOWERS (NOTRE-DAME-DES-FLEURS)
Jean Genet

OUTLAW REPRESENTATION
Richard Meyer

PAMELA, OR VIRTUE REWARDED
Samuel Richardson

PANSIES
D. H. Lawrence

THE PERFUMED GARDEN
Sir Richard Burton, trans.

THE PERKS OF BEING A WALLFLOWER
Stephen Chbosky

PEYTON PLACE
Grace Metalious

THE PHILANDERER
Stanley Kauffmann

POEMS AND BALLADS
Algernon Charles Swinburne

POINT COUNTER POINT
Aldous Huxley

RABBIT, RUN
John Updike

THE RAINBOW
D. H. Lawrence

REPLENISHING JESSICA
Max Bodenheim

SANCTUARY
William Faulkner

SARI SAYS
Sari Locker

THE SATYRICON
Gaius Petronius Arbiter

SEPTEMBER IN QUINZE
Vivian Connell

SERENADE
James M. Cain

SEX
Madonna

SEXUS
Henry Miller

SHANGHAI BABY
Wei Hui (Zhou Weihui)

SIMON CALLED PETER
Robert Keable

*1601—A FIRESIDE CONVERSATION IN YE TIME
 OF QUEEN ELIZABETH*
Mark Twain

SLEEVELESS ERRAND
Norah C. James

SNOW FALLING ON CEDARS
David Guterson

SONG OF SOLOMON
Toni Morrison

SOPHIE'S CHOICE
William Styron

A STORY TELLER'S HOLIDAY
George Moore

STUDS LONIGAN
James T. Farrell

SUSAN LENOX: HER FALL AND RISE
David Graham Phillips

SWEETER THAN LIFE
Mark Tryon

TEN NORTH FREDERICK
John O'Hara

TESS OF THE D'URBERVILLES
Thomas Hardy

THEIR EYES WERE WATCHING GOD
Zora Neale Hurston

THEN AGAIN, MAYBE I WON'T
Judy Blume

THE THIEF'S JOURNAL
Jean Genet

THIS BOY'S LIFE
Tobias Wolff

THREE WEEKS
Elinor Glyn

TOBACCO ROAD
Erskine Caldwell

TRAGIC GROUND
Erskine Caldwell

TRILBY
George du Maurier

THE TRIUMPH OF DEATH
Gabriele D'Annunzio

TROPIC OF CANCER
Henry Miller

TROPIC OF CAPRICORN
Henry Miller

TWILIGHT SERIES
Stephenie Meyer

ULYSSES
James Joyce

VENUS AND TANNHAUSER (UNDER THE HILL)
Aubrey Beardsley

THE WILD PALMS
William Faulkner

WOMEN IN LOVE
D. H. Lawrence

*WOMEN ON TOP: HOW REAL LIFE CHANGED WOMEN'S SEXUAL
   FANTASIES*
Nancy Friday

A YOUNG GIRL'S DIARY
Anonymous

INDEX

Note: **Boldface** page numbers indicate major treatment of a topic; *b* denotes entries located in the biographical section.